ADVANCE PRAISE FOR

SEXUALITIES IN EDUCATION: A READER

"Teachers, activists, and scholars alike will find in this reader both the conceptual tools and the inspiration to invigorate a social justice education practice that embraces sexuality and its myriad intersections. Bolstered by a collection of visual images that will spark desires and provoke intrigues, this courageous collection will provide educators with numerous perspectives and entry points into the complexities of sexuality in education. Locating sexuality within a larger social-cultural context and highlighting its simultaneities with struggles over gender, race, class, sovereignty, disability, and colonialism, this book will occupy an important place in the work of anti-oppressive curriculum workers everywhere."

—*Rubén Gaztambide-Fernández, Associate Professor, Department of Curriculum, Teaching and Learning, Ontario Institute for Studies in Education*

"This book will queer your mind as it increasingly unveils both persistent and situated ways that sexualities matter in education, and demands that we question, act, change. Linking field-defining classics with new voices on norm-criticality, feminisms, and intersectionality, Meiners and Quinn have assembled a stunning collection of scholarship and art that reframes not merely the field of sexualities and education but education itself. Read this today."

—*Kevin Kumashiro,*
Author of Troubling Education: Queer Activism and Antioppressive Pedagogy

"This reader is a must-have for anyone interested in sexuality, education, and social justice. Erica R. Meiners and Therese Quinn have made a unique cross-genred collection of academic as well as political, literary texts and art, highlighting both contemporary and historical perspectives. At its heart is a sharp analysis of the neo-liberal framing of education and the self, informed by an intersectional and queer-feminist approach to the meanings of gender, sexuality, and strategies of change. It brings us closer to understanding the depth of what is at stake, and yet provides inspiration and hopes for change, reminding us of our predecessors' impossible missions and the activists today continuing them."

—*Janne Bromseth, Stockholm University*

SEXUALITIES
IN EDUCATION

Studies in the
Postmodern Theory of Education

Shirley R. Steinberg
General Editor

Vol. 367

The Counterpoints series is part of the Peter Lang Education list.
Every volume is peer reviewed and meets
the highest quality standards for content and production.

PETER LANG
New York • Washington, D.C./Baltimore • Bern
Frankfurt • Berlin • Brussels • Vienna • Oxford

SEXUALITIES IN EDUCATION

A READER

EDITED BY
Erica R. Meiners
and Therese Quinn

PETER LANG
New York • Washington, D.C./Baltimore • Bern
Frankfurt • Berlin • Brussels • Vienna • Oxford

Library of Congress Cataloging-in-Publication Data

Sexualities in education: a reader / edited by
Erica R. Meiners, Therese Quinn.
p. cm. — (Counterpoints: studies in the postmodern theory of education; v. 367)
Includes bibliographical references and index.
1. Sex discrimination in education.
2. Educational equalization. 3. Sexism in education.
I. Meiners, Erica R. II. Quinn, Therese.
LC212.8.S496   370.81—dc23   2011028969
ISBN 978-1-4331-0637-8 (hardcover)
ISBN 978-1-4331-0636-1 (paperback)
ISBN 978-1-4539-0149-6 (e-book)
ISSN 1058-1634

Bibliographic information published by **Die Deutsche Nationalbibliothek**.
Die Deutsche Nationalbibliothek lists this publication in the "Deutsche
Nationalbibliografie"; detailed bibliographic data is available
on the Internet at http://dnb.d-nb.de/.

Cover art by Heather Ault, heatherault.org

The paper in this book meets the guidelines for permanence and durability
of the Committee on Production Guidelines for Book Longevity
of the Council of Library Resources.

Contents

SECTION 2—Contesting Identities in School History

SECTION 3—Self, Sexuality, and Teaching

SECTION 4—Schooling Sexualities and Genders

SECTION 5—Youth and Sexualities

SECTION 6—Citizenship, Nationality, and Culture

SECTION 7—Sexuality, Research, and Representation

SECTION 8—Sexualities Organizing, Activism, and Education

SECTION 9—"Doing It": Sexualities in Education Resources

Acknowledgments

This project is the product of ongoing work and collaborations. We deeply appreciate the many folks who agitate for a more just, feminist, sexually positive and queer world, including countless parents, teachers, students, and community members. In Chicago and beyond we are sustained by artists, abolitionists, poets, beekeepers, nuns, teachers, scholars, bike mechanics, musicians, learners, and more who inspire, challenge and engage us. This beloved community, full of intimates and others whose work we are nourished by, reminds us how to be of use.

A special thanks to all of our absolutely fabulous section editors, for cheerleading and stepping up to the plate throughout the work chronicled in this book—for all their good cheer and help, we are grateful. And for the artists we've worked with throughout this project, we love the world you make. Thank you.

Erica offers a shout of love to her community at the St. Leonard's Adult High School and to the Critical Resistance folks. Therese thanks the School of the Art Institute of Chicago for granting her a Roger Brown Residency in New Buffalo, Michigan, and the Council for International Exchange of Scholars for sending her to Finland through the Fulbright Scholar Program.

We flourish *because of* and *through* communities that sustain us with food, love, art, and ideas. We have deep love for our Chicago-and-beyond family members, including: Ken Addison, Tim Barnett, Erik Bataller, Kari Bradley, Frida Ruckus Bradley, Lisa Brooks, Mollie Dowling, Mona Eid, Gabriela Fitz, Laurie Fuller, Pat Guizzetti, Jean Hughes, Antti Veikko Jauhiainen, Jodi Jensen, Nathan Jones, Shirley Jones, Nic McClelland, Denise Meiners, Elena, Holly May, Heather and Stacia Middlemass, Dennis Quinn, Aza Quinn-Brauner, Mearah Quinn-Brauner, Ajitha Reddy, Balele Shoka, and Tyler Barnett Steinkamp.

For reviewing essays, contributing art, editing prowess, timely feedback and general care and enthusiasm, our team also thanks Bill Ayers, Heather Ault, Lucy Bailey, Shelley Bannister, Kristiina Brunila, David Lee Carlson, Bonnie Fortune, Annette Henry, Amber Jones, Miyoshi Juergensen, Pamela Konkol, Kevin Kumashiro, Catherine Lugg, Irma Nuñez, Bernadette Shade, Brett Stockdill, Daniel Walsh, Gerald Walton, and Susan Woolley.

Credits and Permissions

6. Love Silphium
Heather Ault
Used with the permission of the artist. From the project, 4000 Years for Choice: Celebrating the Reproductive Roots of Contraception and Abortion (4000yearsforchoice.com).

7. Harvey Milk Notes, 1978
Harvey Milk Archives – Scott Smith Collection, San Francisco Public Library.

8. How Sweet It Is!
Jackie M. Blount
Blount, Jackie. 2005. Fit to Teach: Same-sex Desire, Gender, and School Work in the Twentieth Century. Albany: State University of New York Press. "How Sweet It Is? pp. 135–155. Reprinted with permission.

9. The Religious Right and Public Education: The Paranoid Politics of Homophobia
Catherine A. Lugg
Originally published as: Lugg, Catherine A. (1999, May). "The Religious Right and Public Education: The Paranoid Politics of Homophobia." *Educational Policy, 12*(3), 267–283. © Corwin Press, Inc. Reprinted by permission of the publisher.

10. Anti-Briggs Amendment Poster, 1978
Harvey Milk Archives – Scott Smith Collection, San Francisco Public Library.

11. White Trash: Manifesting the Bisexual
Carolyn Pajor Ford
Reprinted by permission of the author.

12. Apple Jumper, Teacher Babe, and Bland Uniformer Teachers: Fashioning Feminine Teacher Bodies
Becky Atkinson
Becky Atkinson's "Apple Jumper, Teacher Babe, and Bland Uniformer Teachers: Fashioning Feminine Teacher Bodies" was published in *Educational Studies, 44*(2), 2008, 98–121, and is used with permission

13. Bound and Gagged: Sexual Silences, Gender Conformity, and the Gay Male Teacher
Eric Rofes
Eric Rofes' "Bound and Gagged: Sexual Silences, Gender Conformity, and the Gay Male Teacher" is from *Status Quo or Status Queer: A Radical Rethinking of Sexuality and Schooling* (Rowman & Littlefield, 2005). © 2005 by Rowman & Littlefield Publishers, Inc. Reprinted by permission of Crispin Hollings, Literary Executor of the Estate of Eric Rofes.

14. Knot a Love Story
Jane Gallop
"Knot a Love Story" appeared in *Anecdotal Theory*, Jane Gallop, pp. 100–111. © 2002, Duke University Press. All rights reserved. Reprinted by permission of the publisher.

15. Girls Are Not Chicks, 2009
Jacinta Bunnell and Julie M. Novack
From *Girls Are Not Chicks Coloring Book*, ReachAndTeach.com / PMPress.org. Reprinted by permission of the artist, author, and publishers.

16. Becoming Mr. Cougar: Institutionalizing Heterosexuality and Homophobia at River High
C. J. Pascoe
Excerpted from *Dude, You're a Fag: Masculinity and Sexuality in High School*, by C.J. Pascoe, © 2007 by the Regents of the University of California. Published by the University of California Press. Reprinted by permission of the publisher.

17. Yogyakarta Principles – For the Rights of Lesbian, Gay, Bisexual and Transgender People.
The Principles are freely available and online in all six United Nations languages at: http://www. yogyakartaprinciples.org/index.html

18. What's Queer Got to Do with It? Interrogating Nationalism and Imperialism
Roland Sintos Coloma
Originally published as: Coloma, R. S. (2003). "Que(e)r(y)ing Nationalism: History, Nation, and Imperialism." *Journal of Curriculum Theorizing* 19(3), 51–70. Used by permission of the author.

19. 41a & b) Barbara Hammer, *Nitrate Kisses*

a. Lorraine and Sally Binford in Nitrate Kisses, 1992 by Barbara Hammer
Used by permission of the artist.

b. Jack Waters and Peter Cramer in *Nitrate Kisses*, 1992 by Barbara Hammer
Used by permission of the artist.

20. 41c & d) Isaac Julien, Looking for Langston
Ref. image 5:
Looking for Langston Series (No.17) The Last Angel of History, 1989
Isaac Julien and Sunil Gupta
Print on gloss paper
20 x 24 cm
Courtesy of Isaac Julien and Sunil Gupta and Victoria Miro Gallery, London

Ref. image 7:
Looking for Langston Series (No.19) After George Platt Lynes Nudes with a Twist 1952, 1989
Isaac Julien and Sunil Gupta
Print on gloss paper
20 x 24 cm
Courtesy of Isaac Julien and Sunil Gupta and Victoria Miro Gallery, London

21. Queer Pedagogy and Its Strange Techniques
Deborah P. Britzman

A longer version of this chapter under the same title was published in *Lost Subjects, Contested Objects: Toward a Psychoanalytic Inquiry of Learning*, by Deborah Britzman (Albany: State University of New York Press, 1998). Reprinted by permission of the author.

22. Christmas Effects
Eve Sedgwick
"Queer and Now" in *Tendencies*, Eve Kosofsky Sedgwick, pp. 1–22. © 1993. Duke University Press. All Rights Reserved. Reprinted by permission of the publisher.

23. Feel Tank
Lauren Berlant
Excerpted from Berlant, L., 2004. "Critical Inquiry, Affirmative Culture." *Critical Inquiry*, (Winter) 30:2, Chicago: University of Chicago Press. Reprinted by permission of the publisher.

24. Utopia Now, 2007
Mary Patten
Used by permission of the artist.

25. Parade, 2004
Lane Relyea
Used by permission of the artist.

26. Gender JUST (Photo)
Used by permission of the artist.

27. Education in the Streets
Deborah B. Gould
Partially excerpted from Deborah B. Gould, *Moving Politics: Emotion and ACT UP's Fight Against AIDS*, University of Chicago Press, 2009. Reprinted by permission of the publisher.

28. Who Is Asian? Representing a Panethnic Continent in Community Activism
Alan Wong
Used with permission of Gay and Lesbian Asians of Montreal.

29. Dive
Andrea Gibson
Used by permission of the artist.

30. The More We Know About Sex, the Better Our Choices
Jeanette May
Used by permission of the artist.

31. Illustration by Suzann Gage. Used by permission of the Federation of Feminist Women's Health Centers.

32. Trans Ally Card. Used by permission of Chances/Dances, Strap-on.org and Trans Youth Resource and Advocacy.

33. Just Like U. Used by permission of Rutgers WPF.

34. Nomy Lamm, 2009. Photograph by Richard Downing. Used by permission.

Ella Flagg Young, date unknown.

Love, Labor, and Learning

Yours in the Struggle

THERESE QUINN & ERICA R. MEINERS

> Certainly, it is important for the growing child to know his own body as it is to know arithmetic.
> ELLA FLAGG YOUNG, 1913[1]

Love, Labor and Learning: Yours in the Struggle

Ella Flagg Young's life and work are inspirations for *Sexualities in Education: A Reader*. A progressive educator and curricular innovator, Young was the first woman elected as president of the National Education Association and to serve as superintendant of a major public school system—Chicago's (Smith, 1979; Moran, 1996; Blount, 1998). As a teacher and administrator Young established a range of new opportunities, including field trips, vocational education, and teachers' councils, and in 1913, after gaining the support of prominent Chicagoans such as Jane Addams, she initiated the nation's first sex education program (Moran, 1996).

Young, a suffragist who promoted a vision of democratic schooling in which students and teachers shared real power, is an apt representative for sexualities education, embodying the presence and absence that is still a hallmark of the field (Smith, 1979). For example, Young put sex on the official map of public schools, but her following ouster encouraged teachers to "'sneak' the subject in first and ask permission later" (Moran, 1996, p. 509). As a feminist and a woman who shared her life with another woman, Laura Brayton, for thirty years, perhaps Young understood the politics of visibility, and how, by naming the centrality of sex, she also put sexualities in the picture.

We invoke Young to highlight themes that are critical to this book: the necessity of intersectional approaches to desire, sexualities, and education; the feminist landscape that supports these dialogs; the queer core of all sexuality work inside and outside classrooms; and finally, the centrality of labor to these discussions.

First, Young's life reminds us that, in a sense, it is always a queer time in the United States.

Uncontrollable sexualities and gender identifications continue to preoccupy those in power. As this book goes to press in spring of 2011 the United States' federal government has gingerly decided it will not defend the constitutionality of the federal Defense of Marriage Act (DOMA); Congress has provided a process for the repeal of the military's ban—*Don't Ask, Don't Tell (DADT)*—on out lesbian, gay, bisexual, transgender, and queer (LGBTQ) men and women; and national attention has focused on queer youth suicides and the school-based "bullying" acts that triggered certain high profile tragedies. Each of these accomplishments is incomplete—DOMA is still being enforced, if not defended; queers are still being ejected from the military; and young people are still targeted for harassment and violence in schools. And defining anti-bullying legislation and the repeal of DADT as "queer successes" makes it easy to overlook other movements bubbling and swirling across the country that center gender and sexuality.

For example, states are pushing to limit women's access to reproductive rights through the refusal of government funds for abortions, support for physicians who, counter to the ethical obligations of their profession, want to "opt-out" of providing any medical procedure to which they are opposed, and through new restrictions on women seeking abortions: 24-hour waiting periods, mandatory counseling, and more. In schools, abstinence-based sex education is still the federal mandate, and teachers are under widespread assault for their "incompetence" and "laziness" while schools are privatized, weakening rights and protections for out LGBTQ educators. Also affecting our view is the knowledge that DADT was repealed the same day that a potential pathway for undocumented youth, the DREAM (Development, Relief and Education for Alien Minors) Act was denied. And, last but not least, 58% of our discretionary federal budget is spent on support for a permanent war economy (National Priorities Project, 2011).

In this context, we are skeptical of the LGBTQ "successes" that media and politicians alike encourage us to celebrate and reminded again of the importance of working through an intersectional lens. For us, as for the 1977 Combahee River Collective, oppressions are not neatly divisible.

> We believe that sexual politics under patriarchy is as pervasive in Black women's lives as are the politics of class and race. We also often find it difficult to separate race from class from sex oppression because in our lives they are most often experienced simultaneously. We know that there is such a thing as racial-sexual oppression which is neither solely racial nor solely sexual, e.g., the history of rape of Black women by white men as a weapon of political repression. (Combahee River Collective Statement, 1977, p. 267)

For the Combahee River Collective, white supremacy is not an adequate frame to name the oppression of Black women. Gender is not simply a problem for women nor is naming white supremacy a central analytic tool only for communities of color. Similarly, for us, it is important to challenge what gets framed as queer issues—to ask, for example, why bullying and pride, but not inflated war budgets or reproductive rights?

Just as suffrage was integral to Young's accomplishments, feminism frames our intersectional analysis and our political educational work. As we survey this educational moment and consider sexualities in particular, feminist tools and perspectives seem needed now, more than ever. For one thing, teaching is always in gender trouble. Still a racialized, heteronormative and feminized field, public education is now being rapidly deskilled and deprofessionalized as teachers are de-unionized and identified as at the root cause of everything from obesity to falling test scores, and their preparation programs are devalued and replaced with a few weeks of summer training. This political assault is possible because teaching *is* women's work.

Also, even as moderate support develops in some school districts and specific schools to address

LGBTQ sexualities and lives, abstinence-based sex education is still the federal policy. Despite the clear value of an analysis of education that includes gender and power, feminist frameworks have never been particularly visible in teacher "training" programs. Yet, feminism, to steal a quote from bell hooks, is for everybody, and we concur with Ella Flagg Young, especially for teachers.

When we survey the work included in this Reader we are pleased that commitment to feminist intersectionality is visible throughout, but we also note what is not as evident in the table of contents as we would have liked. Where is the substantive work on empire? Why is this project so North American centered? It seems now that standpoint epistemology ruled the day—what we solicited reflected our visions, affiliations, and investments, and those of each section's editor. This is, of course, a limitation of all work and a challenge that is partially mitigated by embracing collaborations. Partnering with others pushes us to critically reflect on our assumptions, assertions and actions. We selected people to work with because we were comfortable with and had learned from their analyses and ways of working, and also, because they often offered fresh views that incited, excited and expanded our own.

And we freely admit: this book is queer-centric—queer and other norm-critical perspectives have posed some of the most interesting and urgent questions about sexualities in education and are key here. Often overlooked forms and practices such as art and the ephemera of organizing, poetry, personal essays, and non-academic work also punctuate this collection, illuminating the important place of varied voices and modes of expression in movements for justice and education and inviting us to name the passion that drives our learning and fuels movements. For example, this project includes a page of political notes authored by Harvey Milk and new poetry by queer youth, images from classic films by Barbara Hammer and Isaac Julien and narratives and mission statements by contemporary Chicago artist Coya Paz and youth organizers Gender JUST. These and other excerpts from cultural and political queer and creative lives are interspersed with chapters that offer more theoretical examinations of the complexities of sexualities and schools across the United States, with gestures to their manifestations outside our national borders.

Ella Flagg Young's dedication to improving the working conditions of teachers also reminds us to be transparent about our labor. An unexpected yet formative theme during this book's production was the relationship between authors and publishers. We recognize that many publishers, and particularly independent ones that focus on queer and feminist work, are struggling for cash and support. But these were not the presses that requested hefty reprint fees. Eileen from The Federation of Feminist Women's Health Centers, which holds the rights to *A New View of a Woman's Body*, just asked us to "send what you can." In contrast, some works that we considered influential in our own practices and thinking are not included in this Reader because the requested fees were so high and the authors did not own their copyrights. For example, Kenji Yoshino generously agreed to allow us to excerpt his popular and not lengthy 2006 *New York Times* article, "The Pressure to Cover," but the cost per word totaled over $1,000; as a result, Yoshino's essay is absent here, but we encourage readers to look for it elsewhere.

In the end, we found ourselves writing checks for $50 or $100 for poets and filmmakers who were just as willing to donate their work and haggling unsuccessfully with presses affiliated with wealthy private universities to reduce their publication fees. Like teachers everywhere who supply their art rooms and fill their bookshelves, we paid from our own pockets for this book's permissions, cover art, and more. This is the norm in many occupations now—workers subsidizing, invisibly, parasitic employers. Our participation in this economy reproduces these asymmetrical and problematic constructions and valuations of art and knowledge. There is no neutral ground.

The world of publishing continues to be remade, offering moments of generative chaos and opportunities for radical interventions. With the advent of new technologies, we wonder if publishing companies are even needed anymore. What presses offer—resources, marketing, even copyediting and layout—has diminished so significantly over the years, that their primary contribution is reputation capital, a shell of legitimacy and stature, demarcations that are already available for purchase. We explicate the material conditions of our work because, like Young's support of teacher's unions, economic and political contexts shape labor: materiality matters. Young spent her life negotiating education policy *and* practice, curriculum *and* teacher's rights and did not distinguish one venue as more important to building stronger schools. This is queer educational justice work; it rejects norms that constrain, working across categories to get the job done.

Putting aside our anxieties and self-criticisms about the limitations of all projects and this Reader in particular, we are buoyed by the model of Young's tenacious commitment to staying in the struggle for the long haul. Persistence was a central theme in Young's life; she wasn't sent to school until she was eleven, but continued seeking formal education over decades, and earned a doctorate at age 55 (Smith, 1979). And she was just as resolute in her efforts on behalf of teachers and students. Persistence, tenacity and pleasure are also resonant themes in this Reader, creating a trajectory that links the work of Eve Sedgwick and Catherine Lugg to the newer scholarship of Jillian Ford and Angel Rubiel Gonzalez and connects the provocative pro-feminist pleasure art created by Jeanette May and young radical women to the riotous collectives that produced the transgendered advocacy guide, the TransAlly Card, for local political education. Through snapshots of justice struggles within sexualities and education, these contributors embody the fierceness of Young's loyalties to rigorous and local organizing over the long haul. We offer this Reader as a contribution to that project.

Notes

1. Quoted in Moran, 1996, p. 481.

References

Blount, J. (1998). *Destined to rule the schools: Women and the superintendency 1873–1995.* Albany, NY: State University of New York.

Combahee River Collective. (1983). The Combahee River Collective Statement. In B. Smith (Ed.) *Home girls.* New York, NY: Kitchen Table: Women of Color Press.

Moran, J. (1996, September). "Modernism gone mad": Sex education comes to Chicago, 1913. *The Journal of American History, 83*(2), 481–513.

National Priorities Project. (2011). Federal Discretionary and Mandatory Spending. Retrieved May 9, 2011, from http://nationalpriorities.org/resources/federal-budget-101/budget-briefs/federal-discretionary-and-mandatory-spending/

Smith, J. (1979). *Ella Flagg Young: Portrait of a leader.* Ames, IA: Educational Studies Press and the Iowa State University Research Foundation.

Yoshino, K. (2006, January 15). The Pressure to cover. *The New York Times.* Retrieved April 3, 2011, from http://www.nytimes.com/2006/01/15/magazine/15gays.html

Introduction: Bending the Terrain

Queer and Justice Issues Infiltrate the Education Map

CONNIE E. NORTH

As a graduate student, I had the opportunity to take a sociolinguistics class in which we studied James Gee's (1996) Discourse theory. According to Gee, a Discourse is

> a socially accepted association among ways of using language, other symbolic expressions, and "artifacts," of thinking, feeling, believing, valuing, and acting that can be used to identify oneself as a member of a socially meaningful group or "social network," or to signal (that one is playing) a socially meaningful "role." (p. 131)

This theory illuminates how people create and police boundaries about who is and is not an authentic insider in our manmade social groups ("manmade" not being a slip of the tongue). In class, I asked, "But do all human groups rely on an insider/outsider binary to define themselves? Even if we are talking about a universal phenomenon, given human consciousness and linguistic capacities, could we not decide to organize ourselves differently?" After the professor acknowledged the generalized nature of this theory, I delved into queer, feminist, poststructuralist, critical race, Buddhist, and postcolonial texts that offered alternatives to such exclusive and oftentimes subjugating social grouping practices. In Elizabeth Ellsworth's (2005) terms, I sought membranes "where the brain/mind/body and the 'outside world' touch and interpenetrate, flow into and interfere with each other" (p. 48). The authors in this section contribute to such interpenetration, fluidity, and disruption with their sophisticated renderings of not only what is but also what social arrangements could be in education, U.S. society, and beyond our national boundaries.

Bending the Terrain kicks off with a visual queering of the maps we use to navigate the world. Artist Shannon Kavanagh powerfully reminds us that bodies carrying memories interact and interfere with places, those places holding historicized particularities of their own. Elizabeth Meyer takes up this map in "From Here to Queer: Mapping Sexualities in Education" by explaining how queer theoretical frameworks can help educators question taken-for-granted assumptions about relationships, identity, gender, and sexual orientation. Such inquiries, Meyer argues, can explode rigid social categories, particularly binary categories, and open up possibilities for more expansive social relations and conditions. Meyer further demonstrates how teaching the resistance-provoking knowledges that queer theory demands promises transformative praxes. She particularly describes the potentially liberatory effects of integrating queer concepts, perceptions, and performances into classrooms, asserting that they can help researchers, teachers, and other educators "to creatively work through the current obstacles that prevent teachers from teaching passionately and inclusively" (this volume).

The next chapter takes us beyond the schoolhouse door to interrogate the political and economic forces that perpetuate social injustices and often obstruct transgressive forms of education. In "Sweatshop-Produced Rainbow Flags and Participatory Patriarchy: Why the Gay Rights Movement Is a Sham," Mattilda Bernstein Sycamore examines how a "gaysbian elite" in San Francisco has contributed to misogynist, racist, classist, and ageist struggles, thereby excluding and, at times, violating those who do not assimilate into white, middle-class norms. Bolstering her claim that "[h]omo now stands for homogenous," Sycamore offers illustrations of such exclusions, including gay Castro residents' resistance to the establishment of a queer youth shelter that would offer support to a population with extremely high rates of suicide, drug addiction, and homelessness. She also critiques the gay rights movement's focus on narrow issues such as same-sex marriage, arguing that this move reveals a commitment to obtaining straight privilege rather than challenging U.S.-generated oppression. By exposing the "tyranny of assimilationist norms" (this volume), Sycamore challenges educators, scholars, and activists to examine more critically and reflexively our efforts to transform U.S. society and, in turn, to build more inclusive, anti-imperialist communities and social movements.

Next, Jessica Fields relates some of the "Differences and Divisions" highlighted by Sycamore to educational policies and practices via an examination of school responses to the passage of a Teach Abstinence until Marriage law in North Carolina. In the excerpts included here from her book *Risky Lessons: Sex Education and Social Inequality,* she examines how educators and community members in three middle schools approach sex education. Her analysis reveals students' disparate access to progressive, comprehensive sex education as well as the racialized, gendered, adultist, and heteronormative discourses that shape—and constrain—the sex education they experience in classrooms. Fields also demonstrates how both the rhetoric and policies surrounding school-based sex education contribute to rather than challenge social inequalities and frequently obstruct "a full range of sexual expression in vulnerable young people's lives."

Mel Michelle Lewis then relates the above-mentioned social issues to pedagogy by exploring her teaching of Black queer studies and Black feminist thought as an embodied text in her "Pedagogy and the Sista' Professor: Teaching Black Queer Feminist Studies through the Self." More specifically, she examines how students read the intersections of race, gender, and sexuality through not only foundational written texts but also the body of their Black, lesbian teacher—Lewis. She particularly investigates the pitfalls of engaging identity-based authority in the classroom as well as the possibilities engendered by plunging into the teachable moments that arise when we attend to embodied selves. As Lewis makes clear in this chapter, "the classroom is not a neutral location inhabited only by minds, and void of bodies, identities, and desires." Those desires include not only love for others but also love of our freedom to choose what we do with our bodies. The chapter thus concludes with Heather Ault's celebratory art, which powerfully reminds us that multi-gendered bodies have long sought more expansive environments with which to interact and play.

Although diverse in location and emphasis, the above texts demonstrate their authors' common commitment to bending educational terrains so that they may hold more egalitarian and just social configurations. They also guide us toward viable visions of learning spaces "in which we come to know the world by acting in it, making something of it, and doing the never-ending work and play of responding to what our actions make occur" (Ellsworth, 2005, p. 56).

References

Ellsworth, E. (2005). *Places of learning: Media, architecture, pedagogy.* New York: Routledge.
Gee, J.P. (1996). *Social linguistics and literacies: Ideology in discourses* (2nd ed.). New York: RoutledgeFalmer.

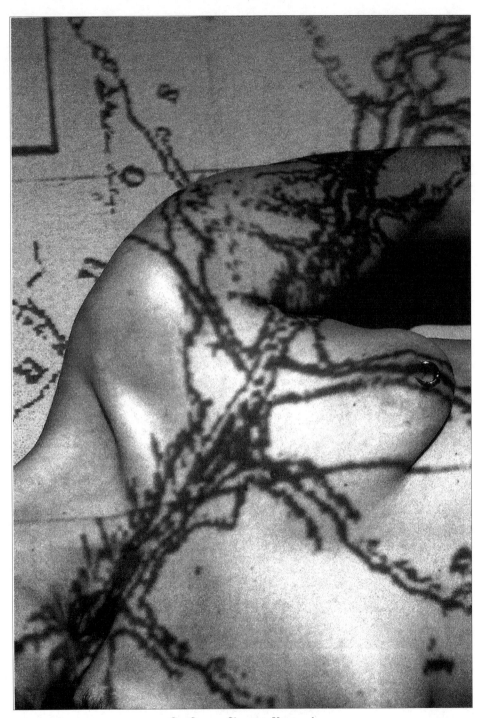

Confluence. Shannon Kavanagh

This photograph is from a series in which I have projected maps onto queer bodies. Maps assist us in navigating, defining, and explaining the world around us, much as the lenses of sexuality and gender identity guide how we navigate and define our environments. Each of these portraits is marked by the experience of a memory tethered to a specific place. Every/body connects with and bends the light of each map in a different fashion, mirroring the process by which we remember. The projection of these maps onto the queer body is an exploration of empowerment of the body over geography—not merely of a place, but also its people, its history, and the memories associated with this place.

CHAPTER ONE

From Here to Queer

Mapping Sexualities in Education

ELIZABETH J. MEYER

Most scholars and educators steer clear of queer theory because "queer" was historically a pejorative term for gays and lesbians or anyone perceived as different. What many people do not understand is that in the past 20 years, scholars and activists have actively reconstructed the term "queer," infusing it with new meanings and applications. Although many individuals still use "queer" with the intent to harm, in scholarly contexts it has come to represent new concepts that, when applied in school settings, can have a liberatory and positive influence on the way schools, and sexualities education in particular, work today.

Another common misunderstanding is that queer theory is a synonym for gay and lesbian studies. Although some queer theory emerged from the work of scholars in this field, it has evolved to become much more broad and encompassing than gay and lesbian studies. Queer theory goes beyond exploring aspects of gay and lesbian identity and experience. It questions taken-for-granted assumptions about relationships, identity, gender, and sexuality. It seeks to explode rigid normalizing categories into possibilities that exist beyond the binaries of black/white, man/woman, disabled/able-bodied, masculine/feminine, student/teacher, gay/straight. Queer theory offers educators a lens through which they can transform their praxis so as to explore and celebrate the tensions and new understandings created by teaching new ways of seeing the world. This chapter will introduce some key tenets of queer theory and describe how all educators can apply these ideas to create classrooms that promote respect for and the inclusion of students, families, and individuals of all races, religions, sexualities, gender expressions, and dis/abilities.

Understanding the Harms of Sexism and Homophobia

In recent years researchers, educators, and the mass media have increasingly paid attention to the important issue of violence in schools. Bullying and harassment are aspects of school violence that have received a significant amount of attention from the media as well as school officials and community members. Although this important issue is getting widespread attention, much of the information about bullying and harassment fails to address the underlying social forces at work. As Martino and Pallotta-Chiarolli (2003) point out in their study of masculinities, bullying has been depoliticized and examined as isolated acts of teasing or violence rather than the enforcement of cultural norms. They explain that "bullying needs to be understood in terms which acknowledge the regime of normalizing practices in which sex/gender boundaries are policed for adolescent boys" (p. 54). These same processes shape adolescent girls' behaviors and relationships as well (Brown, 2003; Duncan, 2004). Since much school-based bullying is discriminatory in nature (California Safe Schools Coalition, 2004; Harris Interactive, 2001; Kosciw & Diaz, 2006; Reis, 1999; Reis & Saewyc, 1999), these behaviors act to create and support a social hierarchy that privileges mainstream identities and behaviors over marginalized ones.

Bullying is closely linked to the problems of homophobia and sexism in schools and has resulted in several court battles over how families, students, and teachers who do not conform to traditional notions of heterosexual masculinity and femininity are allowed to participate in schools. Recent North American cases include the censoring of literature that represents same-sex families in a positive light (*Chamberlain* v. *Surrey School District No. 36,* 2002), educators being fired for being gay, lesbian or bisexual, the right of student groups to meet and discuss issues relating to relationships, sexuality, and sexual orientation (*East High GSA* v. *Salt Lake City Board of Education,* 1999), and students being violently and repeatedly harassed with homophobic taunts and slurs (*Nabozny* v. *Podlesny,* 1996; *School District No. 44* v. *Jubran,* 2005). These cultural battles are being waged every day in schools. Educators need to have accurate information and support to educate their students and communities around issues of gender, sex, and sexuality and how discrimination based on any of these grounds harms everyone in schools. By developing a more critical understanding of these issues, educators can have a profound impact on the way students learn, relate to others, and behave in schools.

Understanding the "Gender Straitjacket"[1]

The first aspect of queer theory that is important for teachers to understand is how traditional heterosexual gender roles reinforce and maintain harmful power dynamics in schools and society. Many people have never questioned how gender shapes our daily behaviors. The invisible nature of gender socialization contributes to its strength and illustrates how hegemony works. Antonio Gramsci (1971/1995) showed how groups in power maintain structures that benefit them by gaining the consent of subordinate groups through subtle, yet powerful, messages that repeatedly permeate daily life. For example, it is not uncommon for students to be told to act more feminine if they are girls or more masculine if they are boys in order to blend in and avoid harassment and discrimination at school.

Judith Butler's (1990) *Gender Trouble* builds on the earlier work of West and Zimmerman (1987) and provides a framework for understanding how gender is constructed through a set of ongoing social interactions. Butler shows how gender has been theorized as a performance of identity and how the matrix of heterosexuality contributes to our existing notions of gender. What this means is that our daily behaviors that signify our gender (separate from but often related to sex) such as clothes, hairstyle, manners of speech and body language, are external representations that are chosen by individuals and fall within a wide spectrum of masculinities and femininities. When these representations adhere to traditional expectations of a masculine male who partners with a feminine female, they are rarely questioned. However, if just one aspect of this equation is changed (for example, two males holding hands or an androgynous or gender non-normative person alone) the individuals are subjected to exclusion, ridicule, violence or other unwanted attention.

Children learn early on in their lives about what cues represent boys and girls. They begin their school careers with this knowledge and work alongside their teachers to practice and perform these gender norms. Children learn that it is not one's sex category noted on a birth certificate that communicates one's gender to the rest of society; rather it is the signifiers we "choose" to wear that will mark us as recognizably male or female. These choices are not freely made, however. They are informed by codes that are explicitly and implicitly taught. Some examples of explicitly taught rules include comments like, "Boys don't wear dresses," or, "Mommies wear makeup to look nice." Implicitly taught dress codes are invisible and pervasive and are communicated through the layout of clothing stores, models in the media, and parental and peer influences. The fact that most people wear clothes and accessories consistent with the gender role expectations for their sex category demonstrates the strength of hegemony in the gender codes we have been taught.

Gender codes constrain all individuals. The strict expectations that accompany them severely limit girls' opportunities to be assertive, physically strong, and competitive and boys' opportunities to be creative, sensitive, and cooperative. A nationwide study conducted in the United States by the Human Rights Watch supports this assertion: "regardless of their sexual orientation or gender identity, youth who violate these rules are punished by their peers and too often by adults" (Bochenek & Brown, 2001, p. 49).

Gendered harassment, which includes homophobic harassment, (hetero)sexual harassment and harassment for gender non-conformity, is one way that society polices and reinforces this heterosexual matrix (Meyer, 2006, 2008). Targeting students who openly identify as gay or dress and act in gender non-normative ways supports patriarchal heterosexual hegemony, and marginalized identities continue to be oppressed. Additionally, when schools fail to intervene by educating *and* punishing perpetrators appropriately, the structure of the school system endorses these dominant ideologies. Schools also frequently and actively silence any discourse that could be seen as positive toward gender and sexual diversity through the official and hidden curriculum, leading us into a discussion of how the use of language and activities of surveillance in schools contribute to creating school climates that are hostile to gender and sexual diversity and reinforce the supremacy of heterosexuality.

Understanding the Hidden Sexuality Curriculum

Language is power. The ability to name and create concepts through discourse is a form of control and domination. Theorists Jacques Derrida (1986a; 1986b), Jacques Lacan (1957/1986) and Michel Foucault (1975; 1980; 1969/1986; 1971/1986) explored the power of words as signifiers to constitute subjects and their experiences as well as the structures in society that police and reinforce dominant ideologies through discursive practices. Critical theorist Peter McLaren (1998) clarifies how these forces work:

> [D]iscourse and discursive practices influence how we live our lives as conscious thinking subjects. They shape our subjectivities (our ways of understanding in relation to the world) because it is only in language and through discourse that social reality can be given meaning. Not all discourses are given the same weight,

as some will account for and justify the appropriateness of the status quo and others will provide a context for resisting social and institutional practices. (pp. 184–185)

Historically, society has constructed homosexuality as an illness, a deviance, and a sin. This discourse was created through psychological research, religious ideologies, and the political and financial privileging of heterosexual and monogamous family structures by the state. The gay and lesbian rights movements that gained momentum in the 1960s and 70s has disrupted and challenged this discourse. Many authors have examined the social, historical, and political forces that worked together to construct the idea of the homosexual and then demonize it (Bem, 1993; Foucault, 1980; Jagose, 1996; Sears, 1998; Weeks, 1985).

Jagose (1996) explains that the concept of homosexuality and, subsequently, heterosexuality is just over a century old. Heterosexism, compulsory heterosexuality (Rich, 1978/1993), the heterosexual matrix (Butler, 1990), and gender polarization (Bem, 1993) are all different terms that seek to explain the discursive practices that present opposite-sex attraction and sexual behavior as the dominant and preferred social practices. The resulting prejudice against those who deviate from these social scripts has been carefully developed through the powerful institutional discourses of organized religion, medicine, sexology, psychiatry, and psychology (Bem, 1993, p. 81). These social discourses are generated through various social institutions, including schools. Educational structures wield extraordinary ideological power due to their role in teaching what the culture has deemed as important and valuable to future generations. Ministries of education, textbook publishers, and teachers determine what lessons are passed on to students and whose knowledge or "truth" is valued (Apple, 1990, 2000). Consequently, schools are important sites for contributing to the normalization of gendered and heterosexual behavior. These acts of surveillance are rooted in Foucault's (1975) concept of the Panopticon—an all-seeing, yet invisible source of power and control. This type of surveillance and control is particularly effective because we all unknowingly contribute to it unless we actively work to make it visible by questioning and challenging it. To expose and critique these acts is part of queer theory's task.

Through the surveillance and control of bodies and language, school structures mandate hyper-heterosexuality using the formal and hidden curriculum as well as extra-curricular activities. The heterosexuality of the curriculum is invisible to many, but some examples include: the exclusive study of heterosexual romantic literature; the presentation of the "nuclear" heterosexual, two-parent family as the ideal, teaching only the reproductive aspects of sexuality; and abstinence-only sex education (Britzman, 2000; Fisher, 2009; Meyer, 2010a; Pinar, 1998). Other forms of relationships and the concept of desire, or *eros,* are completely omitted from the official curriculum. Extra-curricular functions that teach this hyper-heterosexuality include Valentine's Day gift exchanges, kissing booths at school fairs, and proms. Queer youth and their allies have challenged the prom tradition in courts and the media, and this has resulted in schools increasingly granting permission to youth to attend prom in the clothing of their choice with the date of their choice (*Fricke* v. *Lynch,* 1980; *Hall* v. *Durham Catholic District School Board,* 2005; Meyer, 2010b).

Art Lipkin's (1999) book provides in-depth accounts of the discrimination experienced by gay, lesbian, and bisexual educators as well as the painful stories of students who were subject to gendered harassment. In other words, schools are not safe for "guys who aren't as masculine as other guys" or "girls who aren't as feminine as other girls" (California Safe Schools Coalition, 2004). Although the people in control of schools are not directly inflicting the harassment and harm on the non-conforming students (in most cases), their lack of effective intervention (California Safe Schools Coalition,

2004; Harris Interactive, 2001; Kosciw & Diaz, 2006; NMHA, 2002) sends the message that schools do not value, welcome, or even tolerate these borderland identities.

Heterosexism and its more overt partner, homophobia, are very clearly linked to cultural gender boundaries and are informed by misogyny. The most effective challenge to any boy's masculinity is to call him "gay," "homo," "fag," or "queer" (Epstein & Johnson, 1998; Mac an Ghaill, 1995; Martino & Pallotta-Chiarolli, 2003). These slurs challenge his masculinity—his gender code—via accusations of gayness, which is equated with being "feminine." Girls are also subject to similar kinds of policing (Brown, 2003; Duncan, 2004), but research shows that it is much more prevalent among male students (California Safe Schools Coalition, 2004; Harris Interactive, 2001). Continuing to live within prescribed linguistic and behavioral matrices leaves unchallenged the hierarchical binaries of male-female and gay-straight. This work of deconstructing socially invented categories is one strategy to help create educational spaces that are liberatory as opposed to limiting the diversity of human experiences. Understanding the work of liberatory educational theorists is essential to initiating educational practices that seek to transform oppressive educational spaces and create schools that offer a more inclusive and diverse sexuality curriculum.

Understanding Queer Pedagogy and Its Liberatory Effects

South American educator and activist Paulo Freire (1970/1993) is widely recognized for advancing the concepts of liberatory pedagogy and consciousness raising, or *conscientização*. He worked with oppressed groups to critically interrogate and transform social structures. Although some feminists have criticized Freire for his sexist language and assumptions, many thinkers have taken his ideas and built upon them to include anti-sexist and anti-racist work as a form of liberatory pedagogy. In education, feminist pedagogy has built on Freire's concepts to work toward more liberatory educational experiences for all students. However, many scholars of color, lesbian scholars, and Marxist theorists have also critiqued some feminist work as being narrowly centered in the realm of White, middle class, heterosexual privilege. While many poststructural feminists and critical theorists have worked to address these issues, queer theory has learned from this history. Although work in queer theory grew out of lesbian and gay studies, which many scholars critiqued as being dominated by work by and about gay White men, many queer theorists work to understand multiple intersecting layers of dominance and oppression. Liberatory pedagogy and queer pedagogy are thus mutually reinforcing philosophies that share a vision of education as the path to achieving a more equitable and just society.

In April 2004, the Lesbian and Gay Studies Special Interest Group (SIG) voted at the annual meeting of the American Educational Research Association to change its name to the Queer Studies SIG. This action marked an important shift in focus and demonstrates where work in the area of sexuality, gender, and sex education is headed. In her review of queer educational research, Janna Jackson (2001) recorded how the field of gay and lesbian studies has made a shift from studying an imagined, unified experience of being gay in schools to a more broad and open understanding of how categories of sex, gender, and sexuality are learned and experienced in schools.

Queer pedagogues have continued to build on the ideals of critical theory and feminism, but move them further into the realm of the postmodern. The use of "queer" as a more inclusive and empowering word for the gay and lesbian experience emerged in the early 1990s as a controversial and deeply political term (Jagose, 1996, p. 76). "Queer" is understood as a challenge to traditional understandings of sexual identity that deconstructs the categories, binaries, and language that supports them. Butler (1990), Sedgwick (1990/1993) and Anzaldúa (1987/2007) were influential scholars for this emerging school of thought. Jagose (1996) explains that queer theory's most influential achievement is to specify "how gender operates as a regulatory construct that privileges heterosexuality" (p. 83). What the concept of queer seeks to do is disrupt and challenge normalizing modes of thought and, by standing outside them, critically examine and dismantle them.

Kevin Kumashiro (2002) writes, "[L]earning is about disruption and opening up to further learning, not closure and satisfaction" (p. 43) and that "education involves learning something that disrupts our commonsense view of the world" (p. 63). Kumashiro's proposed approach to understanding the learning process is actively queer in that it seeks to question these patterns of normalization and promote creative and alternative ways of thinking in order to work against injustice and social oppression. Although marginalized groups employ new strategies to challenge dominant ideologies, these entrenched discourses push back. The dominant structures of society actively resist forces that try to change them.

Britzman (2000) presents a queer theoretical approach to understanding this opposition in outlining three forms of resistance to sexuality: structural, pedagogical, and psychical. She asserts the need to challenge all three forms of resistance. She specifically addresses how "the curriculum structures modes of behavior and orientations to knowledge that are repetitions of the underlying structure and dynamics of education: compliance, conformity, and the myth that knowledge cures" (p. 35). *Structural resistance* is especially resilient to change as it refers to the "very design or organization of education" (p. 34). In discussing how to challenge *pedagogical* forms of resistance, she encourages educators to recognize the power that *eros* can play in teaching. What this might mean for schools is to integrate discussions of sexuality throughout the curriculum—not just in sexual and health education classes. By integrating lessons relating to sexuality and relationships, students may develop a more complex and multifaceted understanding of sexuality beyond basic medicalized, sanitized, lessons on reproduction and sexually transmitted diseases. Lessons could discuss gender and sexuality in terms of romance, family structures, and other relationships across history and cultures in humanities courses as well as how sexuality is defined and understood through scientific and medical discourses in science classes. Finally, in addressing *psychical* forms of resistance, Britzman advocates working through internal conflicts and ambivalence toward sexuality in order to "raise rather serious questions on the nature of education and on the uses of educational anxiety" (p. 35). Such internal examinations would ask that teachers, administrators, and other educators engage in some active reflection about their own gender expressions and sexual identities, orientations, and behaviors. Such self-study would help make explicit the sources of anxiety and psychical resistance in the educational context in order to more effectively work through them.

This disruption and open discussion of previously taboo issues can be a very difficult one for teachers to navigate. A liberatory and queer pedagogy empowers educators to explore traditionally silenced discourses and create spaces for students to examine and challenge the hierarchy of binary identities that schools create and support such as: jock-nerd, sciences-arts, male-female, white-black, rich-poor, and gay-straight. In order to disrupt these discourses, teachers must learn to see schooling as a place to question, explore, and seek alternative explanations rather than a place where knowledge means "certainty, authority, and stability" (Britzman, 2000, p. 51).

Kumashiro (2002) offers four different approaches to challenge multiple forms of oppression in schools: "education for the Other, education about the Other, education that is critical of privileging and Othering, and education that changes students and society" (p. 23). He advocates most strongly for the application of the latter of these four approaches. In postmodern fashion, Kumashiro explicitly states that his is not a prescriptive program. He explains:

> I do not aim to offer strategies that work. Rather, I hope to offer conceptual and cultural resources for educators and researchers to use as we rethink our practices, constantly look for new insights, and engage differently in antioppressive education. . . . I encourage readers to think of reading this book as an event that constitutes the kind of antioppressive educational practices that I articulate throughout its discussion. It is queer in its unconventionality and it is activist in the changes it aims to bring about. (2002, pp. 25–26)

Through this explanation he is challenging us to find our own ways of creating useful knowledges and understandings of the world. He refuses the position of authority wherein his work will be read unquestioningly and used as a one-dimensional text. Instead he is pushing educators to find new methods to destabilize traditional ways of learning and offers different tools with which we can build that understanding. This is what a queer and liberatory pedagogy is about.

Conclusion

Historically, schools have filled an important cultural role in teaching children to learn what the people in power have deemed important. As a result, children emerge from schools having learned only the language, the history, and the perspectives of the dominant culture. The shifts toward critical pedagogy since the civil rights and feminist movements of the 1960s have begun to raise questions about this type of schooling in search of a way to create students and citizens who will be critical, engaged, independent thinkers. These paradigm shifts hope to move our educational system, and thus our society, in a more egalitarian direction. By better understanding how the forces of hegemony and discursive power work to shape sex, gender, and sexualities, educators will be more equipped to create classrooms that embody the ideals of a queer liberatory pedagogy.

Queer theory is just another step on the road initially paved by critical pedagogy, poststructural feminism, and theories of emancipatory education. In calling on educators to question and reformulate through a queer pedagogical lens (1) how they teach and reinforce gendered practices in schools, (2) how they support traditional notions of heterosexuality, and (3) how they present culturally specific information in the classroom, we will be able to reduce and eventually remove gendered harassment and other related forms of discrimination from schools and, consequently, most realms of society. Schools need to begin to challenge and disrupt traditional ways of knowing and encourage students to question and "trouble" that which is passively assumed and taken for granted in society. In short, institutions of learning must redefine themselves in order to move toward a truly liberatory and emancipatory learning experience.

By doing away with the docile, submissive, "banking" style of learning in schools, we can open up more educational possibilities and socially just experiences for future citizens rather than confine them within ideologies of traditional hegemonic, heteronormative, gender roles. To move in this direction, researchers, teachers, and other educators can benefit from using lenses offered by queer theory to creatively work through the current obstacles that prevent teachers from teaching passionately and inclusively and connecting with their students and communities in meaningful ways.

Note

1. This term is borrowed from William Pollack's (1999) work on boys and masculinities.

References

Aaron Fricke v. *Richard B. Lynch* (U.S. District Court for the District of Rhode Island 491 F. Supp. 381; 1980 U.S. Dist. LEXIS 11770 1980).

Anzaldúa, G. (2007). *Borderlands/La Frontera: The new mestiza.* San Francisco, CA: Aunt Lute Books. (Work originally published 1987)

Apple, M. (1990). *Ideology and the curriculum.* New York: Routledge.

Apple, M. (2000). *Official knowledge: Democratic education in a conservative age* (2nd ed.). New York: Routledge.

Bem, S. (1993). *The lenses of gender: Transforming the debate on sexual inequality.* New Haven, CT: Yale University Press.

Bochenek, M., & Brown, A. W. (2001). *Hatred in the hallways: Violence and discrimination against lesbian, gay, bisexual, and transgender students in U.S. schools.* New York: Human Rights Watch.

Britzman, D. (1995). Is there a queer pedagogy? Or, stop reading straight. *Educational Theory, 45*(2), 151–165.

Britzman, D. (2000). Precocious education. In S. Talburt & S. Steinberg (Eds.), *Thinking queer: Sexuality, culture, and education* (pp. 33–60). New York: Peter Lang.

Brown, L.M. (2003). *Girlfighting: Betrayal and rejection among girls.* New York: New York University Press.

Butler, J. (1990). *Gender trouble.* New York: Routledge Falmer.

California Safe Schools Coalition. (2004). *Consequences of harassment based on actual or perceived sexual orientation and gender non-conformity and steps for making schools safer.* Davis: University of California Press.

Chamberlain v. *Surrey School District No. 36* (4 SCR 710 2002).

Derrida, J. (1986a). Différance. In H. Adams & L. Searle (Eds.), *Critical theory since 1965* (pp. 120–136). Tallahassee: University Press of Florida.

Derrida, J. (1986b). Of grammatology. In H. Adams & L. Searle (Eds.), *Critical theory since 1965* (pp. 94–119). Tallahassee: University Press of Florida.

Duncan, N. (2004). It's important to be nice, but it's nicer to be important: Girls, popularity and sexual competition. *Sex Education, 4*(2), 137–152.

East High Gay/Straight Alliance v. *Board of Education of Salt Lake City School District* (81 F. Supp. 2d 1166, 1197 (D. Utah 1999) 1999).

Epstein, D., & Johnson, R. (1998). *Schooling sexualities.* Buckingham, UK: Open University Press.

Fisher, C.M. (2009). Queer youth experiences with abstinence-only-until-marriage sexuality education: "I can't get married so where does that leave me?" *Journal of LGBT Youth, 6*(1), 61–79.

Foucault, M. (1975). *Surveiller et punir: Naissance de la prison.* Paris: Gallimard.

Foucault, M. (1980). *The history of sexuality, volume I: An introduction.* New York: Random House.

Foucault, M. ([1969] 1986). The discourse on language. In H. Adams & L. Searle (Eds.), *Critical theory since 1965* (pp. 139–148). Tallahassee: University Press of Florida.

Foucault, M. ([1971] 1986). What is an author? In H. Adams & L. Searle (Eds.), *Critical theory since 1965* (pp. 148–162). Tallahassee: University Press of Florida.

Freire, P. (1993). *Pedagogy of the oppressed.* New York: Continuum. (Work originally published 1970)

Friend, R. (1993). Choices, not closets: Heterosexism and homophobia in schools. In L. Weis & M. Fine (Eds.), *Beyond silenced voices: Class, race, and gender in United States schools* (pp. 209–235). Albany: State University of New York Press.

Gramsci, A. (1995). *Further selections from the prison notebooks* (D. Boothman, Trans.). Minneapolis: University of Minnesota Press. (Work originally published 1971)

Hall v. *Durham Catholic District School Board* (ON S.C. 2005).

Harris Interactive. (2001). *Hostile hallways: Bullying, teasing, and sexual harassment in school.* Washington, DC: American Association of University Women Educational Foundation.

Jackson, J. (2001, April 10–14). Come out, come out, wherever you are: A synthesis of queer research in education. Paper presented at the American Educational Research Association Annual Meeting, Seattle, WA.

Jagose, A. (1996). *Queer theory: An introduction.* New York: New York University Press.

Kosciw, J., & Diaz, E. (2006). *The 2005 national school climate survey: The experiences of lesbian, gay, bisexual and transgender youth in our nation's schools.* New York: The Gay, Lesbian and Straight Education Network.

Kumashiro, K. (2002). *Troubling education: Queer activism and antioppressive pedagogy.* New York: Routledge Falmer.

Lacan, J. (1986). The agency of the letter in the unconscious or reason since Freud. In H. Adams & L. Searle (Eds.), *Critical theory since 1965* (pp. 738–756). Tallahassee: University Press of Florida. (Work originally published 1957)

Lipkin, A. (1999). *Understanding homosexuality, changing schools.* Boulder, CO: Westview Press.

Mac an Ghaill, M. (1995). *The making of men: Masculinities, sexualities, and schooling.* Philadelphia: Open University Press.

Martino, W., & Pallotta-Chiarolli, M. (2003). *So what's a boy? Addressing issues of masculinity and schooling.* Buckingham, UK: Open University Press.

McLaren, P. (1998). *Life in schools: An introduction to critical pedagogy in the foundations of education.* New York: Longman.

Meyer, E. J. (2006). Gendered harassment in North America: School-based interventions for reducing homophobia and heterosexism. In C. Mitchell & F. Leach (Eds.), *Combating Gender Violence in and around Schools* (pp. 43–50). Stoke on Trent, UK: Trentham Books.

Meyer, E. J. (2008). Gendered harassment in secondary schools: Understanding teachers' (non)interventions. *Gender & Education, 20*(6), 555–572.

Meyer, E.J. (2010a). *Gender and sexual diversity in schools.* New York: Springer.

Meyer, E.J. (2010b). Gender, class, & proms: High school rites of exclusion [Electronic Version]. *Psychology Today.* Retrieved June 2, 2010 from http://www.psychologytoday.com/blog/gender-and-schooling/201003/gender-class-proms-high-school-rites-exclusion.

Nabozny v. *Podlesny,* 92 F. 3d 446 (7th Cir. 1996).

NMHA. (2002). *"What does gay mean?" Teen survey executive summary.* National Mental Health Association.

Pinar, W.F. (Ed.). (1998). *Queer theory in education.* Mahwah, NJ: Lawrence Erlbaum Associates.

Reis, B. (1999). *They don't even know me: Understanding anti-gay harassment and violence in schools.* Seattle: Safe Schools Coalition of Washington.

Reis, B., & Saewyc, E. (1999). *83,000 youth: Selected findings of eight population-based studies.* Seattle: Safe Schools Coalition of Washington.

Rich, A. (1993). Compulsory heterosexuality and lesbian existence. In H. Abelove, D. Halperin, & M.A. Barale (Eds.), *The lesbian and gay studies reader* (pp. 227–254). New York: Routledge. (Original work published 1978)

School District No. 44 (North Vancouver) v. *Jubran,* 2005 BCCA 201 (BCSC 6 2005).

Sears, J.T. (1998). A generational and theoretical analysis of culture and male (homo)sexuality. In W.F. Pinar (Ed.), *Queer theory in education* (pp. 73–105). Mahwah, NJ: Lawrence Erlbaum and Associates.

Sedgwick, E.K. (1993). Epistemology of the closet. In H. Abelove, M.A. Barale, & D.M. Halperin (Eds.), *The lesbian and gay studies reader* (pp. 45–61). New York: Routledge. (Original work published 1990)

Vriend v. *Alberta* (1 S.C.R. 493 1998).

Weeks, J. (1985). *Sexuality and its discontents.* New York: Routledge.

Weiler, K. (2001). Rereading Paulo Freire. In K. Weiler (Ed.), *Feminist engagements: Reading, resisting, and revisioning male theorists in education and cultural studies* (pp. 67–87). New York: Routledge.

West, C., & Zimmerman, D.H. (1987). Doing gender. *Gender and Society, 1*(2), 125–151.

CHAPTER TWO

Sweatshop-Produced Rainbow Flags and Participatory Patriarchy

Why the Gay Rights Movement Is a Sham

Mᴀᴛᴛɪʟᴅᴀ Bᴇʀɴsᴛᴇɪɴ Sʏᴄᴀᴍᴏʀᴇ

The Assimilation Success Story

As legends go, San Francisco is the place for sexual debauchery, gender transgression, and political deviance (not to mention sexual deviance, gender debauchery, and political transgression). The reality is that while San Francisco still shelters outsider queer cultures unimaginable in most other cities, these cultures of resistance have been ravaged by AIDS, drug addiction, and gentrification. Direct on-the-street violence by rampaging straights remains rare in comparison to other queer-destination cities like New York, Chicago, or New Orleans, but a newer threat has emerged. San Francisco, more than any other U.S. city, is the place where a privileged gay (and lesbian) elite has actually succeeded at its goal of becoming part of the power structure. Unfortunately (but not surprisingly), members of the gaysbian elite use their newfound influence to oppress less privileged queers in order to secure their status within the status quo. This pattern occurs nationwide, but San Francisco is the place where the violence of this assimilation is most palpable.

I first moved to San Francisco in 1992, just before my 19th birthday, and was completely terrified by the conformity, hyper-masculinity, and blind consumerism of the legendary gay Castro district. I quickly figured out that this could never be my "community" and always assumed that it wasn't anyone else's, either. Then one day, just recently, I was walking through the Castro with a friend of mine, whose social group includes a number of gay white men in their fifties, and everywhere guys were smiling at him and reaching out with great big hugs. I realized, then, that the Castro was *somebody's* community, and this was, for a moment, a revelation.

What is sad about the Castro (and similar gay neighborhoods across the country and around the world), and indicative of what gay people do with even a little bit of power, is that these same smiling gay men have failed to build community for queers (or anyone) outside their social groups. Many gay men (even in the Castro) still remain on the fringes, either by choice or lack of opportunity. But as the most "successful" gays (and their allies) have moved from outsider status to insider clout, they have consistently fought misogynist, racist, classist, ageist battles to ensure that their neighborhoods remain communities only for the rich, male, and white (or at least those who assimilate into white middle-class norms). They've succeeded in clamping down on the anger, defiance, flamboyance, and subversion once thriving in queer subcultures, in order to promote a vapid, consume-or-die, only-whites-need-apply version of gay identity. *Homo* now stands more for homogenous than any type of sexuality aside from *buy buy buy.*

In 1992, there were still a few slightly interesting things about the Castro: a gay bookstore with current queer 'zines, and freaks and drag queens on staff; a used bookstore with a large selection of gay books; a cafe with live cabaret shows; a 24-hour donut shop with a rotating cast of tweakers; a tiny chocolate shop filled with delicate creations; a dyke bar; and a cruising park where faggots actually fucked. These meager (and mostly fag-specific) resources have disappeared, as rents have sky-rocketed and corporate chains have replaced local businesses. A glittering Diesel clothing store now dominates Harvey Milk Plaza, the symbolic heart of the Castro, and the historic Castro Theater shows *Eating Out,* a movie about a straight guy pretending to be gay in order to get the girl with the gay friends. (The tagline reads: "The fastest way to a girl's heart is through her best friend.")

Gay bar owners routinely call for the arrest of homeless people, many of them queer youth, for getting in the way of happy hour. Zephyr Realty, a gay-owned real estate company, advises its clients on how best to evict long-term tenants, many of them seniors, people with HIV/AIDS, and disabled people. Gay political consultants mastermind the election of anti-poor, pro-development candidates over and over and over.

In 1998, wealthy gay Castro residents (don't forget lesbians and straight people!) fought against a queer youth shelter because they feared it would get in the way of "community property values." They warned that a queer youth shelter would bring prostitution and drug-dealing to the neighbor-hood. For a moment, let's leave aside the absurdity of a wealthy gay neighborhood, obviously already a prime destination for prostitutes of a certain gender and drug dealing of only the best substances, worrying about the wrong kind of prostitutes (the ones in the street!), and the wrong kind of drug dealers (the ones who don't drive Mercedes!) arriving in their whitewashed gayborhood.

One sign of the power of San Francisco's gay elite is that any successful mayoral candidate must pander to the "gay vote," so it was no surprise when, in February 2003, Gavin Newsom, a straight, ruling-class, city council member representing San Francisco's wealthiest district, hosted a lavish, $120-a-plate fundraiser for the new $18 million LGBT Center. At that point, Newsom was most famous for a ballot measure called "Care Not Cash," which took away homeless people's welfare checks and replaced them with "care." Gay Shame, a radical queer activist group, gathered to protest Newsom's agenda of criminalizing homeless people in order to get ahead at the polls, as well as to call attention to the hypocrisy of the Center for welcoming Newsom's access to cash instead of tak-ing a stand against his blatantly racist and classist politics. Whose Center was this, we asked? Was it a center for marginalized queers, queers of color, homeless queers, trans queers, queer youth, older queers, disabled queers, queer artists, queer activists, queer radicals . . . or a Center for straight politi-cians to hold dinner parties?

Our questions were answered when police officers, called by the Center, began to bash us as soon as they escorted Newsom inside. One officer hit a Gay Shame demonstrator in the face with his baton, shattering one of her teeth and bloodying her entire face. Several of us were thrown face-first into oncoming traffic; one protester was put into a chokehold until he passed out. As four of us were dragged off in handcuffs for protesting outside "our" Center, Center staff stood—and watched—and did nothing to intervene. Neither Newsom nor the Center has ever made a statement condemning the police violence of February 2003. In fact, one year later, newly elected Mayor Gavin Newsom rewarded the powerful gays who stood on the Center balcony and watched queers get bashed. Newsom grabbed national headlines and solidified his San Francisco support base by "legalizing" gay marriage, and throngs of gay people from across the country descended upon City Hall at all hours of the day and night, camping out, sharing snacks and wine, and toasting Gavin Newsom as the vanguard leader of gay civil rights.

I Think We're Alone Now.... Citizenship, Gay Marriage, and the Christian Right

In the fall of 2004, Marriage Equality, a brand new brand of "nonprofit," held two amazing benefits in New York City and Washington, D.C. Called "Wedrock," these star-studded events featured numerous celebrities, major-label activist rockers from Moby to Sleater-Kinney, Bob Mould to Le Tigre. Just to get people all excited about marriage equality, the promotional email for the events concluded by stating, "Get angry, protect your citizenship."

If gay marriage is about protecting citizenship, whose citizenship is being protected? Most people in this country—especially those not born rich, white, straight, and male—are not full citizens. The not-so-subtle demand to "protect your citizenship" evokes images of George W. Bush's screeds against "enemies of freedom." Gay assimilationists want to make sure they're on the winning side in the citizenship wars, and see no need to confront the legacies of systemic and systematic U.S. oppression that prevent most people living in this country (and everywhere else) from exercising their supposed "rights." This willful participation in U.S. imperialism is part of the larger goal of assimilation, as the holy trinity of marriage, military service, and adoption (and don't forget ordination into the priesthood!) has become the central preoccupation of a gay movement centered more on obtaining straight privilege than challenging power.

Gay assimilationists have created the ultimate genetically modified organism, combining virulent strains of nationalism, patriotism, consumerism, and patriarchy and delivering them in one deadly product: state-sanctioned matrimony. Gay marriage proponents are anxious to discard those tacky hues of lavender and pink, in favor of the good ol' stars and stripes, literally draping themselves in Old Glory at every pro-marriage demonstration as the United States occupies Iraq, overthrows the only democratically elected government in the history of Haiti, funds the Israeli war on the Palestinians, and makes the whole world safe . . . for multinational corporations to plunder indigenous resources.

A gay elite has hijacked queer struggle and positioned their desires as everyone's needs—the dominant signs of straight conformity have become the ultimate signs of gay success. Sure, for white gays with beach condos, country club memberships, and nice stock portfolios with a couple hedge funds that need trimming every now and then (think of Rosie O'Donnell or David Geffen), marriage might just be the last thing standing in the way of full citizenship, but what about for everyone else?

Even when the "gay rights" agenda does include issues that matter to a wider range of queers, it does it in a way that consistently prioritizes the most privileged while fucking over everyone else. I'm using the term "gay rights" instead of the more popular term of the moment, "LGBT rights," because

"LGBT" usually means gay, with lesbian in parentheses, throw out the bisexuals, and put trans on for a little window dressing. A gay rights agenda fights for an end to discrimination in housing and employment but not for the *provision* of housing or jobs, domestic partner health coverage but not universal health coverage. Or, more recently, hospital visitation and inheritance rights for married couples, but not for anyone else. Even with the most obviously "gay" issue, that of anti-queer violence, a gay rights agenda fights for tougher hate crimes legislation, instead of fighting the racism, classism, transphobia (and homophobia) intrinsic to the criminal "justice" system. Kill those criminals twice, this logic goes, and then there won't be any more violence.

The violence of assimilation lies in the ways the borders are policed. For decades, there has been a tension within queer politics and cultures, between assimilationists and liberationists, conservatives and radicals. Never before, however, has the assimilationist/conservative side held such a stranglehold over popular representations of what it means to be queer. Gay marriage proponents are anxious to discard generations of queer efforts to create new ways of loving, lusting for, and caring for one another in favor of a 1950s model of white-picket-fence, "we're-just-like-you" normalcy.

The ultimate irony of gay liberation is that it has made it possible for straight people to create more fluid gender, sexual, and social identities, while mainstream gay people salivate over state-sanctioned Tiffany wedding bands and participatory patriarchy. Many straight people know that marriage is outdated, tacky, and oppressive—and any queer who grew up in or around marriage should remember this well. Marriage still exists as a central site of anti-woman, anti-child, and anti-queer violence and a key institution through which the wealth and property of upper-class (white) families is preserved. If gay marriage proponents wanted real progress, they'd be fighting for the end of marriage (duh) and universal access to the services that marriage can sometimes help procure: housing, healthcare, citizenship, tax breaks, and inheritance rights.

Instead, gay marriage proponents claim that access to marriage will "solve" fundamental problems of inequality. This is not surprising, given that the gay marriage movement is run by groups like the Human Rights Campaign and the Log Cabin Republicans, who have more in common with the National Rifle Association than any sort of left agenda, queer or otherwise. These are the same gays who routinely instigate police violence against people of color, homeless people, transgender people, sex workers, and other marginalized queers in their never-ending quest to "clean up" the neighborhoods they've gentrified. Their agenda is cultural erasure, and they want the full Monty.

For a long time, queers have married straight friends for citizenship or healthcare—but this has never been enshrined as "progress." The majority of queers—single or coupled (but not desiring marriage), monogamous or polyamorous, jobless or marginally employed—would remain excluded from the much-touted benefits of legalized gay marriage. Furthermore, in order to access any marriage benefits, those not entirely "male" or "female" would need to accept gender tyranny. As gay marriage continues to dominate the mainstream gay agenda, resources are directed away from HIV prevention, AIDS services, drug treatment, domestic violence services, and other programs desperately needed by less privileged queers—millions of dollars are being poured into the marriage coffin. The fight between pro-marriage and anti-marriage queers is not a disagreement between two segments of a "community" but a fight over the fundamental goals of queer struggle.

Gay marriage proponents are anxious to further the media myth that there are only two sides to the gay marriage/assimilation debate: foaming-at-the mouth Christian fundamentalists who think gay marriage marks the death of Western civilization, and rabid gay assimilationists who act as if gay marriage is the best thing since *Will and Grace*. It is no coincidence that queers who oppose gay marriage are shut out of the picture, since it's much easier for a gay marriage proponent to win an argument with a crazed homophobe than with an anti-marriage queer. And every time some well-meaning straight leftist thinks they're being open minded by taking the gay marriage side, they need to go back to Feminism 101.

Of course, Christian fundamentalists make no distinction between diesel dykes and Diesel jeans, or, to be more direct—they think all queers are gonna burn in hell, Tiffany or no Tiffany (as in, "I think we're alone now . . ."). Every time gay marriage proponents patiently explain to Fundamentalists, "One, two—we're just like you—three, four—we bash queers more!," the Christian Right gains authority. But this false polarization serves gay assimilationists as well by silencing queers who threaten the power that lies behind their sweatshop-produced nylon rainbow flags.

When gay assimilationists cheerfully affirm, over and over again, to lunatics who want them dead, that of course gay identity is not a choice, because who would choose it, they unwittingly expose the tyranny of simplistic identity politics. Not only have the dominant signs of straight conformity become the central goals of the gay assimilationist movement, but assimilationists see a threat to Christian fundamentalist security as a threat to "progress." Forget about choosing our gender, sexual, or social identities; forget about building community or family outside of traditional norms; forget about dismantling dominant systems of oppression—let's just convince the Christian right to accept us on their own terms.

Movement Rights, Civil Community

On January 13, 2005, 22 national LGBT rights organizations (including all the above, and more!) issued a joint statement with the leaden title, "Civil Rights. Community. Movement." Unsurprisingly, this document is filled with empty rhetoric such as, "We, literally, are everywhere," and "Stand up. Spread the word. Share your story." It even quotes gay rights pioneer President George W. Bush from an interview in *People*, where he agrees, in spite of his support for a constitutional amendment banning gay marriage, that a couple joined by a civil union is as much of a family as he and Barbara.

"Civil Rights. Community. Movement." opens by defining "civil rights" as "The rights belonging to an individual *by virtue of citizenship* [italics added]." Here we can already glimpse the exclusionary agenda of the gay rights movement. Instead of calling for universal access to benefits generally procured through citizenship (such as the right to remain in this country), this document seeks to secure a gay place at the red-white-and-blue table of normalcy, on the fashionable side of the barbed wire.

This opening paragraph also attributes the successes of civil rights movements to "the complex interweaving of legal victories, political progress and advances in public opinion." Even a mainstream liberal would agree that many "civil rights" victories came about in large part through mass protests and extensive civil (and uncivil) disobedience campaigns. But the LGBT movement prefers empty terms like "political progress" and "advances in public opinion" to any recognition of direct action struggles. You don't want to frighten the funders!

The document continues by talking about challenging the family values rhetoric of "a small but powerful group of anti-gay extremists" by "[opening] America's eyes to the true family values that LGBT couples, parents, and families are living and demonstrating every day." This is where "LGBT rights" becomes most sinister. In allegedly attempting to challenge the "radical right" (they're not Christians anymore, but worse—radicals!) this document still insists on defining "family values" along heteronormative lines, rolling back decades of queer struggle to create chosen families that do more than just mimic the twisted ones assigned to us at birth.

When the report notes that "Binational LGBT couples and families can be cruelly torn apart by deportation and immigration laws that treat them as legal strangers," we are led to believe that marriage is the only solution to this citizenship dilemma. No mention is made of non-coupled queers who are deported while seeking asylum, of systemic racial profiling in citizenship decisions, or of routine murders of undocumented immigrants on U.S. borders. Instead, the document states, "We must fight for family laws that give our children strong legal ties to their parents." One must infer that this pertains to the cases of lesbian (and gay) parents who lose custody of their children due to homophobic courts, although this is not mentioned. While a shortsighted focus on parental control should be no surprise when coming from a "movement" centered around marriage, it is particularly striking given the extremely high rates of suicide, drug addiction, and homelessness among queer youth, especially those escaping scary families of origin. What about family laws that allow children to get away from abusive parents? What about providing support systems for queer youth, who have extremely high rates of suicide, drug addiction, and homelessness?

The organizations behind this document prefer to talk about the "true family values" of straight-acting gays than to resist the tyranny of assimilationist norms. Apparently, "true family values" call for more inclusive hate crimes legislation but no challenge to the prison industrial complex. "True family values" call for overturning the military's "anti-LGBT" ban instead of confronting U.S. imperialism. "True family values" require all of us to "invest" in the movement, "invest in our future." That's right—send in your check NOW, before you get priced out.

CHAPTER THREE

Differences and Divisions

Social Inequality in Sex Education Debates and Policies

JESSICA FIELDS

In 1997, newspaper readers throughout North Carolina learned that the Franklin County School Board had decided to slice three chapters from its ninth-grade sex education textbook. The book included references to "partners" instead of "spouses" and encouraged young people to postpone sexual activity until they were ready, not until they were married.

Franklin County's decision to censor its textbooks came out of its local debate of "Teach Abstinence until Marriage." In 1995, North Carolina's state legislature enacted House Bill 834, requiring schools to teach students "the risks of premarital sexual intercourse" (1995). Teach Abstinence until Marriage required that school-based instruction focus on "medically accurate" information about sexual danger and risk, including risks of pregnancy, contraceptive failure rates, and the risks of HIV and other STDs. Public schools were also to provide sex education that emphasized "the positive benefits of abstaining from sex outside of marriage and the risks of premarital sex." In the final version of House Bill 834, the legislation's liberal opponents managed to include a stipulation that permitted local districts to teach students about, for example, contraception or abortion if they adopted such learning objectives after first debating them in public school board meetings. The stipulation outlined a particular process: if local education agencies wanted to veer from the required abstinence-only education, as described in state legislation, they had to hold a formal period of community review in which they invited parents to examine proposed materials and curricular objectives. After this public review, school boards would convene for public comment and then vote on their local sex education curriculum. No matter what revisions they made, the abstinence-only message had to remain at the core of their instruction.

In this chapter, I explore varying responses to Teach Abstinence until Marriage in three North Carolina middle schools—two public and one private school in Dogwood and Southern Counties.[1] Sex education routinely focuses on middle school students, reflecting conventional ideas about early adolescence as a time of profound physical, social, and other sexual changes. Teach Abstinence until Marriage required the most substantial changes for the middle school grades, where intensive sex education began in North Carolina's public education.

Dogwood Middle School: Averted Controversy and Unexpected Complications

Dogwood County's sex education debate was swift, primarily because of the efforts of Betty Huffington, an African American woman in her 40s who was Dogwood's health education coordinator. After Teach Abstinence until Marriage went into effect, Huffington met with the Dogwood school board to discuss her plan for implementing the law. Her liberal interpretation of the new requirements required her and her teachers to make few changes to the curriculum. Huffington asserted that the only change required of her and the classroom health educators was to add "until marriage" to their lessons about sexual abstinence.

However, as Huffington described, "Things went fine until we started to talk about who would be involved in classes—whether we were going to have same-sex classes or co-ed classes." Board members believed that the potential for embarrassment was intolerably high for middle school students and that coeducational classes would compromise students'—girls' in particular—comfort in asking questions and seeking information that they needed. In addition, though the girls and boys would be separated for all class meetings, particular classes would have to be entirely single-sex, with a woman teaching the girls and a man teaching the boys. For classes on topics that required explicit discussion of body parts and functions—for example, puberty, abstinence, pregnancy, and STD prevention—the board required that Mrs. Wilkie, the school's trained health educator, turn the boys' classrooms over to Coach Leon Banks, a Dogwood Middle School gym teacher with no formal training as a sex educator.

In Dogwood County, Teach Abstinence until Marriage had limited, if unexpected, consequences for public school sex education. With an understanding of the abstinence-only requirements and of current sex education offerings and with an absence of community constituents organized in opposition to or support of abstinence-only education, the administrator proceeded with little interference from others. Board members' concerns about protecting girls raised an unexpected obstacle to sex education proceeding in Dogwood County; the school board opted for single-sex education and overrode teachers' objections, pedagogical concerns, and students' inconsistent reactions. Single-sex instruction denied boys and girls opportunities to explore important and challenging issues that they might face together, including dating, relationships, rape, sexual harassment, pregnancy, and disease prevention. Governing sex education were conventional adult assumptions about girl-boy relationships and the embarrassment attached to female sexuality, not a commitment to challenging those conventions and the limits they introduce in young people's lives.

Fox Academy: Articulated Alternatives

As a private school, Fox Academy was not accountable to Teach Abstinence until Marriage. The school thus provides a glimpse of an alternative: one form that school-based sex education might assume if not bound by abstinence-only requirements. For an annual tuition of about $10,000, Fox Academy provides an alternative to the prescriptive educations available at local public Dogwood and Southern County schools. Sex education is only one of the many offerings that sets Fox apart. The school emphasizes collaborative relationships between students and teachers and invites students to call their instructors by their first names. Fox's curriculum also encourages students to make choices about their own lives and rejects conventional fear-based lessons about drug use and sex.

There was no debate over middle school sex education at Fox Academy during my time there. The course was an established part of the school's Personal Growth curriculum, and the sex education teacher had the trust and support of her colleagues as she designed classes on puberty, gender roles, media messages, sexual health, and pregnancy. Adults' discussions about sexuality and education at Fox primarily focused on two lesbian, gay, and bisexual (LGB) issues: How do we best support LGB faculty and families? How do we train Fox teachers to challenge homophobia and promote LGB acceptance on campus?

A crowning achievement of Fox's LGB-concerns committee's work was bringing to campus the traveling exhibit "Love Makes a Family," which presents photographs and narratives of families that include lesbian, gay, bisexual, and transgendered members. The LGB committee organized an opening reception and issued press releases to local newspapers and radio programs. A high school teacher explained that Fox would not be inviting others because this was designed as a community event for Fox students, faculty, staff, and families. The press releases were simply to inform others about events at the private school.

I thought about students, teachers, and families who taught and learned down the road in Dogwood and Southern County public schools, people whom Fox teachers excluded from the exhibit and the opportunities it represented. I had never heard discussions at the public schools like those I witnessed at Fox: no teacher talked to me about the importance of advocating for LGB students, parents, or colleagues, and I heard no stories of LGB teachers calling on their peers to provide them with material and emotional support. Dogwood and Southern public schools were full of talk of sex and sexuality, but that talk focused on preventing harassment, pregnancy, disease, and sexual activity altogether. I wondered what it meant for Fox to jealously guard—but still boast about—its actively antihomophobic agenda. I also wondered what happened at the end of the day when Fox students went home to Southern and Dogwood Counties. Would their strikingly different sex educations only affirm existing socioeconomic divides and inequalities? If their paths ever crossed, would these young people be equipped to interact respectfully with one another?

"Children Having Children": The Southern County Sex Education Debates

As Fox teachers addressed homophobia and other LGB issues, the neighboring Southern County's public school system engaged in more than a year's worth of deliberation and community meetings. For fourteen months, advocates of abstinence-only and comprehensive sex education addressed administrators and the county's seven school board members—two African American women, one African American man, three white women, and one white man. Parents, liberals, conservative Christians, African American community leaders, lesbian, gay, bisexual, transgendered, and queer (LGBTQ) activists, clinic workers, and educators lobbied board members and organized letter-writing campaigns.

Midway into the first year under Teach Abstinence until Marriage, the school board had still not come to a decision, so the members appointed a citizen advisory committee to review and recommend sex education learning objectives and curricula. When the school board and system superintendent called for a recommendation from the committee, the conservative white women promoting abstinence-only education constituted only half the committee, but they voted as a bloc. Based on this vote, the committee recommended the purchase of *Sex Respect* (Mast, 1997) and material from Teen Aid, two abstinence-only curricula that are favorites of abstinence-only advocates across the

United States. Researchers and comprehensive sex education proponents have criticized the curricula for their stereotypical depictions of women, girls, and people of color (Trudell & Whatley, 1991; Whatley & Trudell, 1993).

After the committee voted to recommend Sex Respect and Teen Aid, Southern County's comprehensive sex education advocates—a multiracial group, also primarily women—appealed directly to school board members and the school superintendent. Community health educators insisted that school board members and the superintendent look closely at a text that promoted exclusively heterosexual families, featured images of infected and diseased genitalia, and included photographs that overwhelmingly pictured white girls and boys. Their tactics worked. The Southern County school board rejected the recommendation of the citizen advisory committee and adopted a comprehensive curriculum in a five-to-two vote, with the women voting for comprehensive sex education and the men voting against it. In interviews with me, the women members argued that they felt they had to be realistic about the possibility that girls were sexually active and might get pregnant. The men could not bring themselves to imagine—let alone condone—girls becoming sexually active.

The Seductive Rhetoric of Childhood Sexual Innocence

In Southern County, arguments for comprehensive and abstinence-only sex education rested on a shared notion of childhood sexual innocence—a notion imbued with racial, class, and gender stereotypes that rely on and reinforce social inequalities. In sex education debates, the universalizing language of "children having children" obscures social inequalities. Such obfuscation reinforces the very hiddenness that strengthens social inequalities and encourages individualistic explanations of pregnancies and poor adolescent sexual health among young women and girls (Apple, 1999; Bonilla-Silva, 2002). Racism, classism, and sexism are entrenched in part because many of us do not recognize these issues. Recognition of these social divisions and inequalities is crucial to problematizing ideological notions of children as sexually innocent or "at risk." People occupying both positions in the Southern County debate drew on the same discursive repertoire in their accounts of young people's need for sex education.

Despite what universalizing rhetoric might suggest, poor and African American women's and girls' sexuality is central to contemporary debates over the companion issues of abstinence-only sex education. In particular, this centrality reflects a history of controlling myths about African American women's excessive and corrupted sexuality—a history that dates in the United States to the enslavement of black women and men (Collins, 2000; Roberts, 2002; Rose, 2003). Since the 1960s welfare backlash, U.S. conservatives have posited African American mothers as benefiting unduly from government assistance (Levenstein, 2000).

Politically liberal advocates have responded to this conservative rhetoric with racialized notions of their own. With slogans like "children having children" and "babies having babies," many strive to evoke compassion for the mostly low-income, African American, city-dwelling girls who populate dominant images of young women's and girls' pregnancies (Luker, 1996; Nathanson, 1993; Pearce, 1993). This rhetorical strategy claims for poor and African American girls a childhood innocence that has long been the purview of economically privileged, white, suburban girls and boys and that offers limiting conceptions of young people's sexuality. In using this language, advocates of comprehensive and abstinence-only sex education rewrite—and do not rewrite—conventional notions of race, sexuality, and innocence.

Race in Southern County was largely dichotomous: 60 percent of Southern County's residents were white, 37 percent African American, and less than one percent either Asian or Latino/Latina. Six in ten people under 18 years of age were youth of color, and half of those were African American; the pregnancy rate among teens from racial and ethnic minorities was almost twice that among white teens, and 42 percent of the county's youth were enrolled in free or subsidized school lunch programs. Southern County also had a significant number of youth living in poverty. In such a context, ostensibly neutral language about promiscuity, inescapable fates, and the allocation of resources served racialized, classed, and gendered ends.

20–60–20: The Argument for Abstinence-Only Education

For many, school-based sex education is a response to the problem of young people engaging in corrupting and damaging sexual activity (Moran, 2000). Many believe that, without the intervention of sex education, adolescent sexual activity leads to teen pregnancies, children born to ill-prepared teen mothers, and life-threatening STDs, including HIV. This belief presented Southern County's markedly white, middle-class coalition of abstinence-only advocates with a challenge: they had to refute charges that their plan would deny African American and low-income young people information that would likely save lives, and they had to establish that they knew what was best for Southern County's student population.

Throughout the Teach Abstinence until Marriage debate, Southern County community members employed coded imagery that rested on the "subtle, systemic forms of racism" (Neubeck & Cazenave, 2001, p. 6) informing this and other 1990s debates about reproductive health policies in the United States. Abstinence-only advocates focused largely on protecting innocents from the life-threatening influences of those who are sexually active and socially deviant. "Deviant" is ostensibly race-neutral; however, it is also a category that U.S. sexuality educators have too often constructed as comprising African American mothers and poor and low-income people (Booth, 2000; Roberts, 1997; Rose, 2003; Watney, 1987).

According to Wilson (an architect of Teach Abstinence until Marriage) and her allies, teachers' suggestions that condom use rendered sexual activity safe might help the 10 to 20 percent who would inevitably become sexually active. Wilson was also confident that these lessons would not corrupt the 10 to 20 percent of students who were essentially high achieving and whose sexual purity was inviolate. However, she and others advocating abstinence-only instruction claimed that the same messages compromised the health of the 60 to 80 percent of young people who had a chance of falling into either camp: high risk or high achieving, sexually abstinent or sexually promiscuous. While other courses might have future relevance, sex education's impact was immediate: according to abstinence-only advocates, lessons about safer sex would compel students to immediately become sexually active. Thus schools should not adopt a sex education curriculum that sacrificed the well-being—that is, virginity—of the vast majority of students to that of a minority of students who were essentially already a lost cause.

With their 20–60–20 picture of the world, Southern County proponents of abstinence-only education built on a stock of racialized, classed, and gendered assumptions and relied on the tried-and-true strategy of offering numbers as "factual, little nuggets of truth" (Best, 2000; Best, 2001, p. 19). Apparently neutral statistics about young people's propensities for risk taking rendered palatable depictions of the world as composed of girls-who-do and girls-who-don't, good boys and bad boys, students we can save, and those who are unsalvageable. The apparent objectivity of 20–60–20 mystified the moral judgments and racialized and gendered ideology behind these numbers. It also made the educators' decision to protect "the innocent" (and to neglect "the guilty") into a rational, nondiscriminatory calculation.

Innocents at Risk: The Argument for Comprehensive Sex Education

Wearing pins that read "No More Children Having Children" and urging school board members to act in the interest of "at-risk" children, the multiracial coalition of comprehensive advocates rejected curricular approaches that rested on a 20–60–20 picture of Southern's students. They argued instead that, as a gesture of care, the county needed to adopt a comprehensive curriculum that interrupted crises of teen pregnancies and STDs. For these community members, young people's sexual innocence was not a privilege of childhood that warranted preserving; instead, innocence was a state that left children vulnerable to harm. In community meetings, comprehensive advocates routinely reminded the school board that sexual activity often carried steep prices for the "Southern County's at-risk youth."

While abstinence-only advocates spoke of a 20–60–20 divide among students, comprehensive advocates insisted in school board meetings that, for example, "*all* children should be educated," and called on the school board to adopt a curriculum that "reflects the diversity of our students." Consistently, African American and white educators and advocates publicly called for a curriculum that served the needs of all of Southern County's public school students—students whom comprehensive proponents embraced as "ours." In interviews, however, their inclusive visions grew more particular: comprehensive advocates expressed specific concern for struggling African American girls. Like the white, abstinence-only advocates, the multiracial coalition of comprehensive sex education proponents used the language of "children having children." These references to vulnerable youth in Southern County served different ends in this more liberal camp by allowing educators and advocates to speak publicly of their private concerns for African American and low-income girls without claiming those concerns.

Educators' adultifying responses to African American boys' misbehavior deny the boys the protective mantle that childhood offers their white peers. Similarly, mainstream discourse and institutions consistently deny African American girls both the troubled privilege of idealized childhood innocence and the transitional moment of adolescence (Ferguson, 2001; Roberts, 1997). In the late 20th century, unwed white mothers became increasingly common and even accepted; their pregnancies were missteps from which they could recover with the assistance of trusted adults and proper care services. Social rhetoric, however, cast unmarried African American mothers as manifestations of an inherently corrupt sexuality (Kunzel, 1994; Solinger, 2000). As Dorothy Roberts (2002) has argued, many continue to consider African American mothers "inherently unfit and even affirmatively harmful to their children" (p. 179). Too often, contemporary policies governing social programs build on these racialized and gendered understandings to link teenage sexual activity, unwed motherhood, shifting family structures, weakening gender and sexual norms, and welfare dependence (Levenstein, 2000; Mink, 1998; Roberts, 1997). Disenfranchised African American communities find themselves blamed for the very conditions against which they struggle. Like other debates about sexuality and youth sexuality in particular, Southern County's was about more than whether and how young people could engage in sexual behavior safely; this debate was a field on which to struggle over larger politics, anxieties, and moralities.

Ironically, as comprehensive advocates claimed innocence for Southern County youth, they implicitly, if unwittingly, confirmed the guilt of African American and low-income youth and adults. "At-risk" may be analytically specific in epidemiological and other social research, and educators and advocates may speak of "children having children" entirely because of concern for young people. However, the terms have come to function without specific content, relying on ideological codes (Smith, 1999) regarding race, class, sexuality, and innocence and heavy with connotations in lay discussions. "At-risk," for example, assumes "enormous power to identify, explain, and predict futures" for young people in disadvantaged urban schools and neighborhoods (Ferguson, 2001, p. 91; Males, 1999). Similarly, the coded language of "children having children" allows liberals to "talk about African Americans and poor women . . . without mentioning race, gender, or class" (Luker, 1996, p. 86; Males, 1999). Indeed, Southern County comprehensive advocates did not address race or class directly. Their comments were, most often, race and class neutral. However, in Southern County, pregnancy, poverty, and failing public schools were racialized and classed social issues.

Ultimately, this multiracial coalition built its argument for comprehensive sex education on "key myths" (Rose, 2003) about black women's sexuality and corresponding myths about white innocence—in particular, comprehensive sex education proponents built on rhetoric that casts black mothers as bad for their children. Their arguments built on and contributed to a larger discourse about black young people in which "the focus is all too often on individual maladaptive behavior and black mothering as the problem rather than on the social structure" (Ferguson, 2001, p. 78). Rather than confronting the systemic racial inequities that characterized Southern County, comprehensive advocates elided such inequities in their public statements and privately explained girls' missteps as a function of the presumably economically and emotionally impoverished homes they shared with their ill-equipped mothers. Their rhetoric also risked vilifying not only African American women but also African American men, who appeared in their tales only as absent fathers and sexual predators.

Pregnant fifth graders—raceless, vulnerable, and fathomable given "what everybody knows" about irresponsible mothers—were an effective call to action. Pregnant fifth graders were a rarity in Southern County. However, all pregnant young women in Southern County—10 to 19 years old— are twice as likely to be from a racial or ethnic minority than they are to be white. Those promoting comprehensive instruction did not advocate that the school board respond to racial disparities in pregnancies among young women, disparities that existed throughout North Carolina but that were particularly acute in Southern County. They did not insist that the school board adopt a curriculum that either addressed the sexual concerns of boys and young men or involved parents in their sons' and daughters' sex educations. Instead, they stepped into a void that seemed to have been left by Southern's neglectful mothers and predatory men; in doing so, they believed they could save the "little girls" of Southern County.

Conclusions: Constrained Possibilities

With its ostensible universalism, "children having children" obscures the social inequalities that inform debates over school-based sex education and casts young people as innocent of their influence. Although Teach Abstinence until Marriage and the Southern County sex education decision invoked the generic "children," the specter of pregnant African American girls perpetuating a cycle of welfare dependency was consistently implicit in educators' and policy makers' curricular decisions. Unlike their white, male, or middle-class classmates, poor and low-income African American girls contend with adult assumptions that they stand at the heart of a social crisis of teen pregnancy, poverty, and welfare dependency. The rhetoric of African American and low-income girls as sexual innocents is a no-less-constraining possibility, despite its promise of moral standing, social protection, and concern. Claims that girls and women are not sexually guilty but instead innocent leaves them with but two possibilities: they are either hypersexual or asexual—voracious women or chaste children. Through this rhetoric, educators and policy makers in Southern County and elsewhere in the contemporary debate over school-based sex education and adolescent sexuality fail to anticipate full, healthy, adult sexual lives for African American and low-income girls and young women, even as—and perhaps because—they have made these girls and young women the focus of their instruction.

The sexual injustices these girls and women confront are not only attitudinal: girls of color and poor girls are less able than racially and economically privileged girls to avoid unwanted pregnancies or to make them go away through abortion, discreet adoptions, better contraception, and an often greater ability to make change and decisions in their sexual lives and to trust that others will respect such sexual agency. African American girls and women raise African American children in a racist society, and poor girls endure pregnancies and care for children with limited economic resources and prospects. Boys and men, more than even the most privileged girls and women, can and often do walk away from many unwanted consequences of sexual activity. Talk of "children having children" distracts us from these realities, and this rationale allows adults to avoid responsibility for the social conditions in which young people live and that adults have, for the most part, created (Giroux, 2000).

Universalizing and idealizing notions of "children" distract us from the numerous other social inequalities at issue in sex education debates, policies, and practices. Comprehensive sex education is controversial in part because it endorses possibilities other than heterosexual marital sexual activity. Dogwood and Southern counties were overwhelmingly silent on issues of lesbian, gay, and bisexuality. Only Fox, a private school committed to providing an education that responded to and promoted human potential, devoted resources and time to these issues. Without argument, Dogwood and Southern teachers, policy makers, and administrators accepted the legislated requirement that they limit discussion of LGB issues to clarifying that homosexual activity was illegal under the state's sodomy law.[2]

The current social context continues to be characterized by racial, gender, socioeconomic, and sexual inequalities and renders speaking out about young people's sexual lives a risky but necessary task. Educators, researchers, and advocates routinely fail to insist that sex education challenge social inequalities, contribute to a compassionate response, and allow a full range of sexual expression in vulnerable young people's lives. Especially troubling is that the more privileged young people may also be the students attending schools with teachers and institutions addressing the full potential and complexity of their sexual lives.

Notes

1. Throughout this chapter, names of counties, schools, and people are pseudonyms.
2. This restriction no longer stands. The U.S. Supreme Court's 2003 *Lawrence* v. *Texas* decision overturned U.S. sodomy laws. In 2005, North Carolina's General Assembly responded with ratified Senate Bill 602, which corrected a series of state statutes. Among the corrections was the removal of language noting the "current legal status of [homosexual] acts" (North Carolina General Assembly, 2005).

References

Apple, M.W. (1999). The absent presence of race in educational reform. *Race, Ethnicity and Education, 2,* 9–16.

Best, A.L. (2000). *Prom night: Youth, schools, and popular culture.* New York: Routledge.

Best, J. (2001). *Damned lies and statistics: Untangling numbers from the media, politicians, and activists.* Berkeley: University of California Press.

Bonilla-Silva, E. (2002). The linguistics of color blind racism: How to talk nasty about Blacks without sounding "racist." *Critical Sociology, 28*(1/2), 41–64.

Booth, K.M. (2000). "Just testing": Race, sex, and the media in New York's "baby AIDS" debate. *Gender & Society, 14,* 644–661.

Collins, P.H. (2000). *Black feminist thought: Knowledge, consciousness, and the politics of empowerment.* New York: Routledge.

Ferguson, A.A. (2001). *Bad boys: Public schools in the making of Black masculinity.* Ann Arbor: University of Michigan Press.

Giroux, H.A. (2000). *Stealing innocence: Youth, corporate power, and the politics of culture.* New York: St. Martin's Press.

Kunzel, R.G. (1994). White neurosis, Black pathology: Constructing out-of-wedlock pregnancy in the wartime and postwar United States. In J. Meyerowitz (Ed.), *Not June Cleaver: Women and gender in Postwar America, 1945–1960* (pp. 304–341). Philadelphia: Temple University Press.

Levenstein, L. (2000). From innocent children to unwanted migrants and unwed moms: Two chapters in the public discourse on welfare in the United States, 1960–1961. *Journal of Women's History, 11*(4), 10–33.

Luker, K. (1996). *Dubious conceptions: The politics of teen pregnancy.* Cambridge, MA: Harvard University Press.

Males, M.A. (1999). *Framing youth: Ten myths about the next generation.* Monroe, ME: Common Courage Press.

Mast, C.K. (1997). *Sex respect: The option of true sexual freedom.* Bradley, IL: Respect, Inc.

Mink, G. (1998). *Welfare's end.* Ithaca, NY: Cornell University Press.

Moran, J.P. (2000). *Teaching sex: The shaping of adolescence in the 20th century.* Cambridge, MA: Harvard University Press.

Nathanson, C. (1993). *Dangerous passage: The social control of sexuality in women's adolescence.* Philadelphia: Temple University Press.

Neubeck, K.J., & Cazenave, N.A. (2001). *Welfare racism: Playing the race card against America's poor.* New York: Routledge.

North Carolina General Assembly. (1995). *Ratified House Bill 834.* Teach Abstinence until Marriage.

Pearce, D.M. (1993). "Children having children": Teenage pregnancy and public policy from the woman's perspective. In A. Lawson & D.L. Rhode (Eds.), *The politics of pregnancy: Adolescent sexuality and public policy* (pp. 46–58). New Haven, CT: Yale University Press.

Roberts, D.E. (1997). *Killing the black body: Race, reproduction, and the meaning of liberty.* New York: Vintage Books.

Roberts, D.E. (2002). *Shattered bonds: The color of child welfare.* New York: Basic Books.

Rose, T. (2003). *Longing to tell: Black women's stories of sexuality and intimacy.* New York: Farrar, Straus & Giroux.

Sizer-Webb, F.S., Whitney, E.N., & Debruyne, L.K. (2001). *Making life choices: Health skills and concepts.* New York: Glencoe/McGraw-Hill.

Smith, D.E. (1999). *Writing the social: Critique, theory, and investigations.* Toronto: University of Toronto Press.

Solinger, R. (2000). *Wake up little Susie: Single pregnancy before Roe v. Wade.* New York: Routledge.

Trudell, B.N., & Whatley, M.H. (1991). Sex respect: A problematic public school sexuality curriculum. *Journal of Sex Education and Therapy, 17*(2), 122–140.

Watney, S. (1987). The spectacle of AIDS. In D. Crimp (Ed.), *AIDS: Cultural analysis/cultural activism* (pp. 71–86). Cambridge, MA: MIT Press.

Whatley, M.H., & Trudell, B.N. (1993). Teen-Aid: Another problematic school sexuality curriculum. *Journal of Sex Education and Therapy, 19*(4), 251–271.

CHAPTER FOUR

Pedagogy and the Sista' Professor

Teaching Black Queer Feminist Studies through the Self

MEL MICHELLE LEWIS

> For all our students . . . any queer teacher can become the perfect symbol for a variety of meanings . . . we are thought to have knowledge and insight about things they are most eager to know about themselves.
>
> —MICHÈLE AINA BARALE, "THE ROMANCE OF CLASS AND QUEERS"

> The course content serves as the primary text and the gay identity of the teacher is the subtext through which the material, teaching, and classroom experiences are filtered.
>
> —BRYANT KEITH ALEXANDER, "EMBRACING THE TEACHABLE MOMENT"

> The presence of the black woman teacher in the multicultural classroom repositions the location of blacks and women in the academy and . . . repositions the texts of black women in the academic curriculum moving both from a position of margin to center.
>
> —MAE G. HENDERSON, "WHAT IT MEANS TO TEACH THE OTHER WHEN THE OTHER IS THE SELF"

Queer theory, Black studies, and feminist thought recognize the body as a site of experiential knowledge and present frameworks for examining sexualities, identities, and intersections between them, as the quotes above reveal. The pedagogical project of teaching courses and texts that explore the intersections of race, gender, and sexuality from each of these interdisciplinary fields requires that I also interrogate my own body and subjectivities. Drawing from the fields of Black queer studies, Black feminist thought, critical feminist pedagogy, and performance studies, I discuss a pedagogy of embodiment that employs concepts from each interdiscipline. In writing about teaching through my identities, I conceptualize a Black queer feminist pedagogy, a method for teaching intersectionality through the Self.

More specifically, I am concerned with how racist, sexist, and heterosexist ideological dimensions in the classroom marginalize the Black lesbian body. Thus I am committed to constructing a Black queer feminist pedagogy that (1) disrupts pathologized tropes of Black womanhood and black sexuality, (2) discourages a disembodied theorization of intersectional oppressions and identities, and (3) fashions a valuable and constructive way of utilizing body and identity to inspire teachable moments.

In order to render a vocabulary and construct a pedagogical framework, I interrogate three central concepts in this chapter: embodied text, embodied knowledge, and the mind/body split. Alexander's (2005) concept of "embodied text," alluded to in his opening quote, is useful when considering the Black gay body as course content manifested. Similarly, Judith Hamera (2002) deploys the term "embodied knowledge," presenting classroom performance as a possible location for "restor[ing] the knowledge of what we, as bodies in the classroom, are subject to" in relation to "constraint, construction, and situated spectatorship" (p. 129). Both of these concepts consider the reading of the body as text in the classroom and the manifestations of such knowledge. Finally, I critique academic investment in the mind/body split. bell hooks draws attention to how being conscious of one's body as separate from one's self "invites us to invest deeply in the mind/body split" (p. 193). This split creates conditions under which a Black queer woman as teacher is almost always at odds with the existing academic structure, which is unaccustomed to reading the Black female presence, physicality, or sexuality, at least in named ways.

Constructing a Black queer feminist pedagogy that interrogates embodied text, embodied knowledge, and the mind/body split requires that I also consider the pedagogical pitfalls of asserting the embodied self as text in the classroom. As pedagogues, whenever we affirm that the classroom is not a neutral location inhabited only by minds, and void of bodies, identities, and desires, we must also contend with a complex system of pitfalls and consequences. In the following pages, then, I explore the constraints on and possibilities for teaching Black queer feminist studies through embodied texts. But first I must situate my own mind and body in the text.

The Sista' Professor Speaks

As I explore these three (de)constructions of teaching through a Black lesbian embodied text, I draw upon Keith Clark's (2005) conception of the "brother-professor" (p. 267), Joni Jones's (1997) performance of the "sista docta," and Tuesday L. Cooper's (2006) discussion of African American women faculty in the "sista network" (p. 4) to name myself the "sista' professor." I am a young Black woman, in professional attire, aesthetically femme-with-an-edge, and queerly counterculture. I also am cast as an authoritative figure (at least for my students) in the ivory tower of academia. As I perform the sista' professor, many students compliment my fashion sense, discuss their friendships, family, and romantic relationships with me, and consider me a sista' that's got their back. I am the sista'-friend that gives pop quizzes and won't accept late papers. This position allows the complex interplay between the personal, intellectual, and political to flourish.

As sista' professor, a Black lesbian woman, I recognize that students potentially perceive my body, at the intersection of these identities, as "embodied text" in their practice of making connections and identifying silences in course materials. As already noted, Alexander (2005) contends the teacher's body becomes material content in the classroom, an object of inquiry that can "speak" to omissions and absences in the curriculum and signal teachable moments. I utilize this concept of Black gay body as text to generate a feminist analysis of my own pedagogy, acknowledging my text is "always already" racialized, sexualized, and gendered (p. 262). I argue that the question of embodiment can be critical in any classroom and that all teachers (and students) learn with mind and body simultaneously. However, I contend that the body becomes even more saturated with symbolism in courses that center matters of race, gender, sexuality, and other dimensions of "difference."

The teacher marked by otherness, whether by race, gender, and/or sexuality, becomes the perfect symbol for a variety of meanings (Barale, 1994). The queer teacher is thought to have knowledge and insight about body, identity, and sexuality. I assert the Black woman as teacher, who is also a queer "symbol" (Barale, 1994), always already represents deviant sexuality due to constructions of the Black female body as hypersexual and available. In her text *Black Feminist Thought*, Patricia Hill Collins (2000) names and explicates multiple archetypes signaled by the Black female body. She presents the images of mammies, jezebels, the breeder women of slavery, smiling Aunt Jemimas, Black prostitutes, and welfare mothers, as negative stereotypes applied to African American women that have been fundamental to Black women's oppression. She further argues that these racist and sexist ideological weapons permeate social structures and institutions, including the academy, to such a degree that these portrayals become hegemonic, or seen as natural, normal, and inevitable (p. 5). Thus, the Black woman as teacher, whether she identifies as queer or not, represents sexual deviance/difference in the classroom. How then do we contextualize this "symbolic" body, saturated with multiple meanings in the classroom? How might the body and these tropes be used as "course content" to pursue teachable moments?

Identity Politics, Essentialism, and Performative Pedagogy

Identity politics, as characterized by Karen Kopelson (2002), limits the possibility for a multiplicity of subjectivities. The falsely united, exclusionary front of "Black" *or* "woman" *or* "lesbian" is based on assumed static social group identifications. In the classroom, I challenge this notion by simply showing up as a Black lesbian teacher. I also examine with the students how my gender identity and expression, race, and articulated queer identity disrupt common exclusionary tropes and facilitate intersectional inquiries. Kopelson makes note of scholars across a variety of disciplines who are concerned about the risk of naturalizing social identities, warning that to "come out" in the classroom is to "become the representative of an essentialized, preconceived, and wholly dominating queer identity" (p. 21). This essentialization can also occur as more visible markers of race and gender identify us. Kopelson thus asserts a performative framework to contest the narrow identity politics associated with coming out (and having our gender and racial identifiers "read") in the classroom:

> A performative pedagogue, unlike the teacher who comes out in the classroom, allows for and, indeed, actively constructs a self that is multiple, a self in excess of identity per se . . . and allows for multiplicity. [This] is therefore seen as one of the greatest advantages of queer or performative pedagogies over pedagogies of disclosure/coming out, which tend to leave the regulatory and exclusionary work of identity as a system untouched, and to perpetuate confining notions of identities as singular, discrete, and immutable. (pp. 24–25)

Instructors may also deploy performative pedagogies to illustrate how race, gender presentation, and motherhood can obscure lesbianism, especially for women of color like myself whose less visible identities must be asserted in order to complicate monolithic constructions of identity. This strategic assertion of less visible identities into the classroom, as mentioned in the case studies discussed in Kopelson's work, reject tropes of singular construction and push students to apply an intersectional analysis as they consider their course material speaking through the teacher's body as text. Although I recognize Kopelson's preference for performative pedagogies over pedagogies of disclosure/coming out, I do not wish to dismiss coming out discourses entirely. Inserting my Black lesbian self into this gay/non-gay, out/closeted framework is itself an act of "excess" as conceived by Kopelson. Coming out in the classroom, particularly as a Black lesbian whose racial/ethnic presentation and gender expressions also "perform" disruptions, is a performative act that explodes the nexus of "that which is Black" and "that which is queer" (Johnson & Henderson, 2005, p. 7) and a number of other tropes including the feminine, the academic, and the feminist.

Like Kopelson's concern with coming out as the representative of an essentialized queer identity, Henderson (1994) acknowledges the dangers of privileging the Self as Other (for Black women in particular) in an effort to "represent the complex status and condition of the Other in our pedagogy and scholarship" (pp. 433–434). These dangers include navigating the role of a teacher who is expected, by students, to either verify or contest the authenticity of texts authored by or representing the experiences of Black women. Henderson writes that the Black woman instructor must find a way "to enter the classroom with authority without replicating the 'white' and 'male' models of power that excluded and marginalized both black women and their texts from the class and curriculum in the first place" (p. 435). Indeed, the Black woman in a white patriarchal institution speaks to multiple contradictions. For example, I encourage creativity and collaboration between students *and* am responsible for assessing the quality of individually completed work; I encourage the sharing of personal narratives during class and in written assignments *and* insist that those oral and written productions draw upon research to become legitimate scholarly objects. I consider explicitly naming these contradictions as another form of performative pedagogy that disrupts rather than reifies entrenched models of power. I must explore, however, the risks involved in disrupting these models and performing a pedagogy that strategically asserts less visible identities. Asserting the personal and invoking the body in the classroom, which is traditionally conceived of as a neutral, cerebral location, void of bodies and identities, can be professionally (and emotionally) dangerous.

Risk/risqué: The Sexualization of the Classroom

Introducing texts and openly discussing issues of sexuality, desire, and bodies inevitably leads to intellectual exchanges that may be sexually stimulating or lead to risqué conversations in the classroom. Women's studies and queer studies classrooms are often saturated with innuendoes, flirtations, and flushed cheeks. Barale (1994) contends that, at times, the erotic must enter into the classroom as an aid to the learning process; moreover, the presence of a queer instructor may also serve to further eroticize the classroom exchange. Asserting queer identity may be perceived by students, other faculty, and administrators as an act of inappropriately sexualizing the classroom—a classroom that is imagined to be a desexualized and depoliticized zone (Barale, 1994; Clark, 2005). Given the powerful nature of sharing personal stories in the Black studies, queer studies, and/or feminist studies classroom context(s), I do perform an "engaged pedagogy" that includes sharing my own autobiographical material. For example, during a lesson on sexuality and religion, many of my students used either/or statements to name religious and queer identities, such as, "The Christians; the gays; homosexuals; religious people." I shared with them my own queer and religious identities—namely, "I identify as lesbian and Christian." I also once complicated a student's stereotype-laden description of "butch lesbians on motorcycles" by displaying a photo of myself on my own ("very feminine but still kind of lesbian," according to the class) turquoise Harley-Davidson Sportster. However, I often question how far to push my boundaries of comfort and safety, and question how relevant my personal insights are in relation to my students' understandings of race, gender, and sexuality.

Judith McDaniel's (1985) insights assist me in thinking through the question, "Is my sexuality relevant to teaching?" (p. 130). Her vulnerable position as the only out lesbian faculty member on campus teaching lesbian material led her to fear personal attacks from students who responded to the course work with homophobic comments or sentiments. Students who were unsure about their own sexuality or who were exploring its boundaries, also made her investment in the personal dangerous. One student went so far as to spread false rumors regarding affairs with her. Keith Clark (2005) also foregrounds issues related to same-sex desire in the texts that he teaches, yet he is aware that his status as a "brother-professor" (p. 267), who (like the sista' professor) is young, Black, and cool, might be compromised in the eyes of some students should he foreground his own "private" self or teach a course solely devoted to gay and lesbian material.

Although I do fear that students will make homophobic comments (and at times they do), or will in some way harm me personally or professionally, I am often more concerned that my status as "sista' professor" will fall prey to the very stereotypes and assumptions I seek to dismantle in my courses. These articulated assumptions by students include such statements as: all feminists must be lesbians or that Black people are unequivocally homophobic. How do I remain the sista' professor while sharing my private self and my experiences as evidence (Scott, 1991) without reinscribing stereotypes and/or inappropriately sexualizing the classroom? I walk a fine line.

An Uncanny Resemblance: Authenticity, Authority, and Asserting the Other as Self

More specifically, I am troubled that the course materials, and by extension Black women's studies and Black feminisms, will be discounted by my own queer body. My "terrain of the flesh in which meaning is inscribed, constructed, and reconstituted" (Stucky & Wimmer, 2002, p. 3) gives me pause. I am constantly reflecting on my own embodiment as text in the classroom and attempt to interpret the meanings my students are making of my Blackness, femaleness, and queerness. I do not wish to silence myself, my queer students, or misrepresent central ideas in texts or the authors' identities. I intentionally use performative acts to disrupt and provide an embodied example of these intersections without reifying misrepresentations. This intervention includes calling out racism, sexism, homophobia, and heterosexism with equal attention, using both the theoretical and "I," "we," and "us" to denote my status as the "Other." In my classroom, such interruption may sound something like: "Let's not use the term homosexual to name people; it is seen by many queer people as a diagnosis. I prefer the label lesbian; let's use the name people have chosen for themselves"; or, "As Black women, we are often asked for permission to touch, to compare, or to explain our hair to those who are not Black." In the classroom, these statements move theory into the realm of the everyday, honoring experience as evidence.

When I assert the Other as the self in this way, I begin to recognize how my body functions as "text" or as material subject within my classroom. McDaniel (1985) contends that every woman (and, by extension, every-body) who associates with her—faculty or student—must somehow deal with what her material subject, namely her lesbianism, means to him or her. In much the same way, by practicing a Black queer feminist pedagogy, I am asking my students to deal with the many assumptions upon which the academy and other social institutions that we evaluate in class are based. Moreover, I center emotion as a locus of knowing and source of knowledge, drawing on feminist consciousness-raising groups (Weiler, 1991) and the work of Audre Lorde (1984). More specifically, Lorde, a Black lesbian feminist theorist and poet, wrote from the specificity of her own socially defined and shaped life. For Lorde, feelings were a guide to analysis and action. I incorporate emotion as I teach to promote analysis and to integrate vulnerability as a powerful teaching tool into my classroom. For example, I share with my students when I am hurt or disappointed, when things are difficult or complicated to discuss, and when I am excited to share a favorite author, idea, or personal story in class. As I assert body and emotion, I must also ask how the politics of authority and authenticity materialize in the classroom as a result of my uncanny resemblance to the course materials I am teaching on race, gender, and sexuality.

The questions of authority and authenticity are inherent in both Kopelson's (2002) and Henderson's (1994) exploration of performing the Other in the classroom. I critique with my students the notion that I am an "authentic" and/or sole "authority" on Black, queer, and women's subjects in the classroom by virtue of my social locations so as to mitigate the danger in authorizing or rendering a singular viewpoint of these identities or perspectives. Henderson also comments on the authority of the Black woman teacher by saying:

> This authority . . . is not that of the teacher's "standing in" as authenticating text, but rather of privileging the study of black women in such a way that we become the centers and subjects of our own experiences—rather than corollaries of another's. (p. 435)

Like Henderson, I believe teaching the Other as Self allows us to center, and thus, value Black women's experiences and knowledges. She establishes a critical feminist pedagogy that examines the omissions and silences of women's knowledges in dominant discourses, while highlighting women's experiential and shared knowledges that can contribute to a transformation of consciousness for students. This pedagogy also provides students with ways of knowing that enable them to know themselves better and, in turn, live in the world more fully (hooks, 1993).

Although somewhat risky, centering and deepening understandings of the subject matter through the sharing of embodied knowledge located at the nexus of race, gender, and sexuality is critical to the practice of feminist intersectional analysis. When considering these intersections as taught by a Black lesbian instructor, the overdetermined "scandal" of outness, as well as the assumed gender- and race-specific identification with the subject taught, may have the potential to distract students and/or detract from course purposes (Kopelson, 2002, p. 21). Evidence of these assumptions and distractions appear, at times, on my anonymous final evaluations and are familiar to many out queer faculty and faculty of color. I gather from the sentiments shared in evaluations that asserting racial, gender, and sexual identity can run the risk of authenticating or reifying existing identity categories and the narratives that surround and support them (Henderson, 1994: Kopelson, 2002). For example, my evaluations for an introductory women's studies course have included statements like, "The course did not have a Black agenda," and, my favorite, "You're not a ball buster are you? You sound like you could be." (This student then confirmed that she was a "ball buster" herself and seemed somewhat disappointed that there was not more "ball busting" going on in the classroom!) Even so, I seek to explore what is lost when we do not allow our students to know us fully. How can I expect students to undertake this endeavor without being fully present myself? From a Black lesbian performative perspective, I must weigh the risks of engaging the personal and carrying the weight of teaching through one's full, vulnerable self.

Conclusion: My Performance of a Black Queer Feminist Pedagogy

As I perform a Black queer feminist pedagogy I disrupt pathologized tropes of Black female sexuality, insist upon the recognition of embodied intersections, and utilize the body to inspire teachable moments. Although these actions put a great deal of stress on traditional models of authority in the classroom, they productively affect my students as they wrestle with the subjects of identity, power, and oppression. Alexander (2005) assists me in conceptualizing this impact. He comments on the policies and procedures that are cemented in ritual performances of education and writes:

> Issues of sex, gender, and race, come to mediate the educational endeavor . . . the thought of outing one's self in the classroom is always already equated with risk: risk to the physical body . . . but also risk to pedagogical authority. But not to engage the fullness of our character—when necessary, when doing so would make a meaningful impact—is to risk missing the teachable moment. (p. 250)

This meaningful impact is at the heart of my hopes for my students. I invest in knowing students and allowing students to know me. The classroom is not a sterile intellectual environment in which structural oppression and issues of power and identity are left at the door; rather, the classroom is a site for acknowledging and examining these matters in the realm of the personal, which can then be applied by students to institutional spaces beyond the classroom. I have been inspired by students who comment that they have never been asked to consider the Other as "someone," or to connect to a classroom community in which we are all differently located but simultaneously implicated in locations of power and positions of oppression. I imagine their classrooms, workplaces, research, and relationships as fertile ground for transformation as they operationalize this knowledge and perspective in their own lives.

As a teacher, I place myself in conversation with students, sharing my own examples and viewpoints while making clear that my perspective is exactly that—my own. I strategically share the personal, then refer back to assigned texts for additional standpoints or theoretical grounding and ask that my students model this practice. This exchange encourages open dialogue within the classroom and produces a shared knowledge, from which students later draw as they articulate their newfound awareness and insights. Ultimately, my Black queer feminist pedagogy produces a framework that acknowledges and appreciates the intersections of race, gender, and sexuality as a part of the performance of pedagogy. The fullness of our beings and the fullness of our identities serve as the "equipment" with which to teach (Alexander, 2005, p. 254). I utilize my equipment to make connections between ideas and people and to identify silences about our embodied, feeling selves in the classroom. For the sista' professor, performing a pedagogy that speaks my life fully is a refusal to reify the very oppressions that the course curriculum I cover with my students resists. Such performances allow me to revel in the teachable moment.

References

Alexander, B.K. (2005). Embracing the teachable moment: The Black gay body in the classroom as embodied text. In E.P. Johnson & M.G. Henderson (Eds.), *Black queer studies: A critical anthology* (pp. 249–265). Durham, NC: Duke University Press.

Barale, M.A. (1994). The romance of class and queers: Academic erotic zones. In L. Garber (Ed.), *Tilting the tower* (pp. 16–24). New York: Routledge.

Clark, K. (2005). Are we family? Pedagogy and the race for queerness. In E.P. Johnson & M.G. Henderson (Eds.), *Black queer studies: A critical anthology* (pp. 266–275). Durham, NC: Duke University Press.

Collins, P.H. (2000). *Black feminist thought: Knowledge, consciousness, and the politics of empowerment.* New York: Routledge.

Cooper, T.L. (2006). *The sista' network: African-American women faculty successfully negotiating the road to tenure.* Bolton, MA: Anker Publishing Company, Inc.

Hamera, J. (2002). Performance studies, pedagogy, and bodies in/as the classroom. In N. Stucky & C. Wimmer (Eds.), *Teaching performance studies (Theater in the Americas)* (pp. 121–130). Carbondale: Southern Illinois University Press.

Henderson, M. (1994). What it means to teach the other when the other is the self. *Callaloo, 17*(2), 432–438.

hooks, b. (1993). Eros, eroticism and the pedagogical process. *Cultural Studies, 7*(1), 58–63.

Johnson, E.P., & Henderson, M.G. (2005). Introduction: Queering black studies/ "quaring" queer studies. In E.P. Johnson & M.G. Henderson (Eds.), *Black queer studies: A critical anthology* (pp. 1–17). Durham, NC: Duke University Press.

Jones, J.L. (1997). "Sista docta": Performance as critique of the academy. *TDR, 41*(2), 51–67.

Kopelson, K. (2002). Dis/integrating the gay/queer binary: "Reconstructed identity politics" for a performative pedagogy. *College English, 65*(1), 17–35.

Lorde, A. (1984). *Sister outsider: Essays and speeches.* Freedom, CA: Crossing Press.

McDaniel, J. (1985). Is there room for me in the closet? Or, my life as the only lesbian professor. In M. Culley & C. Portuges (Eds.), *Gendered subjects: The dynamics of feminist teaching* (pp. 130–135). London: Routledge & Kegan Paul.

Scott, J. (1991). The evidence of experience. *Critical Inquiry, 17*(4), 773–797.

Stucky, N., & Wimmer, C. (2002). *Teaching performance studies (Theater in the Americas).* Carbondale: Southern Illinois University Press.

Weiler, K. (1991). Freire and a feminist pedagogy of difference. *Harvard Educational Review 61*(4), 449.

Love Silphium. Heather Ault

"Love Silphium" celebrates the 4,000-year history of abortion and contraception practices found around the world and is one of a series of 52 poster designs. In contrast to the mainstream pro-choice narrative defined by "women's liberation" and *Roe* v. *Wade*, 4,000 Years for Choice presents reproductive control as a fundamental human desire that has existed throughout history. Rather than symbols of coat hangers and empowered feminists, these images visualize abortifacient herbs, contraceptive plugs, hand-made condoms, early spermicides, and turn-of-the century barrier methods, as well as the philosophers, physicians, and healers who have documented these practices since the beginning of time. Words such as celebrate, honor, inspire, and love connect reproductive practices to positive emotions and personal actions rather than to rhetoric of struggling, defending, and fighting for reproductive rights.

Introduction: Society Can Only Be as Free and Open as Its Schools

LUCY BAILEY & KAREN GRAVES

In 1978, lesbian and gay school teachers and administrators found themselves fighting for their professional lives in California. Proposition 6, an initiative to bar homosexuals and their allies from working in public schools, became educators' "Stonewall Rebellion" and a significant event at the nexus of lesbian/gay/bisexual/transgender/queer (LGBTQ) and education history. In a declaration opposing the measure, a group of school workers articulated a basic premise: "society can only be as free and open as its schools" ("Proposed Declaration," n.d., p. 1). This salient point suggests why those seeking to understand the intersections between sexuality and education need to take both gay and lesbian history and education history into account. Queer studies scholars need grounding in history, too, not only for the clearer understanding of contemporary issues that comes with historical perspective but also because historical analysis allows one to study (with the benefit of hindsight) the dynamic pulses that flow through political-economic structures, between schooling and dominant ideology. Such analysis helps put school policies and practices into context and discern influential patterns as they develop over time.

The essays in this section focus on LGBTQ education history in the United States over the last quarter of the 20th century.[1] Jackie Blount's analysis of a watershed moment in LGBT teacher activism forms the center of this slice of history and demonstrates the historic vulnerability of teachers who pressed for equality in their profession. Catherine Lugg examines the larger political context that shaped this bold political stand—what might be considered the most significant victory for LGBTQ teachers' rights to date—and also restricted its potential influence. Indeed, Lugg explains how backlash against what was quite modest antidiscrimination legislation intensified as skilled operatives whipped conservative political factions into homophobic outrage.[2] Teacher advocacy stalled in this climate, leaving students to spearhead the next wave of activism for LGBTQ rights. Warren Blumenfeld surveys three decades of student activism, from the gay liberation movement in the 1970s to the proliferation of Gay-Straight Alliances in high schools and middle schools in the

1990s. The overall trajectory of these essays emphasizes the dynamic impact of revolutionary and reactionary activism on school policy in shifting political and historical contexts, a struggle played out by colorful, and in some cases, heroic characters. Clearly, schools have been a key site for dialogue, activism, and change on behalf of sexual minorities.

The field of LGBTQ education history remains rich for study, as education historians have lagged behind other scholars in addressing LGBTQ issues, and educators remain unaware of how sexuality and LGBTQ issues have shaped contemporary policy and practice. Part of the difficulty is that primary sources for this research are extremely difficult to obtain. First, material regarding the private lives of public employees can be scarce. Additionally, people facing a hostile social climate may have felt reluctant to leave traces of their experiences or were selective in recording their thoughts and reflections. Complicating such elusive documentation is that the ways people understand sexuality and sexual identity have shifted over the years. Thus, what might interest contemporary scholars may have had little relevance for women and men in previous generations. Further, papers that an individual kept might be destroyed later or simply not made accessible in archival collections (Freedman, 1998). Although new resources opened up for historians once publishers began to release material on topics regarding sexuality in the 20th century, it was not unusual to find these resources defaced or destroyed in public collections after mid-century (Blount, 2005). Perhaps more troubling, discrimination against the topic and those writing about it within the academy proved another significant barrier to LGBTQ historical scholarship, especially in the early years (D'Emilio, 1989; Kellogg, 2001).

What we now know, thanks in large part to the scholars contributing to this section, is that antigay discrimination in education proved a powerful force in catapulting right-wing politics to prominence in the last decades of the 20th century and fueling LGBTQ activist efforts. Among the LGBTQ population, teachers have been most vulnerable to attack by homophobic forces. This remains true in spite of the critical 2003 *Lawrence* v. *Texas* Supreme Court decision that decriminalized homosexuality (Lugg, 2006). The effect has turned traditional pedagogy on its head, positioning visionary students to lead their teachers in pushing for LGBTQ equity and other social justice issues in education.

Rather than aim for a broad survey of the whole of LGBTQ education history, these essays converge at the moment when lesbian and gay teachers determined, collectively, to confront the oppressive school system that closed ranks against them during the Cold War. Illustrating that "society can only be as free and open as its schools," their actions reverberated throughout the nation, involving students, policies, laws, and other social justice movements (Proposed declaration of unity by California school administrators and school workers, n.d.). But deep-seated assumptions, particularly those connected to gender ideology and sexual identity, take a long time to transform. In this context, writing LGBTQ education history is itself a form of scholarly activism as it substantiates what has been accomplished. As long as schools remain a central site for the expression of homophobia, contemporary educators can turn to history for compelling lessons on how to combat it. Key lessons in this history emerged from the events in California in 1978.

Notes

1. In this section authors use varying terminology regarding sexual orientation. Generally, these historians choose words in common usage during the particular periods under examination.

2. Blount's and Lugg's chapters are excerpts from previously published material, edited here for space considerations. Appreciation is extended to the editorial staff of the State University of New York Press and *Educational Policy* for the use of this pioneering work in LGBTQ education history.

References

Blount, J.M. (2005). *Fit to teach: Same-sex desire, gender, and school work in the twentieth century.* Albany: State University of New York Press.

D'Emilio, J. (1989, September). Not a simple matter: Gay history and gay historians. *The Journal of American History, 76*(2), 435–442.

Freedman, E. (1998). "The burning of letters continues": Elusive identities and the historical construction of sexuality. *Journal of Women's History, 9*(4), 181–200.

Kellogg, A.P. (2001, July 6). Report reveals tight job market for historians of gay topics. *The Chronicle of Higher Education.*

Lugg, C. (2006). Thinking about sodomy: Public schools, legal panopticons, and queers. *Educational Policy, 20*(1), 35–58.

Proposed declaration of unity by California school administrators and schoolworkers. (N.d.) San Francisco Public Library, San Francisco History Center/Book Arts & Special Collections Center, GLC, Box 6.

SUPERVISOR HARVEY MILK
CITY HALL, SAN FRANCISCO

1.

ON ONE HAND THERE IS FREEDOM OF SPEECH, HUMAN RIGHTS, AND THE RIGHT

TO PRIVACY....ON THE OTHER HAND THERE IS PROPOSITION 6 which is a

MISGUIDED, CONFUSED, DANGEROUS, DECEITFULL, FRIGHTENING, AND UN-AMERICAN

ATTACH ON BASIC HUMAN RIGHTS..THE SAME KIND THAT SPAWNED WITCHHUNTS,

NAZISM, MCCARTHYISM.....AND AS EDUCATOR AFTER EDUCATOR, LEGISLATOR

AFTER LEGISLATOR, RELIGIOUS LEADER AFTER REGLISOUS LEADER HAS STATED;

IT IS COMPLELTLEY UNNECCESSARY BECAUSE THERE ARE ALREADY LAWS AND

ENFORCEABLE LAWS ON THE BOOKS TO PROTECT OUR CHILDREN.

IT COMES FROM THE SAME TACTICS THAT NIXON USED TO REACH THE U.S. SENATE...

A SELF SERVING POLITICIAN DREAMING UP A "MORAL" CRUSADE TO RIDE TO POWER..

NIXON CHASES NON EXISTING COMMUNISTS RX OUT FROM UNDER OUR BEDS AND ONLY

ALL TOO LATE WE FOUND OUT ABOUT HIS OWN PERSONAL MORALITY...NOW WE HAVE

A PERSON WHO IS FULL OF CONTRIDICTION AFTER CONTRIDICTION TRYING TO USE

THE GAY COMMUNITY AS RXR SCAPEGOATS   TO SATISFY HIS MORAL CRUSDAE

IN AN ATTEMPT TO RUN FOR HIGHER OFFICE

Harvey Milk Notes, 1978

As the campaign against Proposition 6 intensified, San Francisco Supervisor Harvey Milk engaged John Briggs in debates across California. This page from Milk's notes exposes the base designs of the Briggs Initiative.

CHAPTER FIVE

How Sweet It Is!

JACKIE M. BLOUNT

During the Cold War, lesbian, gay, or "homosexual" teachers hid their identities if they wanted to keep their jobs. This had not always been the case, however. For example, only a few decades earlier schoolmistresses could live with female romantic and/or sexual partners without raising eyebrows. But this state of affairs had changed by the end of World War II as these and other "spinster" teachers were rapidly purged from the nation's classrooms as officials, fearing schools' reputations as refuges for a class of seemingly tainted or possibly even "deviant" persons, sought instead to hire married women teachers and returning male veterans. Matters quickly grew worse for teachers who desired persons of the same sex. By the 1960s states such as Florida and California instituted campaigns, first to identify homosexual teachers and then to revoke their teaching licenses. Teachers had little recourse in such proceedings with laws and public sentiment arrayed so powerfully against them.

The first wave of teachers brave enough to mount legal challenges to this discriminatory status quo were buoyed by the emergence of the modern gay rights movement, which had been triggered in part by the very public and quite sensational 1969 Stonewall Rebellion. Clusters of urban teachers banded together to form grass-roots lesbian and gay teacher organizations that took bold political action, proudly announcing their presence in annual "Stonewall" parades and fighting hard to dismantle discriminatory employment practices. The increasing openness with which lesbian and gay teachers worked for their rights, however, inspired Anita Bryant to make them the centerpiece of her 1977 campaign to overturn newly instituted housing and employment protections for lesbians and gay men in Miami-Dade. Bryant had ignited voters and donors—nationwide—by conjuring images of homosexual teachers seeking to seduce and recruit students.

In the wake of this widely publicized battle, one aspiring gubernatorial candidate in California believed he saw the issue that would catapult him into the spotlight and bring him the flood of campaign donations he would need. He succeeded, but in so doing, he also catalyzed a seismic shift in the fledgling gay rights movement from scattered local efforts to a truly national force. In the end, lesbian and gay teachers in California would be spared a brutal measure designed to rid them and their allies from the classroom. Concern for the rights of lesbian, gay, bisexual, and transgender teachers would fade, though, as activists instead focused their attention in the 1990s and 2000s on the rights and welfare of students. Arguably, some of the fault lines exposed during the battle described in this chapter still reverberate.

Anita Bryant and her supporters gathered in a hotel ballroom to watch the returns from the Miami-Dade ordinance vote. Her guests included California Senator John Briggs, a supporter who had flown in for the festivities. Briggs took pleasure in the emerging landslide vote. "We won! We won!" he told a reporter from KQED, a San Francisco television station. Briggs did not realize it at the time, but that reporter was Randy Shilts, a gay man and former reporter for *The Advocate* who subsequently authored several landmark volumes on pivotal events in gay history. Briggs told Shilts that night that the Miami-Dade victory would aid him in his gubernatorial bid to unseat Governor Jerry Brown. Briggs observed that proportionately as many voters had turned out for a mere referendum as had for the last California governor's race. He described the demographics of California and Miami-Dade as similar, each with significant populations of religious fundamentalists and homosexuals. He indicated that if he were to campaign against homosexuality, he would go from a long shot to a contender for the governorship. He would begin by introducing a bill in the legislature to prohibit homosexuals from teaching. The legislature, he surmised, would refuse to consider it—in which case he would bring the matter to a public referendum like the one he celebrated that night with Bryant (Clendinen & Nagourney, 1999; Shilts, 1982). One week later, Bryant flew to California to support Briggs as he launched his new initiative (Why is gay law needed, anyway?, 1977).

When Briggs returned to California, he quickly introduced a resolution commending Bryant on her Miami campaign, but the Senate Rules Committee refused to allow floor debate on the measure. Then, on June 14, 1977, with police escort, Briggs approached the steps of the San Francisco City Hall where he announced his measure to remove openly homosexual teachers from California schools. Briggs did not choose his hometown of Fullerton, or the state capitol, or even the most populous city in the state. Instead, he introduced his measure in the heart of San Francisco, which he considered "in a captured nation status and wanting to be liberated" from a teeming population of homosexuals. As hoped, journalists, camera crews, and hundreds of vocal gay activists awaited his arrival. He started speaking, but angry shouts of "Stop the New Hitler Now" easily overpowered his words. Barely above the din, Briggs declared that "normal" people should be heard, too. Perhaps as a small concession to gay activists, he explained that his bill would not deny homosexuals the right to housing, jobs, or their sexual lifestyle. Instead, it simply would keep "children from being exposed to homosexual teachers." His voice hardly audible, he quickly finished his remarks and moved toward his waiting car. Immediately he tripped and fell—after which protesters taunted him even more aggressively. Police escorts quickly helped him back into his car, and he sped away (quoted in "Briggs Does His Thing," 1977).

Over the next two months, gay activists and Briggs's supporters alike kept a relatively low profile on the antigay teacher measure as they waited for a Supreme Court decision in the case of James Gaylord, the Tacoma, Washington, teacher dismissed for supposed "immorality." If the Supreme Court decided in Gaylord's favor, then the Briggs Initiative likely would be deemed unconstitutional. On the other hand, if the Supreme Court ruled against Gaylord, the decision probably would inflame public opinion further against the rights of lesbian and gay teachers. Meanwhile, Jean O'Leary, co-director of the National Gay Task Force, concluded, "One thing I know for sure is that in the next two years the focus of debate over gay rights is going to be on teachers and students. . . . It's a hot, rising issue." Not only had Bryant scored a lopsided victory in Miami, but other cities like Wichita and Eugene similarly considered dropping new antidiscrimination ordinances protecting lesbians and gay men. Rhetoric against the supposed threats of homosexual schoolteachers topped the headlines in each case. Yet, as Briggs explained repeatedly over the course of the campaign, his measure would not penalize lesbian and gay teachers who *hid* their sexual orientation. He sought instead to penalize teachers who *publicly* pronounced their sexual orientation—in gay pride parades, at rallies, to the media, through LGBT teacher organizations, and by word of mouth (quoted in Hager, 1977). He wanted all visible and activist LGBT educators to return to the closet.

By this time, the rapidly emerging issue of gay rights had attracted the attention of diverse professional and civil rights organizations. Among them, the American Bar Association decided to consider gay rights during its annual meeting in August 1977. A distinguished panel of speakers lined up to support a resolution urging anti-discrimination legislation regarding housing, employment, and public accommodations, including the U.S. attorney general, the president of the American Psychiatric Association, and Michael Greene, a gay former elementary school teacher from New York. Greene explained, "The whole question of whether or not homosexuals should be allowed in the classroom is academic. We *are* in the classroom, in virtually every school in the country, teaching effectively at every level in both public and private schools." He argued that the central issue instead concerned whether or not homosexuals could claim their identities openly while retaining their teaching positions. Dismissing teachers because of their religious, political, or social views, Greene contended, remained a highly problematic practice. Although Greene reported that members of the American Bar Association seemed sympathetic, they tabled the resolution for action later in the year (quoted in Introduction, 1978). Meanwhile, the Supreme Court decided not to consider the Gaylord case, which meant that the battle in California over the Briggs Initiative would receive neither boost nor hindrance from the nation's highest court. Activists on both sides of the issue then began mobilizing.

On August 3, 1977, Briggs staged a press conference during which he announced that the "California Save Our Children" campaign would seek 312,000 petition signatures. This would remove the decision from legislators and instead place it directly in the hands of voters in a popular referendum—like the Miami Metro referendum. The California attorney general then needed to frame the legal language for the referendum by mid-September, after which Briggs would have 150 days to gather the signatures. The *Lesbian Tide* reported that because the California attorney general planned to run against Briggs in the June 1978 Republican gubernatorial primary, he probably felt no urgency about moving Briggs's proposal through the process. The *Tide* also contended that Briggs's measure might fail on legal grounds because it was "hopelessly unconstitutional" (Cordova, 1977, pp. 13, 35).

In California's largest cities, gay liberation advocates started preparing for a major fight. Although Briggs's measure might be dismissed for technical or legal reasons, early activists wanted to take no chances. The Gay Teachers and School Workers Coalition immediately called on all teachers to build support networks with teachers around the state ("Briggs Goes Bananas," 1977). The group organized a media team specifically to work with journalists and reporters, because "in the past others, both straight and gay have presumed to speak for us; we will speak for ourselves." Although the Gay Teachers and School Workers Coalition enjoyed membership both of lesbians and gay men, several women organized the Lesbian Caucus to assure that the public heard their views. This strategy also made sense to the lesbian school workers who lived as separatists. The Gay Teachers and School

Workers Coalition formed an education committee to challenge "the lies and myths surrounding gay lifestyles and most especially the outrageous stereotypes of those gays who work with children in whatever the capacity." The speakers' bureau sent members to a wide variety of civic groups requesting their services. And finally, the Gay Teachers and School Workers Coalition pressured the influential AFT to go on record in full support of lesbian and gay teachers at this particularly challenging moment (Kurland, 1977).

The long-standing efforts of the Gay Teachers and School Workers Coalition and allied groups around the country such as the New York Gay Teachers Association began paying off. In October 1977, the American Federation of Teachers released an official position statement on the Briggs Initiative—one that left no doubt about its stake in the battle. Don Liles, executive vice president of the AFT, wrote:

> Every individual and organization in California concerned with quality education at all levels should take an unequivocal position opposing the Briggs initiative, the provisions of which would launch a campaign in our schools reminiscent of the red witch-hunts of the late unlamented 1950's.
>
> Because of the initiative, California is about to become a massive test of human rights in a renewed struggle going on in America, as a result of resurgence of the radical right. The issues singled out are: equality for women, abortion, school desegregation, public employees bargaining rights, academic freedom, freedom of the press, gay rights, and federally financed child-care assistance.
>
> The radical right has found that one of the most successful tools is the conversion of civil concerns into moral issues, cloaked in the symbol of the "American family." The easiest issue for mustering broad-based support for the rest of the radical right's campaign is the issue of gay rights.
>
> Senator Briggs has chosen to attack gay women and men, and has singled out a minority within a minority: gay educators. He has shrewdly found a "sitting duck" issue, but his initiative is merely the first in a series of major "moral crusades" supported by the radical right. (Liles, 1977)

Liles made it clear that the AFT viewed the Briggs Initiative not just as a campaign targeted at lesbian and gay educators but rather as a broad attack on the rights of all teachers. Because of the sweeping language of the initiative, *any* teacher who publicly supported the rights of homosexuals could be scrutinized and dismissed. Perhaps of even greater concern to the teachers' union leader, if Briggs's measure passed, its terms would override union contracts. Teachers union members—and, indeed, union members across professions—quickly suspected that Briggs intended to weaken unions with the measure. His previous anti-union stances seemed to confirm this possibility (Hollibaugh, 2000).

Finally, Liles indicated that Briggs mainly focused on lesbian and gay teachers because, as "sitting ducks," they faced a nearly irresolvable dilemma: to fight the Briggs Initiative, lesbian and gay educators needed to identify themselves publicly; however, should the initiative pass, educators who had identified themselves publicly could and probably would be dismissed. The threat of job loss already loomed so large that only a relatively small proportion of lesbian and gay educators in California joined LGBT teacher organizations, marched in pride parades or identified themselves among colleagues, students, and parents. If the initiative passed, that fear would increase substantially.

Gay activists also experienced some initial reticence about fully supporting the rights of LGBT teachers. Some gay activists did not want to "liberate" education without LGBT teachers openly fighting for themselves. An important part of being in the movement was, as the dismissed Maryland teacher, Joe Acanfora, had observed, "If you are homosexual, say it—and get your rights anyway." However, educators notoriously resisted "saying it" because most believed they would *not* get their rights anyway. School districts around the country consistently demonstrated why. For example, the Iowa Civil Liberties Union released a survey indicating that 83 percent of Iowa superintendents surveyed reported that they would not hire a gay teacher ("News from Our Friends," 1978, p. 6). Also, gay activists understood quite clearly that no matter how much credible scientific evidence they offered to suggest that homosexuals molested children proportionately far less often than heterosexual men, the linkage remained strong in public thought. Anita Bryant had capitalized successfully on this potent association in Miami—and she attempted to strengthen it further. To defend lesbian and gay teachers successfully, opponents of the Briggs Initiative would need to confront the gay child molestation bugaboo squarely. They also would need to convince voters that lesbian and gay teachers did not otherwise harm the gender and sexual development of students.

Finally, LGBT activists could reach no agreement about the most effective strategy to employ. Most believed they would lose but that campaigning hard might soften the ground for the future. Some argued that voters might respond best if they viewed the Briggs measure as a civil rights issue. Surely persons of color, women, and persons in other marginalized groups would recognize common elements in the fight for basic rights. Others believed that the real issue in voters' minds concerned homosexuality—and not the specific employment rights of LGBT teachers. To these activists, the best way to gain public support lay in helping voters understand homosexuality better and opening a larger discussion about sexuality in society. Essentially, they maintained that skirting the real issue made no sense. The best path led right to the core of voters' fears and concerns. A few leaders contended that LGBT possessed little clout with voters, so they suggested raising money and hiring allies to conduct the bulk of the campaign. Most activists overwhelmingly rejected this hands-off strategy as playing into the oppression of LGBT persons and accepting their second-class status (Hollibaugh, 2000).

Help in fighting Briggs's measure arrived from unanticipated supporters. For instance, the well-respected national education reporter, John Merrow, wrote a featured article for the September 1977 issue of *Parents' Magazine*. In his provocatively titled piece, "Gay Sex in the Schools," Merrow cited evidence supplied by recent studies of child sexual abuse. He concluded that "my way of answering the question, what do homosexual teachers do to children, is: nothing in particular by virtue of their homosexuality, neither by inclining children toward homosexuality, nor by sexual seduction or molestation. Despite what many parents may fear, homosexuals are almost never child abusers or molesters. Those crimes are nearly always committed by 'straight' males" (Merrow, 1977, pp. 66, 100, 104, 106).

Other national figures weighed in to express their indifference or even their contempt for LGBT educators, however. "I know that there are homosexuals who teach, and the children don't suffer," said then-President Jimmy Carter. Signaling his intention to stay out of the issue, he continued, "But this is a subject I don't particularly want to involve myself in" (quoted in Anonymous, 1977, p. 94). The extremely conservative Max Rafferty, who had served for years as California superintendent of public instruction, also joined the fray. Despite the fact that courts struck down California's sodomy law in May 1975,[1] Rafferty argued in a 1977 issue of *Phi Delta Kappan*, the widely circulated magazine for professional educators, that

Sodomy is against the law everywhere I've ever been or heard of, and its illegality alone should make the matter moot. . . .

For eight clangorous and combative years, I chaired the statewide credentials commission of the most populous state in the nation. Our job in large part was to decide each month whether certain teachers were morally fit to be allowed to teach in California schools. And from the beginning, I do assure you, we took for granted the self-evident proposition that a homosexual in a school job was as preposterously out of the question as a heroin mainliner working in the local drugstore. . . .

School principals and superintendents should refuse to rehire probationary teachers who turn out to be abnormal despite the efforts of preliminary screening. And no one who suffers from this kind of abnormality should be recommended for tenure.

Don't tell me it can't be done. I've been a school administrator for 30 years and I know darned well it can. I repeat: No one has the "right" to be a schoolteacher. It's a privilege, dearly bought and stringently conferred. (Rafferty, 1977, pp. 91–92)

Gay activists understood quickly enough that they had a significant fight on their hands. Even though Briggs, Bryant, Rafferty, and other opponents of the rights of LGBT educators frequently offered arguments that could not be substantiated, they tapped a powerful sentiment among many voters. Such leaders basically played on voters' fear of homosexuality, about which most knew quite little. When reporters asked Briggs point-blank if he knew of any circumstances in California schools when homosexual teachers had cross-dressed, solicited among their students, or promoted homosexuality in classrooms, he reportedly held up what he called a "recruitment booklet," a pamphlet for students that answered their questions about being gay. He never offered any other evidence. When Ellen Broidy and Jan Zobel, two members of the Gay Teachers and School Workers Coalition, appeared on a San Jose television news show with Briggs, Broidy thought things went well at first. The interviewer asked reasonable questions that both Broidy and Zobel handled skillfully. Then Briggs requested permission to "answer." Broidy recounted that Briggs flew into a tirade, using phrases like "sick" and "militant lifestyle." She concluded, "There was little pretense of rational thought on his part during this concluding portion of the show. The demagogue of fear came across loud and clear" (Broidy, 1977, pp. 1, 3). At this early stage, gay activists argued, "We can't look at this thing rationally. . . . California is a big state and we have our share of hysterics." The only way to respond, they contended, was to prepare for "our biggest battle yet" (Cordova, 1977, pp. 13, 35).

That battle took shape quickly. Briggs needed to produce 312,000 signatures by January 1978 to place his initiative in a public referendum. Gay activists feared that if popular vote decided the matter, Briggs would win overwhelmingly. Instead, they hoped technicalities or a ruling on the measure's unconstitutionality would spare them (Teachers' battle looms, 1977). Just in case, however, gay activists organized a statewide conference in Sacramento in September. At this conference, participants unanimously agreed that they should invest fully in campaigning against the Briggs Initiative. Subsequently, they organized a larger conference in mid-December on the campus of the University of Southern California. During this event, activists from around the state coordinated their strategies. They arranged speak-outs that featured such notables as the eminent researcher Evelyn Hooker, and the feminist Gloria Steinem.

Participants in the state activists' caucus articulated their core principles for the campaign. They agreed that strong links existed between oppressions directed at "third world" persons (persons of color), women, lesbians and gay men, and other groups. To work against the oppression of LGBT persons, activists pledged to fight racism, sexism, and other oppressions. The Gay Teachers and School Workers Coalition sent five of its members to the meeting. One teacher reported that "the plenary session was an amazing experience. . . . Over 40 resolutions were presented and passed, mostly by large majorities. The resolutions dealt with many issues, including the rights of Gay people, Third World people, women and other oppressed groups. It was encouraging to hear that most people at the conference agreed that there is a connection between all these oppressions and that it's important not to treat the oppression of gay people as a single isolated issue; we need to support other struggles." Attendees agreed on a representative structure with racial, sex, and geographical balance (Gode-von Aesch, 1978, p. 3). This development both recognized and countered a prevailing tendency in many LGBT organizations in which whites dominated numerically, led proceedings, and demonstrated little commitment to or understanding of issues important to persons of color. Attendees agreed that resisting one oppression meant understanding and resisting kindred oppressions.

The *Lesbian Tide* reported that the Briggs Initiative posed such a serious threat that, despite long-standing differences, lesbians and gay men were beginning to work together. A reporter concluded that "the women's caucus agreed that the majority of men at the [state activists'] conference were making an effort to be friendly and non-sexist." Gay and lesbian conference attendees passed resolutions supporting the Equal Rights Amendment, full custody rights for lesbian mothers, lesbian and gay representatives in media and other public events where possible—or only lesbians if only one representative were permitted, and co-sexual conveners at meetings (Duke, 1977, pp. 13–14).

Meanwhile, Briggs's campaign encountered early problems. One Briggs worker allegedly encouraged signatories to forge their names. Briggs then missed his January deadline for producing 312,000 signatures. Finally, however, on May 1, 1978, Briggs filed over 500,000 signatures—which placed the referendum on the November 1978 ballot ("The Briggs Initiative: Menace in California," 1978). The official wording of the referendum, released by the California attorney general, read:

> One of the most fundamental interests of the State is the establishment and the preservation of the family unit. Consistent with this interest is the State's duty to protect impressionable youth from influences which are antithetical to this vital interest. This duty is particularly compelling when the state undertakes to educate the youth and by law, requires them to be exposed to the state's chosen educational environment throughout their formative years.
>
> A schoolteacher, teacher's aide, school administrator or counselor has a professional duty directed exclusively towards the moral as well as intellectual, social and civic development of young and impressionable students.
>
> As a result of continued close and prolonged contact with schoolchildren, a teacher, teacher's aide, school administrator or counselor becomes a role model whose words, behavior and actions are likely to be emulated by students coming under his or her care, instruction, supervision, administration, guidance and protection.
>
> For these reasons the state finds a compelling interest in refusing to employ and in terminating the employment of a schoolteacher, a teacher's aide, a school administrator or a counselor, subject to reasonable restrictions and qualifications who engages in public homosexual activity and/or public homosexual conduct directed at, or likely to come to the attention of, schoolchildren or other school employees.
>
> This proscription is essential since such activity and conduct undermines that state's interest in preserving and perpetuating the conjugal family unit. (quoted in Donohue, n.d.)

By this time, Briggs knew he would not receive the Republican nomination for California governor. However, he still harbored lofty political aspirations for the future, and he reportedly hoped that his initiative would earn the support he needed. To file the half-million petition signatures, he chose to return to the steps of the San Francisco City Hall because, as he explained, "it is the moral garbage dump of homosexuality in this country." The last time he had spoken there, he had tripped and fallen in front of hundreds of protestors. This time, only around forty demonstrators greeted him—and they kept their distance (quoted in Burns, 1978). From this point forward, Briggs's measure would bear the official title of "Proposition 6," which would appear on the November 7 ballot for all Californians.

When Briggs filed the half-million petition signatures, many gay activists, though preparing themselves for this eventuality, voiced disbelief and pessimism. The editors of *The Advocate* gave in to their sense of foreboding in an unusual lead editorial in the June 1978 issue:

> In the 10½ years *The Advocate* has been published, we pride ourselves in never knowingly telling you untruths, no matter how unpleasant the facts have been. This is one of those times when the truth we have to report is very unpleasant. The bottom line is that it is most unlikely that the Briggs initiative can be defeated in this November's election. We shall have waged a good campaign if the vote ratio is less than the 2 to 1 majority against us that occurred in St. Paul and Miami. We may lose even in San Francisco. We can expect a multimillion-dollar media campaign of lies and hate directed at us. Some gay people probably will commit suicide under this onslaught of hate. Few gay Californians will not experience a lot of pain and anger between now and November. . . . There is not one example in history where a majority has voted for rights of a minority. Despite many people's false beliefs in right triumphing in democratic ways, history clearly shows that success for minority groups has been the result of patient, careful and sophisticated economic and political power applied skillfully and persuasively to rulers and legislatures, not to the votes of the masses. . . . Thanks to many of you, The Concerned Voters of California (CVC) financed an excellent voter survey in California. It told us many things. Among them, the most important is that, except for Boy and Girl Scout leaders, there is no profession Californians wish less open to gay people than teaching. Although they are willing to have us quietly in their midst in many ways, they don't want us near their children. Yes, I know we make superior teachers and that the only people for whom we might be role models are gay children. The public doesn't believe this truth. The issue is too emotional and there isn't time to change their minds. In an election campaign, our truth will have to compete with bigoted lies. Our enemies can and will outspend us, about 10 to 1. Voters who are at all confused will undoubtedly follow their emotional reaction. In short, John Briggs has struck at the weakest point in our line of defense. (Goodstein, 1978, p. 6)

Despite the editor's sense of the futility of the anti-Briggs effort, gay activists and increasing numbers of writers for national media voiced support for defeating Proposition 6. *McCall's* ran an article titled, "Should Homosexuals be Allowed to Teach?" To prepare the story, reporters surveyed 1,300 school officials around the country and interviewed a number of others. Reporters gave the views of Meryl Friedman, co-spokesperson for the New York Gay Teachers Association, considerable weight in the piece, as they did for those of Drs. Jack Weinberg, president, and John Spiegel, former president of the American Psychiatric Association, both of whom supported the rights of lesbian and gay teachers. They reaffirmed the recent studies indicating that heterosexual men molested children proportionately far more often than gay men and lesbians. The piece concluded, "If only the issue could be freed of the exaggerated claims and irresponsible fear mongering, no rational obstacle should stand in the way of letting homosexuals remain and become teachers, subject to those controls and standards of behavior that the profession applies to all teachers" (Hechinger & Hechinger, 1978, pp. 100, 160–162).

By early fall, editors of the *Los Angeles Times* registered their stance on Proposition 6. Although they considered the measure to be "so repugnant to basic American freedoms that we'd prefer to ignore it altogether," they decided to go on record early and strongly in opposition to it. In short, they described it as "an invasion of privacy, and a potential disruption of the education process. It's vicious and mean-spirited, too." If the issue were child molestation, they argued that sufficient laws already existed to remedy problems that might arise. On the contrary, to Proposition 6 supporters, the issue seemed to boil down to opposing homosexuality. Further, editors declared the initiative "so vaguely worded that it would subject teachers to sweeping allegations on baseless charges; it would dignify rumor and innuendo." Any child who disliked his or her teacher would have a powerful weapon for harassing them. For these and other reasons, the editors concluded, "the teachers deserve support now, and the protection of votes against Proposition 6 in November" ("Dignifying Rumor and Innuendo," 1978, sec. 2, p. 6).

As the battle over Proposition 6 played out in state and national media, gay activists worked intensely at the grass-roots level. The recently established Lesbian Schoolworkers organized a demonstration supporting a San Francisco Board of Education resolution opposing Proposition 6 (Lesbian Schoolworkers, 1978). Briggs had successfully staged a number of media events over the early months of the campaign, including speaking on television talk shows and participating in radio interviews. Members of the Gay Teachers and School Workers Coalition decided to protest outside radio and television stations each time Briggs made an appearance. Occasionally, such demonstrations netted activists the opportunity to choose a representative to debate Briggs on the air (Asher, 1978).

Anita Bryant joined Briggs in working for Proposition 6. During the months after her successful "Save Our Children" campaign, Bryant formed a new group, Anita Bryant Ministries. Through this organization, she sought funds from a national audience of conservative Christians to support advertising and other efforts to assure passage of Briggs's handiwork. In one mailing to millions across the country, Bryant claimed:

> Dear Friend: I don't hate the homosexuals! But as a mother, I must protect my children from their evil influence. And I am sure you have heard about my fight here in Dade County, Florida—and nationwide—for the rights of my children and yours.... I cannot remain silent while radical, militant homosexuals are raising millions of dollars and waging a campaign for special privileges under the disguise of "civil rights."... Do you realize what they want? They want to recruit our school children under the protection of the laws of our land! ... And remember, militant homosexuals want their sexual behavior and preference to be considered respectable and accepted by society. They want to recruit your children and teach them the virtues of becoming a homosexual.... We must not give them the legal right to destroy the moral fiber of our families and our nation.... (Bryant, n.d.)

Briggs and Bryant conveyed urgency to their contributors by conjuring images of wealthy gays raising millions of dollars to fund a major media blitz. Contrary to this portrayal, however, gay activists struggled to raise funds to mount a credible campaign. When one organization hosted a large fundraising reception, reporters and photographers showed up to cover the event—which sent closeted guests fleeing. Wealthy allies who sponsored other receptions found that guests resisted attending because they dreaded being seen. Many supporters reportedly refused to wear buttons or place bumper stickers on their cars out of fear that if the measure passed, they might face retroactive punishment. Because the law decreed that political contributions of $50 or more must be reported to the secretary of state, gay activists typically collected checks of $49. Although gay activists had hoped to raise at least $1 million to stage a credible media effort, they only collected around half this amount altogether (Cordova, 1978).

Despite these formidable obstacles, momentum began shifting slightly against Proposition 6. During the 1978 annual summer meeting of its Representative Assembly, the National Education Association approved a resolution affirming its opposition to Proposition 6. The resolution also committed the NEA's legal and legislative resources to defeating this and similar measures (Harbeck, 1997). Then in September, Wilson Riles, the California superintendent of public instruction, announced that Proposition 6 served no useful purpose. "We have enough laws on the books to protect the youngsters," he argued (quoted in "Riles Sees No Need for Prop. 6," 1978, sec. 2, p. 8). A number of prominent state politicians across the political spectrum registered their opposition to Proposition 6 as well, including former governor Ronald Reagan, San Francisco Mayor Willie Brown, and Governor Jerry Brown (Beck, Kasindorm, & Reese, 1978). Entertainers and celebrities including Cher, Jane Fonda, John Travolta, and Norman Lear attended fundraisers to defeat the Briggs Initiative—even though many notable LGBT entertainers stepped away from the spotlight out of fear of career ruin ("To Class or to Court?," 1978; Cordova, 1978). In mid-October, the archbishop of San Francisco went on record against Proposition 6 (S.F. Archbishop opposes passage of Proposition 6, 1978). The Los Angeles Board of Education also officially and unanimously opposed the measure (McCurdy, 1978).

Some of the most sensational events of the campaign included debates between John Briggs and proposition opponents, staged as the referendum approached. One televised debate broadcast in September featured Briggs and Claudia Norby, a lesbian activist, who was assisted by Sandy Lowe, a gay man. Although Norby assumed the role as Briggs's primary debate opponent, cameramen rarely showed her face. Instead, they filmed Lowe, so the debate appeared to be primarily between two men with a woman's voice thrown in. One lesbian, writing for the *Sonoma SCLGA*, complained that this had become a typical pattern in the campaign to defeat the Briggs Initiative. Lesbians' substantial contributions were being marginalized at every turn, she argued. Even though other lesbians sought to debate Briggs after this event, Briggs only chose gay male opponents, particularly Harvey Milk, the first openly gay man elected to the San Francisco Board of Supervisors, and Larry Berner, a little-known gay teacher from Healdsburg (Riggs, 1978). Milk and Briggs frequently tangled in high-profile debates around the state. Briggs reeled off well-practiced lines from cards that he carried. With great regularity, he charged that homosexuals accounted for a third of teachers in San Francisco and a fifth in Los Angeles. "Most of them are in the closet, and frankly, that's where I think they should remain." Hoping to inspire fear, Briggs alleged that "homosexuals want your children. . . . They don't have any children of their own. If they don't recruit children or very young people, they'd die away. They don't have any means of replenishing. That's why they want to be teachers and be equal status and have those people serve as role models and encourage people to join them." Milk, on the other hand, responded to these serious and dogmatic accusations with incisive wit. "How do you teach homosexuality—like French?" or "If it were true that children mimicked their teachers, you'd sure have a helluva lot more nuns running around" (quoted in Shilts, 1982).

Briggs also debated Larry Berner several times. Berner, a shy, tall, bearded, and well-liked second grade teacher, initially wanted no central role in the "No on 6" effort. He had written an article in the *Sonoma SCLGA* describing his experiences as a "spy" in the Briggs petition effort. When his article attracted broad attention, the parents of several children in his class requested transfers. However, Berner enjoyed strong support from colleagues and his school administration. Briggs learned of Berner's activities and decided to make an example of him. Berner rose to the challenge, though, deciding to fight Proposition 6 actively (Sharpe, 1978). In late October, Briggs came to Berner's hometown to debate him in a spectacle that attracted over half of the town's residents—as well as substantial media interest from around the state. The *Los Angeles Times* described the event as "strange" and "weird" because of colorful protests outside as well as the heated rhetoric exchanged inside. During the 90-minute debate, Briggs charged that "we don't allow prostitutes to teach. . . . You can't get married in the state of California if you're a homosexual couple. . . . If they're not good enough to get married, how are we to support the notion that they're to serve as role models (for school children) when they can't bear children themselves?" Briggs made clear the importance he attached to heterosexual modeling for students. After Briggs described the sexual activities of gay men, Berner countered, "Your mind is in the gutter. . . . The children at my school are not obsessed with my sexuality, as you seem to be, senator." The *Los Angeles Times* indicated that around two-thirds of those in attendance appeared to be staunch Berner supporters who applauded his statements vigorously. In the end, Briggs denied that Proposition 6 would require schools to get rid of all homosexual teachers. Instead, once again he maintained he only intended to purge the ones who came out or otherwise vocally supported gay rights. Berner challenged Briggs convincingly, matching him point for point, something Briggs had not anticipated. Berner then became an instant celebrity among gay activists around the state (quoted in McManus, 1978, sec. 1, p. 3).

In the final days before the vote, national media ran powerful editorials encouraging Californians to strike down Proposition 6. For example, the *New Republic* explained that Anita Bryant's "Bible-thumping bombast works well on conservative voters with Dark Age attitudes about job discrimination and equal rights. The California vote will be the first statewide poll on the issue, and its passage would be one of the most damaging and ugly uses of referendum politics in recent memory" ("A California Travesty," 1978, p. 81).

On November 7, when voters filed into their polling places, they received the official voters' pamphlet explaining Proposition 6. At first, the pamphlet warned voters that "the fiscal impact of the proposition would depend on the total number of hearings initiated." Because the total number of cases to be brought potentially could be enormous, state fiscal agents indicated, "we thus conclude that the proposition could result in substantial costs to the state, school districts, and school employees due to an increase in dismissal hearings, plus additional court costs to the state and county governments." The pamphlet then offered brief statements both for and against the measure (Eu, 1978, n.p.).

As votes came in throughout the day, gay activists began celebrating. By evening, reporters announced that Proposition 6 had gone down in a resounding defeat, by a margin of 58 to 42 percent. Less than two hours after the polls closed, Briggs conceded. Meanwhile, Los Angeles Mayor Tom Bradley triumphantly addressed a crowd of 3,000 lesbian and gay activists, telling them, "How sweet it is! You have put on the greatest campaign ever seen in California, uniting all religions, all parties, all minorities. You have carried the message to all. May this be a lesson that Briggs will never forget. The spirit of justice lives in California because of you." Briggs, however, vowed that he would reintroduce the same measure in two years with a better and stronger organization. This would be difficult, though, given that even his conservative home district had rejected it (quoted in "How Sweet It Is!," 1979, pp. 10–12).

Over the weeks following the dramatic vote, activists and editorialists took stock of what had transpired. In assessing the aftermath, however, mainstream media did not call the overwhelming defeat of the bill a victory for lesbian and gay teachers—or even for LGBT rights. Instead, the *San Francisco Chronicle, Los Angeles Times,* and the Associated Press indicated that the defeat was more about resisting governmental interference in personal rights than about homosexuality ("How Sweet It Is!," 1979). A local station, KHJ, aired a similar view with an editorial explaining, "We at KHJ-TV believe that the reason such a majority of voters went against the measure was not necessarily great sympathy for homosexuals in our schools so much as it was a real antipathy for any laws which open the way to serious erosion of the hard won civil rights statutes. Clearly, many felt that this potential loss was greater than any present danger from the sexual preferences of school personnel" (Schaen, 1978). An editorialist for *The Nation* argued that although both "Yes" and "No" forces in the Proposition 6 effort operated with the pretense that the issue mainly concerned LGBT teachers, instead he argued that the central and larger issue was about changing views toward homosexuality in this country. He summarized, "Gay Rights won a victory in the protection of homosexual schoolteachers. The movement won even more by further establishing homosexuality in American culture as a viable sexual alternative" (Gusfield, 1978, pp. 633–635).

In the final analysis, many voters did reject Proposition 6 because it threatened basic free speech rights. It would have provided a point of entry through which further restrictions on basic rights might pass. Although many Californians did not particularly like the thought of LGBT persons working in schools, they also recognized that this measure would have taken away rights from a targeted group of persons. They would not want LGBT persons to gain special rights, but they also did not especially want them to lose them, either. African American voters, the group that most strongly opposed the initiative, expressed grave concerns about a measure that targeted one group for oppression. Latino voters, however, largely supported Proposition 6. Some analysts concluded that this may have been due in part to the influence of rural Catholic churches that staunchly opposed homosexuality. Union members opposed Proposition 6 because it challenged the right of unions to negotiate contracts. For a number of voters, though, the Briggs initiative centrally concerned not basic rights, but homosexuality. The highly public debates inspired by the measure stimulated many to rethink what they thought they knew about persons who desire others of the same sex. And ironically, even though Briggs purportedly introduced the measure to protect students from exposure to homosexuality, the vigorous and very public discussions provoked by the referendum dramatically increased students' knowledge about LGBT persons (Hollibaugh, 2000).

In a retrospective piece, the *San Francisco Examiner* reported that second-grade teacher Larry Berner seemed much happier than he was when Proposition 6 loomed. When he dined in restaurants, he felt freer to hold hands with his male companions. "I don't need to worry any more about what people think of my being gay," he explained. "It's been a joyous experience, being out of the closet. I always expected that something horrible would happen to me if people knew, but the most amazing thing is that absolutely nothing has happened. I'm surviving beautifully." When one of his school board members, a minister, called him a "moral carcinogenic among the tender treasures of the heavenly Father," Berner responded, "That just cracked me up. It was so outrageous that anybody would say that about me" (quoted in Sharpe, 1979, pp. 1, 5). Berner also decided that during the course of the Proposition 6 campaign, Briggs had defamed him by implying and stating outright that Berner could not be trusted with children. Berner eventually won a $10,000 judgment in a defamation lawsuit against Briggs (Associated Press, 1982).[2]

Media reflection on the Briggs vote ended abruptly, however. On November 27, only 20 days after the referendum, San Francisco Supervisor Dan White assassinated Harvey Milk and Mayor George Moscone. White, an anti-gay conservative, quickly confessed to the murders in which he saved a set of hollow-headed, exploding bullets for Milk, who had debated Briggs on a number of occasions. After the news broke, thousands of gay activists and their supporters filled the streets from the Castro district to City Hall, holding lit candles and moving slowly to the sound of a drum (Shilts, 1982). A jury handed White a light sentence: 5 years in prison and parole. It had accepted the defense argument that White's penchant for Twinkies and other junk food had contributed to his depression and the eventual murders (Shilts, 1982).

These proved to be painful months for Briggs as well. Reports emerged that he might face investigation by the IRS (McManus & Leighton, 1979). Then during November 1981, Briggs announced that he would not seek reelection. Echoing an earlier Nixon speech, Briggs said, "You won't have me to kick around anymore." Explaining that he was burned out, he told reporters that he planned to invest in real estate and do consulting work (quoted in "Farewell to Briggs," 1981).

Newly energized activists rallied around the cause of lesbian and gay teachers because figures such as John Briggs and Anita Bryant had identified them as potent fund-raising targets—ones who fought back only at their professional peril. Even though activists rallied to support LGBT teachers, and by extension all LGBT persons, some also resisted championing a class of persons who came out only reluctantly. Before Proposition 6 LGBT school workers rarely stepped forward to identify themselves and resist employment discrimination because they believed they would lose their jobs with little recourse. However, this battle inspired many LGBT school workers to work openly for their own rights as well as those of all oppressed persons. Together with LGBT activists, larger national associations, and other allied organizations, the No on 6 activists waged a formidable campaign. After the vote, though, some activists wanted to distance the larger gay movement from the issue that continued to make it the most vulnerable: the unfounded, yet continued perception that LGBT persons either molested children or influenced them to become "deviant." LGBT school workers still worked at the center of this zone of vulnerability. In the years ahead, they would need to find new bases of support to resist the oppression of LGBT persons in schools.

Notes

1. For a discussion of how the California sodomy law was struck down, see William N. Eskridge, *Gaylaw: Challenging the Apartheid of the Closet* (1999), pp. 106–107.
2. Berner subsequently taught English in Japan for several years. After suffering with AIDS and providing AIDS counseling for others, he died on January 25, 1995, in Tokyo. See Kyodo News Service, Tokyo, "U.S. AIDS Sufferer Berner Dies," January 25, 1995.

References

Anonymous. (1977, October). A homosexual teacher's argument and plea. *Phi Delta Kappan, 94.*

Asher, P. (1978, April). Toe-to-toe, tête-à-tête with Briggs. *Unlearning the lie, gay teachers and school workers coalition.* June Mazer Collection, "Briggs" file.

Associated Press, Domestic News, San Francisco. (1982, September 2). Teacher wins defamation settlement.

Beck, M., Kasindorm, M., & Reese, M. (1978, October 2). Gay teachers. *Newsweek*, p. 56.

Briggs does his thing amid jeers of the gays. (1977, June 15). *San Francisco Examiner.*

Briggs goes bananas. (1977, August/September). *Gay teachers and school workers coalition.* June Mazer Collection, "Briggs" file.

Briggs Initiative: Menace in California. (1978, September/October). *Gay Teachers Association Newsletter,* Eric Rofes's private collection.

Broidy, E. (1977, October/November). A personal reflection: KNTV interview. *Unlearning the lie, Gay teachers and school workers coalition.* June Mazer Collection, "Briggs" file.

Bryant, A. (n.d.) Fundraising/survey letter for Anita Bryant Ministries. June Mazer Collection, "Briggs" file.

Burns, J. (1978, May 2.) Briggs files anti-gay initiative. *San Francisco Chronicle.*

California travesty. (1978, October 28). *The New Republic, 179,* 8.

Clendinen, D., & Nagourney, A. (1999). *Out for good: The struggle to build a gay rights movement in America.* New York: Simon & Schuster.

Cordova, J. (1977, September/October). Teachers may face initiative. *Lesbian Tide.*

Cordova, J. (1978, November/December). Hollywood, Reagan turn out against Briggs. *Lesbian Tide.*

Dignifying rumor and innuendo. (1978, August 21). *Los Angeles Times*, p. C6.

Donohue, P. (n.d.) Initiative measure to be submitted directly to the voters with analysis. June Mazer Collection, "Briggs" file.

Duke, L. (1977, November/December). California goes on orange alert! *Lesbian Tide.*

Eskridge, W.N. (1999). *Gaylaw: Challenging the apartheid of the closet.* Cambridge, MA: Harvard University Press.

Eu, M.F. (1978). California voters pamphlet, General Election, November 7, 1978. June Mazer Collection, "Briggs" file.

Farewell to Briggs. (1981, November 13). *Los Angeles Times.*

Fuchs, J. (1978, August 31–September 6). Briggs targets America's latest scapegoats. *Santa Cruz Independent.*

Gay Teachers Association Newsletter. (1978b, September/October).

Gode-von Aesch, M. (1978, April). Statewide network fights Briggs Initiative. *Unlearning the lie, Gay teachers and school workers coalition.* June Mazer Collection, "Briggs" file.

Goodstein, D. (1978, June). Fighting the Briggs brigade. *The Advocate*, 6.

Gusfield, J.R. (1978, December 9). Proposition 6: Political ceremony in California. *The Nation, 227*(20), 633–635.

Hager, P. (1977, August 29). Gay teachers: Both sides look to high court. *Boston Globe.*

Harbeck, K. (1997). *Gay and lesbian educators: Personal freedoms, public constraints.* Malden, MA: Amethyst Press.

Hechinger, G., & Hechinger, F. (1978, March). Should homosexuals be allowed to teach? *McCall's, 105*(6), 100, 160–163.

Hollibaugh, A. (2000). *My dangerous desires: A queer girl dreaming her way home.* Durham, NC: Duke University Press.

How sweet it is! (1979, January/February). *Lesbian Tide.*

Introduction. (1978a, February). *Gay Teachers Association Newsletter,* Eric Rofes's private collection.

Kurland, D. (1977, September). Gay teachers and school workers coalition. *Plexus.*

Kyodo News Service, Tokyo. (1995, January 25). U.S. AIDS sufferer Berner dies.

Lesbian Schoolworkers. (1978). Announcement of demonstration by lesbian schoolworkers' group. June Mazer Collection, "Briggs" file.

Liles, D. (1977). The Briggs Initiative: Shades of Joe McCarthy. June Mazer Collection, "Schools—Proposition 6" file.

McCurdy, J. (1978, October 19). School board unanimously opposes Prop. 6. *Los Angeles Times.*

McManus, D. (1978, October 26). Briggs debates gay teacher. *Los Angeles Times.*

McManus, K., & Leighton, D. (1979, July 2). Briggs's double life under scrutiny. *New West.*

Merrow, J. (1977, September). Gay sex in the schools. *Parents' Magazine, 52*(9), 66, 100, 104, 106.

News from our friends. (1978, September/October). *Gay Teachers Association Newsletter,* Eric Rofes's private collection.

Rafferty, M. (1977, October). Should gays teach school? *Phi Delta Kappan, 59*(2), 91–92.

Riggs, C. (1978, October). Sexist bias distorts Prop 6 campaign. *Sonoma SCLGA.*

Riles sees no need for Prop. 6. (1978, September 7). *Los Angeles Times*, p. D8.

Schaen, L. (1978, November 20–22). KHJ-TV editorial comment. June Mazer Collection, "Briggs" file.

S.F. Archbishop opposes passage of Proposition 6. (1978, October 12). *Los Angeles Times*, p. B28.

Sharpe, I. (1978, June 25). A gay teacher comes out to fight Briggs. *San Francisco Chronicle.*

Sharpe, I. (1979, April 9). Celebrated Healdsburg gay finds happiness. *San Francisco Examiner.*

Shilts, R. (1982). *The mayor of Castro Street: The life and times of Harvey Milk.* New York: St. Martin's Press.

Skelton, G. (1978, November 1). Voters' opposition to Props. 5 and 6 growing. *Los Angeles Times.*

Teachers' battle looms. (1977, November/December). *Lesbian Tide.*

Teens say "no" to anti-gay discrimination. (1978, September/October). *Gay Teachers Association Newsletter,* Eric Rofes's private collection.

To class or to court? Teachers on the line. (1978, September/October). *Lesbian Tide.*

Why is gay law needed, anyway? (1977, June 12). *Los Angeles Times*, sec. 5.

CHAPTER SIX

The Religious Right and Public Education

The Paranoid Politics of Homophobia

CATHERINE A. LUGG

Introduction

> Homosexual activists are deadly serious about using the education process to teach kids that homosexuality is okay and that anyone who thinks otherwise is a "bigot." If parents are not vigilant in ferreting out such propaganda and countering it, they will witness the rise of a generation hostile to five millennia of Judeo-Christian teaching proscribing homosexual behavior. (LaBarbera, 1996, n.p.)

With the emergence of the Religious Right as a major political force (Bennett, 1995; Diamond, 1995), U.S. public schooling has been subjected to blistering attacks. Whether the area is curriculum, student services, disciplinary policies, or staffing, each has undergone intense scrutiny by the Religious Right regarding its possible moral influence on children (Arocha, 1993; Gaddy, Hall, & Marzano, 1996; Provenzo, 1990). Although this focus is not surprising given public education's prominent role within American society, what is astonishing are some of the conclusions drawn by members of the Religious Right. Some adherents depict public school reform efforts, policies, and practices as promoting homosexuality (Boyd, Lugg, & Zahorchak, 1996; Gaddy et al., 1996; McCarthy, 1996).

These accusations have been leveled whether or not gay/lesbian/bisexual issues are part of a specific educational program or reform. Given most Americans' reticence and occasional hostility in dealing with issues involving sexual orientation and public schooling (Elam, Rose, & Gallup, 1996; Harbeck, 1992; Sears, 1992), this charge has proved to be a fruitful strategy in both thwarting reform (Boyd et al., 1996) and limiting program and service offerings (Gaddy et al., 1996; Harbeck, 1992; McCarthy, 1996). Here I examine the use of *strategic homophobia* by the Religious Right in its quest to "take back America" (Bennett, 1995, p. 421), and discuss implications for educational policy makers and public school personnel.

Early Rumblings

Educational researchers have noted that the Religious Right has played an increasingly significant role in the contemporary politics of American public education (Gaddy et al., 1996; Layton, 1996; Provenzo, 1990). Much of the Religious Right's involvement in school politics has been connected to the broader movement of fundamentalist Christians into the political arena (Diamond, 1995). Prior to the 1970s, involvement in the secular world of politics had been a violation of a basic tenet of fundamentalist ideology (Lugg, 1996b; Skaggs, 1996), and many fundamentalists refrained from even voting (Diamond, 1995). But with the explosion of controversial social issues, such as the civil rights and women's movements, the legalization of abortion, and the U.S. Supreme Court's prohibition of state-sponsored religious practices, fundamentalists perceived that America had become a highly secular and hostile country (Lugg, 1996b; Provenzo, 1990; Skaggs, 1996). Subsequently, for some fundamentalists, political involvement became a religious imperative (Zwier, 1984).

This seemingly hostile environment included the public schools, thanks to various Supreme Court decisions regarding prayer and Bible reading (Lugg, 1996b; Provenzo, 1990; Skaggs, 1996). Given the schools' involvement with children, members of the Religious Right were deeply concerned regarding their possible "immoral influences." Debates over the shape and direction of educational policies and practices intensified during the late 1970s and early 1980s (Gaddy et al., 1996; Provenzo, 1990). As one sympathetic observer explained, "In response to being ignored by politicians and by the education establishment, conservative Christians have finally decided—in the best of the American political tradition—to organize and become active nationally and regionally" (Baer, 1996, p. 8).

One particularly potent issue that mobilized the nascent Religious Right during the 1970s was the emergence of a gay and lesbian rights movement (Bennett, 1995; Diamond, 1995; Miller, 1995; Skaggs, 1996). Many Americans were deeply uncomfortable with the notion of gays and lesbians "coming out," that is, publicly and proudly declaring their sexual orientation (Gross, 1993). For religious conservatives, such announcements indicated just how far American society had fallen away from traditional morality (Murchison, 1994; Skaggs, 1996). Coupled with the belief that homosexuality was intrinsically sinful was the belief that gays and lesbians recruited children (Provenzo, 1990; Skaggs, 1996).[1] For the Religious Right, the greater visibility and outspokenness of gays and lesbians was a political call to arms. As historian Joan Nestle observed, "We were seen as a danger in terms of education, in terms of social policy. Though in a way, it was a recognition of our growing social power" (quoted in Dong, 1995).

The political skirmishes over gay rights began in Florida. In 1977, entertainer and newly born-again Christian Anita Bryant waged a "Save Our Children" campaign in an effort to overturn a Dade County, Florida, municipal civil rights ordinance protecting gays and lesbians from discrimination (Burke, 1993; Harbeck, 1992; Miller, 1995). The campaign played on the old homophobic myths that gays and lesbians were child molesters and recruited children and threatened the already-endangered traditional family (Alwood, 1996; Miller, 1995; Provenzo, 1990; Skaggs, 1996).[2] Nevertheless, Save Our Children was successful; the Dade County civil rights ordinance was overturned. The campaign also held a broader political appeal. Bryant encouraged similar efforts across the country, mobilizing the increasingly significant core of religiously minded political activists in overturning gay rights ordinances in St. Paul, Minnesota; Wichita, Kansas; and Eugene, Oregon (Alwood, 1996; Miller, 1995). As journalist Eric Marcus (1992) noted, "Bryant drew the support of conservative political and religious leaders, including the Reverend Jerry Falwell, a popular television evangelist, and was able to build her crusade on existing networks of fundamentalist churches" (p. 258).

Such political organizing had immediate implications for public education. The following year California state senator John Briggs sponsored a referendum specifically barring gays and lesbians from working in public schools (Alwood, 1996; Burke, 1993; Cannon, 1991; Marcus, 1992; Miller, 1995). Briggs's principal field lieutenant was the Reverend Louis Sheldon, who would later form the rabidly antigay Traditional Values Coalition in 1983 (Bennett, 1995).[3] Not surprisingly, the effort to pass Proposition 6 was marked by a high level of political rancor.

Emotions ran high throughout the fall of 1978, and early polls indicated that Proposition 6 would pass. But the proposal was dealt a political deathblow when the conservative former governor and probable Republican presidential candidate Ronald Reagan attacked the measure (Cannon, 1991; Miller, 1995). To the astonishment of his fellow conservatives, Reagan declared the initiative had

> the potential for real mischief. . . . Innocent lives would be ruined. . . . Whatever else it is, homosexuality is not a contagious disease like measles. Prevailing scientific opinion is that an individual's sexuality is determined at a very early age and that a child's teachers do not really influence this. (as quoted in Harbeck, 1992, p. 129)

Given Reagan's impeccable conservative credentials, as well as mainstream union opposition, the measure was easily defeated, even losing in overwhelmingly conservative Orange County (Burke, 1993).

Yet for the Religious Right a cornerstone of their political agenda was set, and it included public education. Besides pressing for vocal prayer and other devotional activities in public schools and lobbying for public assistance (i.e., "school choice") for those who sent their children to private religious schools (McCarthy, 1996), the Religious Right was committed to ensuring that "traditional American morality" was upheld within the U.S. public schools (Gaddy et al., 1996; Provenzo, 1990). This effort included attacking anything that could remotely be perceived as being pro-gay. In addition, the ideological appeal of denouncing possible state-sponsored sin (Lugg & Boyd, 1996), coupled with the mass-marketed menacing specter of homosexuals in the public classroom, was a proven fund-raiser for many of the more entrepreneurial members of the Religious Right (Alwood, 1996; Miller, 1995). As writer and activist Jewelle Gomez observed, "Large segments of this society are very, very angry that lesbians and gays are more visible" (Difeliciantonio & Wagner, 1995). For many Americans, homosexuality was a topic that engendered more than a measure of discomfort. This ill ease increased during the 1980s with the emergence of a new and terrifying disease, AIDS.

AIDS and "Children at Risk"

Perhaps no other disease reshaped the American social landscape as did AIDS (Gross, 1993). In 1980, medical personnel noticed that gay men were falling ill to particularly virulent forms of infection. Diseases that were rare, such as Kaposi's Sarcoma, or thought to be nonexistent in humans, such as cryptosporidiosis, which affects sheep, appeared with horrifying ferocity (Shilts, 1987). The first to be struck down were gay men, but by 1982 there were similar cases in hemophiliacs, injection drug addicts, women, and children, as well as those who had received blood transfusions. Ample evidence coming from Africa showed AIDS was a blood-borne disease affecting all segments of the population. Nevertheless, in the United States AIDS was initially seen as a gay-only disease (Shilts, 1987).

This misperception had two immediate implications. First, as a public policy issue AIDS was largely ignored until the late 1990s, for it struck down a particularly unpopular political constituency (Shilts, 1987). Officials slashed federal funding for public health programs and basic research under the rubric of reducing wasteful governmental bloat (Cannon, 1991). In addition, most U.S. politicians were leery of lending support to an issue that might be perceived by the electorate as being even remotely pro-gay. According to journalist Randy Shilts (1987), "Official inaction was not a matter of neglect . . . it was elevated to the level of policy" (p. 379).

Second, members of the Religious Right focused on AIDS to raise money and strengthen their political hands. By repeatedly stressing that AIDS was God's wrath visited upon the immoral, religious leaders such as Jerry Falwell, Pat Robertson, and Lou Sheldon took advantage of the public's fear to fill their coffers (Alwood, 1996; Bennett, 1995). Homosexuality was graphically and repeatedly linked with particularly gruesome ways to die (Alwood, 1996). The federal government responded slowly to the widening epidemic in the conservative political climate of the 1980s (Cannon, 1991).

Public educators and policymakers were also placed in an uncomfortable position. Sexuality education was a favorite political target of the Religious Right (Cannon, 1991; Gaddy et al., 1996; Skaggs, 1996). One prominent televangelist, the Reverend Jimmy Swaggart, declared that sex education taught children "how to enjoy fornication without having to feel guilty" (Bennett, 1995, p. 377). Sex education tended to be cursory in many public school districts, and mention of gay and lesbian issues was almost nonexistent (Gibson, 1994). Coupled with the limited political support for sexuality education was educators' own uneasiness with and, at times, overt hostility to homosexuality (Gibson, 1994; Sears, 1992). It was the rare program that addressed the danger AIDS presented to all adolescents (Wright, 1989).

However, two events reshaped the policy response to AIDS. The first was the death of Rock Hudson, an actor and old friend of Ronald Reagan, on October 2, 1985. Hudson had had a long career playing romantic leads in numerous movies and television shows. He repeatedly portrayed the seemingly all-American (and very straight) guy (Cannon, 1991). Prior to Hudson's death, AIDS had been a disease without a face, press coverage, or public policy interest. This all changed with Hudson's death (Alwood, 1996; Cannon, 1991; Miller, 1995; Gross, 1993).

The other event was the release of a report by U.S. Surgeon General C. Everett Koop on October 22, 1986. Koop, a "stern-visaged evangelical Christian," was the unlikely author of the bluntly worded report on the AIDS epidemic (Cannon, 1991, p. 815). Not only did he give three specific public health responses to combat the epidemic—abstinence, monogamy, and condoms—he also called for schools to address the danger of AIDS "at the lowest grade possible" (Cannon, 1991, p. 815). Members of the Religious Right supported the first two recommendations but recoiled at the mention of condoms and discussing AIDS in elementary school (Gaddy et al., 1996). Some rejected the Surgeon General's report out of hand (Alwood, 1996; Bennett, 1995; Shilts, 1987), declaring it fostered a "condom cult" within U.S. public schools (Murchison, 1994, pp. 155–166). That Koop was one of their own contributed to the Religious Right's fury over the report's recommendations (Alwood, 1996; Cannon, 1991; Skaggs, 1996). Koop was savaged for supposedly promoting "grammar school sodomy" (Shilts, 1987, p. 588),[4] and he became an incongruous hero to gay activists (Shilts, 1987). Nevertheless, the strongly worded Surgeon General's report, sent to every household in the United States, legitimated action by public schools in the area of AIDS education.

Although many educators were uneasy with the orientation issues associated with AIDS (Wright, 1989), its inclusion into the at-risk formula was critical, for it encouraged researchers and educators to explore issues facing gay and lesbian students (Cranston, 1992). In 1989, the U.S. Department of Health and Human Services released limited copies of a massive study examining youth suicide (Remafedi, 1994). Although the *Report of the Secretary's Task Force on Youth Suicide* was originally backed by the George H.W. Bush administration, the final version faced numerous political obstacles to publication, for it included a controversial chapter that examined the suicide rates of gay and lesbian youth (Remafedi, 1994). The findings were politically contentious: The report explicitly stated that gay and lesbian youth were at risk.

> Gay youth face extreme physical and verbal abuse, rejection, and isolation from family and peers. They often feel totally alone and socially withdrawn out of fear of adverse consequences. As a result of these pressures, lesbian and gay youth are more vulnerable than other youth to psychosocial problems including substance abuse, chronic depression, school failure, early relationship conflicts, being forced to leave their families, and having to survive on their own prematurely. Each of these problems presents a risk factor for suicidal feelings and behavior.
>
> Gay youth are 2 to 3 times more likely to attempt suicide than other young people. They may comprise up to 30 percent of completed suicides annually. (Gibson, 1994, p. 15)

What was more politically problematic for both the Bush administration in general and Secretary Louis Sullivan in particular[5] were the policy recommendations:

> Public and private schools need to take responsibility for providing all students at the junior and high school level with positive information about homosexuality. Curriculum materials should include information relevant to gay males and lesbians as it pertains to human sexuality, health, literature, and social studies. Family life classes should present homosexuality as a natural and healthy form of sexual expression. (Gibson, 1994, p. 57)

Despite the strongly worded and detailed recommendations, only one state, Massachusetts, subsequently implemented the appropriate policies (Remafedi, 1994).

These responses, limited as they were, triggered a political backlash (LaBarbera, 1996). Fighting against "condoms in our schools" and "immoral lifestyles" became the rallying cries across the country. States (such as Texas) and localities (such as Elizabethtown, Pennsylvania) developed policy statements that were explicitly antigay, in the name of upholding traditional morality (Associated Press, 1996; Gaddy et al., 1996). Members of the Religious Right increasingly viewed public schools as bastions of state-sponsored sin and attacked them as such (Lugg & Boyd, 1996).

By the 1990s U.S. public schools were in the political crosshairs of a broader culture war. Much of the religious and moral ferment was based in the chronic economic anxiety experienced by many Americans. The rhetoric of national sin and redemption held a powerful appeal to those who had suffered lasting economic declines since the 1970s. It was far easier to view one's fate as the result of national and/or personal sin than of individual helplessness in the face of an expanding global marketplace (Lugg, 1996a). Religious-based political activism gave many individuals a voice, particularly at the state and local levels of government. The Religious Right was highly effective in using the symbolic enemy of the "menacing homosexual" to rally the troops to their particular political cause (Edelman, 1988), and the politics of public education became increasingly heated.[6]

Rainbows and Outcomes

In 1992 the chancellor of the New York City Public School System, Joseph Fernandez, found himself embroiled in a particularly nasty controversy regarding a specific curriculum, The Children of the Rainbow (Frankel, 1992). The multicultural curriculum, targeted for the early elementary grades, included brief discussions of gay families (Galst, 1995). One goal of the curriculum was to teach young children to "respect and appreciate gay people" (Berger, 1992a, p. B2).

The public reaction to the curriculum was swift and vitriolic. Although Fernandez received support from the gay community (Alyson, 1992), he ran into staunch resistance from members of the local school board and religious community (Berger, 1992b). Mary Cummins, president of the District 24 school board, attacked the curriculum as "homosexual/lesbian propaganda" and vowed not to implement it (Richardson, 1992, p. A43). Chancellor Fernandez, equally determined, promised to impose the curriculum over a board's and/or community's objections (Myers, 1992). Fernandez was subsequently pilloried for being high-handed and insensitive to local concerns ("Editorial," 1992; Schlafly, 1992).

The ensuing uproar garnered national media attention, with numerous leaders of the Religious Right attacking both the curriculum and Fernandez (Frankel, 1992; Schlafly, 1992). The upheaval over Children of the Rainbow also fostered a political alliance between fundamentalists and conservative Catholics and Jews in New York City (Galst, 1995). All had been outraged by the 1990 Fernandez policy on sexuality education and public health, which included a condom distribution program in the secondary schools (Price, 1993). The new curriculum was perceived as further insult to their deeply held religious values. Fernandez, whose 3-year contract was up for review, was savagely attacked for supposedly fostering immorality within the public schools. When his contract was not renewed in spring 1993 Fernandez lamented, "There's no doubt in my mind that I'm one of the casualties of the battle by religious fundamentalists (Arocha, 1993, p. 12).

Fernandez's analysis of his situation was only partially correct. Conservative religious activists, particularly fundamentalists, used the uproar over the curriculum to push a broader political agenda and widen their political base. According to Frances Kunreuther, executive director of the Hetrick-Martin Institute, "The people who opposed the Children of the Rainbow curriculum were also opposed to the free breakfast program for low-income kids, and favored putting prayer in schools. Basically, they used the issue of homosexuality to push their agenda" (quoted in Galst, 1995, p. 57). One part of the strategy included the production and frequent showing of a 30-minute attack videotape, *Why Parents Should Object to the Children of the Rainbow,* an offspring of an earlier antigay tape, *The Gay Agenda* (Flanders, 1995). The tape was viewed at PTA meetings and private homes, and in some instances with the approval of school principals who opposed Fernandez and the curriculum (Flanders, 1995, p. 108).

Religious Right activists were also inadvertently aided by Fernandez, who placed himself in an extremely vulnerable position by publishing what could be described as a "kick and tell" memoir. His autobiography, published during the height of the curriculum furor, *Tales Out of School: Joseph Fernandez's Crusade to Rescue American Education,* contained scathing references to most political leaders in New York State (Finder, 1992). The book was unlikely to engender support for the embattled chancellor from any political quarter. Nevertheless, the Religious Right played a key role in Fernandez's departure by employing a strategic use of homophobia. By depicting Children of the Rainbow as gay propaganda designed to corrupt the minds of very young public school children, the Religious Right was successful in eroding political support for a chancellor who was already perceived by many as high-handed and spiteful.

In Pennsylvania, the politics of homophobia played out differently. In 1992 the political arena in Pennsylvania exploded over a proposed change in state educational regulations. Outcome-Based Education (OBE) was conceived by the state Board of Education as a means to foster local educational reform (Boyd et al., 1996). Instead of focusing upon standard inputs in determining educational policy, the board shifted its focus to outcomes, that is, from student seat time to demonstrated student competencies. By drawing broad curriculum frameworks and including specific values outcomes, the board hoped to stimulate statewide academic excellence in the pursuit of national and global economic competitiveness (Zahorchak, 1994).

Although the proposal had numerous problems (including its potential costs and that it was an untested plan), the values portion of OBE, which included "tolerance" and teaching children to "appreciate and understand others," was particularly vexing to religious conservatives (Boyd et al., 1996). Ironically, state board members believed the values statements were innocuous. A former board member and businessman, John Dankowsky, recalled:

> I was a boy scout. A scout is trustworthy, loyal, helpful, friendly, curteous, kind, obedient, cheerful, thrifty, brave, clean, and reverent. . . . I've remembered it since I was 11 years old, and I'm 51 now. Now, most religions I know teach that. Now, you have the Peg Luksik's[7] of the world, saying "Oh God, we can't teach that to the children in school." Is she out of her mind? (quoted in Zahorchak, 1994, pp. 80–81)

Nevertheless, opponents of OBE firmly believed that the plan would indoctrinate public school students into adopting "politically correct" values (Zahorchak, 1994).

A key tactic of the Religious Right was to raise the alarm that the new regulations promoted homosexuality. The original 575 outcome statements did not mention sexual orientation, yet the tolerance outcome was quickly construed by members of the Religious Right to mean not only teaching children about homosexuality but also advocating they become homosexual themselves. This very emotional (and paranoid) issue was highly symbolic throughout much of the OBE debate. Proponents of the reform were continually placed on the defensive, thanks to the intensity of the attacks and their own political ineptitude (Boyd et al., 1996). Former executive director of the state Board of Education, Robert Feir, observed that,

> the single best example of how badly we lost control of [OBE] is . . . the debate about homosexuality. In a sense the debate became a . . . debate about things more important than the "Regs," which is really the purpose of public schools, and how do you relate to one another in society. (Zachorchak, 1994, pp. 85–86)

Proponents had not clearly defined what OBE was, and so the Religious Right did it for them. OBE was sin.

Ron Gamble, a pro-family state legislator committed to stopping OBE, launched a particularly potent weapon in summer 1992, the *Gamble-Gram* (Zahorchak, 1994). The *Gamble-Gram* contained an incendiary mix of gay-baiting and dire predictions for Christian parents if OBE were implemented:

- Homosexuals like educational "reform." (June 26, 1992)
- "Voodoo Education" . . . families become obsolete. (July 10, 1992)
- Most self-esteem programs employ techniques used in hypnosis . . . interference with parental roles and responsibilities such as teaching morality. (July 17, 1992)

The Religious Right consistently defined OBE as promoting sin and used homophobic references to reinforce rhetorical points.

For all of the heat and political fury, a scaled-down version of OBE (minus the values outcomes) was enacted into law in 1993 with the help of a pro-family governor, Robert Casey. But OBE was politically dead in Pennsylvania, and the political landscape of the state was transformed. Religious

Right activists would later play key roles in the senatorial campaign of Rick Santorum (Bennett, 1995)[8] and gubernatorial campaign of Tom Ridge (who ran on an anti-OBE platform). Both were subsequently elected. By 1995, OBE was an educational reform that existed only on paper (Boyd et al., 1996), and the Religious Right was one of the most influential political interest groups within the state (Bennett, 1995).

Discussion

For the Religious Right, injecting homophobia into debates over public education policy has been an effective means of hijacking the agenda and reframing the terms of discourse according to their own paranoid rhetoric. In both New York City and Pennsylvania the politics of homophobia played a significant role in shaping the debate over educational change, whether gay and lesbian issues were involved (as they were in New York City) or not (as in Pennsylvania). This strategy is increasingly employed across the country, thanks to the turmoil surrounding students' clubs in Utah, the anxiety over gay marriage, and perhaps most important, the recent Supreme Court decision, *Evans* v. *Romer*, which for the first time in U.S. history acknowledges that gays and lesbians have federal civil rights protections. Given the current cultural and political environment, it is likely that the paranoid politics of homophobia will continue to be played out on the public education stage.

There are important paradoxes regarding the Religious Right, public education, and the paranoid politics of homophobia. The first is the limited presence of gay activists in many of these fights over public education. Although the charges of recruitment and molestation are demonstrably false, they have constrained the involvement of gay and lesbian adults in the politics of public education (Marcus, 1992). As one activist bluntly observed:

> If, in our fear of being labeled pedophiles, we continually glance over our shoulders as we attempt to lend a hand to queer youth, then when we're finally ready to move forward, it will only be to discover that "our children," whom we thought we were helping by staying away from them, have disappeared. The homophobes will have carried the day. (Peck, 1995, p. 224)

The relative absence of gay activists in debates over public education also intensifies the rhetoric of the Religious Right, making gays and lesbians become the immoral and faceless "other." The "invisible homosexual" is reconstructed into the symbolic enemy of children, their parents, and public schools. As the political scientist Murray Edelman (1988) explains:

> Enemies are characterized by an inherent trait or set of traits that marks them as evil, immoral, warped, or pathological and therefore a continuing threat regardless of what course of action they pursue, regardless of whether they win or lose in any particular encounter, and *even if they take no political action at all* [italics added]. (p. 67)

The second paradox is attached to the first: It is the Religious Right, not gay activists, who have demanded that public schools, administrators, teachers, and policy makers address gay and lesbian issues, albeit according to their theological and political agendas. And this has been an explicit component to their political activism since the late 1970s. Although much of their activism tends to be framed in the neutral-sounding terms of standing up for traditional morality and the Judeo-Christian tradition, a vital component has been, and remains, incendiary homophobia.

The legal recognition of same-sex "marriage" has the potential to wreak havoc on an already failing public education system. Without a doubt, it can fundamentally affect every aspect of schooling for children. It will only further erode the moral base on which our society depends and which our young people so desperately need. How ironic that teachers are prohibited by law from sharing their Christian faith, or [that the] school [is prohibited] from even posting a copy of the Ten Commandments at the same time that homosexuals are radically attacking our bedrock institutions. What message are we giving to highly impressionable students regarding our society's most crucial values? (Paige, 1996, n.p.)

There is more than a whiff of paranoid politics (Hofstadter, 1963) in the Religious Right's antigay rhetoric. Because homosexuality is portrayed as a threat to Western civilization, to Christian salvation and, in particular, to school children, any policy or program that can be perceived as being remotely pro-gay is quickly denounced as part of an overarching conspiracy by gay activists to recruit children. The paranoid rhetoric is designed to mobilize parents and concerned citizens to join the battle, for it appears that "our very way of life" is threatened by the evil other. Yet, the incendiary language provides an important theoretical key. As historian Richard Hofstadter (1963) explained long ago:

> The paranoid spokesman sees the gate of this conspiracy in apocalyptic terms—he traffics in the birth and death of whole worlds, whole political orders, whole systems of human values. He is always manning the barricades of civilization. He constantly lives at a turning point: it is now or never in organizing resistance to conspiracy. Time is forever just running out. (pp. 29–30)

It is this deliberately constructed spectacle of fear (Edelman, 1988) that gives the Religious Right potency regarding the politics of public education.

This brings us to the third and final paradox: Given the nearly 20 years of impassioned efforts by the Religious Right regarding gay issues and public education, one would expect the professional literature to analyze this component of their activism and draw both theoretical and policy implications. Yet, for all of the current research examining the Religious Right and the politics of public education, there has been scant mention of the politics of homophobia in the professional educational policy or administration literature. It is a curious omission.

It would appear that given the current political strength of the U.S. Religious Right, educators, administrators, and policy makers will have to confront gay and lesbian issues as they may (or may not) pertain to public education. Yet, much of their work will continue to be defensive, explaining to a viewing public why certain policies, procedures, and curricula do not promote homosexuality. In a profession that professes a commitment to multiculturalism and diversity, it is a highly awkward position in which to be placed.

Notes

1. This has been a very effective scare tactic in raising money for the Religious Right. Televangelist Pat Robertson opined in a fund-raising letter dated May 24, 1994, "Such people are sinning against God and will lead to the ultimate destruction of the family and our nation. I am unalterably opposed to such things, and will do everything I can to restrict the freedom of these people to spread their contagious infection to the youth of our nation" (quoted in a May 23, 1996, press release by the People for the American Way).
2. As community activist Kathleen Sadaat explained, "The myth of harm to children is not a new thing: Gypsies steal them, Jews eat them, we seduce them" (Difeliciantonio & Wagner, 1995).

3. By the mid-1990s, Sheldon would play a significant role in the debates regarding public education and whether or not U.S. public schools "promoted homosexuality." On December 6, 1995, Sheldon appeared before the House Economic and Educational Opportunities Committee, claiming school programs targeted at preventing AIDS, hate violence, and suicide actually fostered homosexuality.
4. Attributed to long-time conservative activist Phyllis Schlafly. Ironically, her son John would be "outed" in 1992 by gay activists (Alwood, 1996; Gross, 1993).
5. Secretary Sullivan had close ties to the Religious Right, and in particular, the Reverend Louis Sheldon. At the time of the report's release, members of Exodus International, an ex-gay group, were soliciting the U.S. Department of Health and Human Services for federal funding for "reparative therapy," a discredited method of supposedly turning gay people heterosexual. See *One Nation Under God*, a film by Teodoro Maniaci and Francine M. Rzeznik (1993), 3Z/Hourglass Productions, Inc. Such therapy was and is widely discredited within the psychology community. Federal funding was not forthcoming.
6. In particular, the viciously homophobic video, *The Gay Agenda*, produced in 1992 by the Traditional Values Coalition, has been very powerful in depicting lesbians and gays as the biggest moral menace facing U.S. society (Difeliciantonio & Wagner, 1995).
7. Two-time candidate for governor, major leader of the Religious Right in Pennsylvania, and OBE's principal opponent (Boyd et al., 1996). She went on to serve as Howard Phillip's (presidential candidate for the U.S. Taxpayer Party) national campaign manager. Its political philosophy is rooted in Christian Reconstructionism, a doctrine that calls for the establishment of an Old Testament theocracy within the United States. Some of the more disturbing teachings of Reconstructionism are that abortionists, blasphemers, homosexuals, and disobedient children should be executed (Diamond, 1995). The USTP also has some linkages with the national Republican Party. Although such political linkages and possible policy implications are fascinating, they are far beyond the scope of this article.
8. According to Bennett (1995), "Over sixty percent of the 600 candidates endorsed by the Religious Right won in November 1994. They included Rick Santorum, who returned to 'stealth campaign' tactics in mobilizing [Christian] Coalition activists in his Pennsylvania senatorial race, while downplaying his extreme views" (p. 420). I viewed both a Coalition 1994 report card and League of Gay and Lesbian Voters Score card regarding Santorum. The Coalition gave him a meritorious 100% on their issues; the League gave Santorum a skull and cross bones.

References

Alwood, E. (1996). *Straight news: Gays, lesbians and the news media.* New York: Columbia University Press.

Alyson, S. (1992, December 30). Fear of the rainbow. *The New York Times,* p. A15.

Arocha, Z. (1993). The Religious Right's march into public school governance. *School Administrator, 50*(9), 8–15.

Associated Press. (1996, October 9). Students protest family values. *Philadelphia Daily News,* p. 19.

Baer, R. (1996). Why did the Religious Right get into politics in the first place? *Politics of Education Bulletin, 23*(3/4), 6–9.

Bennett, D.H. (1995). *The party of fear: The American far right from nativism to the militia movement.* New York: Vintage.

Berger, J. (1992a, November 10). Board is given ultimatum on a gay teaching plan. *The New York Times,* p. B2.

Berger, J. (1992b, November 17). Teaching about gay life is pressed by chancellor. *The New York Times,* p. B5.

Boyd, W.L., Lugg, C.A., & Zahorchak, G.L. (1996). Social traditionalists, religious conservatives, and the politics of outcome-based education: Pennsylvania and beyond. *Education and Urban Society, 28*(3), 347–369.

Burke, P. (1993). *Family values.* New York: Vintage.

Cannon, L. (1991). *President Reagan: The role of a lifetime.* New York: Simon and Schuster.

Cranston, K. (1992). HIV education for gay, lesbian, and bisexual youth: Personal risk, personal power, and the community of conscience. In K.M. Harbeck (Ed.), *Coming out of the classroom closet: Gay and lesbian students, teachers, and curricula* (pp. 247–259). New York: Harrington Park.

Diamond, S. (1995). *Roads to dominion: Right-wing movements and political power in the United States.* New York: Guilford.

Difeliciantonio, T., & Wagner, J.C. (1995). Culture wars. In *The question of equality*. United Kingdom: Testing the Limits production in association with Channel Four Television.

Dong, A. (1995). Outrage '69. In *The question of equality*. United Kingdom: Testing the Limits production in association with Channel Four Television.

Edelman, M. (1988). *Constructing the political spectacle*. Chicago: University of Chicago Press.

Editorial: The parents rebel—III. (1992, November 20). *The Wall Street Journal*, p. A14.

Elam, S.M., Rose, L.C., & Gallup, A.M. (1996). The 28th annual Phi Delta Kappa/Gallup poll of the public's attitudes toward the public schools. *Phi Delta Kappan, 78*(1), 41–59.

Fernandez, J.A. (1993). *Tales out of school: Joseph Fernandez's crusade to rescue American education (with a new Afterword)*. New York: Little, Brown.

Finder, A. (1992, December 14). The Fernandez memoirs color debate on contract. *The New York Times*, p. B3.

Flanders, L. (1995). Hate on tape: The video strategy of the fundamentalist right. In C. Berlet (Ed.), *Eyes right!: Challenging the right-wing backlash* (pp. 105–108). Boston: South End.

Frankel, B. (1992, December 9). Educator's crusade turns NYC nasty. *USA Today*, p. A7.

Gaddy, B.B., Hall, T.W., & Marzano, R.J. (1996). *School wars: Resolving our conflicts over religion and values*. San Francisco, CA: Jossey-Bass.

Galst, L. (1995). Pious moralism: Theocratic goals backed by misrepresentation and lies. In C. Berlet (Ed.), *Eyes right!: Challenging the right-wing backlash* (pp. 50–58). Boston: South End.

Gibson, P. (1994). Gay male and lesbian youth suicide. In G. Remafedi (Ed.), *Death by denial: Studies of suicide in gay and lesbian teenagers* (pp. 15–68). Boston: Alyson.

Gross, L.P. (1993). *Contested closets: The politics and ethics of outing*. Minneapolis: University of Minnesota Press.

Harbeck, K.M. (1992). Gay and lesbian educators: Past history/future prospects. In K. Harbeck (Ed.), *Coming out of the classroom closet: Gay and lesbian students, teachers, and curricula* (pp. 121–140). New York: Harrington Park.

Hofstadter, R. (1963). *The paranoid style in American politics and other essays*. Cambridge, MA: Harvard University Press.

LaBarbera, P. (1996, July 2). "Homosexual correctness" advances in America's school [Policy briefing]. Washington, DC: Family Research Council.

Layton, D.H. (1996). Religion and the politics of education: An introduction. *Education and Urban Society, 28*(3), 275–278.

Lugg, C.A. (1996a). Calling for community in a conservative age. *Planning and Changing, 27*(1–2), 2–14.

Lugg, C.A. (1996b). *For God and country: Conservatism and American school policy*. New York: Peter Lang.

Lugg, C.A., & Boyd, W.L. (1996). Reflection on a Pennsylvania case: Religion and the politics of education reform. *Politics of Education Bulletin, 23*(3–4), 2–5.

Maniaci, T., & Rzeznik, F.M. (1993). *One nation under God*. A 3Z/Hourglass Production.

Marcus, E. (1992). *Marking history: The struggle for gay and lesbian equal rights, 1945–1990*. New York: HarperCollins.

McCarthy, M.M. (1996). People of faith as political activists in public schools. *Education and Urban Society, 28*(3), 308–326.

Miller, N. (1995). *Out of the past: Gay and lesbian history from 1869 to the present*. New York: Vintage.

Murchison, W. (1994). *Reclaiming morality in America: Why traditional morals are collapsing and what you can do about it*. Nashville, TN: Nelson.

Myers, S.L. (1992, December 11). Fernandez tells rebels deadline is today. *The New York Times*, p. B2.

Paige, L. (1996, July 2). *The potential effects on education curricula and policy of homosexual "marriage"* [Policy briefing]. Washington, DC: Family Research Council.

Peck, D. (1995). Making history. In D. Deitcher (Ed.), *The question of equality: Lesbian and gay politics in America since Stonewall* (pp. 196–235). New York: Scribner.

People for the American Way. (1996, May 23). *Ralph Reed v. Pat Robertson* [Press release]. Washington, DC: Author.

Price, J. (1993, February 11). Condom giveaway, gay curriculum lead to ouster of NYC schools chief. *Washington Times*, p. A1.

Provenzo, E.F., Jr. (1990). *Religious fundamentalism and American education: The battle for the public schools*. Albany: State University of New York Press.

Remafedi, G. (1994). The state of knowledge on gay, lesbian, and bisexual youth suicide. In G. Remafedi (Ed.), *Death by denial: Studies of suicide in gay and lesbian teenagers* (pp. 7–14). Boston: Alyson.

Richardson, L. (1992, November 15). Board members offer alternative teaching about homosexuals. *The New York Times,* p. A43.

Schlafly, P. (1992, December 19). Arrogance picks the curriculum. *Washington Times,* p. C3.

Sears, J.T. (1992). Educators, homosexuality, and homosexual students: Are personal feelings related to professional beliefs? In K.M. Harbeck (Ed.), *Coming out of the classroom closet: Gay and lesbian students, teachers, and curricula* (pp. 29–79). New York: Harrington Park.

Shilts, R. (1987). *And the band played on: Politics, people, and the AIDS epidemic.* New York: St. Martin's.

Skaggs, C. (1996). *With God on our side: The rise of the religious right in America.* Lumiere Productions, Inc.

Wright, B. (1989). AIDS and homophobia: A perspective for AIDS educators. *Feminist Teacher, 4*(2–3), 10–12.

Zahorchak, G.L. (1994). *The politics of outcome-based education in Pennsylvania.* Unpublished doctoral dissertation, The Pennsylvania State University, University Park.

Zwier, R. (1984). The new Christian Right and the 1980 elections. In D. G. Bromley & A. Shupe (Eds.), *New Christian politics* (pp. 173–194). Macon, GA: Mercer University Press.

CHAPTER SEVEN

"We're Here and We're Fabulous"

Contemporary U.S.-American LGBT Youth Activism

WARREN J. BLUMENFELD

Introduction

It was a brilliantly sunny, though rather cool, mid-June afternoon. Banners flying, music blasting, people of all walks of life assembled, reuniting, greeting, kissing, embracing, catching up on lives lived in the space between. The signal was given with a contagious cheer rising from the crowd, and for the next few hours the streets would be theirs: Dykes on Bikes revving their engines; shirtless muscled young men dancing to a disco beat atop flatbed floats winding their way down the streets; dazzling drag queens in red and gold and silver; the Freedom Trail Marching Band trumpeting the call; a black-and-white cocker spaniel wearing a sign announcing "DON'T ASSUME I'M STRAIGHT"; lesbian moms and gay dads pushing strollers or walking beside youth of all ages; Gays for Patsy Cline decked out in their finest country duds, two-stepping down the boulevard; AIDS activists falling to the pavement of those same boulevards in mock death to expose governmental and societal inaction, which is still killing so many; married same-sex couples walking hand in hand; Parents, Friends, and Families of Lesbians and Gays (P-FLAG) proclaiming "WE ARE PROUD OF OUR LESBIAN, GAY, BISEXUAL, AND TRANSGENDER SONS AND DAUGHTERS"; alongside political, social, and service organizations, business and religious caucuses of all stripes and denominations, and, of course, bystanders watching the procession, holding court from the sidelines.

And in the midst of this merriment and this protest, the humorous posters and angry placards, the enormous rainbow balloon sculptures arching overhead, and the colorful streamers and glistening "fairy dust" wafting from open windows, amid the shiny black leather and shimmering lamé, the multicolored T-shirts and the drab business suits, came the youth, their radiant faces catching the rays of the sun, marching side-by-side, hand-in-hand, their middle school and high school Gay/Straight Alliance banners waving exaltedly in this storm of humanity, announcing their entry, their solidarity, their feisty outrage, and yes, their pride chanting "Two, Four, Six, Eight, Queer is

Just as Good as Straight, Three, Five, Seven, Nine, LGBTs are Mighty Fine;" then, gaining intensity, singing, "Hey Hey, Ho Ho, Homophobia Has Got to Go," and then, as if hit by an all-consuming revelation, shouting, "We're Here, We're Queer, We're Not Going Back, We're NOT Going Back, WE'RE NOT GOING BACK!"

And indeed, they will not go back into those dank closets of fear and denial that stifle the spirit and ruin so many lives. Oh, they will physically return to their schools and their homes. They will continue to study and play sports, to watch movies, listen to their iPods, and write about their day on Facebook and MySpace. Some will most likely continue to serve as community organizers, and some will go on to become parents, teachers, political leaders once their school days are behind. The place they will go to, though, is nowhere that can be seen. It is a place of consciousness that teaches those who have entered that everyone is diminished when any one of us is demeaned; that heterosexism, sexism, biphobia, transgender oppression (as well as all the other forms of oppression) have no place in a just society.

From the sidelines of the parade, beginning as a whisper and ending as a mighty roar of support: "We are so glad you are here," came voices from the crowd. "We wish we could have done this when we were in high school," cried others too numerous to count. "Thank you so much for your courage!"

From where has this courage come, and how has this change actually come about? It seems that a great many factors have combined to provide the conditions for progressive social change. Researchers are continually unearthing our complex, extensive, and rich history across millennia and cultures (Bérubé, 1990; Blackwood, 1986; Blumenfeld & Raymond, 1993; Boswell, 1980; Bray, 1982; Chauncey, 1994; D'Emilio, 1992, 1983; Faderman, 1991, 1981; Faderman & Eriksson, 1990; Feinberg, 1996; Hinsch, 1990; Katz, 1976; Lauritsen & Thorstad, 1974/1995; Miller, 1995/2006; Steakley, 1982). Throughout this long history, young people have been on the front lines serving as energetic and inspirational pioneering change agents.

Many historians believe that although same-sex attraction and behavior and gender non-conformity have probably always existed in human history, the concepts of sexual and gender identities in general and the construction of these identities and sense of community is a relatively modern Western invention. A historic shift occurred in the early-to-mid-19th century, brought about by the growth of industrialization, competitive capitalism, and the rise of modern science, which provided people with more social and personal options outside the home. As more people moved away from their rural agricultural communities where survival depended upon large, interdependent family units, to cities where individuals entered into employment founded on wage labor, they were given the opportunity to meet and relate to others who recognized their sexual and emotional desires for their own sex (D'Emilio, 1993). It is only within the last 150 or so years that there has been an organized and sustained political effort to protect the rights of people with same-sex and both-sex attractions, and those who cross traditional constructions of gender expression of all backgrounds and ages.

Today, throughout the world, on university and grade school campuses, in communities and homes, and in the media, issues of homosexuality, bisexuality, and transgenderism are increasingly "coming out of the closet." We see young people developing positive identities at earlier ages than ever before. Activists of all ages are gaining important electoral, legislative, and judicial victories. Primarily in academic milieus, greater emphasis and discussion is centering on what has come to be called "sexuality and gender studies" (sometimes referred to as "queer studies") where writers, educators, and students analyze and challenge current notions and categories of sexuality and gender constructions.

While young people have long been integral to the development and success of social movements, due to space constraints this chapter highlights points in contemporary youth activism in the United States since the late 1960s.

Stonewall and Aftermath

There are moments in history when conditions come together to create the impetus for great social change. Although historians trace the origins of the modern movement for lesbian, gay, bisexual, and transgender (LGBT) equality to the early days of the Cold War, the Stonewall Inn, a small bar located at 53 Christopher Street in New York City's Greenwich Village, is widely recognized as the site for a watershed event in LGBT activism (D'Emilio, 1983; Faderman, 1991; White, 2009).

Out of the ashes of the 1969 Stonewall riots, a number of militant groups were formed primarily by young people in their teens and early twenties. One of the first was the Gay Liberation Front (GLF). GLF was not a formalized organization *per se*, but rather consisted of a series of small groups across the United States and other countries. Members held meetings in people's living rooms, basements in houses of worship, and storefronts. They insisted on the freedom to explore new ways of living as part of a radical program of social transformation. GLF adopted a set of principles emphasizing coalition-building with other disenfranchised groups—feminists, ethnic minorities, people of color, working-class people, young people, elders, people with disabilities—as a means of dismantling the economic and social structures they considered inherently oppressive.

It soon became apparent that ideological differences among GLF's members were too significant for all to remain in one organization. Some formed a new organization called the Gay Activists Alliance (GAA), a non-violent militant organization working for the civil rights of homosexuals often through direct actions. Unlike GLF, GAA was a structured organization having elected officials. The organization took its logo from the Greek letter *Lambda*, a symbol for wavelength in quantum physics suggesting dynamism.

While some lesbians remained in GLF and GAA, many women considered their issues and concerns different from those of gay men. Many separated and formed groups, for example GLF Women, Radicalesbians, and Furies, and created publications such as *Dyke*, along feminist principles. They argued that the fight against sexism required all women to band together to challenge male privilege and heterosexual institutions. Others who separated included, for example, transgender activists who founded the group STAR—Street Transvestite Action Revolutionaries—which offered shelter and support to homeless youth.

College and University Organizing

Sparked by the homophile movement of the 1950s and 1960s and energized by the growing gay and feminist movements, the first officially recognized college student group to address LGBT issues organized as the Student Homophile League at Columbia University in 1967, followed closely by groups at MIT, Stanford, Cornell, and others. By the early 1970s approximately 150 groups emerged on campuses throughout the United States. Though a nationwide movement, students founded these groups with differing purposes and various names depending on geographic location or on the groups' primary focus. Examples included the Gay Liberation Front of Rocky Mountain College in Billings,

Montana, "HOPS" (Homophiles of Penn State), and FREE (GLF at the University of Minnesota). Other groups used the name of the Gay Activists Alliance, the Student Homophile League, the Radicalesbians, or names that had special significance to the individual group. As the names of groups varied, to an extent, so did their purposes and operating structures. Some concentrated primarily on political issues while others concerned themselves more with bringing students together at social gatherings.

Although the organic structure of groups varied from campus to campus, many shared similarities. For the most part, groups included elected or volunteer officers or coordinators who facilitated activities and served as group spokespeople. Usually the various groups divided into small committees or collectives to organize social and cultural activities, coordinated speaker bureaus, created and distributed newsletters, and planned political actions. Some sponsored campus gay and lesbian coffee houses like "The Closet Door" at the University of Maryland in College Park that provided college and high school students a supportive social environment.

By 1972 student campus groups organized regional and national conferences around issues of sexuality at Rutgers University, University of Minnesota, University of Texas, University of Massachusetts, and University of Nebraska. In addition, individual organizations sponsored smaller subgroups generally referred to as "consciousness-raising" to discuss issues of "coming out" and internalized oppression. The consciousness-raising groups usually did not have a "leader" or trained psychotherapist and were based on the input of each participant.

University administrators denied official recognition to a number of lesbian, gay, bisexual, transgender, and ally (LGBTA) groups over the years at Sacramento and San José State Universities, Florida State University, Pennsylvania State University, University of Kansas, University of Texas, and others. According to Glen Dumke, chancellor of the California State University system under then-Governor Ronald Reagan the reasons for denial included:

1. . . . the effect of recognition by the college of the Gay Liberation Front could conceivably be to endorse or promote homosexual behavior, to attract homosexuals to the campus, and to expose minors to homosexual advocacy and practices, and
2. . . . belief that the proposed Front created too great a risk for students—a risk which might lead students to engage in illegal homosexual behavior. (Dumke, in Reichard, 2010)

Students in the Society for Homosexual Freedom (SHF) at Sacramento State University, whom the student government represented, sued the chancellor in Sacramento County Superior Court and won the case, forcing the university officially to recognize their group. The court upheld the students' First Amendment rights to free speech and freedom of association by affirming their contention that

> . . . to justify suppression of free speech, there must be reasonable grounds to fear that serious evil will result if free speech is practiced; there must be reasonable ground to believe that the danger apprehended is imminent. (in Reichard, 2010)

After the court decision the group changed its name to Gay Liberation Front (GLF).

Marty Rogers, one of the founding members of GLF at Sacramento State University, described how the denial of recognition and eventual court battle were instrumental in the group's organizing success:

> Being denied recognition, being decreed invisible, reactivated in most group members other similar and painful incidents in their lives. The difference this time was that there was mutual support—from the cam-

pus newspaper and from the student government. Two faculty members openly acknowledged their homosexuality through letters to the Acting College President and the campus newspaper—they insisted on being seen. For once, homosexuals were not running and hiding. Publicly announcing one's homosexuality, an issue which had not really been confronted previously, became an actuality as a result of the denial of recognition. (quoted in Blumenfeld, 1973, p. 16)

Fortified by this precedent-setting case, other campus groups throughout the country waged and won similar battles.

In 1971 the National Gay Student Center (NGSC) became the first nationally focused organization to serve the needs of LGBT students. Today, the organization exists as the National Queer Student Coalition of the United States Student Association. NGSC served as a clearinghouse connecting existing LGBT campus student organizations and published *Interchange,* a nationally distributed newsletter. Community centers also emerged during the early 1970s to address needs and interests of LGBT people on and off campus. One of the first was the "Gay House," run by the Gay Liberation Front chapter at the University of Minnesota. A private foundation funded the three-story house, which offered counseling and other services to the student and larger communities in the Minneapolis/St. Paul area.

Bisexuals, who had worked since the beginning alongside gay and lesbian activists, began to organize in the 1970s. For a number of reasons, neither the gay and lesbian rights movement nor mainstream political movements initially responded to the needs of bisexuals. At first, bisexual women organized themselves in same-sex groups for support and consciousness-raising; bisexual men later followed this example. They coordinated the first National Bisexual Conference, held at Mission High School in San Francisco in June 1990.

By the end of the 1970s a grass-roots network was firmly in place. Activists learned some important lessons during the political battles over anti-discrimination statutes and the Briggs Initiative. They would be sorely tested in the 1980s and beyond.

Organizing around HIV/AIDS

The decade of the 1970s was nearly at an end when a New York doctor discovered a patient with a number of unexplained maladies including an extremely rare form of cancer and pneumonia. By 1980 at least 50 patients had been identified—the overwhelming majority being gay and bisexual men. Not knowing what else to call this constellation of diseases, medical researchers initially gave it the name "Gay-related immune deficiency" (GRID), but soon changed it to "Acquired immune deficiency syndrome" (AIDS) following objections from young gay activists who argued against naming a syndrome of unknown origin after an already stigmatized group. As more became known about this syndrome it was apparent that it was not confined to gay and bisexual men, but rather it was believed to have existed for some time in epidemic proportions among primarily heterosexual populations in areas on the African continent. Its initial entry into the gay and bisexual male community in the United States and other countries, however, profoundly affected the course of political organizing and activism. The epidemic proved to have an enormous political and emotional impact, which tested the very nature and strength of a relatively young movement and forced people to take a hard look at the essential meanings of the concepts of identity and community. Though liberation and civil rights organizing continued as before, the virus injected a new element into the political agenda. On a personal level, virtually everyone had been touched in some ways by the effects of the epidemic. A community-wide bereavement process began as the number of AIDS-related deaths increased. Lesbians, gay men, bisexuals, and transgender people led coordinated efforts to provide care and support for people with AIDS. Existing gay and lesbian community centers expanded services, while establishing new centers dedicated to serving the needs of people with AIDS and their loved ones.

In 1986 young activists formed the direct-action group ACT UP (AIDS Coalition to Unleash Power) to fight governmental and societal inaction. Established in New York City, a network of local chapters quickly emerged in 120 cities throughout the world. Though run independently, the network organized under the theme "Silence = Death" beneath an inverted pink triangle. They reclaimed the pink triangle that had signified ultimate oppression in Nazi concentration camps, and turned it into a symbol of empowerment, to lift people out of lethargy and denial toward a call to action.

ACT UP groups embraced a philosophy of direct, grass-roots actions and nonviolent civil disobedience involving highly visible demonstrations. ACT UP/New York, for example, staged a "sit-in" on Wall Street in 1987 during rush hour to protest price gouging by pharmaceutical companies, particularly Burroughs-Wellcome's high cost of AZT (an antiviral drug). Other actions included a national protest in 1988, which effectively closed down the Food and Drug Administration offices in Bethesda, Maryland; a 1990 action in which over 1,000 people stormed the National Institutes of Health (NIH), also in Bethesda, demanding extended access to government-sponsored HIV clinical trials; in 1991, a disruption of CBS and PBS evening news broadcasts to protest coverage of the Persian Gulf War and negligence in covering the AIDS epidemic; followed closely by a "Day of Desperation" demonstration at Grand Central Station; and visible actions at most of the annual International Conferences on AIDS including, most notably, the VI Conference held in San Francisco in 1990.

AIDS activists, primarily young people, not only challenged traditional ways that scientific knowledge is disseminated, but more importantly, questioned the very mechanisms by which scientific inquiry was conducted, and even redefined the meanings of "science." AIDS activists won important victories on a number of fronts, including assisting people in becoming active participants in their own medical treatment, having greater input into drug trial designs, expanding access to drug trials, expediting approval for certain drug therapies, and forming Community Advisory Boards that hold pharmaceutical companies more accountable for the prices they charge.

Queer Nationalism and the Deconstruction of Sexuality and Gender Categorization

While many activists focused primarily on HIV/AIDS, organizing around other concerns continued. A number of LGBT people in the 1980s and 1990s maintained their focus on coalition building as a major political strategy. Some joined with others in their sustained efforts to end the system of apartheid in South Africa with student groups calling for educational institutions to divest from that country. Others called for an end to U.S. military involvement in Central America, countered the activities of right-wing groups in this country and abroad, lobbied for reproductive freedoms, fought for labor and tenants' rights and the rights of people with disabilities, pushed to end the arms race and to close nuclear power installations, organized to protect the environment, to end poverty and hunger, racism, drug dependency, rape, and other forms of violence and worked to provide equitable educational opportunities for all.

A new generation of LGBT youth activists came of age a decade into the AIDS crisis. Reaping the benefits of increased visibility hard fought by their predecessors, this young and energetic generation was propelled into activism by the incongruities between their concerns for social justice and the reality of their continued second-class status.

Young activists rejected many of the mainstream movement's assimilationist strategies that emphasized a commitment to electoral politics and claims that we were "just like everyone else." Before the Stonewall rebellion, many LGBT people remained closeted for self-protection and because the movement had not yet gained significant visibility to forge links between diverse groups. Young activists emerging within the early AIDS era, though, grew up in a very different social and political climate.

Queer nationals, as many would call themselves, reclaimed the word "queer"—turning a term of oppression into one of empowerment by proudly asserting their difference and by rejecting assimilationist strategies. The term "queer" was expressly chosen as one of inclusion and encompassed lesbians, gay men, bisexuals, transgender persons, intersexuals, and even heterosexual allies who supported liberation efforts for sexual and gender minorities and who actively struggled against the limiting societal notions of "normalcy."

Using direct-action, confrontational strategies similar to those of ACT UP, GLF, GAA, and feminist organizations, the group Queer Nation formed in New York City in 1990 with independent chapters soon appearing in local communities, colleges, and universities throughout the United States and in other countries. Organizing under the motto "We're here. We're queer. We're fabulous. Get used to it!," Queer Nation members stressed "queer visibility" and an end to heterosexual privilege and heterosexism. Organizing strategies combined outrage with feisty and outrageous joy through creative guerilla art and agitprop street theater. Actions included "queers night out," where members "reappropriated" public spaces, such as predominately heterosexual bars and suburban shopping malls, and conducted "kiss-ins," "dance-ins," or other demonstrations of queer visibility. Various chapters also conducted "Save Our Children" actions (the name reclaimed from the anti-gay campaign led by Anita Bryant in the late 1970s) in which members distributed "queer positive" literature, safer-sex information, condoms, and dental dams to high school students as they entered school buildings.

Queer Nation groups were, for the most part, nonhierarchical. Smaller working groups or committees proposed and planned actions. The acronyms of some of these working groups reflected the spirited and witty tenor of the organizations: SHOP (Suburban Homosexual Outreach Program); LABIA (Lesbian And Bisexual Women In Action); GHOST (Great Homosexual Outrage at Sickening Televangelists); Q-Color (Queers of Color); and others. "Urban Redecoration" committees posted and stickered public spaces—trash cans, buildings, buses—with signs announcing "Queers Bash Back," "Homophobia May Be Hazardous to Your Health," "Gay, Lesbian, or Bisexual by Birth, Queer By Choice," "Promote Homosexuality," and "Incite Deviance."

Believing that local police forces were not concerned with protecting the safety of sexual minorities, and in some cases even contributed to their victimization, Queer Nation chapters instituted self-defense squads traveling throughout cities to guard against incidents of queer-bashing and other forms of crime. Under the name "Pynk Panther Patrols," groups patterned themselves after urban anti-crime street groups like the Guardian Angels and trained themselves in self-defense and conflict-resolution techniques.

The rise of queer nationalism in the early 1990s was reminiscent of the "heyday" of the Gay Liberation and GAA movements 20 years earlier. Queer nationalism reinvigorated debates over ultimate movement goals and strategies and also challenged basic assumptions about the definition of community and identity. Proponents of queer nationalism rejected the notion that "we are just like everyone else except for what we do in bed." In fact, some argued the contrary by asserting that virtually all we have in common with straight people is what we do in bed and our oppression and subjectivity—our very way of viewing the world—makes us unlike straight people in many critical ways.

Another significant component of the emergence of queer nationalism is academic scholarship that has channeled major theoretical labor into issues of identity, sexuality, and corporeality on college and university campuses. What has come to be referred to as "Queer Theory," "Gender Theory," and "Queer Studies," with such notable writers as Michel Foucault, Judith Butler, and Eve Kosovsky Sedgwick, among many others, has since had enormous impact in the "academy."

Queer theory is founded on the notion that "identities" are not fixed and are instead socially rather than biologically determined. Queer theorists insist that identities comprise many and varied elements, and that it is inaccurate and misleading to collectively categorize people on the basis of one single element (for example, as "lesbian," "gay," "bisexual," "heterosexual," or as "woman," "man," and others).

Preeminent scholar and social theorist Judith Butler (1990) addressed what she refers to as the "performativety of gender" in that gender is basically an involuntary reiteration or reenactment of established norms of expression, an act that one performs as an actor performs a script that was created before the actor ever took the stage. The continued transmission of gender requires actors to play their roles so that they become actualized and reproduced in the guise of reality, and in the guise of the "natural" and the "normal."

> The act that one does, the act that one performs, is, in a sense, an act that has been going on before one arrived on the scene. Hence, gender is an act, which has been rehearsed, much as a script survives the particular actors who make use of it, but which requires individual actors in order to be actualized and reproduced as reality once again. (Butler, 1990, p. 272)

A variety of theorists argue that the notion of "gender" is a concept that is taught and learned and sustained in the service of maintaining positions of domination and subordination. Not only are the categorical man/woman, heterosexual/homosexual and bisexual, and gender conforming/gender non-conforming binary frames inaccurate and constraining for the complexities and diversity of human bodies and lives, but also they leave no space for intersex people—the estimated one in 2,000 people born with either indeterminate or combined male and female sexed bodies—and transgender, including transsexual, people. In the case of gender, the binary imperatives actually lock all people into rigid gender-based roles that inhibit creativity and self-expression, and therefore, we all have a vested interest in challenging and eventually obliterating the binaries.

Transgender people are increasingly coming out of another closet in large numbers. Many include young people emerging from a new generation of activists who are on the cutting edge in the movement for equality and pride. They are making the links between transgender oppression, heterosexism, and sexism. The increased visibility and activism of transgender activists within popular media and academic discourse has had the effect of shaking up traditionally dichotomous notions of male/female and gay/straight (Catalano & Shlasko, 2010; Stryker, 2008, 2007; Bornstein, 1994; Feinberg, 1996; Wilchins, 2004). They are creating a vision of social transformation as opposed to mere reform by contesting and exploding conventional gender constructions, most notably the limiting and destructive binary conceptualizations and definitions of "masculinity" and "femininity."

The "Gay/Straight Alliance" Movement

Catching the spark from their university and community counterparts, high school and middle school students, aided by supportive faculty, staff, and administrators, responded to an enormous problem on their campuses in the 1990s with the organization of "Gay/Straight Alliances (GSA)." These alliance groups have steadily become important pieces in an overall strategy to ensure that schools fulfill their mandates of providing the best education possible in a safe and welcoming environment for students of all sexual and gender identities. In addition to the GSAs, some schools include parallel Gay/Straight faculty support groups.

GSAs are student-run with faculty advisors who assist the group, offer resources and support, and help to facilitate discussions. Alliance meetings offer participants a space to talk openly about feelings and experiences related to sexual and gender identity and expression and members work to educate themselves and the campus community about issues regarding heterosexism and transgender oppression. Alliances support activities such as attending movies and theater performances; organizing dances, outdoor activities, and field trips; attending political rallies, parades, and marches; hosting speakers, writers, artists, musicians; and sharing meals. As part of their educational mission, GSAs also sponsor "Speaker Bureaus" where members are invited to talk with classes in their schools and sometimes in other community sites regarding issues of heterosexism and transgender oppression, "coming out," becoming and serving as allies, and other topics. Members also help to coordinate and take part in campus-wide "Awareness Days" or "Diversity Days" in which schools set aside the usual daily schedule and sponsor special workshops around issues of multiculturalism.

In addition, students conduct educational efforts around a number of special events, for example the annual National Day of Silence (a day in mid-April each year when students across the nation take a vow of silence to call attention to the epidemic of oppressive name calling, harassment, and violence perpetrated against lesbian, gay, bisexual, transgender, questioning, intersex, queer, and allied students in schools and society); National Coming Out Day (October 11 each year in the United States, October 12 in the United Kingdom, set aside to take further steps in "Coming Out of the Closet" of denial and fear around issues of sexual and gender identity as a personal and community-wide effort to raise awareness); and, No Name Calling Week (based on an idea proposed in the best-selling young adult novel, *The Misfits* (2003) by James Howe, in which four seventh-grade friends suffer the daily effects of insults and taunts. The Gay Lesbian Straight Education Network (GLSEN) collaborates with Simon and Schuster's Children's Publishing and other allies to coordinate a week of awareness activities annually to highlight and work to prevent incidents of name-calling and other types of bullying in schools and communities. Many GSAs work with their local and regional chapters of GLSEN throughout the year. In 1994 Missouri High School teacher Rodney Wilson proposed a National LGBT History Month; it has become a visible and nationally recognized observance of LGBTQ history—October in the United States, February in the United Kingdom.

While student activists have made substantial strides within educational institutions that have had wider implications throughout society, legislatures and the courts have codified many of these gains. Legislators in some states have passed bills to protect people of all ages from gender-based discrimination and sexual harassment and bullying within schools and society. Courageous young people, in their challenging of heterosexism, transgender oppression, and sexuality- and gender-based harassment in the schools have won a number of precedent-setting court cases that have far-reaching implications.[1] In addition, a number of states have passed bullying prevention legislation that includes sexual identity and gender identity and expression as protected categories.

Conclusion

Young people have been and continue to be at the heart of progressive social change movements. Researcher Catherine Corrigall-Brown (2005), in her study of youth participation in social movements, found that activism is directly related with higher levels of self-esteem and self-efficacy, and also associated with verification and crystallization of identity development.

Youth are transforming and revolutionizing the society and its institutions by challenging overall power inequities related to sexuality and gender identity categorizations and hierarchies, and they are also forming coalitions with other marginalized groups. They are dreaming their dreams, sharing their ideas and visions, and organizing to ensure a world free from all the deadly forms of oppression. Along their journey, they are inventing new ways of relating and being in the world. Their stories, experiences, and activism have great potential to bring us to a future where people across the gender and sexuality spectrums will live freely, unencumbered by social taboos and cultural norms of gender and sexuality. It is a future in which all the disparate varieties of sexuality and gender expression will live and prosper in us all.

Note

1. See for example, *Fricke* v. *Lynch* (right to take same-sex partner to high school prom, 491 F. Supp. 381, 1980); *Nabozny* v. *Podlesny* (right to protection from homophobic bullying, U.S. Court of Appeals, Seventh Circuit 92 F.3d 446, 1996); *Vance* v. *Spencer County Public School District* (right to protection against harassment on the basis of sex, sexual orientation, and national origin. 321 F.3d 253, 6th Circuit Court, 2000); *McLaughlin* v. *Puleski County Special School District* (right to personal disclosure of sexual identity in public schools, 2003); *Flores* v. *Morgan Hill Unified School District* (schools must take meaningful steps to address homophobic harassment, 2004).

References

Bérubé, A. (1990). *Coming out under fire: The history of gay men and women in World War II*. New York: Penguin Books.

Blackwood, E. (1986). *The many faces of homosexuality: Anthropological approaches to homosexual behavior*. New York: Harrington Park Press.

Blumenfeld, W.J. (1973). Are you recognized. In *Interchange: The Newsletter of the National Gay Student Center, 1*(3), 14–18.

Blumenfeld, W.J., & Raymond, D. (1993). *Looking at gay and lesbian life*. Boston: Beacon Press.

Bornstein, K. (1994). *Gender outlaw: On men, women, and the rest of us*. New York: Vintage Books.

Boswell, J. (1980). *Christianity, social tolerance, and homosexuality: Gay people in Western Europe from the beginning of the Christian era to the fourteenth century*. Chicago: University of Chicago Press.

Bray, A. (1982). *Homosexuality in Renaissance England*. London: Gay Men's Press.

Butler, J. (1990). *Gender trouble: Feminism and the subversion of identity*. New York: Routledge.

Catalano, C., & Shlasko, D. (2010). Transgender oppression: Introduction. In M. Adams, W.J. Blumenfeld, C. Castañeda, H.W. Hackman, M.L. Peters, & X. Zúñiga (Eds.), *Readings for diversity and social justice* (2nd ed., pp. 423–428). New York: Routledge.

Chauncey, G. (1994). *Gay New York: Gender, urban culture, and the making of the gay male world, 1890–1940*. New York: Basic Books.

Corrigall-Brown, C. (2005, August). Social movement participation among youth: An examination of social-psychological correlates. Paper presented at the annual meeting of the American Sociological Association, Philadelphia, PA.

D'Emilio, J. (1983). *Sexual politics, sexual communities: The making of a homosexual minority in the United States, 1940–1970.* Chicago: The University of Chicago Press.

D'Emilio, J. (1992). *Making trouble: Essays on gay history, politics, and the university.* New York: Routledge.

D'Emilio, J. (1993). Capitalism and gay identity. In H. Abelove, M.A. Barale, & D.M. Halperin (Eds.), *The lesbian and gay studies reader* (pp. 467–476). New York: Routledge.

Faderman, L. (1981). *Surpassing the love of men: Romantic friendship and love between women from the Renaissance to the present.* New York: HarperCollins.

Faderman, L. (1991). *Odd girls and twilight lovers: A history of lesbian life in twentieth century America.* New York: Penguin.

Faderman, L., & Eriksson, B. (1990). *Lesbians in Germany: 1890s–1920s.* Tallahassee, FL: The Naiad Press, Inc.

Feinberg, L. (1996). *Transgender warriors: Making history from Joan of Arc to Ru Paul.* Boston: Beacon Press.

Hinsch, B. (1990). *Passions of the cut sleeve: The male homosexual tradition in China.* Berkeley: University of California Press.

Howe, J. (2003). *The misfits.* Fullerton, CA: Aladdin Books.

Jenny, C., Roesler, T.A., & Poyer, K.L. (1994). Are children at risk for sexual assault by homosexual men? *Journal of Pediatrics, 94,* 41–44.

Katz, J. (1976). *Gay American history: Lesbians and gay men in the U.S.A.* New York: Avon Books.

Lauritsen, J., & Thorstad, D. (1995). *The early homosexual rights movement (1864 1935).* Ojai, CA: Times Change Press. (Original work published 1974)

Miller, N. (2006). *Out of the past: Gay and lesbian history from 1869 to the present.* New York: Vintage Books. (Original work published 1995)

Reichard, D.A. (2010). "We can't hide and they are wrong": The Society for Homosexual Freedom and the struggle for recognition at Sacramento State College, 1969–1971. *Law and History Review, 28,* 629–674.

Steakley, J. (1982). *The homosexual emancipation movement in Germany.* Salem, NH: The Ayer Company.

Stryker, S. (2008). *Transgender history.* Berkeley, CA: Seal Press.

Stryker, S., & Whittle, S. (2007). *The transgender studies reader.* New York: Routledge.

White, C.T. (2009). *Pre-gay LA: A social history of the movement for homosexual rights.* Urbana: University of Illinois Press.

Wilchins, R. (2004). *Queer theory, gender theory.* Los Angeles: Alyson Books.

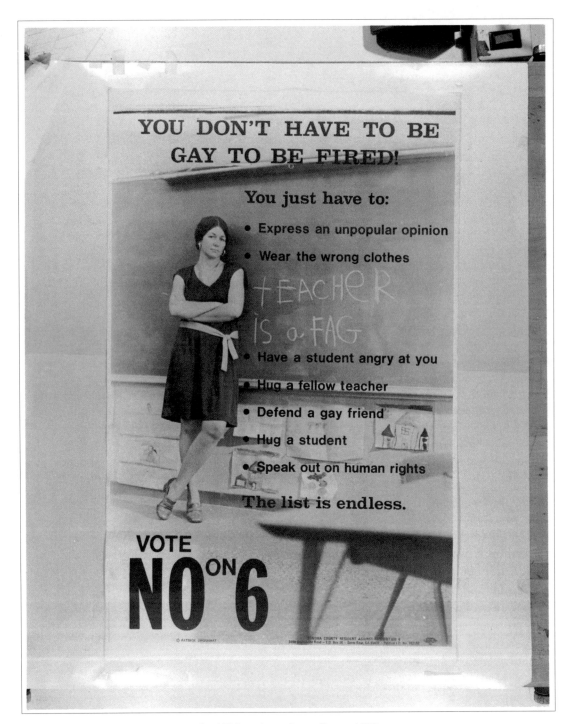

Anti-Briggs Amendment Poster, 1978

The defeat of the Briggs Initiative was a turning point in the battle for equal employment rights in education, the "Stonewall Rebellion" for teachers.

Introduction: Teaching as Whole Self

ISABEL NUÑEZ

That "we teach who we are" stubbornly remains a truism in our field. The current accountability and market-based reform movements can seem determined to remove the person of the individual educator through standardized curricula and scripted lessons. Despite this, scholars continue to acknowledge the centrality of the teacher's unique personality and passion in the educative process. Few of them, however, recognize the role of a teacher's personhood in its entirety.

According to Jung (1923/1949), the human psyche—and each of our personalities—can be understood to involve thinking, feeling, sensing, and intuiting. Though under fire, the intellectual work of the teacher has been ably defended (Schön, 1988), while the value of teachers' emotional engagement is beautifully explored in the educational literature (Michie, 1999). Even with regard to the least examined component of personality in our culture, writers do work to uncover how a teacher's inner world is manifest in their practice (Palmer, 1998; Diller, 1999). It is more challenging, however, to find scholarly work that engages the teacher as a physical being. Even when the students are adults, it is near to taboo to acknowledge the role of teachers' sexuality in their work (Jones, 1996). But if we take the truism seriously, we do teach our sexualities. Sexuality is part of who we are, and it does not go away when we enter our classrooms.

Western societies have long demanded a variety of psychological schisms as a condition of participation as a full and valued contributor. Actions and activities in the private sphere are kept separate from those of the public sphere. Even in a field like teaching, which ideally involves both intellect and emotion, those roles have been distinguished. The division is most often gendered, with men, as principals and superintendents, doing the thinking and women, as teachers, doing the nurturing of their charges (Freedman, 1998). That these bifurcations disserve both individuals and societies should be clear. Whether it is a politician whose hidden actions are discovered to be at odds with his or her public persona and stance, or an experienced nurse whose professional judgment and intuition are dismissed by those with more medical authority, there is a price to be paid when humans cannot be whole.

If such psychic splits are destructive, what are the consequences of outright denial? Repression of any psychological matter does not typically lead to positive outcomes, and a refusal to address something as universal and innate as the drive toward sexual expression, even if such refusal is limited to a particular "sphere" of life, seems downright dangerous. It is probably not a coincidence that U.S. sexual puritanism persists alongside hypersexualized media and an appalling amount of violence toward women. For our individual and societal health, we need to bring teachers' sexuality out of the realm of what Jung terms the psychological "shadow" (Jung, 1934/1968, p. 20).

Thankfully, there are educators and education scholars who are doing just that. The authors in this section present the possibility of teaching with integrity, a word etymologically related to the mathematical integer, or whole number. By integrating emotion, intuition, mind, and body, the essays you are about to read offer teachers the possibility of integrity, of being whole in one's vocation.

Carolyn Pajor Ford, now a high school English teacher, looks back on the evolution of her own sexual identity as a bisexual woman during her adolescence and young adulthood in the opening spotlight text, "White Trash: Manifesting the Bisexual." Her story, while incontrovertibly unique, can also be considered a narrative of experiences that should resonate with many teachers and teachers-to-be. It is worth questioning how welcome Ford, or others with diverse sexualities, felt when entering a vocation that is so tied in with traditional—yet asexual—femininity.

The chapter that follows considers the closely related issue of how women's sexualities are shaped and controlled during their induction into the teaching profession. Prompted by a group of student teachers, Becky Atkinson, in "Apple Jumper, Teacher Babe, and Bland Uniformer Teachers: Fashioning Feminine Teacher Bodies," examines how the norms governing teacher attire reflect the historical appropriation of teachers' bodies as sites of instruction about sexuality and gender. Female teachers' preferred clothing in previous generations emphasized the maternal and the nurturing, reflecting the model of sexuality then desired for students. Frighteningly, the emergent standard appears to erase the physical self entirely, acknowledging not even the constrained sexuality of the traditional teacher body.

Eric Rofes, in "Bound and Gagged: Sexual Silences, Gender Conformity, and the Gay Male Teacher," offers an inspirational portrait of resistance to the forces of control that Atkinson describes. He shares his own work toward the integration of his non-normative sexual self and teacher self in his vocation. More profoundly, he addresses the most primal of human integrations—that of yin and yang or anima and animus—in sharing how masculine energy (order and structure) and feminine energy (receptivity and chaos) are harnessed in his teaching. Seamlessly blending the emotional and intellectual, personal and political, Rofes's chapter is itself a model of wholeness and integrity.

In the following chapter, Jane Gallop also delves into the personal, sexual self through a narrative that she determines to be "Knot a Love Story." Instead, the experience is the impetus for an exploration of the eroticism that she concludes is inherent in pedagogy. She draws on Freud to consider that teaching, like sexuality, may recapitulate formative early experience. Provocatively, she posits that the "naughty" sexual charge from being part of another's transformative experience may well be the heart of good teaching.

Finally, Coya Paz Brownrigg in "Paper Machete" reflects on her problematic, though ultimately possible and extraordinarily rewarding negotiation of sexuality, gender role demands, and parenthood as a lesbian university educator. The essay, this section's concluding spotlight text, charts a continuing path of sexual and vocational evolution. In it, Paz Brownrigg reminds us that the work, both inner and outer, is never complete—but that this should not keep us from celebrating what has been achieved. Together these writers present an alternative vision for wholeness in self, sexuality, and teaching.

References

Diller, A. (1999). The ethical education of self-talk. In M.S. Katz, N. Noddings, & K.A. Strike (Eds.), *Justice and caring: The search for common ground in education* (pp. 74–92). New York: Teachers College Press.

Freedman, S.E. (1998). Teaching, gender, and curriculum. In L.E. Beyer & M.W. Apple (Eds.), *The curriculum: Problems, politics and possibilities* (pp. 230–244). Albany: State University of New York Press.

Jones, A. (1996). Desire, sexual harassment and pedagogy in the university classroom. *Theory into Practice, 35*(2) 102–109.

Jung, C.G. (1949). *Psychological types, or the psychology of individuation* (H.G. Baynes, Trans.). London: Routledge. (Original work published 1923)

Jung, C.G. (1968). *The archetypes and the collective unconscious* (2nd ed.). (W.F.C. Hull, Trans.). Princeton, NJ: Princeton University Press. (Original work published 1934)

Michie, G. (1999). *Holler if you hear me: The education of a teacher and his students.* New York: Teachers College Press.

Palmer, P.J. (1998). *The courage to teach: Exploring the inner landscape of a teacher's life.* San Francisco, CA: Jossey-Bass.

Schön, D.A. (1988). *Educating the reflective practitioner.* San Francisco, CA: Jossey-Bass.

CHAPTER EIGHT

White Trash

Manifesting the Bisexual

CAROLYN PAJOR FORD

This is what it feels like to be bisexual.

You're sixteen and your newest friend has brown hair and brown eyes, and you don't know why but you hope she likes you more than your other friends do. She does. You glide through your sophomore year, writing notes and holding hands on dark buses after basketball games, and only once does the word "lesbian" flash through your mind—only once as you bent down to kiss her warm mouth—because you knew even then that what you were doing had nothing do with her gender. You loved someone and it so happened that she was female; you'd love her if she were a man, if there ever could *be* such a man with brown eyes like bark off a tree, such sweet breath and the kind of skin that you want to touch.

There it was. Now you're 20 and your high school love is just a memory (she dumped you before prom for a swimmer named Champ)—no, not a memory, but an idea. *What happened,* you tell yourself, *is something I'm going to have to figure out one day.* You throw it on the back burner because you're not dying for women—hell, you don't even like any of the feminists in your lit classes 'cuz they all have big mouths and seem, at all times, excessively miffed. You think feminism is unnecessary because you're here and you're bright and nothing has held you back, baby. You yourself don't actually feel like a girl, but a person first and foremost, and you don't feel any great unity to some universal sisterhood. You meet someone with brown hair and brown eyes who is all parts wonderful, who happens to be a man. *If you were a woman,* you tell him in bed one night, *our lives would be much more complex.* He rightly understands this to mean that you'd still be there on his side, on his topside, sometimes on the inside. You wonder what it would be like if he were a girl. You see two lesbians holding hands in the Kroger, unabashed and unshaved. *If that's what it is,* you tell yourself, *I guess I'll never know.*

Now you're 23 and you just got a bad haircut, an $8 mad buzz from Supercuts. And now you work at Kroger. Dykes come through your checkout line and ask you when you're getting off work. This horrifies you, and when you recount this to your roommate, he tells you to wear prostitute red lipstick. Your relationship to All Parts Wonderful turns out to be complex despite his gender. You dump each other after three years of tempestuous devotion.

But your thought remains. Then you meet a girl and she tells you she loves your $8 Supercuts mad buzz. Your heart swells, 'cuz she's beautiful and sweet and has brown hair and brown eyes. She's nothing like the Kroger lesbians. You take it off the back burner. She's strong and soft and a great kisser. *Boy*, you think, *this is really cool*. At night you dream of touching her all over, and when that moment comes, you're not nervous at all.

Now you're girl crazy. You can't get your eyes big enough to take in all the lesbians you allow yourself to see. They're everywhere. You scan the bus and train for them when you get on. If you see one it makes your day. She doesn't have to be cute—that's not what you're after—it's her energy you want. You love how they look, especially the stereotypical ones, the ones whose hair and clothes and body make some wild statement about politics or philosophy or perhaps just plain indifference about the whole beauty myth. You hate Andrea Dworkin, but read her anyway and make snide comments in the margins. You adore Alice Walker. You don't call yourself bisexual, because it seems ridiculous to define yourself by the gender of the person you're close to, when the gender has never been a deciding factor at all. It's the 90s and feminism is now less miffed. So you call yourself a feminist. Feminist, with a hint of fruit.

Then at a basketball game you see a new person in your team's jersey. *What's that boy doing on our team*, you wonder. That boy turns out to be a girl. Her name is AJ. Her legs are hairy and her head is shaved. You think that if she were an animal, she'd be a deer, because her face is soft and beautiful and inviting. She plays basketball exactly the way you do and wears just one tiny crystal earring, the kind you've always wanted. You're enchanted. Her eyes and hair are brown but that's not even it anymore. After two snowy months you can't stand it, you have to kiss her because you never have imagined that such a decent and beautiful person could exist. Then on a blustery January evening, the angels and spirits and saints give you the most exquisite gift of your life, because the deer of a girl with the crystal earring feels exactly the same way you do.

Now you're terrified. You think you want to spend your life with a girl who shaves her head, doesn't shave her pits, and says things like *Fuck the Patriarchy*. She loves Andrea Dworkin. She's the Malcolm X of feminism. Your mother hates her, and your father can't bring himself to look at her. One summer afternoon, in a fit of despair over the choices you've made in life, your mother throws a saltshaker at her. She misses. When she tries to apologize, AJ laughs and says it's a good thing she has such bad aim.

But you appreciate her Malcolm X strength. You need it for when your mother calls. *Are you happy?* she whispers, at the end of each conversation. *Yes, mom*, you say. *Really?* she says, not truly in wonder. You hang up the phone and begin to shake. You've done something terribly wrong. You've fallen in love with a woman, and you had a choice. You chose this. Your heart tightens. You know you're trapped. There's nothing you can do now. You can't imagine your life without her. Yet when you hang up the phone with your mother, the choices you've made terrify you. What will you have when you're 50?

Months pass. You adore AJ, yet more and more you can't bring yourself to touch her. It's not that you don't want to. It's not that you don't think about it. One time, with your hand on her, you were struck with the horrifying realization that this was something you could not do forever. What is wrong with you? Why are you here? Are you not gay enough? You loathe this thought, yet you feel like such an imposter.

Your connection with AJ grows more tenuous daily. She is finding fault in everything you do. You love her, yet you cannot touch her. And ending the connection feels like tearing off a limb from your body. It's unimaginable.

Now you hate your sexuality. It's tangled and messy and filled with too many choices. You wish you were a lesbian. God you should be. You look it. You play basketball. You surround yourself with dykes and go ga-ga when you see one in public. And everyone thinks you're one, anyway. They don't understand the bisexual part. When you try to explain, their eyes glaze over. Then you get paranoid, and wonder what they're thinking. You want to say, *Gender has nothing to do with love.* You want to say, *A person's body is just their shell.* You want to say, *Just because in theory I can fuck everyone doesn't mean that I want to or that I do.*

But you're not fucking anyone now. AJ has left you, and you are sad for two years.

Part II

Years pass. Dykes continue to draw your eye. If you're bisexual, how come you haven't been intimate with a man since the Persian Gulf War? You think it's dormant. Once you figure your gay thing out, you'll be free. The day you decide that you truly want to spend your life with a woman, you develop a raging crush on a man you work with. Is this a story that has no ending?

Then you meet Cherie. She's half Native, half white, a voluminous drinker, an incessant smoker, and a flagrant litterer. *It's my white side,* she says, as she flicks her tenth cigarette butt out your window. Her head is shaved and her muscular arms bear four tattoos of swallows. She wears a heavy silver chain loosely around her neck, boy jeans, a tight shirt. She mocks you for not letting her drink beer in your car. She calls you and everyone else *Baby.* It takes her five hours from the moment you meet her to take you to bed.

I don't even know you, you think, as she's kissing you and pressing her body against yours. You smell her smoke. You want this. It's been so long. But she won't take off her shirt, and won't let you touch her. Her hand is hard and fast and goes to your softest spots too quickly. She won't let you roll to the top. You've never met anyone like her. She's all silver chain, when you want the swallows. You will never come with her, yet she clings to you when she's coming, *baby, baby,* she's coming. Afterwards, she clings to you and rests her stubbly head on your chest. You kiss her forehead and rock her to sleep. You want to be a free bird, too.

You love it that you're falling asleep next to a woman. You like it that's it her. I've just had the worst sex of my life, you tell yourself, but I'm still glad to be here. You will rock Cherie to sleep four more nights, and miss her when she's gone.

This is what you must know about bisexuals: lesbian isn't the only way to be gay. Lesbian isn't the only dyke. You can be 50–50. You can be 70–30. You can *choose* this. And me, I chose this. With my eyes wide and my arms open, this is where I want to be. I'm on the dyky side of bi, a nebulous region where girls are my present, boys are my past, and my future is a strong person with a beautiful heart.

And this is what you must know about the gay community: transgendered people are the second-class citizens, and bisexuals are below even them. We're the white trash of the gay world, a group for whom it's socially acceptable to not accept. Feeling awkward among straights is what it feels like to be bi. Being distrusted among gays is what it feels like, too. So I make my friends and take my lovers in people who transcend the suspicions of their posse. My friends almost always support me, but it's my lovers who will always define me.

CHAPTER NINE

Apple Jumper, Teacher Babe, and Bland Uniformer Teachers

Fashioning Feminine Teacher Bodies

BECKY ATKINSON

A conversation with student teachers just about to begin their professional teaching careers prompted the explorations outlined in this chapter. This group of students embodied the norm of the elementary teaching population in that all five were white, able-bodied, heterosexual, middle- or upper-middle-class young women. They were completing the final semester of their elementary teacher education program at a small, private, conservative, liberal arts, Master's level university located in a suburban community in the Southeast. The students and teachers in the suburban schools in which they were student teaching were predominately white, middle-, and working-class populations. One of the student teachers had been given a pair of "teacher socks," socks decorated with pictures of school buses, books, and pencils by one of her second-grade students. At the after-school group seminar, the young woman expressed dismay at having to wear the socks because of the unwritten rule among the grade-level teachers at her field placement that one had to wear a student's gift immediately. All of those in the seminar group seemed to understand her distress at wearing the teacher socks, as they all viewed this "teacher gear" style of dress as somehow reductive of their image of what a teacher should be.

Although I knew that college-age students dress like college-age students and do not choose more matronly styles of dress like jumpers with turtlenecks, I had not encountered such distress over career-related dress before from student teacher groups I had worked with during the past five years, nor had I heard such a feminist-oriented critique from other groups. I asked them what, exactly, was upsetting about this, apart from questions of personal style, because they had spent the last four or more years of their lives preparing to be elementary school teachers and were halfway through their culminating student teaching experience. They would be full-time teachers in six months or less but were obviously responding to the wearing of "teacher gear" as minimalizing and inevitably constraining.

During several minutes of frank conversation, the women student teachers voiced similar viewpoints about the various forms of teacher dress observed during their clinical placements and the specialized meanings about teaching that each seemed to signify. Their descriptions distinguished three identifiable clothing styles. The first was the teacher gear, or "apple jumper" style of clothing—jumpers, denim shirts, socks, sweaters—often decorated with images associated with school, such as apples or buses. Many of these teachers also demonstrated a propensity to wear clothes displaying images associated with seasons of the year: fall sweaters covered with embroidered leaves or Hallowe'en jack-o'-lanterns, winter snowflake vests, or denim shirts embroidered with tulips and butterflies in spring.

A second category was identified as a "teacher babe" style, characterized by short skirts, low-cut sweaters, and high boots. The student teachers disparaged teachers who chose this type of clothing as unprofessional and "not serious" about the profession. According to one of the student teachers, the quintessential teacher babe at her school wore low-cut sweaters and T-shirts with tight pants to teach her second-grade class. Several other student teachers nodded in agreement about seeing that pattern of dress in teachers at their schools. When asked what they thought was preferable, the young women voiced their preference for a third category, what might be termed "bland uniformer" clothing. This style of professional dress includes modestly fitting pants or skirts with not too closely fitted shirts or T-shirts—no school or seasonal icons or accessories. This style is rather androgynous, and downplays feminine physical characteristics for the sake of comfort and coverage.

This incident and the student teachers' responses to it provide a clear illustration of how one kind of iconic discourse about teachers—as nurturing and maternal—disrupted what a particular preservice teacher saw as a more professional discourse claimed by herself and her peers. Ashley's wearing the teacher socks that publicly marked her as a particular type of teacher, a type she considered unprofessional, illustrates the vulnerability of women teachers' subjectivities to competing discourses constructing women teachers' professional identity. Ashley's subjectivity, "her sense of herself and her ways of understanding her relation to the world" (Weedon, 1989, p. 32), her understanding of what she could see for herself as a practicing teacher, bumped into one of the socially, culturally, and professionally constructed meanings of teaching, materialized as teacher socks.

That conversation and the resulting questions led to my interest in exploring the answers to these questions by a thoughtful consideration of the three styles of teachers' clothing choices as expressions of women teachers' subjectivities, two seen as reprehensible, one seen as preferable, and how this might relate to their identities as white, middle-class, heterosexual, able-bodied young women in the Southeast. This chapter proposes to use a feminist poststructuralist analysis to examine teachers' clothing choices as a discursive practice in which the female teacher body becomes signified in ways that reflect the multiple and often conflicting feminized and professional discourses that permeate women's experience of teaching.

The Apple Jumper Teacher

The jumper as a form of dress evokes cultural, social, and historical construction of teaching as "women's work" (Biklen, 1995; Grumet, 1988), harking back to conventional assumptions about women's "natural" ability to nurture, and her compliance to male leadership, as convincingly proposed by Catherine Beecher to the U.S. Congress in the middle of the 19th century. With the bib-like bodice that covers the chest, and a full, long skirt that masks hips and legs, the jumper's style is reminiscent of housekeepers' full-length aprons or girls' pinafores worn in the past. Indeed, this comparison is not such a stretch in light of the fact that both types of clothing are relatively shapeless and conceal or protect the body and other clothing. This would make jumpers both practical for meeting the physical demands of elementary school teaching, especially when working with young children, as well as the social and moral demands of the role of women teachers in U.S. culture.

The persistent concern with regulating women teachers reflects concerns with controlling the cultural and social contexts of educational institutions, in addition to controlling formalized curriculum and pedagogy. Schools are seen as integral to transmitting what is deemed by the mainstream population to be valuable cultural knowledge, moral values, attitudes, history, myths, and behavioral norms to the youth of the nation. U.S. schools are dominated by European American, middle-class, capitalist, heterosexual interests that are served well by explicit schooling practices that privilege those interests (Apple, 1988; Biklen, 1995; Grumet, 1988; Lather, 1987). Teachers are compelled to enact socially and culturally approved versions of masculinity and femininity that conform to dominant interests. For the apple jumper teacher, then, her body becomes an important site of inscription for discourses of "proper femininity," and a maternal femininity supportive of assumptions related to "women's work." However, discursive processes also produce resistance to the influences shaping subjectivities, as will be discussed in the following analyses.

Discourses of "Proper" Femininity: The Virginal Teacher Body

Historical scholarship on women teachers has shown how public perception of women teachers' morality was quite often linked to their deportment and dress. Teachers performing "proper" femininity were expected to enact a virginal heterosexual femininity but have no relationships, intimate or platonic, with men other than brothers or fathers (Apple, 1988). To ensure this, in the early days of U.S. public education, women teachers were forbidden to wear make-up and instructed to wear several petticoats to ensure that their skirts did not show the shape of their legs (Apple, 1988; Cohen & Scheer, 1997). Because those early teachers were also required to remain single or lose their jobs (Biklen, 1995; Blount, 1996), I suspect that the urge to control women teachers' bodies by requiring them to conceal their bodies for purposes of modeling morality and "proper " femininity, aided local school committees who may have also wanted to minimize these women's attractions in the eyes of men looking for wives.

Commonly understood ideas generated about normative and "model" femininity grow from expectations of women to be heterosexual and suit their practices, behavior, and appearance to the support of hegemonic masculinity. Bartky (1992) writes, "Normative femininity . . . is coming more and more to be centered on women's body—not its duties and obligations—but its sexuality, more precisely, its presumed heterosexuality and its appearance" (p. 86). Women teachers' bodies must be controlled so that the performance of virtuous and moral but heterosexual femininity may be displayed in appropriate pedagogical settings.

Jackie Blount's (1996) scholarship on women educators' employment in the early to mid-20th century proposed that one of the strongest influences shaping schooling practices and policies as they relate to gendered teacher professional identity is the patriarchal focus on maintaining hegemonic femininity and masculinity. As long as single women teachers were viewed as supportive of social expectations through the performance of modesty, morality, and virginity, and their single-minded obedience to the school board rather than a husband, they were preferred candidates for teaching positions. In fact, Blount's research indicates that women teachers and administrators were encouraged to spend time with other women, even live with them, until homophobic concerns emerged about the possibility of lesbianism that was feared might bring about the weakening of male students' "manliness." This fear and the thought that "spinster" teachers would model an incorrect "femininity" and not "educate . . . [young women] . . . in the direction of marriage and motherhood" (Blount, 1996, p. 7) eased marriage restrictions for women teachers. Blount asserted that this emphasis had a profound effect in that it polarized gender stereotypes within the teaching profession and demanded marriage as a demonstration of heterosexual conformity. Furthermore, Blount (1996; 2000) suggested that attention to maintaining this hegemony continues as a strong influence in contemporary schooling practices regulating performances of normative gender behaviors and shaping teaching, especially at the elementary level, as a profession not only for wives, but more so for mothers of children.

Discourses of Maternal Femininity: The Motherly Body

The "feminization of teaching" in the early 19th century initiated the continuing irony of women's involvement with teaching in that they were recruited for their "womanly virtues" and encouraged to think of teaching as preparation for marriage, yet penalized with the loss of their jobs when they decided to marry. Blount's (1996) work, cited previously, highlighted how discourses on "proper" femininity as virginal lost prominence in favor of the idea that "proper" femininity must be demonstrated by marriage. This allowed for conceptions of teachers as mothers, and not just as mothers or wives "in training," to shape women teachers' professional identity.

The downside to this development was that it opened the door for women's "erotic potential" (Richardson, 1985, pp. 15–16) to be present in pedagogical settings. However, in light of the fears of promoting lesbianism through the marriage restrictions, a married woman teacher's permissible opportunities for sexual intimacy, and thereby motherhood, had several benefits. One of these was the performance of "proper" married heterosexual femininity for the socialization of school-age children. The other was that the increased probability of motherhood privileges discourses in which women teachers' bodies signified as maternal and domestic, offering the comfort and nurturing seen as lacking in public institutions but also suggesting the productive orderliness expected of a housekeeper.

The nurturing qualities ascribed to maternal women teachers prescribe a selfless commitment to children and democratic citizenship. Catherine Beecher rested her call to middle-class white women to become teachers to nurture and "civilize" the children of the common school movement with a missionary zeal and nationalistic commitment to the development of American imperialism. Women teachers are compelled by the combination of political and patriarchal discourses that "hail" them to be a "good girl," to enact a missionary zeal for children's development as educated citizens under the mandates of "meeting students' needs" and maintaining "family values" (Ritchie & Wilson, 2000). Several feminist writers have theorized the maternal teacher body as preferred by the schooling enterprise for easing children's entrance into the processes of schooling because the motherly teacher is naturalized as compliant—a characteristic desired by administrators and policymakers—and nurturing—a trait desired by parents and administrators (Biklen, 1995; Davies, 1994; Grumet, 1988; Walkerdine, 1990). Mothers are supposed to give birth and nurturance to children for the continuation of the species. Teachers must reproduce citizens for a democratic society, men and women for a patriarchal heterosexual culture, and differently skilled laborers for a capitalist economy.

A more contemporary version of the apple jumper teacher subjectivity, and perhaps a more extreme one, can be seen in the seasonal wear or holiday-themed clothing worn by many teachers. As the focus of many eyes—those of parents, children, colleagues, administrators, the school board, certifying bodies such as the state, as well as the federal gaze filtered through legislative mandates on teacher quality and accountability—teachers are compelled to act as texts for the culture into which they socialize their students. Women teachers who wear seasonal clothing, such as pumpkin earrings in the fall or snowman-covered sweaters in January, provide a visual illustration of these connections. These "docile" teacher bodies are intentionally inscribed with the icons of mainstream culture in addition to the unacknowledged values, traditions, and knowledge of the culture that they pass on to her students. The individual woman teacher displays the mainstream culture incorporated into these iconic representations, another embodiment of a subjectivity that ironically denies the womanly body but decorates it.

Student Teachers and Apple Jumper Teachers

What, then, did the student teachers find so reprehensible and distasteful in the apple jumper teachers they had observed, and what does that say about their own positionality as inexperienced, young, white, middle-class, heterosexual women in a conservative suburban area in the Southeast? Their positionality would indicate support for this subjectivity. From my own perspective as a middle-aged, white, middle-class heterosexual female teacher educator who had visited dozens of K–6 classrooms, apple jumper teachers had been and still are the norm. The student teachers' critique concerned the professionalism of the apple jumper-type teachers, indicating that this kind of teacher body, although "proper," was too maternal, too domestic, too much of a particular form of femininity that was "unintelligible" to them as professional. The young women talked about apple jumper teachers as if they were an extreme and "not normal" version of a professional educator. Foucault (1977/1995) conceptualized the "intelligible" body as one recognizable and acceptable to aesthetic and cultural representations of the body, in this case the student teachers' conceptions of a professional educator body.

Some of their recoil may have something to do with the age of the majority of elementary teachers. Recently published national statistics about teacher characteristics drawn from a 2003–2004 survey indicate that 54% of teachers were in the 40–60 age group (NCES, 2007). The students could not or refused to see themselves and their futures in the experiences of the teachers they critiqued. One girl's remark about becoming a teacher, meaning "no more college girl," seems to reinforce that speculation.

On the other hand, it could be that this critique was for the teacher identity as the apple jumper teachers had lived it out in their practice. Despite their lack of academic feminist education at the university, this group of young women was voicing a feminist critique of what they saw as a teacher identity that was more womanly than it was professional. This could reflect their own inability to explore—or inexperience with exploring—the various ways of performing as a woman and performing as a woman teacher. From their responses to what they called the "teacher babe," they did not see an intelligible way to be womanly that was also professional, because they rejected the matronly version, as well as a sexy version, of teacher identity. I suggest that their concept of a normative professional identity may have been limited to that of the bland uniformer teacher because of the limited woman teacher subjectivities made available to them within the local schooling context, as well as their inability to or inexperience with mediating their femininity with their professional identity.

Teacher Babe Teachers

In contrast to the apple jumper teacher subjectivity evoking domesticity, nurturance, and "proper" femininity, the subjectivity of the teacher babe offers a more sexualized version of normative femininity as a way to be a woman teacher. Women teachers who choose to dress as teacher babes choose stylish, more form-fitting clothing that accentuates physical features of female bodies, including short skirts, low-cut tops, tight sweaters, and other body-revealing clothing. Although, in one sense, this clothing style reinscribes hegemonic femininity, the performance of this version of femininity is considered transgressive within schooling contexts, if not also outside of school spaces for some women teachers. In fact, one teacher reported that she regulated her clothing, spending very little of her clothing budget on more modestly "sexy" clothes even to wear outside of school, because she did not want to risk students or parents seeing her buxom figure as anything but what she thought of as "professional" (Strickland, 2006). This concern speaks to the fragility and vulnerability of women teachers to unsolicited inscriptions of their bodies as sexualized but at the same time illustrates how women teachers' sexualized bodies can be a powerful form of resistance.

Discourses of Sexualized Femininity: The Teacher Babe as the "Body of Knowledge"

In claiming a "sexy" body through her clothing choices, the teacher babe challenges the limitations on how women mediate their femininity with discourses of professionalism. The teacher babe can be seen as a subjectivity that asks how a woman can perform sexualized femininity and teacher professional identity within the workplace shaped by schools. Teacher babes explore the limits to this merging of femininity with professionalism, putting at risk their professional reputations. Traditional discourses surrounding teaching invoke what bell hooks (1994) and Tara Star Johnson (2006) identified as the Cartesian duality of mind and body. This binary separates the body from the mind, and privileges the mind over the body as if the two cannot operate together. Within the patriarchal culture of schools, the binary of mind and body are overlaid and laminated with norms of heterosexual femininity and masculinity. The teacher's physical body, especially if it is female, must be "erased" to privilege the body of knowledge she is supposed to transmit (hooks, 1994), because the sexual knowledge ascribed to the feminine body is distracting to the male gaze dominating social institutions. For women teachers particularly, the "erotic potential" (Richardson, 1985, pp. 15–16) of their sexualized bodies distracts from the academic and assumed moral purposes of schooling and so must not be present in the classroom. The acceptable female body in the classroom is the "proper" body embodied as the apple jumper teacher, or the "erased" body embodied by the "bland uniformer" teacher. Teacher babe teachers bring into the classroom a transgressive, "improper" female body that competes with school knowledge for students' attention. The teacher's body becomes a sexual text, as opposed to the icon-bearing teacher wearing snowflake sweatshirts embodying a cultural text, or the sexless bland uniformer teacher embodying school texts.

Donna Pendergast's and Erica McWilliam's (1999) paper on home economics teachers and transgression describes a "sexy, groovy" home economics teacher whose attire became a

> means of resisting the identity of the "proper" virginal and motherly teacher, and instead sexualizing the pedagogical persona. . . . The home economics body which refuses to hide its sexuality—which steps out of the asexual, motherly, virginal norms—flaunts this by means of attire. (p. 9)

Such a transgressive female teacher body displaying and performing the "erotic potential" (Richardson, 1985, pp. 15–16) but also performing the body of knowledge that she teaches calls into question the patriarchal beliefs and practices that support the persistence and hegemony of the mind-body binary.

Teacher babes claim their sexuality through their clothing choices and so also bring their sexualized bodies into their classrooms, a risky practice because the body of the teacher is no longer "erased" or sexless, nor is it virginal or maternal. This teacher body must be acknowledged as erotic and "sexy." Teacher babes, in emphasizing their physical presence and sexual potential, demonstrate that they pay attention to themselves as feminine in a way that is not swallowed up by historical and cultural expectations that construct the maternal teacher as selfless and sacrificial in their commitment to their students. Within the institutionalized context of schooling, the sexualized teacher body is seen as irrational (body over mind) and "unintelligible" because it is not seen as belonging in the classroom, as immoral and so unfit to teach.

Discourses of Morality: Teacher Slut and Teacher Predator

Bringing the teacher body into the classroom in a gendered and sexualized performance also makes it possible to envision the teacher body in outside-of-school spaces. This suggests the possibility for nonteacherly behavior in those places, which calls into doubt her morality, especially when linked to work practices. One of the student teachers explained that some of the first-grade teachers in her hall talked about another first-grade teacher as the "teacher slut," who wore short skirts and knee-high boots, arrived at school just before her students did, and was out the door every day five minutes after the students were dismissed. Even though she was married and apparently "respectable," her dress and disregard of the unwritten work ethic about teachers' long hours labeled her as immoral, inappropriately sexual, and unprofessional in her colleagues' eyes.

In recent years, the teacher babe may be more likely to be feared as a sexual predator because of the highly publicized stories of female teachers who have been accused of sexual affairs with, or charged with sexual assault against, their younger male students. At the least, they may be vulnerable to charges of sexual harassment or find themselves victims of sexual harassment, with their clothing seen as "provocative." These possibilities, and the news stories of students as sexual prey, make visible the threat underlying the interest in the control and surveillance of women teachers' bodies, theorized by Sheila Cavanaugh (2004) in her article on school sex scandals and the teacher *femme fatale:*

> The state appointed female teacher who refuses to subordinate her sexuality to a professional sanctioned ascetic dream of motherly love incites anxiety in men who are invested in normative masculinity involving traditional gender hierarchies. Female sexual potence tinged with an intergenerational advantage enabling the teacher-as-mother to adopt a position of power over the male student coded—as son—threatens normative masculine identity development. (p. 316)

The teacher babe's sexuality can also be seen as threatening to hegemonic and normative familial structures, in that her sexuality suggests sexual agency for not only an illicit relationship between younger student and older teacher, but for a relationship that mimics mother/son incest.

Even though the notion of a sexualized femininity performed by classroom teachers is transgressive within the context of schools, it still conforms to normative heterosexual expectations. The femme fatale, or teacher babe version of what is considered feminine, despite her resistance to institutionalized prescriptions for femininity in schools, reinforces heterosexual masculinity so that the polarization of femininity and masculinity historicized within the educational culture as suggested by Jackie Blount (1996, 2000) remains in place.

Student Teachers and the Teacher Babe Teacher

It is important to note here that notions of sexualized feminine dress in the conservative atmosphere of many areas of the Southeast can extend to sleeveless tops that bare the arms (popular in the warm, humid climate) or V-neck shirts that hint at some cleavage. It may be that clothing choices such as these cast some younger women teachers into the teacher babe category without any intention on their part, because even these modest physical revelations make a gendered body visible. A gendered body brings with it "erotic potential" (Richardson, 1985, pp. 15–16) that, in some educational settings, may be enough to render it the sexualized teacher babe. That this can and does occur indicates the permeable and fragile borders between these subjectivities and helps explain the rigid policing this group of student teachers voiced.

On the other hand, the teacher babe teacher was just as unintelligible and unprofessional to the group of student teachers as was the apple jumper teacher. They seemed to see both of these teacher bodies as extreme, almost caricatures of how professional teachers should be, compared to the bland uniformer teacher subjectivity they saw as desirable. This viewpoint is one that positions teaching as a workplace separate from the domestic sphere, perhaps implying more agency for teachers as professionals.

For sure, there are more ways than these three for women teachers to dress that might express other ways of embodying teacher professional identity. I can identify sporty teachers in jogging suits, tomboy teachers in jeans or khakis and T-shirts, and some teachers who wear business-like pantsuits to teach in. The reasons this group of student teachers distinguished the apple jumper, the teacher babe, and the bland uniformer teachers as remarkable might be more indicative of this particular point in their careers. In their teacher education program, they were being groomed as job-seekers and were asked to try to match their professional goals with the schools to which they applied for teaching positions. So, they were engaged in the process of reflecting on and considering goals and purposes for their careers. The teacher babe definitely did not express their professional interests, and bland uniformer teacher did express their interest in what they saw as teacher professionalism.

The Bland Uniformer Teacher

This third category of female teacher dress is one that is less distinctively marked than either of the other two. The student teachers' conversation about the three teacher dress styles conveyed strong conviction that the way of being a teacher indicated by this style of dress was very different from the apple jumper and teacher babe dress they found so reprehensible. The bland uniformer teacher fashions a subjectivity expressed by a bland and unremarkable form of attire that, like the jumper, neutralizes and masks female sexuality. Tara Star Johnson (2006), whose term I have appropriated, characterizes it as "monochromatic combination of sweater or blouse/jacket and slacks or long skirt . . . [a] bland uniform" (p. 259). It consists of serviceable and casual clothing, in that it is loose, modest, and comfortable for bending over, and sitting in small chairs and on the floor. One distinction from the apple jumper style is that this style is even more removed from displays of female sexuality, if possible; its shirts and pants are evocative of the business casual clothing of the male-oriented corporate context. The student teachers saw this way of being a teacher as more professional, unencumbered by the matronly subjectivity they found old fashioned, and the sexuality they found inappropriate and threatening. So, the preferred teacher body is not only desexualized; it is defeminized.

Discourses of the "Erased" Body

Sandra Weber's (1995) book on images of teachers, *That's Funny, You Don't Look Like a Teacher: Interrogating Image, Identity, and Popular Culture,* noted that teachers "know how to dress" (p. 71), referring to most women teachers' realization of the need to desexualize their clothing and, by doing so, desexualizing their bodies. A woman teacher's gendered features must be hidden or minimized and controlled, because "Being a woman in our culture means, among other things, that you live out your life in subjection to the virtually constant demand to police your body, to keep it always under strict mental control. . . . You must master that body and keep it under strict surveillance at all times" (McWhorter, 1999, p. 140). Apple jumper teachers demonstrate this control and regulate their bodies by cloaking them with long skirts and loose tops or conflating them with seasonal or holiday icons. Ironically, this still marks their bodies as womanly.

The bland uniformer teacher models a separation between the domestic as well as the feminine and the workplace, demonstrated by unmarked attire even less feminized, more gender neutral, and asexual than the modest apple jumper attire. Because women teachers are under the scrutiny of students, administrators, parents, and the larger public, bland uniformer teachers express vulnerability to expectations of controlled and subdued sexuality to the point that their bodies become, as bell hooks (1994) theorized, "erased" (pp. 136–149). Erased teacher bodies are inscribed with the various texts and forms of knowledge affirmed by schooling. The bland uniformer teacher body is a docile one that becomes normalized and standardized as the facilitator or transmitter of approved mainstream knowledge. If the complex of discourses works to erase women teachers' bodies and inscribe them with the institutionalized body of knowledge consisting of the content knowledge and skills, values, behaviors, ways of thinking, practices, and habits of the dominant culture, then the woman teacher's body becomes an appropriate site for resisting erasure and unwanted cultural inscription.

Student Teachers and Bland Uniformer Teachers

Why would this group of young women embrace a professional subjectivity embodied as defeminized, even sexless? One way to answer this question is first to reiterate that teachers are implicated in the production of discursively formed norms for masculinity, femininity, the rational and the "normal," national and political interest, and school success and achievement within educational contexts as well as the broader social and cultural context. As pointed out by Cooks and Le Besco (2006):

> the teacher's body shapes and is shaped by institutional bodies of knowledge confirmed to be appropriate for the citizenry. The proper teacher embodies all that the culture/society/nation wishes its people to be, and so her body must be scrutinized, her behavior dissected—held to the dominant standards of (non)conformity. (p. 233)

By performing an "erased" body subrogated and inscribed by cultural, social, historical, and disciplinary forms and texts that are standardized and normalized by school, the bland uniformer teacher can avoid having her feminine body scrutinized and her behavior dissected. In this sense, the bland uniformer teacher subjectivity was appropriated by the student teachers as a form of resistance to the discourses shaping teaching reductively as "women's work." They saw limited options for teachers' professional identity. Of the three they saw as distinctive, two were perceived as too womanly and described as inappropriate and unprofessional caricatures. They either could not understand, and/or felt inadequate to claim or be comfortable with a feminized teacher professional identity. Finally, the student teachers may have also seen that the bland uniformer teacher body conflated with schooling expertise and professionalism was more authoritative. Certainly, their status as novices to teaching would create anxieties about their "classroom management" abilities and skills that might have been eased with claims for what they saw as the normative professional identity.

Implications for Fashioning the Teacher Body

This examination of female teacher subjectivity prompted by a student teacher conversation about teacher apparel suggests several implications. One is that female teacher professional identity cannot and should not be considered monolithic, but as multiple identities that may or may not be expressed in varieties of clothing styles. The student teachers' conversation and the analysis offered in this chapter undoubtedly provoke contradictory opinions and conflicting experiences from its readers. Norms for "proper" femininity or more sexualized femininity may vary in nuance, rigidity, and availability of alternatives depending on the economics, politics, racial, social, and cultural diversity, and even the climate and environment of schooling contexts. This means that these categories are not as stable or clearly defined as the young student teachers seemed to think and are not as limited or limiting as their observations would indicate. What is useful about this analysis is that the conversation does serve as a starting point for richer and more varied conversations about female teacher professional identities, how they are discursively shaped by a multitude of influences, and how women teachers make choices about how they relate to their profession.

Another implication suggests avenues of resistance or innovation for those who see the wisdom in expanding the varieties of female teacher professional identity. More inquiries that make visible the multitudes of women teachers' subject positions enable more focused and intentional resistance to the narrowing of those subjectivities. Scholarship on clothing as a discursive practice, as well as other discursive practices, is encouraged as a way to share the varieties of ways in which women teachers shape professional identities.

Teachers who choose to transgress and resist erasure can explore ways to bring their bodies into the classroom as a visible presence, the "return to the body" called for by hooks (1994, pp. 146–148). Yet it is important that women teachers develop strategies to accomplish this in ways that enhance the profession, not provoke more policing. An obvious way to draw attention to the body is by clothing. Discursive practices such as clothing choices work in at least two ways. They shape how others view the person wearing the clothes; they also shape the person's sense of who she is relative to her context. This relationship offers space for resistance and agency. As Finkelstein (1997) observed, "Whenever . . . styles are toyed with, then fashion is reiterating its ability to influence human subjectivity. . . . Fashioning the body becomes a practice through which subject positions are also fashioned" (p. 157).

The final implication is the need for more research in this area. For example, how do discourses of race, class, and ability shape women teachers' identities in ways that are not the white, middle-class, able-bodied, heterosexual varieties presented in this article? Are there intersections and/or conflicts? Is there a lesbian teacher identity? Is that more transgressive than the teacher babe subjectivity? How do questions and criteria for "good teaching" shape considerations of women teachers' professional identities? What are the conditions in which women teachers mediate satisfying professional identities that are also compelling to young women teachers entering the field? How is teacher professional identity represented in teacher education programs?

These questions and others no doubt stimulated by the limitations of this article provoke further inquiry and reflection on the discursive qualities of women teachers' subjectivities and pedagogy, and demand more nuanced deliberations in thinking about the purposes for and consequences of how teachers' bodies in the classroom are constitutive of their pedagogy and not separate from it.

References

Apple, M. (1988). *Teachers and texts: A political economy of class and gender relations.* New York: Routledge & Kegan Paul.

Bartky, S. (1992). *Revaluing French feminism: Critical essays on difference, agency, and culture.* Bloomington: Indiana University Press.

Biklen, S. (1995). *School work: Gender and the cultural construction of teaching.* New York: Teachers College Press.

Blount, J. (1996). Manly men and womanly women: Deviance, gender role polarization, and the shift in women's school employment, 1900–1976. *Harvard Educational Review, 66,* 318–338.

Blount, J. (2000). Spinsters, bachelors, and other gender transgressors in school employment. *Review of Educational Research, 70,* 83–101.

Cavanaugh, S. (2004). Upsetting desires in the classroom: School sex scandals and the pedagogy of the femme fatale. *Psychoanalysis, Culture and Society, 9,* 315–332.

Cohen, R., & Scheer, S. (1997). *The work of teachers in America: A social history through stories.* Mahwah, NJ: Lawrence Erlbaum Associates.

Cooks, L., & LeBesco, K. (2006). Introduction and the pedagogy of the teacher's body. *Review of Education, Pedagogy & Cultural Studies, 28,* 233–238.

Davies, B. (1994). *Poststructuralist theory and classroom practice.* Geelong, Victoria, Australia: Deakin University Press.

Finkelstein, J. (1997). Chic outrage and body politics. In K. Davis (Ed.), *Embodied practices: Feminist perspectives on the body* (pp. 150–167). London: Sage Publications.

Foucault, M. (1995). *Discipline and punish: The birth of the prison* (2nd ed.). New York: Vintage Books. (Original work published 1977)

Grumet, M. (1988). *Bitter milk: Women and teaching.* Amherst: University of Massachusetts Press.

hooks, b. (1994). *Teaching to transgress: Education as the practice of freedom.* New York: Routledge.

Johnson, T.S. (2006). Performing a/sexual teacher: The Cartesian duality in education. *Review of Education, Pedagogy and Cultural Studies, 28,* 253–266.

Lather, P. (1987). The absent presence: Patriarchy, capitalism, and the nature of teacher work. *Teacher Education Quarterly, 14,* 7–14.

Llewellyn, K.R. (2006). Performing post-war citizenship: Women teachers in Toronto secondary schools. *Review of Education, Pedagogy & Cultural Studies, 29,* 309–324.

McWhorter, L. (1999). *Bodies and pleasures: Foucault and the politics of sexual normalization.* Bloomington: Indiana University Press.

National Center for Education Statistics. (2007). *Context of elementary and secondary education: Characteristics of full-time teachers.* Accessed at http://nces.ed.gov/programs/coe/2007/section4/ indicator33.asp

Pendergast, D., & McWilliam, E. (1999). Marginal pleasures, teachers and transgression. Paper presented at The Australian Association of Research in Education annual conference, Melbourne, November–December.

Richardson, L. (1985). *The new other woman: Contemporary married women in affairs with single men.* New York: The Free Press.

Ritchie, J., & Wilson, D. (2000). *Teacher narrative as critical inquiry: Rewriting the script.* New York: Teachers College Press.

Strickland, C. (2006). A teacher knowledge study: Five female teachers' understanding of gender. Ph.D. diss., University of Alabama.

Walkerdine, V. (1990). *Schoolgirl fictions*. London: Verso.

Weber, S. (1995). *That's funny, you don't look like a teacher: Interrogating image, identity, and popular culture*. London: Falmer Press.

Weedon, C. (1989). *Feminist practice & poststructuralist theory*. New York: Basil Blackwell.

CHAPTER TEN

Bound and Gagged

Sexual Silences, Gender Conformity, and the Gay Male Teacher

ERIC ROFES

In my current role as a university professor, I find myself curious about the relationship between two things I hold dear: my sex life and my life in classrooms.

It sometimes seems impossible for me to put these lives together or to understand that my identity as an educator is intertwined with my identity as a sexually active gay man. I spend most of my teacher life grading papers, counseling students, preparing and teaching classes, and observing in classrooms. I attend conferences focused on contemporary school reform initiatives, and I engage in rowdy debates focused on school choice, equity, and multicultural educational practices. I am immersed in ongoing study focused on historical constructions of childhood, urban youth identities, and the effects of charter schools on public education.

At the same time, I have an academic gay life that is partially focused on my historical research into gay men's sexual cultures of the 1970s, HIV prevention, and gay men's sexual health, and the experiences of lesbian and gay schoolteachers. Not only do I participate in academic and community-based conferences on these topics, but I also participate in ongoing work as a community organizer in lesbian, gay, bisexual, and transgender communities. I currently focus energy on organizing a national gay men's health movement. The week after I finished writing this chapter, I traveled to Washington, D.C., to meet with the leadership of major gay organizations to discuss how to address sexual scandals when they arise and how to combat the Right's intense sexualizing of lesbians and gay men.

Beyond my academic work, my everyday life reflects similar tensions; my body carries these contradictions. I may go from a three-hour block focused on preparing a new course to an exciting erotic assignation with a new friend. My mix of identities and lives forces questions on me. Is it possible to be immersed in gay male cultures without picking up the habit of intense cruising in all social situations? How does my immersion in gay male cultures translate to my behavior at teacher conferences or my visits to local schools? Once, when I was having sex with a new partner, he asked me to "turn off the teacher rap" for a while. I had been using direct instruction—a formal pedagogical method I had used the week before with my credential students—in an entirely different, and perhaps inappropriate, arena.

Living in two very different places exacerbates this split. During most of the school year, I live half of each week outside a town called Blue Lake, deep in the redwoods of Humboldt County. My everyday life in the communities surrounding my university seems quite separate from gay culture, separate from gay and lesbian people. I am openly gay in my job, but because I have met very few gay men in Humboldt County, my gay identity there seems less sexual and more political or rhetorical. This is not a place where I regularly pick up strangers or spend a great deal of time socializing with other gay men. While there are informal social networks of men in this area, I mostly use my time in Humboldt County to focus on my work, not my libido or my social life.

My other home is in the heart of the Castro, the primary gay neighborhood in San Francisco, considered by many to be the primary gay city in the United States. My lover and I own a cottage just a few yards down from Eighteenth and Castro, the crossroads of the gay world. During the school year, I spend about half of each week in San Francisco. While there, I hang out at some of the local coffee shops with other gay male habitués. In the evening, I am likely to visit gay male bars in the South of Market neighborhood. During the days, I occasionally plan a "sex date" with a friend, or I find myself cruising and meeting a handsome man on the street and then going to his place or my place for a tumble.

My political views lead me to deeply probe the relationship between my life as a teacher and my life as a gay man. I have been active in gay liberation for more than 25 years and have worked in gay community centers, AIDS organizations, and the lesbian and gay media. While I have certainly engaged in mainstream gay rights work, my primary interests have focused on aspects of gay liberation that chart directions far afield from mainstream heteronormative cultures and social formations. I am not interested in a gay rights agenda that argues that lesbians and gay men are the same as heterosexuals and therefore deserving of equal rights. I am committed to a gay liberation agenda that argues that queer cultures have much to teach mainstream America about sex, gender, democratic social networks, and equitable relationships.

While the gay movement in the 1990s moved politically from the Left to the center (and some would say to the Right), I have maintained ongoing activism based in what some would characterize as the "Left fringe" of gay liberation. While I do some work on gay marriage, I am more interested in developing, exploring, and affirming patterns of kinship that are not based on a nuclear family structure or a traditional, "committed," gendered dyad. Gender-nonconforming men and women have been shunted aside by a gay rights movement hungry for "respectable" leaders who have mass appeal because they do not threaten the status quo; however, I am fixated on the social and cultural power emerging from troubling, subverting, and violating gender norms. During a time when AIDS has served as a convenient excuse for social critics to declare an end to a "failed" sexual revolution, I continue to immerse myself in communities that value and prioritize sex, and I organize my social and sexual practices in ways that can be described as "nonmonogamous," "promiscuous," or (drawing on Whitman's poems) profoundly "democratic" in spirit.

Each day when I wake up, at least two people move in me: the teacher and the lover. I do not view these two aspects of my life as contradictory or paradoxical, though I know others might. During most of my career in education I have juggled two public identities—the educator and the gay liberationist—and I have attempted to understand their intersections and explore the tensions that emerge from their simultaneity. For a long time I have suspected that some people with whom I work in schools and on educational policy matters would find problematic those aspects of the way I enact my sexual identity. I have also noticed that some colleagues in gay and lesbian movement work discount my work in schools or have no interest at all in my educational efforts.

At times, I feel deeply divided, ricocheting between extremes. I might check my answering machine at home in San Francisco on a Sunday afternoon, and there will be a student calling with questions about white racial formations or the purpose of public education in a democracy, questions for the following day's midterm examination. The next message might be from my lover, who is calling to inform me he will be late for dinner as he is meeting his boyfriend for a late-afternoon romp. I might do an Internet search under my name and turn up seemingly paradoxical listings: a selection of explicit sex writings from my latest book precedes a report from an education newspaper about my charter school research.

Although I may feel as though my life is split down the middle, intellectually I believe my work in education and gay liberation emerges from the same source: a commitment to creating sites that resist, undermine, and throw off institutionalized forms of oppression that have become endemic to life in the United States. My interest in school reform is motivated by a desire to see urban schools become places that expand the critical consciousness of poor young people and that provide tools for social and political change. My interest in undermining gender as a normalizing and oppressive construct emerges from my awareness of the continuing power of patriarchy to limit the life chances of girls, women, and gender-nonconforming boys. Although sexual freedom is a problematic term, especially when bandied about in post-AIDS America, for me it offers insights into the transformative possibilities of pleasure in an advanced capitalist system that has succeeded in commodifying and gaining monopoly over most forms of leisure, play, and pleasure (Bronski, 1996).

Ultimately, I believe my work as a teacher is about supporting students as they become agents of transgression and activists for social and political change. My mission as an educator is best captured by bell hooks in the introduction to her book *Teaching to Transgress: Education as the Practice of Freedom* (1994):

> The classroom remains the most radical space of possibility in the academy. . . . I add my voice to the collective call for renewal and rejuvenation in our teaching practices. . . . I celebrate teaching that enables transgressions—a movement against and beyond boundaries. It is that movement which makes education the practice of freedom. (p. 12)

Classroom Predicaments No. 1: Enacting Masculinity

At various times in my college teaching career, I have become almost paralyzed with uncertainty about what to wear, how to speak, how to walk, how to sit, how to move. I neurotically obsess on these questions or repress them fully. I sometimes find myself spending as much time struggling over questions of appearance, voice, and movement as I do over the content of a day's lesson. Occasionally, on mornings when I teach, I open my closet and find not my clothes for the day but issues of whiteness, class status, gender performance, and sexual-identity enactment unleashed in a manner that threatens to overwhelm me and make me late for work.

When I am teaching my class "Gay and Lesbian Issues in Schools," I am hyperaware of how I represent myself as a gay man to my students. I wonder how my queer students would like to see me perform gender and what my heterosexually identified students take away from their time with me.

Should I look and act like a stereotypical fag, or should I provide an alternative vision of gay manhood? Is it okay to use camp, wit, and biting irony, or should I eschew the affectations of fagdom and provide an alternate vision? Is it okay to cross my legs, move my hands, raise my eyebrows? Can I call my gay students "honey"? Is it okay for me to refer to male colleagues as "girlfriends"? What image should I project when I walk across the room?

I feel as if biology has situated me in a somewhat privileged position to grapple with these questions. I possess key attributes that resonate with traditional masculinity in American culture: I am six feet four; I have thick facial and body hair; and I am built like a linebacker. I have taken what genetics has offered and made decisions that affix my position within masculine norms: I wear a beard, speak in a deep voice, keep my hair in a crew cut, and work out at a gym. I can easily perform a white ethnic masculinity common among working-class and lower-middle-class men. At times I look more like a stevedore than a schoolteacher.

Yet I am acutely aware that the masculinities I perform are cut through with political issues that can trigger a range of problematic responses. I may put on a performance of machismo at a local leather bar on a Saturday night, playing the big, tough butch man as a sexual strategy to signal a range of erotic activities and roles to the men I desire. Yet that same Village People macho man might make me seem intimidating and unapproachable to my undergraduate students and might suggest the affirmation of patriarchal norms that I actually aim to undermine. In one-on-one counseling situations with gay male students, I may cross my legs, affect a gentle voice, and make expressive hand gestures in an attempt to dissipate any sense of threats the students may feel from me. Yet the same display of "femme" energy might alienate many of my heterosexual students or confirm stereotypes. It also might undercut my ability as a teacher to structure the classroom, present expectations, and enforce standards for classroom discourse and student work. Should I resist affirming to students the typical stereotypes that say some gay men are effeminate?

When I first began to teach college, I found that the energy I project has a powerful influence on the response of students. I attempted to initiate empowering student-focused conversations utilizing my best critical pedagogy skills. Students worked with me to frame questions and organize classroom time. We planned format and process to maximize participation. Yet when time for discussion came, few students would participate. It sometimes felt as if I were pulling nails out of walls to get the majority of students to check in as part of the conversation.

One of the students—a women's studies major—was kind enough to approach me after one of my early failures at facilitating and encouraging a lively, engaged conversation. "The class is intimidated by you," she said matter-of-factly, shaking her head. "You say all the right things and clearly understand how these discussions are supposed to happen. Yet your energy—it's all wrong. It sends a very different message than the words you actually speak. You give off profoundly mixed signals."

I turned to colleagues for advice—lesbian colleagues, actually—who talked to me about gender performance in the classroom. They enlightened me about putting to work in my pedagogy my "butch" energies and my "femme" energies. At first I did not know what they meant, but I listened intently, took a lot of notes, and mulled their comments for quite a while. I realized that they were asking me to apply a valuable lesson to my undergraduate teaching, a lesson I had learned early in my career as a gay activist.

I have chaired many public forums, tense community meetings, and crisis-sparked town hall discussions where people of divergent views come together for debate, conflict, and resolution. When facilitating these events, I have learned to draw on different energies at different times. My butch energy, when channeled appropriately and nonabusively, is useful in setting limits, confronting participants who violate collectively made discussion rules, and keeping the group on task. I draw it from a place within me seeking to control, direct, and order. Although the gestures, inflections, and movements that accompany it may or may not look traditionally masculine, the energy definitely taps into that particular source within me.

My femme energy is employed to open up access, invite participation, and cut through and deflate tension. It employs humor, self-deprecation, campiness, and gentler qualities. I have become adept at recognizing when my femme energy will bring me things that my butch energy will not; I have some ability to dance between the two in a subtle but intricate performance of diversely gendered energies. I am also aware that my femme energy, when released properly, can be used effectively to set limits and keep an agenda on task.

I recognize that the use of constructs such as "butch" and "femme" can reinscribe essentialist views of gender. This is not my intent. I see neither term as natural or genetic nor assigned by biology to one sex or the other. I share in Joan Nestle's understanding of the distinction between these terms and naturalized gender constructs:

> For me, "fem" has a very problematic relationship to "femininity"; perhaps because I spent my early lesbian years as a butchy-looking fem, perhaps because I have lived my whole adult life within lesbian communities, or perhaps because my mother wanted me to be more her missing husband than her sexually competitive daughter and thus gave me only rudimentary instruction in how to be a girl—wear a girdle or your ass will look like the side of a barn, wear lipstick so you don't look like death, always be a good fuck. (Nestle, 1998, p. 129)

Hence while aware that such performances do not spring naturally from my maleness (Butler, 1993), I deliberately and self-consciously have carried butch/femme energies into my classroom pedagogy. My women's studies student proved to be correct: When I introduce a class discussion gently, with openness and playfulness, and leave space for silences, humor, and the flexibility needed to accommodate last-minute student-initiated changes, my students respond enthusiastically. When I default to butch energies due to fear, disorganization, or mindlessness, the students usually are silent, frozen, sometimes even withholding.

I began to consider anew the male teachers I had known who had been explicitly effeminate, including music and drama teachers I had had during my high school years and one social studies teacher whose hands danced before him uncontrollably whenever something truly excited him. His enthusiasm proved infectious, and we students would become caught up in whatever passion he was creating in the classroom at that moment. Only after class, behind his back, would we mock him, call him names, and ridicule his style of teaching. Was this simply a case of his teaching methods' successfully capturing his students' interest, or was there something we truly loved about his campy gestures and queeny voice? Did these instances—moments of authentic pedagogical magic—allow teacher and students to collectively break out of constricted gender roles and, for at least a few minutes, violate patriarchal dicta?

Educators have started to write about how sexist and heterosexist practices in classrooms harm gender-nonconforming children, including boys and young men (Boldt, 1997; Sedgwick, 1993; Thorne, 1993). Mairtin Mac an Ghaill (1994) has described schooling as a "masculinizing agency" and the "way in which dominant definitions of masculinity are affirmed within schools, where ideologies, discourses, representations and material practices systematically privilege boys and men" (p. 4).

R.W. Connell (1989) has argued that "a degendering strategy, an attempt to dismantle hegemonic masculinity, is unavoidable; a degendered rights-based politics of social justice cannot proceed without it" (p. 232). He argues that schools must play a critical role in a move toward these politics:

> The importance of education of masculinity politics follows from the onto-formativity of gender practices, the fact that our enactments of masculinity and femininity bring a social reality into being. Education is often discussed as if it involved only information, teachers tipping measured doses of facts into the pupils' heads; but that is just part of the process. At a deeper level, education is the formation of capacities for practice. (p. 239)

Clearly, gay male teachers have a great deal at stake in developing a "degendering strategy." Yet we are wrong if we pretend that our mere presence in the classroom is counterhegemonic. Being transgressive because we are openly gay while being compliant because we affirm traditional masculinities may do little to alter the sex-gender system that wreaks havoc in our everyday lives.

Classroom Predicaments No. 2: Sex, the Body, and the Classroom

It is frightening to think about the relationship between one's sex life and one's classroom, between one's embodied identities as a teacher and a lover. Many gay men maintain sharp divides between the two, insisting one's sex life is personal and private and that it has no bearing on one's students. Yet the erotic circulates in any classroom and is often harnessed as a source of power that drives teaching pedagogies.

Like gay-identified men working in other mainstream cultural institutions—such as religious organizations, the health care industry, and the political arena—we as gay male teachers are offered two options: take a lover and perform with him a type of relationship that approximates hetero-coupledom, or desexualize ourselves, stifle our erotic energies, and disprove the stereotypes of the sex-obsessed homosexual. Gay male teacher identities rarely allow men room to construct personas that do not suppress the erotic and that allow them to avoid becoming leering, harassing letches who are inappropriate in a workplace. I worry that our performances within these narrow options present our gay male students—and others—with examples of gay identities that are neither helpful nor relevant to their lives and to the difficult choices they must face in integrating sexual identity, sexual orientation, and sexual energies into their personhood. Yet I take seriously concerns about power and consent that inform certain feminist thinking on sexual harassment (Dines, Jensen, & Russo, 1998; Dworkin, 1988; Frye, 1983), and I believe that professors who address sex overtly in a classroom setting must be mindful of abuses and must be committed to self-scrutiny.

What possibilities exist for the creation of new kinds of gay male identity that acknowledge the value some of us place on the erotic and the ways in which it enters not only our classrooms and teaching practices but the classrooms and practices of all effective educators? If I take seriously many students' experiences of sexual harassment or abuse, it seems critical to examine my own sexualized persona rigorously and with tremendous sensitivity. Do we want to present ourselves to students as whole human beings—not simply as a mind but as a body, a spirit, and a sexuality? Is it possible to be seen by students as a sexual being without pandering to stereotypes or imposing one's comfort with sex onto students who maintain different values or who may have experienced harassment from teachers? As students struggle with their own sexual concerns, will I ever be able to find a way to support them without stifling my own struggles and silencing my own stories? How can a teacher from any vulnerable marginalized population even consider such questions without undermining her or his job and putting a career at risk?

I have faced a range of issues about sex, the body, and erotic desires during the three spring semesters in which I have taught my gay studies class:

- What do I do when I find in my mailbox on Valentine's Day a single long-stemmed rose that a staff member insists was placed there by "an unknown male undergraduate" who tried to deliver it surreptitiously?
- How do I respond when a student asks me if I will be dropping by the Bondage à Go-Go sex club on Wednesday night?
- When the weather gets warm and I am feeling good about my body, is it ever okay to wear a Lacoste shirt to class that shows my big arms? What about a tank top or simply a sleeveless vest?
- What should I do when I am cleaning up after a workout in the university recreation center's showers, and two of my undergraduate gay male students walk in and proceed to shoot quick glances in my direction as I quickly finish showering and toweling off?
- How do I react when I recognize a former or current student at a bathhouse, sex club, or while I am in a chat room on America Online?

The only conversations in this arena of which I have been a part have focused on the ethics of college teacher-student liaisons. I answered that question years ago for myself—deciding I did not need the risk and the headaches such interactions could bring—so perhaps this has allowed another series of questions to emerge for me. If I believe that there are many diverse and ethical ways for people to structure their social and sexual practices, is it important or educative to affirm various options within the classroom? Is it possible to affirm one pattern of sexual organization without undercutting others or violating critical boundaries that are intended to shield students from sexual harassment? What responsibility do gay male teachers who enjoy and intellectually support casual, nonmonogamous sexual relations have to our gay male students?

My students know that I have a lover and that I live with him in San Francisco. I introduce this tidbit—appropriately, I believe—during the first class, when I ask them not to call me at home after 9 P.M. Several have met Crispin, either when we have run into students on the street or at gay community festivals and street fairs or when he has dropped in at our class potluck suppers. I am always acutely self-conscious of how I interact with my lover when students are around: I want to be "appropriate," but I do not want to fully stifle the attraction and physicality between us, nor do I want to elevate the erotic element of the relationship over others. When he visits me in class, I give him a peck of a kiss when I first see him, and I am conscious not to stifle touching his arm or holding his hand. If I run into students on the street when we are wearing tank tops or leather armbands, I become quite self-conscious, but I do not avoid greeting them nor do I feel ashamed to be seen or known to participate in gay male sexual cultures.

A few years back, a student drew an analogy in class that used my relationship with Crispin in a way that revealed how the student believed we were in a monogamous relationship. I cannot recollect the precise context for this incident, but it was something similar to a discussion I had recently had with students about President Bill Clinton's affair with Monica Lewinsky. During a heated discussion on this topic, one focusing on the role of Hillary Clinton, a student asked me, "How would you feel if Crispin were to have an affair with some other guy?"

In fact, I know how I would feel because our relationship is not sexually exclusive, and we regularly discuss our feelings about each other's "extramarital" liaisons. But how do I answer this question when it comes from undergraduate students who assume that being in a couple is automatically equated with monogamy?

When a student, Brenda, first raised a similar question in class and displayed her assumptions about the nature of our relationship and the boundaries about sex we had constructed, I paused for a moment and considered my response. It seemed as though an important, teachable moment had arrived, but one fraught with all kinds of risks. Through my mind raced a number of scenarios: the dean confronting me with evidence that I had flaunted my sexual promiscuity to my students; a lawsuit where a group of students sue me for sexually harassing them by responding to Brenda's statement with anything other than "my sex live is my personal private business"; the newspaper headlines declaring, "He teaches at the university, but at night, he wallows in the sexual gutters of the naked city."

I paused before responding, then I downshifted energy and spoke directly to Brenda. "This might sound strange for you to hear, but I feel as if I should correct an assumption that seems to lie behind your statement," I said calmly. "You seem to believe Crispin and I have structured our relationship in a manner that parallels traditional monogamous heterosexual relationships. Many couples—of all sexual orientations—choose other ways of organizing their relationship. It has been documented that gay men in particular often maintain what are known as open relationships. I just wanted you to know that your assumption doesn't fit our relationship design because we do not maintain monogamy in our relationship or believe we should control what our partner does with his body and his time. Open relationships surely have their challenges, but we've found it works best for us."

When I finished, there was total silence in the room. A few hands slowly were raised; additional students put forward some questions; I offered responses; then we returned to the lesson at hand. I felt conflicted between wanting to fully exploit a teachable moment and wanting to place what I believed were necessary boundaries on the discussion. Over the next few weeks, I heard from several students that they had appreciated my candor and the respect with which I held them, indicated by my disclosure. From that point forward, I believed that the class had become an intimate site for teaching and learning and that the rigid role of teacher had flexed in a way that promoted the critical pedagogy of the class.

I have had other encounters with my undergraduates that have challenged my commitment to including sex and the body in my teaching as something more than a distanced, depersonalized intellectual exercise. I have run into students at San Francisco's Folsom Street Fair, an annual event celebrating the leather and fetish communities, when we have all been dressed in sexualized clothing. Afterward, I have always believed it to be important to acknowledge the encounter before class in a casual, informal manner. Here I aim to show that participation in such activities is neither embarrassing nor a "big deal." One lesbian graduate student once referenced her interest in sadomasochism in a personal reflective paper, indicating that her own middle school students could deal with her lesbian identity but not her sexual interests. I thought it was appropriate and valuable to affirm her situation by sharing an incident from my own years as a middle school teacher, when students on the playground who were playing with handcuffs jokingly asked me if I had ever seen a pair. I indicated that I, too, owned a set of handcuffs and left it at that.

As I consider my own classroom predicaments, I realize that my aim in confronting issues of desire, sex, and love in my pedagogy and relations with students is not to get into trouble, violate valuable boundaries protecting students from harassment, or earn a reputation as a particularly transgressive or radical educator. Instead I believe that the stigmatizing, silencing, scapegoating, and attacks that commonly surround the appearance of sex in the classroom are social practices that contribute to producing a populace that experiences sex and desire in a manner best characterized by confusion, frustration, pain, and abuse. If critical pedagogy is about collectively gaining a deep understanding of how social and political forces interact with all of our everyday lives and help to produce our identities, social practices, and communities, then silencing, avoiding, or depersonalizing/disembodying sex may function powerfully to affirm and reify a dangerous and oppressive status quo.

Reproducing or Recreating the Body Politic

Silin (1997) argues that "Americans are alternately expansive and silent about the place of sexuality in the early childhood classroom" (p. 214). The intense obsession with sex and schooling and the profound silences associated with it are part of an ideology that is effective at, as James Sears (1992) has aptly stated, "reproducing the body politic" (p. 15). Keeping sex private and silencing discussion of desire, bodies, and erotic practices in classroom discourse effectively ensures the continued marshaling of sex as an effective form of social control. As Sears states:

> Sexuality, then, is more a construct of ideology and culture than it is a collection of information about biology and the body; power and control are central to our modern understanding of sexuality and ourselves as sexual beings.... How we define and express our sexuality has significant political implications.... There is, then, an integral relationship between the learning of human reproduction and reproduction of social relations. Understandings of gendered and sexual arrangements, teenage pregnancy, and child sexual abuse further illustrate this relationship. (pp. 18–19)

As teachers, we all teach a great deal about sex, whether we acknowledge it or not. What we say and what we do not say, what is voiced and what is silenced create knowledges for our students with tremendous ramifications. Gay male teachers—whose bodies, desires, and practices may transgress heteronormative constructs and patriarchal paradigms—could be a source of startling new learnings. This chapter represents an initial attempt to trouble the comfortable notions of gay male teachers that circulate within liberal educational discourse. I have attempted to examine ways in which gay male identities and cultures might be useful in our pedagogical practices.

For too long, gay men have understandably fought a narrow battle, seeking admittance into the classroom as openly gay educators. Likewise, queer students of all genders and sexualities have worked to achieve a relative degree of safety in public schools throughout the United States. All too often, as we have made these efforts, we have made compromises and sacrifices that have gone unspoken and unacknowledged. We have gained limited entry into the classroom by denying authentic differences between many gay men's relationships to gender roles, sexual cultures, and kinship arrangements and those of the heteronormative hegemony.

This chapter is a call to dialogue about the sacrifices we have made and the implications they have for democratic education and social change.

References

Boldt, G. (1997). Sexist and heterosexist responses to gender bending. In J. Tobin (Ed.), *Making a place for pleasure in early childhood education* (pp. 188–213). New Haven, CT: Yale University Press.

Bronski, M. (Ed.). (1996). *Flashpoint: Gay male sexual writing.* New York: Masquerade Books.

Butler, J. (1993). *Bodies that matter: On the discursive limits of "sex."* New York: Routledge.

Connell, R.W. (1989). Cool guys, swots, and wimps: The interplay of masculinity and education. *Oxford Review of Education, 15*(3), 291–303.

Dines, G., Jensen, R., & Russo, A. (1998). *Pornography: The production and consumption of inequality.* New York: Routledge.

Dworkin, A. (1988). *Letters from a war zone.* London: Secker and Warburg.

Frye, M. (1983). *The politics of reality.* Freedom, CA: Crossing Press.

hooks, b. (1994). *Teaching to transgress: Education as the practice of freedom.* New York: Routledge.

King, J. (1998). *Uncommon caring: Learning from men who teach young children.* New York: Teachers College Press.

Mac an Ghaill, M. (1994). *The making of men.* Buckingham, UK: Open University Press.

Nestle, J. (1998). *A fragile union: New and selected writings by Joan Nestle.* San Francisco, CA: Cleis.

Sears, J. (1992). Dilemmas and possibilities of sexuality education: Reproducing the body politic. In J. Sames (Ed.), *Sexuality and the curriculum: The politics and practices of sexuality education* (pp. 7–33). New York: Teachers College Press.

Sedgwick, E. (1993). How to bring your kids up gay. In M. Warner (Ed.), *Fear of a queer planet* (pp. 69–81). Minneapolis: University of Minnesota Press.

Silin, J. (1997). The pervert in the classroom. In J. Tobin (Ed.), *Making a place for pleasure in early childhood education* (pp. 214–234). New Haven, CT: Yale University Press.

Thorne, B. (1993). *Gender play: Girls and boys in school.* New Brunswick, NJ: Rutgers University Press.

CHAPTER ELEVEN

Knot a Love Story

JANE GALLOP

Half a dozen years ago, new to Rice University and anxious to find students to work with, I agreed to an independent study that a graduate student proposed. We would meet for half an hour once every two weeks; he would read psychoanalytic theory and write six short papers. Readings were structured around my undergraduate course on Freud and my just-published book on Lacan, so that this supplementary course would not demand much time or effort on my part. Commuting weekly from home in Milwaukee to Rice in Houston, trying to get my next book done, although I wanted students, in fact I had little time to give them.

A few weeks into the semester the student turned in his first paper as I was off to the airport for my Thursday evening commute. Reading it on the plane, I couldn't see what he was trying to say; so, disappointed, I gave it a B-. Back at Rice on Tuesday morning, I put it in his mailbox so he would have time to read my comments before we met that afternoon. Over the weekend—through research time, social life, and family time—I had in fact completely forgotten about the grade, so I was at first puzzled when he showed up in my office the next day, obviously agitated.

I could see agitation, but it was only later that I learned how angry he actually was. In retrospect I recognize that graduate students usually are offended by a B-, but trying to fulfill my teaching duties despite an impossibly busy schedule meant I got the work done (preparation, grading, advising) but didn't have time to reflect on its effects. He walked into my office and demanded to know—in a hypercontrolled voice through which a certain shaking nonetheless appeared—what I was doing. I didn't know what he was talking about. He asked point-blank why I had given him a B-. Then I remembered and replied that that is the grade I give to papers where the writing is so bad I don't understand the point. Recognizing one of those never-pleasant situations when a student protests his grade, I braced myself to stand my ground.

After a few back and forths between his challenge and my reiterated position, he asked if we could read through the paper together. I resisted: that would take hours. He stood by his demand; my resistance fixed upon the time it would take, time I did not have. Finally, as a way out of deadlock, I agreed to begin going through the paper, thinking that beginning would demonstrate how impossible his demand was, how much time it would take. I know now that he believed if he could get me actually to read the paper with him I would be confronted with its excellence and forced to recognize my error.

So we began—with adversarially opposed agendas. I would read a sentence aloud, then say what I understood and indicate portions I did not understand. He then would explain what he had been trying to say. This was, as I had imagined, a very time-consuming activity: the full discussion of a sentence took ten minutes or so; in the half hour allotted to our meeting we had gotten through the first paragraph.

At first this exchange had quite a bite; underlying the discussion were mutual accusations of blindness. As I indicated what I didn't get, it was as if to say: "See, your writing fails, you deserve a B-." When he explained what he meant, it was as much as saying: "This is so obviously a worthy and interesting idea; you are prejudiced, stupid, or crazy if you can't see that." But by the time we had gotten through the first paragraph, something had changed. We were no longer fighting each other; we were in fact working together.

In retrospect, I am amazed that he could give up not only his challenge but the sort of defensiveness a writer usually exhibits in discussion of his less-than-successful writing. He had moved from trying to "show" me to trying to see the paper as I saw it. The going was slow and difficult, but there were little breakthroughs. I would come to understand what he had been trying to say; he would realize how and why the sentence did not communicate what he thought it meant. Progressing sentence by sentence, each working hard to explain or grasp, we moved slowly but thoroughly through the text with what seemed a shared double understanding: of what he had been trying to say and of what the paper actually said.

This painstaking work, the sense of laboring together and building understanding, was enormously satisfying and totally engrossing. Partway through the second page, I realized an hour had gone by; it was 5:30. I called the friend I was to meet for dinner at six, told her something had come up and asked if we could reschedule. Looking back, that phone call (and the decision behind it) feels like some sort of turning point. My resistance had specifically focused on how much time he was demanding; this commitment to pursue to the end of the paper represented a dramatic giving up of that resistance. When I phoned my friend, I was giving the student what he had demanded, but now I, too, wanted this.

At seven P.M., after two and a half hours, we reached the end of the paper, neither until then letting up concentration, the concerted effort to understand and communicate. We were both exhausted, but I for one felt a pleasure in that. He seemed overwhelmed and silenced. He had gotten what he demanded—my full attention and explanation—but the angry young man who had walked in challenging my judgment had come to see the paper as I did, as a B- paper, in graduate school terms, a failure. He sat there huddled over and seemed very vulnerable. I wanted to comfort and reassure him, imagined patting him on the head. What I did was lean over so I was actually looking up at his lowered head in order to make eye contact. He was amused and, I believe, lifted from his despond.

Since we had not had a chance to discuss the readings, I offered to meet again for a half hour on Thursday. We agreed upon a time and parted. I went home, had a drink, and ate dinner in a strangely agitated state. Unable to concentrate on anything, I retreated into TV watching and then sleep. Normally an extremely sound sleeper, I woke up in the middle of the night, agitated, thinking about this student, about the extraordinary time passed in my office. Unable to fall back to sleep,

I turned my energy to grading a batch of papers from my undergraduate Freud class, allowing me to return them earlier than I had promised. I felt, excitedly, like a really good teacher, finding unsuspected pockets of time for my students.

All the next day, I thought of the graduate student, obsessively. By afternoon, these thoughts had become recognizably erotic. By Thursday I suspected I had a crush on him and began to talk about it with friends, feeling the need for help in dealing with this. My obsessive thoughts, my sexual fantasizing, were real sources of pleasure, but within a few days I went from feeling like a wonderful teacher to feeling myself a very bad teacher indeed.

As well as I can judge, I was both. He learned in that session to see his writing more clearly, to recognize when it did not say what he wanted it to. His writing improved steadily: his next paper earned an A-; by the end of the semester he was writing excellent papers. I continued to devote time to meeting with him and was particularly eager to go over his writing, trying in fact to reproduce that extraordinarily pleasurable experience. My desire for him also grew steadily: by the end of the semester I felt as if I were in love.

I am in fact convinced that not only was I both a good and a bad teacher (by most any standard I am aware of for such evaluations), but that I became both at one and the same time, in one and the same move—in that moment when I called my friend to cancel dinner, when I decided to give him the time he needed but also when I wanted to stay with him until we finished. I suspect that what made me a good teacher was precisely what made me a bad teacher.

It is this apparent paradox that I propose to examine in this essay. I do not use the word "paradox" blithely here; it marks an experience of nearly unbearable ethical conflict as my psyche swung between a manic sense of my beneficent power and a horrifying image of myself as dirty old lech. I was aroused in fact by the sense that I was a "good teacher," by feeling my power to help someone reach his fullest. Yet the arousal meant I was getting off on being his teacher, using him for my own perverse gratification. Although I have felt the weight of that paradox tear at my affects and my self-esteem, I term the paradox "apparent" in the hope of rethinking our pedagogical morality.

In deciding to write and publish this essay, I am wagering that I am not a pervert, that this incident, although perhaps clearer and more dramatic, is in its ambiguity fairly representative of a broad range of pedagogical experience. The remainder of the essay will attempt to work through this incident, to analyze what happened and why, and to articulate some of the theoretical questions posed by it. But before going on to that work, out of consideration for the reader I should negotiate the dissolution of our implicit narrative pact. This is not a love story, rather a story of falling in love. Narrative convention leads us to take "falling in love" as the opening scene of a drama, which will unfold so as to determine whether that scene should be, retrospectively, interpreted as "love" or "fall," or even, most compellingly, as both. Here, however, it is not the opening scene but the whole story. Recounting it, I feel the pull toward conventional closure: did we do it? what happened? Half a dozen years ago, living the story, I felt—much more powerfully—the same pull: felt impelled against my better judgment to push for consummation or rejection. But in fact, from the point of view of narrative promise, "nothing happened": we neither had sex nor damaged our pedagogical relation.

My urge—as reader, writer, or protagonist—to turn this into a love story is massive. Whether the story then had a happy or disastrous ending, it would in any case remove us from the scene of pedagogy, would definitively interpret what happened not as teaching but as love. Yet the tale I need to tell—from grade protest to the full bloom of my crush—is a story of desire arising within the scene of pedagogy, where it is troublingly unclear whether this is really teaching or really sex. Narrative convention directs us to decide whether this story belongs to romance or accounts of teaching experience. To make that generic decision is also to decide whether I was a good or a bad teacher: the good teacher could conquer this and put it to pedagogical use; the bad teacher would give in to desire and abandon duty.

The pressure to decide whether the scene belongs to romance or to professional experience asserts itself not only in the drive to find out how it ended, but also in the stylistics of my account. Some of the language, the agitation, the not-realizing-until-later, the rhythm, clearly derive from romantic convention. Other portions of the account, the stress on labor, words like "communicate" and "understand," seem to derive from the equally conventional discourse of the good teacher. Not only are there two different discursive styles, but the narrating subject is temporally split; two narrative points of view interlace: what I experienced then and what I know now. This temporal splitting of the first-person narrator can be heard in two voices: the voice of the romantic heroine (impelled by the story, not knowing what will happen), and the older but wiser teacherly voice (not only a knowing subject but she who transforms experience into lesson).

Writing and rereading the narrative, I find myself embarrassed not, as I had imagined, by the romantic confession, but much more by the "goody-goody," naively idealistic language of the teacherly voice. Readerly pleasure pulls toward the romantic interpretation. The only language I can summon to describe a powerful experience of doing exactly what I imagine to be good teaching seems bankrupt. Perhaps recognizably conventional discourse seems more appropriate for an impelled, ignorant heroine, more foolish for a knowing, teaching subject. But I also suspect that my preference for romantic over pedagogical cliché is knotted to my persistent urge to interpret this experience and this relation as erotic rather than professional, as love story rather than teaching experience.

∗ ∗ ∗

For months, whenever I thought about those hours in my office, it was like remembering going to bed with someone. I felt we had shared something intense and intimate, that during that time I was totally focused, totally there with him. I found myself speaking of that session in embarrassed, excited, inadequate periphrasis. In memory, the scene became deeply eroticized: by that I do not mean that I revised it with sexual content (touching or innuendo), but the memory had an aura of treasure around it. Thinking about my relation to this student, I began to refer to that afternoon in my office as "the primal scene."

"Primal" because it felt like some sort of origin point. In two decades of teaching, I have had various intense relations with students: friendships, enmities, even—in my younger, wilder days—actual affairs. I choose to consider this scene, not because the relation is unique, but because the scene is unique. Of all the various ambiguous and charged relations with students, this is the only one where I feel I can locate the beginning of my erotic investment. Into my office that afternoon walked a student with an obvious interest in working with me to whom I gave little thought; when he walked out two and a half hours later, he had moved to the center of my thoughts, where he stayed for many months. Because this event has for me something like the magical status of an origin, I persist in believing (despite familiarity with the technique for "deconstructing" origins) that if I could analyze this event I would understand how and why I invest erotically in students.

Because I have a fix on where this cathexis arose, I feel certain, in a way I cannot be about any other of my relations with students, that the erotic charge arose not alongside of the pedagogical relation (not coincidentally because I liked X body type or Y personality or because Z was going on in my psychosexual life), but that the desire arose as part and parcel of a scene of pedagogy. The eros was not a deviation, a distraction, an addition, an aside; it arose in the center of what was a purely pedagogical exchange, as pure as any such can be.

What precisely was so erotic about the scene that had taken place in my office? Recalling it for this account, I am struck by the drama of resistance and vulnerability. The backdrop of his initial anger and challenge give particular piquancy to my sense of his placing himself, undefended and vulnerable, in my hands, trusting it would do him good. I feel as if he let me put his balls in my mouth.

As this image makes clear, eros here is tied to gender. Both the anger against which I stand my ground and the vulnerability that so moves me are gendered masculine in my account. The transformation of masculine threat into male vulnerability is certainly part of the pleasure: what might be understood as a turn from figurative "balls" to corporeal ones.

This drama of resistance and subsequent capitulation, fantasy resolution of the battle of the sexes, is the most sensational representation of the eros; it's what strikes my fancy, what I prefer to imagine and recount. What happened after he ceased resisting, after I too gave up my resistance, is less dramatic, less sexy to recount, to imagine, but is in fact where not only the teaching but also "the sex" happened. The intimacy of working together without barriers between us was, I believe, the sensation I desired to repeat, was the experience that felt like sex. But it is also what occasions the goody-goody prose and is in imagination or in the telling not erotic. Something about erotic representation pushes me toward locating the eros in the power struggle, which is its necessary but not sufficient precondition. In the narrative, what happens when the power struggle is over seems prissy, teacherly. But I do believe that what aroused me in the scene was this moment when we were being good together and not—as imagination would recount—a hot, bad drama of violence and power.

While that intimate experience of being good together seems to have little to do with gender, the preliminary battle and the fantasy repetitions that insistently frame that experience are hypergendered. Whether in my idealistic utopian mode or in my bad-girl fantasies, I would like to separate and choose one of these erotics and discard the other. But to my embarrassment I find I cannot disentangle an erotic that I believe to be gender-irrelevant from hypergendered scenarios. I thus find myself in the apparently contradictory position of claiming this scene as generally representative of pedagogical relations, regardless of gender, while at the same time emphasizing the particular gendering of female teacher and male student.

This contradictory position impels me to attempt to disentangle the two, but I nonetheless say "apparently contradictory" out of an inkling that the specific gender configuration here may actually help make the scene generally representative. Although I have in fact had more fantasies about, sex with, crushes on, female students than male students, I have chosen here to look at this scene because I suspect the particular gendering of female teacher and male student makes it possible to see an erotic play of pedagogy that is usually overlaid by oppressively real power relations. Here gender hierarchy crosses pedagogical position: teacher's power runs counter to male prerogative. The contradiction between the two hierarchies destabilizes the positions, makes each position seem, at least in part, play-acting.

I used to play school when I was a child, after I had started going to the real one. I would play with my brother, my only younger sibling, who was not yet himself in school. During those games where I was always the teacher, I believe I really taught him to read.

I go back to my infantile pedagogy because I imagine it tells something about why and how I wanted to be a teacher. Probably most teachers who care about teaching, probably many who are good teachers, wanted to be teachers. And behind the guidance counselor's phrasing, we might recognize something like the drive to be the teacher, the teacher's desire.

The phrase "infantile pedagogy" is meant to allude to the Freudian notion of "infantile sexuality." Freud thought that in order to understand what we usually call sexuality, we must recognize its first flowering in childhood. Adult sexuality takes its shape and its force by being an unconscious—and therefore conflicted and contorted—repetition of certain childhood relations and configurations. I am suggesting, analogously, that to understand (adult) teaching, we might posit it as a conflicted and contorted repetition of certain childhood configurations. I am not saying that playing school with my brother was sexual but that the repetition of the infantile in the adult activity sexualizes the latter.

Going back to my own childhood, I hope to understand things of wider application than just to those teachers who started out as big sisters instructing their little brothers. In proposing the concept of infantile pedagogy, I am imagining that teaching in general is informed by largely unconscious reactivations of powerful childhood pedagogical configurations, which, of course, in their specific forms vary with the individual.

Fifteen years after playing school with my brother, I started to teach "for real." My last year of graduate school, I taught my first (and second) class: the same course both semesters, but the second semester one student became particularly interested in things I was saying about the books we were reading; one young man wanted to learn what I wanted to teach. We started meeting for coffee and talk outside of class. I began to burn with desire for him, applied my wits to seducing him, and—although I got nowhere sexually—we had a lot of great conversations.

Mike was smart and good-looking, but I don't believe that's what led me to chase him all over campus. What overheated me was the fit between some fantasy I had and the way he responded to me. It is probably very much to the point that I was at the time still a student, with my own very strong cathexes onto teachers. Mike took me for a teacher and appeared to be learning from me in the very way I was still learning from my teachers. I remember often thinking that he must be the same age as my brother: I was still "playing teacher."

In relation to Mike, I was not only playing the teacher but was specifically playing my teachers, my dissertation committee, who were all male. In this fantasy-like reversal, Mike was not the student, but was me as student. The positions that I thought of as real were me-female-student and my male teachers. In this seeming reality, gender and pedagogical hierarchy relayed each other and I could not disentangle the one who had the knowledge from the one who had the balls. Finding myself in an analogous relation to Mike but in the opposite role, I felt I had switched genders. My concurrent sense of our "real genders," however, caused me to experience the pedagogical positions as drag performance, role-playing.

Although "being the teacher" felt like a masquerade, I am convinced that Mike learned a lot from me. An academic himself today, he supports this sense of the real pedagogical value of our encounter. This ambiguity between play and real teaching goes back beyond Mike to my infantile pedagogy. I believe I actually did teach my brother to read. Both of these primal scenes take on formative force precisely by combining playing teacher with really teaching. The fantasy sense of being in a role that was not by rights mine made me feel very powerful, but it is the apparent "real" effect of the game that was so totally intoxicating. This knot of pretense and reality is, I believe, the very paradoxical heart of my pedagogy. I was, and from the beginning, at one and the same time, a fake teacher and an effective one. I am—after twenty years of teaching literally hundreds of students, as a "full professor"—still getting off on "playing teacher" even or especially while I actually teach.

* * *

As I work my way through this material, it keeps organizing itself into opposed pairs: teaching/sex, understanding/conflict, duty/gratification, experience/representation, gender-blind/hyper-gendered, reality/pretense, labor/play. A strong moralizing impulse would reduce each pair to the opposition between good and bad, demand we separate them and choose. But not just the moralizing impulse. My erotic fantasies, my romantic daydreams, and my narrative pleasure would likewise also disentangle the two strands. My wish to be good and my fantasy of being bad would both claim one strand and disavow the other. These impulses to separate are radical: the strands represent competing interpretations of the scene, of self, of life. But, working my way through the material of this scene, over and over, I sense that these strands are inextricably entangled.

One more opposed pair of terms before I close, this one, in the actuality of writing this essay, the most troubling: theory and story. What I wanted to do in this essay was tell this story; to justify that, I felt it must do a lot of theoretical work. Throughout this writing, I have feared that there is too much story, at the same time as I found myself continually falling back into story, adding more stories in the latter part, which is supposed to be theory. If story is not subordinate to theory, then I have fallen short of duty, given in to my own (exhibitionist) gratification.

The protagonist of this essay fantasized and feared betraying her identity as teacher, but by the time I chose to write this up, I knew the outcome and was pretty confident I had maintained my identity. But the drama of professional identity repeats itself in the scene of writing. Choosing to write this for a professional journal meant worrying about whether the writing is professional, scholarly, academic. Although the dry, negative connotations of those terms urge me to transgress and disavow this identity, my choice of this context signifies a wish that this essay be taken as writing that serves the pursuit of knowledge. Although I do not like writing with a teacherly voice, to be included in this professional journal this writing ought to turn life to lesson for more general application (for the benefit of others), to subordinate story to theory.

On the level of greatest actuality, in today's scene of writing rather than the pedagogical scene from my past, the real moral knot, the question that tears me is not about falling in love but about falling into story, not whether or not this is a love story, but whether or not this is a story.

CHAPTER TWELVE

Paper Machete

C OYA P AZ B ROWNRIGG

My partner and I are having a brief discussion about what Ida, our daughter, should wear to the Dyke March, and I remember that today is the 10-year anniversary of the first time my partner and I had sex, a torrid, alcohol-fueled affair that involved three other people and an awkward, eye-averting brunch the next morning. Back then, I was a short-haired sex educator who wore shirts that said Dyke, wrote a sex advice column called I Heart My Clit, and offered workshops on how to use a vibrator, some more hands-on than others. Now I'm a college professor with a brand-new Toyota Scion, a fancy stroller, and a standing date at Wiggleworms, which is a dance and music class for babies 12–24 months old. I write lip gloss reviews on Twitter (shameless plug), and I know that later today, when I'm marching in the Dyke March, I'll stay as far away from the young women wearing tape on their nipples and proudly proclaiming "Resistance Not Assimilation" as I can. The 24-year-old version of me is probably shaking her head in disgust.

But let's get real. In our current anti-immigrant hysteria, I'm way more worried about the fact that my daughter is half-Mexican than about the fact that her parents are two moms. So far, no one has hurled insults, religious pamphlets, or even dirty looks our way. The opposite, in fact.

For example, at our local playground, the playground mommies gather in groups, staking out territory with blankets, diaper bags, and carefully appraising looks. They don't give me the time of day—I like to think it is because my Barbie-doll ponytail and exuberant cleavage is out of place in their sea of yoga pants and sensible shoes, but more likely they just aren't that interested in me. Gorgeous shiny lips aside, I look like any other mom at the playground. But my partner, butch as hell and covered in tattoos, is a big hit. Yuppie moms love her. She is on a first-name basis with all of them and their kids, regularly giving me updates: Henry got a haircut; Lisa can count to 20 in Spanish! On the train, when Nina holds our baby, people offer up seats and baby advice while I stand, bored, looking at advertisements. Gray-haired men in Cubs shirts ask her about teething, and even police offers smile encouragingly and ask to hold the baby. It is like living in an alternate universe, where everybody loves the gays.

I don't want to paint an overly rosy picture of gay parenting. There are some challenges. People are obsessed with whether my child is a boy or a girl, and this is where my gender politics get a headache. Once, a woman came over to pick up something we were giving away on Freecycle. When we'd talked on the phone, I'd mentioned my daughter, and when the woman got to our house she looked at Ida, dressed in gray leggings and a navy T-shirt, confused. "This is a girl?" she asked. "Mmm . . . hmmm," I replied. She looked at us for a moment and then brightened. "Oh," she said, "already a tomboy, I guess!"

Another time, shopping at H&M, a woman said, "Oh, your son is so cute!" "Thanks," I said. "What's his name?" "Ida!" "Oh," she asked, "so this is a girl?" What I wanted to say was, "Yes—for now!" But instead I just said my usual "Mmm . . . hmmm." And good thing, too, because about 12 seconds later she freaked out: "It's not my fault I thought she was a boy. I mean, you dress her like a boy! She looks like a boy! You're shopping in the boys' section. It's not my fault!" And on and on and on. I guess that was a prime opportunity to do some kind of gender education/intervention, but the truth is, I never take the opportunity when it arises.

At Wiggleworms, there is a mom who LOVES my daughter. And I love her son. He's sweet and charming and a great dancer. So when she inevitably says, every class, something like "Oh, here comes your girlfriend!" or "Someday they'll go to prom together," I resist the urge to say, "Unless one of them is gay." I just say, again, "Mmm . . . hmmm," because to do otherwise would make this well-meaning mom uncomfortable. That would cut out, for eternity, the possibility of a play date: a hot commodity with the under-2 set. And when it comes down to it, what I want more than anything is to be the parent of a child who feels liked and loved and accepted. So I bite my tongue.

Recently, though, during a morning trip to Target, the cashier kept cooing at my child: "Oh, he's so cute! He's so cute! What a cute baby!" She looked at me, and then at Ida. "Oh! So cute!" Looked back at me. "He must look like his daddy, right?" I shrugged and didn't answer. "Does he?" "Does he what?" "Does he look like his daddy?" I could have inserted an easy "Mmm . . . hmmm" and ended it right there. I could have. But I didn't. Not because I wanted to stage an intervention but because I was totally and completely insulted that this woman assumed that my gorgeous, incredibly cute child could not possibly look like me. So instead I said, "Oh, I don't know what her 'daddy' looks like." She stared at me, confused, probably wondering what kind of slut can't even guess what her baby's father looks like. So I smiled. "I don't know what her daddy looks like because we made her at a sperm bank!" The cashier's mouth literally dropped open and the woman behind me started laughing hysterically. "Well," she shrieked, "you don't hear that every day! Nope! That's awkward! Don't hear that every day!" I just shrugged. But even this has a happy ending. The woman leaned in toward my child and said, "Well, no matter who you look like, you're beautiful." That I could agree with. Mmm . . . hmmm.

I could go on and on, but my daughter is carefully marching around our living room wearing one of my high heels and she is wrapping a bag of blocks around her neck. My partner is dressed and looking askance at the stained old Ani DiFranco T-shirt I'm wearing. It is our 10-year sexiversary, and while this morning hasn't exactly set the mood, we've got a babysitter tonight. I don't have to worry about whether I'll get lucky, though. Looking around at half-chewed crackers ground into the floor, dolls hanging from the television and coffee table, and a suspicious brown lump in the corner of the room, I'm pretty sure I already have.

Introduction: Schooling Students in Gender and Sexuality Expectations

DARLA LINVILLE

The situation for lesbian, gay, bisexual, trans(gender), queer, and questioning (LGBTQ) youth in America's high schools, although not perfect yet, seems to some observers to be improving. Students are advocating for gay-straight alliances (GSAs), teachers are naming themselves as allies or queer adult supporters, and administrations are being pushed to be responsive to students' pleas for help when they are being bullied (*L.W.* v. *Toms River Regional Schools, Board of Education,* 2007; *Nabozny* v. *Podlesny,* 1996). Although students report name-calling, bullying behavior, and resulting academic and social difficulties in nationwide surveys, these same surveys report that in schools that offer administrative support for student organizations such as GSAs and have a clearly enumerated disciplinary code that punishes harassment on the basis of gender expression or sexual orientation, students feel much safer (Kosciw, Diaz, & Greytak, 2008). In the national media it has been reported that teens are coming out at younger and younger ages (Cloud, 2005) and that even some elementary schools have changed their policies to accommodate gender-variant second-graders (Brown, 2006). And *The New York Times* reported in November 2010, "Last month, the federal Department of Education told schools they were obligated, under civil rights laws, to try to prevent harassment, including that based on sexual orientation and gender identity. But the agency did not address the controversy over more explicit classroom materials in grade schools" (Eckholm, 2010, p. A16).

Conversely and concurrently, acts of violence have been recorded against LGBTQ and gender-variant young people over the last 10 years. Some of these stories have gotten little or no media coverage, and some have been national events. In one school district in Minnesota, seven students have committed suicide in the past year as a result of harassment, and two teachers are on leave for harassing students based on their sexual orientation. Since the beginning of the 2010–2011 school year, the media have covered five student suicides from middle school to college. In central Maine, students report that the worst harassment happens around sexual orientation and body size/appearance.

While these events seem to counteract or contradict each other and induce confusion about the social reality for queer and gender-variant youth, they are all part of the larger discursive struggle about sexuality and the sanctity of differential gender valuation in contemporary U.S. culture (Sedgwick, 1990). Schools have been the sites for these struggles since the end of the 19th century, and both teachers' and students' bodies have been closely regulated within educational settings (Blount, 2000, 2005; Foucault, 1977; Lugg, 2003, 2005; Luschen & Bogad, 2003; Pascoe, 2007; Weiler, 2006). Disputes over the content of the curriculum, the appropriate gender and sexual behavior of teachers and students, and the role of schools in teaching about sexuality have raged throughout the 20th century (Fields, 2008; Fine & McClelland, 2006; Irvine, 2002; Perrin & DeJoy, 2003; Reese, 1986; Spring, 2004; Urban & Wagoner, 2000; Zimmerman, 2002). These arguments have often questioned the rights of students who do not conform to gender and sexuality regulations to an education, taken away the rights of non-heterosexual or gender-variant adults to be in physical proximity to children, and denied the non-heterosexual evidence in curriculum subjects' lives in order to keep homosexuality or gender variance out of the classroom. Underlying these efforts are some of the contradictory discourses about sexuality and gender that form the foundation of modern society. These are the contradictions that Foucault (1978) pointed out and that many others have built on: that although heterosexuality is the presumed natural and superior half of the heterosexual/homosexual binary, its boundaries are quite unstable and must be enforced and reinforced throughout one's life, and that gender performance and sexual behavior or object choice get conflated and define a certain type of person—the homosexual.

Although we no longer overtly present girls with instruction on becoming a "young lady," and boys may be allowed to cry sometimes, schools still create and uphold a very traditional gender binary and the expectation that heterosexual dating and marriage are in the future of all students. The texts in this section highlight just what adults in schools do and do not do to create opportunities for young people to cross the boundaries of traditional expectations. In Jacinta Bunnell's drawing of a fairy/girl, at the beginning of this section, we see the attributes that the artist recognizes in girls but that are often not celebrated in them by adults. While toys and stars marketed to girls often affirm beauty, style, and sweetness as girls' qualities, Bunnell celebrates girls' creativity, assertiveness, self-love, and unlimited potential. She makes visible and audible the expectation that girls can be more than the limited "princess" image they are often offered.

Erica Boas, in "Walking the Line: Teaching, Being, and Thinking Sexuality in Elementary School," examines the ways in which gender and sexuality lines are monitored and buttressed in elementary classrooms, even by progressive teachers grappling with notions of "appropriateness." Teachers find expressions of sexuality in elementary school children to be unnatural and perversions of childlike behavior, assuming that the children who engage in expressions of sexuality must be inappropriately exposed to it in neglectful or abusive homes or through older peers. Their denial of sexual expression among children upholds the notion that young children are innocent of sexuality themselves and maintains the belief that talking about sexuality in elementary classrooms introduces children to a topic they would otherwise have no experience of.

In "Becoming Mr. Cougar: Institutionalizing Heterosexuality and Homophobia at River High," C.J. Pascoe unmasks the ways in which heterosexism and sexism underlie many of the common rituals and interactions in high school. Teachers and students alike reference gender normativity and heterosexuality to make sense of one another and understand the concepts being taught in class. Boys who fail to conform to gender and sexuality standards, even if only in verbal representations of themselves, are subject to ridicule by both teachers and peers. Like the teachers in Boas's chapter, Pascoe's teachers swim in a sea of sexism and heterosexism, and for the most part they do not realize the role they play in creating the discursive environment in which the roles for young men are always already understood, and the limitations about being sexual or speaking about sexuality in public change according to a student's social locations.

Similarly, in "The Right Way to Be Gay: How School Structures Sexual Inequality," Katie Elliott describes the gender, racial, class, and sexuality performances that allow a gay student to be accepted and embraced by students at Midwest High. The student who embodies the "right way" does not advocate for political changes in the school, dresses in preppy clothes, and performs gender in the ways other white boys in the school do. Students with other class locations, with a political agenda for LGBTQ visibility, or who are not white do not easily find acceptance in the school, and their gayness is considered to be too "in your face" by other students. As in the other articles in this section, here race, class, gender expression, and sexuality converge to create meanings about both identities and behaviors—to determine if they are acceptable or unacceptable, within the boundaries of appropriateness, or over the lines.

Finally, Dave Glick rebels against the traditional model of high school altogether, finding that in some (often rural and socially conservative) locations students who cannot or are unwilling to conform to gender and sexuality expectations never get relief from the harassment they experience. Unwilling to wait for the leaders of those districts to create a different environment for LGBTQ students, or anyone perceived to be different, he took the lead in creating an online alternative environment for students. In his GLBTQ Online High School, he hopes to address the social and academic needs of students in far-flung places.

References

Blount, J.M. (2000). Spinsters, bachelors, and other gender transgressors in school employment, 1850–1990. *Review of Educational Research, 70*(1), 83–101.

Blount, J.M. (2005). *Fit to teach: Same-sex desire, gender, and school work in the twentieth century.* Albany: State University of New York Press.

Brown, P.L. (2006, December 2). Supporting boys or girls when the line isn't clear. *The New York Times,* p. 1.

Bunnell, J., & Novak, J. (2009). *Girls Are Not Chicks Coloring Book.* Oakland, CA: PM Press.

Cloud, J. (2005). The battle over gay teens. *Time, 166*(15).

Eckholm, E. (2010, November 7). In efforts to end bullying, some see agenda. *The New York Times,* A16.

Fields, J. (2008). *Risky lessons: Sex education and social inequality.* New Brunswick, NJ: Rutgers University Press.

Fine, M., & McClelland, S.I. (2006). Sexuality education and desire: Still missing after all these years. *Harvard Educational Review, 76*(3), 297–338.

Foucault, M. (1977). *Discipline and punish: The birth of the prison* (1st American ed.). New York: Pantheon Books.

Foucault, M. (1978). *The history of sexuality: An introduction.* New York: Random House.

Irvine, J.M. (2002). *Talk about sex: The battles over sex education in the United States.* Berkeley: University of California Press.

Kosciw, J.G., Diaz, E.M., & Greytak, E.A. (2008). *2007 national school climate survey: The experiences of lesbian, gay, bisexual and transgender youth in our nation's schools.* New York: GLSEN.

L.W. v. *Toms River Regional Schools, Board of Education,* PQ07IE-02596 (New Jersey Supreme Court 2007).

Lugg, C.A. (2003). Sissies, faggots, lezzies, and dykes: Gender, sexual orientation, and a new politics of education? *Educational Administration Quarterly, 39*(1), 95–134.

Lugg, C.A. (2005). Thinking about sodomy: Public schools, legal panopticons, and queers. *Educational Policy, 20*(1),

35–58.

Luschen, K.V., & Bogad, L. (2003). Bodies that matter: Transgenderism, innocence and the politics of "unprofessional" pedagogy. *Sex Education, 3*(2), 145–155.

Nabozny v. *Podlesny,* 92 F.3d 446 (7th Circuit 1996).

Pascoe, C.J. (2007). *Dude, you're a fag: Masculinity and sexuality in high school.* Berkeley: University of California Press.

Perrin, K.K., & DeJoy, S.B. (2003). Abstinence-only education: How we got here and where we're going. *Journal of Public Health Policy, 24*(3/4), 445–459.

Reese, W.J. (1986). *Power and the promise of school reform: Grassroots movements during the Progressive Era.* Boston: Routledge & Kegan Paul.

Sedgwick, E.K. (1990). *Epistemology of the closet.* Berkeley: University of California Press.

Spring, J.H. (2004). *The American school, 1642–2004* (6th ed.). Boston: McGraw-Hill.

Urban, W.J., & Wagoner, J.L. (2000). *American education: A history* (2nd ed.). Boston: McGraw-Hill.

Weiler, K. (2006). The historiography of gender and progressive education in the United States. *Paedagogica Historica, 42*(1/2), 161–176.

Zimmerman, J. (2002). *Whose America?: Culture wars in the public schools.* Cambridge, MA: Harvard University Press.

1- creativity
2- assertiveness
3- self-love
4- unlimited potential

Girls Are Not Chicks, 2009. Jacinta Bunnell.
From the *Girls Are Not Chicks Coloring Book*, 2009. Jucinta Bunnell and Julie Novak, p. 23

CHAPTER THIRTEEN

Walking the Line

Teaching, Being, and Thinking Sexuality in Elementary School

ERICA M. BOAS

> In appearance, we are dealing with a barrier system; but in fact, all around the child, indefinite
> lines of penetration were disposed.
>
> —FOUCAULT (1978/1990, P. 42)

What would elementary school be without lines? Parents line up to fill out paperwork to enroll their kindergartners into schools before (sometimes long before) the start of the school year. Yellow buses and cars line up outside of the school building to drop off children at the beginning of each day. Children stand in lines awaiting the arrival of their teachers as the first bell rings, and they likely sit in lines on the rug or in desks as they receive instruction. They line up again each time they go out to recess or lunch and each time they come back into the classroom from the yard. In assemblies they sit in lines and walk to their classes in lines. There are also the lines upon which grades, the concept of "age appropriateness," and instructional levels rely. These lines of human development are oriented toward a naturalized progression of learning and socioemotional stages.[1] We think of such lines as a mark of order. Lines epitomize organization—they are neat, manageable, and safe. They signify boundaries, and teachers depend upon them to keep order at school. At the end of the school day these lines dissolve into something less systematic, less knowable, looser, until the opening of the next school day. But what happens when lines blur, as they do in the following excerpts, into something unusual to an elementary school day? Something like kissing, perhaps?

Mark	Once I was walking up to the other field, and the kindergarten class was lined up against the fence as part of the PE activity. And there was a g–. Oh, I can't remember if it was a girl or a boy. But one of them was all up on the other one kissing them.
EB:	What were you thinking at that moment?

Mark   Oh, you mean when I first saw it? To be honest, I was like, "Damn!" You know? I can't remember if it was the boy or the girl now, but I was like, "Whoa! That kid's all up on that other one." You know what I mean? They were like, "Mmmmm" [makes kissing gesture], and I was like, "Whoa! I didn't know they did that kind of thing in Kindergarten." [Laughs.] (Mark, personal communication, March 28, 2008)[2]

Likewise Monica, a kindergarten teacher at a public charter school, shows bafflement at the sexual behavior she observes in the classroom.

It's like they're doing it subconsciously or something. I don't know. . . . I'm just like, "Let's keep our bodies to ourselves. Don't lay on top of each other, you might hurt each other. . . ." It's not like they're even aware of what they're doing. But it's weird how they will do, little kids who I don't think have ever seen someone have sex or even really know what it is, what I would consider to be sexual things. . . . I don't think they have any awareness that this is a sexual thing. . . . But I'm also just a lot of time wondering in my head, like, "I wonder if there is really a young awareness of sex?" (Monica, personal communication, March 2, 2008)

These are not isolated examples. There are many teachers like Mark and Monica, teachers who demonstrate that there is still much to learn about sexuality, especially in elementary schools. Sexuality, a topic rarely thought to be a meaningful aspect of elementary school life, is a topic largely absent from the official discourse on and in elementary schools. However, having spent years working in elementary schools, and after speaking with many teachers on the subject, it is clear that sexuality is a significantly palpable, living energy in elementary schools. This energy, while diffuse, becomes visible through the realization of lines that organize elementary schools and the management of such contentious subjects as sexuality.

Accordingly, this chapter is an interpretive representation of narratives and thoughts such as Mark's and Monica's about sexuality as conveyed by teachers who work in elementary school spaces. It treats the lines that derive from sexuality in the elementary schools and attends to two questions designed to deepen an understanding of the ways in which sexuality plays out in this context: What are the lines of thought that guide teachers' interpretations and subsequent management of sexuality in the elementary school? How do these lines provide insight into the ways in which normativity is created? Following these lines can help educators obtain a more robust understanding of how we manage and produce sexuality. It looks to the ways in which we adults, like the kindergartners about whom Monica speaks, don't "even really know what it is" when we talk about sexuality. And one way to view the ways in which elementary schools manage sexuality is to hear from teachers.

Methodological Lines/Lines of Communication

"I'm not sure I'll have anything to tell you. I can't think of any examples of sexuality right now," Dahlia warned me while we were setting up our interview in March 2008 (Dahlia, personal communication, April 3, 2008). I assured her that we would find something to talk about, because even if she could think of nothing, I would provide examples from my own experiences teaching and working in elementary schools, and we could work together to interpret them. A teacher for five years, I had witnessed the ubiquity of sexuality in school life. I realized, however, as I spoke these words to Dahlia, that in some ways my intellectual foray into sexuality and the elementary schools was a test of the normality of my own experiences. I arrived at this project with the assumption that sexuality is perceptible in primary schools. Therefore, part of my reason for conducting such a study was to see if my teaching experience resonated with that of others, and if, in fact, there was a "there" there. In effect, I was merging my own lines of engagement as a teacher and as a researcher, a tension that often left me feeling pulled in opposite directions.

In the spring of 2008 I set out to find elementary school teachers willing to speak with me on the subject, beginning by contacting a couple of teachers whom I knew and then asking them to provide me with references and to ask their colleagues if I could interview them. I had worked on a professional basis with three of the teachers and was an acquaintance of three others. The remaining four teachers were strangers to me before the interviews. Eight of the ten teachers taught in public schools populated mostly by low-income students of color. The other two, not represented individually in this chapter, taught in a private school. The interviews, which I recorded and transcribed, ranged from 1 hour to 2 1/2 hours. I met with each teacher one time and then followed up by phone or by email.

These conversations establish that there *is* something there, and that it is significant. In the interviews I asked teachers to tell me "critical incidents" of the times they thought sexuality had become salient in the school and to work with me to analyze these moments. While not all of the teachers' responses are directly represented in this chapter, all of the teachers with whom I have spoken have helped me to better comprehend how sexuality is talked about, lived, and managed in elementary schools; their intellectual footprints are embedded into these pages. They have helped me conclude, for example, that the perceived invisibility of sexuality arises out of a complex interaction of forces that conspire to keep it out of sight. It is squelched dialogue and constrained expression; yet it is palpable. The few studies of sexuality in elementary schools that have been published also show this to be true (Thorne & Luria, 1986; Ferguson, 2001; Renold, 2005). Once we open our eyes and our mouths to see it and to speak of it, we find that sexuality is omnipresent. For this reason Renold (2005) asserts that there is a "need to address the ways in which the adult world treats, recognizes, regulates, punishes and ultimately creates children's sexualities" (p. 22). I take up her challenge and look to teaching adults to guide us in understanding how sexuality organizes and produces the conditions of life for people of *all* ages.[3]

I seek to open lines of communication, as teachers and I did when we spoke, with other parties interested in the operation of sexuality in a space where it is not supposed to occur. This analysis is, and can only ever be, what Philip Brian Harper (2000) calls "critical speculative knowledge," insight that accepts the ultimate inevitability of subjective interpretation that aims, primarily, to inspire thoughtful and critical intellectual (ex)change. I approach this theoretical examination in this spirit of "critical speculative knowledge" by analyzing the statements of real people who teach real children. These statements have been constructed through memory; furthermore, that teachers share thoughts on a politically sensitive subject knowing that I am a researcher with the objective of presenting my work to the public complicates the analysis. I recognize that such a tangle throws out a great challenge. I thus offer the analysis that follows as an exploration of theoretical possibilities in a world in which the nuanced operation of sexuality, inflected by other domains of power, cannot be understood in absolute terms or in totality. In my attempt to represent the statements, interpretations, and ways of seeing of teachers in combination with my own, I undertake the social constructionist work that challenges the linear trajectory and aim of scientific inquiry that has held sway in academia.[4] A social constructionist approach is, in practice and in interpretation, a somewhat messy method of inquiry in that it endeavors to show that we inhabit a world we make collectively for ourselves.

Theoretical Lines

In this chapter I explore the lines that become intelligible when teachers talk about sexuality in elementary school. Conceptually, a line connotes something organized and direct, certainly straight, with an exact geometry. Sexuality, therefore, acts in contrast to a line and attempts to define it prove elusive. In fact, the analytic category of sexuality, perhaps *because* it is so unwieldy, allows us to see through and past what might otherwise be presumed to be straight lines. There are few "straight" answers in teaching, in human development, and in sexuality, at least in part because dialogue about sexuality is maintained as "wondering in [the] head."

Yet when elementary school teachers do talk about sexuality, they speak from and across lines. First, teachers are asked to walk the "party line" in support of heterosexuality and heteronormativity, the ideological-material system that normalizes and naturalizes the indivisibility of woman and man as reproductive partners in social processes. Even when (and maybe especially when) they are silent on issues of sexuality do they invoke a presumed heterosexuality. They also participate in a trajectory of human development in which individuals move through a linear progression of childhood to adolescence to adulthood. Second, they occupy the line of the liminal space between the public and the private spheres; they mediate between the school and the home. Finally, when teachers talk about sexuality in the elementary school, they speak through binaries to make sense of this unwieldy and charged subject.

Collectively, these lines become oriented toward a "normalizing mission," (Chatterjee, 1993) with aims to create "normative" children; that is, schooling directs students toward heterosexual, middle-class[5] norms and values.[6] Following the lines of the normalizing mission and the ways in which they dissolve, disappear, deviate, and become disoriented in teachers' statements about sexuality in the elementary school opens up different ways of thinking about the power of elementary schools in the production of society. In this essay I pair Foucault and Althusser to illuminate the ideological underpinnings of sexuality in schooling. While Foucault provides us with a robust theory of sexuality and normalization, Althusser gives analysis of the role of schooling in the creation of ideology.[7] Ideology is a necessary focus in attempts to comprehend why certain ways of thinking, and therefore of being, become normalized. Students and teachers as imagined subjects become important actors in the creation of schools as complex apparatuses for reproducing national ideology, an ideology that upholds the middle class as sacrosanct guardians of capitalist society (Althusser, 1971). Following Marx in his theory of the reproduction of the relations of production in capitalism, Althusser argued that the school (both public and private) is a primary Ideological State Apparatus of the present, having replaced the role of the church of a few centuries ago. It performs the task of reproducing relations of power through "an apprenticeship in a variety of know-how wrapped up in the massive inculcation of the ideology of the ruling class" (Althusser, 1971, p. 157). In short, according to Althusser, the middle classes reproduce the ideology of the upper class through tangled processes of indoctrination largely executed through schools.

Placing Althusser and Foucault in conversation, it becomes clear that such ideology is inscribed, enacted and created, in part, through sexuality. Foucault (1978/1990), in contrast to Freud, argued that sexuality is not innate to humanity. Rather, it is a socially constructed instrument for the deployment of power that has been created over time through a "web of discourses" (p. 30) and is a "dense transfer point for relations of power: between men and women, young people and old people, parents and offspring, teachers and students, priests and laity, and administration and a population" (p.

103). Following this line, Foucault argues that the deployment of sexuality creates an understanding of "normal" behaviors and practices, which operate recursively on interpersonal and social levels. Intimate relationships, he asserts, produce a distinct middle class, or bourgeois, conception of sexuality in family (or private) life that takes on a normalizing power, which in turn regulates the broader social (or public) life. Foucault explains that sexuality "compares, differentiates, hierarchizes, homogenizes, excludes. In short, it *normalizes*" (Foucault, 1977, p. 183). The discourse of sexuality, therefore, is a terrain of power—in Foucauldian terms, the site of struggle for control of bodies and souls. Sexuality is a "regime of power-knowledge-pleasure" (p. 11) that must be understood not as a "thing," a natural human possession toward which an individual is oriented (in the sense of libido à la Freud), but as a "vector of power" (Rubin, 1993), a composite of lines of power, knowledge, and pleasure that produce the conditions of life. Thus, the social and political significance of sexuality cannot be undermined by its apparent invisibility or assumed insignificance in elementary schools—these are simply deterrents to understanding the intrinsic power present in sexuality, discourse in the service of ideology.

Discourse that gives way to insights into ideology can be revealed by following the points and lines in teachers' words and interpreting them through theories on discourse and ideology offered by Foucault and Althusser. And while they provide a broad analytical framework for understanding the major concepts in this chapter, others assist in elucidating this rather elusive topic. For example, Ariès (1962), Ferguson (2001), and O'Connell Davidson (2007) help me to think about the position of the child with regard to sexuality, and Stoler (2006) allows for clearer insight into binaries. Together, the teachers and the published social theorists introduced here show elementary schools to be agents fundamental in producing sexuality through the construction and maintenance of these discursive and ideological geometrical configurations.

Living the Line: Model Citizens

Just as teachers constantly watch their students, teachers also know that their students and the parents of their students watch them, too. They are public servants, and in the service of creating citizens they are themselves expected to exhibit all the qualities of a good citizen. In one example of this, Mark explains that he observed second graders kissing one another at the end of lunch recess when the rest of the students were lining up to return to the classroom.

> I mean, I think that's natural two kids kissing because they like each other, and so I told their teacher, "Um, I saw your students kissing over there. Just thought you might want to know." Because I thought he should know, not because I wanted the kids to get in trouble. That kind of stuff is normal, but it's just not appropriate at school. That kind of behavior just doesn't belong in school. I mean, I wouldn't kiss my partner or hug for an extended period of time in the halls or in the classroom, so I figure students shouldn't either, right? I mean, I wouldn't want them to think that that's what we do in a public place. I want to model good behavior, and I don't think kissing and that kind of thing is good behavior for kids to see at schools. (Mark, personal communication, March 28, 2008)

Because teachers are agents of the state, they must embody the type of citizen that the state desires. As Mark points out, they must be models for the children, and such modeling has much to do with how they manage their own sexuality. However, if they want their students to do the same, teachers are not supposed to exhibit sexuality. The self-regulation of their own bodies, usually acts of de-sexualization, instructs their students. Yet in their efforts to hide sexuality, they succeed in maintaining heterosexuality inasmuch as the default sexuality is heterosexuality, as is evident in this statement by Greta, a fourth-grade teacher, in response to my question about the ways in which she responded to a female student's repetitive sexualized behaviors.

> I always feel like this . . . over-protective person like an outsider, right? And then I know this isn't true, but I do have a voice in my head that says, "Well, if they knew that you were a dyke, well, then it would even be worse because it would be, just like whatever you did, people would interpret that as trying to discourage females from being with males." That's just a lot of . . . baggage from stuff. Reading, experiences, and stuff like that. And I know that that's not true of me personally, but it does make me cautious, and it does make me double-check myself in terms of what do I say, or what does that sound like? How could it be interpreted? (Greta, personal communication, March 14, 2008.)

Both Greta and Mark present the situation of many teacher respondents—sexuality is consistently on their minds, informing how they manage their bodies, interact with their students, and how they interpret students' behaviors. They are cognizant of ways in which, in their positions as teachers, sexuality facilitates the regulation of their own bodies and speech; that is, they negotiate their own possibilities and limitations through the prism of sexuality, which they weigh against the judgments of the parents and the state.

Walking the Line: Between Spheres

Public elementary school teachers walk the unmarked heteronormative line as they simultaneously straddle a major line between the school and the home. As actors in state institutions who instruct and care for children, they are inevitably intertwined in the lives of these children during the school day and beyond; their power in schools reaches into homes. Althusser (1971) explicates the significance of transgressing this perceived binary. For Althusser, schools are indoctrinating entities that carry out the dictates of the bourgeoisie, dictates that sustain them as the ruling class; they "constitute the dominant Ideological State Apparatus" (p. 157). But indoctrination is not carried out by schools alone; he asserts that it is not solely the school, but the "School/Family couple" that plays a "determinant part in the reproduction of the relations of production . . ." (p. 157). In Althusserian theory, this determinant part is the inculcation of ideology, and it is best done through a conflation of the school (public) and home (private).

In friendlier language, McKay (1998) writes that schools instruct us in "the skills, social norms and values that allow us to successfully integrate into society," (p. ix). If this is so, then teachers are the unnamed actors in this statement and the conduits through which students learn ideology. They are actors who serve as bridges connecting the school and the family. Therefore, the actions and speech of teachers can provide insight into the social operation and proliferation of ideology, processes well captured through ethnographic methods that attend to micro-processes in local sites. Through interviews with teachers, we can also identify *which* skills, norms, and values society privileges; they provide us a "way in" to exploring the processes through which society then goes about distinguishing who is permitted to inhabit these values. For example, when Monica asserts, "Kissing and hugging and doing other things like that is for home or somewhere else. Not for school" (Monica, personal communication, March 2, 2008), she avers that a perceived boundary exists between the public and private sphere for sexual expressions that should not be transgressed. Such unspoken rules become official when they become punishable, like the "no kissing policy" that kindergarten teacher Greta mandated in her classroom after two girls kissing each other became a distraction (Greta, personal communication, March 14, 2008). As Josie, a third-grade teacher, points out, noticing and talking about sexual expressions by children require that teachers interact with parents (Josie, personal communication, April 8, 2008). Sexuality thus operates as a mechanism for differentiating "appropriate" behaviors from those that are not, and this distinction is grounds for the public institution of schooling to enter into the private sphere of the family.

In another instance, Cassie, a second-grade teacher, talks about a male student who was poking girls in the bottom with pencils and making "sexual sounds" during class time:

> I've sat down with him personally and talked with him about, there's obviously areas on peoples' bodies that you're not allowed to touch. . . . I know that his mom and dad have had those conversations with him. I know that he lives in a small apartment with his mom and step-dad. And as a child I remember hearing my mom have sex. I mean, I think that especially as an eight- or nine-year-old, very familiar with what that sounds like. . . . If you talk about low-income families and parents are always at work, and children are going home to kick it by themselves for a while, and they're turning on that TV, or they're listening to "Superman that Ho" on the radio, you are getting that exposure. (Cassie, personal communication, March 8, 2008)

A comment such as this shows that teachers are eyes that see into the private sphere of the home, but because they cannot see everything that happens, they are left to theorize the remaining possibilities. Cassie perceives low-income families as exposed to inappropriate education. Because she has had experiences that may be similar to those of her low-income students, she can empathize with them, and it supports her assertion that poor children are improperly educated. But as a teacher, she is in a position to correct the perceived dysfunctions of the home through the power bestowed by the state.

In more severe cases, or with "probable cause," teachers are mandated by law to report to Child Protective Services (CPS). Through this "line" as well, teachers become participants in the (perceived) private sphere of the home. Mandating reporting requires that teachers become the "eyes" of the state and as such do the state's work in regulating the private sphere. They thus straddle the perceived division that demarcates the public and private spheres. They are in a prime spot to regulate both the state and the domestic spheres.

Thinking with the Line: Binaries

When talking about sexuality, teachers speak through lines. They make sense of sexuality by conjuring up imagined social binaries. These lines ultimately help them to accept that which is developmentally appropriate, appropriate for school and normal, and what is not. The reification of particular binaries that emerged from the interviews illuminates the perceived dichotomous relationships of public/private and child/adult, and these become commonsense frameworks for understanding child sexuality even as the explanations teachers give undermine the fixedness of the oppositions. This study, then, allows us to see how the category of sexuality illuminates the project of maintaining binaries—binaries regulated and reinforced by teachers and schools in support of prevailing conceptions of normal. It is an attempt to link what might otherwise be considered banal to larger-scale ideological and discursive projects. In this section I attend to these two main dualisms highlighted in the interviews which, as Foucault argued in *The History of Sexuality* (1978/1990), are both negotiated through constructs of "normal." While these particular dualisms have been well attended to across disciplines, my concern in this section is to illustrate how they become reified, put to use, and made socially significant with regard to sexuality and elementary schools.

Public/Private

The home-school connection is a significant area of education studies.[8] Curriculum, sociology, psychology, and policy concerned with education do a great deal in attempts to bridge this perceived divide. Much of the research is based on the assumption that homes and schools are distinct spheres, but attention to the relationship between the school and home confirms that schools *and* homes are part and parcel of the normalizing project. Schools and homes thus mutually contribute to the political project of national ideology insofar as these public and private spheres act in tandem to shore up political ideologies to maintain national cohesion. Take, for example, the following interview excerpts: Monica, a kindergarten teacher, supplies rationale as to why she believes kissing to be inappropriate for the school context. And Grace, another kindergarten teacher, explains why she established a "no kissing policy" in her class after repeated incidents of children kissing became a distraction to others (Grace, personal communication, March 23, 2008). Cassie indicates why she tells her students that their actions are inappropriate.

> *Monica:* It's not something that school is about. Kissing and hugging and doing other things like that are for home or somewhere else. Not for school. (Monica, personal communication, March 2, 2008)

> *Grace:* I know kids come in [to kindergarten] with all kinds of behaviors that they do just because they're little kids. But they have to learn that in school, or in any public place, they can't do that. They just can't, you know? (Grace, personal communication, March 23, 2008)

> *Cassie:* [Girls] can't be all sexy and stuff running around the classroom. (Cassie, personal communication, April 8, 2008)

In these teachers' statements there is a clearly defined division between the school (public) and the home or "somewhere else" (private). Recall Mark's assertion, "That kind of stuff is normal, but it's just not appropriate at school. That kind of behavior just doesn't belong in school." Monica, Grace, Cassie, and Mark illustrate that schools should be sexless spaces, distinct from the home or "somewhere else." Monica and Grace make explicit the line between the school and the home. The statement exemplifies Althusser's (1971) argument that the modern Ideological State Apparatus (ISA) is upheld through a coupling of schools and families; it demonstrates that when the connection between the school and home is improper, teachers draw a clear line between them, pointing to spaces outside the school where inappropriate learning occurs. Consequently, the responsibility for those children who are behaving improperly at school lies, at bottom, with home life; the home is to blame when children do not succeed. Problems with children in school lead teachers to look to the home as both the cause and their correction, and the culprits are largely low-income ones.

To justify blaming the home for failure, teachers must first draw a distinct line between the home and the school. They look to behaviors that transgress norms of the school. Sexual expressions provide a clear window through which to categorize these behaviors. Teachers reported that students in their schools kiss, touch, or speak with sexualized language, and each of them leaned on the notion that school is a public place wherein sexual behaviors are inappropriate. While such an understanding of these behaviors seems reasonable, the point I seek to make is not whether the teachers are right or wrong but rather to show the ways in which sexuality clarifies the perceived line between homes and schools. Yet paradoxically, the category of sexuality also challenges this binary. That is, when children behave in particular ways in schools, the messages that schools impart to the children regarding this behavior will also logically be taken into the home and vice versa. That teachers frequently see and regulate sexual expressions *in* schools demonstrates that sexuality *is* a major issue *in* schools and is not simply something that happens or is learned in the home, thereby illustrating that these binaries are less stable than we think. But binaries are useful constructs in the maintenance of the status quo because they allow for categorization. If binaries aid in creating and perpetuating categories that support hierarchies of power, then sexuality can help to deconstruct the myth of binaries by illuminating the power dynamics and relationships that inhere in our modern social assumptions, as can be seen in these teachers' words. Binaries are epistemologies, the ways through which we take for truth that we know that which we know. The Western ontology of the "taxonomic gaze" (Stoler, 2006) renders natural knowledge based in categories, taxonomies, classifications (Foucault, 1978/1990) that serve to differentiate and sort people into mostly static hierarchies of power. A social system relying upon hierarchies of difference—race, class, gender, and sexuality (to name just a few)—depends on categorization.

These epistemological projects support dualisms and are mainly concerned with matters of difference, and these differences inform and direct the ongoing construction of social binaries and their consequences. The public/private binary is integral to the formation of the social system and, therefore, of national ideology. Historically, the issue of privacy in the United States has been inextricably linked to questions of freedom, and the importance of freedom to the nation cannot be understated. Yet poor people quite literally cannot afford middle-class privacy/freedom, which ultimately creates the conflation of public and private life for them.[9]

The public/private division permits homes to be constructed as simultaneously separate from, and linked, to schools, as is portrayed in Cassie's imaginings of her student's home life. Constructing the school/home relationship in this way allows for families to be blamed for social failures (separate), and it also permits school agents to enter into the home (linked). In a case regarding another male student, Cassie tells me that she was constantly in touch with this boy's mother and that they had, together, come up with a behavior modification strategy in which he was not allowed to hang out with his friends if he misbehaved in school.

> I've had to talk to with his parents about this student really needs to learn boundaries. . . . You know what gets taken away from him that's been completely effective? His mom just won't let him kick it with all the boys in the hood that are talking about "your teacher's a fox." And "come over to my house and let's watch MTV all night." Like they should not be watching "Flavor of Love." I should not hear third graders going "Flavor Flav!" and you're looking at women with all their business hanging out and 20-year-old women macking on one 50-year-old dude who used to rap in '85. Like, it's just gross. (Cassie, personal communication, April 8, 2008)

Because of Cassie's concern about this boy's behavior, which appears in the public space of the school but is perceived as learned in the domestic sphere of the home, Cassie and the boy's mother together created a disciplinary plan, which demonstrates one approach in which teachers enter and influence the private sphere. Yet it is the presumed faith in the public/private binary that ultimately provides justifications for the line to be crossed.

Child/Adult

Cassie's concern with what a third grader should and should not be doing highlights another binary pronounced in the interviews—that of child/adult. The child/adult dichotomy rests on an assumption of linear development and difference. The categories adult and child are social constructs that serve political projects. The assumption that children are (and should be) essentially different from adults emerged, as Phillipe Ariès (1962) established in his eminent work *Centuries of Childhood*, between the 15th and 18th centuries as class divisions widened. He argued that childhood is a social construct and that Western conceptions of childhood are constructed by adults through adult ideas of adulthood.[10] Childhood, it then follows, is not a "natural," universally occurring phase of life; it is created, in context, toward political, economic, or social goals (Prout & James, 1997). In this way, "culture, morality, sociability is written on children in an unfolding process by adults (who are seen as fully 'developed,' made by nature) in institutions like family and school" (Ferguson, 2001, p. 80). And, as adults, "we look to 'the Child' to give meaning and coherence to our lives, to tell us who we are and what we hold dear, to provide a bulwark against the encroaching tides of change . . ." (O'Connell Davidson, 2007, p. 10). Thus adults depend on the maintenance of the separate category of child to give direction to our lives.

Maintaining a clear line between child and adult creates circumstances under which children whose behavior is perceived as adult gives rise to alarm. Transgressions of this binary that occur on the terrain of sexuality create situations in which teachers feel they must intervene. For example, in reference to girls dressing "sexy," Cassie relates, "I tell girls straight up that they can't act like they're 19 when they're 8" (Cassie, personal communication, April 8, 2008). Cassie's comment suggests that an 8-year-old child who is acting like she is "supposed to" cannot exude sexuality that is reserved for adults. Children who do demonstrate sexualized, "adultified" (Ferguson, 2001) behaviors are deemed in need of rescue.[11] Children are easily molded into stereotypes of victimized childhood because they are seen as passive and helpless. According to O'Connell Davidson, children are often used to promote political projects that rely on the image of children as needing rescue.[12]

Cassie's statement evokes rescue narratives that have normalization as their aim. The rationale for these normalizing missions is also contingent on the reification of the child/adult binary made more transparent through issues that cohere around sexuality. Sexuality illuminates the difference between a "normal" child and one that may not be properly (de-)sexualized. Children who are "too knowledgeable" at a certain age, like the child described by Cassie, possess an understanding of sex that is seen as too adult, or not keeping within the lines of childhood. O'Connell Davidson (2007) writes:

> In contemporary Western societies, we *need* children to be passive, helpless and dependent, to be objects not subjects, for only then can they serve as conduits for our relationships with others; we *need* them to be empty, evacuated of individuality and agency, innocent and trusting, for only then can we inscribe on them the meaning that is lacking in the rest of our lives. And yet this fetishized view of "childhood" as a state of dependency, innocence and vulnerability is difficult to sustain, especially when children themselves often refuse to cooperate with it. (p. 22)

Therefore a girl who is "running around the class all sexy" does not exemplify appropriate child behavior—"sexy" is reserved for adults—and this is the rationale behind Cassie's educational intervention. That the boy in her classroom learns inappropriate sexuality from watching adult TV provides Cassie with a rationale for why this child exhibits disruptive and inappropriate sexual behaviors—his source of knowledge corrupts the child/adult binary.

Cassie's line of thinking reflects the ideology that provides rationale for civilizing missions that compel child rescue interventions. Child rescue interventions, which appear to be benevolent manifestations of humanitarian care, underscore the ideology that directs corrections in human behaviors. Charged with the task of correcting behaviors deemed deviant or inappropriate, teachers carry out the tasks of present-day civilizing missions of child rescue interventions, which could more accurately be called "normalizing missions" in the context of public schooling. These normalizing missions, then, rely on solidified notions of difference, which are maintained through dichotomizing binaries. The "taxonomic state," which Stoler (2006) uses to describe our ontology of categorization, equips us with ways of making natural differential treatment based on what we believe to be good and right for children—to wit, Mark's assertion that he "wouldn't want [kids] to think that [kissing] is what we do in a public place." And in another interview Grace, a third-grade teacher, asserts: "But they have to learn that in school, or in any public place, they can't do that." The interviews point to a pattern of response when children demonstrate that which is considered deviant or inappropriate sexuality.[13] The first thing teachers say they do is speak with the child exhibiting the behavior, as demonstrated by Monica's instruction on appropriate and inappropriate behaviors for school:

> Um, and I feel like in terms of what I feel like I've told kids, like, "This is inappropriate for school." Um, I've told them kissing is inappropriate for school. Even though I'll tell them there's nothing wrong with it, it's ok, but school is not the place for that. Because it's not. I wouldn't kiss, you know. Even if one of my loved ones was at school, I wouldn't sit there and kiss on the workplace or at school or . . . um . . . anything around nakedness. If they're like showing their underwear. I tell them that's totally inappropriate. And I feel like other things I've told them are inappropriate for school are touch—if anything physical is happening between two kids with any parts of their bodies, like, you know, their butt, or like their private. Or if another kid was touching another kid's nipple. I would feel like I would have to teach them that that's not appropriate. Like parts of the body that are just, like, you know, I'm not going to tell that to another kid if they're touching the kid's foot. You know? Unless they were doing it in a way that was like, "Maybe that's sexual!" It's not to me, so, like, I don't know. (Monica, personal communication, March 2, 2008)

There is then an informal conversation with parents to correct the undesired behaviors of the children, as noted in Mark's interview:

> First, I would talk to the student to try to figure out what was going on. And, you know, then I would let their parents know. And I would try to let their parents know in a non-punishment judgmental kind of way. (Mark, personal communication, March 28, 2008.)

Correcting behaviors seen by teachers as sexual establishes which acts are considered inappropriate, a process which Monica explains in detail. The process allows the children committing the acts, and those watching, to construct a repertoire of behaviors that should or should not be performed or spoken, as the case may be. The act of disciplining, and especially of calling on the parents to participate in tandem with teachers in the disciplining, has as its core a normalizing mission. Therefore, children who do not exhibit adultified sexual behaviors are seen as well-adjusted, normal children not in need of rescue (Ferguson, 2001; O'Connell Davidson, 2007).

Closing Lines

Attention to normalizing processes is essential to better understand operations of power. This is a political project in itself. Elementary schools, seen as benevolent and pure public spaces but wholly informed by and instructing of "an ideology which represents the School as a neutral environment purged of ideology" (Althusser, 1971, p. 156)—normalizing institutions that separate those who cannot achieve normal from those who appear to. But as Foucault (1978/1990) reminds us, attempting to achieve "normal" is a laborious project that is "bound to fail" (p. 42). So whether it is agreed that normalization should be a purpose of schooling or not, the processes that ensure that some children come out recognizably "normal," while others are identified as deviant, cannot be blamed on the children themselves. Normalizing missions require highly involved political and social labor, rooted in historical processes, and they have severely consequential outcomes. Therefore, to accept the role of schools as normalizing institutions, we must also accept them as institutions that serve to differentiate through dualisms and punitive tactics to identify deviance.

Sexuality highlights cultural and political tensions, and these tensions play out in our real and imagined worlds, and certainly in the context of schools. As McKay (1998) writes, "Because sexuality and the societal norms related to it carry such significance for the shape of society itself, sexuality has become the site of considerable social and moral conflict" (p. 20). Consequently, teachers are in a precarious and challenging position as thinking, critical actors in state institutions. They must constantly "walk the line" when dealing with the controversial issues that surround sexuality because it is not a socially accepted aspect of elementary school practices. They navigate, or walk the line, between the state (public) and the home (private). In doing so, they must also negotiate the meanings of children and sexuality, two categories that rely upon enforcing binaries.

As has been shown, there is little room for teachers to talk about sexuality as part of an official discourse, which means that discussions about sexuality are pushed to the peripheries of the school day. And because the concept of sexuality lacks concrete definition in common parlance, many of us often speak of sexuality without an agreed-upon understanding of its meaning. For example, Monica's comment that the sexuality of children often remains as "wondering in the head" articulates the amorphous quality of sexuality as a constant struggle to comprehend and put words to it; sexuality's tensions and challenges are evident in our vocabulary. For teachers who do see the significance of sexuality in elementary school life, institutionally they cannot enter into a conversation without risk of confusion or punitive repercussions, thus limiting possibilities for those who do not yet see its importance. Rendering visible some of these "lines of penetration" is necessary because only then will the silence and secrecy that now constrains our social condition be opened to (re)construct ways of being (and therefore knowing) that may cultivate more freedom.

Notes

1. Jean Piaget's (1969/2000) stages of cognitive development and Erik Erikson's (1950/1983) theory of socioemotional development hold the foundations of educational theory in elementary schools. These theories maintain that there is a natural development of human growth that progresses in stages through the life cycle.
2. All names have been replaced by pseudonyms to protect the privacy of the respondents.
3. If sexuality is understood as a "vector of power," then the term "children's sexuality/ies" is misguided. While children and adults may perform sexuality differently and be differently judged for their sexual expressions and while sexuality may have distinct effects on children and adults, sexuality as an organizing principle should be understood as a system similar to race. We would not differentiate adult race from children's race because race is a system of power that affects all.
4. Donna Haraway's text "Situated Knowledges: The Science Question in Feminism and the Privilege of Partial Perspective" has been pivotal in contesting the scientific method in intellectual inquiry. She instead argues for the "partial perspective" of "knowing subjects" as an acceptable basis for knowledge claims.

5. Undoubtedly, these lines also point toward whiteness. This paper, however pertinent the subject, does not account for a race analysis even though there are pronounced instances wherein race becomes salient (though admittedly understated). Future iterations of my writings will attend to the articulation of race and sexuality.

6. Foucault (1978/1990) discusses the regulation of children's sexual behavior through the intervention of doctors and teachers. He writes that the sexual behaviors of children became a "prop" that supported efforts to define that which was allowed visibility and that which would be relegated invisible (p. 42). The control of children's bodies, however, did not have the aim of eradicating sexual behaviors in children; on the contrary, what this management allowed for was the proliferation of a powerful "medico-sexual regime" with children as its support and the family as the object. In effect, this produced "indefinite lines of penetration" that enabled the construction of the acceptable and unacceptable as children and adults alike crossed these lines, thus marking themselves as either normal or abnormal (Foucault, 1978/1990, p. 42).

7. According to Althusser, ideology "represents the imaginary relationship of individuals to their real conditions of existence" and therefore has a "material existence." It interpellates, or hails, all individuals, and so we are always-already its subjects (pp. 109–119).

8. See *Funds of Knowledge* (2005) by Gonzalez, Moll, and Amanti for an in-depth look at the ways in which the home-school connection may be thought. Discourse on the home-school connection currently proliferates.

9. Consider the use of home visits by teachers and social workers to predominantly poor households. Moreover, living in a "small apartment" with multiple people creates a bodily proximity not experienced in more spacious (and expensive) accommodations, and the closeness of apartment units creates a loss of privacy. In this, and probably many other ways, privacy is "afforded."

10. Conceptually, childhood is perceived as a developmentally natural period of life distinct from adulthood. In this period, young people are supposed to be disabused of the corruptive burdens of adulthood.

11. In no way do I intend to assert that intervention should not happen under circumstances in which children have been sexually abused or harmed sexually. However, as O'Connell Davidson (2007) and Weis and Fine (1993) point out, the mainstream way in which youth sexuality has been theorized is through a narrative of victimization.

12. See also Aries, P. (1962), Prout and James (1997) for socio-historical accounts of child rescue narratives.

13. Many teachers admitted that there were times when they did not say anything at all to that which they categorized as sexual behaviors. Usually these behaviors were classified as "natural" by the teachers and therefore not in need of correction. Yet there were other times when teachers confessed that they turned away because they didn't want to deal with the ramifications. As Greta put it, "[T]here might be differences in culture, and I wouldn't want to impose my beliefs on the kids or make parents upset and have them come in all angry" (Greta, personal communication, March 14, 2008).

References

Althusser, L. (1971). Ideology & ideological state apparatuses. In *Lenin and philosophy and other essays* (pp. 127–186). New York: Monthly Review Press.

Apple, M. (2006). *Educating the "right" way: Markets, standards, God and inequality.* New York: Routledge.

Ariès, P. (1962). *Centuries of childhood: A social history of family life.* New York: Alfred A. Knopf.

Chatterjee, P. (1993). *The nation and its fragments: Colonial and postcolonial histories.* Princeton, NJ: Princeton University Press.

Erikson, E. (1993). *Childhood and society.* New York: W.W. Norton & Co. (Original work published 1950)

Ferguson, A.A. (2001). *Bad boys: Public schools in the making of black masculinity.* Ann Arbor: University of Michigan Press.

Foucault, M. (1977). *Discipline and punish: The birth of the prison.* New York: Pantheon.

Foucault, M. (1978/1990). *The history of sexuality: An introduction* (Vol. I). New York: Random House. (Original work published 1978)

Gonzalez, N., Moll, L.C., & Amanti, C. (Eds.). (2005). *Funds of knowledge: Theorizing practices in households, communities, and classrooms.* New York: Routledge.

Haraway, D. (1991). Situated knowledges: The science question in feminism and the privilege of partial perspectives. In *Simians, cyborgs and women: The reinvention of nature* (pp. 183–202). New York: Routledge.

Harper, P.B. (2000). The evidence of felt intuition: Minority experience, everyday life, and critical speculative knowledge. *GLQ: Journal of Lesbian and Gay Studies, 6*(4), 641–657.

McKay, A. (1998). *Sexual ideology and schooling: Towards a democratic sexuality education.* Albany: State University of New York Press.

O'Connell Davidson, J. (2007). *Children in the global sex trade.* Malden, MA: Polity Press.

Piaget, J., & Inhelder, B. (2000). *The psychology of the child.* New York: Basic Books. (Original work published 1969)

Prout, A., & James, A. (1997). A new paradigm for the sociology of childhood? In A. Prout (Ed.), *Constructing and reconstructing childhood* (pp. 7–33). New York: RoutledgeFalmer.

Renold, E. (2005). *Girls, boys and junior sexualities: Exploring children's gender and sexual relations in the primary school.* New York: Routledge.

Rubin, G.S. (1993). Thinking sex: Notes for a radical theory of the politics of sexuality. In H. Abelove, M.A. Barale, & D.M. Halperin (Eds.), *The lesbian and gay studies reader* (pp. 3–44). New York & London: Routledge.

Stoler, A. (2006). *Haunted by empire: Geographies of intimacy in North American history.* Durham, NC: Duke University Press.

Thorne, B., & Luria, Z. (1986). Sexuality and gender in children's daily worlds. *Social Problems, 33*(3), 176–190.

Weis, L., & Fine, M. (1993). *Beyond silenced voices: Class, race, and gender in United States schools.* Albany: State University of New York Press.

CHAPTER FOURTEEN

Becoming Mr. Cougar

Institutionalizing Heterosexuality and Homophobia at River High

C. J. PASCOE

Cheering students filled River High's gymnasium. Packed tightly in the bleachers, they sang, hollered, and danced to loud hip-hop music. Over their heads hung banners celebrating 50 years of River High's sports victories. The yearly assembly in which the student body voted for the most popular senior boy in the school to be crowned Mr. Cougar was under way, featuring six candidates performing a series of skits to earn student votes.

Like the other four Mr. Cougar candidates, Brent and Greg—both handsome, blond, "all-American" water polo players—paraded around the gym while students cheered in what looked a lot like a marriage ceremony. As Brent's name was announced, a female student emerged from the back of the gym holding up a poster board sign decorated with his name and his water polo number. Behind her, Brent, dressed in a tuxedo and flanked by his mother and a formally attired female escort, stepped out into the auditorium of raucous students. The quartet proceeded around the gym, pausing at each of three sets of bleachers so the students could applaud. Brent and his escort waved to their friends. His mother beamed as she held tightly to his arm. Brent stopped at the third set of bleachers to deposit her in a row of chairs specially designated for the mothers of the Mr. Cougar candidates. (No seats were provided for fathers or other relatives, who presumably sat behind them in the bleachers.) Brent planted a kiss on either cheek and proceeded around the remainder of the gym with his teenage escort. After all members of the "Top Six" (the six candidates who had received the most votes in the Mr. Cougar contest) had engaged in this procession, they disappeared behind a screen to ready themselves for their skits.

Moments later Brent and Greg entered the stage dressed like "nerds" to perform their skit, "Revenge of the Nerds." They wore matching outfits: yellow button-down shirts; tight brown pants about five inches too short, with the waistbands pulled up clownishly high by black suspenders; black shoes with white knee socks; and thick, black-rimmed glasses held together with white tape. As music played, the boys started dancing, flailing around comically in bad renditions of outdated dance moves like the Running Man and the Roger Rabbit. The crowd roared in laughter when Brent and Greg rubbed their rear ends together in time to the music. Two girls with long, straight hair and matching mini skirts and black tank tops, presumably the nerds' girlfriends, ran out to dance with Brent and Greg.

Suddenly, a group of white male "gangstas" sporting bandannas, baggy pants, sports jerseys, and oversized gold jewelry walked—or, more correctly, gansta-limped—onto the stage. They proceeded to shove Brent and Greg, who looked at them fearfully and fled the stage without their girlfriends. The gangstas encircled the two girls, then "kidnapped" them by forcing them off the stage. After peering timidly around the corner of the stage, Brent and Greg reentered. The crowed roared as Brent opened his mouth and, in a high-pitched, feminine voice, cried, "WE have to get our women!"

Soon a girl dressed in a sweat suit and wearing a whistle around her neck carried barbells and weight benches onto the stage. Greg and Brent emerged from behind a screen, having replaced their nerd gear with matching black and white sweat pants and T-shirts. The female coach tossed the barbells around with ease, lifting one with a single hand. The audience hooted in laughter as the nerds struggled to lift even the smallest weight. Brent and Greg continued to work out until they could finally lift the weights. They ran up to the crowd to flex their newfound muscles as the audience cheered. To underscore how strong they had become, Brent and Greg ripped off their pants. The crowed was in hysteria as the boys revealed, not muscled legs, but matching red miniskirts. At first Greg and Brent looked embarrassed, then they triumphantly dropped the skirts, revealing matching shorts, and the audience cheered.

Brent and Greg ran offstage as a stagehand unfurled a large cloth sign reading "Gangsta's Hideout." Some of the gangstas who had kidnapped the girlfriends sat around a table playing poker, while other gangstas gambled with dice. The nerds, who had changed into black suits accented with ties and fedoras, strode confidently into the hideout. They threw the card table in the air, causing the gangstas to jump back as the cards and chips scattered. Looking frightened at the nerds' newfound strength, the gangstas scrambled out of their hideout. After the gangstas had fled, the two miniskirted girlfriends ran up to Brent and Greg, hugging them gratefully. Several African American boys, also dressed in suits and fedoras, ran onto the stage, dancing while the former nerds stood behind them with their arms folded. After the dance, the victorious nerds walked offstage hand in hand with their rescued girlfriends.

This scene highlights the themes of masculinity I saw during a year and a half of fieldwork at River High School. The Mr. Cougar competition clearly illuminates the intersecting dynamics of sexuality, gender, social class, race, bodies, and institutional practices that constitute adolescent masculinity in this setting. Craig and Brent are transformed from unmasculine nerds who cannot protect their girlfriends into heterosexual, muscular men. This masculinizing process happens through a transformation of bodies, the assertion of racial privilege, and a shoring up of heterosexuality.

Like a wedding, this popularity ritual marks a transition to adulthood (Modell, 1989). The Top Six are handed off from an opposite-sex parent to an age- and gender-appropriate escort. In this case, the mother's relinquishing of her son to a female date, while receiving a chaste but sexualized sign of goodbye, the kiss, symbolizes the way certain heterosexual practices denote adulthood. As in a wedding ritual, the starring couple is dressed up in costume, cheered by others and posed for pictures so that the two remain linked in students' minds for years to come.

Though teenagers and sexuality are almost redundant concepts, schools are not necessarily thought of as sexual institutions. However, as indicated by this school-supported skit, schools themselves are organizer(s) of sexual practices, identities, and meanings. Beginning in elementary school, students participate in a "heterosexualizing process" (Renold, 2000) in which children present themselves as "normal" girls or boys through discourses of heterosexuality (see also Kehily, 2000; Robinson, 2005). Schools . . . regulate sexual meanings . . . in ways that are heteronormative and homophobic (Walford, 2000; Walters & Hayes, 1998). The ordering of sexuality from elementary school through high school is inseparable from the institutional ordering of gendered identities. This heterosexualizing process as organized by educational institutions cannot be separated from, and in fact is central to, the development of masculine identities.

While school rituals such as Mr. Cougar are a prime site for the affirmation and definition of normative sexual and gender identities, seemingly neutral areas of academic instruction also draw upon and reinforce normative definitions of heterosexuality (Letts & Sears, 1999). Heteronormative discourses permeate sex education curricula, which often feature a heterosexual married couple as the model for teen sexuality (Moran, 2000; Trudell, 1993) and biology classes, in which gendered metaphors are used to explain the fertilization process (Martin, 1996).

Formal and informal sexuality curricula, or the way sexuality is constructed at the level of the institution through disciplinary practices, student-teacher relationships, and school events (Trudell, 1993) encouraged students to craft normative sexual and gendered identities in which masculinity and femininity were defined by heterosexuality (Neilsen, Walden, & Kunkel, 2000). Through these institutional practices of heterosexuality, River High provided the scaffolding for an adolescent masculinity constituted by interactional rituals of heterosexuality and homophobia. Through school rituals, pedagogical practices, and disciplinary procedures, River High set up formal and informal sexual practices that reflected definitions of masculinity and femininity as opposite, complementary, unequal, and heterosexual (Butler, 1993).

Pedagogy: The Unofficial Gender and Sexuality Curriculum

The junior and senior social science classroom belonging to Ms. Macalister (whom students affectionately called Ms. Mac) was a shrine to heterosexuality. Ms. Mac was one of the most popular and effective teachers at River High. Short in stature, sporting high heels and an enormous personality, Ms. Mac infused the learning process with life and laughter. Walking into her room, students saw a row of floor-to-ceiling cabinets decorated with long, laminated ribbons designed to look like film from a movie reel. Down the center of these film rolls ran pictures of River students from proms and Winter Balls of years past. While a senior picture or two occasionally interrupted the parade of formal dresses and tuxes, the vast majority of the pictures showed boy-girl pairs dressed in their formal best. This had the effect of creating an environment in which a gender-differentiated heterosexuality was celebrated and made a focal point.

Ms. Mac established a comfortable rapport with her students through lighthearted teasing. Much of this teasing revolved around students' romantic relationships. One morning, as usual, friends Jeremy and Angela walked in late, chatting amiably. Ms. Mac looked at them and shook her head, sighing, "Ah, the couple of the year coming in late." Jeremy and Angela rolled their eyes and laughed as they took their seats. Ms. Mac's comment effectively transformed a cross-gender friendship into a heterosexualized pairing. In commenting on Jeremy and Angela this way, she turned them into a pair who would fit right in with the normative images on her wall.

Like other teachers, Ms. Mac frequently drew on and reinforced concepts of heterosexuality in her teaching. One day she was trying to explain to the students the "full faith and credit clause" of the U.S. Constitution, which states that one state has to honor another state's laws. Using marriage as an example, Ms. Mac was explaining that "if a state makes a law that twelve-year-olds can get married without their parents' permission . . ." when she was quickly interrupted by students yelling out things like "That's gross!" Ms. Mac presumably used marriage as an example to which all students could relate because of its assumed universality and ahistorical nature. However, she could have drawn on timely, social justice-oriented examples such as the Defense of Marriage Act and movements for gay marriage. She instead reinforced a narrative of heterosexuality that depends on a similar age of the two partners, involves the state sanction of that relationship, and encourages procreation as central to such a relationship.

Teachers at River High often felt the need to control a potentially out-of-control sexuality in the classroom, even though they drew on imagery of this same sexuality in their pedagogical practices. Invoking sexual examples and metaphors was a useful pedagogical tool that allowed teachers to communicate with students and hold their attention, but because teen sexuality was perceived as potentially explosive, teachers constantly sought to corral these same discussions. Ms. Mac for instance, walked this delicate line as she managed a class project in which students were supposed to create a political party. The students needed to outline a platform, design campaign goals, and develop fundraising strategies. Student groups created parties ranging from those that addressed serious issues, such as the Civil Rights Party and the Environmental Party, to fanciful parties such as the Party Party (devoted to—what else?—partying) or the Man Party, dedicated to ending women's suffrage.

The members of the Safer Sex Party, Jenny, Stephanie, and Arturo, planned to encourage condom use by handing out free condoms they had picked up at the local Planned Parenthood office. Jenny, to illustrate their point, held up a paper bag from which she withdrew a handful of multicolored condoms to show me. When the Safer Sex Party presented its project the next day, Ms. Mac panicked as they began to pass out condoms taped to pieces of paper with their party's slogan on them. Ms. Mac cried, "Oh, my goodness!" and looked at me wide eyed. Arturo read their statement of purpose, saying they had formed their party to "prevent HIV and AIDS." Chaos swept the class as students laughed and made jokes about the condoms. Ms. Mac sighed dramatically and repeatedly, muttering, "No, no no no no." Chad asked, "Can we have an example of safe sex?" Students laughed. Ms. Mac announced, with a note of pain, "Ladies and gentlemen, I'm just a little bit shocked by this. I could get fired. School board policy prevents the distribution of them. I'm going to have to collect these afterwards."

In this instance the condom served as a symbol around which social anxieties about teen sexuality coalesced. The condom was a "cultural object," or something that tells a story about the culture in which it is found (Griswold, 1994). It represented students' real or potential sexual practices. Ms. Mac certainly followed the school board's edict in her concern about students' sexual behavior and reflected the River High administration's general anxiety about it. This panic around the condom was ironic, as the students were acting, in this instance, as responsible sexual agents. Their political party was dedicated to promoting safer sex practices and stemming the spread of sexually transmitted diseases. With this goal they challenged River High's orthodoxy that students were not responsible enough to control their own sexual behavior by asserting that, in spite of their sex education curriculum, they did know about condoms and actually cared about their own and other students' sexual health.

The condom, as a cultural object, also illustrated the importance of heterosexual activity to masculine identities. While the girls tittered and laughed, it was the boys in the class for whom the link with sexual activity was important. For boys the condoms served as evidence of masculinity in that they were a proxy for heterosexual success. The boys were the ones who held on to the condoms instead of handing them back, made sure other students knew they held on to them, and attempted to gather more condoms. Chad also demonstrated his heterosexuality in a way that no girl did by requesting an example of "safe sex." Even Ms. Mac acknowledged the importance of condoms as symbols of virility when she specifically addressed the boys in the classroom as she tried to manage the condom distribution frenzy—"so all you guys who put them in your wallets, give them back." The condoms became concrete symbols of masculinity through their signification of heterosexual activity. The condoms both threatened the stability of the classroom (in the minds of the teachers and the school administrators) and symbolized masculinity by indicating sexual activity.

In addition to teaching practices built on shared understandings of heterosexuality, mild discourses of homophobia permeated student-teacher interactions. Homophobic jokes between teachers and students, usually boys, figured prominently in River High's unofficial sexuality curriculum. Such interactions were especially frequent in mostly male spaces such as the weight room or the auto shop classroom. While Ms. Mac worried about the potential sexual activity of the boys in her class (and seemingly ignored the sexism of the boys who formed the Man Party), other teachers teased boys for an obvious lack of heterosexual experience. Huey, a large, white junior who sported an outdated hightop haircut and walked with an oafish, loping gait, was a regular recipient of these sorts of homophobic taunts. His unfashionable clothing and sluggish interactional style marked him as an outcast. He wore his pants high on his waist, as opposed to the low-slung style favored by most boys, and tight-fitting shirts tucked into his pants, cinched by a belt. Other boys usually wore oversized shirts and certainly didn't tuck them neatly into their pants. Looking for approval from the other boys in auto shop, Huey continually pulled stunts of stunning stupidity, usually at the urging of other boys. One day when I walked into auto shop, the entire class was in an uproar, screaming about how Huey had run and dived headfirst into the hood of the old Volvo that sat in the center of the room. The boys frequently joked about Huey's hypothetical girlfriend. Mr. Ford, the art teacher, and Mr. Kellogg, the auto shop teacher, also teased Huey about his lack of heterosexual success. One afternoon, after school let out, Mr. Ford walked across the quad from the art room to stand with Mr. Kellogg in front of the auto shop room. He pointed across the quad at Huey, who was slowly loping toward them. Mr. Ford turned to Mr. Kellogg, saying, "I had to teach him a lesson. I turned around and caught Huey flipping me off. I said, 'You should be doing that to girls, not to me.'" Both Mr. Kellogg and Mr. Ford laughed as Mr. Kellogg said, "I don't even know if Huey knows what that is yet! But I'm sure somebody has told him." Although, like most gestures, flipping someone off or giving someone "the finger" has multiple meanings, and generally means one is simply disregarding another, in this instance Mr. Ford invoked its literal meaning—"fuck you." In doing so Mr. Ford invoked commonsense notions of masculinity in which, because Huey was a boy, he should be "fucking" girls, not Mr. Ford. This sort of interaction reaffirmed that, as a boy, Huey should be participating in masculine behavior such as engaging in sexual activities with girls. The comment also drew on a mild homophobia by reminding Huey that he should be "fucking" girls, not men.

Teachers commonly tuned a deaf ear to boys' homophobic and sexist comments. Ignoring or passively watching boys' sexist and homophobic comments often occurred in primarily male spaces where, if a teacher were to address every offensive comment students uttered, very little learning would take place. Mr. Kellogg, the auto shop teacher who had teased Huey, primarily ignored the boys' off-color comments about sexuality. One hot afternoon he sent the students out to disassemble lawn mowers as a way to practice dismantling car engines. A group of boys grabbed rubber mallets and began pounding away at the tires and other parts of the mowers instead of quietly dismantling them with screwdrivers the way they had been instructed to do the previous week. Presumably this wouldn't be how they would actually dismantle car engines. I laughed along with the boys, who had formed a circle around those who were ferociously beating a lawn mower. Colin, standing next to me in the circle, said, "We have a whole class of retards who hit like girls." Surprisingly, this was one of the few times I heard a boy insult another by comparing him to a girl (or to someone who was developmentally disabled). Before each hit, the boy wielding the mallet yelled out in a deep affected voice, "One time!" to indicate that he would remove a given piece of the lawn mower by hitting it only one time instead of requiring multiple tries. Sufficient destruction with one hit indicated a given boy's strength and competence. As Jayden positioned himself to swing the mallet, Mr. Kellogg, who stood next to me and rolled his eyes, gently reminded Jayden to move his ankle away from the mallet so that he wouldn't shatter it. After yelling "One time!," Jayden hit the lawn mower, but apparently not to his satisfaction. So he turned around, switched hitting hands, and cried in a high-pitched voice, "I'm a switch hitter." The circled audience laughed and chanted, "Switch hitter! Switch hitter!" Swishing his hips and lisping, Jayden continued, "I'll show you a switch hitter!" Josh yelled, "I bet you will!" The session concluded as Josh, disgusted and surprised, yelled, "Dude, you hit like a girl!" The boys in auto shop drew on images of both femininity—"you hit like a girl"—and bisexuality—"I'll show you a switch hitter." (A bisexual man was often referred to as a "switch hitter" or as someone who "played for both teams.") Mr. Kellogg not only ignored these comments, but seemingly wrote them off to "boys will be boys" behavior, for he shook his head and laughed at their antics.

None of this is to say that Mr. Kellogg meant to be homophobic. Rather, this sort of collective affirmation of masculinity provided one of the few ways in which teachers could build rapport with their students, though it replicated definitions of masculinity as homophobic and sexist. Joking about sexuality was a way for teachers to cross generational boundaries, illustrating to their students that they were not rendered completely irrelevant by their age. In this way teachers in both mixed- and single-sex classrooms curried boys' favor by catering to their senses of humor, often at the expense of girls' dignity.

While teachers must have heard students use derogatory words such as *fag, gay, dyke,* or—as in the previous instance—*switch hitter,* with one exception I never heard any reprimands. Mr. McNally, the drama teacher and the exception, instructed his students not to call things they thought were stupid "gay," comparing it to calling a pair of shoes they didn't like "Mexican." When I was explaining my research to his class, they asked me what sorts of things I took notes about. Among other things, I said that I took notes on situations in which it looked like "guys were being not guy enough." A slight male sophomore to my left asked, "You mean gay, like homosexual?" Mr. McNally piped in with:

> That's something we haven't talked about in this class yet. You guys have been really good and I haven't seen the need to talk about this, but we might as well, since we're on the subject. You know how people use the word *gay* and they're usually calling something stupid, right? Well I have a lot of friends who are gay and they aren't stupid. So when you call something gay and mean stupid, you're really calling my friends stupid! It's not like I go around saying, "Oh, that so Italian" or "Oh, that's so Mexican" or "Oh, that's so people-who-wear-blue-shirts!" So that sort of language is really not acceptable in this class, okay?

The students laughed at Mr. McNally's comparisons and seemed to receive this admonition seriously. Mr. McNally was the only teacher I saw specifically address this issue in or out of the classroom. But even Mr. McNally, who prided himself on creating a classroom environment in which homophobic slurs were not tolerated, let pass boys' sexualized insults and sometimes participated in these jokes. Consider Mr. McNally's interaction with Rob during his advanced drama class. Rob walked to the stage preparing to perform that day's assignment, a dramatic enactment of a song. He wore a black tank top, jeans, and black wrap-around glasses. His hair was cropped short and spiked up. He looked as if he had just stepped off the set of the movie *The Matrix*. Mr. McNally commented, "Rob's lookin' sharp with those glasses." This comment was followed by a short pause as the class grew silent. Then Mr. McNally asked, raising his eyebrows suggestively, "What are you doing after class, Rob?" The class cracked up. "It was on everybody else's mind!" Mr. McNally defended himself, laughing along with them. Although Mr. McNally had previously lectured the class on the inappropriateness of homophobic insults, he easily participated in a masculinized homophobic ritual in which he pretended to hit on Rob in order to make the class laugh, as if to remind them that they should laugh at men who hit on other men.

Heterosexist and homophobic discourses about masculinity permeated the educational process at River High. Heterosexual discourses were embedded in the physical environment of the classroom, teachers' instructional practices, and students' classroom behavior. Teachers used these discourses to illustrate instructional concepts in ways that presumably resonated with male students. That same sort of balancing act maintained by the administration between knowing about student sexual practices and discouraging any acknowledgment of such practices was reflected in these interactions between teachers and students, in which teachers used sexually loaded discussions to relate to students while simultaneously discouraging sexual activity. These sorts of practices primarily centered on boys; thus messages about sexuality were simultaneously messages about gender.

School Rituals: Performing and Policing Gender and Sexuality

As most students at River High would report, the major rituals of the school year were the Homecoming Assembly and football game, the Winter Ball, the Mr. Cougar Assembly, and the prom. Whether students loved them, hated them, or professed indifference, these rituals shaped and organized much of their school-based social lives. The centrality of ritual to social life in high school is little different from the centrality of ritual to social life in general. Sociologists and anthropologists have long noted that ritual is key to the formation and continuation of a society (Durkheim, 1995; Turner, 1966). Through rituals, members of a society reaffirm shared morality and values. School rituals are symbolic, bodily performances that affirm "in" and "out" groups, the normal and the abnormal (Light, 2000; Quantz, 1999), reproducing dominant understandings of race, gender, and class (Foley, 1990). School rituals don't just reflect heteronormative gender difference; they actually affirm its value and centrality to social life.

Performing Masculinity and Heterosexuality: Mr. Cougar

Years in advance, Mr. Cougar hopefuls talked about the election. John, a junior, spoke with me extensively about becoming Mr. Cougar. "It's neat," he told me with a smile on his face. "You wait for it all through high school. When you are a freshman you wait till you are a senior just to do it." Eric emphasized that Mr. Cougar was a "popularity contest." He expressed his frustration that he didn't qualify for the "Top Six," saying, "People want to be Mr. Cougar. Yeah, I wanted to be Mr. Cougar. But all it is is a popularity contest based on sports figures." This dual attitude toward the ritual echoed most boys' approaches to Mr. Cougar. They both wanted to become Mr. Cougar and rejected the whole endeavor because of its impossible standards. The Mr. Cougar ritual began toward the end of the basketball season when each student received a list including the names of every senior boy. Through a series of votes, the list was whittled down over the next few weeks to the six candidates referred to as the Top Six. From their freshman year on, students talked about the Top Six. Many set achieving membership in the Top Six as a goal early on in high school. During the weeks before the Mr. Cougar Assembly, candidates were featured prominently around school, with the Mr. Cougar nominees competing in lunchtime games. The day of the final election, an assembly was held in which all the candidates participated in skits in front of the entire student body. A panel of four teachers judged the skits. After the assembly the students voted for Mr. Cougar. That night the winning skit and the winner of the Mr. Cougar title were revealed at the basketball game.

Mr. Cougar skits, such as the "Revenge of the Nerds" skit that opened the chapter, illustrate the relationships between heterosexuality and masculinity, with girls often framed as a reward for masculine feats of strength. Randy Green and Freddy Martinez squared off in a similarly masculinized contest in their skit, "Wrestling World." The skit began with two boys carrying out a sign reading "Wrestling World, River High School 7:00 November 5." Loud music blared, and four boys emerged, sparring, onto the stage. Randy mouthed as a deep voice boomed over the speakers, "You ready to do this?" Freddy answered with an equally deep voice, "I'm totally ready." Two other wrestlers, wearing turquoise and white to indicate that they were from River's rival high school, Hillside, responded in high-pitched female voices, "Let's do this!" The student body laughed at the whiny "girl" voices. As in the "Revenge of the Nerds" skit, male imitations of seemingly female behavior drew laughter and derision from the audience.

Twenty girls ran out on stage to dance a choreographed routine while the wrestlers changed offstage. The girls' shirts indicated which team they supported, with the River supporters in gold and the Hillside supporters in turquoise. Freddy and Randy emerged in loose-fitting, white T-shirts and gym shorts. They warmed up by jumping rope, performing push-ups, and sparring with each other. Their Hillside opponents appeared, not in workout clothes, but in red long johns, cowboy boots, and cowboy hats, riding broomstick "ponies." They performed "girl" push-ups from their knees rather than their feet and made a big show of not being able to jump rope, instead tangling themselves up in the short rope. They concluded this fantastic display of incompetence and femininity by slapping each other in a manner students referred to as "girl-fighting," rather than sparring with each other like real boxers, as Freddy and Randy did.

As soon as the boys finished their warm-ups, the chorus to the disco hit "It's Raining Men" played over the speakers. Presumably leaving their competition aside, the boys from each team threw their arms over each other's shoulders and proceeded to high-kick together like a line of Rockettes. The crowd roared in laughter at this imitation of femininity. Suddenly the music switched to the theme song from the movie *Rocky* as the stagehands set up a wrestling ring. The wrestlers ran behind a screen to change into their outfits. Freddy and Randy emerged in sweats stuffed to make them appear huge and well muscled. As the music changed from the *Rocky* anthem to the "Oompah Loompah" chorus from the movie *Willy Wonka and the Chocolate Factory,* the Hillside team emerged skipping instead of strutting, and wearing bathrobes instead of sweat suits. They soon dropped the bathrobes, revealing tiny tight spandex wrestling singlets, at which point the audience laughed.

As the match began, surprisingly, the weaklings from Hillside High began to beat the River team. The crowd laughed hysterically as the supposed underdogs started to win the match. However, the River team soon recovered, and the match ended as Freddy picked up the skinniest Hillside wrestler and swung him around before tossing him out of the ring. After this sound defeat, Queen's "We Are the Champions" started to play. The dancing girls reappeared, and those wearing turquoise shirts ripped them off, revealing gold shirts, thus indicating that they were now aligned with the winning team from River. They ran up to Freddy and danced around him to a song repeating the lyric "What does it take to be number one?"

Much like the "Revenge of the Nerds" skit, "Wrestling World" tells a story of masculinity and heterosexuality at River High. The skit fostered and encouraged masculinity as heterosexual, with women as rewards for a job well done. Like Brent and Craig, Freddy and Randy showed that they were men deserving of the Mr. Cougar crown through their deep voices, their physical strength, and their recognition of femininity. More importantly, "hicks" from Hillside were held up as an object lesson. The audience was supposed to, and did, laugh at them for their "hick" (read poor) clothing, their lack of physical strength, and their high-pitched voices. Additionally, the audience was encouraged to laugh at all displays of male femininity when the boys threw their arms over one another's shoulders to perform high kicks as if they were Rockettes. School officials vetted these skits, so presumably they encouraged, agreed with, or at least saw as unproblematic these definitions of masculinity. By providing the space and institutional support for such rituals, the school, in effect, endorsed normative masculinity as heterosexual and dominant.

Policing Gender and Sexuality

While the school administrators, in dealing with the Mr. Cougar skits, seemingly turned a blind eye to overt displays of heterosexuality, they didn't do this in all situations. While expressions of sexuality were often encouraged or at least tolerated for white boys, for certain groups of students, especially African American boys, they were especially discouraged.

At River High, African American students, both boys and girls, were disproportionately visible, and the boys were disproportionately popular. This in-school status conflicted with their social status in the outside world, in which black men are disproportionately poor, jobless, and homeless. As James Earl Davis (1999) describes this seeming contradiction, "Black males are both adored and loathed in American schools. They are on the vanguard of hip-hop culture and set the standards of athleticism. On the other hand, they experience disproportionate levels of punishment and academic marginality" (49). African American boys move from the unjust disciplinary system of high school to a racist social and economic system. They are frequently under stricter disciplinary scrutiny than their white counterparts (Ferguson, 2000; Majors, 2001; Price, 1999). Black men in America are consistently seen as hypersexual and hypermasculine (Ross, 1998). Accordingly, at River High differential treatment often coalesced around African American boys' sexualized behaviors. The reclaiming of white women from the clutches of the gangstas in the Mr. Cougar sketch illustrates the assumed destructive potential of black male sexuality. This fear of black male heterosexuality is also revealed in the informal disciplinary regimes deployed around school rituals.

Each year River High School put on a dance show. During my fieldwork the show "Music Brings the People All Together" consisted of 24 different dance routines, some by individuals, most by groups, and a grand finale featuring the entire cast. Many of the dances were rather sexual. The dance show started off with a "can can" routine in which a line of girls dressed in period costume rapidly and repeatedly flipped up their skirts in the front and back, showing their underwear. It seemed that the entire point of the routine was to show their underwear as many times as possible.

The last routine was an ensemble piece (one of the seven mixed-gender dance routines) to "I've Had the Time of My Life," the theme song to the movie *Dirty Dancing*. The routine drew from the story line of the move, in which teenagers at an upscale resort in the 1950s are prohibited from dancing "dirty." Dancing in such a way that one's pelvis meets with another's in a grinding motion is forbidden. At the end of the movie the teenagers triumph at the resort's annual talent show in which the male lead, Johnny, and female lead, Baby, rebel against their parents' stodgy ways to dance "dirty" to the song "I've Had the Time of My Life." In the beginning of this routine, Ricky and Samantha stood in the middle of the stage facing each other and staring intently into each other's eyes, as do Baby and Johnny in the movie. Also, as in the movie, Ricky's hands ran seductively up and down Samantha's arms and sides as they began to gyrate their hips simultaneously in time to the music. The two continued to perform sexually evocative moves accompanied by sexually charged looks. Several minutes into the song all of the performers joined them to execute a final group dance, spilling out onto the floor of the theater in a celebration of "dirty dancing."

However, not all students were given free reign to dance this seductively. The 18th dance number was put on by the Pep Club, the name given to a group of primarily African American students, much to their frustration, by the school administration. The Pep Club, or Bomb Squad, as they renamed themselves, had formed to give black students a presence at school assemblies and games. The cheerleading squads, as at other schools, were primarily composed of white girls (Adams & Bettis, 2003). There were no African American members during my time there. African American girls at River were keenly aware of this, frequently noting the whiteness of the cheer squad as they performed at assemblies. One particular group of African American girls, many of whom were on the Bomb Squad, danced and sang through many of the assemblies. As the mostly white cheerleading team took the floor at the Fall Sports Assembly, one of these girls, Trisha, yelled out, "I don't see no black cheerleaders!" She was right: there were no black cheerleaders. They were mostly white and Asian, with a smattering of Latina girls. At another time I heard a white cheerleader make a similar comment when Sarah told me that African American girls who were talented dancers tried out for cheerleading but never made the squad.

The Bomb Squad had similar problems appearing on stage at school events. According to the Bomb Squad members, they often had trouble getting the school administration to let them perform at rallies and assemblies, even though the student body went wild as they performed their high-energy dance, step, and chanting routines.

The Bomb Squad's performance to an initially slow hip-hop song that picked up tempo as it continued opened with the six boys sitting in chairs and the girls dancing in front of them, gyrating their bottoms in front of the boys' faces. The boys eventually stood up to dance behind the girls, rotating their hips, but never touching the girls. At the end of the song, the group ran off the stage, the boys high-fiving and hugging each other, each yelling over the others, "I didn't touch her!" "I didn't either!" K.J. stopped to explain to me, "We'd get suspended if we touched the girls."

The next day in weight lifting, several of the boys explained to me that before the dance show several of the vice principals had come to watch the dances in order to give them official approval. While three of the dances were relatively sexual—the can can, the "dirty dancing" finale, and this routine—only the African American boys were singled out and given strict instructions not to touch the girls. The dancers in the finale were white, and in the can-can there were no boys. So while sexuality was certainly on display and approved of in the dance show, it was the relationship between race, gender, and sexuality that rendered black boys so potentially dangerous to the delicate balance of the (hetero)sexual order established by the school.

The problem here is not heterosexuality but a particularly racialized and gendered heterosexuality. Teenagers are seen as inherently sexual, and black men are seen as extremely sexual. So the sexual behavior of African American teenage boys is taken much more seriously than that of white boys.

In her study of sixth-grade African American boys, Ann Ferguson (2000) argued that teachers and administrators attributed an intentionality to African American boys' misbehavior that they did not attribute to white boys' misdeeds. When white boys misbehaved, teachers excused them with a resigned "boys will be boys" response. However, when African American boys joked, spoke out, or otherwise misbehaved in the classroom or schoolyard, adults at the school Ferguson studied assumed that they were doing so on purpose. This assumption of an adult intentionality results in harsher punishments for African American boys. By setting up a logic of institutionalized racism, this sort of treatment stunts their educational development. When white boys danced sexually with (usually white) girls, the administration didn't take note of it, possibly regarding it as a normal teenage behavior. It is highly unlikely that, much like the adults at the school Ferguson studied, the administrators at River saw African American boys' sexual behavior as adult and intentional. African American boys embodied contradictions in that they were both profoundly threatening and profoundly disempowered in the world of River High.

Gender and Sexuality Regimes

The social space of River High was a complex cultural arena in which students, teachers, and administrators invested in and reproduced larger cultural meanings around gender and sexuality. Because of that, River High's structuring of gender and sexuality was, in the end, unremarkable but important because it provided the context in which boys and girls forged gendered and sexual identities. As teachers and administrators told me when I first entered the school, it indeed felt like a school out of Middle America. It wasn't just that the school was objectively average, it was that the students and administrators saw it that way. Students often spoke of "Cougar Pride" or "tradition" without embarrassment. I expected to hear sarcasm, but instead I heard an earnest passion in their voices as they talked about what they liked about River. Some even talked about returning to teach at River like Mr. McNally, the drama teacher, or Mr. Hobart, the principal. Their ordering of the heterosexual matrix was interesting precisely because it was the stuff of everyday life. In time-honored high school rituals, masculinity and femininity were produced as opposite and unequal identities primarily through heterosexual practices, metaphors, and jokes.

River High's administrators, like many parents and policymakers, were wary of teens' burgeoning sexuality. They feared that too much information or too much discussion of sex might encourage the students to engage in all sorts of irresponsible behaviors. In a nation that views teenage pregnancy rates as a sign of its moral worth, refuses to provide single and unemployed mothers with sufficient financial support, and is deeply divided about abortion, sex is indeed a scary subject. Ms. Mac's terror about the loss of her job in the face of students' distribution of condoms illustrates how seriously school boards, parents, and some teachers take the issue of teen sex. However, teachers must also navigate the everyday educational process. They somehow must engage students in learning about things that seem foreign to their own lives, such as the Interstate Commerce Act or the Fourteenth Amendment. To this end, Ms. Mac took a path several other teachers do: she used examples about sex. That way she could forge rapport with students by catching their attention (wow—my teacher is talking about sex!) and relating a seemingly esoteric subject to topics that permeated much of student life—sex and romantic relationships. But the way she deployed sexual talk in her pedagogy was not neutral. That is, her sex talk was directed primarily at boys—assuming, for instance, that they were the ones interested in condoms. It seemed that girls' subjectivity was tangential to course work—as when a group of boys formed the Man Party, literally dedicated to rolling back women's citizenship rights, with no repercussions. Similarly, male teachers curried boys' attention by allowing sexist and homophobic conversations and practices to go unchecked.

River High School rituals mirrored society's expectations of a dominant, white heterosexual masculinity and a sexually available femininity. Boys were represented in these rituals as heterosexually successful and physically dominant over girls and over weaker boys. They repeatedly emphasized their masculinity by losing their feminine voices, beating other boys into submission, and validating their heterosexuality by "winning" girls. Girls, conversely, were represented as sexually available in both the yearbook pictures and the homecoming skits. The administration, for all of its fear about teen sexuality, organized and funded school rituals that fostered a sexist heterosexuality, with girls as sexual objects or rewards.

It seemed that the administrators, the teachers, and the kids were trying to accomplish the task of education and socialization in the best way they knew. This task and the way these students were taught to become adult men and women illustrate not just the particularities at River High but the ambivalence and anxieties we, as a society, feel about issues of gender, sexuality, and race.

References

Adams, N.G., & Bettis, P.J. (2003). *Cheerleader! An American icon.* New York: Palgrave Macmillan.

Butler, J. (1993). *Bodies that matter.* New York: Routledge.

Davis, J.E. (1999). Forbidden fruit: Black males' constructions of transgressive sexualities in middle school. In W.J. Letts IV & J.T. Sears (Eds.), *Queering elementary education: Advancing the dialogue about sexualities and schooling* (pp. 49–59). Lanham, MD: Rowman & Littlefield.

Durkheim, E. (1995). *The elementary forms of religious life.* New York: The Free Press.

Ferguson, A. (2000). *Bad boys: Public schools in the making of black masculinity.* Ann Arbor: University of Michigan Press.

Foley, D. (1990). The great American football ritual: Reproducing race, class and gender. *Sociology of Sport Journal, 7,* 111–135.

Griswold, W. (1994). *Cultures and societies in a changing world.* Thousand Oaks, CA: Pine Forge Press.

Ingraham, C. (1999). *White weddings: Romancing heterosexuality in popular culture.* New York: Routledge.

Kehily, M.J. (2000). Understanding heterosexualities: Masculinities, embodiment and schooling. In G. Walford and C. Hudson (Eds.), *Genders and sexualities in educational ethnography* (Vol. 3, pp. 27–40). Amsterdam: JAI.

Letts, William J. (2001). When science is strangely alluring. *Gender and Education, 13*(3), 261–274.

Letts, W.J., & Sears, J.T. (Eds.). (1999). *Queering elementary education: Advancing the dialogue about sexualities and schooling.* Lanham, MD: Rowman & Littlefield.

Light, R. (2000). From the profane to the sacred: Pre-game ritual in Japanese high school rugby. *International Review for the Sociology of Sport, 35*(4), 451–463.

Majors, R. (2001). Cool pose: Black masculinity and sports. In S. Whitehead and F. Barrett (Eds.), *The masculinities reader* (pp. 208–217). Cambridge: Polity.

Martin, K. (1996). *Puberty, sexuality and the self: Boys and girls at adolescence.* New York: Routledge.

Modell, J. (1989). *Into one's own: From youth to adulthood in the United States, 1920–1975.* Berkeley: University of California Press.

Moran, J. (2000). *Teaching sex: The shaping of adolescence in the 20th century.* Cambridge, MA: Harvard University Press.

Neilsen, J.M., Walden, G., & Kunkel, C.A. (2000). Gendered heteronormativity: Empirical illustrations in everyday life. *The Sociological Quarterly, 41*(2), 283–296.

Price, J. (1999). Schooling and racialized masculinities: The diploma, teachers and peers in the lives of young, African American men. *Youth and Society, 31,* 224–263.

Quantz, R.A. (1999). School ritual as performance: A reconstruction of Durkheim's and Turner's uses of ritual.

Educational Theory, 49(4), 493–513.

Renold, E. (2000). "Coming Out": Gender, (Hetero)Sexuality and the Primary School. *Gender and Education, 12*(3), 309–326.

Robinson, K. (2005). Reinforcing hegemonic masculinities through sexual harassment: Issues of identity, power and popularity in secondary schools. *Gender & Education, 17*(1), 19.

Ross, M.B. (1998). In search of Black men's masculinities. *Feminist Studies, 24*(3), 599–626.

Trudell, B.N. (1993). *Doing sex education: Gender politics and schooling.* New York: Routledge.

Turner, V. (1966). *The ritual process: Structure and anti-structure.* Ithaca, NY: Cornell University Press.

Walford, G. (2000). Introduction. In G. Walford & C. Hudson (Eds.), *Genders and sexualities in educational ethnography* (Vol. 3, pp. 1–6). Amsterdam: JAI.

Walters, A.S., & Hayes, D.M. (1998). Homophobia within schools: Challenging the culturally sanctioned dismissal of gay students and colleagues. *Journal of Homosexuality, 35*(2), 1–23.

Warner, M. (1993). Introduction. In M. Warner (Ed.), *Fear of a queer planet: Queer politics and social theory* (Vol. 6, pp. vii–xxxi). Minneapolis: University of Minnesota Press.

CHAPTER FIFTEEN

The Right Way to Be Gay

How School Structures Sexual Inequality

KATHLEEN O. ELLIOTT

This chapter reports on findings from 18 months of ethnographic research conducted at Midwest High School, a large public high school with approximately 2,000 students, located in a mid-sized midwestern city. The city is known as a socially and politically liberal place, and, as a school, Midwest reflects these perspectives. Many students consider themselves "liberal," and the school officially supports numerous diversity initiatives, including those related to sexual diversity. The surrounding community is predominately white, a fact that was once mirrored in the student population at Midwest. However, as the area has grown, school demographics have become more diverse. While most teachers and staff are white, as are 56% of students, there are growing and increasingly visible numbers of African American and Latino students. Thirty-two percent of all students at Midwest receive free and reduced-priced lunch. Just as racial demographics have changed, so too have sexual demographics. During my time at the school, there was a small but significant number of out LGBT students, a fact that some faculty commented on as a relatively new phenomenon. While the majority of these students were white, there was also a small number of queer students of color who were out at the school. Changes in student demographics, whether related to race, social class, or sexuality, brought increased awareness of diversity to the school and also created new divisions among students. This chapter will discuss these processes as they relate to students' intersecting sexual, gender, and racial identities and will sketch the contours of the fluctuating lines of inclusion and exclusion within school culture.

School Culture at Midwest: The Middle Ground

There are few better places for an educational researcher studying gender and sexuality to be than in the hallways of a high school. One can learn a lot by hanging out in the hallway—about social groups and how they interact, about teacher-student relationships, about what is going on and who is important on any given day in the social life of a school. The hall at the main entrance to Midwest High School—centrally located at the intersection of the two main wings of classrooms, close to the library and the main office—was perhaps the best place to see and be seen. I spent a great deal of time there during the months I spent at Midwest working with diverse students to examine how youth construct and experience their gender and sexual identities in relation to the school. This informal, transient space was a rich arena within which students negotiated school culture and where the meanings of sexuality, identity, inclusion, and exclusion were culturally produced and reproduced.

While it took a great deal of time to get to know the deeper workings of social life within Midwest, it did not take long at all to get an initial sense of what this life entailed, what characteristics were valued or derided, how to gain and retain status in the building. On my first trip through the entryway, making my way through the crowd of students moving from one side of the building to the other, I could clearly hear it all around me. "You're such a fag!" a white male student yelled at another as they passed each other. "That's so gay," another student exclaimed in response to her friend's story. As the year progressed, the cacophony of homophobic language continued. Homophobia was central to students' modes of interacting, and it was not limited to language. As is common in schools across the country, homophobic behavior was also widespread. The great majority of the LGBT students I worked with at Midwest described experiences of harassment, isolation, and/or discrimination at school. This behavior was sometimes explicit and even violent. Other times it was more subtle, more "under the table," as one freshman described it. The ubiquity of homophobic language and behavior marks the centrality of sexuality, specifically heterosexuality, to social life at Midwest. It also illustrates the power of particular structures and expressions, particular ways of understanding masculinity, femininity, and sexuality, that support continuing sexual inequality, discrimination, and violence.

Unfortunately, it is not unusual to find homophobic language being used in a U.S. high school. In this way, Midwest was representative of a national culture in which homophobic discourse, discrimination, and violence continue unabated. However, in other ways, perhaps most notably in its policies regarding sexual inequality, Midwest stood out from the norm. Midwest promoted an official culture of tolerance aimed at increasing support for LGBT students at the school. I enter into a broader examination of the struggles over school policy that were involved in the production of this culture of tolerance elsewhere (Elliott, 2010). In general, the school, as a community, relied on the concept of "tolerance" to guide its understanding of creating a diverse and inclusive school environment, a concept that has been critiqued by scholars of anti-racist and anti-homophobic education for failing to address the complexities and structural roots of inequalities related to race, class, and sexuality (Agid & Rand, 2007; Brown, 2006; Nieto, 2006). At Midwest, administrators, faculty, and students repeatedly described the school as "tolerant" or "open." The school had policies in place for responding to homophobic harassment, taught comprehensive sexuality education that included information about LGBT health and sexualities, had a visible and very active Gay-Straight Alliance (GSA), and had a small but visible number of out LGBT students, some of whom occupied leadership positions within the school. In addition, the district employed an LGBT resource specialist to serve as an advocate for LGBT students and act as liaison between schools and families. As Casey, a sophomore girl, explained, "I really think the majority of people are really understanding and very, very chill about the whole thing," a description that I heard from the majority of students, including some LGBT students. Casey's description references the increasing comfort with queer sexuality that some argue exists among a new generation of young people who are more knowledgeable about and more open to sexual diversity than previous generations (Cloud, 2005; Savin-Williams, 2005).

As these brief descriptions indicate, Midwest occupied a space in between the often dichotomous illustrations of schools as either welcoming or dangerous places for LGBT youth. And, similar to what Linville (2009) found in her work with youth in New York City, Midwest students inhabited ground between understandings of youth as unprecedentedly accepting and rigidly homophobic. At Midwest, students lived in the space between absolute acceptance and total derision of sexual diversity. They viewed themselves as tolerant yet still used anti-gay language. LGBT students said that their school was accepting and then described experiences of homophobic harassment. Linville explains, "LGBTQ teens may sense that school is fine and free of homophobia and, at the same time, that the least safe place they find themselves is school, without this being a contradiction" (Linville, 2009, p. 155). In this way, school becomes both a source of support and a dangerous space for LGBT students. At Midwest, district policies and school practices that aimed to promote a more tolerant school environment, together with the increasing visibility and acceptance of sexual diversity in the broader community and in the school, did lend support to some LGBT students and had a positive impact on school culture. However, these policies and institutional support mechanisms did not eradicate homophobic behaviors and attitudes, and they did not support all LGBT students equally. The impact of policies like these was mediated by entrenched structures of gender, social class, and race that influenced diverse LGBT students' experiences in different ways. Indeed, increased acceptance and continued discrimination represent opposite but simultaneous aspects of the culture at Midwest.

Utilizing queer theory, researchers like Linville have provided tools for examining this in-between space and for understanding the complexity of students' experiences and perceptions of sexual inequality in their schools (Linville, 2009; Kumashiro, 2001; Rasmussen, 2006). They stress the importance of using the deconstructive project of queer theory to look beyond the binary descriptions that promote simplistic understandings of schools and the youth they serve. Queer theory enables the recognition of fluidity in students' identities and understandings, fluidity that may play a central role in creating greater acceptance of sexual diversity and breaking down old gender and sexual hierarchies. These insights are important for understanding the complexity of students' experiences and of the processes of social change that can occur among youth in schools. It is important to recognize that changes surrounding the acceptance of sexual diversity among young people do not occur in a simple progression, for example from homophobic attitudes to more accepting, equity-oriented perspectives, but rather are negotiated and contested within the fluid middle space that I found in my work at Midwest. It is equally important to explore how this fluidity, and how students' identities, experiences, and attitudes, are mediated by institutions like schools and structured by other aspects of their own and each others' negotiated identities. In this chapter, I discuss what this in-between space looked like in one school and how students' diverse experiences of sexuality were structured within the institutional school setting. I explore the realities for diverse LGBT students of a school that fostered both increased acceptance and continued homophobia. Ultimately, I examine the way that sexual inequality was structured at Midwest and how, as new acceptance of sexual diversity opened among students, new borders of exclusion were also drawn along both new and familiar lines.

The Diverse Experiences of LGBT Students at Midwest

As I conducted this research and got to know LGBT students at Midwest, I found the diversity of their experiences striking. Much of the literature on LGBT youth in schools seeks to illuminate the injustices these students face in educational institutions structured by homophobia. These studies document the harsh realities of many queer youth in schools, including harassment, assault, and isolation (Bochenek & Brown, 2001; Filax, 2003; O'Conor, 1995). This is important work. Yet as others have pointed out (Savin-Williams, 2005), there is a danger in the narrow representation of all LGBT youth as homogeneous and as victims. It is important to tell a more complete story of queer youth in school, one that accounts for the complexity of real lives. Some researchers have recently begun a "movement away from a focus on abjection and survival" (Rasmussen, 2006, p. 3), exploring the ways in which LGBT students across the country respond to homophobia with organizing, activism, and pride, rather than with isolation and self-hatred (Mayberry, 2007; Mayo, 2004; Miceli, 2005). Others have shed light on the diversity of LGBT students' experiences and how the intersections of other identity markers, particularly race and social class, affect these experiences in different ways (Kumashiro, 2001; McCready, 2001).

At Midwest, diverse LGBT students experienced the school and their intersecting identities very differently. While Midwest promoted a culture of tolerance that, in some ways, was successful in improving the school's climate for LGBT students, tolerance and acceptance were not extended to all LGBT students. For example, not all of them experienced homophobic harassment in the same way or to the same extent. They also dealt with these experiences in different ways. Some sought to fit in with the school's dominant, heterosexual norms. These students tried to make their queer sexuality invisible. Others became activists, directly challenging the school's culture. At Midwest, whether an LGBT student experienced acceptance or derision depended significantly on her/his racial, social class, and gender identities, as well as on the level of activism she/he engaged in against homophobia at the school. The diverse experiences of the LGBT students I worked with demonstrated the limits of tolerance at Midwest and how the culture of tolerance incorporated traditional norms that had been slightly modified in ways that reinforced, rather than dismantled, dominant discourses of gender and sexuality. As the experiences of the students whose stories follow illustrate, at Midwest, there was a right way—and many wrong ways—to be gay.

Fitting into the Culture of Tolerance

At Midwest, those LGBT students who were socially successful and accepted were white, middle-class boys who identified as gay and exhibited gender identities that aligned closely with the norms of dominant white, middle-class masculinity at the school. These students often occupied leadership positions at the school and participated in activities such as athletics and student government that were valued highly in school culture. Because of their participation in school activities, these students, though small in number (I knew or knew of five or six such students) were relatively visible. Though out at school, they attempted in most other ways to fit into the dominant, hetero-centric culture. These students described Midwest as tolerant and said that they did not experience any harassment or discrimination because of their sexual identities. Dan exemplified this type of student at Midwest.

Dan was one of the most traditionally "successful" LGBT students at Midwest. A white, middle-class freshman, he came out as gay the summer before his freshman year. He was a high-achieving student, president of the freshman class, and a member of the track team. He described enjoying school and said that he did not experience any homophobia or harassment. He said, "I don't get made fun of at all. Nobody ever, I mean, nothing. People may say stuff behind my back, but they're not going to make fun of me openly, um, they just see me and, I mean, I'm pretty normal." In fact, Dan was often heralded by his peers for being more "normal" than some other LGBT students and for not being "in your face" about his sexuality. When the students I worked with described Midwest as tolerant, they often used Dan as the primary example to illustrate their point. He was the student most often mentioned by heterosexual students when they described having LGBT friends, and his position as the freshman class president was often cited as an example of how accepting the school was of sexual diversity.

Significantly, Dan downplayed his sexual identity and adhered closely to norms of dominant, white masculinity at the school. He dressed in a preppy manner, usually wearing jeans or khakis and a sweater or button-down shirt. In fact, he was part of a group of popular students referred to simply as the "preps." He was a member of the track team, participated in school functions, and even used the sexist and homophobic language common among heterosexual male students. He used words like "fag" in disparaging ways and sometimes participated in the name-calling and verbal harassment of his LGBT peers. His appearance and behavior allowed Dan to fit into the culture of tolerance at Midwest. He was gay and officially out; however, aside from adopting this public label, he minimized all other aspects of his sexual identity. Unlike many students at Midwest, both heterosexual and queer, he did not exhibit his sexuality at all. He did not talk about sexual attraction or relationships, and he did not date or act on any potential sexual or romantic feelings. Rather, he adopted a sexual identity that was almost completely non-sexual. At the same time, he emphasized those aspects of his identity, such as his athleticism and clean-cut, masculine appearance that adhered to norms of dominant, white masculinity at the school. Still, Dan was out as gay at the school. In this way, he was not "passing" as or pretending to be heterosexual. Rather, by emphasizing his dominant gender identity and effectively negating most aspects of his sexual identity, he exemplified the "safe" gay student—one who was gay and out but who did not threaten or transgress the boundaries of dominant constructions of gender or sexuality. In this way, Dan created an identity that fit within the bounds of the culture of tolerance, which allowed him to be accepted by his school community.

For Dan, fitting into the dominant culture at Midwest involved downplaying his sexual identity and adhering to dominant gender norms. It also required him to differentiate himself from some of the other LGBT students who adopted a visible, activist position at the school. He explained, "So, like, I'm gay and, um, well, I don't really have any friends here who are gay, but I know of people who are gay and there's a big difference between me and them." He saw these students as drawing unnecessary attention to themselves through their appearance, behavior, and/or activism. He said, "So the people who are gay here, many of them that I see are very, I mean, they go to GSA, they are very into rights and [here he adopted a high-pitched, demanding voice to impersonate these "other" LGBT students] 'you need to change, I want my rights, you guys all need to do this for me because I'm being,' you know, and they kind of get up in people's faces." He continued, adding, "And then, these people, many of them, like, you know, dress differently, a lot of them dye their hair, they talk differently." Dan attributed the homophobic harassment that some LGBT students experienced to these students' behavior and appearance. He explained, "You need to expect to get made fun of if you're going to act that way." In this way, he individualized the homophobia that some students experienced, attributing it to personal decisions regarding dress or behavior and effectively pathologizing those students who did not fit within the culture of tolerance at the school.

Outside the Limits of Tolerance

In many ways, Dan and students like him can be seen as a success story. He was an out gay student who was accepted by his school community, occupied a leadership position in the school, and said that he did not experience any homophobic harassment from his peers. However, not all LGBT students at Midwest experienced this kind of acceptance. In fact, the majority of LGBT students I worked with described experiences of homophobic harassment or discrimination and occupied less visible, and less powerful, positions at the school than their heterosexual peers or students like Dan. In fact, for most out LGBT students, their peers were far from being "very chill about the whole thing." As Ryan, a freshman who identified as bisexual, put it, "Everyone always says, oh, it's really tolerant. Well, it's really tolerant in that . . . well, as long as you keep it to yourself it's tolerant." Failure to "keep it to yourself" could take many forms at Midwest. LGBT students who exhibited non-conforming gender identities, expressed their sexualities, or engaged in activism against homophobia at the school were often described as being too "in your face" about their sexualities, a description that marked these students as falling outside the boundaries of tolerance at the school. Queer students of color also encountered less acceptance than their white LGBT peers. Sam, a white sophomore, and Tara, a Latina junior, were two students who illustrated the boundaries of tolerance at Midwest.

When students talked about LGBT students who were "in your face" about their sexualities, they often used Sam as their illustrative example. Like Dan, Sam was white and middle class, and he came out as bisexual in the eighth grade. Sam was also a high-achieving student, but unlike Dan, he exhibited a non-conformist gender identity. He often wore tights under shorts or torn pants with a long coat. He wore multiple pieces of hemp jewelry and had long hair that he often kept deliberately shaggy. Sam was very politically active both in and out of school. He was the president of the school's Gay-Straight Alliance and was involved in queer youth organizations. He identified with the wider gay community and was active in social and political movements for sexual equality. At school, Sam had experienced significant homophobic harassment, both verbal and physical, although he did not like to call himself a "victim" of harassment. During his freshman year, he experienced daily abuse from a classmate that left him feeling isolated and angry. When he approached one of the school's guidance counselors about the issue, he was told that he needed to "learn to deal with it," a recommendation that echoed Dan's effort to individualize structural homophobia. It was not until his parents complained to the school and contacted the district's LGBT resource specialist that the school intervened. Sam rearranged his class schedule and the harassment stopped.

While Sam described Midwest as relatively tolerant—"better than lots of places"—he was quick to add, "People do have their homophobia ingrained in them. And, like, with masculinity and femininity, you have to prove it. You have to prove what you are." Here, Sam explained the importance of gender norms to students' experiences of sexuality and the culture of tolerance at Midwest. Many LGBT students did not differentiate between discrimination based on their sexuality and that based on their non-conforming gender identities. In this way, gender norms emerged as a proxy for the limits of tolerance at Midwest. While students' declarations of sexual identity could be "tolerated" within the school's cultural norms, the expression of their sexualities through alternative gender expressions or activism was not. Such failure to "keep it to yourself" placed LGBT students outside the boundaries of the culture of tolerance (Elliott, 2010).

Tara was a Latina junior who identified as a lesbian. Unlike both Dan and Sam, Tara was not a high-achieving student. In fact, she had a history of discipline problems and truancy, and she struggled with isolation and anger resulting from years of harassment and even abuse. She was considered by many teachers to be a problem student. Tara exhibited a masculine gender identity. She dressed in baggy T-shirts and jeans in the style popular among Latino boys at the school and wore her long hair pulled back in a low ponytail. She was friends with a group of Latino students known to be a bit "rough" as some teachers described them to me. During my time at Midwest, Tara had recently joined the GSA, but was not involved in any other school activities. She described the school as "50/50 accepting of homosexuality" and said that she experienced verbal and physical harassment, though she tended to downplay both. "I hear things a lot in school. Like people will yell, 'There goes the faggot.' People don't say it right to me, but I hear it. I try not to let it hurt me." She also described instances wherein a group of boys would physically harass her. "Guys would be feelin' on me and saying, like, does this make you straight? How about this? I'd just be like, no, you look like a chick and try to get them to stop. They were doing it to be funny in front of people. Let's make the lesbian straight, you know?" Situations like these, the violence of which cannot be understated, marked Tara's experience at Midwest and illustrated how her experiences were racialized, gendered, and sexualized in ways that those of white queer boys were not.

Unlike Sam's, Tara's parents did not intervene with the school on her behalf. It was not until her behavior problems necessitated intervention from district officials that any adult learned about or became involved in her situation. Tara was a middle-class Latina; however, she was adopted and her parents were both white. As educated professionals, they may have had the ability to intervene on her behalf had Tara shared her experiences with them. However, Tara's parents reacted negatively when she came out to them as a lesbian and were uncomfortable with her gender identity. In fact, Tara initially continued to date boys in an attempt to force herself to be heterosexual. While she and her parents were working to improve their relationship, their lack of support made her reluctant to turn to them when she experienced problems at school related to her sexuality. Her example illustrates the importance of parental support for LGBT students' access to institutional support mechanisms.

Like Sam's, Tara's non-conforming gender identity and activism as a member of the GSA placed her outside the bounds of tolerance at Midwest. Her status was compounded by her racial identity, which reinforced constructions of her as a problem student within the dominant white culture at the school. In these ways she failed to fit within the confines of accepted queer sexuality, and she experienced both verbal and physical harassment. Along with Sam and the majority of out LGBT students at Midwest, Tara exemplified the "wrong" way to be queer at the school.

New Lines of Exclusion at Midwest

The diverse experiences of the LGBT students I worked with illustrate the realities of tolerance at Midwest and demonstrate its limits. Although the majority of the administration, faculty, and even student body described the school as tolerant and could offer tangible evidence of school policy or student experience to support their claim, ultimately, the culture of tolerance at Midwest reinforced, rather than dismantled, dominant structures of gender and sexuality. The slight redefinition of dominant norms of sexuality that allowed some LGBT students to be out and accepted by their school community relied on the reification of other dominant structures, such as gender and race. This process opened the boundaries of tolerance just enough to allow a minority of LGBT students inside, further marginalizing the majority of LGBT students at the school.

In the process of redefining the boundaries of tolerance at Midwest, there was a restructuring of power dynamics within the school. For example, on the one hand, dominant structures of sexuality became slightly less powerful, allowing greater comfort and familiarity with sexual diversity in general. On the other hand, gender emerged as a more dominant organizing principle at the school. The most traditionally successful queer students at the school—those who were socially accepted, involved in school activities, and/or occupied leadership positions—were white, middle-class boys who, like Dan, adhered closely to dominant gender norms and expressions. Their constructions of dominant masculinity included the use of sexist and homophobic language and required the silencing of their queer sexualities. Like Dan, these students adopted non-sexual LGBT identities that did not challenge dominant gender frameworks or disrupt the school's heterosexist culture. These students' traditional gender identities, together with their white, middle-class status, allowed them access to other structures of power within the school that made it easier for them to transgress sexual boundaries while still being accepted within the culture of tolerance.

However, if LGBT students expressed their queer sexual identities, adopted non-conforming gender identities, or were outspoken about homophobia in the school, this tolerance was withdrawn. This is evident in the experiences of gay male students who expressed less traditionally masculine gender identities, like Sam, as well as masculine lesbians, like Tara. These students' "in your face" sexual identities, non-conforming gender identities, and activism around LGBT issues explicitly challenged dominant structures of gender and sexuality at the school and, therefore, set them outside the boundaries of tolerance. These students described experiences of harassment, and they occupied less powerful academic and/or social positions within the school than students like Dan.

There were important distinctions among the experiences of all of the LGBT students with whom I worked at Midwest. They experienced different levels of acceptance or derision and of access to institutional support structures. Many factors contributed to this variance in LGBT student experiences, from family support and personal relationships to individual personality to larger structures such as gender, race, and social class. However, despite these differences, when students or school officials described the school as tolerant, they offered a specific example, that of Dan, as representative of both the LGBT student community at Midwest and the school's acceptance of sexual diversity. In this way, the culture of tolerance obscured the distinctions among the experiences of different LGBT students, as well as the continued entrenchment of structural homophobia and gender policing.

With Dan as its proof, the culture of tolerance at Midwest effectively concealed structural homophobia at the school through the comfortable individualization of homophobic behavior. The example of Dan supported the idea that all LGBT students had the option of being accepted and that choosing not to be was, therefore, the fault of the individual student. School officials, teachers, and students, including some LGBT students like Dan, consistently blamed LGBT students themselves for the harassment and discrimination they experienced. In this familiar homophobic discourse, these students were faulted for choosing to perform their gender, sexuality, and/or activist identities in non-normative ways. These "choices" were seen as unnecessary, flamboyant, and even arrogant rejections of the acceptance offered to some LGBT students. Defining individual choices regarding dress, behavior, or expression of gender and sexual identity as the cause of homophobic harassment obscures structural homophobia and reduces deep patterns of social inequality to irregularities in personal taste or style. The culture of tolerance at Midwest strengthened this process by stretching the bounds of accepted sexual diversity just far enough to include students like Dan. He provided students and school officials with a clear example of an LGBT student who chose to be "normal" and was, therefore, accepted, reinforcing conceptions of the school as tolerant.

Conclusion

As the diverse experiences of LGBT students indicate, there was a clearly defined "right" way to be gay at Midwest. The boundaries of accepted sexual identities had been redrawn to include a specific version of queer sexuality—one that fit within the bounds of dominant white, middle-class masculinity. In this way, sexual orientation was co-opted into existing structures of dominance, creating a "less dangerous" form of homosexuality that did not challenge these broader frameworks. This slight redrawing of the boundaries allowed some LGBT students, specifically white, middle-class gay males, to be accepted and successful, provided they conformed to these new definitions. However, the majority of LGBT students at the school remained outside these new boundaries, further marginalized from their "normal" heterosexual peers and, now, their "tolerated" queer classmates. Ultimately, school culture obscured the distinctions among the experiences of different LGBT students (including differences associated with gender, race, and social class), as well as the continued entrenchment of structural homophobia. The school's culture of tolerance actually circumscribed structures of intolerance by allowing slight modifications to traditional norms of gender and sexuality that served to marginalize most LGBT students at the school.

References

Agid, S., & Rand, E. (2007). Teaching beyond tolerance. *Radical Teacher, 80,* 2–5.

Bochenek, M., & Brown, A. (2001). *Hatred in the hallways: Violence and discrimination against lesbian, gay, bisexual, and transgender students in U.S. schools.* New York: Human Rights Watch.

Brown, W. (2006). *Regulating aversion: Tolerance in the age of identity and empire.* Princeton, NJ: Princeton University Press.

Cloud, J. (2005). The battle over gay teens. *Time, 166,* 15.

Elliott, K. (2010). Gender, sexuality, and social change in high school. Unpublished dissertation. University of Wisconsin-Madison.

Filax, G. (2003). Queer invisibility: The case of Ellen, Michael, and Oscar. In S. Books (Ed.), *Invisible children in the society and its schools.* Mahwah, NJ: Lawrence Erlbaum Associates.

Kumashiro, K. (2001). Queer students of color and antiracist, antiheterosexist education: Paradoxes of identity and activism. In K. Kumashiro (Ed.), *Troubling intersections of race and sexuality: Queer students of color and anti-oppressive education* (pp. 1–25). Lanham, MD: Rowman & Littlefield.

Linville, D. (2009). Queer theory and teen sexuality: Unclear lines. In *Theory and educational research: Toward critical social explanations.* New York: Routledge.

Mayberry, M. (2007). The story of a Salt Lake City gay-straight alliance: Identity work and LGBT youth. *Journal of Gay & Lesbian Issues in Education, 4*(1), 13–31.

Mayo, C. (2004). Queering school communities: Ethical curiosity and gay-straight alliances. *Journal of Gay & Lesbian Issues in Education, 1*(3), 14.

McCready, L. (2001). When fitting in isn't an option, or, why black queer males at a California high school stay away from Project 10. In K. Kumashiro (Ed.), *Troubling intersections of race and sexuality: Queer students of color and anti-oppressive education* (pp. 37–53). Lanham, MD: Rowman & Littlefield.

Miceli, M. (2005). *Standing out, standing together: The social and political impact of gay-straight alliances.* New York: Routledge.

Nieto, S. (2006). Affirmation, solidarity and critique: Moving beyond tolerance in education. In *Beyond heroes and holidays: A practical guide to K–12 anti-racist, multicultural education and staff development* (pp. 7–18). Washington, DC: Teaching for Change.

O'Conor, A. (1995). Who gets called queer in school? In G. Unks (Ed.), *The gay teen: Educational practice and theory for lesbian, gay, and bisexual adolescents* (pp. 95–101). New York: Routledge.

Rasmussen, M. (2006). *Becoming subjects: Sexualities and secondary schooling.* New York: Routledge.

Savin-Williams, R. (2005). *The new gay teenager.* Cambridge, MA: Harvard University Press.

CHAPTER SIXTEEN

Virtual, Welcoming, Queer, School Community

An Interview with Dave Glick

DARLA LINVILLE

I approached Dave Glick, founder of the GLBTQ Online High School with some skepticism about the project, specifically with a question about why non-heterosexual students should leave their local, face-to-face schools for another educational experience. Why did we let their schools and their classmates and administrators off the hook that way? Why not press harder for change? On the other hand, I understand Dave's sense of urgency and his desire to proclaim that while we should continue to push for social and policy changes, we cannot sacrifice today's youth. We must offer them another situation right away. In this interview Dave explains the benefits of a GLBTQ Online High School for those students who can take advantage of it. Dave uses GLBTQ or glbtq in speaking about a non-heterosexual youth population. For the purposes of this interview I have standardized all instances of the acronym to GLBTQ.

Dave Glick taught in Minnesota in a small, rural, mostly Christian district and was shocked at the discrimination he experienced for being Jewish. Although he was conscious about discrimination and oppression before that time, living through it brought home to him the ways that GLBTQ youth ask for help from schools to address harassment and violence often to find that the administrators' responses are ineffective and that most people wish they would just "get over it." These experiences led him to imagine starting a school in a different format, to create a welcoming space for students who didn't feel they fit in to their home community, and feared they might never find safety or acceptance there. The GLBTQ Online High School opened for students in January 2010.

Darla Linville (DL): How are your students' face-to-face schooling options failing to meet their needs?

Dave Glick (DG): It's hard to generalize, but we've had students who had been so harassed at school that they developed anxiety disorders and suffered from post-traumatic stress syndrome. We have students who came to us after having dropped out of school because they felt so little connection to the social scene or the curriculum. Others have little opportunity to identify or develop friendships with other GLBTQ youth, leaving them isolated and unsupported. Certainly some schools do a fine job serving their GLBTQ students, and we applaud them. Unfortunately, that's not true everywhere.

DL: Many high school experiences happen through extracurricular activities and rituals. Do you think students miss something by attending high school through an online format?

DG: Our school includes extracurricular activities and social discussion areas, so opportunities for non-academic interactions are plentiful. As we grow, we anticipate having face-to-face social and academic gatherings wherever we have clusters of students, and we're also planning to have a summer camp and travel experiences as the school matures.

I think it's just as valuable to think about what "regular" high school students miss by not taking online classes. Online students, including ours, have the opportunity to take classes with students from all over the country or world. In our case, that means students can find a supportive community no matter their location, even if they live in the smallest, most isolated town in Kansas.

Finally, it's sometimes those social rituals that provide the most painful experiences for GLBTQ youth. Consider the recent situation where the lesbian student who wanted to take her girlfriend to the prom was denied that opportunity or the countless stories of kids who pretend to be something they're not or even harm themselves due to the pressures to be straight. These things happen frequently, and for many GLBTQ youth represent the dark side of those extracurricular activities and rituals.

DL: Is social critique (of anti-GLBTQ discrimination, of the constructs and confines of adolescence, of heteronormativity, of gender normativity, of sexism, of the intersections of oppressions, etc.) built into the curriculum and discussions in your school? How?

DG: Yes, we're working on it. We are creating a GLBTQ Studies course for high school students that will include aspects of those topics as well as various cultural views of gender and sexuality variances. Once created, that course will be available for all students nationwide, not just those formally enrolled in our school. We are also continually revising our curriculum to include references to the contributions of GLBTQ individuals throughout history. This will help provide our students with numerous positive role models in their chosen fields.

Introduction: *Realidades*realities, *Palabras*words, y*and *Estudios*studies

LGBTQIQ Youth in Schools

JILLIAN FORD

Queer is a verb—an action—a way of living that is in complete harmony with who I am. It is a label that implies the absence of labels almost to the point of rendering itself obsolete.
—MIKAELA SHELDT

We are currently living—and dying—in the midst of an epidemic of violence in the United States. At unprecedented rates, young folks are committing suicides that they and their families tie directly to anti-gay bullying endured at school. Over the course of September and October 2010, the number of teen suicides reported in the national media skyrocketed. And while the likelihood is high that the national media are just now catching up to a problem that has existed for a long time, an attendant consequence of such attention is the long-overdue willingness of more classroom teachers, administrators, and policymakers to learn about the struggles and successes of lesbian, gay, bisexual, transgender, queer, intersex, and questioning (LGBTQIQ) youth inside and outside of formal school structures. This section includes chapters that address these struggles and successes from two different angles, as well as a chapter about the implicit challenges that face researchers seeking to investigate sexuality in schools.

We chose the title *Realidades*realities, *Palabras*words, y*and *Estudios*studies because these words frame the snapshots of queer youth lives in schools offered in this section. In "Queer and Transgender Youth: Education and Liberation in Our Schools," Anneliese A. Singh and Ken Jackson give a brief history of the Safe Schools movement and discuss the realities of public school environments for queer youth in the United States. They also suggest myriad strategies for educators to create safer schools for all youth (*realidades*realities). In "'Being Queer Is the Luckiest Thing': Investigating a New Generation's Use of *Queer* Within Lesbian, Gay, Bisexual, Transgender, and Queer (LGBTQ) Student Groups," Jane Bryan Meek presents results from an empirical study in which she focuses on the ways LGBT-identified students at a Midwestern university think about and relate to the word "queer" (*palabras*words). And in "Let Me In!: The Impact of the Discourse of Impossibility on Research and Curricular (Re)formation," Sandra J. Schmidt contemplates the obstacles that face scholars who aim to conduct research about sexuality in schools (*estudios*studies).

Clearly, it is not only LGBTQIQ students who are negatively affected by the anti-gay harassment and violence that plagues schools today; hostile climates affect all members of the community. This is particularly true when other students, teachers, and administrators do not address bullying. In settings where harassment and bullying are left unchecked, all students—including the perpetrators—are learning that homophobia and heterosexism are acceptable forms of individual and group interaction. The high level of aggression toward youth who are perceived to be gay both indicates and perpetuates the systemic oppression that maintains a social hierarchy and keeps queer youth in the margins. In this section, we also address the complexities of intersectional identities, oppressions, and gifts; we understand fully that race, class, sexuality, gender, ability, ethnicity, nationality, and religion are only some of the identities that are inextricably linked.

A note about terminology: The authors in this section have thought and talked and thought some more about the most appropriate language to use for the youth we wish to highlight. I use the acronym LGBTQIQ for the Introduction as a broad—though admittedly inaccurate—term for sexualities. That is, some transgender and intersex youth identify as straight, and questioning youth may be questioning their gender, not their sexuality. Though the word queer is often used to connote these nuances, not all sexually marginalized youth identify as queer. And while much of our research explores explicitly intersectional identities, a great deal of previous research on related topics is limited strictly to gay and/or lesbian. Finally, and perhaps most importantly, the youth with whom we work are most certainly innovators, and we understand that language and identities are morphing as new understandings are reached.

*****

I open this section with a spotlight text from a young friend of mine, Mikaela Sheldt, who is a talented blend of self-learned and highly trained artistry-in-action. Recently, she set up space in a nonprofit community art gallery that serves as a site for visual and performing arts, lectures, and film screenings. Her "showing," which was actually more like a "sharing," was 30 days of making the process of her art-creating public. Each day for a month, Sheldt spent several hours in front of a large canvas, painting a piece that grew organically from the energy, love, questions, and discussions she shared with members of the public who came to view her art. By the end of the month, she had created a breathtakingly beautiful painting. What follows is an excerpt from her original statement about the project, titled "30 days," and a poem she wrote as she reflected on her experience.

Una joven amiga mía, Mikaela Sheldt, es una talentosa mezcla de auto-aprendida y sumamente entrenada artista en acción. Recientemente, ella estableció su espacio en un centro comunitario que es una galería dinámica de arte local y regional. Su "muestra," que en realidad fue mas una "aportación," consistió en treinta días de hacer público el proceso creativo de su arte. Cada día, durante un mes, Sheldt pasó varias horas frente a un lienzo, pintando una obra se desarrolló orgánicamente de la energía, amor, preguntas, y discusiones que ella compartió con el público que visito su espacio artístico. Al final del mes, ella creó una impresionantemente hermosa pintura. Lo que sigue es un poema que ella escribió mientras reflexionaba acerca de su experiencia.[1]

What Lovers Do

by Mikaela Shelt

I'm certain someone is trapped inside my painting.
I cannot sit in front of it,
I sit with it.
Listen to it.
Respond with devotion, dedication, and
Singular attention.
On opening night,
The people have no faces
But my painting is beautiful.
She follows my every move
And I
Notice every person who looks at her,
Talks to her,
Touches her.
I want the people to leave so that we can be alone together.

I am convinced a woman is trapped inside my painting.
Company to my thoughts,
She pushes me,
Keeps me honest,
Uses all the weak spots I didn't know I had,
She has no patience for my ego,
Breaks me down
Only to piece me together again
Just the way she wants me.
I let her do it.
How could I stop her?
She is too quick.
If I try to control her,
She makes sure I am miserable.

A woman is trapped inside my painting,
I am certain of it.
The fact that she has camouflaged herself—Expertly
Does not surprise me.

It fits her personality
Perfectly.
If you knew her,
Like I do,
You would understand
She doesn't want to be this way.
People taught her
How to paint walls.

I am in love with the woman in my painting
It is agony.
Purely mental.
I cannot hold her,
See her,
Hear her.
It is as though I've created her—That she is myth
A figment of my imagination.
I cling to every morsel.
She feeds me just enough
I keep coming back.

I love her,
Cannot imagine existing without her.
If only she would come out of hiding.
Leave her painting
I have cut open my chest
To let her climb in.
It would only take a moment
No one would have to see,
Or even know she is there.
I would keep her secrets
Just to feel her inside me.
Close to me,
Breathing,
Heart beat,
Next to mine.

She is my love,
My painting.
And I will wait for her,
Patient—Cut open and vulnerable,
Because that is what lovers do.

Sheldt's project challenged the meaning of artist, art, and audience. Over the course of 30 days, she created not only the painting, but also a community of people, an exchange, and an experience. The process itself became the thing that was created: the art.

El proyecto de Sheldt desafía el significado del artista, el arte, y la audiencia. Durante el periodo de 30 días, ella creo no solo una pintura sino también una comunidad de gente, un intercambio, y una experiencia. El proceso se convirtió en la misma cosa que se creó: el arte.

I use her insight to set the stage for Section V: *Realidades*realities, *Palabras*words, yand *Estudios*studies. I am grateful for her willingness to be decidedly public in her art-making. Her level of intentional vulnerability—perhaps an attempt to demystify one method of liberatory practice—can help us all learn to trust one another a bit more.

*Utilizo su percepción para introducir la Sección V: *Realidades*realities, *Palabras*words, yand *Estudios*studies. Agradezco su disposición a ser decididamente publica con el desarrollo de su arte; su nivel de transparencia—tal vez un intento de desmitificar un método de practica oscilatoria—puede ayudarnos a confiar un poco más los unos en los otros.*

Note

1. Lucia Vidable (Spanish translation)

CHAPTER SEVENTEEN

Queer and Transgender Youth

Education and Liberation in Our Schools

ANNELIESE A. SINGH & KEN JACKSON

> Last year, I was just another gay student trapped in the proverbial closet. Silenced by the hostility of my peers and the indifference of my teachers, I became invisible. I sacrificed the authenticity of my emotions for a false sense of acceptance. In spite of my pain and isolation, denial seemed easier than the alternative. It was familiar and safe. Yet even in denial, my sexuality was questioned. I was bullied and called a "faggot." I faced harassment in the hallways and was forced to change my route to class.
> —AUSTIN LAUFERSWEILER, 16-YEAR-OLD QUEER YOUTH, GEORGIA

This chapter identifies practices for educators developing safe school environments for LGBTQQ (lesbian, gay, bisexual, transgender, queer, questioning) youth and those who are perceived as LGBTQQ so there is a more humanizing school environment for all youth. The authors acknowledge that all school environments are not the same and that educators must determine the best applications for practices in creating affirmative environments for LGBTQQ youth and those perceived as LGBTQQ, in addition to identifying the effective advocacy necessary for their particular school setting. Effective advocacy occurs as one first understands practices that create supportive climates for queer and transgender youth within the unique contexts of one's setting, and then follows this understanding with program implementation and assessment. To assist in gaining this understanding of effective practices, the authors review the current literature on LGBTQQ youth in schools, from bullying and violence studies to the unique resilience literature. The authors provide a brief historical perspective to contextualize school policy with LGBTQQ youth in the United States and globally, including statistics on LGBTQQ youth and the various challenges and opportunities existing within schools to support their academic, social, and personal well-being. The authors also examine the history of safe schools activism, the critical role of youth in this activism, and the specific advocacy role educators may take in school settings with regard to supporting LGBTQQ youth. The chapter concludes with a list of innovative and effective strategies and resources educators may implement immediately in schools to develop positive academic and personal support systems for LGBTQQ youth in school settings. Throughout the chapter, an emphasis on intersecting identities for LGBTQQ youth (e.g., race/ethnicity, gender, social class, etc.) are specified, and the confluence of both oppression and resilience LGBTQQ youth experience due to heterosexism and other systemic forces (e.g., racism, ableism, etc.) is explored. An extensive discussion of language and terminology related to queer and transgender youth is outside of the scope of this chapter (see Georgia Safe Schools Coalition for an in-depth glossary). For this chapter, we use the term "queer" as an umbrella term to include lesbian, gay, bisexual, questioning, asexual, and other sexual and affectional orientations that are not heteronormative. We use the term "transgender" to encapsulate gender identities and expressions that are gender nonconforming.

Why (Re)vision Education for Queer and Transgender Youth Is Needed

The topic of queer and transgender youth is rarely acknowledged within education settings (Singh & Burnes, 2009). There is more often silence on queer and transgender identities within the school curricula, administrative activities, and the daily practice of education. The biannual survey of 7,261 LGBTQQ high school and middle school students conducted by the Gay, Lesbian and Straight Education Network (2009) found that almost 90% of queer and transgender youth were verbally and/or physically bullied at school. Because of the fear these youth experienced, a third of the students surveyed skipped school and attributed a decline in their academic performance to bullying based on sexual orientation and gender identity and expression. In addition, all youth in schools are vulnerable to this type of bullying. Youth who are heterosexual and cisgender (cisgender defines those whose sex assigned at birth is in alignment with their gender identity and/or expression) hear epithets such as "faggot" and "dyke" commonly throughout the day (D'Augelli, Grossman, & Starks, 2006). Phrases such as "that's so gay" intimate for youth that non-heteronormative identities are not only not valued and validated but are also undesirable and unworthy (Singh, 2010). Research has additionally shown that queer and transgender youth have the highest rates of suicide for youth ages 15–24 due to societal experiences of homophobia and transphobia (D'Augelli, Hershberger, & Pilkington, 2001). Other long-term studies of queer and transgender youth have also shown high rates of substance use (Grossman & D'Augelli, 2005) and homelessness (Consolacion, Russell, & Sue, 2004) related to their sexual orientation and gender identity and expression.

In addition to escalating rates of victimization in schools and other stressors, queer and transgender youth also experience a lack of support from educators from within the school (Komosa-Hawkins, et al., 2008). The American School Counselors Association (ASCA) has set standards of advocacy and developed an ethical code that provides expectations that school counselors should be trained for and engage in advocacy for students who are from historically marginalized groups (ASCA, 2007a, 2007b; ASCA, 2004). However, many school counselors continue to report feeling unprepared from their training programs to address issues concerning queer and transgender youth in their settings (Dillon, et al., 2004; Pollock, 2006). Recent research on social justice advocacy in education (Singh, Urbano, Haston, & McMahon, 2010) has encouraged educators to actively incorporate positive, active, and ongoing discussions about queer and transgender issues at all levels of education. A major challenge to instituting such transformation of educational environments is related to opposition to such work from conservative groups that frame discussions about supporting queer and transgender youth in terms of "inappropriate" or "encouraging homosexuality" for youth

(Russell & McGuire, 2008). Suddenly, the discussion of developing safe environments for all youth to develop positive thoughts and feelings about their sexual orientation and gender identity and expression shift to being "about sex" and not about safety. Much of advocacy in creating safe school environments for queer and transgender youth, therefore, involves educators taking personal and professional risks in creating affirming environments for these youth. For instance, Valenti and Campbell's (2009) study of advisors of Gay-Straight Alliances (GSAs) suggests the hesitations in choosing to sponsor a GSA included fears of job loss, credibility, and accusations of recruiting. These fears were shared by both advisors who identified as LGBTQQ and those who were heterosexual and cisgender.

With the high rates of bullying and the lack of prepared educators to support queer and transgender youth, interventions are typically remedial, reactive, and lack foresight and intentionality in learning about queer and transgender identities in schools. In the next section, we explore the history of safe schools activism to identify how educators and school advocates have addressed systemic oppressions of heterosexism, homoprejudice, and transprejudice within school settings.

History of Safe Schools Activism

> President Obama has appointed Kevin Jennings, founder of GLSEN (Gay, Lesbian, Straight Education Network)—which sponsored the conference that produced the notorious "Fistgate" scandal (in which young teens were guided on how to perform dangerous homosexual perversions including "fisting")—to head up "Safe Schools" efforts at the Department of Education. Jennings is a vicious, anti-religious bigot who once said "[F–k] 'em" to the "Religious Right." He supports promoting homosexuality and gender confusion as normative to even young students.
> —ATLAS SHRUGS, PAMELA GELLER [ULTRA-CONSERVATIVE] BLOG, JUNE 7, 2009

Just as President Barack Obama appointed Kevin Jennings—the former executive director and founder of GLSEN (Gay, Lesbian and Straight Education Network)—to the post of Assistant Deputy Secretary for Safe and Drug-Free Schools—the religious right in the U.S. mounted a backlash to his appointment. This type of backlash is a common story in the history of safe schools activism. Safe schools activism on behalf of and by queer and transgender youth has persisted in the United States and globally despite continued assaults from the religious right, as demonstrated by Geller's quote above. The success of this activism has been on multiple levels and has included both street-level protest and intra-school advocacy. Often, this history has included the establishment of non-profit and community-based organizations that are able to not only develop resources for supporting queer and transgender youth in schools but also to create accountability networks through coalition building and advocacy. Although a full history of safe schools activism is outside the scope of this chapter, it is important to note that this movement has grown both national and local grassroots activists. For instance, the Gay, Lesbian and Straight Education Network (GLSEN) is one of the most well-established non-profit organizations engaging in safe schools activism. The organization grew out of local teacher activism within the Gay and Lesbian Independent School Teachers Network in 1990 (GLSEN, 2006, 2009). Five years later, GLSEN hired Kevin Jennings as executive director, and the organization gained a national focus. Local chapters of GLSEN began to form across the United States with the support of GLSEN educational resources geared toward increasing school awareness about the needs of queer and transgender youth.

Currently there are numerous national resources for educators to advocate for queer and transgender youth and for students to initiate their own activism within their school. Some of this activism has involved national movements to identify a day to recognize and highlight issues influencing queer and transgender youth. For example, on the national Day of Silence (held in April each year) students take a vow of silence in school to challenge the silence on queer and transgender issues within schools and the continued homoprejudice and transprejudice youth experience in school settings. There are also one-day events such as Coming Out Day (October 11), when students and educators in schools stage creative ways to develop awareness and action to affirm queer and transgender students (e.g., by building a large door where queer and transgender students can come "out" to honor their sexual orientation and/or gender identity and expression, or by scheduling educational panels on queer and transgender issues).

> A lot of students talked about how they hated them—faggots—and stuff. And I did not even want a part of that, so I just kind of sat in the corner and minded my own business. I was afraid to tell anyone anything about it . . . It's changed me a lot.
> —MARC (PSEUDONYM), COLLEGE STUDENT IN METRO ATLANTA, GEORGIA

While queer and transgender adults have shouted, "We're here, we're queer," schools struggle to "get used to it." Queer and transgender youth also struggle to find school communities that are both safe and affirming. From Gay-Straight Alliances (GSAs), to coming out identification and integration into the life of the school, queer and transgender students endeavor to find their places. Schools with GSAs are more likely to have cultures and environments that are supportive of queer and transgender students as students hear fewer homophobic comments, experience less harassment, and feel safer (GLSEN, 2006, 2009). GSAs improve the school climate of queer and transgender students even if the student does not attend meetings (Kim, 2009). However, while there are as many as 3,000 GSAs in the United States, fewer than 25% of the middle and high schools have GSAs, and many regions have fewer than 10% of their schools with this vital support (Fetner & Kush, 2008; GLSEN, 2006).

Students in more rural locations or in lower socioeconomic settings have a decreased chance of finding GSA support, with fewer GSAs in Southern and Midwestern states than Northern or Western states (Fetner & Kush, 2008; Kim, 2009). Under the Equal Access Act of 1984, a law heavily supported by conservative Christian groups in order to allow Bible and religious clubs on campus, students are legally permitted to form GSAs if the school allows any kind of non-curricular club. Ironically, it has been conservative opposition that has made formation of GSAs difficult for many queer and transgender students. As a result, students often face resistance, rejection, and harassment as they begin to exercise their rights for equitable school organizations. For example, students at Berkmar High School in Lilburn, Georgia, had "point/counter point" editorials offered by their student journalists in which one writer suggested, possibly facetiously, that having a GSA could well lead to clubs promoting prostitution (Youth Journalism, 2005). One wonders if students of the Bible Club or service clubs had the same scrutiny or what such debate does to devalue a climate of safety and affirmation not only for queer and transgender students, but for all students. As reflected in Florida's (2002) book *The Rise of the Creative Class*, there is a correlation between areas that promote tolerance for queer and transgender individuals and the creativity and growth of those areas.

> Talented people seek an environment open to differences. Many highly creative people, regardless of ethnic background or sexual orientation, grew up feeling like outsiders, different in some way from most of their schoolmates. When they are sizing up a new company and community, acceptance of diversity and of gays in particular is a sign that reads "non-standard people welcome here." (Florida, 2002)

Florida notes that this has less to do with queer and transgender people being the creative ones and more to do with the type of environment that is created when tolerance and support is extended even to the queer and transgender community.

Other instances of safe schools activism have used the Internet and social networking tools to confront discrimination. The "pink shirts" movement advocating for safe schools was begun by two seniors in a Canadian high school (CBS News, 2007). A freshman boy at their school had attended the first day of the school year wearing a pink shirt. He was called anti-gay epithets and physically harmed by several members of the senior class. On the same day as these homophobic hate crimes within the school, the two seniors used MySpace and Facebook to communicate with their peers in school and asked students to challenge homophobic bullying by wearing pink shirts to school the following day. Indeed, a "sea of pink" was seen in the school the next day with nonviolent protest and demands for safe school environments. Currently, there are "pink shirt days" and "pink shirt movements" across the United States and Canada to creatively continue safe schools activism for queer and transgender youth.

Transgender youth have been an important component of safe schools activism. Although many of their stories are lost and/or not identified, one of the most effective national instances of activism on transgender issues was the development of a glossary and transgender activism in schools guide—for example Bending the Mold: An Action Kit for Transgender Youth (Lambda Legal, 2008). In this resource, transgender youth have self-defined words such as transgender and genderqueer. They also have compiled school policies and legislation important for transgender youth to be aware of as they engage in advocating for their rights regarding gender identity and expression in schools. A school self-assessment template is also included, which looks at the existence of accessible restrooms, school paperwork, education training, non-discrimination policies, and other aspects of the school that hold the potential of transforming schools into safe, supportive environments for transgender youth. While queer and transgender youth are often silenced in schools, these youth and their allies are making their voices heard with increasing frequency in schools as we discuss in the following section.

Coming Out as Activism

> My high school counselor loved me, but I was the straight, Christian boy who did everything right; got straight A's, was always happy but could never really be myself; so on the inside that was just— just horrible.
>
> —ADAM (PSEUDONYM), COLLEGE STUDENT, METRO ATLANTA, GEORGIA

Beyond having a place of recognition and the support such an environment creates, queer and transgender students have used identity disclosure (coming out) as an inadvertent means of activism. While many students lack the safety for such, some students in unlikely areas have made the decision to come out with various results. Athletics and sports teams are often places students find particularly homophobic. Corey Johnson, a co-captain of his high school football team, came out with the support of his teammates, coaches, and family. When facing harassment from other teams, his teammates were most supportive, allowing Johnson to speak on ABC's *20/20* and become GLSEN's Visionary Award recipient (Cassels, 2000). On the other hand, Greg Congdon, a football player a couple hundred miles from Johnson, lived in a rural town and had a much different experience. A failed suicide attempt resulted in his being "outed" (identity disclosure against his will) to the school. Greg faced rejection and torment at his school, was threatened not to play sports again, and received no support from his teachers and counselor. He skipped classes, staying in his car or at a nearby creek or cemetery, rather than face the harassment at school. In all of this, no one from the school called his parents to inform them that anything was wrong (Woog, 2002).

Both students represent the experiences of queer and transgender youth in schools who desire to represent themselves honestly. In all cases, whether willingly or not, the students and school personnel who come out as queer or transgender, or queer or transgender allies, are activists and social change agents. The unknown is whether schools will continue being settings of oppression or become refuges of affirmation and use strategies to (re)vision school cultures so that queer and transgender youth may not only survive, but thrive.

Strategies for Making Schools Supportive of Queer and Transgender Students

> It's amazing how much a brochure . . . outside the counselor's office—saying about like being open and accepting LGBT students—would have made so much of a difference in the high schools because visually seeing that instead of wondering and getting up the guts to ask—that's two very different things.
> —SARA (PSEUDONYM), COLLEGE STUDENT, METRO ATLANTA, GEORGIA

In order to (re)vision schools as settings where queer and transgender youth are valued for their identities, there are several strategies on which educators may take immediate and long-term action within their schools. In this section, we discuss general strategies that may be addressed across grade levels as important steps toward developing queer- and transgender-positive school environments. We encourage educators to find ways to collaborate with queer and transgender youth and their allies both within and outside of the school settings when using any of the strategies discussed below. In addition, there is much injustice that must be addressed in school. However, each strategy should be used in tandem with the recognition of not only the barriers queer and transgender youth face, but also with the recognition of resilience these youth demonstrate in their everyday lives at school.

Enumerate Categories of Sexual Orientation, Gender Identity, and Gender Expression in Non-Discrimination and Anti-Harassment Policies

Educators and youth activists can begin advocacy to develop safer environments in their school settings for queer and transgender youth by ensuring that sexual orientation and gender identity and expression are enumerated or listed as protected categories in school policy. Ideally, state and federal governments should enumerate these categories through legislation; however, this does not always occur. Education scholars have suggested that when these categories are not included, school faculty and staff who may or may not be queer or transgender may not feel safe speaking up about issues that affect queer and transgender youth if their own jobs may be at risk as educators. As a result, students also lose the chance for valuable role models.

> I think it's so sad that these people that could have been our mentors, these people who could have helped us out so much, are prevented by fear.
> —ANNIE (PSEUDONYM), COLLEGE STUDENT, METRO ATLANTA, GEORGIA

If a school and/or district's non-discrimination and anti-harassment policies include these categories, then safe schools activists have a foundation upon which to develop the following strategies we discuss below. If these are not enumerated categories, activists should use the other suggested strategies to bring awareness to the need for school policies to be revised accordingly.

Conduct School Climate Survey on the Environment of Queer and Transgender Students

To help schools develop a climate of affirmation, the community must first see the need. One effective way to accomplish this is through a School Climate Survey. While these can be created or borrowed from other sources, the Gay, Lesbian and Straight Education Network (GLSEN) has implemented them nationally, and variations are available to the public (see www.glsen.org). Comparing one's school data to state and national results can prove helpful, but whether one creates an original survey, uses an existing survey, or modifies one for one's own situation, all can bring the conversation of queer and transgender harassment to everyone's attention. Teachers, parents, and administrators become more engaged when they see the needs and hear the voices of their own students. Adapting the surveys to include a variety of oppressed groups can serve the purpose of enlarging the scope of the need, as well as broadening the scope of support for creating affirming schools for all students. In addition, it is helpful to develop surveys in which students may self-identify by writing in the words they want to use instead of checking boxes with predetermined categories—not only with regard to sexual orientation or gender identity and gender expression, but also with regard to race, religion, gender, ability, etc. A critique of this approach is that schools are mandated to collect information about students based on certain identities they have, and these must be specific categories. However, even in these situations, educators can ensure that additional space is provided for students to identify the words they would like to use to describe themselves.

Students will need a safe, semi-private opportunity to respond to the survey if they are to give their most forthright responses. After the survey, educators must create an appropriate response for the community. Whether done during a faculty meeting or student advisory period, presenting the results to faculty, staff, and administrators by simply posing the question "What do you notice in these results?" provides an environment for others to participate in creating the solutions needed. When looking at the results, it is helpful to have faculty participants respond to the question "What groups might feel the least safe in our school?" It is not uncommon that they will note that LGBTQ students feel unsafe and unwelcome based on the school's survey. Likewise, when asked "What derogatory words do you hear the most?" faculty members are likely to note that they hear "fag" and "That's so gay" quite frequently. In addition, if the survey has a section for students to write in their responses, the community can hear voices often silenced. One such survey asked students, "If you like, share any incident or event related to diversity or acceptance that you have seen or experienced." Student responses included "I get called a fag at least once or twice a day" or "[My teacher] is homophobic and makes homophobic remarks in class. He told his class if they let gay people marry they'd have to let people marry goats. Very disappointing. . . ." When these responses and comments are presented to the community, it can move people to understand not only that there are queer and transgender people in "our" school, but that they feel isolated and unsafe. Moreover, as the survey reveals intersections of identity, the process begins for understanding that oppression for some is oppression for all.

Provide Professional Development on Queer and Transgender Issues in the School

A critical component of supporting queer and transgender youth is ensuring that all levels of educational professionals (e.g., school counselors, faculty, administrators, custodial staff) are participating in ongoing professional development on queer and transgender issues. This professional development should not be a onetime event, but rather provide ongoing educational opportunities throughout the year. Ideally, there should be a daylong training on queer and transgender issues that integrates attention to the intersections of heterosexism with other systems of oppression (e.g., racism, sexism, ableism, etc.) in addition to providing education on basic terminology and dispelling myths about queer and transgender issues. Having this solid foundation of training in the pre-planning period before the students arrive can then be followed up by monthly updates of professional development. Queer and transgender youth should be central to all professional development. Inviting youth (from the school itself and/or the community, depending on the grade level) to collaborate in planning professional development topics helps ensure that the focus is not only on the challenges they face, but also on the resilience they have so educators can understand how to build more empowering environments in their classrooms.

Respond to Aggression toward Queer and Transgender Students

After the school determines where it stands on non-discrimination and harassment, develops an understanding of the need, and trains and communicates with the community, it must then be prepared to act. In even the most supportive of environments, there will be incidents that reflect the more hateful aspects of society; likewise in places where a school is moving to a more affirming place, there will be instances of resistance that will at times manifest in oppressive and aggressive acts. The school leadership must be prepared to respond quickly and thoughtfully. Referring back to its mission statement, harassment policies, and professional organizations (e.g., Just the Facts Coalition, 2008), educators can set the tone for the environment they wish to create. Officials will be tested, and advance planning response options that include both discipline and counseling can make an adverse situation into one of growth and affirmation for individuals and the community. Leaders need to understand the multiple roles that community members may play. Those who harass need both consequences and counseling follow-up. Those who are victims need counseling and affirmation and recognition of the hurt they experience and the resiliency that they demonstrate. In addition, those who are observers of hateful acts often exhibit signs of stress and need affirmation, as well as instruction in advocacy strategies. While hate incidents traumatize, they can also be an opportunity for the community to reaffirm who it is and what it believes.

Integrate Queer and Transgender Issues Visibly into the School Culture

In addition to positively reacting to aggression, schools can be proactive in helping queer and transgender students survive and thrive on campus. Providing opportunities for queer and transgender students and their allies to integrate seamlessly into the school culture allows for education, self-advocacy, and needed social supports. Being able to live authentically arises from knowing that one is safe. As has been mentioned, students feel safer and report fewer incidents of harassment at schools with GSAs (GLSEN, 2006, 2009). Such organizations and activities implicitly state to queer students and the school culture that queer and transgender students have a right to exist, be supported, and participate fully in the life of the school. As students create and participate in a variety of activities and functions within the school year, the inclusion of queer and transgender affirmative activities can be a natural extension in the life of the school. Experiencing queer and transgender functions such as the Day of Silence, National Coming Out Day, and No Name Calling Week not only allows queer and transgender student expression but also provides forums for discussion that can increase student body support and understanding. While at times advocates feel they must operate under a "better to ask forgiveness than permission" paradigm, operating under the adage of "administrators do not like surprises" builds long-term relationships for whole school culture shifts. Moreover, by gaining the support of the school's social and political leaders (student government and senior class presidents), these events move from the peripheral of school life into foundational character education opportunities. Research has indicated that the motivation for GSA mentors advocating for queer and transgender students was (1) a protective attitude toward queer and transgender youth and their situations and (2) a personal connection with queer and transgender youth and their issues (Valenti & Campbell, 2009). Providing education and interaction with queer and transgender students and their allies allows future allies to arise and participate in establishing a school climate of affirmation. Therefore, when future aggression or new students arrive at the school, the understanding of the culture becomes "this is not who we are," and an ethos of affirmation for all students becomes more of the norm.

Include Queer and Transgender Content Authentically into the Curriculum and Library

Authentically allowing queer and transgender participation in the school social structures parallels authentically integrating diversity understandings and queer and transgender visibility in the curriculum. Schools can move past the "assembly of the month" mentality and begin allowing students to engage in discussions within the places they spend the majority of their time within schools—the classrooms. As literature teachers strive to develop higher order thinking skills in their students, ignoring the queer and transgender sensibilities of Tennessee Williams or James Baldwin reduces the educational opportunities of all students and the affirmation and support of queer and transgender students. History teachers who lead engaging presentations on historical revolutions in human history or on civil rights leaders from Mohandas Gandhi to Dr. Martin Luther King Jr. would do well to include the past and current struggles/resiliency of queer and transgender people. Science teachers who seek to communicate relevancy in their subject have opportunities to discuss the latest in research (e.g., gene research, queer and transgender expression in the animal kingdom) and ethics within their fields.

Inclusion and discussion within existing units requires teachers to have queer- and transgender-affirming attitudes as well as the knowledge and resources to provide quality instruction. Professional teacher organizations can provide resources that offer rigor and relevance for all students. (The National Council of Teachers of English, for example, offers resources for its members on professional responsibilities and resources for supporting LGBTQ students. (See http://www.ncte.org/search?q=gay.)

Besides classroom teachers, media specialists/librarians can provide safe havens for students who are questioning and needing unconditional supports. Students often turn to the people in their school who have demonstrated openness and affirmation, and often the same people in the building who present the danger of banning books are the ones who understand the need for diversity and affirmation. Wise librarians understand that due to stigmatization, questioning students may be hesitant to ask for help with queer and transgender materials, much less check them out. Schools who allow such books to be "borrowed" without checking them out and returned under an honor system provide resources that the student might not otherwise find available. Like other professional educator organizations, the *School Library Journal* provides numerous resources for media specialists seeking to be allies for all students (see http://www.schoollibraryjournal.com). They and classroom teachers who allow queer and transgender students to "see themselves" in their studies help them validate their existence and worth in a world that is often hostile and abusive.

As schools integrate queer and transgender activities into existing units, they can also provide unique lessons and units that focus on diversity and affirmation for all. Schools can see the benefit of developing the community and moral sensitivities of their students. Such conversations can help students synthesize, analyze, and evaluate higher order skills that educators seek in their students. Natural places within the school structure could include health, advisory, social studies, and peer counseling courses. Since Israel and Hackett's study (2004) in adults indicated that short-duration LGBTQQ attitudinal training was less effective than simply providing information on LGBTQQ people and could even increase homonegativity, it seems likely that the same is true for students. Creating an affirming culture for all requires continuous opportunities for knowledge and discussion. Some schools have special diversity, tolerance, or community skills courses for all of their students. The content can include a variety of diversity issues and groups and is built on the foundation that understanding others increases empathy and that one is responsible for treating others respectfully— even if one does not fully agree with or understand the other person. Running from six weeks to a full semester, these courses allow students to grapple with complex issues vital to the school community with the same rigor and engagement as their other classes. They can provide a foundation for creating a school climate that affirms all students.

Engage Informative Outreach to Parents about Queer and Transgender Issues

Because educators often cite their fear of parents' reactions to any education or attention to queer and transgender issues in school, it is helpful for safe schools activists to proactively address their fear through outreach to parents. Often, parents are unaware of the school's mission and/or non-discrimination and anti-harassment policies. Using these school policies as a foundation, safe schools activists can work with administrators to hold in-person meetings and use letters and email communications to share why these policies are important and how they will be used within the school. These communications can also include school promotional material, such as school handbooks, admission forms, websites, and other school forms.

Collaborate with Community Organizations that Serve Queer and Transgender Youth

Many educators are interested in building safer environments for queer and transgender youth, but they may feel unsure about what basic terminology to use and/or may feel uncomfortable identifying the most salient issues schools should work on with regard to supporting queer and transgender youth. Collaborating with community organizations that serve queer and transgender youth is a helpful way to provide basic education. In addition, these organizations can recommend strategies of activism that should be incorporated by safe schools activists based on the typical issues they see queer and transgender youth manage. Working with community organizations can also create an accountability and feedback loop, so it is important that these collaborations be ongoing throughout the school year. Once recommendations are made, meetings with stakeholders in both the school and community organizations can collaboratively evaluate the school's progress and make further recommendations for change within the school. Again, queer and transgender youth should be central to these collaborations if they are to be most effective.

Conclusion

This chapter has discussed the need for a (re)visioning of school settings so that they become environments in which queer and transgender youth are valued and invested stakeholders in the school community. While there is a long-standing history of oppression within schools regarding queer and transgender issues, there is also a rich, vibrant, and creative history of advocacy, activism, and significant social change. Supporting queer and transgender youth may be as simple as demonstrating a Safe Zone rainbow sticker indicating an educator's commitment to the safety of these youth. However, such individual actions must go further and build collective momentum toward making deep, institutional changes in the way in which all students are supported in the expression of their sexual orientation and gender identity and expression.

References

American School Counselor Association. (2004). *ASCA national standards for students.* Alexandria, VA: Author.

American School Counselor Association. (2007a). *ASCA national model: A framework for school counseling programs.* Alexandria, VA: Author.

American School Counselor Association. (2007b). *The professional school counselor and LGBTQ youth.* Alexandria, VA: Author.

Cassels, P. (2000). A brave athlete, supportive school: The Massconomet Regional High football team's co-captain comes out and finds a world of support. Bay Windows Magazine (http://www.baywindows.com). Retrieved from http://www.outsports.com/gaymassplayer.htm

CBS News. (2007). Bullied student tickled pink by schoolmates' T-shirt campaign. CBSNews.ca. Retrieved from http://www.cbc.ca/canada/nova-scotia/story/2007/09/18/pink-tshirts-students.html

Consolacion, T.B., Russell, S.T., & Sue, S. (2004). Sex, race/ethnicity, and romantic attractions: Multiple minority status adolescents and mental health. *Cultural Diversity and Ethnic Minority Psychology, 10*(3), 200–214.

D'Augelli, A.R., Grossman, A.H., & Starks, M.T. (2006). Childhood gender atypicality, victimization, and PTSD among lesbian, gay, and bisexual youth. *Journal of Interpersonal Violence, 21,* 1462–1482.

D'Augelli, A.R., Hershberger, S.L., & Pilkington, N.W. (2001). Suicidality patterns and sexual orientation-related factors among lesbian, gay, and bisexual youths. *Suicide & Life-Threatening Behavior, 31,* 250–264.

Dillon, F.R., Worthington, R.L., Savoy, H.B., Rooney, S.C., Becker-Schutte, A., & Guerra, R.M. (2004). On becoming allies: A qualitative study of lesbian-, gay-, and bisexual-affirmative counselor training. *Counselor Education and Supervision, 43*(3), 162.

Fetner, T., & Kush, K. (2008). Gay-straight alliances in high schools: Social predictors of early adoption. *Youth & Society, 40*(1), 114–130.

Florida, R. (2002). The rise of the creative class: Why cities without gays and rock bands are losing the economic development race. Retrieved from http://www.washingtonmonthly.com/features/2001/0205.florida.html

Gay, Lesbian and Straight Education Network. (2006). From teasing to torment: A report of school climate in Georgia. New York: Gay, Lesbian and Straight Education Network. Retrieved from http://www.glsen.org/binary-data/GLSEN_ATTACHMENTS/file/000/000/695-1.pdf

Gay, Lesbian and Straight Education Network. (2009). The 2009 National School Climate Survey. New York: Gay, Lesbian and Straight Education Network. Retrieved from http://www.glsen.org/cgi-bin/iowa/all/library/record/2624.html?state=research&type=research

Georgia Safe Schools Coalition. (2010). Glossary. Retrieved from http://www.georgiasafeschoolscoalition.org/
    index.php?option=com_content&view=article&id=26&Itemid=30

Grossman, A.H., & D'Augelli, A.R. (2005). Recreational substance use among lesbian, gay, and bisexual youth:
    Frequency and predictors. In J. Caudwell & P. Bramham (Eds.), *Sport, active leisure and youth cultures* (pp.
    55–72). Eastbourne, UK: LSA Publications.

Israel, T., & Hackett, G. (2004). Counselor education on lesbian, gay, and bisexual issues: Comparing information
    and attitude exploration. *Counselor Education and Supervision, 43*(3), 179.

Just the Facts Coalition. (2008). *Just the facts about sexual orientation and youth: A primer for principals, educators, and
    school personnel.* Washington, DC: American Psychological Association. Retrieved from www.apa.org/pi/lgbc/pub-
    lications/justthefacts.html

Kim, R. (2009). A report on the status of gay, lesbian, bisexual and transgender people in education: Stepping out of
    the closet, into the light. National Education Association Research Department. Retrieved from ERIC data-
    base.

Komosa-Hawkins, K., Saldaña, E., Thomas, G.M., Hsiao, C., Rauld, M., Miller, D., & Fisher, E.S. (2008). Promoting
    school success for lesbian, gay, bisexual, transgendered, and questioning students: Primary, secondary, and ter-
    tiary prevention and intervention strategies. *California School Psychologist, 13,* 79–91.

Lambda Legal and National Youth Advocacy Coalition. (2008). *Bending the mold: An action kit for transgender youth.*
    Retrieved from www.lambdalegal.org/ . . . /bending-the-mold/order-bending-the-mold.html

Mahan, W., Varjas, K., Dew, B.J., Meyers, J., & Singh, A.A. (2007). School and community providers' perspectives
    on gay, lesbian, and questioning bullying. *Journal of LGBT Issues in Counseling, 2,* 45–66.

Pollock, S. (2006). Counselor roles in dealing with bullies and their LGBT victims. *Middle School Journal, 38*(2), 29–36.
    Retrieved from ERIC database.

Poteat, V.P., & Espelage, D.L. (2005). Exploring the relation between bullying and homophobic verbal content: The
    homophobic content agent target (HCAT) scale. *Violence and Victims, 20*(5), 513–528.

Russell, S.T. (2005). Beyond risk: Resilience in the lives of sexual minority youth. *Journal of Gay & Lesbian Issues, 2*(3),
    5–18.

Russell, S.T., & McGuire, J. (2008). The school climate for lesbian, gay, bisexual, and transgender (LGBT) students.
    In M. Shinn & H. Yoshikawa (Eds.), *Toward positive youth development: Transforming schools and community pro-
    grams* (pp. 133–149). New York: Oxford University Press.

Singh, A.A. (2010). It takes more than a rainbow sticker! Using the ACA Advocacy Competencies with queer clients.
    In M. Ratts, J. Lewis, & R. Toporek (Eds.), *Using the ACA Advocacy Competencies in counseling* (pp. 29–41).
    Alexandria, VA: American Counseling Association.

Singh, A.A., & Burnes, T.R. (2009). Creating developmentally appropriate, safe counseling environments for trans-
    gender youth: The critical role of school counselors. *Journal of LGBT Issues in Counseling, 3*(3–4), 215–234.

Singh, A.A., Urbano, A., Haston, M., & McMahon, E. (2010). School counselors' strategies for social justice change:
    A grounded theory of what works in the real world. *Professional School Counseling, 13,* 135–145.

Valenti, M., & Campbell, R. (2009). Working with youth on LGBT issues: Why gay-straight alliance advisors become
    involved. *Journal of Community Psychology, 37*(2), 228–248.

Woog, D. (2002). Life was hell for a gay teen jock: I lost everything I thought was my life. In his *Jocks 2: Coming out
    to play.* Los Angeles: Alyson Books. Retrieved from http://www.outsports.com/entertainment/20020920
    jocks2.htm.

Youth Journalism in the News from *The Atlanta Journal-Constitution* (2005). Gwinnett opinions: The Berkmar con-
    troversy: Student editorials present two sides of the issue of a school club for gay students. Retrieved from
    http://www.highschooljournalism.org/Content.cfm?id=65&mode=1&newsid=220

CHAPTER EIGHTEEN

"Being Queer Is the Luckiest Thing"

Investigating a New Generation's Use of Queer within Lesbian, Gay, Bisexual, Transgender, and Queer (LGBTQ) Student Groups

JANE BRYAN MEEK

Lesbian, gay, bisexual, and transgender (LGBT) young adults have grown up alongside the reappropriation of the term queer, although it is likely their first encounter with it may have been through popular culture's *Queer Eye for the Straight Guy, Queer Duck,* or *Queer as Folk*—a far cry from political use of the term by radical activist groups like Queer Nation in the 1990s. Since queer people in the West began reclaiming the word in the late 1970s, the embodiment of queerness has taken many shapes, inspiring critical theories within the academy and signifying various sexual and political practices. But at the large Midwestern university where this study was conducted, it is uncertain what exactly informs young people's use of this controversial term. This chapter is dedicated to exploring how members of LGBT (and sometimes Q for queer or questioning) student organizations at an urban, public university in the Midwest think about and relate to the term queer in their sense of identity, community, and activism. The following excerpts are taken from a larger ethnographic study that was inspired by my experiences working with these diverse students as the university's LGBTQ coordinator.

Considering the lack of a cohesive or consistent definition of queer in the United States, in addition to the term's pejorative history and its association with radical activists, one could argue that it is an unlikely identification for teens and young adults from rural or conservative Midwestern towns and public school systems that fail to offer comprehensive sex education, LGBT history curriculum, or Gay-Straight Alliances. Yet, as this study reveals, queer is being taken up by many students as they begin questioning binary-based identities and as they strive for a more inclusive sense of community. This chapter explores how student group members engage with queer and contextualizes these students' voices within some current ideas of queer research from various fields.

Debates over the term queer often embody the most contentious issues within social movements organized around sexual orientation and gender—issues over the notion of an essential or fixed identity and "the policing of that identity's boundaries and the concomitant exclusion of the gay community's 'others,' be they female, nonwhite, working class, or transgendered," as queer theorist Thomas Piontek (2006, p. 3) articulates. My discussions with these students revealed that they are highly aware of this exclusion of "others," labeled by one student "misfits," within the so-called gay community. As articulated by my study's participants, such "misfits" often employ queer to represent their distinct positions as the marginalized within a minority, while elsewhere the term is used to critique the gender binary of hetero/homosexual discourses, to highlight gender nonconformity in various cultural contexts, or to remain ambiguous when identifying one's sexual orientation. Queer thus yields a provocative power to critique, re-envision, and evade; this potential for multiple meanings and usages has kept queer a relevant and controversial term for decades, especially among some LGBTQ youth cultures.

The concept of queerness may have taken on additional significance in the United States with the cultural and political rise of a new homonormativity, a recent phenomenon that queer historian Lisa Duggan (2002) defines as a "depoliticized gay culture anchored in domesticity and consumption" (p. 179), which sets a standard for respectable gay behavior that reflects the values of upper-middle-class whiteness. Duggan (2002) is quick to point out, however, that her use of *homonormativity* does not suggest it exactly compares with heteronormativity since "there is no structure for gay life, no matter how conservative or normalizing, that might compare with the institutions promoting and sustaining heterosexual coupling" (p. 191). But many students in this study seemed highly aware of and affected by the cultural standards set by homonormativity, and the majority of the comments excerpted in this chapter focus on students' sense of homonormative trends and the oppositional stance to such trends that queer often represents.

In critiquing the normalizing trends within dominant LGBTQ culture, other queer theorists (Cohen, 1997; Gamson, 1995; Goldman, 2004) have described how homonormativity as a cultural and discursive force downplays differences between LGBTQ peoples or even erases these differences in order to bolster those images and expressions that have gained some level of social acceptance in recent years. Many self-identified queers reject this normalization of their sexual and gender identities, but their voices are not often documented in current sexuality research. In my review of LGBTQ youth research studies and their methodologies, I found a noticeable lack of queer theoretical considerations of identity, as well as outdated uses of language, linear notions of identity development, and attempts to define what counts as "legitimate" sexual identities. One example is sociologist Ritch Savin-Williams's (2005) research published in the book *The New Gay Teenager*, in which he exerts his institutional power to claim that there are debates over the legitimacy of certain identities: "Current controversies over identity labels include whether transexuality reflects a sexual or a gender identity, whether 'sexual fluidity' and 'unlabeled' are sexual identities, and whether idiosyncratic contemporary terms (e.g., 'queerboi') are legitimate" (p. 35). Failing to contextualize these so-called debates, I would challenge his discourse as being grounded in a homonormative and institutionalized perspective that has become all too common in academic research of LGBTQ youth. In fact, in the Editor's Note of a recent issue of the *Journal of LGBT Youth*, James T. Sears (2008) claims, "As younger people identify themselves queerly and act through the phenomenological selves of sex, gender, identity, and desire, our adult understanding is next to nil" (p. 1).

Although some educational researchers apply queer theory to their research methodologies (Talburt & Steinberg, 2000; Rofes, 2005), many studies from the field of education focusing on

LGBTQ college students have been critiqued for their "pre-millennial social and methodological constructs" (Sears, 2008, p. 2)—the most apparent being the various identity development models (e.g., the Cass, Klein, or D'Augelli models) that have overly determined how LGBTQ people are studied and represented and which are unable to account for the intersections of race, ethnicity, class, gender identity, ability, and nationality. Therefore, my aim in using open-ended focus group discussions was to encourage participants to proclaim and "compete for their preferred cultural scripts," as detailed in the scripting theory of C. Lynn Carr (1999), and in my questioning I avoided making assumptions about participants' use of common identity labels and instead prompted them to clarify taken-for-granted terminology.

As my participants' use of queer depended greatly on their cultural context, I must acknowledge the ways in which the context of an urban public university both limits and focuses this study. For instance, conducting the study within a public educational institution takes advantage of the ways in which a school is a "concentrated site of contestation around issues of power and identity" (Rasmussen, Rofes, & Talburt, 2004, p. 2), which was especially evident in the comments of those students who had completed coursework in the Department of Women's, Gender, and Sexuality Studies. But attending a university with such course offerings represents an educational privilege that not all LGBTQ young adults have. Furthermore, some LGBTQ-identified student group members are able to participate in these groups in part because they have the luxury of recreational time and feel welcomed in predominantly white spaces, both reflective of class and race privileges. However, many of these participants prioritize their participation in their group and make time to attend meetings even though they also work part-time jobs, exist without financial or emotional support from family, come from working-class backgrounds, and deal with racial and class inequalities. I also must point out, as Rofes (2005) does, that LGBTQ student groups might not appeal as much to queer youth of color who might identify more strongly with their racial, ethnic, or religious identities and thus feel more legitimized in groups with such a focus (p. 59). This surely influenced my self-selected sample of participants, but in an attempt to remain sensitive to the racial and class diversity of my participants, I asked all participants to fill out anonymous questionnaires about their multiple social identities. Of the 41 questionnaires returned, 7 people identified themselves as racial minorities, and the majority of participants (35 out of 41) identified as middle or upper-middle class.

I distributed the questionnaires prior to the discussion of queerness in hopes that these demographic questions would prompt participants to explore how multiple identity categories are at play both in their individual lives and within the collective, but participants did not directly address the influence of their own race, class, nationality, or ability on their ideas. Some students did, however, assert that they understood how the race and class of others could potentially influence their association with gay- versus queer-identified groups. This line of reasoning was especially pronounced as they discussed how gay-identified groups are often dominated by white gay men of a certain class who, as one student said, "can easily assimilate because they have a level of visibility and social acceptance." Even though comments like this did touch on racial and class inequalities, I acknowledge the ways in which these aspects were not more thoroughly interrogated and discussed, and I call for further research that can more accurately account for the diversity of LGBTQ, queer, Same-Gender Loving, intersex, Two-Spirit, and allied communities, and the way "racial discrimination and marginalization, immigration, poverty, cultural and linguistic alienation, and isolation" influence the use of queer in different cultural contexts (Driver, 2008, p. 6).

Analysis of Focus Groups

Although there are several LGBTQ student groups at this university (at least five on the main campus), I chose to focus on the three groups that have the most membership and overall activity—GenderBloc, LGBT People of Medicine, and Out On Campus. To give a brief description of each, GenderBloc defines itself as "a radical queer activist organization" that "use[s] grassroots action, performance art, activism, and educational programming to work for queer rights [and] for recognition of queer people in society, especially focusing on gender non-conformity" (GenderBloc, 2008, para. 1). LGBT People of Medicine functions more as a professional association group composed of a loose network of LGBTQ and allied medical students and faculty, as well as practicing physicians from the community, who organize monthly potlucks "for fellowship among current and future healthcare workers of all sexual orientations" and conduct or assist "with activities intended to help future physicians understand how they can best care for their patients of the LGBT population" (College of Medicine, 2008, para. 1). Out On Campus is the oldest LGBTQ student group on campus. Its leaders at the time of this study were encouraging their diverse members to become more activist-oriented, since in the past the group was devoted almost solely to organizing social events such as going to nightclubs, films, pool parties, and LGBTQ-related campus events.

Although these organizations are distinct in the way they define, organize, and educate themselves, broad themes about queerness developed within and across the groups. In debating which people in which contexts use queer rather than the more traditional labels of gay, lesbian, or bisexual, students discussed the social and political implications of identity labels, and each focus group described the factors that they believe determine how one identifies, such as social status or whether one's gender identity and expression could be easily assimilated. For the purposes of this chapter, however, I must limit my discussion to the central theme that students discussed with the most detail and enthusiasm, namely how queer represents to them an engaged and questioning stance that resists assimilation to the dominant culture and through which they feel empowered to explore new structures for their personal relationships and communities.

The ability of queer to simultaneously unite diverse populations as well as trouble the notion of rigid, binary-based identities makes it appealing to some LGBTQ people and dangerous to others, and thus queerness can expose ideological differences and power dynamics within LGBTQ and allied populations. In my interview with queer-identifying GenderBloc member Rita, she identifies, based on her experiences, certain societal factors that might lead a gay-identified person to resist the term queer:

Researcher: Who do you think tends not to use queer and why?

Rita: White, middle-class gay men. I feel like when you reach a certain level of privilege in mainstream society, you tend to not want to be dragged down by the other people who cannot assimilate. Usually, white gay men can easily assimilate because they have a level of visibility and social acceptance. Their sexuality has been assimilated into their entire being and it's no longer the main thing defining who they are. It's become like just another part of them. But for others in the queer community, they don't have that privilege, and their queerness is what defines them.

This student explains that for genderqueer people who cannot or will not "pass" as normatively gendered or monosexual,[1] queer can act as more than an inclusive label: it can signify the need to resist rigid taxonomies that categorize people based only on one aspect of their multiple and shifting identities.

At the root of this kind of anti-identity identification is an embodied critique of the traditional foundations of sexual and gender identities based on binary systems and notions of a fixed and unified self. Queer theorist Ruth Goldman (2004) classifies such people as the "queer queers," explaining that this oppositional use of queer does indeed destabilize the traditional concept of identity: "The term 'queer' emphasizes the blurring of identities . . . and offers a way in which to express many intersecting queer selves—in my case, to name just a few, as a bisexual, a Jew, a feminist, an anti-capitalist, an anti-racist—all of which stand in opposition to powerful societal norms" (p. 84). Goldman contemplates the oppositional stance of queer queers as contrasted with other uses of queer that signify a less intersectional perspective, such as queer as simple shorthand for lesbian and gay. In this regard she cautions against the commodification of queer as yet another identity label appealing to those with privilege and capital: "As 'queer' gains currency, it is increasingly being appropriated and commodified, and thus increasingly risks collapsing into another term for white lesbians and gays, and ultimately white gay men" (Goldman, 2004, p. 85).

According to Rita and echoed in the following experiences of Out On Campus students, however, queer has in recent years often been rejected by more privileged white, cisgender[2] gay men and embraced by genderqueer and transgender people whose non-normative expressions have led to their marginalization within some LGBTQ contexts:

Ned: I kind of see queer as more non-normative. Like queer to me means more, I don't want to say transgender, but not gender normative—like a masculine dressing woman or a feminine dressing man, or someone who doesn't present a typical gender expression.

Shannon: I use the word queer to identify who I am as far as sexuality and as far as my gender identity because . . . it's been forced on all of us from an early age that there's a binary of gender, there's a binary of sexuality: that you're straight or gay, you're a girl or a boy. And for me there exists so much fuzziness in all of those spectrums that I don't necessarily feel that I identify with any of the terms, but for me queer kind of embodies that you don't have to decide: you don't have to make a decision, that it's okay for there to be a fuzziness.

Lacy: I've found that when it comes to non-normative gender identity and bisexuality or pansexuality,[3] that [using queer] is a little more common. And also with the questioning people or those who don't like labels.

This exchange is an example of how some students see queer as encouraging their critique of the binary system of gender and sexuality and the identities, or mere labels, defined by such a rigid system. Shannon later emphasizes that without this implicit critique, queer as yet another identity category would not be as appealing: "I don't need the word queer, but that's finally one term that the larger definition is more inclusive. So it's not really the word queer, it's the concept of inclusivity that the word implies."

Although Shannon appreciates how queer legitimizes her personal sense of the innate ambiguity or "fuzziness" of sexuality and gender, she and other students also acknowledge how fuzzy and unclear this term may seem to the general population when they use it as an identity label. Describing a typical negotiation that occurs in such conversations, Lacy says she is often met with a "blank stare" when she identifies as queer, and the inevitable follow-up questions include, "What do you mean? Do you like boys or girls?" But two students from Out On Campus claim that this confusion can be productive, leading to much more complex and educational dialogues about the nature of sexuality and gender:

> Lacy: Well, more so once they're like, "Queer? Oh, okay, so what specifically?" And I'll say, "Well, bi." And they'll be like, "Well, how does that work?" Then I have to specify like, monogamous, polyamorous, and on and on. It just gets ridiculous, but you know, hey, educate them more now, less a pain for me later.

> Shannon: Yeah, I've had the same kind of experience where if someone asks, "Well, are you gay?" Or if I said to someone who I didn't know or who I did know for that matter, like, "I'm a lesbian," then I feel like that kind of ends their question process, that kind of puts the brakes on where they're going to go further, not all the time but usually. And then they have a preconceived notion based on the way I'm dressed and different things like that: they're probably going to assume that I like feminine women, and that's the only type of people that I'm sexually attracted to, which is not the case at all. So using the word queer for me, kind of, it leaves a lot of people kind of dumbfounded, but it opens up an arena for discussion, which is really like you said, it can be kind of aggravating. But . . . you know people are misinformed and uninformed by no fault of their own because it's not something that's talked about in our culture, but I feel like using the word queer for me kind of helps to open that up for more discussion.

These students have thus come to expect the challenge of educating others when they identify as queer, which can be both empowering and "aggravating." But as both students infer, it seems to be part of the queer territory.

While queer has remained "in itself an unstable term, one whose effectiveness depends upon it remaining unstable" (Carlin & DiGrazia, 2004, p. 198), Shannon alludes to the consistent cultural assumptions attached to the identity terms of lesbian or gay in terms of gender expression and attraction. Other students discussed their awareness of and grappling with this "mainstreaming of gay and lesbian culture" (Halberstam, 2008, p. 35), which has involved a commodification that Out On Campus members described in this way:

> Ned: When I think of gay culture, I kind of think of bars and flashing lights and rainbow flags. When I think of queer culture, again I associate queer in my mind with not being gender normative; I kind of think of younger queer people just hanging out and walking around and doing non-gender-normative things.

> Javier: As odd as it sounds, I think I might have that same thought. It's like with gay you think of rainbows and Pride in general, and then when it comes to queer, it seems more of a natural, low-profile kind of setting.

> Paul: I think based on what everybody said, it's kind of like the heterosexual world sees it as gay and they only understand the word gay. And queer is what we understand and how we see it. And maybe the ones that are in the gay community that don't understand the word queer, maybe are living too much of a heterosexual life, I don't know.

> Javier: They need to be gayer.

Queer theorist Michael Warner (1993) explains that the commodification of gay culture has had clear class- and age-related effects: "In the lesbian and gay movement, the institutions of culture-building have been market-mediated: bars, discos, special services, newspapers, magazines, phone lines, resorts, urban commercial districts," and thus "dominated by those with capital" (pp. xvi–xvii). He goes on to describe the "nonmarket forms of association" that other identity movements have utilized— "churches, kinship, traditional residence"—as being "less available for queers" (p. xvii). For young people like Javier who come from rural, small towns, the LGBTQ student organizations at this university have been, in his words, "kinda like a family, especially for me 'cause my family is usually kind of a horrible thing to be around," and several other students agreed that these organizations play a vital role in their lives. Since financially unstable young people are often not included in institutions of culture-building that are geared toward those with capital, such commodified cultural systems do not take account of the difficulties facing young queer people: "Heterosexual ideology, in combination with a potent ideology about gender and identity in maturation, therefore bears down in the heaviest and often deadliest way on those with the least resources to combat it: queer children and teens" (Warner, 1993, p. xvi).

But as youth studies researcher Susan Driver (2008) claims, these same factors are inspiring some queer youth to "become innovative participants in do-it-yourself media projects, popular cultural narratives, local drag performances, anti-oppression activisms, online communities, and music subcultures," and such youth "push us to become nuanced in the ways we read, watch, and listen to young people telling their own stories and envisioning their futures" (p. 1). The activities of the explicitly queer-identified group GenderBloc exemplify this point as members publish a quarterly zine called the *Queer Canon* and regularly host and perform in drag shows on and off campus, the proceeds of which they sometimes donate to national organizations like the former Gender Public Advocacy Coalition. These students have also compiled curricula on gender and sexuality they call the Queer Education Program, which they are advocating to become a unit within the university's Peer Education Program; and the group has recently produced a Trans Survival Guide for "transgender and genderqueer students at the university" (GenderBloc, n.d., para.1). At least for this particular group, filling the void left by a commodified gay culture has led to the creation of a dynamic queer subculture grounded in activism, education, and creative expression.

Analyzing these focus group discussions has impressed upon me the practical utility of queer for many in this particular age group, and I agree with Driver's (2008) idea that

> In many ways, youth as a time of transition and flux, in between childhood and adulthood, renders the status of "queer" highly resonant to young people pressured by normative developmental ideals of self and reproductive narratives of maturation. . . . [Y]outh articulate themselves in polyvalent ways . . . [and] they use "queer" as an adjective to suggest a rich and layered sense of self, evoking a transitional process, refusing to define themselves once and for all. (pp. 11–12)

Not only can *queer* promote alternative modes of development, it can also bring into focus the normalizing strains of homonormative gay culture that several students alluded to, such as Hamilton's idea that "there are ways to be gay that are really easy in conservative areas," and Paul's sense that "the ones that are in the gay community that don't understand the word queer, maybe are living too much of a heterosexual life" and, as Javier added, "need to be gayer." Students expressed varying levels of insight regarding this homonormative identity or set of standards, but it surfaced as a relevant topic in every focus group.

In these discussions, students identified some examples of homonormativity to include a privileging of the monosexual gay and lesbian identity over the non-monosexual identities of bisexuals, pansexuals, and others; traditional masculine and feminine gender expressions; monogamous and long-term relationships deserving of marriage rights; and other assimilationist values that reinforce cultural stigmas against genderqueer, liberationist, non-monosexual, and sex-positive people and their identities. Furthermore, the promotion of homonormative behavior intersects with other dominant images of LGBTQ people in national media as white, middle to upper class, fully abled, traditionally gendered, and possessing full citizenship status. These intersections construct an imaginary community and culture that prove Goldman's (2004) point that there are "ways in which we manage to establish norms even when we are struggling to resist and challenge them" (p. 93).

In trying to decipher what exactly makes a hypothetical queer culture different from a gay culture, these students described various examples of homonormativity and its gesture toward traditional respectability, especially in the structuring of relationships:

Chloe: I feel like you have a lot of really like traditional gay relationships where they still adhere to a lot of the social norms in terms of, you know, gender roles and monogamy . . . you know, that whole idea that if you're in a gay relationship, it's like people have to do everything that they can to like show that it's not any different, you know, than like straight relationships. So I see, like, queerness as like a rejection of that—being like, we can be whatever we want and be in relationships however we want to.

Hamilton: I think that's interesting 'cause I think there are, like, emerging structures for gay relationships and lesbian relationships now. And I feel like as those become more, you know, mainstream, maybe they won't be included in queer anymore because of the radical nature of queer.

According to these students, queerness resists this homonormative pressure of social assimilation and, instead, legitimizes what Chloe described as "the new avenues that people are exploring" in their relationships. In this vein, Out On Campus member Paul concluded that people who use or identify as queer tend to embrace their non-normative social status and feel empowered to resist norms: "Queer is definitely used by the people who are more comfortable with themselves. They are fine with being queer; they're fine with being gay. They don't have anything to hide; they don't have anything to hide from anyone else."

Emerging from these conversations is a sense that queerness can represent an oppositional stance to heterosexism and homonormativity, and even the youngest members of Out On Campus expressed an understanding of "being queer" as synonymous with having an analytical and socially engaged perspective.

Javier: I think that being queer is like the luckiest thing that ever happened. I feel like we are all—people who identify as queer—are like gifted, you know? I feel like it's one of my favorite things is to be able to talk to people who try to understand and feel . . . like there are so many questions about gender and sexuality that can't be answered, but I feel like I'm having those conversations with people and like sharing that experience and that my mind is open to that, you know? It's like my mind has expanded a little bit in kind of figuring it all out. I feel lucky and I wouldn't want it to be any other way.

Paul: I would agree with what you're saying. I feel like queer, even though in the beginning I would-
            n't have thought that way, but queer has been the best thing that ever happened to me. It
            leaves the opportunity for you to take it, but it opens so many doors.

Shannon: And it's so much fun.

Paul: It is.

Bayard: It opens so many doors, that's interesting—as opposed to shuts a lot of doors.

Paul: I'm just saying being queer with yourself opens up doors so that you can actually question
            things. Too many people who live in the heterosexual world don't have to question anything,
            and they might even live their entire lives without questioning anything. And I feel like being
            queer gives you the opportunity to look at norms and see what you think is right and
            wrong, other than just following what everyone else is doing because you're already outcasts
            anyway and have to stand on your own two feet and make up your mind what's best for you.

Ned: Like it opens doors to personal growth rather than like more tangible job opportunities or
            something.

Javier: I mean this as a queer community, as we are becoming stronger and more prominent in the
            world, then we are making others question themselves, which adds to our community
            because they're finding things about themselves, because they are questioning . . . we need
            to enforce the fact that other people should question themselves.

Paul: So you're saying, though, queer not just in the gay community, but queer opens up other doors
            for straight people too?

Javier: Possibly, they could.

Articulating a queer, questioning stance allowed these students to acknowledge how they have ben-
efited from analyzing social norms of sexuality and gender, and their hope that heterosexual allies will
join them in this practice reflects their desire for queerness to be as inclusive of and helpful to as many
people as possible. They clearly do not want another rigid identity category that encourages the policing of its boundaries, but instead appreciate *queer*'s ability to expose heterosexism and develop an oppositional perspective to dominant norms.

Queerness, for most of these students, is thus not only desirable but vital to maintaining their
sense of agency and diversity within their community. Their discourse of queerness contrasts with
the discourses of pride and legal power that more mainstream (and sometimes apologetic) LGBTQ
communities use, and some of these students are using a queer lens to critique and resist hetero/homo-

normativities. Warner (1993) suggests one potential outcome of such a queer oppositional perspective: "Heteronormativity can be overcome only by actively imagining a necessarily and desirably queer world" (p. xvi). In his book *The Trouble with Normal: Sex, Politics, and the Ethics of Queer Life*, Warner (1999) continues his argument that such a necessary and desirable queer world would not prioritize same-sex marriage and other gestures toward normalcy, but would expose such heteropatriarchal values as based on a "false morality" that promotes a culture of sexual shame, among other things (p. 36).

Warner (1999) turns the assimilationist logic on its head through promoting a queer culture in which "a relation to others, in [queer] contexts, begins in an acknowledgment of all that is most abject and least reputable in oneself," where "abjection is understood to be a shared condition" (p. 35). This rejection of hetero- and homonormativity and embrace of abjection offers "dignity in shame," which he claims is "a premise of queer culture, and one reason why people in it are willing to call themselves queer—a word that, as Eve Segdwick notes, 'emblazons its connection to shame in a way that still roils the moralists'" (Warner, 1999, p. 36). As Paul from Out On Campus said, "We are all in the same [queer] umbrella because of our struggles, because of our denials, because of our oppression, because of hate." Lacy agreed, saying, "I'd like to add the whole self-identification factor of being queer 'cause I think that's the root of it. It's how you feel; it's a reflection of how society treats you and how you feel your place in society." But Warner (1999) insists that this "dignity in shame" is the basis for a queer ethic: "Queer scenes are the true salons des refusés, where the most heterogeneous people are brought into great intimacy by their common experience of being despised and rejected in a world of norms that they now recognize as false morality" (pp. 35–36).

In seeking to explore how young people relate to the ideas of queerness in their cultural contexts and through analyzing their discussions and stories, I have found what Driver (2008) suggests to be accurate: "Embracing queer notions as a living language responsive of their ongoing insubordination to heteronormative codes, youth claim the term 'queer' to accommodate their shame, fear, doubts, rage, and curiosities . . . as a heuristic device that helps them navigate adult reasoning and regulations" (p. 12). I would also add that queerness goes far beyond the "Gay? Fine by me"[4] mantra and offers these young people an oppositional perspective from which they can critique heterosexism, gender stereotypes, and what Warner (1993) calls "the regimes of the normal" (p. xxvi), including homonormativity. This queer oppositional perspective is rooted in "not an identity, but a questioning stance, a cluster of methodologies that let us explore the taken for granted and the familiar from new vantage points," as Piontek (2006) has defined it (p. 2).

Although this oppositional stance and desire for an inclusive community is not unique to queer youth, it is clear that many of my participants are beginning to understand at an early age the problems of policing identities and are responding by actively queering identity-based community and culture. Such early engagement with concepts of identity and community is a provocative outgrowth of people coming out at younger ages during a dramatic cultural shift regarding sexuality and gender. This study has revealed that some LGBTQ young adults already possess a sophisticated knowledge and experience of both homo- and heteronormativity and are seeking out new ways to educate and express themselves that challenge these norms. Their work thus deserves more attention and support not only from their LGBTQ elders but also from their school communities.

Notes

1. Monosexual refers to the binary-based categories of hetero/homosexuality that limit one's sexual object choice to a single gender (James, 1996, p. 220).
2. Cisgender is defined by the Division of Diversity and Community Engagement (2008) at the University of Texas at Austin as "provid[ing] a name for a gender identity or performance in a gender role that society considers to be a match or appropriate for one's sex. The idea of cisgender originated as a way to shift the focus off of a marginalized group, by defining not only the minority group [transgender] but also the majority" (para. 14).
3. The members of GenderBloc define pansexual in their zine as "A person who has potential emotional, physical, and/or sexual attraction to any person irrespective of sex or gender" (Queer Canon, n.d., p. 6).
4. A slogan made popular by students from Duke University in 2003 who used the phrase as part of a T-shirt project to address homophobia on the campus after the *Princeton Review* had named the university one of the nation's least unfriendly campuses in the nation for LGBTQ students ("Gay? Fine by Me," n.d., 2010).

References

Carlin, D., & DiGrazia, J. (Eds.). (2004). *Queer cultures*. Upper Saddle River, NJ: Pearson Prentice Hall.

Carr, C.L. (1999). Cognitive scripting and sexual identification: Essentialism, anarchism, and constructionism. *Symbolic Interaction, 22*(1), 1–24.

Cohen, C.J. (1997). Punks, bulldaggers, and welfare queens: The radical potential of queer politics. *GLQ: A Journal of Lesbian and Gay Studies, 3*, 437–465.

College of Medicine. (2008). Lesbian, gay, bisexual, and transgender people in medicine. Retrieved March 17, 2009, from http://medonestop.uc.edu/ MedOneStop/Organizations/StudentOrg.aspx?OrgID=44

D'Augelli, A.R., & Grossman, A.H. (2006). Researching lesbian, gay, and bisexual youth: Conceptual, practical, and ethical considerations. *Journal of Gay & Lesbian Issues in Education, 3*(2/3), 35–56.

Driver, S. (2008). Introducing queer youth cultures. In S. Driver (Ed.), *Queer youth cultures* (pp. 1–18). Albany: State University of New York Press.

Duggan, L. (2002). The new homonormativity: The sexual politics of neoliberalism. In R. Castronovo & D.D. Nelson (Eds.), *Materializing democracy: Toward a revitalized cultural politics* (pp. vii–xxxi). Durham, NC: Duke University Press.

Gamson, J. (1995). Must identity movements self-destruct? A queer dilemma. *Social Problems, 42*, 390–407.

Gay? Fine by me. (n.d.) Retrieved November 23, 2010, from http://www.williams.edu/ MCC/resources/qrTShirt.php

GenderBloc. (2008). Flyers and ads. Retrieved November 7, 2008, from http://homepages.uc.edu/~southaea/genderbloc/index.php/Flyers_and_Ads

GenderBloc. (n.d.). Trans survival guide. Retrieved April 26, 2009, from http://homepages.uc.edu/%7Esouthaea/genderbloc/images/a/a8/ Trans_survival_guide.pdf

Goldman, R. (2004). Who is that queer queer? In D. Carlin & J. DiGrazia (Eds.), *Queer cultures* (pp. 83–97). Upper Saddle River, NJ: Pearson Prentice Hall.

Halberstam, J. (2008). What's that smell? Queer temporalities and subcultural lives. In S. Driver (Ed.), *Queer youth cultures* (pp. 27–50). Albany: State University of New York Press.

James, C. (1996). Denying complexity: The dismissal and appropriation of bisexuality in queer, lesbian, and gay theory. In B. Beemyn & M. Eliason (Eds.), *Queer studies: A lesbian, gay, bisexual, and transgender anthology*. New York: New York University Press.

Meek, J.B. (2008). Lose the radicals, wear a suit, and meet me in the Rose Garden: A critique of the Human Rights Campaign's gay agenda. *Intersections: Women's and Gender Studies in Review across Disciplines*. Forthcoming.

Piontek, T. (2006). Queering gay and lesbian studies. Champaign-Urbana: University of Illinois Press.

Queer canon (n.d.). [electronic version]. Retrieved April 11, 2009, from http://homepages.uc.edu/%7Esouthaea/genderbloc/images/a/a8/Queer_Canon_0 08.pdf

Rasmussen, M.L., Rofes, E., & Talburt, S. (Eds.). (2004). *Youth and sexualities: Pleasure, subversion, and insubordination in and out of schools*. New York: Palgrave Macmillan.

Rofes, E. (2005). *A radical rethinking of sexuality and schooling: Status quo or status queer?* Lanham, MD: Rowman & Littlefield.

Savin-Williams, R.C. (2005). *The new gay teenager*. Cambridge: Harvard University Press.

Sears, J.T. (2008). Editor's note: The (re)searching of queer youth. *Journal of LGBT Youth*, *5*(3), 1–3.

Student activities and leadership development. (n.d.). Retrieved April 11, 2009, from https://www.uc.edu/sald/OrgListing.aspx

Talburt, S., & Steinberg, S.R. (Eds.). (2000). *Thinking queer: Sexuality, culture, and education*. New York: Peter Lang.

Warner, M. (1993). Introduction. In M. Warner (Ed.), *Fear of a queer planet: Queer politics and social theory* (pp. vii–xxxi). Minneapolis: University of Minnesota Press.

Warner, M. (1999*). The trouble with normal: Sex, politics, and the ethics of queer life*. New York: The Free Press.

Notes

1. Monosexual refers to the binary-based categories of hetero/homosexuality that limit one's sexual object choice to a single gender (James, 1996, p. 220).
2. Cisgender is defined by the Division of Diversity and Community Engagement (2008) at the University of Texas at Austin as "provid[ing] a name for a gender identity or performance in a gender role that society considers to be a match or appropriate for one's sex. The idea of cisgender originated as a way to shift the focus off of a marginalized group, by defining not only the minority group [transgender] but also the majority" (para. 14).
3. The members of GenderBloc define pansexual in their zine as "A person who has potential emotional, physical, and/or sexual attraction to any person irrespective of sex or gender" (Queer Canon, n.d., p. 6).
4. A slogan made popular by students from Duke University in 2003 who used the phrase as part of a T-shirt project to address homophobia on the campus after the *Princeton Review* had named the university one of the nation's least unfriendly campuses in the nation for LGBTQ students ("Gay? Fine by Me," n.d., 2010).

CHAPTER NINETEEN

Let Me in!

The Impact of the Discourse of Impossibility on Research and Curricular (Re)formation

SANDRA J. SCHMIDT

I recently attempted to undertake a research project with high school students asking them to make visible where they received messages that shaped their sexual identity(ies). The purpose was to learn from students how schools shape their sexual identities and imaginations. Unable to gain immediate access through local school districts, I posted a message to other members of the AERA Queer SIG, an organization that stretches across the United States and Canada and beyond North America, asking for advice about how to pose the inquiry to schools. I received a flood of replies from researchers in the United States, every one of them discouraging. From seemingly liberal to conservative states and institutions, I was repeatedly told that no school district would give me access to its schools/students. It was too controversial for administrators to undertake given the potential for internal disruption and/or community repercussions. Each response, though, acknowledged the need for such work. If we know the research is important, why don't we do it? Are these respondents correct, or are we so mired in a discourse of impossibility that we cannot imagine the possibilities for research?

Although administrators and parents might argue that sexuality has no place in schools, Stephen Thornton (2003) proposed that gay and lesbian issues in schools are a "hidden curriculum that everyone sees." He argues that schools do not explicitly address gay and lesbian issues in the (social studies)[1] curriculum; therefore, schools claim that they do not teach about sexuality. The formal curriculum, ripe with opportunity to show the influence of gay persons and cultures on society and policy, refuses to make such people and issues available to students. Thornton counters, "Although unmentioned in the publicly announced curriculum, all young people learn that sex role deviance, actual or perceived, exacts a heavy price. It is surely one of the most successful exercises in social training that schools perform" (p. 277). Noting the detrimental impact of the loud silence on the curriculum, Thornton proposes a more inclusive curriculum as well as inquiry into the impact of the silence.

The critiques offered by Thornton and others contribute to a field of literature concerned with the efficacy, imagination, and identity of young people, especially lesbian, gay, bisexual, transgendered, transsexual, queer, questioning, and intersex (LGBTQQI)[2] youth. They deconstruct the heteronormative underpinnings of research. Other research cites a hostile school climate that alienates LGBTQQ youth and youth identified by their peers as LGBTQ. There is research about/on/of curriculum, but there is a dearth of empirical research about the relationship between curriculum/learning/school climate and youth identities, achievement, and efficacy. An examination of the primary journal whose mission is to link LGBTQ youth and schools reveals the limitation of available research. Even in a journal whose goal is to address LGBTQ issues in schools, there are few empirical articles about this relationship. In 2008, after publishing fifteen issues, *The Journal of Gay and Lesbian Issues in Schools* became *The Journal of LGBTQ Youth*. While I do not know the reason behind the title change and regenerated mission, the purview of articles reveals a shortage of research directly related to schools and far more attention to youth and higher education. Of the 98 articles published in the journal in the last seven years, 21 consisted of research conducted on college campuses, 16 of research conducted outside the U.S., and 8 of research conducted on P–12 teachers. Of the 16 articles addressing U.S. LGBTQ school-age youth, fewer than half were about schools and even fewer were conducted in schools. This is a curious dilemma since we repeatedly claim the necessity for such research.

If we know there is a need for school-based research about LGBTQQI issues and that it is not being done, we need to examine the reasons for this absence. This chapter explores the possibility that at least a portion of the answer lies in unaligned discourses. I propose that the discourse of LGBTQQI issues available to schools via scholars does not speak with the discourse of policy imperatives to which schools must attend. The manner in which we, queer scholars, frame issues writes us out of the dominant discourse of accountability. As such, schools never need to consider the "appropriateness" of the research; they can limit access by deeming this research as unnecessary in the current policy climate. The chapter is organized around a query of four literatures—that of policy; that of critical multicultural education, from which LGBTQQI claims to education arise; theories that disrupt heteronormativity; and literature that seeks to solve the problem of marginalized youth—to explore the resulting discourses. The last two literatures, which examine queer discourses, are the core of the chapter, as they help us understand the problem of absences in research.

A Theoretical Interlude

The discussion in this chapter relies on two theoretical concepts—discourse and queer theory.

Discourse makes explicit the embeddedness of language in social structures (Fairclough, 2001; Foucault, 1978/2000, 1981; Mills, 2004). Words are not merely language; the political, historical, and cultural contexts around those words give them meaning. A word has limited meaning unto itself but has extensive meaning within a broader network of ideas. Many of these meanings are specific to a group, whether that group is a nation or a community of academics. In each context, language is used in a particular manner to achieve a particular end. Critical theorists attend to the power of discourse as a mechanism for dictating how we understand the world (Britzman, 1995; Lather, 1991; Mills, 2004). They argue that what we can know exists through the discourses we have access to. In my academic community, a coffee shop has a particular meaning that helps me make decisions about how to use its space. My uses differ from people who define the place differently. They look strangely at anyone who spends hours sipping a cup of tea in front of their computer. Applied to identities of people, such discourse is powerful because it identifies proper and improper ways to be. The assignment of attributes to language creates categories that affect how we identify and behave, and our actions reinforce that meaning.

Queer, as a theory, interrogates how performances of sexuality and gender are normalized. Queer theorists argue that the production of norms/standards of sexuality regulates behavior and identity (Britzman, 1995; Butler, 2004; Dilley, 1999; Jagose, 1997). A standard arises when a term like heterosexual acquires a set of attributes that define what is socially acceptable. Heterosexual is not merely a word but rather a concept imbued with a set of characteristics by which to define normal and allow individuals to assess and monitor themselves and others. By consistently referring to sexual identities through this language, the "normal" center is retained. The power of the center is reaffirmed through the use of binaries such as masculinity/femininity and heterosexual/homosexual, through which words acquire meaning. The use of opposing ideas makes them interdependent for meaning. In relation to discourse, queer theory examines the performances and mechanisms that stabilize discursive meanings. The theory of normalization has influence beyond gender and sexuality.

Understanding queer theory and discourse are fundamental to reading this chapter. The chapter has no methods section or discussion of how the literatures are read. The tools described here are utilized to describe the discourses that emerge when a set of literature is considered together. It draws attention to the implications of that discourse and the social meaning and norms they produce.

Policy: The Discourse of Accountability

Research, even that conducted by unaffiliated researchers, exacts a toll on public school resources. Independent researchers must be able to rationalize the way(s) in which the research will benefit the school. Schools are more likely to support projects that parallel the research and evaluation demands/needs of the school or those that tie to larger educational discourses. Although education policy is ostensibly determined locally, recent federal initiatives have ushered in an era of reform that has tied the hands of local institutions. The 2002 reauthorization of the Elementary and Secondary Education Act as No Child Left Behind (NCLB) reshaped the influence of federal policy on states by requiring schools to adopt federal goals and setting priorities for major funding organizations. Since 2009, states unable to internally meet their needs in funding public education have been invited to supplement their funding/reform of their education program with money from the "Race to the Top Fund." These monies affect how a national discourse of accountability and standards has become locally embedded.

The four-pronged test of the "Race to the Top Fund"—adopting standards, building data systems, rewarding/retaining effective teachers, and turning around low-achieving schools—are consistent with the mandates of NCLB (U.S. Department of Education, 2009). The federal government claims that common standards, increased assessment, and improved data collection will make schools more accountable to the populace. Enter the age of accountability (Ravitch, 2010; Rothstein, 2008). Accountability addresses hiring and retaining highly qualified teachers, but its core focus is measuring the impact of their teaching. This has largely been done by the adoption of state curriculum standards and statewide, high-stakes tests that measure students' achievement of/teachers' teaching of those standards. As the pressure and consequences attached to these tests increase, so does the pressure to alter curriculum and school structures to help students perform better on these tests. Some states assess different content areas, but all states must test and report reading, writing, and numeracy achievement. Schools need researchers to help them evaluate curriculum and programs in these areas to improve test scores. Funding organizations such as the Institute of Education Sciences (IES) and the National Science Foundation (NSF) respond by putting out calls to develop intervention strategies to assist in the alignment of learning and testing in these areas.

The federal government has the ability to offer research money to scholars and incentive monies to schools and, recently, dole out consequences based upon its accountability mandates. Historically, states and localities have controlled their educational agendas. This means that school change must be consistent with the ideologies of the people with power in communities. While the federal government can hold schools accountable for their test scores, how schools get there is determined locally. Different localities adopt different curricular programs and materials. This has long been identified as the strength of the U.S. school system in adapting to a large, diverse nation. Local control appeals to federalist notions, but may allow localities to implement measures that are incongruent with national trends. If the politics of a local area do not support a particular justice issue, there is no pressure to alter practices except through a lawsuit (Birden, Gaither, & Laird, 2000). It was the federal courts, not localities, that upended racial segregation in local school districts. Local players have the power to make particular issues relevant to their localities and give them attention in the schools. As Birden, Gaither, and Laird (2000) purport, this means that in the Bible Belt South, communities that are strongly religious and anti-gay will ensure that LGBTQ issues are not addressed in their schools.

This discussion of policy is intended to raise awareness about some of the ways in which policy discourses and mandates affect the types of research done in schools. The national agenda has created a discourse of accountability. While the concept is actually quite broad, its relatively narrow usage in policies and accompanying research has produced a common cultural understanding of the word and its attributes—testing, school choice, standards, teacher merit. It pervades the education discourse of the government as well as the general populace. These ideas normalize what constitutes a meaningful education. It places standards, testing, and curriculum development at the forefront of entryway into schools. Locally, this means that accountability is the priority to which schools allocate their resources and what is determined to be an important research need. Presently, the emphasis is on particular curricular areas and the content and methods related to developing and implementing that curriculum to improve state and national test scores. Secondary in this discussion is that research interests and allowances are strongly affected by the will of the local community. Schools are less likely to embark on a project that is inconsistent with the views of the local community either because school leaders share in that view or because they fear consequences from that community. After all, school boards ultimately hire all school officials, and school boards are elected by the populace. The discourse and reality of school policy are important in considering how we (re)shape the discourse to make LGBTQ issues relevant and important to schools.

Critical Multicultural Education: The Need for Recognition and Redistribution

Political philosopher Nancy Fraser (1995, 2003) argues that justice for oppressed groups depends upon both recognition and redistribution. Central to her argument is the notion that while individuals may be oppressed, it will ultimately be groups that receive justice (see also Young, 2004, for further discussion of group identity and Appiah, 1996, for a counterargument). Recognition attends to the marginalization, absence, or domination of groups. The remedy in this case is legal and social recognition of marginalized groups. Redistribution addresses issues of access to resources. Remedies of maldistribution involve providing resources to marginalized groups or transforming structures that limit access by marginalized groups. Although few people categorize remedies as recognitive or redistributive, her call for both is consistent with the work of multicultural educators who recognize that students of color, LGBTQ youth, students from families with low incomes, students who speak English as a second language, and students with emotional or physical disabilities suffer from both a failure to be recognized as differentiated and a lack of access to particular but necessary resources in and through education.

Much of the work for justice in the education arena evolves under the umbrella of multicultural education. James Banks's (1993) five-tiered hierarchy for redressing race, gender, and class inequality birthed the field of multicultural education. At the rudimentary level are ways to recognize women and people of color in curriculum and classroom activities. At higher tiers are suggestions about how to dissect social structures that maintain injustice/racism/sexism. More recent work by Banks (2001) and others (Kozol, 2005; May, 1999; McLaren, 1994; Sleeter & Grant, 1999) have pushed even more the need for schools, not just the curriculum, to transform the institutional and structural injustices that are embedded in the education system and maintain a two-tiered educational system. Although the push may be for systemic change, these scholars do not advocate this at the expense of group identity (Vavrus, 2002; Williamson, Rhodes, & Dunson, 2007). They do not advocate for the assimilation of marginalized groups into the mainstream but draw upon pluralistic cultural understanding and awareness of the individuals and groups affected by these power shifts. The tenets of multicultural education are consistent with the understanding that social transformation requires both recognition and the restructuring of access to social resources.

Locating LGBTQ Issues in/for Schools

The literature about the best and proper ways to address LGBTQ issues in schools arises out of, but is distinct from, multicultural education. As in any academic field, there is no single conversation in this literature. What is common is the identification of the problems. While there are a variety of problems (and solutions) explored in the literature, there is some agreement about LGBTQQI students and issues in school curriculum and policy. There is a general acknowledgment that schools reinforce and support heterosexual identities. From here it is possible to divide the field into two conversations. Although these fields overlap in that each would agree with the issues raised by the others, the substance of how they frame problems and solutions differs. Discussion of these literatures and their audiences promotes a fuller understanding of the discourses that shape the field and present possibilities. Making these explicit allows us to understand the context in which research and development projects are being put forward. This section highlights two discourses. The first critiques the heteronormative nature of schools by drawing attention to the messages of school culture and curriculum. The second, working from a framework that LGBTQ students are marginalized, proposes school-based remedies. Rather than create division, this chapter purports that the variation in discourse is significant and that all camps (supportive of change and inclusion) must be recognized.

Disrupting Heteronormativity

Epstein, O'Flynn, and Telford (2000), in their review of literature on sexualities in schools, cite queer theory as a literature that "concerns questions of identity, performance, and fluidity" (p. 129). This literature tries to understand and assess the heteronormative structure of schools. In short, it evaluates the way in which schools assume the heterosexuality of students, teachers, and parents and create policies, rules, and curriculum to facilitate this. These heterosexual underpinnings are often unconscious. Hence, the sense of and attention to the concept of a norm—a practice or standard embedded in our actions and worldview (Butler, 2004; Ewald, 1990). Queer theorists draw particular attention to how the labels we give ourselves and those with whom we identify are made possible or impossible by norms that bind these groups. Research using this theory largely examines identity politics, the many influences on the student and teachers' identities, and how schools require students and teachers to negotiate these identities (Pinar, 1998). Such work may examine the autobiography of a lesbian teacher and how she negotiates her identity in and through school. It may examine the ways students learn to resist oppression and develop activist identities in an arena that does not facilitate this. Empirical and theoretical work in this vein comprises the field of queer theory. These researchers and theorists understand "queer" as a discourse that queries and/or disrupts normality, not a means for simplifying the LGBTQ acronym. Inside this discourse community, language such as "performance," "identity," and "interruption" take on central and particular meanings. Rather than take "research" or "curriculum" as accepted terminology, queer (and other critical) theorists turn these words back on themselves to expose how meaning has become normalized. Perusal of the chapters in Pinar's (1998) edited volume or articles in the *Journal of LGBT Issues in Education/Journal of LGBT Youth* provides examples of scholars and researchers "queering" common understandings of education and its components. In another journal, Sumara and Davis (1999) note that their intentions in writing of heteronormativity in schools is not to propose specific curricular change but to stir readers so that they might become more conscious of sexual norms in the work of schools. The disruption caused by these queries of the familiar is comfortable to scholars in this intellectual realm.

Like the work that it criticizes, queer theory has adopted its own normalizing discourse that warrants disruption in the consideration of its use in school-based research. Queer theory belongs to a particular (elite) community of scholars (Meiners, 1998). Epstein, O'Flynn, and Telford (2000), in propelling this critique of the literature, note: "At times, it may lean, from our perspective, overly much toward a concentration on the verbal and textual at the expense of the material" (p. 129). Much of the work in this arena comes from and is written for other scholars in the field. Participants in this community understand the play on language and the possibilities they present; outsiders find this odd.

In addition to Pinar's work, journals such as *Social Text, Curriculum Inquiry,* and *Journal of Homosexuality* contain much of the scholarship that links heteronormativity, queer theory, and education. The missions of these journals reveal a scholarly audience. *Social Text* (2010) identifies itself as "A daring and controversial leader in the field of cultural studies" that "consistently focuses attention on questions of gender, sexuality, race, and the environment, publishing key works by the most influential social and cultural theorists." Speaking to the lack of materiality, the editors of *Curriculum Inquiry* note: "This leading international journal brings together influential academics and researchers from a variety of disciplines around the world to provide expert commentary and lively debate." The debates and conversations inspired by these articles and authors are essential to the field and broadly affect research and scholarship in education; they are not independent of the field in which teachers practice. But this is a line of argument that, while useful for deconstructing curriculum and practice, understanding how students understand schools, space, and selves, and removing essentialist ideas from research, is not yet prevalent in (and possibly relevant to) the research and dialogue within P–12 schools. The ideas and methods described here are largely incongruent with the intention of policy-makers and evaluation offices.

Solving the Problem of Marginalized Youth

The second literature that forms a discourse related to LGBTQQI issues and schools is that surrounding LGBTQ youth. Drawing from studies conducted outside of school, research on mental health, and curricular queries, this discourse encourages school leaders and teachers to address the marginalization and at-risk status of these youth. Schools have long been cited as dangerous places for students who identify as or are perceived to be LGBTQ (Crocco, 2002; Kosciw & Diaz, 2006; Russell, McGuire, Lee, Larriva, & Laub, 2008). Research highlights the hostile hallways where anti-gay epithets, name-calling, and physical bullying toward LGBTQ youth or youth perceived to be LGBTQ are common currency. One study, citing the hate directed at LGBTQ youth, indicated that being called "gay" was the most feared name a student could hear (Levstik & Groth, 2002). The February 2008 shooting of a gay middle school student and a number of high-profile suicides by bullied students in 2009 and 2010 reflect the increasingly hostile environments of U.S. schools. Congruent with Thornton's observations, the literature cites a general absence of visible LGBTQ people, issues, and events anywhere in schools—the curriculum, school policies, sex education classrooms, or posters on the walls (Ferfolja, 2007). Schools fail to acknowledge or account for the sexual diversity of their students (or staff and parents/guardians), an indication of the heteronormative culture of schools. Without explicitly referencing heteronormativity, the marginalization that reinforces the "abnormal" status of LGBTQ issues and justifies bullying, name-calling, and fear result from this positionality. LGBTQ youth are at risk in a culture that bullies and fails to recognize them.

Research about the negative culture in schools and high suicide rates has produced materials and interventions to help educators change this culture. This literature is presented to inservice and pre-service teachers as actions they can take to produce a safer school climate for LGBTQ youth and students who have LGBTQ parents. The audience for these materials is people who have the most direct influence on the everyday experience of LGBTQ youth. Some of these programs are being implemented, but their impact is rarely evaluated. Looking closely at these remedies and how they are framed provides insight into how they are contributing to the discourse about LGBTQ youth and how they might create space for research. The remedies are broken apart in the section below but then analyzed as a whole in terms of the discourse they produce.

Identifying Gay People, Events, and Issues.

The remedies closest to the classroom are remedies that propose ways to expand the formal curriculum. Books such as *Overcoming Heterosexism and Homophobia: Strategies That Work* (Sears & Letts, 1997), *Queering Elementary Education: Advancing the Dialogue about Sexualities and Schooling* (Letts & Sears, 1999), *The Gay Teen* (Unks, 1995), and special editions of *Theory and Research in Social Education* (March 2002) and *English Journal* (March 2009) are largely written for teachers and educators and contain direct reference to materials, programs, and methods aimed at reforming the curriculum to include LGBTQ issues, people, and events. These range from changes in the sex education curriculum to specific talk about gay and lesbian sexual identities, references to the sexuality of writers and historical figures who are gay, books for children about a diversity of family structures, inclusion of LGBTQ-themed policies and issues in civics classrooms, songs that contain LGBTQ-friendly lyrics in music classes, acknowledgment in biology that the animal kingdom is not exclusively heterosexual and monogamous, and inclusion of same-sex couples in household simulation activities. Each writing is an effort toward a more inclusive curriculum.

The discussion in this literature positions LGBTQ issues as external to the curriculum. These activities are designed to supplement the curriculum rather than alter the core of it. Drawing from queer theory, the literature could argue that the formal and hidden curriculum be deconstructed for their assumptions/teachings about sexuality rather than merely propose the addition of people and events. Further, the identification of sexuality only in conjunction with LGBTQ individuals suggests that heterosexual people don't have sexuality. We are encouraged to raise sexuality as something that affects the way Whitman approaches his poetry because he is gay but not how Thomas Paine wrote *Common Sense*. Whitman, being gay, has sexuality that affects his writing; Paine, being straight, does not. Sexuality is part of everyone's identity, not an attribute that belongs only to the Other.

School Programs that Confront Homophobia and Bullying

Some schools take advantage of packaged programs developed to address homophobia (Lipkin, 1995; Mager & Sulek, 1997; Marchman, 2002; Myers & Kardia, 1997). These programs may be addenda lessons in the classroom, videos shown during homeroom, or a presentation at a school-wide assembly. Overall, they try to give a face to an LGBTQ person, confront homophobia, disrupt the view held by some students, and ultimately change the hostile school climate. Some of these programs specifically tackle bullying. In response to violence in schools, some states have passed laws requiring schools to address bullying through programs that teach youth to recognize bullying and see its effects (Cahill & Cianciotto, 2004). The aforementioned lessons and programs are external to the formal curriculum and other "regular" functions of school. Their location reifies LGBTQ issues as external to the curriculum and discussion of accountability.

Issues surrounding bullying are increasingly viable for and visible in schools due to media coverage and parental pressure. The recognition of the prevalence and impact of bullying is important, but the manner in which it is contextualized deserves attention. Common (anti)bullying programs largely address the bullying and seek to correct the actions of students. They fail to address the structures that produce the bullying; behavior is removed from social context. While there are a number of root causes of bullying, one root is the heteronormative and masculine underpinnings of schools and their social structures. The language used to bully is often anti-gay, reinforcing the fear of gay epithets. The conditions are often more severe for boys who are asked to conform to the rigid structures of masculinity. Youth who are bullied are often physically smaller or more emotional. These features, combined with not being able to fight back, defy the traditional view of masculinity to which young boys should adhere (Connell, 1995; Kimmel, 2000). Bullying is effective because it demasculinizes the target while reinforcing the masculinity of the perpetrator. The underlying structures addressed largely by gender theorists are essential for real change. Choosing to address only the symptoms—the words or bruises—does not change the culture of schools. The assemblies themselves and the power they demonstrate in the abuser reinforce bullies' dominant position in the building. Further, the emphasis on learning to fight back or learning to protect oneself from bullying to those who are bullied places them in the wrong. While the school will protect them, they are also being told they are not real men. Together these messages give credence to a masculinity defined by physical strength, emotional fortitude, and heterosexuality and the social dynamics it creates in schools.

Bullying and the discussion of homophobia inherent in it rightfully depict the at-risk and vulnerable position of youth who push at gender boundaries and assert marginalized sexualities. But as the only consistent engagement of marginalized gender (and gender performance) and sexuality in schools, it also perpetuates the association between LGBTQQI identities and negativity/victimhood (Rofes, 2004). Gay must be bad if the only images and discussions we can find are negative. Hence, the fear is perpetuated; even if I think that might be me, why would I want to be that if life is so unpleasant? Negative associations as the only visible representations serve an unintended consequence of perpetuating LGBTQ as undesirable categories of gender and sexual identification.
Gay-Straight Alliances

LGBTQQ and Allied Youth

(LGBTQQA) often find themselves isolated in schools. Noting the combination of isolation and a hostile climate, the Gay Lesbian Straight Education Network (GLSEN) sought to support and connect youth leaders who were claiming positive spaces for students in schools. Taking advantage of the Equal Access Act of 1984, GLSEN advocated for Gay-Straight Alliances (GSA) as safe spaces for LGBTQ youth and their allies. Although individual GSAs have unique characteristics, the basic premise is that "A Gay-Straight Alliance (GSA) is a student-run club in a high school or middle school that brings together LGBTQ and straight students to support each other, provide a safe place to socialize, and create a platform for activism to fight homophobia and transphobia" (GSA Network). Many GSAs are part of the national network of GSAs. As such, they participate in the National Day of Silence or work with other area chapters to organize an "alternative prom."

The mission of GSAs is to counter the victim and marginalization narrative of gay teens in schools by offering a proactive and inclusive space for students (Cahill & Cianciotto, 2004; Griffin, Lee, Waugh, & Beyer, 2003; Rofes, 2004). In contrast to the unsafe culture during the day, the GSA offers safety and recognition. Students often meet in the classroom of a supportive teacher, reaffirming that physical space affects safety and identity. A primary function of the GSA is to allow LGBTQQA youth to meet others. Following a school day of disunity and isolation, the meeting provides community and familiarity. It is a reminder to students that they are not alone. It also allows students to talk about being gay, lesbian, or bisexual in developing their sexual identity, an aspect absent from the health/sex education curriculum. GSAs also encourage students to be activists in their school or community, bringing visibility to LGBTQ people via a fight for rights. Students may learn to be politically engaged in their social studies classrooms but rarely discuss the impact of homophobia or transphobia on the political community. Throughout these purposes is a call for safety and visibility for youth in schools.

The discourse surrounding the problem of marginalized youth

Each of these remedies is unique; together they produce an understanding of LGBTQ issues in schools. They form a common language or discourse and its use is both freeing and reifying. The most recognizable element in the discourse is the negative connotation of being LGBTQ (see also Rofes, 2004). Each remedy and the literature that supports it relies on the idea that being LGBTQ is a hardship. It uses claims about the difficulty of being a person who is LGBTQ to argue that schools must be safer for these students. This is in contrast to the multicultural literature that presumes there are unjust and inequitable structures—lack of group recognition and access to resources. Schools as institutions are not implicated. The focus on individual actions and needs means that the remedies schools implement only need address individual behaviors and safety, issues that are distinct from schools themselves and the central purposes of education, particularly in an age of accountability.

Schools are dominated by the formal curriculum to which students and teachers are accountable. The citations above do not re-center LGBTQ issues (or justice) in this curriculum. Instead, it renders them extracurricular. Either they are extra to the central curriculum—in the form of an aside mention of one person's sexuality or an extra unit of study—or they occur outside the regular school day—in the form of after-school activities and assemblies that reorganize the school day. The location of LGBTQ issues in the extracurricular is significant. This relegation presents a hidden message about the importance of LGBTQ issues. They are kept in the margins, outside the curriculum through their primary location in these external spaces. They are not valuable enough to be included in the studied curriculum and never challenge the hidden message of the formal curriculum.

The discussion of how and where to locate LGBTQ issues in schools is important. One element of multicultural education is the need for recognition in contrast to silence. But the manner of inclusion being interrogated in this section warns of the danger of keeping recognition in the margins. Consider the complicated message sent via the creation of GSAs as clubs. While it is clear that these spaces are necessary for youth to find others and to be supported, the very need for the club perpetuates the margin. LGBTQ identities are distinct from the sexual identities that are acceptable during and in other school activities. This implication reinforces the "gay is bad" discourse that seems to be the only one available to students in schools. The placement of LGBTQ issues in the extracurricular has implications for research and assessment in today's policy world. The movement places them outside the range of issues important to schools today.

Where and how sexuality is framed by and within schools has a direct impact on students. While schools are not the only arena in which young people learn about social norms and the categories through which they can identify themselves, schools are strong forces. As young people, students spend many of their waking hours in school. This is partially required because schools provide social training (Thornton, 2003). They are a common arena available to most youth in society that teaches social norms/rules. By normalizing heterosexuality, one sexuality becomes more legitimate than others. Heterosexuality as a norm delegitimizes and marginalizes other categories and even variation within the dominant category. Some of this occurs through official policies; much happens less intentionally. By inundating students with some references and excluding or othering different possibilities, schools affirm heterosexuality as normal. Students are schooled in a proper sexual discourse, one that marginalizes LGBTQQA youth and the research that might reshape the nature of schools.

Contrasting Discourses: The Challenge of Making LGBTQ Research Matter

This is not a paper about the impact that being a member of the LGBTQ community has on youth but about the potential to research this impact in P–12 schools in the United States. Examining the discourse, we can imagine the influence. But much of what we write is conjecture. Research that examines the ways schools affect sexuality come largely from England, Australia, and New Zealand, and even then, much of this research is conducted in private schools (Epstein & Johnson, 1998; Ferfolja, 2007; Mac an Ghaill, 1994). The research about youth in the United States is largely conducted outside of schools (Kosciw & Diaz, 2006; Sears, 1990). Participants are contacted via community groups or online networks or asked to participate as adults reflecting back on school. We need more research in schools that directly examines the school context, its influence on young people, and the impact of interventions. The discourse around sexuality in schools limits the possibilities for conducting this important research.

Sexuality remains outside the inroads that other multicultural issues have achieved in current policy measures. Schools, in their achievement reporting, must disaggregate data according to race, gender, and socioeconomic status. They must also ensure that English-language learners and students with learning and emotional disabilities take and pass the high-stakes tests. These emphases mean that research funding and research projects designed to eliminate gaps and propose or evaluate remedies receive high priority. Some groups, through the multicultural lenses of increased identification of the differentiated group and a redistribution of education resources toward these groups, have made their issues matter in local and national policy debates. Why have LGBTQ as a group(s) not received the same status?

One critical difference is that LGBTQ issues appear to be remedied through extracurricular measures, something that requires fewer and different education resources. The focus on the at-risk status—school violence, bullying, and suicide rates—is real and important in preserving the lives and well-being of LGBTQ youth and should not be abandoned. But it also places research and intervention in the hands of law enforcement, mental health, and social work personnel rather than education scholars. It also largely individualizes the hard-to-define group and removes the need for group recognition that justice theorists argue is vital. The group status piece is largely advocated for with organizations such as GSAs. While membership in a GSA may help individuals build a safe social network throughout the school day, most adults in and outside of schools see this as a club for students rather than a demand for group recognition within a hostile environment and heteronormative culture.

The remedies also propose curricular inclusion but as supplemental to the existing standards. Efforts to make space for curricular change as a remedy to absence manifest as add-ons to—rather than substantive change of—the existing curriculum. Although queer theorists want to disrupt the heteronormative function of the curriculum and make major changes to the structure of curriculum and its function in schools, most of the literature written to educators appeals to ways of carving out space within the existing curriculum for a queer moment in a straight school year.

The way in which recognition is advocated and the changes that are suggested impact how we conduct research on LGBTQ youth. Recognition, as noted by multicultural and justice theorists, is important but not sufficient. The small changes that occur in the extracurricular spaces have the potential to create systemic change because they help the group begin to achieve a differentiated status. But the remedies proposed largely rest with recognition and fail to advocate for the redistribution of educational resources to LGBTQ youth. The statistics collected about LGBTQ youth suggest that the affected students are a relatively small portion of the school population. More importantly, the data focuses on the at-risk measures, not achievement measures, indicating that the problems are centered on what peers do to one another rather than on the curriculum and testing in which schools must invest their attention. It may be that the problems lie only in the distribution of non-academic resources; we do not yet have the data to support or contradict this. But the question arises of how to make this matter in education if we want to do research in schools about LGBTQ issues. Otherwise, talking to students in GSAs or those who are victimized becomes sufficient for telling the whole story.

Another important feature in the discourse that limits research is the representation of the word sexuality. Two issues presented above confine the inclusiveness of the word sexuality. First, sexuality is often connoted with "sex." While the two are distinct, the perceived relationship and taboo nature of sex in schools creates fear among administrators and parents. Second, the limited relationship between sexuality and LGBTQ limits the breadth of potential research. Researchers wanting to conduct research on sexuality should seek to consider the sexuality of all students. The normalizing processes described above likely have greater conscious impact on LGBTQ youth who find their identities delegitimized, but such claims also require investigation of the production of heterosexuality. The willingness to see schools in the entirety of their social functions, including the production of sexuality, must be addressed to allow this research to take place. Many schools see themselves as the shapers of one identity—citizenship. This has led scholars to suggest that the production of this citizenship identity mandates that citizens act in a heterosexual manner; LGBTQ individuals can be citizens as long as they do not simultaneously proclaim their sexual identity (Bickmore, 2002; Loutzenheiser, 2006; Macintosh & Loutzenheiser, 2006). This relationship is also largely unexplored in empirical spaces and does not seem to carry over into a broader examination of all sexual identities and the space made for them in schools and society.

Schools, in this or other discursive climates, do not see the value of the research we seek to do. Evaluating the discourse we promote and use within our community highlights a divergence with national agendas and rhetoric to which schools attach their resources. These discourses are examples of the difficulties in conducting the research needed to follow up on the challenge that Thornton and others have offered. Much of the writing available about LGBTQ issues in schools is related to remedies that draw loosely from research in schools. The access to schools by researchers is just as limited as the curricular access students find. Schools like to hide the role of sexuality in the curriculum and in the process are able to create discourses that serve as barriers to all sorts of remedy and research.

Conclusions

There is a dearth of research about sexuality in schools even within the rich fields of Queer Theory and LGBT Studies. Studies of heteronormativity and personal accounts from teachers reveal some of the inner workings of schools. But speaking to policy and even presenting our agendas and ideas within our own research organizations requires more and different kinds of inquiries, kinds that are not yet dominant in the field. The discourse that these powerful groups use, hear, and perpetuate is problematic because it affects the worldview they hold and limits the possibilities they can imagine. It is important to address the realness of the different languages we speak. The inquiry above highlights the manners in which we speak apart from policymakers but also some of the troubles within our discourse frames. This chapter specifically identifies a divergence from the discourse of accountability, but the consideration is relevant for whatever era comes next. There is a need to find the commonality of interest.

This inquiry focuses largely on discourse, but I do not begin to presume this is the lone factor at play. This chapter does not account for the ever-present homophobic tone of U.S. culture. People's underlying fears and prejudices shape what they value, and homophobia interferes with the work we are trying to do. Homophobia arises internally and socially. People's experiences in organizations and communities shape their prejudices and determine how they express these prejudices publicly. The repetition of negative images in relation to LGBTQ sexualities is internalized and leads to some of the suicides and violence highlighted by the media. The dominance of homophobia in individuals and societies constrains our actions in very real ways. People respond to this fear and make decisions for themselves and others based upon it. Homophobia itself and the actions it produces are also discursive. Fear causes people to perform their sexuality in a certain way, thus building boundaries that constrain our view of sexuality. For example, it is difficult within the boundaries constructed to imagine the positive and everyday experiences of many LGBTQ people. It is written outside the discourse and our imaginations. Discourse reflects the cultural environment, but it also effectively confines behavior and dialogue. By bounding sexuality to LGBTQ issues and by bounding LGBTQ issues around the normal process of schools or part of the central functions of schools, schools effectively undermine the ability to create adequate response or space to queer schools.

I do not pretend to have answers. Looking back at the study I have planned, I feel compelled to do as others have done and work on a college campus, as Meek did in the previous chapter, or have college students look back at high school. This study will be helpful and provide something for us. But this work reifies the margins and the distance that I critique in this chapter. There is a rich queer academic culture, but we still need to find better routes to recognition in P–12 education if we want to truly transform the sexual normalizing of schools. We need to teach policymakers that there is value in learning to think queerly.

Notes

1. Thornton (2003) writes specifically about the social studies, but his argument resonates through research about any content area. His work is about curriculum, but written in this case for social studies educators whom he argues have opportunity for explicit inclusion of LGBTQ issues.
2. I recognize the same struggle with terminology that was discussed in the introduction. The identities at the core of the literature vary throughout this chapter, and I am often not as inclusive as I would like to be. It is difficult in each instance to imagine all who are affected by the policies and discourses I cite. Following from Meek (previous chapter), I do not want to use queer as an umbrella term because it is an identity taken intentionally by some youth and not others. I will move between acronyms in this chapter, often intentionally and always problematically.

References

Appiah, K.A. (1996). For racial identities. In K.A. Appiah & A. Gutmann (Eds.), *Color conscious: The political morality of race* (pp. 74–104). Princeton, NJ: Princeton University Press.

Banks, J.A. (1993). *Multicultural education: Issues and perspectives* (2nd ed.). Boston: Allyn and Bacon.

Banks, J.A. (2001). *Cultural diversity and education: Foundations, curriculum, and teaching* (4th ed.). Boston: Allyn and Bacon.

Bickmore, K. (2002). How might social education resist heterosexism? Facing the impact of gender and sexual identity ideology on citizenship. *Theory and Research in Social Education, 30*(2), 198–216.

Birden, S., Gaither, L., & Laird, S. (2000). The struggle over the text: Compulsory heterosexuality and educational policy. *Educational Policy, 14*(5), 638–663.

Britzman, D.P. (1995). Is there a queer pedagogy? Or, stop reading straight. *Educational Theory, 45*(2), 151–165.

Butler, J. (2004). Gender regulations. In her Undoing gender (pp. 40–56). New York: Routledge.

Cahill, S., & Cianciotto, J. (2004). U.S. policy inventions that can make schools safer. *Journal of Gay & Lesbian Issues in Education, 2*(1), 3–17.

Connell, R.W. (1995). *Masculinities*. Berkeley: University of California Press.

Crocco, M.S. (2002). Homophobic hallways: Is anyone listening? *Theory and Research in Social Education, 30*(2), 217–232.

Dilley, P. (1999). Queer theory: Under construction. *International Journal of Qualitative Studies in Education, 12*(5), 457–472.

Duke University Press (2010). Social Text. Retrived March 21, 2011, from http://www.dukeupress.edu/Catalog/ViewProduct.php?viewby=journal&productid=45631

Epstein, D., & Johnson, R. (1998). *Schooling sexualities.* Buckingham: Open University Press.

Epstein, D., O'Flynn, S., & Telford, D. (2000). "Othering" education: Sexualities, silences, and schooling. *Review of Research in Education, 25,* 127–175.

Ewald, F. (1990). Norms, discipline, and the law. *Representations, 30,* 138–161.

Fairclough, N. (2001). *Language and power.* Harlow, UK: Pearson Education Ltd.

Ferfolja, T. (2007). Schooling cultures: Institutionalizing heteronormativity and heterosexism. *International Journal of Inclusive Education, 11*(2), 147–162.

Foucault, M. (1981). The order of discourse. In R. Young (Ed.), *Untying the text: A poststructuralist reader.* Boston: Routledge.

Foucault, M. (1990). *The history of sexuality: Volume 1: An introduction.* New York: Vintage Books. (Original work published 1978)

Fraser, N. (1995). From redistribution to recognition? Dilemmas of justice in a "post-socialist" age. *New Left Review, 212,* 68–93.

Fraser, N., & Honneth, A. (2003). *Redistribution or recognition? A political-philosophical exchange* (J. Golb, J. Ingram, & C. Wilke, Trans.). London and New York: Verso.

Gay-Straight Alliance Network. Retrieved June 20, 2010 from http://gsanetwork.org/what-we-do

Griffin, P., Lee, C., Waugh, J., & Beyer, C. (2003). Describing roles that gay-straight alliances play in schools. *Journal of Gay & Lesbian Issues in Education, 1*(3), 7–22.

Jagose, A. (1997). *Queer theory: An introduction.* New York: New York University Press.

Kimmel, M. (2000). Masculinity as homophobia: Fear, shame, and silence in the construction of gender identity. In M. Adams et al. (Eds.), *Readings for diversity and social justice.* New York: Routledge.

Kosciw, J.G., & Diaz, E.M. (2006). The 2005 school climate survey: The experiences of lesbian, gay, bisexual, and transgendered youth in our nation's schools. New York: GLSEN.

Kozol, J. (2005). *The shame of a nation: The restoration of apartheid schooling in America.* New York: Three Rivers Press.

Lather, P. (1991). *Getting smart.* New York: Routledge.

Letts, W.J., & Sears, J.T. (Eds.). (1999). *Queering elementary education: Advancing the dialogue about sexualities and schooling.* Lanham, MD: Rowman & Littlefield.

Levstik, L., & Groth, J. (2002). Scary thing, being an eighth grader: Exploring gender and sexuality in a middle school U.S. History unit. *Theory and Research in Social Education, 30*(2), 233–254.

Lindblom, K. (Ed.). (2009). *English Journal, 98*(4).

Lipkin, A. (1995). The case for a gay and lesbian curriculum. In G. Unks (Ed.), *The gay teen: Educational practice and theory for lesbian, gay, and bisexual adolescents* (pp. 31–52). New York: Routledge.

Loutzenheiser, L.W. (2006). Gendering social studies, queering social education. In A. Segall, E.E. Heilman, & C.H. Cherryholmes (Eds.), *Social studies—The next generation* (pp. 61–75). New York: Peter Lang.

Mac an Ghaill, M. (1994). *The making of men: Masculinities, sexualities and schooling.* Buckingham: Open University Press.

Macintosh, L.B., & Loutzenheiser, L.W. (2006). Queering citizenship. In G.H. Richardson & D.W. Blades (Eds.), *Troubling the canon of citizenship education* (pp. 95–102). New York: Peter Lang.

Mager, D.N., & Sulek, R. (1997). Teaching about homophobia at a historically Black university: A role play for undergraduate students. In J. Sears & W. Letts (Eds.), *Overcoming heterosexism and homophobia: Strategies that work* (pp. 182–196). New York: Columbia University Press.

Marchman, B.K. (2002). Teaching about homophobia in a high school civics course. *Theory and Research in Social Education, 30*(2), 302–305.

May, S. (1999). *Critical multiculturalism: Rethinking multicultural and antiracist education.* Philadelphia: Falmer Press.

McLaren, P. (1994). White terror and oppositional agency: Towards a critical multiculturalism. In D.T. Goldberg (Ed.), *Multiculturalism: A critical reader* (pp. 45–74). Cambridge, MA: Blackwell.

Meiners, E. (1998). Remember when all the cars were Fords and all the lesbians were women? Some notes on identity, mobility, and capital. In W.F. Pinar (Ed.), *Queer theory in education* (pp. 121–140). Mahwah, NJ: Lawrence Erlbaum Associates.

Mills, S. (2004). *Discourse*. London: Routledge.

Myers, P., & Kardia, D. (1997). "But you seem so normal!" Multidimensional approaches to unlearning homophobia on a college campus. In J. Sears & W. Letts (Eds.), *Overcoming heterosexism and homophobia: Strategies that work* (pp. 197–208). New York: Columbia University Press.

Ontario Institute for Educational Studies (2010). *Curriculum Inquiry*. John Wiley & Sons. Retrieved February 15, 2011, from http://www.wiley.com/bw/journal.asp?ref=0362–6784

Pinar, W.F. (Ed.). (1998). *Queer theory in education*. Mahwah, NJ: Lawrence Erlbaum Associates.

Ravitch, D. (2010). *The death and life of the great American school system: How testing and choice are undermining education*. New York: Basic Books.

Rofes, E. (2004). Martyr-target-victim: Interrogating narratives of persecution and suffering among queer youth. In M.L. Rasmussen, E. Rofes, & S. Talburt (Eds.), *Youth and sexualities: Pleasure, subversion, and insubordination in and out of schools* (pp. 41–62). New York: Palgrave Macmillan.

Rothstein, R., with Jacobsen, R.J., & Wilder, T. (2008). *Grading education: Getting accountability right*. New York: Teachers College Press.

Russell, S.T., McGuire, J.K., Lee, S., Larriva, J.C., & Laub, C. (2008). Adolescent perceptions of school safety for students with lesbian, gay, bisexual, and transgender parents. *Journal of LGBT Youth, 5*(4), 11–27.

Sears, J.T. (1990). *Growing up gay in the South*. New York: Haworth Press.

Sears, J., & Letts, W.J. (1997). *Overcoming heterosexism and homophobia: Strategies that work*. New York: Columbia University Press.

Sleeter C.E., & Grant, C.A. (1999). *Making choices for multicultural education: Five approaches to race, class, and gender* (3rd ed.). New York: Macmillan.

Sumara, D., & Davis, B. (1999). Interrupting heteronormativity: Toward a queer curriculum theory. *Curriculum Inquiry, 29*(2), 191–208.

Thornton, S.J. (Ed.). (2002). *Theory and Research in Social Education, 30*(2).

Thornton, S.J. (2003). Silence on gays and lesbians in social studies curriculum. *Social Education, 67*(4), 226–230.

U.S. Department of Education (2009). *Race to the Top program executive summary*. Washington, DC: Author.

Unks, G. (Ed.). (1995). *The gay teen: Educational practice and theory for lesbian, gay, and bisexual adolescents*. New York: Routledge.

Vavrus, M. (2002). *Transforming the multicultural education of teachers: Theory, research, and practice*. New York: Teachers College Press.

Williamson, J.A., Rhodes, L., & Dunson, M. (2007). A selected history of social justice in education. *Review of Research in Education, 31*, 195–224.

Young, I. (2004). Five faces of oppression. In L. Heldke & P. O'Connor (Eds.), *Oppression, privilege, & resistance* (pp. 37–63). Boston: McGraw-Hill.

Introduction: Crossing Borders

Jukka Lehtonen

Sexuality is not a universal, consistent phenomenon that people adopt in a vacuum. It is constructed like gender as part of the cultures in which we live. Gender and sexualities are not objects but the products of different kinds of practices, policies, and power relations. They are constructed and sustained in regions, spaces, communities, and interaction—with one of the most central forums being educational contexts, policies, processes, and institutions.

The construction of sexuality is part of the national political framework. States and societies define boundaries, conditions, and possibilities for what type of education is organized, who is allowed and in which way to raise and educate children and young people, and what kinds of aims are established for the politics of education. At schools, children and young people are educated to become citizens and members of their societies. They are educated as political citizens: the kind who know how to vote in elections and are aware of their rights and responsibilities, or the kind who learn or choose to become more passive subjects. They are raised to become citizens of the labor market, the kind who adopt the skills and talents necessary to succeed in working life or the kind who adopt, for instance, educational and professional fields appropriate for a woman or a man. They are trained to become consumer citizens, citizens who defend their country, and also religious citizens. In educational processes, molding young people into citizens occurs normatively toward the desired type of citizenship, and boundaries related to gender, sexuality, and ethnicity are intertwined in these processes. Awareness of this can lead us to question the understanding of citizenship as universal membership defined through rights and responsibilities (see Pateman, 1988; Yuval-Davis, 1997). In different countries and regions, the processes of educating citizens and being educated as a citizen are emphasized in different ways, and there is also variation in how conscious or concealed the educational functions of raising citizens are (see Gordon, Holland, & Lahelma, 2000).

The process of being raised as a citizen is gendered and racialized (Anthias & Yuval-Davis, 1992; Lister, 1997; McClintock, 1995; Walby, 1994) but also sexualized (Bell & Binnie, 2000; Cooper, 1995;

Cossman, 2007; Evans, 1993; Plummer, 2003; Richardson, 1998; Waites, 2005; Weeks, 1998). In some countries or regions, only boys are offered opportunities for education or to receive preferential treatment in the educational system. Girls may be raised to become future mothers; boys future soldiers. As part of a school's open or more hidden processes, children learn, or are supposed to learn and internalize, the idea that girls should adopt heterosexual femininity and boys heterosexual masculinity in order to succeed in their lives and to achieve societal acceptability. Revealing the naturalization and invisibilization of heterosexuality can work as a strategy when attempting to seek new ways of conceptualizing and constructing citizenship (Cooper, 1995; Duggan, 1995).

In some schools or in the educational systems of some countries, equality and non-discrimination are emphasized more than in others. In these institutions and policies, ways of dismantling unfair societal practices and challenging stereotypical assumptions related to gender and sexuality are sought out. On the other hand, some countries have attempted to control how one can speak about sexuality and especially homosexuality in schools, going so far as legislating the matter. Clause 28 used to be in force in the U.K.; it was used to attempt to prevent teaching non-pejoratively about homosexuality in schools (see Stacey, 1991). In Lithuania, discussion of comparable legislation took place in the 2000s. For a long time, Finland and Austria also had laws that prevented the dissemination of non-pejorative information about homosexuality. In the United States, debate has been stimulated by, for instance, the "No Homo Promo" campaigns that characterize homosexuality as contagious as well as by other attacks by conservative religious groups (see, e.g., Duggan, 1995). There has been opposition to teaching non-pejoratively about homosexuality, using the arguments of moral decay, the decline of the family, and the corruption of children, as well as the collapse of society. In countries where sex between members of the same gender is forbidden, sometimes under pain of death, there are not necessarily any specific laws or discussion of opinions related to sexual orientation as touched on in schools. In places such as these, it may well be experienced as obvious that one does not provide instruction on the matter, at least in a factual or positive light.

A parallel phenomenon tightly bound to the educational assignment of raising citizens is the construction of an image of nation and nationality—one's own and others'. Nationality is conceptualized as an imagined community (Anderson, 1991) that is produced through a variety of processes, including education. This understanding raises questions such as, what kind of conception of what it means to be American is constructed through schools in the United States? Or, what kind of image of Finnishness, Russianness, or Swedishness is offered to children and young people in my native country of Finland as part of school and school cultures? In what ways is the image of Asians perceived in European educational institutions? Or the image of Americans in Southeast Asian schools? Or the image of Africans in North American schools? Immigration for reasons of education, work, family, or refugee status affect these perceptions—in both the countries accepting the arrivals as well as the countries from which they have departed—among those who make the move and the people around them.

Images of one's own nation and other nationalities are constructed in gendered and sexualized ways. The cavalcade of male military heroes defending their countries, self-sacrificing mothers who lean on God for strength, kings who radiate glory, and the scientists and artists who have put their countries on the map are recorded in the history textbooks used in schools. In these stories, men are the foremost builders of nations; women are presented primarily as the mothers, wives, and daughters of these male heroes. The heterosexual family and an ideal masculinity are emphasized.

Countries can be personified as people. Finland's neighboring countries are seen as mother countries by their inhabitants (*Svea mamma* in Sweden and Mother Russia in Russia). Finland, on the other hand, is often described as the Maiden of Finland, an innocent virgin that brave Finnish lads need to defend against threatening military forces. Ethnic and national otherness, for their part, are often sexualized and gendered into an opposite against which one's own idealized national image can be reflected (Ahmed, 2000). In Finland, for instance, Swedish men are often perceived as more effeminate and more homosexual than Finnish men. This cultural image has been used to build the image of the honorable Finnish man. The oversexualized, dangerous African man; the exotic, submissive Asian woman; the sexually and monetarily avaricious Russian woman—otherness based on stereotypes—is constructed in schools, the media, and in youth cultures. And in which ways are the masculinity, femininity, and sexuality of the groups in possession of power constructed? Who is suitable to represent a normal citizen and on what terms? In Finland as well as in many other "Western" countries, a white-skinned, middle-class, well-educated, healthy, non-disabled man is acceptable for this purpose, along with—in line with the current national image of gender equality and heterosexuality—a similar wife. What does this mean for the non-citizens living in the country and for those citizens who do not fit into the position of normative citizenship? Phelan has described the status of such people—especially lesbians and gays—as "marginal citizens" (Phelan, 2001). How do normalizations and marginalizing processes like this reflect on and formulate teacher education, teaching methods and curricula, and student interactions?

This section focuses on various perspectives on diverse sexualities regarding citizenship, nationality, and regional differences at the national level, as well as differences among the regions of a globalized world. Diane Richardson analyzes the concept of citizenship and its relation to sexuality, examining how citizenship is founded not only on an assumption of maleness but also on that of a certain type of heterosexuality. Roland Sintos Coloma analyzes nationalism from a historical perspective, applying a queer reading to elicit dimensions related to gender and sexuality. Jay Poole and C.P. Gause examine the construction of sexuality in rural America. Their analysis of this theme relies on the binary of rural and urban and draws on a representation of the American construction worker, in their view a culmination of an iconic American masculinity. Peter Dankmeijer discusses experiences from educational programs and the premises of educational strategies that have been used to attempt to increase equality and rights linked to sexual diversity in different regions of the world. In his analysis, it becomes apparent that despite globalization, the intertwining of sexuality in local cultures is meaningful not only for people who live in different regions but also in terms of the educational programs used to attempt to reinforce their rights and fair treatment. In her article, Irina Schmitt analyzes Swedish school policies in relation to nationality and sexuality, demonstrating how Christian traditions and values are linked to the educational processes of producing Swedish ethnicity and heteronormativity.

Gender and sexuality are constructed differently in different contexts, both globally as well as within national boundaries. Regional traditions and rural and urban surroundings limit and open up different kinds of circumstances and conditions. The suitability and possibility of various sexualities are limited by these preconditions. International media, films, fashion, and music, increasing travel, and the ubiquitous products of multinational corporations reflect on and construct the images that children and young people have of themselves. The Internet opens up a channel for accessing information and images of sexuality and gender. It easily seems as if the world is growing smaller, as if everyone belongs to the same global community. But is this the case? Perhaps words, thoughts, and images are interpreted in different ways and result in different consequences in the minds and actions of people who live in different places. As far as sexuality and gender are concerned, the unifying world remains a diverse place and in constant movement.

References

Ahmed, S. (2000). *Strange encounters: Embodied others and post-colonialism.* London & New York: Routledge.

Anderson, B. (1991). *Imagined communities: Reflections on the origin and spread of nationalism.* London: Verso.

Anthias, F., & Yuval-Davis, N. (1992). *Racialized boundaries: Race, nation, gender, colour and class, and the anti-racist struggle.* London: Routledge.

Bell, D., & Binnie, J. (2000). *The sexual citizen: Queer politics and beyond.* Cambridge: Polity Press.

Cooper, D. (1995). *Power in struggle: Feminism, sexuality and the state.* Buckingham: Open University Press.

Cossman, B. (2007). *Sexual citizens: The legal and cultural regulation of sex and belonging.* Stanford, CA: Stanford University Press.

Duggan, L. (1995). Queering the state. In L. Duggan & N. Hunter (Eds.), *Sex wars: Sexual dissent and political culture* (pp. 178–193). New York: Routledge.

Evans, D. (1993). *Sexual citizenship: The material construction of sexualities.* London: Routledge.

Gordon, T., Holland, J., & Lahelma, E. (2000). *Making spaces: Citizenship and difference at school.* London: Macmillan.

Lister, R. (1997). *Citizenship: Feminist perspectives.* London: Macmillan.

McClintock, A. (1995). *Imperial leather. Race, gender and sexuality in the colonial contest.* London: Routledge.

Pateman, C. (1988). *The sexual contract.* Cambridge: Polity Press.

Phelan, S. (2001). *Sexual strangers: Gays, lesbians and dilemmas of citizenship.* Philadelphia: Temple University Press.

Plummer, K. (2003). *Intimate citizenship: Private decisions and public dialogues.* Seattle: University of Washington Press.

Richardson, D. (1998). Sexuality and citizenship. *Sociology, 32*(1), 83–100.

Stacey, J. (1991). Promoting normality: Section 28 and the regulation of sexuality. In S. Franklin, C. Lury, & J. Stacey (Eds.), *Off centre: Feminism and cultural studies.* London: Unwin Hyman.

Waites, M. (2005). *The age of consent: Young people, sexuality and citizenship.* Basingstoke: Palgrave Macmillan.

Walby, S. (1994). Is citizenship gendered? *Sociology, 28*(2), 379–395.

Weeks, J. (1998). The sexual citizen. *Theory, Culture and Society, 15*(3–4), 35–52.

Yuval-Davis, N. (1997). *Gender nation.* London: SAGE.

CHAPTER TWENTY

Citizenship and Sexuality

What Do We Mean by "Citizenship"?

DIANE RICHARDSON

The answer to this question owes a great deal to the influence of the work of T.H. Marshall (1950), a British sociologist who shaped post-war thinking about citizenship. Marshall defined citizenship in terms of three sets of rights: civil or legal rights, political rights, and social rights. Civil or legal rights are institutionalised through the law and include things such as the right to own property; freedom of speech, thought and faith; liberty of the person and the right to justice. Political rights are institutionalised in parliamentary political systems and councils of local government and include the right to vote and participate in the exercise of political power. Social rights include the right to a certain level of economic welfare and security as well as the right 'to share to the full in the social heritage and to live the life of a civilised being according to the standards prevailing in the society' (Marshall, 1950, p. 10). These are rights that are institutionalised in the welfare state, for example, unemployment benefits and provision for health and education. According to Marshall, these rights evolved historically in a certain order, civil rights emerging first in the 18th century, political rights in the 19th century, and social rights in the 20th century.

In this and in subsequent analyses, the primary focus has been on the relationship of social class and citizenship (Marshall, 1977), with some discussion of nation/ethnicity. The question of the relationship of citizenship to gender, until recently, has been largely absent from much of the debate within the social sciences and in the case of sexuality almost non-existent. However, this is no longer the case as new work in citizenship studies has interrogated and critiqued traditional understandings and conceptual concerns. Over the last two decades what has been termed a 'gender-blind' understanding of citizenship has been challenged by, in particular, feminist analyses (Phillips, 1991; Lister, 1997; Walby, 1994, 1997; Voet, 1998). Thus, for example, Sylvia Walby criticises, along with other aspects of his analysis, Marshall's conception of three stages in the attainment of citizenship on the grounds that it is contradicted by the history of the development of women's rights. That is, 'for first world women political citizenship is typically achieved before civil citizenship, the reverse of the order for men.' (Walby, 1997, p. 171). Underlying this body of work is the assumption that access to citizenship is a highly gendered process and that, despite claims to universality, a particular version of the normal citizen/subject is encoded in dominant discourses of citizenship. Historically, citizenship has been constructed in the 'male image.' Indeed, in ancient Greece, where concepts of civil and political citizenship have their origins, women, along with children and slaves, were excluded from the status of citizenship and, it is argued, have continued to be marginalised in contemporary accounts where the paradigmatic citizen is male (Wilton, 1995). Traditional accounts of citizenship have also been much criticised, again often by feminist writers, for neglecting to consider how ideas of citizenship are racialised, as well as gendered (Anthias & Yuval-Davis, 1992; Alexander, 1994; Taylor, 1996).

In part reflecting these critiques, the Marshallian notion of citizenship as a set of civil, political, and social rights has been more broadly criticised in recent years as much too simplistic. Other definitions have emerged in response to social changes in the family and the economy, in particular the idea of citizenship as social membership; as common membership of a shared community. Bryan Turner (1993a, p. 2), for example, suggests that citizenship may be defined as 'that set of practices (juridical, political, economic, and cultural) which define a person as a competent member of society, and which as a consequence shape the flow of resources to persons and social groups.' Within this framework citizenship has been most commonly understood in terms of national identity: citizenship as a set of practices which define social membership in a particular society or nation-state. A citizen is someone who belongs, who is a member of a given nation or a member of a given city or particular region within a nation-state. By implication, those who are perceived as not belonging to the city-state or the nation-state can be excluded from the rights of citizenship. They are non-citizens, denied the right of membership of, or belonging to, a particular community with an assumed shared identity.

Such an analysis of citizenship raises the question of how 'nationhood' is defined. Rather than understanding 'nation' as an unproblematic, timeless, given, it is argued that most modern nations are of recent invention. For example, Benedict Anderson (1991) argued that nations are 'imagined communities,' systems of cultural representation whereby we come to imagine a shared experience of belonging to a particular community. Although the idea of nation as an invention has received wide theoretical attention, there has been relatively little discussion about how assumptions about gender or sexuality are implicated in the representation and creation of such 'imagined communities.' Joanne Sharp (1996, p. 99), for example, argues that gender difference is in-built into Anderson's notion of nations as imagined communities: 'Anderson's thesis of imagined communities assumes an imagined citizen, and this imagined citizen is gendered. . . . Women are scripted into the national imaginary in a different manner. Women are not equal to the nation but symbolic of it.'

Anne McClintock (1995) similarly argues that the concept of nationhood tends to emphasise unity, while manifesting itself as masculine and sanctioning institutionalised gender differences and inequalities:

> All nations depend on powerful constructions of gender. . . . No nation in the world gives women and men the same access to the rights and resources of the nation-state. Rather than expressing the flowering into time of the organic essence of a timeless people, nations are contested systems of cultural representation that limit and legitimise peoples' access to the resources of the nation-state. (p. 353)

This idea that nations are gendered and, as I shall go on to argue, sexualised 'fictions' reproduced across space and time through shared representations and practices, is therefore important to understanding how citizenship status is dependent on practices through which social difference is produced.

Definitions of citizenship as national identity have increasingly been brought into question as a result of social and political changes which have challenged traditional boundaries of nation-states, in particular processes of globalisation as well as changes in eastern and central Europe (Turner, 1993b; Outhwaite, 2008). New modes of electronic communication have also enabled and encouraged the development of shared communities that go beyond regional or national identities. It is changes such as these that have prompted discussion of whether we might need to think about citizenship developing within the context of larger forms of social membership than nation-states. In a 'post-national' context, and what is increasingly referred to as a 'post-secular' age, what becomes the basis for unity or belonging? What is the basis for common membership of a shared community? We might, for instance, consider citizenship as grounded in a notion of a union across various nation-states, as in the 'European Union,' or alternatively in terms of religious unity, for example in speaking of the Islamic or Christian 'world.' We may even consider citizenship as social membership in a more fundamental sense, in terms of belonging to the human race—of being a part of 'humanity.' There are already shifts, connected with new forms of governance associated with neoliberalism (Richardson, 2005), toward 'rights being linked to the status of human beings (human rights), rather than citizens of the state' (Pakulski, 1997, p. 84; McLaughlin, Phillimore, & Richardson, 2011). In this respect it is important to recognise that 'human being' is a concept which, while seemingly abstract and universal, would appear to be, along with 'citizenship' and 'nation,' both gendered (Phillips, 1991) and—as will be discussed later—sexualised (Richardson & May, 1999).

The concept of cultural citizenship has also been part of recent debates on citizenship. Along with civil, political, and social aspects of citizenship, it has been suggested that a cultural dimension to citizenship should be included (Pakulski, 1997; Stevenson, 2000). Although the concept of cultural rights is not new, it has tended to be understood within broader debates on social rights rather than as a separate dimension of citizenship. Indeed, as Turner (2000) points out, sociologists generally have not addressed the issue of cultural rights and cultural citizenship, despite the fact that these are issues that are intimately connected to the processes of multiculturalism, globalisation, and the development of mass education and communication systems. The emergent debates in cultural citizenship seek to establish cultural rights and obligations as a new set of citizenship claims, in particular in the spheres of education. It can be conceptualised broadly in terms of 'the capacity to participate effectively, creatively and successfully within a national culture' (Turner, 2000). Cultural rights, institutionalised through the 'culture industries,' would include the right to participate in the culture of a particular society and to representation in the media and popular culture. In these terms social exclusion can be understood partly in terms of the denial or relative lack of cultural space accorded to certain groups in society. This is recognised by Pakulski (1997), who analyses cultural citizenship in terms of the right to symbolic presence and visibility (vs. marginalisation); the right to endignifying representation (vs. stigmatisation); and the right to propagation of identity and maintenance of lifestyles (vs. assimilation).

Finally, it is important to acknowledge a shift in recent years to defining citizenship in terms of consumerism (Evans, 1993; Bell & Binnie, 2002). This representation of the citizen as a consumer is related to the emphasis on individual choice and commercialism associated with the free market economy that since the 1980s has dominated government policies in the U.K. and the United States, as well as elsewhere. Increasingly, the focus is on the rights of citizens as consumers of goods, commodities, and services in the public and private sector.

This use of citizenship as a concept is about membership based on the consumption of certain lifestyles: consumer communities. As David Evans, in one of the first books to be published on the theme of sexuality and citizenship, argues: 'As consumers we are unique individuals with needs, identities and lifestyles which we express through our purchase of appropriate commodities' (Evans, 1993, p. 45). However, the ability to exercise the right to consume depends on money or other resources to trade with as a prerequisite for citizen membership. Thus, as with the other forms of citizenship that have been considered, behind the appeal to universal rights lies a citizenship machinery which excludes some from full citizenship. Lister (1997) makes a similar point to Evans in relation to gender, arguing that women's position in the labour market and the disproportionate role women play in caring work places them at a disadvantage in access to income, limiting their effective participation in consumer citizenship.

These, then, are some of the key ideas and debates about the contested concept 'citizenship.' In the following section I want to examine these different definitions of citizenship in relation to sexuality.

Sexuality and Citizenship

The relationship between sexuality and citizenship, and the construction of concepts of sexual and intimate citizenship, has become an important theme in studies of sexuality across a number of disciplines, including legal theory (e.g., Cooper, 2004; Cossman, 2007), political theory (e.g., Phelan, 1995, 2001; Wilson, 1995), geography (e.g., Bell & Binnie, 2000, 2002), literary criticism and cultural studies (e.g., Berlant, 1997; Isin & Wood, 1999) and sociology (e.g., Evans, 1993; Plummer, 2003; Richardson, 2000a, 2004; Weeks, 1998, 2007). The question of how citizenship is constituted through heterosexual norms and practices is an important theme within this body of work. It is argued that the 'normal citizen' has largely been constituted as heterosexual and, consequently, that heterosexuality is a necessary if not sufficient basis for full citizenship (Richardson, 1998; Phelan, 2001). To illustrate this interconnection, I will give an example under each of the different definitions of citizenship that I have previously outlined.

Within the traditional and dominant model of citizenship as a set of civil, political, and social rights, it can be argued that in many parts of the world lesbians and gay men are still only partial citizens, insofar as they are excluded from certain of these rights. This is evidenced by attempts by lesbian and gay movements and campaigning groups to get equal rights such as, for example, formal marriages, civil partnerships, parenting rights, and similar legal status within the armed forces as heterosexuals. A further aspect of civil citizenship, which relates to Marshall's conception of the right to justice, is the lack of protection in law from discrimination or harassment on the grounds of 'sexual orientation.'

Turning to political citizenship, although lesbians and gay men are not denied the vote and are a part of the electorate, their ability to exercise political power is delimited. The knowledge that someone is lesbian or gay has long been seen as a positive disadvantage, if not a disqualifier, for political office. Although the fact that since the 1990s a number of 'out' politicians have successfully fought seats in parliament in British general elections, and similarly have done so in other parts of Europe and the United States, suggests that this is beginning to change (Richardson & Monro, forthcoming).

Social citizenship tends to be interpreted in terms of the social rights of welfare, including education, and once again lesbians and gay men have highlighted their disadvantaged position. For example, in many parts of the world same-sex relationships are not officially recognised or sanctioned, affecting pension rights, inheritance rights, as well as denying lesbian and gay couples the rights that married heterosexual couples are often entitled to. Nevertheless, it is important to recognise that the dominant ideology of liberal citizenship in the west has been increasingly receptive to certain lesbian and gay rights claims.

Since the 1990s, a rights-orientated assimilationist agenda has dominated lesbian and gay movements (Waites, 2005). The primary goal is normalisation, and citizenship is the key concept appealed to in demands for social change (Phelan, 2001). Within such discourses lesbian and gay men are represented as oppressed minorities seeking access to core institutions such as marriage, family, and the military, as 'good' citizens who want to be included and share in the same rights and responsibilities as heterosexuals (D'Emilio, 2000). Many would claim that through deploying discourses of citizenship such rights-based approaches have been successful (Weeks, 2007). Certainly, it is the case that in many parts of the world gains have been made in relation to age-of-consent laws, access to healthcare, rights associated with social and legal recognition of domestic partnerships, immigration rights, parenting rights, and so on. The significance of such changes has been questioned on the grounds that homophobia, discrimination, marginalization, and hostility toward lesbians and gay men continues, and that any progress that has been made is slow and uneven (see, for example, Warner, 1999; Bell & Binnie, 2000). Also, there are apparent contradictions in this policy environment, with nation-states seeking to continue to reinforce a heterosexual/homosexual binary, for instance in the U.K. by the fact that marriage continues to be defined as a specifically heterosexual privilege. A more fundamental critique of rights-based claims for equality, and the political goal of assimilation and integration as 'normal citizens,' is that it will only achieve an imaginary equality and the illusion of progress (Vaid, 1995; Phelan, 2001).

If we take citizenship to mean social membership of a nation-state, it would appear that even though lesbians and gay men are legal citizens of different 'nations,' they have historically had ambiguous citizenship status, neither fully accepted nor totally excluded; their place in the national imaginary has been as marginal citizens (Phelan, 2001). According to Taylor (1996), citizenship carries with it

> not just the formal membership of a nation-state, but a whole set of socio-economic and ideological practices associated with nationalism. These amount to mechanisms of exclusion and inclusion of particular groups and categories of individual. These have included, most notably, those without property, women, racialised groups and the differently abled, children and lesbians and gay men. (p. 162)

David Sibley (1995) has similarly argued, in relation to Britain, that we can recognise a number of 'key sites of nationalistic sentiment, including the family, the suburb and the countryside, all of which implicitly exclude black people, gays and nomadic minorities from the nation' (p. 108). That is, it is implicitly the heterosexual (as well as white and non-nomadic) citizen that, he argues, has come to symbolise an imagined national community and which underlies the construction of a notion of a shared collective national identity.

Historically, this is evidenced in a variety of ways. For example, the term 'homosexual' has long been associated with the charge of treachery and treason (Edelman, 1992), usually 'justified' with the claim that homosexuals are liable to blackmail (Ellis, 1991). This image of 'the homosexual' as a potential traitor has been used to signal fear of a threat to national security. Hence, this particular historical construction of homosexuality, based upon a presumed risk of betrayal, has undermined the position of 'homosexuals' as legitimate members of a particular nation-state.

Homosexuality has been perceived as a threat to the nation-state in other respects. A common version of this is the claim that the preferably married, stable cohabiting heterosexual nuclear family, conceptualised as both natural and necessary for the good of the nation, is at risk of being undermined by the emergence of different sexualities and family networks. The traditional (heterosexual) family in this scenario is represented as in need of defending against lesbians and gay men, who supposedly pose a threat to it (Stacey, 1991; Richardson, 2004). Appealing to such arguments, some politicians and policymakers justified the introduction of laws that were hostile to lesbian and gay relationships. For example, David Wilshire, the member of the British parliament responsible for introducing Section 28 of the 1988 Local Government Act, which outlawed the 'promotion' of homosexuality in local authority schools, claimed that his actions were motivated by the principle of supporting normality: 'Homosexuality is being promoted at the ratepayers' expense, and the traditional family as we know it is under attack' (as quoted in Carabine, 1992, p. 32). This amendment was subsequently repealed, but not until 2000 in Scotland, and 2003 in the rest of the U.K.

Other examples of attempts to deny lesbians and gay men inclusion within national boundaries in the past include the attempts by the United States government, in the aftermath of the Second World War, to control homosexuality. As Lee Edelman (1992) describes it: 'those efforts responded to the widespread perception of gay sexuality as an alien infestation, an unnatural because un-American practice, resulting from the entanglement with foreign countries—and foreign nationals—during the war' (p. 269). A more recent attempt to confound the categories of nationalism and (hetero)sexuality was evidenced in the resistance offered by the Romanian government to campaigns to decriminalise same-sex relations. (For an account see Baciu, Cimpeanu, & Nicoara, 1996.) Thus, for instance, speaking at the CEPES-UNESCO Conference in Bucharest on the justification of homosexuality as a human right in 1995, a representative of the Romanian Ministry of Justice asserted that homosexuality was not Romanian: 'the nature of the Romanian does not admit this unnatural law [homosexuality], this immorality' (Report of the Conference Proceedings, May 31, 1995).

Related to this, it would seem that very often the role of sexuality in the construction of concepts of nationality has not merely been linked to heterosexuality, but to a form of heterosexuality that to varying extents is anti-gay and lesbian. Speaking of nationalisms in the United States, Henry Louis Gates, Jr., claimed that: 'national identity became sexualised in the 1960s, in such a way as to engender a curious subterranean connection between homophobia and nationalism' (Gates, 1993, p. 234).

This association between homophobia and nationalism, as Gates puts it, may be interpreted as politically expedient in contexts where traditional concepts of national boundaries are being challenged, with the consequent threat to the construction of national identities and national publics. That is, if we regard citizenship as a set of social practices which 'define social membership in a society which is highly differentiated both in its culture and social institutions, and where social solidarity can only be based upon general and universalistic standards' (Turner, 1993a, p. 5), then in some contexts heterosexuality, conceptualised as universal, natural, and normal, may indeed serve as an important unifying principle, a means of achieving social solidarity among different and differentiated groups.

Insofar as the nation-state has normatively been constructed as heterosexual, this does not mean that all forms of heterosexuality have been regarded equally as representing 'normal' citizenship status. It is heterosexuality as a specific form of married coupledom, more specifically among the middle classes, that is commonly held up as a model of good citizenship, necessary for ensuring national security and a stable social order. By implication, other forms of heterosexuality, for instance young, unmarried women who are single mothers, have in the past been seen to 'imperil the nation' (Williams, 1997). Also, as I have already indicated, the association of heterosexuality and nation also intersects with concepts of race. Historically it is a white heterosexuality that has been privileged, and we can find many examples, both in the past and more recently, of the construction of black as well as working-class heterosexual relations as a supposed threat to the nation-state (Alexander, 1994; Weeks, 2010).

Heterosexuality is often implicit in the 'right' to other forms of social membership, for instance based on religious or ethnic identifications. For example, in 1995 the organisers of the annual St. Patrick's Day Parade in Boston successfully sought a court order banning Irish-American lesbians and gay men from marching in the parade under their own banner. In previous years, lesbians and gays had also been denied the right to march as a distinct contingent in the St. Patrick's Day Parade in New York City (Davis, 1995). Such controversies were essentially battles over the definition of Irishness (and what it means to be Irish American) and the inclusion or exclusion from such membership.

Finally, if we take citizenship as social membership to mean 'humanity,' belonging to what is called the human 'race,' even then it can be argued that citizenship has been premised within heterosexuality. Historically, there is a long tradition of understanding what it is to be human in essentialist terms. The term human is commonly used to refer to group membership based on biological criteria: the belonging to a particular species. Although this way of thinking continues to exert influence, within social theory the view has emerged that humanity should be thought of as socially constructed. In other words, we become human through the process of social interaction whereby the categorisations 'person' and 'human' are attributed to individuals (Shotter, 1993; Richardson & May, 1999).

This is significant in terms of understandings of citizenship as social membership, for it suggests that, even at the most fundamental levels of social inclusion, the boundaries of membership are a cultural construction. Thus, it is possible for people to be constructed as 'other' through relegation to the borders of human existence. One example of this process of dehumanisation is through the claiming of animal attributes for certain groups, thereby legitimising exclusionary practices on the grounds that they are less than human. This has been particularly evident in relation to the representation of colonised peoples, especially Australian Aborigines and African slaves, as well as other groups such as Jewish and Gypsy communities (Sibley, 1995).

Such dehumanising processes of exclusion can also be observed in relation to gender and sexuality. Insofar as women have often been identified as closer to 'nature,' they have also been at risk of exclusion from 'civilised' society. The interaction of gender with race, ethnicity, and class has been important in this respect; it is particular groups of women—for example black and working class women—who have traditionally been represented as closest to nature and therefore lower ranking in a 'hierarchy of being' (Sibley, 1995). Interestingly, whereas in the examples cited above the processes of dehumanisation operate through the exclusion of those deemed to be closest to nature and, therefore, more 'animal-like' and less 'civilised,' in the case of sexuality it also operates to exclude those who are not a part of nature so defined (as heterosexual), who are constructed as un-natural (as homosexual). In other words, in the case of homosexuality, disenfranchisement was facilitated by a complex construction of homosexuality as both 'unnatural' and as too close to a state of nature, expressed in the stereotypic highly sexualised understandings of lesbians and especially gay men (Terry, 1999).

The naturalisation of heterosexuality has not only served to dehumanise lesbians and gay men, it has also provided a context in which the right to existence of lesbians and gay men may be questioned. Indeed, the connection between (hetero)sexuality and humanity is reflected in those who would go so far as to question the right to life of lesbians and gay men. In some parts of the world such views are institutionalised through laws that recommend the death penalty for homosexuality, such as, for example, in Yemen, Sudan, and Mauritania. In countries where homosexuality is legally 'tolerated,' homophobically motivated hate crimes including murder continue to occur ('War on Want,' 1996; Amnesty International, 1997; Richardson & May, 1999).

At an institutional level, processes of de-personalisation and de-humanisation can have important implications for access to rights. For example, despite appeals to universalism in speaking of basic human rights, conventional human rights frameworks have been selective in their use of this term. The struggle to get lesbian and gay rights recognised as human rights reveals the way in which the concept of 'human rights' has historically developed in ways that have often failed to recognise many of the abuses perpetrated against certain social groups. It also raises the question of whether such discourses serve not only to authorise which human rights claims are recognised as basic to humanity, but also to actively shape the social meaning and construction of what it means to be a 'person' who is recognised, to greater or lesser extent, as 'human.' In this sense we can understand the demand for lesbian and gay rights as a struggle not only about rights *per se*, but also about what those rights signify; as 'a struggle for membership in the human community' (Herman, 1994, p. 19).

Definitions of citizenship in terms of cultural citizenship also raise questions about the sexualised, as well as gendered, nature of social inclusion and access to 'rights and entitlements' (Richardson, 2000b). Historically, lesbian and gay relationships have been systematically denied and ignored in popular culture; existing only in covert or disguised articulations or, in the rare cases where lesbian and gay themes were made explicit, in highly negative and unidimensional representations. Critiques of such stereotyped and negative representations have been an important concern of both feminist and gay movements since the 1970s (Marshment, 1997). Although rarely expressed in terms of rights to cultural citizenship, such resistance has led to the production of more positive images and texts in a range of cultural sites. In recent years, there has been a gradual increase in the participation and representation of lesbians and gay men in the media and popular culture, perhaps most noticeably on television, for instance in primetime 'soaps.' The significance attached to such sociological shifts is that whereas previously the focus of lesbian and gay representation was largely subcultural, as a result of cultural efforts by and for lesbians and gay men themselves, it is now increasingly mainstream (Cottingham, 1996).

At one level, it is possible to regard the inclusion of lesbian and gay images and narratives in popular culture as constituting an important form of recognition and access to cultural citizenship. However, such an interpretation is questioned by those who argue that the greater visibility of lesbians and gay men in mainstream cultural life is less an acknowledgement of cultural rights than evidence of a process of commodification and assimilation into dominant culture (Chasin, 2000). Paradoxically, it is when we come to define citizenship as consumerism that non-heterosexuals seem to be most acceptable as citizens, as consumers with identities and lifestyles that are expressed through purchasing goods, commodities, and services (Bell & Binnie, 2002).

Also, as with the other aspects of citizenship that have been considered, access to the right to consume is both a gendered and sexualised experience. Lesbians and gay men may be free to consume but only within certain spatial and cultural boundaries. The boundaries of citizenship as consumerism are the limits to where, when, and how we can consume lesbian and gay 'lifestyles'—that is, the boundaries of (heterosexual) tolerance and of 'public spaces' in which consumer communities can exercise their right to consume (Binnie, 1995). It is also important to recognise, in considering the role of the market in sexual cultures, that consumer citizenship is significantly structured by access to time and money.

Conclusion

In this chapter I have highlighted how certain forms of citizenship status are closely associated with normative forms of heterosexuality. In this sense we can understand the concept of citizenship to be sexualised, rather as others have talked of the 'racialisation' of citizenship (Taylor, 1996) and of how citizenship is gendered (Lister, 1997; Walby, 1994, 1997). The argument that the 'normal citizen' has largely been constituted as heterosexual (Duggan, 1995; Richardson, 1998; Bell & Binnie, 2000), would, however, appear to be queried by responses to lesbian and gay demands for 'equal rights,' social changes that have led to new forms of citizenship status for (some) lesbians and gay men. However, as I have argued, we need to set against this the question of how far these changes actually reinforce dominant constructions of citizenship, rather than challenge them, insofar as these are constituted through heteronormative assumptions and practices. Lesbians and gay men were previously constrained by representations of themselves as mad, bad, or sad; now they are being shaped through normative constructions of responsible and respectable sexual citizenship.

References

Alexander, M.J. (1994) Not just (any) body can be a citizen: The politics of law, sexuality and postcoloniality in Trinidad and Tobago and the Bahamas. *Feminist Review, 48,* 5–23.

Amnesty International United Kingdom. (1997). *Breaking the silence: Human rights violations based on sexual orientation.* London: Amnesty International United Kingdom.

Anderson, B. (1991). *Imagined communities.* London: Verso.

Anthias, F., & Yuval-Davis, N. (1992). *Racialized boundaries: Race, nation, gender, colour and class, and the anti-racist struggle*. London: Routledge.

Baciu, I., Cimpeanu, V., & Nicoara, M. (1996). Romania. In R. Rosenbloom (Ed.), *Unspoken rules. Sexual orientation and women's human rights*. London: Cassell.

Bell, D., & Binnie, J. (2000). *The sexual citizen: Queer politics and beyond*. Cambridge: Polity Press.

Bell, D., & Binnie, J. (2002) 'Sexual citizenship: marriage, the market and the military,' in S. Seidman and D. Richardson (eds.) *The handbook of lesbian and gay studies*. London: Sage.

Berlant, L. (1997). *The queen of America goes to Washington City: Essays on sex and citizenship*. Durham, NC, and London: Duke University Press.

Binnie, J. (1995). Trading places: Consumption, sexuality and the production of queer space. In D. Bell & G. Valentine (Eds.), *Mapping desire. Geographies of sexualities*. London: Routledge.

Carabine, J. (1992). 'Constructing women': Women's sexuality and social policy. *Critical Social Policy, (12)*23, 23—37.

Chasin, A. (2000). *Selling out. The lesbian and gay movement goes to market*. New York: St. Martin's Press.

Cooper, D. (2004). *Challenging diversity: Rethinking equality and the value of difference*. Cambridge: Cambridge University Press.

Cossman, B. (2007). *Sexual citizens: The legal and cultural regulation of sex and belonging*. Stanford, CA: Stanford University Press.

Cottingham, L. (1996). *Lesbians are so chic . . . that we are not really lesbians at all*. London: Cassell.

Davis, T. (1995). The diversity of queer politics and the redefinition of sexual identity and community in urban spaces. In D. Bell & G. Valentine (Eds.), *Mapping desire. Geographies of sexualities*. London: Routledge.

D'Emilio. J. (2000). Cycles of change, questions of strategy, the gay and lesbian movement after fifty years. In C.A. Rimmerman, K.D. Wald, & C. Wilcox (Eds.), *The politics of gay rights*. London: University of Chicago Press.

Duggan, L. (1995) 'Queering the State,' in L. Duggan and N. Hunter, *Sex Wars: Sexual Dissent and Political Culture*. New York: Routledge.

Edelman, L. (1992). Tearooms and sympathy, or, the epistemology of the water closet. In A. Parker, M. Russo, D. Sommer, & P. Yaeger (Eds.), *Nationalisms and sexualities*. London: Routledge.

Ellis, C. (1991) 'Sisters and citizens,' in G. Andrews (ed.), *Citizenship*. London: Lawrence and Wishart.

Evans, D. (1993). *Sexual citizenship: The material construction of sexualities*. London: Routledge.

Gates, H.L., Jr. (1993). The black man's burden. In M. Warner (Ed.), *Fear of a queer planet: Queer politics and social theory*. Minneapolis: University of Minnesota Press.

Herman, D. (1994). *Rights of passage: Struggles for lesbian and gay equality*. Toronto: University of Toronto Press.

Isin, E., & Wood, P. (1999). *Citizenship and identity*. London: Sage.

Lister, R. (1996). Citizenship engendered. In D. Taylor (Ed.), *Critical social policy. A reader*. London: Sage.

Lister, R. (1997). *Citizenship: Feminist perspectives*. London: Macmillan.

Marshall, T.H. (1950). *Citizenship and social class*. Cambridge: Cambridge University Press.

Marshall, T.H. (1977). *Class, citizenship and social development*. Chicago and London: University of Chicago Press.

Marshment, M. (1997). The picture is political: Representation of women in contemporary popular culture. In V. Robinson & D. Richardson (Eds.), *Introducing women's studies* (2nd ed.). Basingstoke: Palgrave.

McClintock, A. (1995). *Imperial leather. Race, gender and sexuality in the colonial contest*. London: Routledge.

McLaughlin, J., Phillimore, P., & Richardson, D. (2011). *Contesting recognition*. Basingstoke: Palgrave Macmillan.

Outhwaite, W. (2008). *European society*. Cambridge: Polity Press.

Pakulski, J. (1997). Cultural citizenship. *Citizenship Studies, 1*(1), 73–86.

Phelan, S. (1995). The space of justice: Lesbians and democratic politics. In A.R. Wilson (Ed.), *A simple matter of justice? Theorizing lesbian and gay politics*. London: Cassell.

Phelan, S. (2001). *Sexual strangers. Gays, lesbians and dilemmas of citizenship*. Philadelphia, PA: Temple University Press.

Phillips, A. (1991). Citizenship and feminist theory. In G. Andrews (Ed.), *Citizenship*. London: Lawrence and Wishart.

Plummer, K. (2003). *Intimate citizenship: Private decisions and public dialogues*. Seattle: University of Washington Press.

Richardson, D. (1998). Sexuality and citizenship. *Sociology, 32*(1), 83–100.

Richardson, D. (2000a). *Rethinking sexuality*. London: Sage.

Richardson, D. (2000b). Extending citizenship: Cultural citizenship and sexuality. In N. Stevenson (Ed.), *Cultural citizenship*. London: Sage.

Richardson, D. (2004). Locating sexualities: From here to normality. *Sexualities, 7*(4), 391–411.

Richardson, D. (2005). Desiring sameness? The rise of a neoliberal politics of normalisation. *Antipode, 37*(3), 514–534.

Richardson, D., & May, H. (1999). Deserving victims? Sexual status and the social construction of violence. *Sociological Review, 47*(2), 308–331.

Richardson, D., & Monro, S. (forthcoming). *Sexuality, diversity and social change.* Basingstoke: Palgrave Macmillan.

Sharp, J.P. (1996). Gendering nationhood: A feminist engagement with national identity. In N. Duncan (Ed.), *Bodyspace: Destabilizing geographies of gender and sexuality.* London: Routledge.

Shotter, J. (1993). Psychology and citizenship: Identity and belonging. In B.S. Turner (Ed.), *Citizenship and social theory.* London: Sage.

Sibley, D. (1995). *Geographies of exclusion. Society and difference in the West.* London: Routledge.

Stacey, J. (1991). Promoting normality: Section 28 and the regulation of sexuality. In S. Franklin, C. Lury, & J. Stacey (Eds.), *Off centre: Feminism and cultural studies.* London: Unwin Hyman.

Stevenson, N. (Ed.). (2000). *Cultural citizenship.* London: Sage.

Taylor, D. (1996). Citizenship and social power. In D. Taylor (Ed.), *Critical social policy. A reader.* London: Sage.

Terry, J. (1999). *An American obsession: Science, medicine and homosexuality in modern society.* Chicago: University of Chicago Press.

Turner, B.S. (1993a). *Citizenship and social theory.* London: Sage.

Turner, B.S. (1993b). Contemporary problems in the theory of citizenship. In B.S. Turner (Ed.), *Citizenship and social theory.* London: Sage.

Turner, B.S. (2000). Outline of a general theory of cultural citizenship. In N. Stevenson (Ed.), *Cultural citizenship.* London: Sage.

Vaid, U. (1995). *Virtual equality: The mainstreaming of gay and lesbian liberation.* New York: Doubleday.

Voet, R. (1998). *Feminism and citizenship.* London: Sage.

Waites, M. (2005). *The age of consent: Young people, sexuality and citizenship.* Basingstoke: Palgrave Macmillan.

Walby, S. (1994). Is citizenship gendered? *Sociology, 28*(2), 379–395.

Walby, S. (1997). *Gender transformations.* London: Routledge.

Warner, M. (1999). *The trouble with normal: Sex, politics and the ethics of queer life.* New York: The Free Press.

War on Want (1996). *Pride world-wide. Sexuality, development and human rights.* London: War on Want.

Weeks, J. (1998). The sexual citizen. *Theory, Culture and Society, 15*(3–4), 35–52.

Weeks, J. (2007). *The world we have won.* London: Routledge.

Weeks, J. (2010). *Sexuality* (3rd ed.). London: Routledge.

Williams, F. (1997). Feminism and social policy. In V. Robinson & D. Richardson (Eds.), *Introducing women's studies* (2nd ed.). Basingstoke: Palgrave.

Wilson, A.R. (Ed.). (1995). *A simple matter of justice? Theorizing lesbian and gay politics.* London: Cassell.

Wilton, T. (1995). *Lesbian studies: Setting an agenda.* London: Routledge.

CHAPTER TWENTY-ONE

What's Queer Got to Do with It?

Interrogating Nationalism and Imperialism

ROLAND SINTOS COLOMA

On October 11, 2001, the Associated Press posted a photo, which it later pulled, illustrating the critical relevance of sexuality in discourses of war and nationalism. The photo caption read:

> A Navy officer signs a bomb attached to the wing of an aircraft on the flight deck of the USS Enterprise in the Arabian Sea, Thursday, Oct. 11, 2001. The USS Enterprise is one of the ships involved in the attacks in Afghanistan. Complete writing on spare fuel tank reads, "War Party." (AP Photo/Jockel Finck)

The reason the photo was controversial was the content of the Navy officer's message, which read, "HIGH JACK THIS FAGS." The bomb functions as obvious retaliation by the U.S. government and military against the Afghanis for the horror of September 11th. Animating this act of retribution for America's double castration as signified by the destruction of the Twin Towers is an explicit homophobic masculinity that renders the United States as an offensive dominator penetrating its victim with the bomb as its phallic apparatus of vengeance. It is thereby difficult to divorce nationalism from the operations of sexuality.

In our heterosexist and homophobic society, according to queer theorist Eve Sedgwick (1990),

> Our culture still sees to its being dangerous enough that women and men who find or fear they are homosexual, or are perceived by others to be so, are physically and mentally terrorized through the institutions of law, religion, psychotherapy, mass culture, medicine, the military, commerce and bureaucracy, and brute violence. (p. 58)

The inscription of the homophobic message on the phallic equipment of the military brings together nationalism, imperialism, and sexuality and intersects them with race and gender. This chapter examines nationalism as a form of resistance, in particular as a form of anti-imperial resistance (often in response to the imperialist brand of nationalism). It outlines the consequences engendered by nationalism as well as the critiques of and alternatives to nationalism. While this chapter sustains a discussion on gender, history, and nation, it extends this discussion to focus on sexuality by putting queer theory to work in deconstructing nationalism and the reproduction of history and nation. While nationalism has been successful in waging revolutionary struggles against imperial rule, the "liberation" of the nation at the expense of non-elites, women, and queers cannot be simply dismissed as a price that needs to be paid.

Nationalism and Anti-Imperialist Resistance

Benedict Anderson (1991) defines the nation as a limited and sovereign imagined community that is undergirded by the cultural production and circulation of print capitalism. The nation is a politically free state with "finite, if elastic, boundaries" whose members share "a deep, horizontal comradeship" (p. 7), even though they will not know, meet, or interact with all of their fellow-members. These communities are distinguished from earlier configurations "not by their falsity/genuineness, but by the style in which they are imagined" (p. 6). Print capitalism—through novels, newspapers, magazines, and other circulars—emerges as the source of nationalism with the decline of premodern religious and dynastic systems beginning in the early 1800s.

Nationalism is a powerful strategy for anti-imperial resistance, since "nations inspire love, and often profoundly self-sacrificing love" (Anderson, 1991, p. 141). This "fraternity" love, based on a bond of brotherhood, enables millions of people "not so much to kill, as willingly to die for such limited imaginings" (p. 7). The types of national liberation movements against imperialism can be generally categorized under three headings: politico-economic, socio-cultural, and subaltern. Political movements generally arise from defeats of the colonized elite's insistence on being properly represented in governments in the colony and, more importantly, in the metropole. The U.S. complaint of taxation without representation in the British parliament and the War in the Colonies in the 1770s, for example, illustrate how economic and political movements can lead to military struggles and eventual independence. In an example from the Philippines, some *ilustrados* (Western-educated, propertied elites from mixed Spanish or Chinese backgrounds) joined the largely peasant-based revolutionary movement after failing to gain recognition from the Spanish legislative house in the late 19th century (Ileto, 1979). In addition, since "culture is the vigorous manifestation on the ideological or idealist plane of the physical and historical reality of the society" (Cabral, 1994, p. 54), it is neither complete nor totalizing but an inherently contested terrain.

Cultural movements shaped by artists, writers, performers, scholars, and other activists produce not only a national literature and culture that the people can call their own, they mobilize their nationalist projects to build alliances and resist imperial impositions. Ideological resistance through the labor of cultural producers and critics works in tandem with the literal armed struggle against colonial aggression. Edward Said (1993) depicts the three projects of resistance culture: to insist on "the right to see the community's history whole, coherently, integrally" in order to "[r]estore the imprisoned nation to itself"; to conceptualize resistance not solely as a reaction to imperialism but as "an alternative way of conceiving human history"; and to "pull away from separatist nationalism toward a more integrative view of human community and human liberation" (pp. 215–216). The by-products of these projects are the "restoration of community, assertion of identity, [and] emergence of new cultural practices" (p. 218) that transform the outlook and configuration of the society.

The political and cultural liberation movements against imperialism also gain support from the everyday acts of subaltern resistance. The "weapons of the weak" include "foot dragging, dissimulation, false compliance, pilfering, feigned ignorance, slander, arson, sabotage" (Scott, 1985, p. 29). This form of liberation movement requires minimal or no coordination, relies on institutional invisibility, and hides behind the mask of public acquiescence. With "its implicit disavowal of public and symbolic goals," it is "informal, often covert, and concerned largely with immediate, de facto gains" (p. 33). Wielded separately and collectively, the politico-economic, socio-cultural, and subaltern forms of liberation movements serve as potent nationalist strategies to resist continuous imperial authority and encroachment in the colonies.

Critiques and Alternatives to Nationalism

"Like all stereotypical notions, the notion of the masses has both an upgrading connotation and a degrading one" (Trinh, 1989, p. 12). The masses are imagined as fellow citizens in their homogeneity and bond as people of the same geopolitical territory, socio-cultural affiliation, as well as ontological and epistemological frameworks. They share similar desires, aspirations, and goals. The invocation of the numeric and symbolic strength of the masses as a literal entity or as a trope for collectivity functions to demonstrate pride in one's heritage and background or legitimacy as a representative of a constituency. However, the "masses" is readily juxtaposed against the "elites," and within such a dichotomy the elites almost always occupy the superior position. The "masses" here becomes a pejorative signifier of a people who are backward, dimwitted, lazy, and docile. Nationalism as a mechanism for representing the masses can be effective and successful for anti-imperial resistance, but it is not innocent. Its operations are imbued with selectivity and violation. Critiques against nationalism raise questions regarding its elitist, mimetic, and patriarchal character.

Frantz Fanon (1963) indicts particularly the native bourgeois whose nationalist interest is complicit in the propagation of Western ideals and culture and in the continuous subjugation of the colonized people. Since the colonial middle class generally does not own or control the economic mode of production, it highlights instead the professionals who are derisively characterized by Fanon as parasitic intermediaries and controlled puppets of Western capital and governments. Through tourism and other "economic development" projects, the native bourgeois caters to Western consumption and pleasure by exploiting its country's natural resources, labor, and people. By harvesting the gains from its own land and people, it "comes to power [and] uses its class aggressiveness to corner the positions formerly kept for foreigners" (p. 155). The nationalism of the native elite, according to Fanon, is a sedimentary legacy of the colonial period and seeks to replicate similar material structures and governing hierarchies, thereby advancing their class interests and continuing the oppression of the masses.

As a prescription for the elimination of the "bourgeois phase," Fanon articulates that "the combined effort of the masses led by a party and of intellectuals who are highly conscious and armed with revolutionary principles ought to bar the way to this useless and harmless middle class" (p. 175). In its place, instead, are "people's parties" that nurture and further the plight of the common folk and that marshal "honest intellectuals" (p. 177) and political education in the development of social consciousness. Since Fanon does not clarify the content and delivery of political education, different interpretations open up. Is Fanon calling for a political education similar to grassroots organizing that culminates visible mass action and mobilization? The book *The Wretched of the Earth* also functions as political education in that Fanon aims to uncloak people's false consciousness. His examination of violence and spontaneous movements, his critiques of the bourgeois and nationalism (such as the pan-Africanist Negritude), and his studies of colonial mental disorders are lessons that can be read and learned by the literate members of the society. Thus, are printed texts and literacy required elements of political education? Or does political education take place in the Freirean process of conscientization in which people are able to read the word and the world (Freire, 1997)? Similar to feminist consciousness-raising, which invokes the personal as political, conscientization as a localized literacy and political strategy enables one to connect one's lived experiences to broader societal issues and problems. Fanon's disdain for hegemonic nationalism points to this third and last interpretation—local and small scale, accessible and egalitarian—as his likely strategy for political education. Political education can definitely become a mechanism that develops the social consciousness of the people, establishes a more collective-based governance, and holds the government responsible and accountable.

Nationalism has also been critiqued as being Eurocentric, especially since nationalism among the colonized peoples of color has been framed as mimetic. Eurocentric chauvinism can be clearly detected in the work of E.J. Hobsbawm's (1992) redeeming of "beneficial" aspects of European imperialism, since it has supposedly produced anti-imperial resistance and nation-building. He states that

> apart from a few relatively permanent political entities such as China, Korea, Vietnam, and perhaps Iran and Egypt which, had they been in Europe, would have been recognized as "historic nations," the territorial units for which so-called national movements sought to win independence, were overwhelmingly the actual creations of imperial conquest, often no older than a few decades, or else they represented religio-cultural zones rather than anything that might have been called "nations" in Europe. Those who strove for liberation were "nationalists" only because they adopted a western ideology excellently suited to the overthrow of foreign governments, and even so, they usually consisted of an exiguous minority of indigenous évolués. (p. 137)

He characterizes the three anti-imperial movements "of any significance" under three categories: elite nationalism derived from Western models, anti-Western xenophobia, and militaristic tribalism.

Partha Chatterjee (1993) incisively takes to task such Eurocentric understanding. "If nationalisms in the rest of the world have to choose their imagined community from certain 'modular' forms already made available to them by Europe and the Americas," he contends,

> what do they have left to imagine? History, it would seem, has decreed that we in the postcolonial world shall only be perpetual consumers of modernity. Europe and the Americas, the only true subjects of history, have thought out on our behalf not only the script of colonial enlightenment and exploitation, but also that of our anticolonial resistance and postcolonial misery. Even our imaginations must remain forever colonized. (p. 5)

While Chatterjee concedes that colonialism has made a tremendous impact on the life, psyche, culture, and economy of the colonized, there is still a certain part that is left untouched, the part that truly fuels the nationalist fervor. Anticolonial nationalism partitions the society into two distinct domains: the material or outside realm where the Western hegemony of money, politics, science, and technology dwells and the spiritual or inside realm that bears the Eastern cultural essence and precolonial values. Anticolonial nationalism in which the spiritual is sovereign thus becomes "a project of mediation" (p. 72) that is aided by the appropriation of popular tastes, the creation of a traditional past, and the eradication of colonial difference. By focusing on the cultural aspects of nationalism, resistance and liberation movements can be recognized as having a longer history of people who have not been considered overtly political.

Another major criticism is the patriarchal aspects of nationalism that do not take into consideration the impact of colonialism and nationalism on women. Anne McClintock (1995) comments that "[w]omen are typically constructed as the symbolic bearers of the nation, but are denied any direct relation to national agency" (p. 354). She maps out a feminist theory of nationalism that deals with:

> (1) investigating the gendered formation of sanctioned male theories; (2) bringing into historical visibility women's active cultural and political participation in national formations; (3) bringing national institutions into critical relations with other social structures and institutions; and (4) at the same time paying scrupulous attention to the structures of racial, ethnic and class power that continue to bedevil privileged forms of feminism. (p. 357)

Putting her theory into practice, McClintock reveals the unmarked gendering in the writings of male nationalists as well as the acts of courage and resistance performed by African women. She criticizes Fanon in particular for setting up a framework in which the colonized male fantasy is to take the white man's place by seizing and possessing white women while remaining silent about the position and suffering of colonized women. When colonized women are active participants within the revolutionary movement, Fanon depicts them as providing service to the nation as instructed by men, thus leading McClintock to remark that "[p]rior to nationalism, women have no history, no resistance, no independent agency" (p. 367), in Fanon's articulation. She also finds Anderson's print capitalism insufficient as a form of inciting and circulating nationalism, especially since literacy and access to books and newspapers privilege the educated, economic elites, and mostly men. She posits, instead, that nationalism is a fetish spectacle whose invention of tradition and nation is theatrically performed and visually consumed. In such rendition, men "embody the political and economic agency of the volk, while women were the (unpaid) keepers of tradition and the volk's moral and spiritual mission" (p. 377). McClintock's interpretation coincides with Chatterjee's, as both scholars set up an oppositional binary between the material-public-Western-male and the spiritual-private-Eastern-female.

Feminist scholars have led the way in demonstrating the criticality of gender as an analytic category, unpacking the absence-presence of patriarchal masculinity in men's writings and revealing women's agency and experiences (Scott, 1988). Feminists of color and in the Third World, in particular, have demonstrated their ability to act on their own behalf and speak for themselves, and often do not separate women's emancipation from anti-colonial nationalist movements. Ketu Katrak (1992) shows how Gandhi utilized the symbolic myth of submissive female sexuality as a driving force behind his non-violent opposition to British rule that simultaneously encouraged women to join the independence movement and bolstered the repressive mechanisms that continue to restrict women's activities within and outside of their homes and families. Although there is growing recognition of women's issues, Delia Aguilar (1998) notes that women face indirect, if not overt, hostility and antagonism, even in "radical" Marxist circles. Aguilar contends that reconciling feminist and (male) nationalist agendas means not subsuming women's issues under the umbrella of the nation but recognizing the interconnection among gender, racial/ethnic, and class issues and the various roles women play within nationalist movements. She further questions how Western feminist ideologies impose upon Third World women and women of color to think and act as feminists in ways that reinforce analytical and political divisions between nation and gender.

For many indigenous women who lead nationalist movements, the divisions between nation and gender are not as pronounced or even as important in comparison to white feminists. Their survival as indigenous peoples against social, cultural, economic, and political genocide mandates not hierarchizing issues but confronting them simultaneously, since they are intertwined and affect one another.

The critiques against nationalism—that nationalism is elitist, mimetic, and patriarchal—have spawned interest in alternatives for collective action and identification. While numerous formulations abound, two strands dominate: those that work beyond the nation and those within the nation. The alternatives that work beyond the nation include the notions of Black Atlantic, Balkanism, and cosmopolitanism. Paul Gilroy's (1993) concept of Black Atlantic is a transnational, racialized configuration that triangulates and connects the historical and contemporary experiences of peoples of African descent through trans-Atlantic movements throughout and between Africa, Europe, and the Americas. Gilroy critically brings together earlier Francophone Negritude and Anglophone pan-African solidarities and examines the cultural and political manifestations of slavery, colonialism, and resistance that go beyond national boundaries. Maria Todorova's (1997) concept of Balkanism does not offer a description of how people within a section of eastern Europe named their regional histories and cultures but rather how the region has been interpellated with unfair, insensitive, and oppressive generalizations. She explicates how the Balkans have been constructed through (Western) European accounts and how the people of Greece, Bulgaria, Albania, Romania, and the former Yugoslavia have represented themselves and resisted demeaning characterizations. The notion of cosmopolitanism has also emerged as a transnational identity that frames the diasporic perspectives and experiences of the migrants, exiles, refugees, and other world travelers at the height of global capitalism. Aihwa Ong (1998), for example, addresses the flexible citizenship of "international managers and professionals [who] have the material and symbolic resources to manipulate global schemes of cultural difference, racial hierarchy, and citizenship to their own advantage" (p. 135). Aware of the shortcomings and violence inflicted by nationalism, Jusdanis insists that the nation is still necessary. In his formulation, the civil and cultural matters are in the hands of the national, while the federal takes care of military, economic, and intergovernmental affairs. Even within the beyond-nation alternatives of Black Atlantic, Balkanism, and cosmopolitanism, the nation remains an integral entity, especially since transnational and transcontinental movement and migration still continue to be mediated by the juridical laws of the nation.

With the nation still a viable contender for people's sense of identification and community, it might be more fruitful, then, to explore more inclusive and perhaps less destructive configurations of solidarities. Within the United States, scholars have offered various models, such as panethnicity, multinationalism, and new tribalism. Yen Le Espiritu (1992) describes the panethnicity model as a strategic way in which a race-based governmental categorization has been co-opted by Asian Americans in order to galvanize people of various ethnic and national backgrounds into political alliances. As a way to pay attention to increasing globalization and to resist ethnocentrism, Maria Koundoura (1998) posits the idea of multinationalism, as opposed to assimilationist and liberal multiculturalism, which situates various racial, ethnic, and cultural backgrounds as fragments of the national whole. In Espiritu's panethnicity and Koundara's multinationalism, remaining intact is the substance of ethnicity and nation. Gloria Anzaldúa's (2000) new tribalism provides a multifaceted notion of identity, "a kind of mestizaje that allows for connecting with other ethnic groups and interacting with other cultures and ideas" (p. 185). New tribalism begins with the premise that traditions adapt and share with those they come in contact with; thus, they are inherently dynamic, porous, impure, and hybrid. It rethinks the relationships between individual and community and community and nation, in a global society in which "[t]he 'we' becomes singular and the 'I' becomes plural" (p. 222). Such a position recognizes the multiplicity of individual experiences and the solidarity needed in building and imagining a community or nation.

Nation, History, Woman

A critical project of nationalist movements is the writing of the nation's history. In order to imagine a community, the writing and telling of the past are galvanized so that "national history secures for the contested and contingent nation the false unity of a self-same, national subject evolving through time" (Duara, 1995, p. 4). History with a capital "H" appropriates and sutures the fragments, excess, and heterogeneity in order to narrativize coherence, unity, and linearity. However, if identity refers "to a subject position produced by representations in relation to other representations," and the self "is constituted neither primordially nor monolithically but within a network of changing and often conflicting representations" (p. 7), the concepts of nation, national identity, and nationalism need to be revised.

> Nationalism is rarely the nationalism of the nation, but rather marks the site where different representations of the nation contest and negotiate with each other. . . . Although nationalism and its theory seek a privileged position within the representational network as the master identity that subsumes or organizes other identifications, it exists only as one among others and is changeable, interchangeable, conflicted, or harmonious with them. (p. 8)

Although dominant national histories may privilege and proliferate a particular narrative, competing and alternative constructions are never completely eliminated. Even though we may "critique the nation as the subject of History," it is almost "impossible to radically displace the nation as the locus of history, if for no other reason than that our values, whether as historians or individuals, have been intimately shaped by the nation-state" (p. 6). For these reasons, the nation as an entity may be insufficient, at the same time that it is also indispensable.

In representing a nation, historians of the United States, particularly social, ethnic, feminist, and lesbian and gay historians, have recovered and written about experiences and conditions that disrupt, compete against, align with, or parallel hegemonic narratives in History. While they have demonstrated the multiplicity, heterogeneity, and hybridity of history, they have also illuminated the various strategies used particularly by the state to contain the differences within the nation. Governmental apparatus such as immigration laws, police and public health officials, and Americanization programs such as education and training have been utilized in order to minimize difference and project a national whole (Ngai, 1999). By highlighting their "difference" in relation to the dominant History, historians have brilliantly shown that history is contested, dynamic, and multiple. For example, ethnic and immigration historians demonstrate that the United States as a nation is not "pure." Its dominant Anglo-Saxon traditions have been infused by "foreign" peoples and cultures within and outside of geopolitical boundaries (Jacobson, 2000). Scholarship on whiteness (particularly Irish and Jews), "in-betweens," interracial relations, and multiethnicity testifies that racial hierarchy among, between, and within whites and people of color are constantly in dispute (Roediger, 1991; Brodkin, 1998; Leonard, 1992). Moreover, historians of women have sustained generative discussions on the question of "difference" and its impact on identity, community, and even nation. Women's history functions as a description and analysis of women's experiences as well as an intervention to traditional male-dominant narratives and historiography. It provides empirical, theoretical, and discursive spaces to explore the unexamined, recuperate the voices of the silenced, and trouble the commonly accepted renditions of particular stories, people, events, and settings. Working within and against their traditional and interdisciplinary intellectual lenses and research methodologies, scholars of women's history have forged multiple and often divergent paths of studying, analyzing, and presenting their work (Gordon, 1978; Scott, 1988).

Feminists have underscored the ways in which nation, nation-building, and nationalism are intrinsically gendered. Women's historians, for example, have shown how female sexuality and prostitution, women's organizations and spiritual motherhood, and the racialization of whiteness and the gendering of policies bring together women's experiences and the construction of the nation (Guy, 1991; Bederman, 1995; Hoganson, 1998). Another major area foregrounded in feminist scholarship is the construction of nation as a woman. McClintock (1995) cites Nira Yuval-Davis and Floya Anthias' identification of five aspects in which women and nationalism converge: (a) "as biological reproducers of the members of national collectivities"; (b) "as reproducers of the boundaries of national groups (through restrictions on sexual or marital relations)"; (c) "as active transmitters and producers of the national culture"; (d) "as symbolic signifiers of national difference"; and (e) "as active participants in national struggles" (p. 355). The trope of nation as woman is marshaled in order to bolster a sense of family and familial love and to assemble and bind heterogeneous and even conflicting people together. For instance, Christina Klein (2000) shows how the notion of familial love through maternal care and adoption has operated to enable the United States to personalize its political commitments to Asia during the Cold War period. The nation, therefore, has often been invoked as a woman, especially in the configuration of a motherland.

While the nation as woman and mother is conceived as loving, nurturing, and giving, on the other hand "she" is also threatened by conquest, abuse, and power by masculinized forms of transgression and imperialism. The metaphors of colonial narratives represent the colonized victim as female and passive and the colonial aggressor as male and dominant. The violence of rape has been the most common literal and metaphorical symbol to describe and analyze the invasion and penetration of imperial forces in their attempts to pry open the country and ravish its resources.

This gendered narrative takes on a particularly racialized and orientalist form in examining the relations between the West and the non-West. Edward Said (1978), for example, argues that the geographical region currently called the Middle East has been historically, culturally, and politically imagined and constructed as an oriental (woman)—exotic, mysterious, irrational, and alluring—a perfect and convenient Other against which the West defines itself. In the Chicana/o and Latina/o context, scholars analyze the representation of Malinche, who served as the guide and mistress of Spanish explorer and conqueror Cortez. Depicted as La Chingada (or the "fucked one"), Malinche functions within the Chicano male ideology as a race traitor and a willing whore who initiated the breeding of mestizos, the emblems of racial mixing, which supposedly diluted the Aztec blood and signaled the decline and eventual demise of the Aztec empire and civilization. Both Malinche and mestizos are marked as threats and pariahs in this patriarchal discourse. Chicana feminists, on the other hand, recuperate Malinche as a race savior who, in the name of Aztec cosmology, saw in Cortez the revitalization of her people and civilization (Anzaldúa, 1999). Thus, within the racialized and gendered narratives of colonialism and nationalism, the (heterosexual?) woman who bears children plays an important, albeit complicated, role in malleable desires and imagined configurations.

Putting Queer to Work

In scholarship regarding nation and nationalism, race, gender, and class have been utilized as analytical categories, either individually or intersectionally. What has been grossly neglected and needs to be continuously interrogated is sexuality as a category for analysis. A productive starting point in utilizing sexuality as a category of analysis is to make tentative distinctions among the terms "sex," "gender," and "sexuality." Conventional understanding of sex or "chromosomal sex" is based on the "irreducible, biological differentiations between members of the species Homo sapiens who have XX and those who have XY chromosomes" (Sedgwick, 1990, p. 27). On the other hand, gender is "the cultural meanings that the sexed body assumes" and is performative, "constituting the identity it is purported to be. In this case gender is always a doing, though not a doing by a subject who might be said to preexist the deed" (Butler, 1999, pp. 10, 33). However, "the association of 'sex' . . . through the physical body, with reproduction and with genital activity and sensation" situates sex beyond the chromosomal framework and into socio-cultural relations, thus complicating the sex/gender distinction (Sedgwick, 1990, p. 28). The realities of intersex and other transgender people and the performativity of sex also call into question the chromosomal basis of "sex" (Butler, 1999). The biological foundation of sex, of who is (considered) a man or woman, is therefore no longer tenable. The meanings and performances of both sex and gender must then be understood as cultural constructions. This affirms Simone de Beauvoir's position: one is not born a woman; one becomes a woman (Beauvoir, 1953). Moreover, sexuality denotes the "array of acts, expectations, narratives, pleasures, identity-formations, and knowledges, in both women and men, that tends to cluster most densely around certain genital sensations but is not adequately defined by them" (Sedgwick, 1990, p. 29). To use sexuality as a main analytic frame implicates sex and gender, as well as their intersections with race, class, and nation. These categories constitute and are constituted within each other: "No social category exists in privileged position; each comes into being in social relation to other categories, if in uneven and contradictory ways" (McClintock, 1995, p. 9). What this last section aims to accomplish is to foreground an interrogation of sexuality in order to unpack the underlying patriarchal heteronormative culture and economy that support the concepts and practices of nation, nationalism, and imperialism.

Queer theory anchors many of the discussions regarding sexuality and draws its analysis from feminist, anti-racist/race-conscious, Marxist, poststructuralist, and psychoanalytic frameworks (Jagose, 1996). The fluidity and contingency of queer theory serve as its strength: "That it can become such a discursive site whose uses are not fully constrained in advance ought to be safeguarded not only for the purposes of continuing to democratize queer politics, but also to expose, affirm, and rework the specific historicity of the term" (Butler, 1993). The primary subjects and objects of lesbian, gay, bisexual, transgender, and queer scholarship have been sexual minorities and their histories, cultures, productions, and practices (Leong, 1996). History as a discipline has slowly produced gay and lesbian narratives, and has generated discussions on the role of theory in its work and profession (Duggan, 1998). Feminists have led the exploration of sexuality, particularly women's sexuality, in myriad ways. Although most of their projects fall within the un(re)marked heterosexual matrix, an increasing attention is being paid to the heterosexist constructions of nation, family, and history. A number of postcolonial feminists are interrogating the heterosexual nature of the nation, for example through the governmental surveillance of the non-procreativity of its lesbian and gay citizens (Alexander, 2000). Feminists in Ethnic Studies are reexamining the Asian American history of bachelors and male sojourners from mid-19th and early 20th centuries that challenges the conjugal nuclear family as the natural unit and the heterosexist categories of thinking about conjugal and non-conjugal sex (Yanagisako, 1995). Jennifer Ting (1995) posits the notion of "deviant heterosexuality" to simultaneously trouble the monolithic structure of heterosexuality and implicate it within dynamics of knowledge and power. She argues that

> to say "heterosexuality" is determined by more than object choice is to say that not all heterosexualities will be equally privileged by heterosexism, precisely because sexualities are implicated in power relations and cultural logics. In other words, the particular kind of heterosexuality constructed within the historiographic tradition of the bachelor society is working, at the level of representation, to develop, secure, and reproduce certain cultural logics (such as those underpinning the racial and class meanings of Asians and Asian Americans or ideas of U.S. national identity). (pp. 277–278)

Ting provides a useful direction to instigate an investigation into the workings of the conjugal and patriarchal family as well as of male heteronormative sexuality. Queer theory, thus, addresses not only sexual minorities but also race, masculinity, and heterosexuality (Thomas, 2000).

Putting queer to work is a project of the insurrection of subjugated knowledge and power that resides in perverse strategies of readings and that opens and proliferates enabling praxis. For example, Lauren Berlant (1997) considers the construction and effects of queer nationalism. By interrogating the production of nation, citizenship, and subjectivity, Berlant examines the political strategies deployed by queer Americans to both resist and subvert hegemonic heteronormativity through parody and camp. She analyzes lesbian and homoerotic performances and images; "queeritual" prayers such as "I praise life with my vulva" and "I praise God with my erection"; in-your-face tactics such as Pink Panthers, queer nights out, mall visibility actions, and public kiss-ins; and queered fashion and commodities such as Queer Bart Simpson and "gay"-ing Gap advertisements. Such strategies develop an insider queer nation, thereby consolidating a sense of belonging, legitimacy, and expression of difference and enfranchising queer citizens to define themselves in relation to their Other—the heterosexual outsiders. These nationalist strategies, however innovative, effective, and affective, must be interpreted as mere reversals of binaries, as turning things upside down, in this case queers over straights, safety over violence, visibility over marginalization. Juxtaposing feminist and deconstruction frameworks, Berlant questions the political utility of "separatist withdrawal" and "counterspectacle." She calls instead for "a negative space, a space where suddenly the various logics of identity that circulate through American culture come into contradiction and not simple analogy" (p. 169). Using lesbian fanzines as icons of "counterproductivity," she rotates the meaning of consent, goes beyond the analytic move of under erasure and provides "a space of politics in which to be 'out' in public . . . [is] to be out beyond the censoring imaginary of the state and the information culture that consolidates the rule of its names" (pp. 172–173). Berlant's work demonstrates both the pleasure and pain in working within and against institutions and representations that symbolize our belonging and exclusion.

Putting queer to work is an anti-homophobic project that directs attention to the un(re)marked patriarchal heteronormativity that functions as a legitimating factor in historical representations of the nation, nationalism, and imperialism. It also highlights the resistance offered by gay, lesbian, bisexual, and transgender individuals and communities, while remaining cognizant of its simultaneous non-innocence and efficacy. The operations of patriarchal heteronormativity center, but not exclusively, on women. The production and reproduction of nationalism heavily relies on the trope and literal embodiment of a woman functioning as a national symbol and operating within patriarchal and, in the case of colonialism in Asia, orientalized frameworks. What happens if the symbol changes into a man, or more specifically into a queer man? Or if it changes into a lesbian? How, then, are nation and nationalism reconfigured? What possibilities open up, and how are earlier interpretations foreclosed or revised? This line of questioning might seem absurd; however, it is precisely this absurdity that renders the intersection between nation and (non-hetero)sexuality unintelligible and that fortifies heterosexism and homophobia in many nationalist movements. Nationalism centers on a heterosexist patriarchy that relies on women to be the bearers of children, culture, and nation. Queers who do not subscribe to heterosexual conjugal sex and (re)production of children and nation or to the patriarchal consumption of unidimensional (read: male) gaze, desire, and pleasure destabilize the commonsensical notions and intersections of sex, gender, and nation. The deviance of queers signifies their uselessness within the culture and economy of heterosexist patriarchy. However, their deviance becomes useful in interrogating and disseminating its gaps, fissures, contradictions, and discontinuities and in providing alternative spaces for different interpretations, productions, performances, and configurations.

The deployment of queer theory is neither a mere call for inclusion nor a dilution of "real" issues. The intervention of queer theory in discussions of nationalism and imperialism underscores that the "contests for discursive power can be specified as competitions for the material or rhetorical leverage required to set the terms of, and to profit in some way from, the operations of such an incoherence of definition" (Sedgwick, 1990, p. 11). The nation as family brings up questions such as: Who belongs in the family? What kind of family is it? Who becomes parent or child in such a setting? By asking such questions, queer theory highlights the limits of customary understanding, urges the acknowledgment and proliferation of various meanings and configurations, and implicates such discussion within contested relations of power and knowledge. Furthermore, while feminists have explored the trope "nation as woman," a queer feminist reading of the same trope situates it within "a hegemonic, homoerotic/homophobic male canon of cultural mastery and coercive erotic double-binding" that "can be only part of the strategy of an antihomophobic project" (Sedgwick, 1990, p. 58). The battle over the nation (as woman) needs to be understood as primarily a battle between men. Using Sedgwick's (1990) insight on gender and sexuality, nationalism and imperialism produce "oppressive effects on women and men of a cultural system in which male-male desire became widely intelligible primarily by being routed through triangular relations involving a woman" (p. 15). What happens when the analysis of imperial relations shifts from a heterosexual matrix of male-female rape to a particularly male homosexual matrix? How do the terms "top," "bottom," and "missionary position" gain different outlooks and valences in queering imperial encounters? Is the top always in control, and does the one on the bottom necessarily surrender his power and desire? Does this shift change the dynamic of anti-imperialist nationalism from violence to pleasure? Can we simply dismiss the "positive" consequences of colonialism, such as public education, improved infrastructure, and health care, as beneficial accidents or as planned mechanisms for people's acquiescence? While the violent history and consequences of nationalism and imperialism on the body, mind, and psyche cannot be erased and must always be remembered, an openly queer framework can at the very least direct our attention to the homophobic operations of both nationalism and imperialism and ensure that heterosexism and its manifestations in our theories and praxis come out of the closet.

References

Aguilar, D. (1998). *Toward a nationalist feminism.* Quezon City, Philippines: Giraffe.

Alexander, M.J. (2000). Not just (any) body can be a citizen: The politics of law, sexuality and postcoloniality in Trinidad and Tobago and the Bahamas. In C. Hall (Ed.), *Cultures of empire: Colonizers in Britain and the empire in the nineteenth and twentieth centuries: A reader.* New York: Routledge.

Anderson, B. (1991). *Imagined communities: Reflections on the origin and spread of nationalism.* London & New York: Verso.

Anzaldúa, G. (1999). *Borderlands/la frontera: The new mestiza* (2nd ed.). San Francisco, CA: Aunt Lute/Spinsters.

Anzaldúa, G. (2000). *Interviews/entrevistas* (A. Keating, Ed.). New York & London: Routledge.

Beauvoir, S. de (1953). *The second sex.* New York: Knopf.

Bederman, G. (1995). *Manliness and civilization: A cultural history of gender and race in the United States, 1880–1917.* Chicago & London: University of Chicago Press.

Berlant, L. (1997). *The queen of America goes to Washington City: Essays on sex and citizenship.* Durham, NC: Duke University Press.

Brodkin, K. (1998). *How Jews became white folks and what that says about race in America.* New Brunswick, NJ: Rutgers University Press.

Butler, J. (1993). *Bodies that matter: On the discursive limits of "sex."* New York: Routledge.

Butler, J. (1999). *Gender trouble: Feminism and the subversion of identity.* New York & London: Routledge.

Cabral, A. (1994). National liberation and culture. In P. Williams & L. Chrisman (Eds.), *Colonial discourse and postcolonial theory: A reader.* New York: Columbia University Press.

Chatterjee, P. (1986). *Nationalist thought and the colonial world: A derivative discourse.* London: Zed.

Chatterjee, P. (1993). *The nation and its fragments: Colonial and postcolonial histories.* Princeton, NJ: Princeton University Press.

Duara, P. (1995). *Rescuing history from the nation: Questioning narratives of modern China.* Chicago: University of Chicago Press.

Duggan, L. (1998). The theory wars, or, who's afraid of Judith Butler? *Journal of Women's History, 10*(1), 9–19.

Espiritu, Y.L. (1992). *Asian American panethnicity: Bridging institutions and identities.* Philadelphia, PA: Temple University Press.

Fanon, F. (1963). *The wretched of the earth.* New York: Grove.

Freire, P. (1997). *Pedagogy of the oppressed.* New York: Continuum.

Gilroy, P. (1993). *The Black Atlantic: Modernity and double consciousness.* London: Verso.

Gordon, L. (1978). What should women's historians do?: Politics, social theory, and women's history. *Marxist Perspectives, 3,* 128–136.

Guy, D.J. (1991). *Sex and danger in Buenos Aires: Prostitution, family, and nation in Argentina.* Lincoln: University of Nebraska Press.

Hobsbawm, E.J. (1992). *Nations and nationalism since 1780: Programme, myth, reality.* Cambridge: Cambridge University Press.

Hoganson, K.L. (1998). *Fighting for American manhood: How gender politics provoked the Spanish-American and Philippine-American Wars.* New Haven, CT: Yale University Press.

Ileto, R.C. (1979). *Pasyon and revolution: Popular movements in the Philippines, 1840–1910.* Quezon City, Philippines: Ateneo de Manila University Press.

Jacobson, M.F. (2000). *Barbarian virtues: The United States encounters foreign peoples at home and abroad, 1876–1917.* New York: Hill & Wang.

Jagose, A. (1996). *Queer theory: An introduction.* New York: New York University Press.

Jusdani, G. (2001). *The necessary nation.* Princeton, NJ: Princeton University Press.

Katrak, K.H. (1992). Indian nationalism, Gandhian "satyagraha," and representations of female sexuality. In A. Parker, M. Russo, D. Sommer, & P. Yaeger (Eds.), *Nationalisms and sexualities.* New York & London: Routledge.

Klein, C. (2000). Family ties and political obligation: The discourse of adoption and the Cold War commitment to Asia. In C.G. Appy (Ed.), *Cold war constructions: The political culture of United States imperialism, 1945–1966.*

Amherst: University of Massachusetts Press.

Koundoura, M. (1998). Multiculturalism or multinationalism. In D. Bennett (Ed.), *Multicultural states: Rethinking difference and identity*. London & New York: Routledge.

Leonard, K. (1992). *Making ethnic choices: California's Punjabi Mexican Americans*. Philadelphia, PA: Temple University Press.

Leong, R. (1996). *Asian American sexualities: Dimensions of the gay and lesbian experience*. New York: Routledge.

McClintock, A. (1995). *Imperial leather: Race, gender and sexuality in the colonial contest*. New York & London: Routledge.

Ngai, M.N. (1999, June). The architecture of race in American immigration law: A reexamination of the Immigration Act of 1924. *Journal of American History, 86*, 67–92.

Ong, A. (1998). Flexible citizenship among Chinese cosmopolitans. In P. Cheah & B. Robbins (Eds.), *Cosmopolitics: Thinking and feeling beyond the nation*. Minneapolis: University of Minnesota Press.

Roediger, D. (1991). *The wages of whiteness: Race and the making of the American working class*. New York & London: Verso.

Said, E.W. (1978). *Orientalism*. New York: Vintage.

Said, E.W. (1993). *Culture and imperialism*. New York: Vintage.

Scott, J.C. (1985). *Weapons of the weak: Everyday forms of peasant resistance*. New Haven, CT: Yale University Press.

Scott, J.W. (1988). *Gender and the politics of history*. New York: Columbia University Press.

Sedgwick, E.K. (1990). *Epistemology of the closet*. Berkeley: University of California Press.

Ting, J. (1995). Bachelor society: Deviant heterosexuality and Asian American historiography. In G.Y. Okihiro, M. Alquizola, D.F. Rony, & K.S. Wong (Eds.), *Privileging positions: The sites of Asian American studies*. Pullman: Washington State University Press.

Todorova, M.N. (1997). *Imagining the Balkans*. New York: Oxford University Press.

Trinh, T.M. (1989). *Women, native, other*. Bloomington: Indiana University Press.

Thomas, C. (Ed.). (2000). Straight with a twist: Queer theory and the subject of heterosexuality. Urbana: University of Illinois Press.

Yanagisako, S. (1995). Transforming orientalism: Gender, nationality, and class in Asian American studies. In S. Yanagisako & C. Delaney (Eds.), *Naturalizing power: Essays in feminist cultural analysis*. New York: Routledge.

CHAPTER TWENTY-TWO

Under Construction

Sexualities in Rural Spaces

JAY POOLE & C. P. GAUSE

Introduction

One of the most iconic images of American masculinity and male sexuality is the construction worker. He is often imagined and (re)presented as an independent male: muscular, virile, and replete with brute strength. He is able to form something out of nothing with ease and style. The construction worker, with his hard hat and his tool belt always at the ready, captures the American ethic of hard work. Stereotypes situate the construction worker as lacking in formal education and with little interest in obtaining more schooling and often as someone from a rural area or with family roots in rural spaces. Construction workers, despite the fact that women are represented in the occupation, are contextualized in traditional masculine roles, with emphasis on the use of the male body as a tool for work. Popular culture has traditionally constructed males in the construction industry, regardless of race/ethnicity, as crude and bawdy. The attachment of a sexualized edge often commenting on and posturing "bad boy" behavior, particularly toward women, is evident in historic and current media (re)presentations (Freeman, 1993; Gause, 2008). Indeed, the image of the construction worker has been sexually objectified in the media both in masculine and feminine forms. Males are usually portrayed as shirtless and wearing jeans and a hard hat, with sweat dripping down a muscular body. These images are often made more dramatic by showing the male construction worker maintaining a provocative pose, with camera angles revealing a chiseled body and breadbasket filled with bread (slang for a crotch filled with a sizable penis). Females, meanwhile, are often portrayed wearing a hard hat with a bikini or other minimal clothing to raise the sexual awareness of the viewer. Even as many immigrant workers now fill the ranks of the construction industry, the image of the sexy construction worker, usually a white male, is still predominant in American culture. Rugged, strong, and determined, the American construction worker exists in the foundations of what many historically think ensures America's presumed greatness: its industry.

As industrialization exploded in America in the late 19th and early 20th centuries, the call to work resounded, and ordinary men and women answered by leaving the farm behind for work in the emerging factories, which were often located in what we now know as urban areas. Indeed, the construction of industry relied on the hard work of the common man, with women either staying at home with the children and/or working in the factories being built by the men. Rural, agrarian ways of life began to be decentered as people shifted into an urban existence, which included schooling as a means of enhancing the workforce.

On the farm, men and boys were responsible for working the fields, and women and girls took care of the house and vegetable garden. The nuclear family held a sacred location in traditional rural culture; marriage and sexual monogamy for the purpose of reproduction were dominant in terms of being together sexually (Little, 2007; Johnston & Longhurst, 2010). However, in the city, women began to find opportunities to work for wages, as did children, though child labor, among other labor practices, became incredibly abusive. Women could earn their own money and not depend on men for sustenance. Ways of being sexual were imagined and practiced as recreational rather than reproductive. Schooling was emphasized as a way in which America could train future workers; thus, education became a central means of instilling discipline and the work ethic (Spring, 2005). As 20th-century urbanization progressed, no longer were the roles of men, women, and children so clearly defined.

Questions of "being" emerged and eventually would be taken up as sociopolitical through the women's movement and other social movements. Yet what seems to have remained steadfast is the notion that men and women are supposed to be together in particular ways. Opposite-sex sexuality had long been and continues to be the dominant way of being sexual with another person. In fact, those who do not conform to traditionally defined opposite-sex sexuality are marginalized and are often perceived to be deviant, immoral, and/or diseased. Indeed, those who locate themselves in the margins often continue to engage in heteronormative sexual and gender practices, resulting in the exclusion of those who do not conform to such practices, e.g., gay couples functioning in dominant/subordinate binaries (Kendall & Martino, 2006). How do we get to these impasses of what is acceptable and not acceptable with regard to gender and sexuality? And how is sexuality and gender identity defined by social and cultural rules and practices? These questions are not framed to elicit answers; rather, they are intended to be provocative as one considers intersections of sexuality, gender, and education, particularly in rural spaces.

Theoretical Perspectives

Here the lenses of critical and queer theories are used in the context of deconstruction in order to consider the intersections of sexuality, gender, and education within and among the so-called rural. Deconstruction assumes that something has been previously built, and our construction worker— being the "real" man that he is—simply tears it down in order to eliminate whatever "it" is. As we examine sexuality and gender within and among educational and rural spaces, we employ deconstruction as a method; however, we do not simply tear down what has been previously constructed. Rather, we examine constructions in order to raise questions and provoke possibilities. A beginning point is an assumption that much of what we know is the product of complex social and cultural interactions that serve to construct beliefs and practices, which some have called social constructionism.

Many have taken up discussion of sexuality within a notion of social constructionism; namely, that sexual identities are formulated through a complex interaction among social, cultural, personal, and perhaps geographic locations. Much like the construction worker uses various materials to build something where nothing was, sexualities and gender identities seem to draw on many aspects of human existence as it is constructed. One of the foundations in the construction of sexualities and gender identities rests in the notion of the binary. Stemming from ancient Greek ideology, binaries are exclusive, as they lack identification of possibilities beyond pairings of particular and presumably related concepts. For example, male and female are paired as opposite and complementary in the binary, excluding the possibility that there are other sexes. Similarly, masculine and feminine are paired, excluding other expressions of gender. It is within these reified binaries that we may locate oppressive beliefs, values, and practices that serve to exclude those who do not fit within their perimeters. As we are educated, we learn that these binarial constructions are to be held as truth. What we learn about sexualities and gender is no exception.

Education, including schooling, becomes a pathway for learning how to be sexual and how to express gender. As Spring (2005) points out, American public schooling has been and continues to occupy a space in which the norms of society are taught and reinforced; thus, one often learns how to *be* vis-à-vis the social curriculum that is present in educational spaces. In rural locations, social and cultural boundaries are grounded in more traditional approaches, e.g., males are strong, independent, self-sufficient, and focused on caring for their families, while females are nurturing, dependent, maternal, and supportive of their husbands. Urban identities, though grounded in traditionally masculine and feminine constructs, may blur the rigid boundaries that are found in the rural. Pretty (2002) asserts that community identity impacts one's self-identity. Presumably, teachers whose identities are grounded in particular community standards and practices will reiterate particular identities in the classroom. Thus, if one's identity is based in rural beliefs, values, and practices, it is likely that those will be directly or indirectly conveyed to students, affecting their perspectives. Critical theorists in education assert that educators must identify and disrupt structures and practices that perpetuate oppression and discrimination.

Noted critical theorists/educators such as Freire, Greene, hooks, Purpel, and Shapiro call for teachers to carefully consider the impact of personal, social, and cultural values, beliefs, and attitudes, asserting that education should call into question oppressive systems and practices rather than reinforce them. In order to engage in what Purpel and McLaurin (2004) call the prophetic voice in education, one must call into question what is grounded in truths constructed through and within social and cultural spaces. In other words, we must work to deconstruct what has been constructed. As educators we must, like the construction worker, often tear down in order to create possibilities for building. One of the theoretical spaces that can be engaged as questions arise rests in what has been called queer theories.

While no single theoretical concept is identified as queer, the notion of queer theories rests in the idea that the practice of codification and classification is exclusive (Jagose, 1997; Hall, 2003). In order to transcend the bounds of labeling and classifying, one must engage in practices that push beyond the limits set forth through social and cultural construction. Complementing critical approaches, queer lenses enable the disruption of beliefs, value systems, and practices that serve oppression. There is an inclusive quality to queerness in this context. Thus, when one considers sexual and gender identities from queer points of view, one may be able to disrupt dominant constructions of identities, usually conceived in the binary, that serve to oppress, e.g., males and females are "normally" heterosexual.

Here, working from and through the image of the American male construction worker as representative of what is masculine, traditional constructions of gender and sexuality are considered through critical and queer lenses, with particular attention paid to how sexuality has been and is constructed in spaces that have been identified as rural. First, what is meant by "rural," particularly to 20th- and 21st-century American culture, is carefully considered. Second, sexual identities in the context of rural spaces are taken up. Finally, possibilities for how one might imagine rural sexualities are considered. The hope is that educators might, in the spirit of the prophetic voice, call their own beliefs and practices into question so that they and the students whose lives they touch may be encouraged to disrupt oppressive or potentially oppressive practices.

Deconstructing Rural

Just what is imagined when "rural" is used to define spaces? Perhaps now you are imagining any variety of things: large fields, lots of trees, farmhouses, dogs lying on porches of small and perhaps run-down homes where an impoverished family may reside. . . . The images go on. What is important is that rural is imagined. Rural images emerge from perception, and perception is shaped by experiences. Currently, in the United States, rural locations are often romanticized and represent escape from the grinding routines of daily work. A drive through the country is thought to be refreshing, and a stop at a small country store to buy old-fashioned candy is such a treat! City dwellers retreat to the country to rejuvenate in bed-and-breakfasts fashioned from old farmhouses. Owning a place in the country becomes the dream for many middle-class suburban dwellers, many of whom have lost track of the ancestors who only a few generations ago languished and toiled in the very fields passed on the country drive. As urban centers grew in America, fueled by rural dwellers' moving to the city for a better life, boundaries between rural and urban began to be more clearly defined. Urban and rural represent a binary that has now been culturally reified to have particular meanings. For example, the city is a location for business and commerce while the country is a place for tranquility and, in some areas, agriculture; those with wealth and power often conduct business in the city, have a residence there, and also have a country estate or a gentleman's farm; cities are places for experiencing culture and art, while the country provides restful and creative spaces for artists whose work is exhibited in the city; country life is simple, while city life is complicated; the city is more receptive to those in the margins, while the country represents a place of exclusion; the list goes on. Centers of human activity have existed, of course, for thousands of years. Yet in America, it has been the rural that historically propelled wealth and material success.

History books in most schools point students toward the importance of agriculture as the foundation of America's greatness, with the glaring absence of the importance of "black" and Asian masculinities in the production of American goods and services (Gause, 2008). Indeed, the colonial and pre-Civil War South was a center of agricultural prosperity as rice, cotton, indigo, sugarcane, tobacco, and trees for lumber were grown and harvested on lands that were cleared of forests to make way for cash crops (Ball, 1998). The wealth of white plantation owners was unsurpassed and of course constructed on the backs of slave labor. Indeed, the poor white farmer and his family could not compete with the wealth and resources of the planter and often became relegated to a life of struggle. In the late 19th century, as the factories of the northern United States emerged as productive and powerful, the dominance of the South as the economic powerhouse of America dimmed.

Class began to be re-examined and aligned with education as those with material wealth and those without were delineated largely through what was and was not owned, and what school was or was not attended. According to Sowell (2005), the majority of illiterate whites in the United States resided in the South, despite the fact that southern whites represented only one-third of the entire population prior to the Civil War. Additionally, southern white children, prior to the Civil War, were disadvantaged with regard to schooling, as northern areas had four times as many schools attended by four times as many students. Children of all races in the North went to school approximately twice as long as those in the South, and patents for inventions such as the cotton gin went mostly to northerners (Sowell, 2005). The struggle for ownership plays out racially and ethnically with education positioned as a catalyst for propelling one into possibilities for achieving material wealth (Spring, 2005). Even today, success in America is defined through levels of education and what one is ultimately able to own. Thus, our construction worker, uneducated and dependent on his body rather than his mind, has little hope of being materially wealthy. Much like the construction worker represents American masculinity and hard work, the post-Civil War southern United States became representative of the rural as the region struggled to compete with opportunities offered in urban and industrialized locations.

Indeed, those struggling to make a living in the southern United States in the late 19th and early 20th centuries played out fear, anger, and frustration largely through racial, ethnic, and social conflicts. White working-class southern culture as well as African American working-class culture began to take shape. White and African American working-class southern cultures are based on economic, political, intellectual, social, and religious stratification couched in patriarchy that clearly defines expected cognitive, social, and behavioral characteristics and roles. Conservative political ideologies that privilege, at least rhetorically, small government, fiscal responsibility, and social values based in morality, defined within traditional contexts, dominate this cultural space. Schooling is valued for its ability to promote earning potential in the job market, not as a location for intellectual discourse. Higher education is viewed as elitist and potentially threatening to values that hold hard, usually physical work in high esteem. Social status is measured against those who are economically advantaged and, within the white and African American southern working class as well as the emerging immigrant working class, those who own property are ascribed higher status compared to those who do not (Benokraitis, 2001; Capparell, 2007; Roebuck & Hickson, 1982). Religion, contextualized as conservative Protestant and Christian based, is central in white working-class southern culture and other non-white racial and ethnic cultures. For many, religion offers hope from the perils of sin, which is fundamentally emphasized in doctrines that typify churches that represent conservative Christian values such as Southern Baptists, Churches of God, and Pentecostal Holiness (Conser & Payne, 2008; Roebuck & Hickson, 1982). The term "redneck" is used to describe people who are identified as or who identify as white working-class southerners. Additionally, the term "black redneck" has been used, though not popularly, to describe African Americans who live in poverty in so-called rural locations. Recently, the media have pointed out the hostility surrounding immigrant workers, historically often called "wetbacks," particularly those who do not have legal documents affirming their right to be in the United States (Norquest, 1972). The effect of poverty on those in rural locations, particularly African Americans, is profound, with those living in the so-called "black belt" of the South among the poorest and most disadvantaged of any group in America (Bateman Driskell & Embry, 2006; Lichter & Parisi, 2008). Perhaps one of the greatest frustrations for the poor white person (the redneck) and other non-whites is an apparent inability to become successful as defined by the dominant culture (Goad, 1997).

Additionally, traditional value systems that privilege heteronormative ways of being together create many opportunities to exclude and marginalize those who do not or cannot conform to the hegemony of being rural. Thus, the perception that one must flee to the city becomes pervasive as otherness is identified and defined in rural spaces and, while some do move to town, others stay in the country, so to speak, and seemingly maintain rural identities—a notion that should be challenged if one is to more fully understand the complexity of the rural (Gray, 2009).

Perhaps the image of the construction worker—strong, independent, and sexually in charge, emerging from working-class roots within a legacy of poverty despite hard work—begins to form a narrative of rural that exists within traditional and historic sociocultural frames rather than simply a place on a map that is considered the opposite of urban. Value systems that privilege maleness, celebrate traditionally performed femininity, and outwardly promote heteronormatively constructed sexualities (emphasis on dominant and subordinate sexual roles) form the structure for locating in rural spaces despite where one is geographically. One can be rural in any locale, and rural may take on many aspects of being. Indeed, rural is shaped and reshaped as we push against boundaries that have been constructed by social systems, cultural traditions, hegemonic practices, and those whose lives have impacted ours. Thus, sexuality in rural spaces may be considered beyond the bounds of geography and within the confines of the performance of the boundless aspects of rural.

Sexualities in Rural Spaces

Thinking about sexualities, much like considering what constitutes rural, conjures up many representations of ways to be sexual. Certainly, modernity has created opportunities for sexual behavior to be defined and codified, yet, acting sexually with someone else remains a very personal endeavor. Our construction worker, functioning as the epitome of traditional masculinity, is presumed to be sexually attracted to females who are as feminine as he is masculine. He is presumed to be sexually exciting, virile, and able to perform above expectations. However, what we do not know lies within non-public spaces that he may occupy sexually, and certainly we have seen how those who occupy nontraditional sexual identities engage in the performance of very traditional gender roles, e.g., the "clone" identity or "bear" identity in gay male subculture (Kendall, 2006). As Kinsey (1948/1998; 1953/1998) pointed out to us in his groundbreaking work on sexualities in males and females, people are engaged in any number of sexual ways of being despite the perception that there is a "normal" and "natural" way to be sexual. Indeed, sexualities are often defined within a context of normal, and heterosexual sexualities are dominant in American culture. The construction worker is framed as a normal and natural male—strong, tough, virile, and desired by women. Thus, in the binary, women are framed as "naturally" soft, dependent, emotional, and ready to please men. What has become dominant in American and other cultures is the notion that what is "natural" and "normal" with regard to sexuality is the coupling of men and women as defined within the traditional.

Rasmussen, Rofes, & Talburt (2004) point out that "Normative frameworks, including heteronormative frameworks, are the scaffolding that holds in place an entire system of power and privilege that endeavors to regulate young people, people of color, queers, and women to the symbolic fringes of society" (p. 3). Indeed, it is so-called normal that allows the creation of so-called abnormal, which sets in motion an incredible system of oppression contextualized in hierarchy and binarial paradigms, with gender and sexuality being prominent in the discourse of what is and is not normal. Moral codes support this framework of normal and natural, and morality is often constructed from and through religious traditions.

It is impossible to discuss sexualities within rural spaces without discussing religion and its impact on what many believe to be moral behaviors and decision making. Indeed, Christianity, particularly in fundamentalist Christian traditions, is built upon a biblical narrative that emphasizes obedience, concern for others (though this has become selective), and the promise of an eternal life if one conducts one's self in a moral fashion. Interestingly—and of upmost importance—the Bible is a guide for how to live a moral life, particularly for those who adhere to fundamental perspectives. Geographically, there are many areas that may be considered non-urban in the United States; however, one region in particular bears the distinction of being the "Bible Belt": the South.

The southern United States is as synonymous with religious fundamentalism as it is with rural geography. As Sears (1991) points out, southerners as a group are predominately Christian and "often are more orthodox, their reading of the Bible is more literal, and their religious rituals are more flamboyant" (p. 24). It is not surprising that religion is a dominant thread in the tapestry of the lives of most southerners, and this is no exception for those southerners who claim any variety of sexual and gender spaces. The Southern Baptist denomination is predominant in the South, with well over 42,000 churches nationwide according to the Southern Baptist Convention (http://www.sbc.net /aboutus/default.asp). Southern Baptists and United Methodists together account for the majority of the church population of the South, as they have for nearly two centuries (Sears, 1991). Most importantly, the location of dominant models of gender roles and sexuality resides in religious spaces that have been constructed within the hegemony of the Christian church, and in the South the church represents orthodoxy and fundamentalism. Additionally, the foundation of morality is built upon the church, and in the South the moral code is reiterated through immersion in the teachings of the Bible as interpreted by preachers and the family. For people who begin to negotiate normative and alternate gender and sexual identities, the clash with religion-based ideals occurs early in the process, resulting in a constant sense of avoiding deviance, shame, and isolation from what has been deemed natural and/or normal according to the moral code (Krondorfer, 2009). Keep in mind that sex for pleasure continues to violate fundamental moral codes, which emphasize the role of sex as primarily reproductive. Those who do not or cannot identify within "normal" and "natural" frames must negotiate being unnatural, abnormal, and immoral (Downs, 2007). Since 20th- and 21st-century American cultural ideals and practices, particularly moral codes associated with rural spaces, are often contextualized within religious structures, the link between identity and morality exists within spaces that are defined by religion and religious doctrines and practices; thus, shame is again given space to exist and grow. Indeed, the very creation of humans, according to fundamentalist Christian doctrine, relied on a male and female formed by a higher being.

Interestingly, the creation story recounted in Genesis, which so many who are reared in fundamentalist Christian environments hear over and over, emphasized the supposition that Adam and Eve had no knowledge of their nudity prior to Eve's consumption of the fruit of the Tree of Life; thus, they were filled with shame about nudity and presumably sex once the fruit had been consumed. It is this linking of nudity (awareness of the physical body), sexuality, and shame that becomes intriguing and important as one reflects on how one may become shameful about one's body and its engagement with others sexually.

Inerrant in the fundamentalist Christian creation story is the "natural" sexual coupling of males with females for the purpose of procreation in order to establish God's greatest creation—humans.

Adam's partner, after all, was Eve, not Steve. Thus, heterosexuality, whose primary purpose is to produce offspring, is established as natural and normal, and gender roles are clearly defined, with males being physically and mentally superior to females, who are contextualized within a shadow of contempt for breaking the rules set forth by the King James version of the Holy Bible, the foundational text often cited by fundamentalist Christians regarding the position of man and woman within American society (Pagels, 1988). Within the frame of rural, if one presumes that rural includes moral codes grounded in fundamental and traditional Christian-based sexual and gender roles, sexuality is bound by roles that emphasize male dominance, reproduction, and adherence to gender roles. Abandoning normal and natural sexualities and gender identities becomes a very serious matter and often a location for much angst and shame. Indeed, we see what happened to Adam and Eve when they disobeyed God: they were banished from the Garden of Eden (a rural space) into the cold cruel world where they faced lives of hardship.

To abandon particular beliefs and practices in the South is to abandon God and his son, Jesus. Doing this will jeopardize eternal life, according to many Christian teachings. Currently, religious fundamentalism and evangelical Christianity play major roles in American politics and education, with an emphasis on keeping a moral code that does not embrace differences (Feldman, 2005). Indeed, the family in America is often structured around Christian-based ideals and, as we have discussed, rural frames emphasize the nuclear family structure. The so-called family-values concept emerged in the 1990s in the political discourse surrounding morality and has remained a player on the political stage (Jakobsen, 2000).

For those with rural points of view, the family unit is central, and the hegemony of the family is structured within a heteronormative frame. "Alternative families" are not easily conceptualized or practiced in rural spaces; thus, sexualities that do not promote alternative families are not acceptable. Schooling reinforces the notion that the family, defined in particular ways, is the location of moral education, and when one has a supposedly immoral family, one is at risk of becoming immoral.

Those who are nonconformist with regard to sexual and gender identities often find it difficult and sometimes impossible to carve out an existence in spaces that adhere to conservative and fundamental ideologies (Adamczyk & Pitt, 2009; Goldfarb, 2006; Kendall & Martino, 2006). Indeed, many people do exist in non-urban environments where they engage in a variety of sexual and gender practices; however, visibility of such "deviance" is often minimal (Bell & Valentine, 1995; Gray, 2009). Indeed, Gray (2009) points out that "metronormativity" contributes to the notion that gays/queers in the country are somehow incomplete and in need of escape to the metropolis in order to fully realize their gayness/queerness. Certainly there are gays, lesbians, trans-people, queers, bears, etc., who live happily in rural locales, just as there are people in such locales who struggle with shame, anxiety, and isolation.

In Fellows's (1996) work *Farm Boys*, readers encounter the lived experiences of men who grew up on Midwestern farms struggling with identities that did not fit into conservative and fundamental frames. The impact of gender roles contextualized in the rural is evident as one reads about "farmwork" and "housework" and the struggles many of the people interviewed had with negotiating their positions in and among these expected ways of being productive on the farm. Also, readers of *Farm Boys* will note that there was common silence about sexuality associated with life in a rural space; thus, one was left to negotiate sexuality within one's own mind or within dark, experimental spaces with a friend, neighbor, or family member. Much like our construction worker, the classroom of rural culture, where men act/acted in particular ways, influenced boys on the farm. Straying from the bounds of traditional masculinity and sexuality was taboo and not fodder for conversation. Of course, not all is silent in the world of rural sexual deviance, as evidenced by such social/political groups as the Radical Faeries, who embrace antiestablishment perspectives while adapting rural and environmentally sustainable stances in the politics that members promote. Yet the voices of sexual and gender nonconformists in rural spaces are often minimized or silenced. The construction of what and how one should *be* remains grounded in frames that do not embrace diversity, and this has become a location for social and political discourse as the 21st century unfolds.

Constructing the Future of Sexualities in Rural Spaces

Is there any hope for our construction worker to be seen in a different way? Does he need to be? These questions certainly beg other questions about how we might (re)consider his identity and possibilities that may exist not only for him, but how he is read. Educational spaces offer promise with regard to (re)reading how and what we believe about particular phenomena, and sexuality is no exception. Certainly, no one can say that sexualities will become drastically different in rural spaces or any other space for that matter; indeed, human sexual practice seems to have remained consistent throughout time. What does seem to change is the codification and level of visibility sexual and gender identities enjoy within any given historical period (Bolin & Whelehan, 2009; Foucault, 1978; Jefson, 2005).

In America, nonconforming sexual and gender identities have become increasingly visible over the past forty years with momentum building as the 21st century passes its first decade. Mainstream print and electronic media include numerous representations of people who are sexually and gender nonconformists. Stereotyped characters abound on television, and political debates are fueled with discussions about "gay marriage," gays in the military, and gay families. Even geographically rural spaces enjoy enhanced visibility of sexual and gender nonconformity through television and the Internet.

As Gray (2009) points out, youth in rural locations are exploring queer sexual and gender spaces through the use of new and mass media. Indeed, the queer youth of today are probably no queerer than youth 50 or 100 years ago, yet they enjoy the ability to easily access each other and those outside their geographies, enabling liberatory experiences. Explorations of sexualities on the Internet are seemingly endless as people engage in cyberspace unbounded by physical limits. One can simply close the bedroom door and *be* anything one can imagine via the Internet (Rebchook & Curotto, 2007; Ross, 2005). However, if one's perspective is grounded in traditional, fundamental, and/or conservative frames, one is not likely to stray too far into experimental sexualities or gender identities without guilt and angst and certainly not in any public way. Indeed, the public face of rural sexualities remains steadfast in its heteronormative foundations, even for those who are nontraditionalist, e.g., the happy gay/lesbian couple (Valverde, 2006). Alarmingly, evidence suggests that among African American teens, those in rural areas are likely to have sex more often, more likely to have unprotected sex, and more likely to contract STDs than their counterparts in urban areas (Sexually Transmitted Diseases, 2003). It is not clear that similar studies have occurred for white or other non-white teen groups. One may presume that silence about sex and sexualities is an underlying cause of the apparent discrepancy between teens in the country versus teens in the city. Certainly, this area of inquiry raises questions and demands more research. The discourse between traditionalists and nontraditionalists is evident in American cultural and social spaces as well as political spaces. Foundations rooted in puritanical belief systems reinforced by Victorian-era silence run deep, and even in the new millennium many find it difficult to abandon tradition.

As Ferber and Kimmel (2004) point out, conservative and right-wing positions emphasize the building of America by white men, and the modern militia movement is demonstrative of efforts to reclaim so-called rural values, including masculinity (and femininity) contextualized in traditionalism. Ferber and Kimmel (2004) use an illustration that appeared in *WAR* magazine in 1987 that depicts a white man wearing a hard hat and a workman's vest with a caption that reads, "White men *Built* this nation!! White men *Are* this nation!!!" Indeed, racism, sexism, and nationalism abound in this image, and, of course, the image depicts a construction worker. Despite his association with what many deem extremist positions, our construction worker still represents what is believed by many to be good in America: hard work, grit, independence, and determination. He continues to represent values and beliefs that are grounded in male-dominated systems of being, together with particular emphasis on heteronormative identities. His whiteness reflects the notion that to be successful and productive, you must work for what you want, and what you have reflects your commitment to hard work. According to the dominant work ethic, those who suffer from poverty simply have not or will not work hard enough to pull themselves out if it. Traditionalism and conservatism thrive in the rural.

Thus, sexualities and gender identities in the rural reflect traditional and often conservative frames that are located in perceptions, values, and beliefs rather than on maps. Obviously, one cannot dismiss the impact of the country—or the city, for that matter—on how one perceives; indeed, it is perception that opens up possibilities for new ways of being. Educators bear the responsibility of teaching what is believed to be important in forming life paths, and one must consider the importance of a critical perspective in lesson plans. If we as teachers simply reiterate what has gone before us, we do not create opportunities for imagining other possibilities. Without a critical perspective, our construction worker, though he may elect to stay just where and what he is, has no hope of doing or being anything else. Additionally, if educators do not open spaces for the disruption of the status quo, our construction worker will be read in particular ways regardless of what he may or may not be. Perhaps the promise of the future truly lies in the abilities of people to critique and question what is known, how it became known, and what can be known. In imaginative spaces, sexualities and gender identities may take on shapes, forms, and practices that are not bound at all by rural, urban, or any other space.

References

Adamczyk, A., & Pitt, C. (2009). Shaping attitudes about homosexuality: The role of religion and cultural context. *Social Science Research, 38*(2), 338–351.

Ball, E. (1998). *Slaves in the family.* New York: Random House.

Bateman Driskell, R., & Embry, E. (2006, August 11). Rural communities in the South: Persistent black belt poverty. Paper presented at the annual meeting of the American Sociological Association, Montreal Convention Center, Montreal, Quebec, Canada. Retrieved May 25, 2009, from http://www.allacademic.com/meta/p104326_index.html

Bell, D., & Valentine, G. (1995). Queer country: Rural lesbian and gay lives. *Journal of Rural Studies, 11*(2), 113–122.

Benokraitis, N. (2001). *Contemporary ethnic families in the United States: Characteristics, variations, and dynamics.* New York: Prentice Hall.

Bolin, A., & Whelehan, P. (2009). *Human sexuality: Biological, psychological, and cultural perspectives.* New York: Routledge.

Campbell, H., Bell, M., & Finney, M. (2006). *Country boys: Masculinity and rural life.* University Park: Pennsylvania State University Press.

Capparell, S. (2007). *The real Pepsi challenge: The inspirational story of breaking the color barrier in American business.* New York: The Free Press.

Conser, W., & Payne, R. (2008). *Southern crossroads: Perspectives on religion and culture.* Louisville: University Press of Kentucky.

Downs, A. (2007). *The velvet rage: Overcoming the pain of growing up gay in a straight man's world.* Cambridge, MA: Perseus Books.

Feldman, G. (Ed.). (2005). *Politics and religion in the white South.* Lexington: University Press of Kentucky.

Fellows, W. (1996). *Farm boys: Lives of gay men from the rural Midwest.* Madison: University of Wisconsin Press.

Ferber, A., & Kimmel, M. (2004). "White men are this nation": Right-wing militias and restoration of rural American masculinity. In A. Ferber (Ed.), *Home-grown hate: Gender and organized racism.* New York: Routledge.

Foucault, M. (1978). *The history of sexuality: An introduction, volume 1.* New York: Random House.

Freeman, J. (1993). Hardhats: Construction workers, manliness, and the 1970 pro-war demonstrations. *Journal of Social History, 26*(4), 725–745.

Gause, C.P. (2008). *Integration matters: Navigating identity, culture and resistance.* New York: Peter Lang.

Goad, J. (1997). *The redneck manifesto.* New York: Simon and Schuster.

Goldfarb, E. (2006). A lesson on homophobia and teasing. *American Journal of Sexuality Education, 1*(2), 55–66.

Gray, M. (2009). *Out in the country: Youth, media and queer visibility in rural America.* New York: New York University Press.

Hall, D. (2003). *Queer theories.* New York: Palgrave Macmillan.

Jagose, A. (1997). *Queer theory: An introduction.* New York: New York University Press.

Jakobsen, J. (2000). Why sexual regulation? In K. Sands (Ed.), *God forbid: Religion and sex in American public life* (pp. 104–123). New York: Oxford University Press.

Jefson, C. (2005). A review of the social construction of sexuality. *American Journal of Sexuality Education, 1*(1), 183–188.

Johnston, L., & Longhurst, R. (2010). *Space, place, and sex: Geographies of sexualities.* Lanham, MD: Rowman & Littlefield.

Kendall, C. (2006). Pornography, hypermasculinity, and gay male identity: Implications for male rape and gay male domestic violence. In C. Kendall & W. Martino (Eds.), *Gendered outcasts and sexual outlaws: Sexual oppression and gendered hierarchies in queer men's lives* (pp. 105–130). New York: Harrington Park Press.

Kendall, C., & Martino, W. (2006). Introduction. In C. Kendall & W. Martino (Eds.), *Gendered outcasts and sexual outlaws: Sexual oppression and gendered hierarchies in queer men's lives* (pp. 5–16). New York: Harrington Park Press.

Kinsey, A., Pomeroy, W., & Martin, C. (1998). *Sexual behavior in the human male.* Bloomington: Indiana University Press. (Original work published 1948)

Kinsey, A., Pomeroy, W., Martin, C., & Gebhard, P. (1998). *Sexual behavior in the human female.* Bloomington: Indiana University Press. (Original work published 1953)

Krondorfer, B. (2009). *Men and masculinities in Christianity and Judaism.* London: SCM Press.

Lichter, D., & Parisi, D. (2008, Fall). Concentrated poverty and the geography of exclusion. Rural Realities. Retrieved June 7, 2010, from ruralsociology.org/ . . . /Ruralrealities/pubs/RuralRealitiesFa112008.pdf

Little, J. (2003). Riding the rural love train: Heterosexuality and the rural community. *Sociologia Ruralis, 43*(4), 401–417.

Little, J. (2007). Constructing nature in the performance of rural heterosexualities. *Environment and Planning D: Society and Space, 25,* 851–866.

Norquest, C. (1972). *Rio Grande wetbacks: Mexican migrant workers.* Albuquerque: University of New Mexico Press.

Pagels, E. (1989). *Adam, Eve, and the serpent: Sex and politics in early Christianity.* New York: Vintage.

Pretty, G. (2002). Young people's development of the community-minded self: Considering community identity, community attachment and sense of community. In A.T. Fisher, C.C. Sonn, & B.J. Bishop (Eds.), *Psychological sense of community: Research, applications, and implications* (pp. 183–203). New York: Kluwer Academic/Plenum.

Purpel, D., & McLaurin, W. (2004). *Reflections on the moral and spiritual crisis in education.* New York: Peter Lang.

Rasmussen, M.L., Rofes, E., & Talburt, S. (2004). Transforming discourses of queer youth and educational practices surrounding gender, sexuality, and youth. In M.L. Rasmussen, E. Rofes, & S. Talburt (Eds.), *Youth and sexual-*

ities: Pleasure, subversion, and insubordination in and out of schools. New York: Palgrave Macmillan.

Rebchook, G., & Curotto, A. (2007). Sexual networks online. In G. Herdt & H. Cymene (Eds.), *21st-century sexualities: Contemporary issues in health, education, and rights.* New York: Routledge.

Roebuck, J., & Hickson, M. (1982). *The southern redneck: A phenomenological class study.* New York: Praeger.

Ross, M. (2005). Typing, doing, and being: Sexuality and the Internet. *Journal of Sex Research, 42*(4), 342–352.

Sears, J. (1991). Growing up gay in the South: Race, gender, and journeys of the spirit. Philadelphia, PA: Haworth Press.

Sexually transmitted diseases; Rural black teens have riskier sex than urban counterparts. (2003, August). *Medical Letter on the CDC & FDA,* 43. Retrieved June 7, 2010, from Research Library. (Document ID: 384186781).

Sowell, T. (2005, April 26). Crippled by their culture: Race doesn't hold back America's "black rednecks." Nor does racism. *The Wall Street Journal.*

Spring, J. (2005). *The American school 1642–2004* (6th ed.). New York: McGraw Hill.

Valverde, M. (2006). A new entity in the history of sexuality: The respectable same-sex couple. *Feminist Studies, 32*(1), 155–162.

CHAPTER TWENTY-THREE

LGBT, to Be or Not to Be?

Education about Sexual Preferences and Gender Identities Worldwide

PETER DANKMEIJER

Based on an assessment of global needs for education in LGBT issues and experiences generated from expert meetings and projects by the Global Alliance for LGBT Education (GALE), this paper proposes that most educational programs take goals such as "we need to combat homophobia" for granted. However, a cross-cultural analysis of resources and needs for education about sexual diversity shows that this goal, with its focus on "gay identity," is heavily influenced by a Western perspective on gay emancipation. In other regions, different perspectives—such as dealing with machismo, conflict resolution, promoting respect, and diversity management—are more relevant for effective education, and respect for "being gay" may not be the most dominant aspect of emancipation and education strategies in those regions. However, such differences in perspective do not imply the impossibility of collaboration on the international level. On the contrary, international comparison can be an important contribution to more effective ways of learning and teaching.

This article concludes that there is a need to develop more concrete but also more culturally sensitive objectives for education about people who are Disadvantaged because of their Expression of Sexual Preference Or Gendered Identity (DESPOGI) as well as for better grounding of educational methods on evidence-based expectations for effect on attitudes and behavior. It is recommended that the effects of educational tools and training be monitored and that cross-cultural comparison be encouraged.

Contested Educational Objectives and Strategies for Emancipation

To educate effectively about sexual orientation and gender identity, it is essential to be clear about the ultimate objectives in areas such as knowledge, attitudes, and behavior (Bartholomew et al., 2006). Most current programs state their objectives in rather general ways, for example "to combat homophobia," "to eradicate prejudice," or "to prevent discrimination." In the field of education about LGBT issues, there is as yet little thought about concrete goals. There is also limited information about what kinds of education and training on LGBT issues really work. From the experiences of the Global Alliance for LGBT Education, it became clear that many activists and educators take for granted the common goal "to combat homophobia." But what does this mean? There is a lot of variety in the interpretation of this (seemingly) common goal.

GALE is a global network of educators and trainers who have joined to identify, enhance, and share educational expertise on gender and sexual orientation. GALE, supported by the Dutch development organization Hivos, investigates what has been done in the field, explores best practices, and facilitates experimentation with enhanced practices among its members. These enhanced practices are published on the GALE website (www.lgbt-education.info) and in open-format tool kits. Between 2003 and 2005, a global needs assessment was carried out to lay the foundation for this work (Dankmeijer, 2005). In the following years, regional strategy meetings were held, and further quick reviews of interventions, projects, stakeholders, and quick scans on the right to education and training were conducted in Latin America and Europe. More quick-scan research will follow. Currently, concrete projects focusing on schools and several methods of storytelling are under way in ten countries across four continents. This article offers an exploratory review of goals and methods and perspectives based on this work.

In exploring goals and practices on a deeper level, a series of implicit but differing views tend to surface, especially in the Global South. There is a diversity of ideas about the significance of sexual orientation or preference and gender identity across cultures as well as across people who are disadvantaged because of their orientation, gender identity, or their expression. In some cultures, gender tends to be seen as a rigid psychological or social category, in others, it seems to be quite changeable or may fall in between the gender identities of the male/female binary. From the global perspective, gender identity is increasingly seen as a continuum, notwithstanding that local communities may not agree with this view. These varying perspectives make us consider what should be the proper objectives for emancipation: acceptance that people may be born in the "wrong" body, tolerance for nonbinary gender expressions, crushing/queering the binary, or something in between?

Sexual orientation or preference is also multifaceted in its appearance. There may be same-sex attraction and practices (not always in conjunction with each other), there may be age-old traditional and modern same-sex partner arrangements (with not much evidence of whether they always involve sex or romantic relations), and there may or may not be self-identification as same-sex-attracted individual, partners, or subcultures. Different conceptions in this area intersect and make the picture more complicated. In some countries, notably in Africa and Asia, self-identification as "gay" or "lesbian" has been linked with Western discourses on sexuality, and some label "identity" and the promotion of "coming out" strategies as Western and even as postcolonial. In the Global South, self-identification as "gay/lesbian" is often considered middle-class (read: rich), individualistic, and dismissive of family and social responsibilities. Apart from this, coming out would often endanger someone's personal safety. At the same time, in most countries of the Global South, there are now lesbian, gay, bisexual, transgender, intersex and queer (LGBTIQ) groups forming, with openly LGBTIQ leaders who are both celebrated for their courage in taking a stand for human rights and considered weird or even despised by less well-off local people who cannot or do not want to embrace such strategies. It is clear from this short sketch that formulating concrete objectives for mutual tolerance and respect, equal treatment, or even full implementation of human rights and social dignity is no easy task. One may wonder if it is possible at all, as seen from the global level.

(While writing this article, I found it difficult to describe the phenomena and the target groups who should benefit from the education GALE wants to offer. Therefore, with a slight touch of humor, I introduce a new acronym, which is more useful for educators who want to improve the situation of people who are Disadvantaged because of their Expression of Sexual Preference Or Gendered Identity: DESPOGI.)

When we add the educational dimension to the spectrum of behaviors and identities and look not only at objectives but also at methods, the picture gets even more complicated. In countries where the government is or has been dictatorial for a long time, people are taught to keep their mouths shut. The basic democratic freedom to develop and voice one's own opinions is not there. As a consequence, people are used to educational methods in which they are told what to do by high-status teachers or speakers, often without practical application. Examples include learning the Qur'an by heart, learning the grammar of a language but not how to speak it, learning duties but not freedoms, learning biological aspects of sex (if one is lucky) but not how to meet someone, experience pleasure, or deal with difference and stigma. Countries with a longer tradition of democracy or debate have developed models of learning by debate, the sharing of experiences, and interactive exercises to explore attitudes and learn practical skills. Research in Europe and the United States shows that the more interactive the methods, the more effective they are at changing attitudes and behavior, for example in work toward preventing HIV or stigma (Zimmerman & Schunk, 2001; Fulpen et al., 2002). It remains unclear whether such research is biased and therefore generally valid only in (Western) Europe and the United States or whether it may have more intercultural validity.

In sum, the nature of oppression and exclusion differs across cultures, as do the perspectives of better worlds. Different views lead to different conceptualizations of what kind of education is needed (Dankmeijer, 2008).

Theoretical Background and Methods

In order to make sense of our work-floor experience, I will contextualize our work by using theoretical frameworks from different academic fields. First, GALE is aiming to enhance the quality of educational work on emancipation of DESPOGI people. For theory on effective education about emancipation and antidiscrimination, we are looking toward theories on stigma in general and on queer studies specifically (symbolic interactionism: Goffman, 1959, 1968; heteronormativity: Schwarzer, 1975; Rich, 1980; Foucault, 1976, 1984a, 1984b; Rubin, 1992; Adam, 1998; Warner, 2000), theory on how to set educational goals (taxonomy theory: Bloom & Krathwohl, 1956; Anderson & Krathwohl, 2001), theories on pedagogy (pedagogy of diversity: Prengel, 1995), and health promotion theory on effective interventions (the revised versions of the health belief model: Green & Kreuter, 2005; Bartholomew et al., 2006).

First we look at how to analyze stigma. There is a lot of research and related theory that documents discrimination and homophobia, but much of it focuses on a descriptive level and singles out only statistical categories of people who discriminate or are discriminated against. It is by now well known that even cross-culturally people who are younger, less educated, male, more religious, and think along rigid lines of good and bad tend to be more homophobic (Warwick, 2004; Takács, 2006). But this kind of research is not very helpful in getting an idea of how stigma works in practice and how it can be combated. For this we look to symbolic interactionism as developed by Erving Goffman. Symbolic interactionism argues that the self is social and the social arises from the interaction of individuals. Goffman postulates that people enact "performances" to give meaning to their social interaction. Through their performances people justify themselves as *selves* before others, who can be regarded as the audience. This interaction and socialization process compels the individual to construct his/her own social identity and serves as a self-making process (Goffman, 1959). In such an analysis, identity and the public performance of identity become extremely important to both self-esteem and social status. This is especially the case for people unable to achieve high-status identities because their emotions, behavior, or physical appearance contain elements of identities and performance that are stigmatized because of their low status or are completely discredited. Goffman distinguishes between stigma based on discredited identities (where the stigma is visible and unavoidable) and discreditable identities (where the stigma is invisible and has to be revealed before the person in question is discredited). Discrimination against gay and lesbian identities is an example of discreditable stigma (Goffman, 1968).

For educational purposes, it is important to learn from the general processes of stigmatization and to be aware that discrimination against gay and lesbian people is different from discrimination based on, for example, sex, race, or age. Many people will maintain that showing a discreditable stigma is a social provocation. Also, since education about DESPOGI people is still not accepted in many countries, the first attempts to develop specific educational interventions in this area have been carried out by LGBT organizations rather than by educators. This is bound to have an influence on the content of the resources. Goffman explains how the stigmatized often join in-groups to achieve a sense of belonging or authenticity. Militant activism is seen by such grassroots groups as a way to challenge "normals" and to politicize their stigmatized life rather than attempt normality. Militancy can involve a demand to be seen as fully human, rather than as a category, but it is a delicate balance between being accepted as "normal" while at the same time not denying difference (Goffman, 1968).

Second, to make sense of the concrete experiences of DESPOGI people, we analyze these experiences according to theories that have emerged around the concept of heteronormativity. The German feminist Alice Schwarzer (1975) first analyzed relationships between women and men as problematic and described the norms and values around heterosexuality as a set of attitudes and behaviors that interact with each other in order to maintain the dominant position of men over women. In her work, focused mainly on heterosexual relationships and the position of women, she calls women "slaves of men" and explores issues like sexual abuse of women, the right to abortion, and the freedom of women to work. Adrienne Rich took this notion a step further by postulating the concept of "compulsory heterosexuality," analyzing the set of norms and values centered on heterosexuality as an intentional plot by powerful men to make the heterosexual norm and lifestyle compulsory for lesbians (Rich, 1980).

However, the notion that powerful mainstream elites were purposefully oppressing small minorities had already been opposed by Norbert Elias (1969) and later in a more pronounced way by Michel Foucault (1976) and a school of followers who call themselves "constructionists." Elias analyzes the development of European social "civilized" behaviors as a continuously growing network of intricate interactions needed to control increasingly large and specialized societies. The control of citizens by local knights, regional counts, national kings, and later nation-state and federal bureaucracies was first managed by brute force but has become increasingly complex, with citizens adapting themselves to behaviors and norms that may raise their status in society. Elias states that individual citizens are unable to really steer this civilizing process because larger social forces are at work. The ongoing development of larger government bodies and specialization in societies forces a historical need for monopolies of power and control that are neither completely purposeful by the elite nor changeable by the less powerful. Elias also showed convincingly that these large social developments are affecting state apparatuses but are also reflected in day-to-day citizen behaviors such as how we eat, how we talk, how we interact, and how we show gendered behaviors. In this way Elias shows how daily routines and public identities and performances relate to large political and social developments. Elias never got to analyzing gendered roles.

Michel Foucault (1976, 1984a, 1984b) does not relate directly to Elias's work, but he does also analyze "oppression" as an intricate process driven by historical developments and power struggles. In his analysis of the contemporary situation of "homosexuals," he points out that the "homosexual" identity and even more recent concept of "fighting homophobia" rely heavily on typical Western European historical developments. Much of his work focuses on showing that "homosexuals" did not exist before the word "homosexual" was coined in 1869. Although there were same-sex behaviors and attractions, social interaction and identities concerning this were not framed in a *discourse* about homosexuality and oppression but were unique to every time period and culture. Also—and quite important in its implications for educational purposes—Foucault explains the importance of "coming out" as a typically European/Catholic custom, mirroring a need to confess and to always speak the truth. This is seen as not only an individual need but also as a reflection of the social control exerted by the church, state, and fellow citizens to keep individuals in line. By analyzing the identity and social performance of "homosexuals" as a historically and socially constructed phenomenon that is unique to Europe and the 20th century, Foucault opposes academics and activists who maintain that some people are born "homosexual," that they are intentionally "oppressed" by heterosexual elites, and that confessing one's "homosexual identity" (coming out) is the only way to fight this oppression. This is called the "coming out" or "identity" strategy (Seidman, 2003). On the contrary, Foucault says, publicly performing this identity and making continuous testimonies about it (coming out) will push people into a discourse about social categories, will position oneself as an everlasting victim, and will limit one's choices. Foucault has been interviewed several times about his ideas for education and was found to be critical of what he called "repressive normalizing practice" (Palermo, 1994). By asking for "tolerance" and explaining that gays and lesbian are "normal," the educator puts herself/himself right in the middle of the heteronormative discourse (Warner, 2000). Foucault's analysis has become the basis for a new, more radical "queer" movement of people who want to resist the limitations of self-identification. However, Western society seems to be so strongly organized around self-identification and confession that even European radical queers cannot resist the temptation to create a discourse about themselves.

The cultural anthropologist Gayle Rubin also looked at sexuality but from a more feminist perspective. She coined the concept "heteronormativity" and noted how mainstream society creates a hierarchy between the sexes and between different sexual practices that denounces the female-gendered role and downplays or demonizes some non-normative sexual practices. The hierarchy places reproductive, monogamous sex between committed heterosexuals as "good" and any sexual acts and individuals who fall short of this standard as lower and ultimately in the "bad sex" category (Rubin, 1992). The concept of heteronormativity, which connects the analysis of gender with an analysis of sexuality, has been taken over in several educational packages for education about LGBT issues, as we will see later on.

Third, we need to look for ways to translate earlier analyses into concrete and effective interventions. Priority is set on concrete and clear objectives. Generalized goals such as "combating discrimination, prejudice, and homophobia" are vague and need to be more precisely defined to be able to tailor interventions towards measurable effects. For this, we look in two directions: toward educational taxonomy theory and toward health promotion theory. Krathwohl and Bloom developed a theory on how to set objectives for schools (Bloom & Krathwohl, 1956; Anderson & Krathwohl, 2001). Their theory is called a "taxonomy theory" because it proposes a hierarchy of goals. They distinguish between a cognitive and an affective domain. This division is important for education about DESPOGI people. It would not be sufficient to teach the facts about DESPOGI people without addressing the more important social and emotional needs of the affective domain. The hierarchy of the affective domain describes how the educator must first gain attention and then interest, how the education process would progress to the formation of opinions, framing them in wider existing frameworks of norms and values, and how finally the student would learn to act automatically on the enhanced values and norms. The Pedagogy of Diversity follows this up with a set of principles that point out the inseparable connections among culture, affections, and cognitions (Sheets, 2005). It distinguishes between teacher pedagogical performances and student cultural performances. By being aware of (sub)cultural identities and performances, educators can consciously intervene and help students to deal with diversity. Part of this is reevaluating existing values and norms and related social status. The Pedagogy of Diversity has as a starting point the premise that individuals can learn to deal with diversity and that social change can be enacted by citizens.

The Pedagogy of Diversity is an instrument for enhancing the individual performance of educators, but it does not help very much in developing effective interventions. For this, GALE is looking toward health promotion theory and specifically to "intervention mapping" (Bartholomew et al., 2006). Bartholomew and colleagues have developed this method to prepare campaigns and interventions in an evidence-grounded way. Because the field of LGBT education is still in its early phase, there has been almost no evidence-based work. In this case especially, intervention mapping can help to create a more focused development process of strategies, trainings, and resources. Intervention mapping proposes to map the challenges, needs, and underlying behavioral and environmental factors, and to use this information to establish very specific objectives and choose potentially effective methods. Guided by health promotion theory, this attempt to make a review of educational interventions worldwide is guided by the notion that we need to be more specific about concrete behavioral and environmental factors and about objectives and didactic methods to be effective in education. This leads us to questions such as: Is coming out a necessary requirement to stopping violence or diminishing social distance toward DESPOGI people? When extreme masculinity, sexism, and heteronormativity seem to play an important role in homophobia, what kinds of methods will be effective in changing the attitudes and behaviors of males who identify as heterosexual? Of course, the answers to such questions will have to be contextual. When "gayness" or "masculinity" is defined differently in various cultures and situations, the answers will also be different. But we remain curious about the possible global similarities. In many ways heteronormativity seems to be a dominant trait of most cultures.

In the next section we will review some examples of educational interventions in different parts of the world, and we will try to assess what can be improved so as to enhance their effects.

Coming-out Panel Sessions and Antidiscrimination Resources

In Europe and North America, most resources developed by gay and lesbian activist organizations tend to focus on combating unjust discrimination. The general analysis is a concept of oppression: a majority of heterosexuals are repressing the self-expression of gay, lesbian, bisexual, or transgender-identified people. As such, gays, lesbians, bisexuals, and transgenders have become conceptualized as a kind of cultural minority, outside the norm of heterosexuality, rather than a fairly diverse set of people with marginalized sexual orientations. The purpose of Western education and training about LGBT issues is to obtain approval or at least tolerance for gay, lesbian, bisexual, or transgender-identified people. The push for this acceptance is usually far greater for gay men than for lesbians, bisexuals, and transgender people. As a consequence, in education resources and training, there is often a stronger focus on combating homophobia in particular than on combating heteronormativity in a wider sense. "Combating homophobia" is considered to encompass all non-heterosexual "identities" by many Western-oriented educators who often fail to fully integrate the significance of lesbophobia, biphobia, transphobia, heterophobia, and the social context of heteronormativity and related negative behaviors. Also, there is a great divergence between educators who adhere to the Pedagogy of Diversity and those who primarily promote acceptance of homosexuals as "normal."

In Western Europe and French-speaking Canada, a widespread model of education about LGBT issues is the panel session with volunteer gay and lesbian speakers. Local gay and lesbian groups offer panel sessions to secondary schools. Based on preliminary results of a European quick scan on educational interventions by GALE, we estimate that 10–15% of the targeted schools accept this offer; we estimate that there are over 3,000 volunteer educators in Europe. The gay and lesbian speakers tell their coming-out story, answer questions, and engage in a discussion about homophobia. This model is typical for Western Europe; it started in the Netherlands (Dankmeijer, 1994), Germany (Timmermans, 2003), and the Scandinavian countries almost 40 years ago.

In the last ten years, a number of teacher-training strategies have been developed in the Western world (Uliasz, 2008). These are also offered by LGBT organizations, usually by professional trainers. There seem to be two kinds of programs. In the Anglo-Saxon countries (the United States and the UK), "five-step" programs are popular.

1. Warm-up: diagnostic exercise and sensitization of the participants
2. Sharing of stories and statistics about discrimination to convince participants that LGBT issues are worthwhile
3. Exploring strategies and concrete interventions
4. Exploring intentions for follow-up action by participants in their schools
5. Exercises about facing challenges

In these programs, gay, lesbian, or transgender identity and explicit rights for people with such an identity are of central concern. From the resources, it also appears that the Swedish "All Clear" program (RFSL/All Clear EQUAL Project, 2006) follows a similar format. Here the background theory context is heteronormativity rather than homophobia, but it is unclear to what extent other issues besides discrimination against gays and lesbians are discussed. In the Netherlands, Germany, and Italy, trainers seem to use a more open-program format, using more abstract concepts (such as "the norm of heterosexuality," "the gender system," "the sexual interaction career," or "a taxonomy of educational goals for tolerance") or mind maps as anchors, around which they build a program with a tailored variation of exercises. In these programs, "gay" identity is still a central concern, but it is usually located within a wider context of gender, heteronormativity, sex education, and diversity and discrimination issues in general.

Playing with Full Sexual and Gendered Citizenship

Many Latin American respondents who were interviewed during the needs assessment for GALE (Dankmeijer, 2005) mentioned machismo and sexuality as central issues (see also Caceres et al., 2004). Erotic and sexual role-play between "macho" men and "take me /don't touch me" women are crucial in the way heterosexual norms are mediated. In a game of attraction and repulsion, men and women (and also feminine and butch women, transvestites, transgenders, macho men who have sex with men, and effeminate men) test who has the power. Don't mistake the term "role-play" with innocent games. This "play" is sometimes more fight than game. Women, who were traditionally the weaker players in this game, are increasingly gaining ground, but in their own feminine way. The rise of the "transgender" movement in Latin America, with its extremely feminine leaders, reflects this heteronormative emancipation in the LGBT movement. However, it is still extremely dangerous to "play" in the "wrong" way: when non-heterosexual or atypical gender or sexual behavior is exhibited, it can provoke both excitement and a violent reaction. Although the context is highly heteronormative and discussion of sexuality largely taboo, there is paradoxically much room for erotic behavior that is not heterosexual or limited to typical gender roles. It is not uncommon for people to perform different gendered behavior during the day and the night, to shift roles during sex, or to be the penetrating partner while being dressed as a woman or the other way around. This phenomenon, as occurs in Brazil, has been labeled "fluid sexualities" (Parker, 1999).

In Latin America it seems, therefore, to be more logical to give wider attention to sex education than to a solidified "gay" identity. In a wider context of sex education with a focus on sexual citizenship, respect for different identities and behaviors that do not comply to traditional roles can be better integrated. With the campaign against AIDS, opportunities to develop such sex education programs opened up. In some cases, the LGBT movement actually took responsibility for providing this. For example, the sex education program of Parana in South Brazil was developed by CEPAC, a sex education organization initiated by the LGBT organization Dignidade. The CEPAC program consists of several modules and starts with creating awareness about citizenship and making one's own choices. It goes on to technical sex education, the social context of sexuality (like machismo), and respect for marginalized behaviors. In the last sessions, speakers from an LGBT organization may be invited to answer questions from students.

The recent development of the LGBT movement in Latin America is characterized by more interaction on the global level. Examples of interventions, curricula, and training programs from the United States, Europe, and by UNAIDS are considered and sometimes more or less copied. This introduces the focus on coming out and identity to Latin American countries. But attention to "LGBT" identity is not only imported. The strengthened self-awareness of the LGBT movement, the greater acceptance of civil rights for all in a growing number of Latin American countries, and the need to advocate for rights in politics also contribute to more visibility. Currently there is an interesting mix of images in educational resources, ranging from hetero-normalized gay young people to very expressive and sexy transgender women.

The development of educational resources and training about LGBT issues is still in its early stages in Latin America. It will be interesting to see what direction these take and what models of emancipation will be underlying these interventions. It is also interesting to see that in Latin America not only "gay" organizations are developing resources, but also governments, municipalities, and lesbian feminist organizations. It is obvious that such stakeholders will have different perspectives.

Coping with Social Diversity, Inequality, and Shame

Many Asian countries have ancient cultures and social traditions that are not "liquid" in any sense. Social relationships are often prescribed in detailed ways. It is important to have respect for people with a higher status and to avoid shame. The traditional social systems are usually organized in a heteronormative way. For people with feelings of same-sex attraction or who feel they are not born with an appropriate gender, there are really only two choices: they can shift into a particular (low) social class or caste in which same-sex or transgender behavior is common, or they may lead double lives. In most Asian countries there are groups of "third sex" people who have a traditional way of life. These social classes or castes are highly visible in society and have always been visible. For example, in Thailand, it is completely credible to have a *kathoey* ("third sex") volleyball team in a secondary school[1] or possible to have separate toilets for *kathoey*.[2] But this does not mean life is happy and uncomplicated for "third sex" people. They are usually part of the lowest levels of societies. They often have traditional functions like blessing heterosexual marriages and births and are sometimes ascribed magical powers that can also be used to curse people. In modern societies, these functions become less important and lower paid, but "third sex" people are still blocked from other jobs, which forces many into prostitution, begging, and extortion ("pay or be cursed"). Being of a lower stratum of society, poor, and potentially a threat, "third sex" people are not popular with the general public.

Sexuality is traditionally not a great taboo in Asia, although there are rules and restrictions relating to the social hierarchy and religious cleanliness/purity. However, conservative Asian governments who promote an anticolonial "return to the original Asian culture" paradoxically take over the British colonial taboos about sexuality (Narrain, 2003). In practice this means that the Victorian rejection of sodomy gets combined with the more traditional fear and rejection of lower-class "third sex" subjects. This is an active resistance. For example, in India, a sex education manual was banned because its cover showed explicit sex scenes from a famous Hindu temple (personal interview with Edwina Pereira, Bangalore, India, 2004). Modern shame is more prevalent than traditional frankness.

In Asia there is hardly any education about sex, same-sex relationships, or gender. Only in the last few years, due to increasing need for HIV prevention efforts, has debate begun over the need for sex education. The public shame of talking frankly about sexuality is a major limitation. Available sex education is often still limited to international schools, and even then U.S.-oriented "abstinence only" programs are usually implemented, doing nothing to counter the culture of shame. But even within such a context, education about gender and DESPOGI is (potentially) possible.

Culturally sensitive information about gender and DESPOGI people does align with the central values of mutual respect and tolerance for diversity as formally upheld in most Asian countries. The Philippines, for example, has implemented an education act that makes it mandatory to teach about diversity (personal statement by Anna Leah Sarabia during a workshop in 1998). Meanwhile, a secondary school in Bangalore offers respect-centered sex education in which lessons are based on learning self-respect and respect for others (personal interview with Anu Monga and Raji Amarnath, Bangalore International School, India, November 2004). The program is partly based on a U.S. model and combines abstinence education toward marriage and respect for people with different lifestyles, including *hijras* (India's "third sex"). The students go back to their families in the countryside on weekends and are told to teach their parents and neighbors about these values. Teachers identify the major problem with the program as how to deal with the fact that almost all of the students will have sex before marriage anyway. Although sexuality is not discussed in a frank way, this program still represents the exception. Some sex education organizations, for example Talking About Reproductive

Health Issues (TARSHI) in New Delhi and International Services Association (INSA) in Bangalore, are influenced by global organizations such as the International Planned Parenthood Federation, SIDA (Sweden), and the World Population Fund (Netherlands), and offer programs in which sexuality is discussed a bit more frankly. But in most cases gender is only discussed in a heterosexual context, and same-sex behavior is avoided. There are isolated interventions to educate "gay" and "lesbian" young people, for example, in Japan, China, and Indonesia. These consist of magazines, CD-ROMs, and short videos with stories, often made by young and internationally oriented people.

African Models: Discussing Democracy and Marginalization

In Africa, education about LGBT issues in mainstream institutions remains largely unexplored. In most African countries, both authorities and populations fiercely oppose any sexual diversity. The cultural and historical existence of same-sex relationships is denied or labeled as "imported Western decadence." Some countries legally forbid any hint of same-sex attraction. This situation makes any education very difficult. The two major exceptions that we know of are South Africa and Namibia.

Especially since the abolition of apartheid, South Africa has experienced a wave of progressive policies, legally combating all forms of discrimination. However, personal attitudes do not change just because laws change: a majority of the South African population still holds negative attitudes toward same-sex relationships. Local LGBTIQ groups have recently started to experiment with educational interventions, such as by publishing personal life stories, organizing panel discussions in schools, and starting a teacher training program (personal interviews, 2004). All of these are in their early stages. In Namibia, the LGBT organization The Rainbow Project (TRP, now defunct) developed training for medical practitioners and teachers. Unlike in South Africa, in Namibia it is not acceptable to offer formal teacher training about LGBT issues. Instead, TRP traveled around the country offering open workshops to teachers in different ethnic regions (Uliasz, 2008). There are many ethnically different tribes and regions in Namibia, and most of them feel not completely included in society because of a lack of civil rights or because of cultural and social exclusion. In some tribes, same-sex relations are normal or at least acceptable in certain contexts, while in others and in the most dominant Namibian tribe, such relationships are not. The TRP workshops are offered as an afternoon gathering with a dinner. The meetings start with a discussion of democracy and citizenship and go on to discuss the marginalization of different tribes, cultures, and behaviors. Although same-sex relationships as such are not discussed in-depth, all participants know that the workshop is also about this issue. However, it is never discussed outside of the broader context of general Namibian citizenship concerns.

One of the main priorities of African LGBT grassroots organizations is to make the general population and the authorities aware that same-sex relationships are indigenous to Africa and not a threat to national security or "African" masculinity. A certain visibility of LGBT issues will be necessary to attain this goal, but this kind of visibility needs to be balanced with the level of acceptance by local populations and authorities. This promises to be a slow and careful process, starting with basic capacity building by local LGBT people themselves. It will be very difficult in the coming years to work in schools.

Storytelling is an important tool for communicating and educating in Africa. In the absence of formal schooling, oral storytelling by elders has traditionally been—and still is—a major educational method. Because most Africans still don't have access to the Internet but do have mobile phones, a number of projects have been launched to share stories between young people on HIV prevention and living with HIV. Saskia Wieringa and co-workers did a series of interviews with women having sex with women. These stories are in most cases not about being labeled "lesbian" but about a diversity of indigenous sexual and cohabitation arrangements with labels like "Tom Boys," "lesbian men," and "ancestral wives" (Morgan & Wieringa, 2005). But there are also LGBTIQ organizations that adopt the coming-out model to a certain extent. The Johannesburg-based project Behind the Mask also uses storytelling as its core method. Its website, www.mask.org.za, offers information on sexual diversity in African countries and has featured hundreds of personal stories. Local people are trained to tell and write their stories. These stories are about people who identify as being gay, lesbian, or transgender. People with more traditional sexual and cohabitation arrangements are not featured on this site. There is some debate as to what extent people who identify as gay or lesbian or transgender can be truly considered as representative of other citizens with more indigenous sexual and cohabitation arrangements. This, of course, also poses a dilemma for education: When Africans want to promote the notion that same-sex arrangements are also traditionally part of African cultures, how can they credibly do this without really representing them? Seen from this angle, education through storytelling presupposes a strong and representative grassroots fundament. This fundament is often not yet available and difficult to organize in the African context (Kiragu & Nyong'o, 2005; ICC/GALZ, 2004; Johnson, 2007).

Acceptability in the Face of Islam

Similar fierce resistance can be found in Arabic countries and countries where Sharia is part of the legal system. Here, the basis of rejection of same-sex relationships is the Qur'an and its teachings. Public education about same-sex relationships is not possible in most of these countries, especially in contexts where the words of the Qur'an are taken literally. We are talking here about same-sex relationships rather than DESPOGI, because there may be more tolerance for sex changes since Ayatollah Khomeini issued a fatwa (1987) that sex reassignment surgery is acceptable in the face of Islam. Still, the last decade has seen some significant new voices. U.S.- and European-based organizations have started discussions on DESPOGI issues in the Arabic world. The U.S.-based LGBT organization Al-Fatiha (http://www.al-fatiha.org) focuses on the capacity building of gay Muslims abroad. An important aspect of this is the development of novel Qur'an interpretations, which allow some space for LGBT individuals to carve out an identity. In the Netherlands,[3] Belgium,[4] Germany,[5] and the UK,[6] Muslim gay and lesbian activists have joined the debate and are looking for models to create more acceptance of sexual diversity. This needs to be made clear before they can embark on educational efforts. One debate is whether gay and lesbian Muslims should focus on justification of sexual diversity through Qur'an-based interpretations or appeals to cultural tolerance. Another debate is whether same-sex behavior or feelings can be justified at all. After much debate in recent years, a kind of consensus seems to be emerging: to focus on respect and to rely on Qur'anic references that only Allah is allowed to judge people.

In the last few years, a range of grassroots organizations in the Middle East and North Africa has also formed. Within these organizations, there is much less debate about the relationship between same-sex relations and the Qur'an. Their priority is survival and self-organization. Formal education in the mainstream is still far away. One of the first visible educational resources is the 2009 storybook publication *Bareed Mista3jil* by the Lebanese organization Meem.[7]

But even here there are some careful mainstream developments. In Europe, and in some isolated cases, such as Azerbaijan, workshops are given to health professionals, teachers, and secondary school students on respect toward people who have same-sex feelings. In these workshops, the relationship between the reality of human emotions and behaviors on one hand, and the guidelines associated with the Qur'an and cultural pressure on the other, are central concerns. Among Muslims in general, a discussion is starting about the need for sex education and how it relates to Islam and to the state policy. Professor Abdessamad Dialmy of Morocco has probably been the most progressive voice in this debate, speaking openly in 2010 about the need to discuss premarital sex and homosexuality (Dialmy, 2010). This is part of a broader discussion about civil rights and the right to education for women and young people. It is recognized that the Muslim world will forfeit many opportunities with the current restrictions on women and young people, and that parents have increasing problems in raising respectful children in a globalized world. On the other hand, Qur'an-oriented guidelines and traditional family structures are difficult to reorganize.

Discussion

One of the notable aspects of this review is the difficulty in assessing the situation in different regions without making comparisons with the United States/Europe or referring to U.S./European theory and academic literature. Indeed, this very publication is part of the Western academic way of thinking and disseminating information. In addition, the Western academic and activist traditions are rapidly spreading across the world. Other traditions, which may be extremely worthwhile, may be more local, less visible, or may have a lower status. A nonbiased overview of educational interventions on DESPOGI seems impossible. Even a concept like heteronormativity, which—contrary to (for example) "homophobia" may claim a cross-cultural understanding—is probably heavily influenced by the Western genesis of it. But whatever way we look at it, a global movement is on its way and we have to come to grips with the different performances of DESPOGI and the discourses that surround it.

From the GALE needs assessment, research, and projects up until now, it seems clear how local opportunities and limitations regulate the access of young people and professionals to education about DESPOGI. This is the major factor determining options for DESPOGI education. In Western Europe, coming out and testimonials have been a dominant form of education for decades now, made possible by the greater openness created in the 1960s and the focus by gay and lesbian grassroots organizations on identity and coming out as a social emancipation strategy. It is unclear why the panel session method did not take off in Anglo-Saxon countries. Maybe the access to schools was too limited due to the influence of conservative parents. Parents have more control over the school content in the United States and the U.K. than in continental Europe, and they have often codified their objections in national or local legislation. But even when such restrictions are absent, storytelling by gay and lesbian volunteers has not been a major intervention in these countries—in contrast, for example, with the popularity of panel sessions in Quebec, Canada. It would be interesting to do cross-cultural research on this or to cross culturally experiment with seemingly cultural interventions such as panel sessions and (until now U.S.-based) Gay/Straight Student Alliances.

In the Global South, the HIV epidemic has created opportunities for education about sexuality and citizenship, including DESPOGI issues. However, these formal opportunities have to be implemented with much care because of public prejudice and resistance. Still, this trend is gaining strength. For example, in 2008, the ministers of education of Latin American countries issued the joint Mexico City Ministerial Declaration "Educating to Prevent: Addressing Homophobia in Schools" (Ministerial Declaration, 2008; SIECUS, 2008). In late 2009, UNESCO issued "Technical Guidelines" for sex education that explicitly include the need to educate about same-sex relationships (UNESCO, 2009). In early 2010, NGOs presented a thorough report on stigma and discrimination that concluded that discrimination hampers HIV prevention (NGO Delegation to the UNAIDS Board, 2010), and a few months later the Special Rapporteur on the Right of Everyone to the Enjoyment of the Highest Attainable Standard of Physical and Mental Health issued a report that condemns the criminalization of same-sex relations because of its destructive effect on HIV prevention (Human Rights Council, 2010). Note how the need for effective HIV prevention remains the major argument; the case for applying human rights to LGBT people as a moral value is currently still too weak to stand on its own. It would be worth researching how the political status of upholding human rights and especially the rights of DESPOGI people can be prioritized as a theme of its own.

A second factor influencing the content of education about LGBT issues is the opinion of the developers. Apart from the prejudiced and religiously oriented programs by churches condemning homosexuality (which we did not discuss here), almost all positive programs have been developed by gay and lesbian grassroots organizations in the Western world. Most activists are self-identified gay and lesbian, and some are self-identified transsexual, so identity strategies are at the forefront of their thinking and prevalent in their resources, even when local (sub)cultures have different concepts and definitions. This seems to be partly due to the need to advocate for equal treatment, which requires a comparison between the better treated and the stigmatized. But it clearly also relates to the import of Western and sometimes specific U.S. concepts and interventions. Often, the Western concepts are adapted to a certain extent to regional cultures and trends. But in many cases educational resources are mere translated copies with different pictures as opposed to input that has been critically considered in terms of cultural usability. New interventions and resources would benefit in quality if researchers and resource developers were to make a more in-depth analysis of the needs and specific objectives and teaching/learning methods of each country or (sub)culture.

One question that remains is whether it is possible to imagine human rights education about DESPOGI without implying that all people with non-heterosexual preferences or non-mainstream gender identities should consider this an essential part of their personal identity and discuss it to enable social change. LGBT—to be or not to be? It depends. Personally, I think there are ways to emancipate and to educate without a central focus on coming out and personal identity. In EduDivers, the Dutch Expertise Centre on Education and Sexual Diversity, a two-year intervention mapping project has led to the proposal to focus new concrete performance objectives for heterosexual-identified students on diminishing social distance from and increasing social support for DESPOGI (Kamps & Dankmeijer, 2010). Concrete objectives would be formulated—say, students who know each other's differing sexual preference or gender self-image sit next to each other in class, eat lunch together, go to camp together, and sleep in the same tent together. The "knowing each other's differing sexual preference or gender self-image" does not necessarily involve an obvious coming out or even a clear "sexual" public identity. It would be interesting to discuss to what extent such concrete objectives may be cross-cultural, although the feasibility of reaching them would differ very much, and intermediate objectives would need to be formulated for situations in which a direct approach would be a bridge too far.

It remains a major problem that same-sex relationships and non-mainstream gender identities are discriminated against and socially marginalized. To challenge this situation, it is necessary to highlight the inequalities and the suffering it brings to people. However, in the end, we look forward to a situation in which there is no inequality or social distance, even when there will always be differences. *Not* labeling may be typical for taboos, but it may also be an aspect of situations in which labeling does not really matter anymore. In the West, the current "queer" debate about labels and labeling definitions may be typical of the transition between these two situations. In other regions, a more relaxed way of dealing with sex, same-sex relationships, and gender may not need a transition with a "confession" mode. A more general discussion about civil rights, machismo, tolerance, and sexuality may be more effective. It is the challenge for educational resource developers across cultures to discover how this can be done effectively and through culturally sensitive approaches.

References

Adam, B. (1998). Theorizing homophobia. *Sexualities, 1*(4), 387–404.

Anderson, L.W., & Krathwohl, D.R., et al. (Eds.). (2001) *A taxonomy for learning, teaching, and assessing: A revision of Bloom's taxonomy of educational objectives.* Boston: Allyn & Bacon.

Bartholomew, L.K., Parcel, G.S., Kok, G., & Gottlieb, N.H. (2006). *Planning health promotion programs. An intervention mapping approach* (2nd ed.). San Francisco, CA: Wiley Imprint/Jossey-Bass.

Bloom, B.S., & Krathwohl, D.R. (1956). *Taxonomy of educational objectives: The classification of educational goals, by a committee of college and university examiners. Handbook I: Cognitive domain.* New York: Longmans, Green.

Caceres, C., Frasca, T., Pecheny, M., & Terto, V. (2004). *Cuidadanía sexual en América Latina: Abriendo el debate* (Vol. 1, no. 4). Lima: Universidad Peruana Cayetano Heredia.

Dankmeijer, P. (1994) Gay and lesbian education in Dutch schools. *Promotion & Education* (Vol. 1, No. 4).

Dankmeijer, P. (2005). *Needs for education about LGBT issues. Report of a global need assessment for a global network on sexual diversity education.* Amsterdam: GALE. Retrieved March 21, 2011, from http://www.lgbt-education.info/en/about_us/history/report_of_the_needs_assessment

Dankmeijer, P. (2008). International challenges for education regarding sexual diversity. In I. Dubel & A. Hielkema (Eds.), *Urgency required. Gay and lesbian rights are human rights* (pp. 229–235). The Hague: Hivos.

Dialmy, A. (2010). *The importance of sex education for young Muslims. A study project.* Presentation at the 3rd World Congress of Muslim Philanthropists in Doha. Unpublished document.

Elias, N. (1969). *The civilizing process, Vol. I. The history of manners.* Oxford: Blackwell.

Foucault, M. (1976). *Histoire de la sexualité. Vol. I: La volonté de savoir.* Paris: Gallimard.

Foucault, M. (1984a). *Histoire de la sexualité. Vol. II: L'usage des plaisirs.* Paris: Gallimard.

Foucault, M. (1984b). *Histoire de la sexualité. Vol. III: Le souci de soi.* Paris: Gallimard.

Fulpen, M. van, Bakker, F., Breeman, L., Poelman, J., Schaatsma, H. & Vanwesenbeeck, I (2002). *Vmbo-scholieren, seksualiteit en seksuele vorming: Een effectonderzoek naar de vernieuwde versie van het lespakket 'Lang leven de liefde.'* Utrecht: Rutgers Nisso Groep.

Goffman, E. (1959). *The presentation of self in everyday life.* Garden City, NY: Doubleday.

Goffman, E. (1968). *Stigma: Notes on the management of spoiled identity.* London: Pelican Books.

Green, L.W., & Kreuter, M.W. (2005). *Health program planning: An educational and ecological approach* (4th ed.). New York: McGraw-Hill.

Human Rights Council. (2010). *Report of the special rapporteur on the right of everyone to the enjoyment of the highest attainable standard of physical and mental health, Anand Grover.* A/HRC/14/20. New York: United Nations General Assembly. Retrieved August 14, 2010, from http://www2.0hchr.org/english/bodies/hrcouncil/docs/14session/A.HRC.14.20.pdf

ICC/GALZ. (2004). *All Africa Symposium on HIV/AIDS & Human Rights—Official report.* Johannesburg: International Capital Corporation Limited.

Johnson, C. (2007). *Off the map. How HIV/AIDS programming is failing same-sex practicing people in Africa.* New York: IGLHRC/GM Printing.

Kamps, L., & Dankmeijer, P. (2010). *Wat moeten we doen om scholen echt homovriendelijker te maken? Intervention mapping toegepast op homo-emancipatie in Nederlandse scholen voor voortgezet onderwijs.* Amsterdam: EduDivers.

Kiragu, J. & Nyong'o, Z. (2005). *LGBTI organizing in East-Africa: The true test for human rights defenders.* Nairobi: Urgent Action Fund/Regal Press.

Ministerial Declaration. (2008). *Education to prevent.* Retrieved August 14, 2010, from http://data.unaids.org/pub/BaseDocument/2008/20080801_minsterdeclaration_en.pdf

Morgan, R., & Wieringa, S. (2005). *Tommy boys, lesbian men and ancestral wives. Female same-sex practices in Africa.* Johannesburg: Jacana Media.

Narrain, A. (2003). *Queer: "Despised sexuality," law and social change.* Bangalore: Books for Change.

NGO Delegation to the UNAIDS Board. (2010). *Stigma and discrimination: Hindering effective HIV responses.* Retrieved August 14, 2010, from http://unaidspcbngo.org/wp-content/uploads/2010/05/2010_NGO_Report _Final_website.pdf

Palermo, J. (1994). *I'm not lying, this is not a pipe: Foucault and Magritte on the art of critical pedagogy.* Buffalo, NY: Buffalo State College. Retrieved August 14, 2010, from http://www.ed.uiuc.edu/EPS/PES-Yearbook/ 94_docs/PALERMO.HTM

Parker, R. (1999). *Beneath the equator. Cultures of male homosexuality and emerging gay communities in Brazil.* London: Routledge.

Prengel, A. (1995). *Pädagogik der fielfalt: Verschiedenheit und gleichberechtigung in interkultureller, feministischer und integrativer pädagogik.* Opladen: Leske+Budrich.

RFSL/All Clear EQUAL Project (2006). *All clear. Lesbians, gays & bisexuals at work.* Sweden: Norra Sk ne Offset (www.frittfram.se).

Rich, A. (1980). Compulsory heterosexuality and lesbian existence. *Signs: Journal of Women in Culture and Society, 5,* 631–660.

Rubin, G. (1992). Thinking sex: Notes for a radical theory of the politics of sexuality. In C. Vance (Ed.), *Pleasure and danger: Exploring female sexuality.* London: Pandora Press.

Schwarzer, A. (1975). The *"little difference"* and its big consequences. Women on the subject of themselves [Der "kleine Unterschied" und seine großen Folgen. Frauen über sich]. Frankfurt am Main: S. Fischer.

Seidman, S. (2003). *Beyond the closet: The transformation of gay and lesbian life.* New York: Routledge.

Sheets, R.H. (2005). *Diversity pedagogy: Examining the role of culture in the teaching-learning process.* Boston: Allyn & Bacon.

SIECUS (2008). *Mexico City Ministerial Declaration—"Educating to prevent." Addressing homophobia in schools: How key stakeholders can ensure safe and inclusive schools.* Retrieved August 14, 2010, from http://www.msmasia.org /tl_files/2010%20resources/10—06_resources/PAHO_Anti-homophobia_factsheet_FINAL_ENG.pdf

Takács, J. (2006). *Social exclusion of young lesbian, gay, bisexual and trangender (LGBT) people in Europe.* Brussels: ILGA Europe & IGLYO.

Timmermans, S. (2003). *Keine angst, die bei en nicht! Evaluation schwul-lesbischer aufklärungsprojekte in schulen.* Aachen: Jugendnetzwerk Lambda NRW e.V.

Uliasz, L. (2008). *Report. Teacher training expert meeting: Warsaw, November 10–13, 2008.* Warsaw: GALE/Campaign Against Homophobia.

UNESCO. (2009). *International technical guidance on sexuality education. An evidence-informed approach for schools, teachers and health educators. Volume I: The rationale for sexuality education. Volume II: Topics and learning objectives.* Geneva: UNESCO.

Warner, M. (2000). *The trouble with normal.* New York: The Free Press; Cambridge, MA: Harvard University Press.

Warwick, I., Chase, E., & Aggleton, P. (2004). Homophobia, sexual orientation and schools: A review and implications for action. London: Thomas Coram Research Unit, Institute of Education, University of London. http://www.education.gov.uk/research/data/uploadfiles/RR594.pdf

Zimmerman, B.J., & Schunk, D.H. (Eds.). (2001). *Self-regulated learning and academic achievement: Theoretical perspectives.* Mahwah, NJ: Lawrence Erlbaum Associates.

Notes

1. http://en.wikipedia.org/wiki/The_Iron_Ladies_(film)
2. http://news.bbc.co.uk/2/hi/asia-pacific/7529227.stm and http://www.youtube.com/watch?v=YBGepP_XYfc
3. YOESUF Foundation, now defunct
4. Merhaba, www.merhaba.be
5. MILES, http://www.berlin.lsvd.de/cms/index.php?option=com_content&task=view&id=22&Itemid=64
6. al-Bab, http://www.al-bab.com/; Safra Project, http://www.safraproject.org
7. http://www.bareedmista3jil.com/about.htm

CHAPTER TWENTY-FOUR

Sexuality, Secularism, and the Nation

Reading Swedish School Policies

IRINA SCHMITT

> The inviolability of human life, individual freedom and integrity, the equal value of all people,
> equality between women and men and solidarity with the weak and vulnerable are all values that
> the school should represent and impart. In accordance with the ethics borne by Christian tradi-
> tion and Western humanism, this is achieved by fostering in the individual a sense of justice, gen-
> erosity of spirit, tolerance and responsibility.
>
> (SKOLVERKET 2006A, 2011, P. 3)[1]

Sweden is often seen as a good-practice example when it comes to pedagogy and educational outcome (Seemann 2009), and as earning good results in international tests of students' abilities, even
if the two recent PISA studies show less pleasing figures (Skolverket 2007; OECD 2010).[2] Sweden
is also renowned as a gender-equal society with a system for day care that allows parents to work and
that produces fathers who are more active in family care than their European counterparts. On the
other hand, feminist researchers especially critique what is perceived as Swedish complacency with
these accomplishments as it disallows critical reflections on the limitations of domestic efforts
toward gender equality, as seen in the prevailing gender pay gap or the racialization of some forms
of violence (de los Reyes, Molina et al. 2003). Much less discussed is the historically close relationship between church and state in Sweden. Until 2000, the Church of Sweden, an Evangelical
Lutheran church, was a state church, and its leaders still hold a prominent position in public debates,
such as the debate over "gay marriage."

In my analysis of recent revisions to Swedish school policy texts, I look for traces of this relationship, reading school policy texts as the materialization of notions of national belonging. For this
analysis, I engage discussions that question the secularity of secularism and critique notions of futurity and universal childhood.

School policies are fascinating documents. Beyond their direct educational implications, they are
the materialization of notions of belonging in fundamental yet often rather implicit ways. They are

both the reflection of a societal status quo and a vision of a future-in-the-making; they are normative statements of the policymakers' notions of societal problems and their solutions (Bacchi 2009). Thus, they are inscriptions of normal/ized bodies that engage in particular interactions, based on understandings of normal/ized citizens. I argue that young people are also implicitly constructed as heterosexual citizens-to-be and that the learning processes of citizenship are embedded in these normative understandings of belonging within the nation-state.

School policies are interesting documents also for their position in time. They are by necessity images of past conceptualizations of education and national belonging, while casting future citizens. I aim to trace this processuality by analyzing policy texts and curricula in the light of the recently passed new school law.

Border Work—Sexualities and the Nation

The borders of nation-states are primarily controlled as geographic spaces. Often these borders lie at the heart of a nation, at the main airports situated near national capitals. Research on the sexuality of migration (Cantú, Naples et al. 2009; Luibhéid 2002, 2008) has during the last ten years or so shown how the drawing of national borders is intimately linked to understandings of sexualities and gender informed by notions of "national identities."[3] Yet this border control is also done through internal negotiations of belonging that find one manifestation in legal documents. In light of ongoing critiques against the exclusivity of nation-states, I am puzzled by the strength of "the nation" to inform the materiality and imaginary of people's lives and how these reflect implicit and explicit definitions as well as conditions of belonging.

In the texts I analyze, both "sexuality" and "the nation" are invoked in various ways. Sexuality can be understood as sexual activity or as sexual orientation, yet it also figures in references to family formations and gendered social roles. The analysis of the interrelation of gender and nation is a central moment in postcolonial feminist research and has gained renewed interest for queer researchers critical of homonationalism (Yuval-Davis 1997; Puar 2007). In her discussions of the interrelations of "the nation," gender, and sexuality, Tamar Mayer (2002 [2000]) reminds readers that the "empowerment of one gender, one nation or one sexuality virtually always occurs at the expense and disempowerment of another" (p. 1).

The construction of sexually liberal "Western" nations is used to create further othering and violent exclusion of "non-Western"—imagined as "Muslim"—societies and of individuals coming to "the West" as migrants. The problematic role of hegemonic queers in "the West"—multiply privileged but sexually othered—and our possible implication in discourses and acts of violent normalization, nationally and internationally, is a painful reminder of the interrelatedness of concepts and experiences of "national identity," ethnification, racialization, and sexuality/sexualization (Haritaworn 2008).

In the context of education, critical researchers engage the interdependences of gender, ethnification/racialization, and class with postcolonial, antiracist, and feminist theories (Frosh, Phoenix et al. 2002; Phoenix 2009; Hoerder, Hébert et al. 2005; Thorne 1993; Eilard 2009; Ambjörnsson 2003). Other researchers are acutely aware of the need to focus on interdependences of racializations and sexualizations (Martinsson and Reimers 2008; Rasmussen, Rofes et al. 2004; Epstein, O'Flynn et al. 2003; Meyer 2009; Kumashiro 2002).

What's God Got to Do with It? Finding the Not-Quite Secular

Rather than mapping school policies for (the invisibility of) statements that more or less clearly link sexuality-as-sexual-orientation and national belonging, I would like to focus this text on a seemingly curious aspect by looking for god—references to Christian norms and values—in Swedish school policy texts. I do this in light of ongoing processes of re-inscription of societies such as Sweden with notions of modernity, gender equality, and inclusion of sexual minorities, and the ascription of national, cultural, and religious others with traditionality, inequality, and homophobia.

For my analysis, I engage discussions of secularism and its limitations. Ann Pellegrini's and Mary Lou Rasmussen's discussions of "Christian secularism" are helpful (Rasmussen 2010; Pellegrini 2008). Joan W. Scott (2009), with her "slip of the finger" coinage of the term "sexularism," suggests reading Western secularisms as historically implicated in current attempts to other sexism and homophobia (p. 1). Scott's analysis of the history of secularism and enlightenment arguments as inherently sexist is highly relevant to understanding how we need to complicate the simplifying juxtaposition of so-called modern and secular against assumedly religious and traditionalist positions. She argues for a nuanced analysis of the heredity and current uses of the notion of secularism:

> But I want to take the argument further and suggest that it is not at all clear that secularism is a sufficient historic explanation for the admittedly more open, flexible kinds of sexual relations that have gained acceptance in some countries of the West in recent years. When we begin to untangle the strands that are these days taken to be the whole package, we find a much more complex story than the one that ties secularization inevitably to sexual emancipation. (Scott 2009, p. 6)

Rather than accept the completeness of the project of secularism in Western nation-states and its unquestioned interrelation with gender equality, I follow Pellegrini, Rasmussen, and Scott in the discussion of the obvious traces of a specific Christian religious tradition. By undermining notions of Sweden as a secular society, I reflect on equally implicit understandings of "children" and "youth" as universal.

Inscribing the Future—Seeing the Particular in Universalizing Notions of "Youth"

> The future is only the stuff of some kids. Racialized kids, queer kids, are not the sovereign princes of futurity. . . . It is important not to hand over futurity to normative white reproductive futurity. (Muñoz 2007, p. 365)

In this critique of Lee Edelman's almost angry argument against an inscription of queerness in a mode of reproduction and child/future-orientation, José Esteban Muñoz argues for the careful analysis of notions of "children" and "youth" (Edelman 2004; Muñoz 2007). The attachment of children and young people to the future, by necessity an ill-defined time that is emotionally charged with visions of progress and improvement, needs to be understood as limited to some specific young people and is cruelly complemented by the death—figuratively or literally—of those young people who do not figure in this image of the future. While Muñoz's reading might underscore discussions of queer young people as victims, he does not engage a simplifying discourse of some proponents of rights-based approaches to discrimination (see Cooper 1995). Muñoz (2007) argues that theories of queer temporality that fail to factor in the relational relevance of race or class merely reproduce a crypto-universal white gay subject that is weirdly atemporal—which is to say a subject whose time is a restricted and restricting hollowed-out present free of the need for the challenge of imagining a futurity that exists beyond the self or the here and now. (p. 364)

Here Muñoz takes up antiracist feminists' call to analyze societies, experience, and subjectivities as inhabiting the interrelational space informed by diverse power relations. At the same time, it would be counterproductive to read normative discourses as stable and stagnant; indeed, they are constantly challenged, disrupted, and "unbelieved" (Atkinson and DePalma 2009). I hope to engage this understanding of the messy interdependencies of power relations to my analysis of school policy texts.

Working with School Policies

My analysis of Swedish school policy texts aims to understand the sociopolitical references that are inscribed in them. Engaging Judith Baxter's feminist poststructuralist discourse analysis, I analyze one specific aspect of the texts in question, traces of Christianity (Baxter 2003). Another angle that would lead to productive discussions is the analysis of neoliberal notions of "choice," which is given more space in Swedish education through the advance of independent schools (*fristående skolor*), or the growing focus on national and international tests in schools. By analyzing representations of Christianity as a cultural given in Swedish education, I obviously decontextualize this aspect of the texts, yet such limitation seems appropriate for creating a "readable" story with a focus on the production and representation of sexualized bodies and positions in the policy texts. I also limit this analysis by leaving out other relevant texts such as nongovernmental contributions to the debate. Such contestation of hegemonic discourses is important to take up in the analysis of policies (Bacchi 2009). For this text, however, I am intrigued by the documents that can be understood as the foundation for school education and a reflection of national imaginaries and intentions.

Catherine McGregor (2008) points out that the

legislative genre's communicative intent is invested in rationality, intentionality and consciousness, creating a single speaking voice that is authorized to speak with legitimate authority. . . . Semiotic tools convey particular meanings, particularly in their ability to convey authority; in the world of policy, authority to prescribe and enact flow from legislated and/or governance structures, and such intentions can also be conveyed through policy texts. (McGregor 2008, pp. 11–12)

While policies gain their discursive role through implementation, they are also representative and informative of social praxes. School policies concern young people's negotiations of sexualities in schools, partly through the exclusion and invisibility of non-normative subjectivities or relationships. Getting ahead of myself, I would argue that this invisibility can paradoxically lead to hypervisibility, as Judith Butler (2009) points out:

Gender norms have everything to do with how and in what ways we can appear in public space; how and in what way the public and private are distinguished, and how this distinction is instrumentalized in the service of sexual politics; who will be criminalized on the basis of public appearance; who will fail to be protected by the law or, more specifically, the police, on the street, or on the job, or in the home. Who will be stigmatized; who will be the object of fascination and consumer pleasure? (Butler 2009, p. ii)

Carol Bacchi problematizes how education policies are often seen as preventive or remedial measures for all kinds of societal problems—from ill health caused by social disadvantage to crime—and points to the need to investigate the assumptions of "problems" that can be read as indicators of societal norms (Bacchi 2009). Yet school policies are not focused on a single issue; rather, they map a societal space marked by generational difference. In Bacchi's terminology, the problem represented by school policies is the need to manage a societal group that is differentiated primarily by age. I will read the selected texts both synchronically and diachronically (Baxter 2003) and adapt Baxter's methodology that focuses on spoken word to the more stable genre of policy texts and policy suggestions.

The Material—Swedish School Policies under Reconstruction

Three kinds of texts directly govern Swedish schools: the school law (*skollag*), the general curriculum (*läroplan*), and topic-specific course plans (*kursplaner*).[4] On June 22, 2010, the Swedish parliament passed a new school law that was implemented on July 1, 2011 (July 1, 2012, for adult education). Aims for the new curriculum had been clearer competency goals and a clearer grading scale (Skolverket 2009).

My analysis is in part a reflection of this process (working mainly with parts of the documented discussion available until the summer of 2010). The texts I use here are the old law and general curriculum for obligatory schooling, preschool, and day care (Skolverket 2006b, 2006a),[5] the final suggestions and comments for the new law entitled "The new school law—for knowledge, choice and security" (*Den nya skollagen—för kunskap, valfrihet och trygghet*) (Government of Sweden 2009; Skolverket 2010c), as well as the final school law and the new general curriculum (Skolverket 2011; Government of Sweden 2010).[6] I accessed all these texts on the homepage of the Swedish National Agency for Education, *Skolverket*, and *Regeringskansliet*, the Government Offices.[7]

The old law, dating from 1985, has been updated a number of times. The decision-making process toward the new law has been long and, especially in the months leading up to its passage, not always smooth. The government's law commission (*Lagrådet*) remarked critically on the length and complexity of the text as well as on some structural and conceptual inconsistencies (Lagrådet 2010). A number of institutions and persons have been active in the revision process; interestingly, among the groups invited to act as reviewers are *Samarbetsorgan för etniska organisationer i Sverige*, the umbrella association for ethnic organizations in Sweden, and *Riksförbundet Kristen Fostran*, the national organization Christian Upbringing. Thus, members of non-Christian religious groups are mainly represented through ethnic groups (which might be predominantly Christian, or not) (Government of Sweden 2009). The Swedish Federation for Lesbian, Gay, Bisexual and Transgender Rights, *Riksförbundet för homosexuellas, bisexuellas och transpersoners rättigheter*, has participated in the process by submitting comments.

Analysis—"Our Swedish, Nordic, and Western Cultural Heritages"?

Both the old Swedish general curriculum from 1994 and the new version to be enforced starting in fall 2011 (Skolverket 2006a, 2011) open with a chapter on "Fundamental Values" that reads:

> The inviolability of human life, individual freedom and integrity, the equal value of all people, equality between women and men and solidarity with the weak and vulnerable are all values that the school should

represent and impart. In accordance with the ethics borne by Christian tradition and Western humanism, this is achieved by fostering in the individual a sense of justice, generosity of spirit, tolerance and responsibility. Education in the school shall be non-denominational.

As it stands, this passage reads as a contradiction in terms. It is interesting alone for the equation of Christianity and Western humanism to the exclusion, for example, of Jewish or Muslim humanism. While it could be argued that all three are "Western" Abrahamic faiths, the current positioning of Islam as culturally oppositional to Christianity demands at least a reflection of the inclusiveness or exclusiveness of the notion of "Christian humanism." To embed education in a specific cultural-religious tradition and at the same time demand nondenominational education invites careful critique; the obvious tension remains unnamed and unquestioned.

In the remaining introductory section in both the old and new texts, there is a direct intertextual reference to antidiscrimination legislation (including mention of transgender identity in the new curriculum) (Baxter 2003; Skolverket 2006b). Yet the old curriculum marks the national situatedness of this cultural reference: students shall be "familiar with central parts of our Swedish, Nordic and Western cultural heritages" (Skolverket 2006b, 2006a). Indeed, as Lotta Björkman (2010) points out, curriculum demands that teachers give students knowledge about the norms that surround them. The "us" defined in this brief passage is a classic interpellation of those who belong to the Swedish nation as those who can read themselves into the Swedish, Nordic, and Western cultural heritage.

The change in the new curriculum is seemingly minimal: students shall now have "knowledge and understanding of *the* Swedish, Nordic, and Western cultural heritage," thus opening up the earlier interpellation of a national "us." In exchange, it seems, the new curriculum demands that students also acquire "basic knowledge of the Nordic languages" (Skolverket 2011, my translation and emphasis).

Similarly, the texts teach us how to understand gender, sex, and sexuality:

> The school should actively and consciously further equal rights and opportunities for men and women. The way in which girls and boys are treated and assessed in school as well as the demands and expectations that are placed on them, contributes to their perception of gender differences. The school has a responsibility to counteract traditional gender roles and should therefore provide pupils with the opportunity of developing their own abilities and interests irrespective of their sexual identity. (Skolverket 2006a, 2011) [8]

The use of the term "sexual identity" is, unfortunately, misleading here; the Swedish original reads "*könstillhörighet*," which directly translates as belonging to a sex, and is thus a longer term for "*kön*," sex. While a clear commitment to gender equality is important in the recognition of existing inequalities, this text implies a limitation of gendered and sexed bodies, referring to a model that allows only two options to the exclusion of those who do not match this prescription.

The old school law does not have a reference to Christian traditions, although it offers references to gender equality similar to the school plan and also refers to "basic democratic values" (Utbildningsdepartementet 1985). In 1999, a demand for "those who work in schools" to "actively counteract all types of insulting treatment such as bullying or racist behaviour" was added (Utbildningsdepartementet 2000, 1985):

> School activities shall be structured in accordance with fundamental democratic values. Each and every person active in the school system shall promote respect for the intrinsic value of every human being and for our common environment. (Utbildningsdepartementet 2000, p. 1).

Both in the proposition and in the new school law, the equivalent passage reads:

> Education shall be structured in accordance with fundamental democratic values and human rights such as the inviolability of human life, the freedom and integrity of the individual, the equal worth of all humans, gender equality and solidarity between people. (Government of Sweden 2009, 2010, my translation)

At first glance, there is no reference to Christian values in this proposition. This is where the analysis of (parts of) the policymaking process is productive. The proposition is accompanied by the comments of the referral groups and a constitutional commentary (*författningskommentar*) (Government of Sweden 2009). In this commentary, the policymakers explicitly refer to the old general curriculum, Lpo 94 (Skolverket 2006a):

> According to Lpo 94, this happens through bringing up the individual with a sense of justice, generosity, tolerance and responsibility in accord with the ethics held by/managed by Christian tradition and Western humanism. These values are central moments in learning and are therefore directly expressed in the law. (Government of Sweden 2009, my translation)

While the referral groups generally supported the proposition, two institutions, the Equality Ombudsman (*Diskrimineringsombudsman* [sic!]) and the Delegation for Human Rights in Sweden (*Delegationen för mänskliga rättigheter i Sverige*) considered the reference in the commentary "unfortunate" and suggested that it be deleted from the constitutional commentary (Government of Sweden 2009).[9] Despite these debates, the new general curriculum indeed keeps the reference to Christian ethics and Western humanism (Skolverket 2010a, 2010c).[10]

The intertextuality of these texts in this process is striking and serves to ground the new text in the old policy texts, creating continuity in their inherent logic and value statements. This continuity is complicated by the reference to human rights and the revised antidiscrimination legislation (Government of Sweden 2009). The *Diskrimineringslag* specifies seven grounds for nondiscrimination: sex, transgender identity or expression, ethnicity, religion, or other belief, disability, sexual orientation, or age (Government of Sweden 2008).[11] In the proposal for the new school law, the government suggests avoiding the listing of grounds for discrimination, arguing that such a list would create confusion and limit the work against offensive behavior. While this reasoning has its merits, it would be complicit in the not-naming of bodies, identifications, and practices that are beyond the binary options given by the text's emphasis on gender equality. While the final version of the curriculum does indeed mention the seven grounds of nondiscrimination defined in Swedish antidiscrimination legislation, I argue that within the Swedish framework of gender equality, sexuality is related to binary notions of sex and gender (Skolverket 2011). Subjectivities that do not match this religiously coded Swedish/Nordic/Western gender-equal conceptualization remain hidden in the tension between this conceptualization and the references to antidiscrimination.

Conclusion—"Christian Secularism" and the "Universal" Child

How can such a seemingly eclectic reading of school policies be useful, queer, and usefully queered? Looking at the role of children and young people in political argumentation might offer insights into the loaded-ness of the task. As Elspeth Probyn (1996) argues, "childhood as event requires that attention be paid to the modes in which it is articulated: as original, as nostalgic, as quintessential, as anecdotal, as fiction, as fact" (Probyn, 1996, p. 96). Probyn's claim is a useful reminder to scrutinize our motivations and strategies as researchers. Writing about school policies might seem like writing about children and young people from a distance. It does, however, give some understanding of the position of children and young people in a society and about basic notions of being and belonging that are invested in such policies.

The education researcher and pedagogue Sharon Todd (2001) claims that

> Curriculum is central in educating students to become certain kinds of people, individuals or citizens . . . there is an underlying assumption about what it means to learn and be "educated"; indeed, who educators think students should become frequently defines the aims and purpose of educational practices. (p. 1)

It is possible to abstract that school laws are informed by how policymakers think about the people students are going to be(come) in the future, and, as McGregor reminds us, these policymakers are invested with legitimacy and authority through the discursive creation of a "macro-actor" (McGregor 2008). In that sense, school policy documents are future oriented and construct young people entirely as students and as citizens-to-be, in the future tense. This also implies that young people are not seen as full subjects "right now," but can only wait for "the future" to be able to fully participate in the society they are trained for. This is reflected also in the diverse laws and regulations that exclude young people from full societal participation and cast them as in need of protection.

Pellegrini (2008), with reference to Muñoz and Edelman, underlines the specificity of that future-orientation, critiquing that it is the "universal" child who is inscribed in this future.[12] This universalism is, however, specifically embedded in the sense of Pellegrini's Christian secularism, and the intertextual insistence on the importance of "Western humanism" we find in the (discussion of) Swedish policy texts shows this interrelation. Or, in Muñoz's (2007) words, "all children are not the privileged white babies to whom contemporary society caters" (p. 363).

I set out to understand how this ephemeral "society" "caters" to specific children and to look for traces of Christian secularism and the production of specifically sexualized (Rasmussen 2006) and racialized subjects. This production lies in the paradoxical naming of and, at the same time, leaving unnamed subjectivities in the school laws. The relative invisibility of non-heteronormative sexualities in school laws juxtaposes the statement of antidiscrimination legislation.

The new school law and the new general curriculum both indeed include the seven grounds of nondiscrimination (Government of Sweden 2010; Skolverket 2011). Still, the new Swedish general curriculum, as well as the new school law via the intertextual references in the commentary, might be problematized as an example of Christian secularism, conflating "Christian tradition" that is neither defined nor analyzed for its problematic history with a notion of "universal" belonging. The construction of a Christian secular framework is obvious. Embedding these texts in notions of universal values that are in turn based on Christianity defines students (and teachers) as subjects who embody these values—or as their other. It is here that heteronormativity and specifically Swedish ethnicity are constructed as normal markers of school students. Here, the maybe-not-so-surprising exclusion of non-heteronormative subjectivities in schools "happens"—or, rather, is done.

In these school policy texts, the conceptualization of the nation as grounded in a Christian and Western cultural context creates paradoxical tension by engaging both notions of the liberated West and continuities of exclusive Christian humanist traditions regarding national belonging. School laws inscribe a national future. They are written for "our children," thus producing a "we" through the inexistence of "others."

Notes

1. Taken from the English-language version of the old general curriculum (Skolverket 2006a); the passage in the new general curriculum is identical in Swedish (Skolverket 2011).
2. An earlier version of this text was presented at the European Social Science History Conference 2010 in Ghent, Belgium. I thank my colleagues who critically informed my thinking through the various stages of writing and especially Gerald Walton, Jukka Lehtonen, Kristiina Brunila, and the anonymous reviewer for their productive comments.
3. Of course, this discussion has been going on much longer (Probyn 1996), for example in the negotiations of conflicting understandings and meanings of "queer diaspora" (Binnie 2004). The recent dramatization is interesting, as the historicity of questions often is equally interesting as the historicity of the answers.
4. In addition, every municipality writes a school plan (*skolplan*) that defines a pedagogical framework and specific aims. Following the new law, the municipal school plans will no longer be mandatory (Government of Sweden 2009).
5. An English-language version exists, which will be the text I use here for citations, though I have read and analyzed the Swedish original of the text. Otherwise, I translated the texts and present them in inverted commas to remind the reader that the quote is interpreted by translation.
6. The Swedish term *trygghet* is only poorly translated as "security," since it can be read as a representation of a Swedish sense of feeling secure that includes economic and social stability and personal integrity.
7. My selection excludes the texts for the options of higher secondary schools, Sami schools, special schools for children who are hard of hearing or have visual impairments, and special schools for children with learning impairments.
8. Taken from the English-language version of the old general curriculum (Skolverket 2006a); the passage in the new general curriculum is identical in Swedish (Skolverket 2011).
9. The Equality Ombudsman is a public authority working against discrimination. Until December 31, 2008, there were several separate authorities for antidiscrimination, such as the equal rights ombudsman and the ombudsman against discrimination based on sexual orientation. The Delegation for Human Rights in Sweden is an organization established to support public authorities, municipalities, and county councils in their human rights work.
10. At the time of revision of this text in November 2010, both the general curriculum for the comprehensive *grundskola* (grades 1–9), including the subject-specific curricula (Skolverket 2010a), and propositions for upper secondary school, *gymnasieskola*, were available. While a reading of the propositions would be beyond the scope of this paper (students can choose from 19 different programs, each with various subjects), a glance at the curriculum for civics suggests that the old antidiscrimination legislation was used as a reference; as categories for groups and identities, sex, nationality, religion, ethnicity, and class are mentioned for the basic course (Skolverket 2010b). Even the final version of the general curriculum includes this passage (Skolverket 2011).
11. While activists were pleased that trans people are included, many would have preferred that the text read "gender identity or expression," not limiting the law to trans experiences.
12. By introducing Edelman's position to question the political value of future- and child-orientation, Pellegrini (2008) brings up a complex issue for education researchers, one that I have not quite resolved. Being interested in education, we are "in the business" of future-orientation.

References

Ambjörnsson, F. (2003). *I en klass för sig. Genus, klass, och sexualitet bland gymnasietjejer.* Stockholm: Ordfront Förlag.
Atkinson, E. & DePalma, R. (2009). Un-believing the matrix: Queering consensual heteronormativity. *Gender and Education 21*(1), 17–29.
Bacchi, C.L. (2009). *Analysing policy: What's the problem represented to be?* Frenchs Forest, NSW: Pearson.
Baxter, J. (2003). *Positioning gender in discourse. A feminist methodology.* Basingstoke: Palgrave Macmillan.

Binnie, J. (2004). *The globalization of sexuality.* London: Sage.

Björkman, L. (2010). En skola i frihet–med "misstagens" hjälp. In J. Bromseth & F. Darj (Eds.), *Normkritisk pedagogik. Makt, lärande och strategier för förändring* (pp. 155–182). Centrum för genusvetenskap, Uppsala universitet.

Butler, J. (2009). Performativity, precarity and sexual politics. *AIBR: Revista de Antropología Iberoamericana 4*(3), i-xiii.

Cantú, L., Naples, N.A. & Vidal-Ortiz, S. (2009). *The sexuality of migration: Border crossings and Mexican immigrant men.* New York: New York University Press.

Cooper, D. (1995). *Power in struggle: Feminism, sexuality and the state.* New York: New York University Press.

de los Reyes, P., Molina, I. & Mulinari, D. (2003). Introduktion–Maktens (o)lika förklädnader. In P. de los Reyes, I. Molina & D. Mulinari (Eds.), *Maktens (o)lika förklädnader. Kön, klass & etnicitet i det postkoloniala Sverige.* Stockholm: Atlas.

Edelman, L. (2004). *No future: Queer theory and the death drive.* Durham, NC: Duke University Press.

Eilard, A. (2009). Att skildra mångfald i läromedel. Hur en inkluderande intention kan skapa underordning. *Tidskrift för Genusvetenskap 4:* 96–115.

Epstein, D., O'Flynn, S. & Telford, D. (2003). *Silenced sexualities in schools and universities.* Stoke on Trent and Sterling: Trentham Books.

Frosh, S., Phoenix, A. & Pattman, R. (2002). *Young masculinities: Understanding boys in contemporary society.* Basingstoke: Palgrave.

Government of Sweden. (2008). Diskrimineringslag (SFS 2008:567). Retrieved July 20, 2010, http://www.do.se/Documents/pdf/diskrimineringslagen.pdf?epslanguage=sv.

Government of Sweden. (2009). Regeringens proposition 2009/10:165. Den nya skollagen–för kunskap, valfrihet och trygghet. Retrieved July 20, 2010, http://www.regeringen.se/content/1/c6/14/23/68/25bd4959.pdf.

Government of Sweden. (2010). Skollag SFS 2010:800. http://62.95.69.3/SFSdoc/10/100800.Pdf.

Haritaworn, J. (2008). Loyal repetitions of the nation: Gay assimilation and the "war on terror." *darkmatter 3–Postcolonial Sexuality.* Retrieved July 20, 2010, http://www.darkmatter101.0rg/site/wp-content/uploads/pdf/3-haritaworn_loyal_repetitions_of_the_nation.pdf.

Hoerder, D., Hébert, Y.M. & Schmitt, I. (Eds.). (2005). *Negotiating transcultural lives: Belongings and social capital among youth in comparative perspective.* Göttingen: V&R Unipress (2nd ed., 2006: Toronto: University of Toronto Press).

Kumashiro, K. (2002). *Troubling education. Queer activism and antioppressive pedagogy.* New York: RoutledgeFalmer.

Lagrådet. (2010). Den nya skollagen–för kunskap, valfrihet och trygghet. Utdrag ur protokoll vid sammanträde 2010–02–24. Retrieved July 20, 2010, http://www.lagradet.se/yttranden/Den%20nya%20skollagen%20-%20for%20kunskap,%20valfrihet%200ch%20trygghet.pdf.

Luibhéid, E. (2002). *Entry denied: Controlling sexuality at the border.* Minneapolis: University of Minnesota Press.

Luibhéid, E. (2008). Queer/migration. An unruly body of scholarship. *GLQ: A Journal of Lesbian and Gay Studies 14*(2–3), 169–190.

Martinsson, L. & Reimers, E. (Eds.) (2008). *Skola i normer.* Malmö: Gleerups.

Mayer, T. (2002 [2000]). Gender ironies of nationalism: Setting the stage. In T. Mayer (Ed.), *Gender ironies of nationalism: Sexing the nation* [e-book] (pp. 1–24). London: Routledge.

McGregor, C. (2008). Norming and <re>forming: Challinging heteronormativity in educational policy discourses. *Canadian Journal of Educational Administration and Policy 82.* http://www.umanitoba.ca/publications/cjeap/articles/mcgregor.html.

Meyer, E.J. (2009). *Gender, bullying, and harassment. Strategies to end sexism and homophobia in schools.* New York: Teachers College Press.

Muñoz, J.E. (2007). Cruising the toilet. LeRoi Jones/Amiri Baraka, radical black traditions, and queer futurity. *GLQ: A Journal of Lesbian and Gay Studies 13*(2–3), 353–367.

OECD (2010). PISA 2009 Results: Executive summary. Retrieved July 10, 2010, http://www.pisa.oecd.org/dataoecd/34/60/46619703.pdf

Pellegrini, A. (2008). "What do children learn at school?" Necropedagogy and the future of the dead child. *Social Text 26*(4), 97–105.

Phoenix, A. (2009). De-colonising practises: Negotiating narratives from racialized and gendered experiences of education. *Race Ethnicity and Education 12*(1), 101–114.

Probyn, E. (1996). *Outside belongings.* New York: Routledge.

Puar, J.K. (2007). *Terrorist assemblages. Homonationalism in queer times.* Durham, NC: Duke University Press.

Rasmussen, M.L. (2010). Secularims, religion and "progressive" sex education. *Sexualities 13*(6), 699–712.

Rasmussen, M.L. (2006). *Becoming subjects. Sexualities and secondary schooling.* New York: Routledge.

Rasmussen, M.L., Rofes, E. & Talburt, S. (Eds.). (2004). Youth and sexualities. Pleasure, subversion, and insubordination in and out of schools. New York: Palgrave Macmillan.

Scott, J.W. (2009). *Sexularims.* Paper presented at the RSCAS Distinguished Lectures, Ursula Hirschmann Annual Lecture on Gender and Europe. http://cadmus.eui.eu/dspace/bitstream/1814/11553/1/RSCAS_DL_2009_01.pdf.

Seemann, M. (2009). *Geschlechtergerechtigkeit in der Schule. Eine Studie zum Gender Mainstreaming in Schweden.* Bielefeld: Transcript.

Skolverket. (2006a). Curriculum for the compulsory school system, the pre-school class and the leisure-time centre Lpo 94. Retrieved July 20, 2010, http://www.skolverket.se/publikationer?id=1070.

Skolverket. (2006b). Läroplan för det obligatoriska skolväsendet, förskoleklassen och fritidshemmet Lpo 94. http://www.skolverket.se/publikationer?id=1069.

Skolverket.(2007). PISA 2006–15-åringars förmåga att förstå, tolka och reflektera-naturvetenskap, matematik och läsförståelse. Stockholm. http://www.skolverket.se/publikationer?id=1760.

Skolverket. (2009). Ny läroplansstruktur och ny betygskala. Retrieved July 20, 2010, http://www.skolverket.se/sb/d/2627.

Skolverket. (2010a). Del ur Lgr 11: Läroplan för grundskolan, förskoleklassen och fritidshemmet: kapitel 1 och 2. Retrieved July 20, 2010, http://www.skolverket.se/content/1/c6/02/21/84/Lgr11_kap1_2.pdf.

Skolverket. (2010b). Samhällsvetenskapsprogrammet. Samhällskunskap 1a:1, 50 p. Retrieved July 20, 2010, from http://www.skolverket.se/sb/d/3414.

Skolverket. (2010c). Sammanfattning av skollagens 29 kapitel (2 July 2010). Retrieved July 20, 2010, http://www.skolverket.se/sb/d/3885/a/20552.

Skolverket. (2011). Läroplan för grundskolan, förskoleklassen och fritidshemmet 2011. Retrieved July 20, 2010, http://www.skolverket.se/publikationer?id=2575.

Thorne, B. (1993). *Gender play: Girls and boys in school.* New Brunswick, NJ: Rutgers University Press.

Todd, S. (2001). "Bringing more than I contain": Ethics, curriculum and the pedagogical demand for altered egos. *Journal of Curriculum Studies 33*(4), 431–450. Retrieved July 20, 2010, http://www.informaworld.com/smpp/content%7Edb=all%7Econtent=a713807095.

Utbildningsdepartementet (1985). *Skollag (1985:1100).* Retrieved July 20, 2010, http://www.riksdagen.se/webbnav/index.aspx?nid=3911&bet=1985:1100.

Utbildningsdepartementet (1999). *Lag om ändring i skollagen (1985:1100).* Retrieved July 20, 2010, http://www.notisum.se/rnp/sls/sfs/19990886.pdf.

Utbildningsdepartementet (2000). *Education Act (1985:1100).* Retrieved July 20, 2010, http://www.sweden.gov.se/content/1/c6/02/15/38/1532b277.pdf.

Yuval-Davis, N. (1997). *Gender & nation.* London: Sage.

CHAPTER TWENTY-FIVE

Drama Performances Address Stigma, Discrimination of MSM and HIV/AIDS Prevention

SILJA RAJANDER & PHAL SOPHAT

In response to the high rates of HIV among men who have sex with men (MSM) and the stigmatisation and discrimination of MSM in Cambodia, Men's Health Social Services (MHSS), a community-based organisation, was established in 2004 with the aims of preventing HIV/AIDS and sexually transmitted infections (STI) among MSM, providing social support and counselling to MSM, and advocating for an enabling environment for MSM. This work has proved challenging, for homosexuality is criticized as unnatural, and knowledge of safe male-to-male sex practices is poor, country director of MHSS Phal Sophat observes. Responding to these challenges, MHSS has conducted varied programs and campaigns, including workshops, seminars, and drama performances, has met with local authorities to lobby for their support and developed and distributed printed materials and condoms.

In Cambodia, MSM are often divided into two groups on the basis of bodily appearance: "short hair" and "long hair" MSM. It is the latter cross-dressing transgender MSM who are often subjected to sexual harassment and violence, Sophat explains, describing "when we say we work with MSM, some people think 'oh, transgender!' because they are visible. For other MSM, nobody knows [their sexual identity] and it's easier for them." Indeed, "short-hair" MSM are often referred to as "hidden MSM," and many get married in response to their parents' expectations. MHSS has thus educated students on safe sex practices from a bisexual perspective and has advocated for the equal right to social recognition of MSM.

In 2006 and 2007, MHSS organised drama performances by volunteers, presentations, and peer educator sessions on HIV prevention and stigma and discrimination of MSM, in three universities and one high school in Phnom Penh. Sophat describes these activities as having been "very successful and a lot of fun." Students posed many questions and took part in lively discussions following the drama performances and presentations. Sophat states:

The students asked the presenter questions like why he'd become an MSM, how about sexuality, what about the partners of MSM, what do MSM look like, what their life is like, where MSM come from, you know all these things, and can they make themselves not MSM? Some people reject MSM because they have a particular image of them. They think that they will get MSM, that they can become affected and that it can affect their school image, that because they have a friend or are friends with someone and they spend a lot of time together that they can become gay. And also they think that because of the culture, because the foreign culture, men become MSM, and they think that chemicals in food can make them MSM. So they think that it's not natural, because they think that it comes from different environments. We discussed what they think about MSM, and why they think about MSM as they do.

Views of gender are solidly body-based in Cambodia, and it is considered important to achieve a coherent masculine or feminine bodily appearance and not appear as "half a man and half a woman," as Sophat describes. While teachers and students have embraced the importance of addressing sexual health issues, Sophat asserts, the stigmatisation of homosexual identity has rarely been interpreted by their audiences as a human rights issue:

They think the issue is not that MSM don't have rights; "why don't you really try to be a man?" [laughs]. During one of the campaigns we had to explain a lot, to teach people who said "oh, stigma and discrimination [also] come from the MSM, they make us discriminate against them," and that became a long question and discussion session, you know.

For information on MHSS, see http://www.khana.org.kh/images/OD/Men1.htm.

Drama Education for HIV/AIDS Prevention in Phnom Penh, 2007. Phal Sophat

Yogyakarta Principles—For the Rights of Lesbian, Gay, Bisexual, and Transgender People

JUKKA LEHTONEN

The Yogyakarta Principles on the Application of International Human Rights Law in Relation to Sexual Orientation and Gender Identity is a set of international principles relating to sexual orientation and gender identity. The principles are used as a tool to fight for the rights of lesbian, gay, bisexual and transgender people. Following an experts' meeting held in Yogyakarta, Indonesia, November 6–9, 2006, these principles were adopted, and they are refereed in various international institutions such as the United Nations.

Included in the Principles are the following education-related topics:

- States shall undertake programmes of education and awareness to promote and enhance the full enjoyment of all human rights by all persons, irrespective of sexual orientation or gender identity. (Yogyakarta Principles, p. 10)
- States shall take all appropriate action, including programmes of education and training, with a view to achieving the elimination of prejudicial or discriminatory attitudes or behaviours which are related to the idea of the inferiority or the superiority of any sexual orientation or gender identity or gender expression. (Yogyakarta Principles, p. 11)

More on Yogyakarta Principles:
http://www.yogyakartaprinciples.org/principles_en.pdf
http://www.yogyakartaprinciples.org/principles_en.htm

Introduction: Another Telling Representational Effect

KARYN SANDLOS

When sexuality takes up space in education, it often does so under the guise of settling controversy, celebrating difference, and teaching for tolerance. Yet, contemporary debates on the politics and pedagogy of sexuality have moved well beyond thinking about sexuality as a stable representation of experience or place of self-recognition. Something more volatile is being theorized; namely, sexuality is being imagined as an ambivalent, open-ended, and conflictive process of making identifications. The concept of identification foregrounds both the contradictions between lived experiences and dominant discourses of identity and the differences within individuals and communities. According to Deborah Britzman, in her speculations on the qualities of a queer pedagogy in this section, "to shift from an insistence upon identity to an exploration of identifications allows pedagogy to consider the problem of how the self reads itself." One place to focus an inquiry into reading practices is on the unpredictable and destabilizing effects of our encounters with representations, objects, and other people.

What would it mean for education to cultivate practices of reading that unsettle the stability of sexuality, race, gender, and other markers of identity and draw attention to our ambivalent experiences of self and other? How do representations of sexuality provoke new forms of educational inquiry into the more radical possibilities of identification, desire, and misrecognition? In this section, film stills, essays, documentary images, and political interventions invite us to explore these questions in a variety of contexts (the cinema, the academy, community-based research, and on the street), and across a spectrum of theoretical and practical orientations (psychoanalytic pedagogy, participatory research, queer theory, and theories of human development). Works by artists, academics, researchers, and cultural producers take up issues of pedagogy and sexual difference in order to address the historic invisibility and repression of queer desire and as a means to transgress the stabilities of the representational.

The section opens with a series of stills from the films of Barbara Hammer and Isaac Julien. Hammer's films of the late 1970s—*Dyketactics, Multiple Orgasm, Double Strength, Women I Love,* and *Superdyke*—juxtapose realist images of lesbian lives and bodies with abstract, metaphoric images of sexuality and freedom. While these films were subject to charges of essentialism in the emerging context of semiotics and feminist film theory, Hammer (1993) describes the sense of strategic urgency that propelled her work: "A marginalized and oppressed group must make a mark first, define a form, and make a statement that they exist. . . . There could be no semiotics if there were no sign" (p. 71). In this section, images from *Nitrate Kisses* (1992)—elderly lesbians in an intimate embrace, and an erotic tryst between an interracial gay male couple—hint at Hammer's method of juxtaposing "unauthorized" LGBTQ historical narratives with images of queer desire in the creation of "perceptual, intellectual and emotional configurations that provoke pain and give pleasure" (Hammer, 1993, p. 73). In this way, Hammer positions her audience as active producers of personal, political, and emotional meanings.

The strategic use of images to provoke a cultural discourse on sexuality and desire also characterizes the work of British independent filmmaker Isaac Julien. In 1984, Julien cofounded the Sankofa Collective, a group of artists and filmmakers committed to exploring queer history, masculinity, and racial and sexual difference. In an interview, Julien describes the work of the Sankofa Collective as both an aesthetic and pedagogical project: "We had three ambitions: first to make films, second to create an intellectual context for their reception, and third to generate a discourse in that space" (Latil, 2000). The Sankofa Collective positioned independent film as an important context for theorizing the homoerotic structures of the gaze and the aesthetic possibilities of representing queer desire. Sankofa's purpose, however, was not simply to fill in gaps in the field of mainstream representation, where images of black gay male identity and sexuality were stereotypically pathologized or absent but also to create conditions for understanding how desire is constituted through what Sedgwick has termed "the fractal intricacies of language, skin, migration, state" (this volume). Julien's 1989 film *Looking for Langston* examines the life, politics, and sexuality of Harlem Renaissance poet Langston Hughes. As the images in this section will suggest, this lush black-and-white film alternates between the aesthetic of documentary realism and dreamlike scenes constructed from Hughes's poetry. Julien himself plays the role of Hughes lying in his funeral coffin, in an elegiac meditation on the loss and enduring significance of this black gay cultural icon.

Deborah Britzman, in her germinal essay "Queer Pedagogy and Its Strange Techniques," explores the relations among queer theory, psychoanalytic reading practices, and pedagogy. For Britzman, education raises the problem of how we learn to recognize and call into question the conceptual boundaries that structure our intellectual landscapes and shape our perceptions of self and other. This sort of learning would struggle against the normalizing structures of education, including the desire for harmonious relations, the wish for knowledge to become the royal road to attitudinal change, and the pedagogical insistence on empathy as a solution to the problem of difference. Britzman writes:

> The normal view is that one should attempt to "recover" authentic images of gays and lesbians and stick them into the curriculum with the hope that representations—in the form of tidy role models—can serve as a double remedy for hostility toward social difference for those who cannot imagine difference, and for the lack of self-esteem of those who are imagined as having no self. However, the question that cannot be uttered is, Just how different can these different folks be and still be recognized as just like everyone else?

Paradoxically, while our educational narratives of inclusion and tolerance construct sexuality as a place of affirmation and moral certainty, these same narratives also produce LGBTQ sexuality as other to or outside of "the norm." By calling attention to the pedagogical wish for representations to serve as a corrective for intolerant attitudes, Britzman invites us to consider the complex processes through which students and teachers grapple with and resist giving up old ideas in order to make space for new ones. The problem that Britzman brings into focus has to do with how a queer pedagogy might unsettle conceptual binaries (e.g., inside/outside, self/other), make room for uncertainty, and move us in the direction of implication. The study of implication risks seeing classrooms as places where identifications can be allowed to wander in unpredictable directions, where meaning can break down and struggle against the limits of thought, and where attention to habits of reading can become "a practice of the self that can exceed the self."

Francisco Ibáñez-Carrasco, in his essay "Making the AIDS Ghostwriters Visible," turns our attention to problems of implication and the conceptual limits that structure contemporary approaches to participatory research involving persons living with HIV/AIDS. He focuses, in particular, on the emerging sexual micro culture of "sex pigs"—gay men who practice adventurous and risky sex—to explore the complex perceptions of queer sexuality that come both from outside of queer communities and from within them. According to Ibáñez-Carrasco, sex pigs "are lightning rods for emotionality, excess, exhilaration, envy, and scorn," and so they present an opportunity for inquiry into the tensions of in/visibility of gay men in participatory HIV/AIDS research. Ibáñez-Carrasco cautions that HIV/AIDS researchers are learning to translate the intricacies of gay men's sex, sexuality, and emotionality into the clinical language of epidemiology, while their own education in sexuality goes unexamined. The essay offers a preliminary pedagogical framework for thinking about and clarifying the investments, blind spots, and biases of the next generation of HIV/AIDS researchers.

Brian Casemore, in his essay "'A Different Idea' in the Sex Education Curriculum: Thinking Through the Emotional Experience of Sexuality," offers another view of implication in a qualitative research project on the emotional world of sexual health education. He brings the aesthetic representation of adolescent female sexuality found in a documentary film to a focus group discussion with middle school students. The first version of implication has to do with the students' struggle to express and understand their responses to one character in the film, an African American single mother. Their conversation suggests the difficulty for the students of thinking about the emotional experience of sexuality, a difficulty manifested in the identificatory practices and defenses typical of adolescent development. Casemore provides a psychoanalytic reading of the conversation and demonstrates how the focus group participants negotiate the emotional terrain of encountering sexuality and racial difference, and risk a reparative reading. In a second version of implication, Casemore refuses the position of the researcher as omniscient observer by making explicit his research protocol and questions, and his own complex emotional response to the troubling ideas of his research participants.

The section closes with a return to the productive possibilities of reading and identificatory practices by way of a memorializing gesture to queer theorist and literary scholar Eve Sedgwick (1950–2009). While Sedgwick's books *Epistemology of the Closet* (1990) and *Novel Gazing: Queer Readings in Fiction* (1997) are widely considered to represent her most important contributions to the field of queer studies, for me, Sedgwick's personal, poetic, and scholarly collection of essays, *Tendencies,* is an evocative meditation on the "open mesh of possibilities, gaps, overlaps, dissonances and resonances, lapses and excesses of meaning" (this volume) that make up a queer life. In the excerpt "Christmas Effects," Sedgwick enacts a playful and incisive critique of how the meaning of this cultural holiday coheres in the image of the personal, institutional, religious, capitalist, and heteronormative system known as "the family." She asks: "What if the richest junctures weren't the ones where *everything means the same thing?*" and she brings this question to teasing out and listing the many contradictory and conflicting meanings that constitute queer possibilities for crafting one's sexual identity. *Tendencies* is a provocative testament to Sedgwick's practice of writing queer desire through "performative acts of experimental self-perception and filiation" (this volume).

Sedgwick's turn toward the performative within queer politics and thought finds resonance in the example of Feel Tank, a Chicago-based collective of activists, artists, and academics. Currently, Feel Tank includes Lauren Berlant, Debbie Gould, Mary Patten, Matthias Regan, and Rebecca Zorach. In Feel Tank's "Parades for the Politically Depressed," pajama-clad collective members carry protest signs with slogans such as "Don't Just Medicate—Agitate!" and "Exhausted? It Might Be Politics." Through performance, criticism, art, and activism, Feel Tank explores our political attachments to difficult emotions such as hopelessness, apathy, anxiety, fear, numbness, despair, and ambivalence. According to the group's loosely written manifesto, "we are also interested in hope" (Mary Patten, personal communication, December 27, 2010).

References

Hammer, B. (1993). The politics of abstraction. In M. Gever, J. Greyson, & P. Parmar (Eds.), *Queer looks: Perspectives on lesbian and gay film and video* (pp. 70–75). Toronto: Between the Lines.

Latil, F. (2000). Interview with Isaac Julien. Retrieved December 20, 2010, from http://newenglandfilm.com/news/archives/00may/julien.htm

Sedgwick, E. (1990). *Epistemology of the closet.* Berkeley and Los Angeles: University of California Press.

Sedgwick, E. (1997). *Novel gazing: Queer readings in fiction.* Durham, NC: Duke University Press.

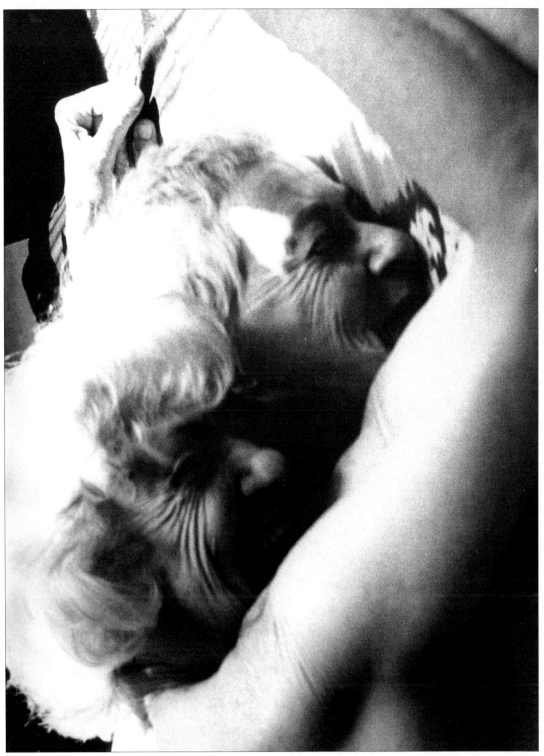

Frances Lorraine and Sally Binford in *Nitrate Kisses*, 1992. Barbara Hammer

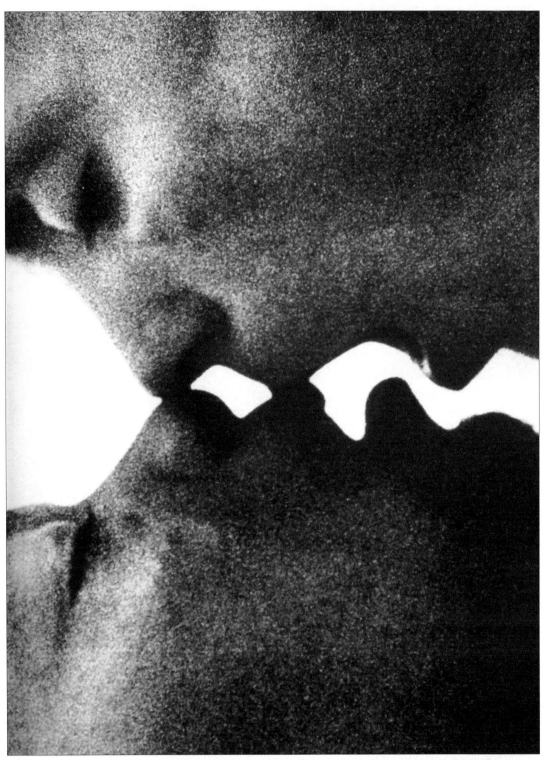

Jack Waters and Peter Cramer in *Nitrate Kisses*, 1992. Barbara Hammer

Looking for Langston Series (No. 17) The Last Angel of History, 1989. Isaac Julien and Sunil Gupta

Looking for Langston Series (No. 19) After George Platt Lynes Nudes with a Twist 1952, 1989.
Isaac Julien and Sunil Gupta

CHAPTER TWENTY-SEVEN

Queer Pedagogy and Its Strange Techniques

DEBORAH P. BRITZMAN

In an essay that rethinks the historicity of identity politics and the situated question of what is at stake (and for whom) when identities are at stake, Gayatri Chakravorty Spivak (1992) worries about education. She asks repeatedly, 'What is it to learn and to unlearn?' The call is to think about what institutional education as a set of discourses and practices has to do with the self-determination *as well as* the subordination of global subaltern populations. Spivak is not asking that 'identity' be restored to a nice ontology, a site of uniqueness or comfort, a font of self-esteem, or a celebration of individuality. In fact, by centering the question of learning and unlearning, it is precisely the unthought of these sorts of regulatory declarations that she takes as a problem. What does learning and unlearning mean when one considers both "cases of exorbitant normality rather than disease [and] cases of confounding the instituted laws?" (p. 776). Can the project of education become the gathering ground for 'deconstructive revolts?' Can pedagogy provide ethical responses that can bear to refuse the normalizing terms of origin and of fundamentalism, those that refuse subjection?

The concern for 'cases of exorbitant normality' and how such 'cases' are produced in education is not new.[1] Near the end of *Civilization and Its Discontents*, Freud (1930/1975) addresses a footnote to educators. Having already deemed education as one of the impossible professions, he notes one of its fault lines: "In sending the young out into life with . . . a false psychological orientation, education is behaving as though one were to equip young people starting on a polar expedition with summer clothing and maps to the Italian Lakes" (p. 71). The phrasing, 'false psychological orientation' can be read as a critique of the way education disavows the complexities and treacherous conflicts of 'civilization': of education's repetitious offer of tidy stories of happiness, resolution, and certainty as if life were something to be overcome and mastered with as little disturbance as possible. Freud's concern is with how education came to conduct itself without a theory of conflict and otherness and how education might think about making selves interested in life as a state of emergency. As with Spivak's call one might read Freud as saying that there is a problem with narratives that promise the normalcy of life, that presume a life without difference, without a divided self.

What makes normalcy so thinkable in education? How might pedagogy think the unthought of normalcy? To allow such questions, three different forms of practice will be set in tension: those of queer theory, those of pedagogy, and those of psychoanalytic reading practices. Queer theory transgresses the stabilities of the representational; pedagogy situates the problem of normalcy in classroom sites and worries about the social production of the learning self; and psychoanalytic theories of reading refuse knowledge as certainty in order to call into question three forms of subjection: the subject-presumed-to-know, the capacity of the subject's response to be unencumbered by that which it cannot tolerate; and the subject's own 'passion for ignorance.'[2] Taken together, these practices make one curious about the means by which normalcy becomes the great unmarked within classroom sites and the means by which pedagogy itself might intervene to agitate the limits and fault lines of normalcy. Once normalcy is constructed as a historical problem of pedagogy and marked as a production of pedagogy itself, a further question is raised: Can the reading of normalcy be a queer reading practice?

Each part of this chapter depends upon the assumption that education is a structure of authority even as it structures the very grounds of authority required for its own recognition. As a practice and as a discourse, education intimately disciplines the conceptual needs of students and teachers. Some of these needs concern a desire for a transparent truth, for stable communities and identities, and for a pedagogy that ignores contradictions. And even those needs that desire an oppositional or critical practice bear the traces of these first demands. At the same time, all these contradictions compete with the ways discourses of affectivity and intellect are organized and differentially lived. In bringing into dialogue queer theory, psychoanalytic reading practices, and pedagogy, and by using these three terms to consider the problem of how knowledge of bodies and bodies of knowledge become a site of normalization, this chapter is an attempt to practice the kinds of deconstructive revolts raised earlier by Spivak; to take apart the conceptual orderings that conceal the very difficult question of what difference difference makes. If, then, every learning is an unlearning, 'what is it to learn and unlearn?'

My attention to these tensions is part of an attempt to imagine a queer pedagogy (as opposed to a queer pedagogue), a pedagogy that worries about and unsettles normalcy's immanent exclusions, or, as many now pose the problem, normalcy's passions for ignorance.[3] It is a pedagogy that attempts to provoke what Gary Wickham and William Haver (1992) term "the very proliferation of alternative sites of identification and critique" necessary if thought is to think the limits of its own dominant conceptual orders, and if new desires are to be made. This means thinking a pedagogy whose grounds of possibility require risk, uncertainty, and implication in traumatic times. It means imagining a pedagogy prepared to exceed the doubled Foucauldian (1990) subject: "subject to someone else by control and dependence; and tied to his own identity by a conscience or self knowledge" (p. 420). And while it may be difficult to conceive of self-knowledge as a site of subjection, much of my argument is meant to unsettle old centrings of the self in education: to unsettle the myth of normalcy as an originary state and to unsettle the unitary subject of pedagogy. However, rather than offer a 'how to' manual of pedagogy, I am trying to imagine a queer pedagogy along the lines of what Sue Golding (1993) calls 'technique,' "a route, a mapping, an impossible geography—impossible not because it does not exist, but because *it exists and does not exist exactly at the same time*" (p. 166).

In thinking a queer pedagogy, I wonder if the terms of queerness can exceed and still hold onto its first referent, namely transgression and an economy of affection and practices of desire, that, in its hesitations, both speaks and departs from its relational name. And by holding to this tension can a queer pedagogy implicate everyone involved to consider the grounds of their own possibility, their own intelligibility, and the work of proliferating their own identifications and critiques that can exceed identity as essence, explanation, causality, or transcendence? The shift, then, of a queer pedagogy is one that becomes curious about identifications and how identifications constitute desires (Borch-Jacobsen, 1982). The move is meant to pose a question concerning how it is that one decides the desirability and relevancy of representation itself. It is a movement, akin to Lee Edelman's (1994) curiosity, toward "the way in which identity turns out to be a trope of representation" (p. 16).

Whether one looks for one's own image in the other and hence invests in knowledge as self-reflection and affirmation, or whether, in the process of coming to know, one invests in the rethinking of the self as an effect of and condition for encountering the other as an equal, is the problem this chapter engages. And in claiming as desirable the proliferation of identifications and critiques necessary to imagine sociality differently, can a queer pedagogy wander, along with Samuel Delaney (1991), "the margin[s] between claims of truth and the claims of texuality" (p. 28), between what is taken to be real and what is constituted as experience, between the immediacies of expectation and the afterthought of (mis)recognitions? Can pedagogy move beyond producing essentialist subject positions and ponder the fashioning of the self that occurs when attention is given to the performativity of the subject in queer relationality?

I

Queer Theory proposes to think identities in terms that place as a problem the production of normalcy and in terms that confound the intelligibility of the apparatuses that produce identity as repetition. As deconstructive revolts, queer theories acknowledge the intrusion of exorbitant normalcy and the ways such normalcy ignores the everydayness of queer identifications, pleasures, practices, and bodies. The concern here is in thinking the cost of narrating identities and the cost of identities itself.[4] Queer theory is not an affirmation but an implication. Its bothersome and unapologetic imperatives are explicitly transgressive, perverse, and political: transgressive because it questions the regulations and effects of binary categorical conditions such as the public and the private, the inside and the outside, the normal and the queer, and the ordinary and the disruptive; perverse because it turns away from utility even as it claims deviancy as a site of interest;[5] and political because it attempts to confound instituted laws and practices by putting into place queer representations on their own everyday terms.[6]

Queer theory, then, becomes queer when, as Teresa de Lauretis (1991) notes, it "conveys a double emphasis on the conceptual and speculative work involved in discourse production, and on the necessary critical work of deconstructing our own discourses and their constructed silence" (p. iv). Queer theory takes up that queer space of simultaneously questioning and asserting representations and in outing the unthought of normalcy. The attempt is to provoke yet-to-be-made constructions of subjects interested in confronting what Peggy Phelan (1993) terms as "the not all" of representation (p. 32). As an unruly collection of discursive strategies of reading and of narrating bodies and histories and as performative street politics that refuse to think straight, queer theory engages what Alexander Duttman (1993) terms "a supplement of impertinence" (p. 112), or the dissimilitude within representation: what cannot be recuperated, said, or managed; what becomes undone despite a promise of certainty.

Where queer theory meets pedagogy is in how it conceptualizes normalcy as negation.[7] It constitutes normalcy as a conceptual order that refuses to imagine the very possibility of the other precisely because the production of otherness as an outside is central to its own self-recognition. This orientation to normalcy as the pernicious production of such binaries as the self/other and the inside/outside may be quite significant to the conceptualization and the transformation of the education of education.[8] This is so because within contexts of education the pointing to normalcy as exorbitant production allows one to cinder simultaneously the relations between and within those who transgress and undress the normal and those whose labour is to be recognized as normal. When pedagogy meets queer theory and thus becomes concerned with its own structure of intelligibility—with the education of education—and when pedagogy engages its own impertinence, the very project of knowledge and its accompanying subject-presumed-to-know become interminable despite the institutional press for closure, tidiness, and certainty.

And yet, to get to the space where difference and not similitude is the space of pedagogy, a detour into the question of identify is necessary. To notice that 'identity' has become what Michel Foucault (1990) has termed 'an incitement to discourse,' perhaps slides too easily over the very problem articulated within the field of queer theories. As an incitement the concept of identity seems to mobilize and regulate whole sets of epistemic anxieties over such agitated relations as identity and politics, narrations and practices, history and representation, identity and identifications. What seems common to queer theory is an insistence on understanding identity as both a social and historical production and as a relational ethic: identity as neither transcendence nor equivalence.

In queer theory, talk about identity has moved well beyond old formulas of accepting experience as telling and transparent and as supposing that role models are the transitional object to self-esteem. Something far less comforting is being put into place: namely, identity is examined as a discursive effect of the social and as being constituted through identifications. The self becomes a problem of desiring a self and hence in need of a social. It is identification that allows the self-recognition and misrecognition. And it is through identification that desire is made. But because identification is a partial, contradictory, and ambivalent relation with aspects or dynamics of others, it may be thought of as a means to make and direct desire. Many positionings are possible: identification of, identification with, identification against, over-identification, and so on.[9] Diana Fuss's (1995) working definition suggests the tensions of identificatory relations: "Identification inhabits, organizes and instantiates identity. . . . [It can be considered] as the play of difference and similitude in self-other relations [and] does not, strictly speaking, stand against identity but structurally aids and abets it" (p. 2). To shift from an insistence upon identity to an exploration of identifications allows pedagogy to consider the problem of how the self reads itself.

In discussing the debate between identities and politics Douglas Crimp (1992) poses the problem of relationality:

> Identification is, of course, identification with an other, which means that identity is never identical to itself. This alienation from the self it constructs . . . does not mean simply that any proclamation of identity will only be partial, that it will be exceeded by other *aspects* of identity, but rather that identity is always a relation, never simply a positivity . . . perhaps we can begin to rethink identity politics as politics of relational identities formed through political identifications that constantly remake those identities. (p. 12)

If identity is not identical to itself but only a possibility in relation to another and if such a relation is one of difference within as well as difference between identities, what might it mean for pedagogy to think about identity as a problem of making identifications in difference? Such a question is *not* one that requires a naïve empathy. For, as Freud (1925) reminds educators, the project of empathy is actually a projection of the self into the conditions of the other. This projection becomes forgotten with the hope that it is possible, in Freud's words, 'to feel our way into people.' And yet, because feelings are contradictory, historical, ambivalent, and a statement of need, feelings are a response to something and hence are already constitutive of relations. To feel one's way into someone else, then, cannot be an originary moment, and to act as if it were means one must shut out both the infinite variations and slippages of affect and the fact that feelings are also contradictory and ambivalent forms of thought or structures of intelligibility that depend upon historically specific spheres.[10] In other words, feelings are not capable of transcending history and the relations already supposed. As Freud (1925) remarks, "We shall always tend to consider [we can imagine] people's distress objectively—that is, to place ourselves, with our own wants and sensibilities, in their conditions, and then to examine what occasions we should find in them for experiencing happiness or unhappiness" (p. 26). Yet, even in this very imagined moment, one can only imagine the self.

If one cannot feel one's way into people without, in actuality, representing the self as the arbitrator and judge of the other's actions and possibilities, perhaps it is time to question what one wants from empathy and whether the educational insistence that feelings are the royal road to attitudinal change is how identificatory structures actually work. Instead, one might consider feelings as constituting ignorances, ambivalences, and knowledge, and thus as that which cannot exist without narrative conventions and their own structures of intelligibility and unintelligibility. The argument here is not that feelings do not or should not matter or that one should not work with perspectives and conditions that are not own's own. It is to suggest that feelings are symptomatic of more than the individual's intentionality. Indeed, precisely because feelings are matters of history, of location, and of bodies, one might consider feelings as symptomatic of contradictory pushes and pulls of relationality and need. In the context of a queer pedagogy, a more useful way to think about feelings requires attention to what it is that structures the ways in which feelings are imagined and read. This means constituting feelings for another as a curious reading practice, as a problem of ethical conduct, and as a symptom of identificatory engagement. That is, pedagogy might provoke the strange study of where feelings break down, take a detour, reverse their content, betray understanding, and hence study where affective meanings become anxious, ambivalent, and aggressive. Rather than invoking a discourse of empathy that cannot explain itself, pedagogy might become curious about what conceptual orders have to do with affectivity and with what reading practices have to do with proliferating one's identificatory possibilities and modes of critique.

II

In questioning the question of reading practices, linking reading practices to forms of sociality, and hence to the very structuring of intelligibility, identifications, modes of address, and civic life, I mean to signal not just how one comes to recognize, imagine, and contain signs. Rather, in education the problem becomes how one comes to think, along with others, the very structures of signification in avowing and disavowing forms of sociality and their grounds of possibility; to question, along with others, one's form of thinking, one's form of practice. Reading practices, then, are socially performative. And part of the performance might well be the production of normalcy—itself a hegemonic sociality—if techniques of reading begin from a standpoint of refusing the unassimilability of difference and the otherness of the read. This case of 'exorbitant normality,' or passion for ignorance, occurs when 'the other' is rendered as either unintelligible or intelligible only as a special event and hence as never entitled to an everyday. Exorbitant normality is built when the other is situated as a site of deviancy and disease, and hence, as if in need of containment. Such cruel reading practices, all too common, may well be a symptom of what Michael Warner (1993) calls heteronormativity (p. xxi).[11]

Reading practices might well perform something interesting, and this has to do with producing social selves whose thinking about their own structures of intelligibility recognizes and refuses the confinement of sameness and the seduction of affirmation that has as its cost the expulsion of otherness. Reading practices might be educated to attend to the proliferation of one's own identificatory possibilities and to make allowance for the unruly terms of undecidability and unknowability. One might think about the proliferation of identifications as a means to exceed—as opposed to return to—the self. What if one thought about reading practices as problems of opening identifications, of working the capacity to imagine oneself differently precisely with respect to how one encounters another, and in how one encounters the self? What if how one reads the world turned upon the interest in thinking against one's thoughts, of creating a queer space where old certainties made no sense?

In naming reading practices as having the capacity to be queered, I am offering not so much a remedy for the ways reading practices can construct normalcy. The production of normalcy, as Foucault (1990) points out, is not "a history of mentalities" (p. 152) or one of meaning, but rather 'a history of bodies' and is hence a problem of how sociality can be lived and how politics can be imagined. To focus the question of reading practices as activities central to classroom pedagogies one might consider reading practices as social effects of something larger than the one who reads—a different order of time than the moment of reading might suggest. My concern is with constituting reading practices as symptomatic of relations of power, as capable of both expressing a desire that exceeds subjectivity and as provoking deconstructive revolts: reading practices as a technique for exceeding auto-affectivity and the accompanying investment in pinning down meanings, in getting identities 'straight.' My interest is in thinking of reading practices as possibly unhinging the normal from the self in order to prepare the self to encounter its own conditions of alterity: reading practices as an imaginary site for multiplying alternative forms of identifications and pleasures not so closely affixed to—but nonetheless transforming—what one imagines their identity imperatives to be. Then pedagogy may be conceived within two simultaneous terms: as an imaginative way to think about and to perform reading practices that still manage, however precariously, to be overconcerned with practices of identification and sociality; *and* as a technique for acknowledging difference *as the only condition of possibility for community.*

The problem I am trying to get at is something different than a plea for inclusion or merely adding 'marginalized voices' to an overpopulated curriculum. Inclusion, or the belief that one discourse can make room for those it must exclude, can only produce, as Judith Butler (1993) puts it, "that theoretical gesture of pathos in which exclusions are simply affirmed as sad necessities of signification" (p. 53). The case of how gay and lesbian studies has been 'treated' in a sentimental education that attempts to be antihomophobic serves as my example of where arguments for inclusion produce the very exclusions they are meant to cure. Part of the tension is that there tends to be only two pedagogical strategies: providing information and techniques of attitude change.[12] The normal view is that one should attempt to 'recover' authentic images of gays and lesbians and stick them into the curriculum with the hope that representations—in the form of tidy role models—can serve as a double remedy for hostility toward social difference for those who cannot imagine difference and for the lack of self-esteem for those who are imagined as having no self. However, the question that cannot be uttered is, just how different can these different folks be and still be recognized as just like everyone else? Or, put differently, given the tendency of the curriculum to pass knowledge through discourses of factuality and morality, how can difference be different? And, different from what?

The liberal desire for recovery and authenticity that takes the form of inclusion in the curriculum, perhaps as an add-on, certainly in the form of a special event, attempts two contradictory yet similar manoeuvres. On the one hand, the strategy constructs an innocently ignorant general public. Here, I want to signal how the normal of the normative order produces itself as unmarked sameness, and as if synonymous with the everyday even as it must produce otherness as a condition for its own recognition. For those who cannot imagine what difference difference makes in the field of curriculum, the hope is that the truth of the subaltern might persuade these normative folks to welcome the diversity of others and maybe feel their way into people in order to transform, at the level of these very transferable feelings, their racist, sexist, heterosexist attitudes. But how, exactly, is it possible to feel one's way into what can only be imagined as difference without producing, in that very act, the same? On the other hand, this strangely estranged story of difference requires the presence of those already deemed subaltern. Here, the recovery being referenced is the recovery of what the norm supposes these different folk lack, namely the self-esteem of the same. The originary myth of self-esteem, or a self-knowledge that assumes the self as lack, actually works to shut out the very conflictive operations that produce the self as lack and incapable of desire.

These liberal hopes, these various narratives of affirmation that are lived, however differently, as conceptual needs—and oddly, as one-way instances of empathy—are, however, really about the production of sameness. Certain subalterns might be invited into the curriculum but not because they have anything to say to those already there. Indeed, if these textualized folks began to talk to one another, what would they actually say? Could they even make sense? The problem is that the lived effects of 'inclusion' are a more obdurate version of sameness and a more polite version of otherness. David Theo Goldberg (1993) puts it this way: "The commitment to tolerance turns only on modernity's 'natural inclination' to *in*tolerance; acceptance of otherness presupposes as it at once necessitates delegitimation of the other." Pedagogies of inclusion, then, and the tolerance that supposedly follows, may in actuality produce the grounds of normalization. Lived at the level of conceptual needs, such hopes are only able to offer the stingy subject positions of the tolerant normal and the tolerated subaltern. Put differently, the subject positions of US and THEM become recycled as empathy.

Returning to the double subject of Foucault, what does this subject precisely know about itself in talk about the other? Is there a form of self-knowledge that can untie the self from gender, racial, and sexual centerings? How is it that talk about queerness might refuse such binary oppositions like the public and the private or refuse to produce a chain of signification that Toni Morrison calls 'the economy of stereotypes,' and instead, in the words of Peggy Phelan (1993), make talk that "upset[s] representational economies" (p. 26). How might pedagogy address what Eve Sedgwick (1992) terms the great divide of homo/hetero and thus begin to confront the question of everydayness: "In whose lives is homo/heterosexual definition an issue of continuing centrality and difficulty?" (p. 40). Can pedagogy admit, as Judith Butler (1991) advises, "the different routes by which the unthinkability of homosexuality is being constituted time and again?" (p. 20). Or put a bit differently, can pedagogy admit to the unthinkability of normalcy and how normalcy 'is being constituted again and again'?

These questions might provoke a different take on discourses of information in terms of their centrality to the intelligibility of education design and in terms of addressing the trauma it invokes.

Along with cultural activists such as Cindy Patton doing AIDS education work, I assume the failure of the old information discourses of education: knowledge of 'facts' does *not* provide a direct line to the real, to the truth, and to the righteous conduct.[13] As a discourse of knowledge, 'information' cannot account for things like affective investments as recalcitrant and as conflictively fashioned within particular narratives. It has nothing to say about how such information produces a hierarchy of addresses and therefore constitutes authority and modes of passions for ignorance. The information model is not capable of thinking how authorization is imagined and lived in classrooms. Nor can reliance upon the evidence of information account for the confusion when one's own sense of cohesiveness becomes a site of misrecognition or the trauma unleashed when the discourses borrowed to work upon and perform the fictions of subjectivity stop making sense. Indeed, the reliance upon facts as the transitional object to attitude change provides no pedagogical theory of negation or the way ideas and facts can become unattached from and even work against emotional ties.

There are at least two regulating fictions about information as the direct line to knowledge that need to be deconstructed. The first is that receiving information, acquiring 'just the facts,' is no problem for the learner. The myth is that information neutralizes ignorance and that learners and their teachers will rationally accept new thoughts without having to grapple with unlearning the old ones. The second fiction is that information is a mirror of the real and hence an antidote for ignorance. The reasoning goes something like this: If people had the real facts, they might rationally decide to act better toward the 'victims' of ignorance or view their own ignorance as self-victimization. This view safely positions the knower within the normative, as a sort of volunteer who collects knowledge not because one's social identity is at stake or even only made possible through the subjection of others but rather because such information might protect one from the unintelligibility of others. Thus this discourse called information purports to construct compassion and tolerance as the correct subject position but in actuality performs the originary binary opposition of US/THEM in more elaborate and normalizing terms.

At this point, it is helpful to ask whether discourses of information and discourse of feelings discussed earlier are actually different from each other. Information models of education assume that facts are an objective corrective to ignorant feelings. Feeling models of education attempt a subjective corrective to the distancing mechanisms of objectified knowledge. But as a corrective, what must be ignored is that feelings are not rational techniques of self-adjustment nor is knowledge 'un-implicated' in its own sets of ignorances. However, to maintain itself each discourse depends upon the very inside/outside distinctions that provoke new forms of US/THEM. These discourses might be understood best as two kinds of social effects that spring from positioning classroom subjects as lack: as either lacking the proper feelings, whether these feelings be those of toleration or self-esteem or as lacking knowledge, either the knowledge of the other or the intelligence of information. What cannot be considered however, is the question of cathexis and negation: where affect either meets the idea or becomes untied from the idea. The problem here is not one of abolishing either affectivity or intellect from the classroom. The problem is one where the valorization of either diminishes the very possibility of thinking about what happens when affectivity is imagined as constitutive of conflictive identificatory strategies and when conflictive discourses are imagined as mapping neatly onto desire. The problem is for pedagogy to insist upon affectivity and intellection as dialogic, as desire, and as implication.

Exploring how experiences of those deemed subaltern are imagined, then, means taking a second look at the everyday normative and rethinking the normative as producing the grounds of estrangement and new forms of ignorance. For some, such a second look means embodying the fear that these queer terms may well decentre the very terms of their own identity and hence the grounds of intelligibility upon which the self is supposed, coalesced, and recognized. At the same time, when the normative order is already lived as a site of estrangement, as it is for those always already positioned as subaltern, something different happens when listening to how one's identity gets pinned to estrangement: this has to do with not recognizing oneself in the discourses of otherness, of not living one's life as a stereotype, and of having to uncouple oneself from the regulations of stereotypes as the only condition of talk. Can pedagogy unleash new terms, new subject positions that move beyond voyeurism, social realism, spectatorship, and the metaphysics of presence, and onto ones that take into account the historicity—as opposed to the psychology—of social difference?

III

If, as suggested early on, the only condition of community is difference, which forms of sociality are allowed (and which prohibited) when difference is, however contradictorily, imagined? Consider how two different stories of ignorance are produced when pedagogy stalls within the humanistic faith that representation can deliver what it promises: unmediated access to the real. And consider how everyone involved gets caught "in the margin[s] between claims of truth and claims of textuality" (Delaney, 1991, p. 28). The first instance is drawn from the work of Cindy Patton. Patton (1990) analyses how U.S. governmental discourses of information both construct and exhaust subjects. The specific crisis of education Patton addresses is how AIDS education becomes organized when there is no direct relation between acquiring the facts about viral transmission and fashioning safer sex practices.

Patton examines how purportedly inclusive governmental campaigns of information as a discourse actually work to produce the basis of exclusion, discrimination, and social policing. The addressee of these 'facts' are actually two: the 'general public,' who might get the virus, and 'risky communities' who spread the virus. She argues that the general public is positioned as having *the right to know*, whereas communities placed at risk have the *obligation to know* not to spread the virus and to confess their relation to HIV. Precisely because such discourse claims are tied to varying contexts of self-knowledge, or identity, all that can be produced are identities that are either suspected or innocent. The limits of this campaign stall in the argument over the right to know as opposed to universalizing of safer practices of the body. The general public is thus constructed as composed of innocent bystanders who, with facts in hand, might be able to protect themselves, and this officially inclusive discourse, in and of itself, is anti-discriminatory: if safety can be constituted as if outside the epidemic, then there is nothing to fear. Thus, with nothing to fear, the general public has no 'reason' to discriminate and is safely positioned within the realm of rationality.

This dynamic of subjection becomes even more elaborate in the recent AIDS information discourses of 'No One Is Safe.' While ostensibly producing inclusivity, at the level of social effects, new forms of exclusivity are being performed. In Cindy Patton's (1990) words: "Far from breaking down the sharp dichotomy between 'risk groups' and the 'general public,' the rhetoric of 'no one is safe' produced a policing of identity borders as well as community borders: 'no one is safe' because you can't tell who is queer" (p. 101).

The No One Is Safe campaign supposes queerness as the social virus and heteronormativity as being at risk, in that heteronormativity can become a site of misrecognition, however vehemently it is performed. What can happen to anyone is that anyone can be queer. Two kinds of social policing, then, are provoked: (1) the normal must suspect both the self and the other; and (2) in a queer turn, one might consider that far from being an originary state, the normal, too, requires a pedagogy. In such a campaign Foucault's doubled subject is alive and anxious: to be normal is to be tied to self-knowledge and subject to dependence upon others for recognition. But while, as Patton suggests, the No One Is Safe campaign works to set in motion a policing of identity borders, something anxious is also produced in that the campaign unleashed, in part, the unthinkable: no place of safety, no stable comparisons, and the struggle with the fear of being mistaken, of not knowing or being known. Sometimes something queer happens when the categories of US/THEM scramble for articulation even as they are disrupted.

But the disruption of identity, in its anxious attempts to coalesce, can take a different form. In the second story of the passion for ignorance, even when identities are asserted, however one imagines their emancipatory possibilities there is no guarantee that representation can instantiate its desires to know and be known. Eve Sedgwick (1992) describes the flip side of No One Is Safe as it is lived in education. In this case a graduate seminar composed of men and women attempt to read gay and lesbian literature. Sedgwick reports her own discomfort in the course: originally, she and the women of the seminar situated the discomfort "to some obliquity in the classroom relations between [women] and the men. But by the end of the semester it seemed clear that we were in the grip of some much more intimate dissonance" (p. 61). And this had to do with the differences between and within women. In discussing gay and lesbian literature, readers—from whatever position—were confronted with their own self-knowledge. They were, at the same time, subjected to someone else's control even while they scrambled to become tied down to their own identity. In Sedgwick's words:

> Through a process that began, but *only* began, with the perception of some differences among our mostly explicitly, often somewhat uncrystallized sexual self-definition, it appeared that each woman in the class possessed (or might, rather, feel we were possessed by) an ability to make one or more of the other women radically doubt the authority of her own self-definition as a woman; as a feminist; as a positional subject of a particular sexuality. (Ibid.)

Here, the problem is not that no one was safe, because in this case one could tell who was queer. Rather, telling queerness in the context of identity politics seemed to set up new forms of authority and new hierarchies of knowledge and identity that called into question old forms of authority, namely categories such as woman, feminist, and sex. At the same time newly inverted forms of US and THEM emerged from reading gay and lesbian texts, and consequently the boundaries of the inside and the outside were maintained. These positions were neither implicitly pedagogical nor emancipatory in that, in this case, identification remained tied to self-knowledge, to identity. Evidently, and perhaps in spite of the curriculum, gay and lesbian literature was read as a special event—perhaps a vicarious means to learn something about the other, perhaps a vicarious means for 'others' to affirm their otherness and berate those who are imagined as the same. So even when the course material has gestured to difference, there still remains the question of how difference is to be read and ethically engaged. The 'facts' of gay and lesbian literature were not telling, and acquiring the 'facts' was a problem for all involved. No one is safe, not just because anyone can be called queer but because something queer can happen to anyone when one attempts to fix and unfix identity.

As Sedgwick reminds us, this 'intimate dissonance' should not be read as a social effect of bad pedagogy but rather as the beginning of pedagogy. If hierarchies must first be inverted, rendered as already estranged, in order to draw attention to themselves, this first move is a tricky beginning. Any inversion, after all, is what should provoke pedagogy to do something more: to engage its own impertinence and imagine what it might mean to be a social subject in a place called the classroom. But if pedagogy is to do something more with inverted hierarchies, it must not fall into the cul-de-sac of merely reversing the place of expertise, shutting down identifications with epistemological privilege, and providing a stage for what Foucault calls the 'speaker's benefit,' or the pleasure that is made from fleeing power (Agamben, 1993, p. 189). Instead, pedagogy might consider the problem of engaging its own alterity, of staying in that space of difference described by Samuel Delany as within 'the margin[s] between claims of truth and the claims of textuality.' Within these margins everybody might begin to consider the fact that representations and the identities they assume to serve, however emancipatory, cannot provide access to an unmediated real, or even invoke, in and of themselves, thought that can think against itself.

Now Patton's reading of governmental AIDS information discourses shows how the normal subject-presumed-to-know and the deviant subject-obligated-to-confess are both discursively produced. Both positions require boundary policing, although such policing does not work in the same way, and each demands different degrees of subjection. But these networks of power—discursively lived at the level of bodies and disciplined by normative educational practices—depend upon an insistence of stable and hence predictable identities that can then be contained. This, of course, is the authorship of normalization. Then we have Sedgwick's description of her seminar, where differences within, say, the category 'woman' disrupt the impossible promise of sameness, the promise of a community whose very basis depends upon subjects who presume but cannot know the same. In Sedgwick's seminar the identity hierarchy is upset, although epistemological privilege is still dependent upon the fashioning of bodies into stable identities whose knowledge is thought to spring from an unambivalent identity. In both instances, then, although in different ways, identity disciplines bodies and cannot articulate its own identificatory structures. The cost of 'difference' is thus the very acknowledgment necessary for political practices, for what Giorgio Agamben (1993) names as "the idea of an inessential commonality, a solidarity that in no way concerns an essence" (cited in Felman, 1987, p. 23).

The two examples, however singular, point out two divergent directions provoked by the same problem: namely, the social effects of identity when identity claims take on an aura of verisimilitude and hence are taken as if they can exist outside of the very historicity that provokes such claims, and their attendant feelings in the first place. What is left unthought, then, is the very reading practices that structure intelligibility and that make identity possible even as these practices perform impossible identities. If a pedagogical project is to move beyond the repetition of identity and the only two subject positions allowed when identity is understood as one of the self versus others, then pedagogy itself must become a problem of reading practices, a problem of social relations, and a problem of the means to refuse to think straight.

IV

Shoshana Felman's (1987) exploration of the pedagogical practices of Lacan's return to (and rereading of) Freud offers a way to rethink reading practices beyond the impulse to instantiate identity as the repetition of sameness. Her concern is psychoanalytic: to consider techniques of thinking 'beyond one's means,' to consider the possibility of exceeding the self by becoming interested in questioning the impulse to normalize. Felman notes three analytic practices of critical interpretation: those having to do with alterity; those having to do with dialogue; and those having to do with theory. Taken together, these three techniques may allow one to create new strategies for reading. While I will briefly outline Felman's practices, they will be elaborated by rereading some of the issues raised earlier by Patton and by Sedgwick.

Reading for alterity begins with acknowledgment of difference as the precondition for the self. One begins not by constructing resemblances with another, but the reading necessarily passes through the other, and in the other reads not identity (other or same) but difference and self difference (Ibid., 24). Reading as an interpretive performance, then, may become an imagined means to untie self knowledge from itself if the self can be encountered as split between recognition and misrecognition. In this way no category is sufficient, final, or total, and no category can be mastered or known as sheer positivity.

A second reading practice is provoked in dialogue. Here Felman borrows Freud's recognition of dialogue as a 'structuring condition of possibility.' To read is automatically to construct a dialogic relation with a self and with a text to allow for something more. But in making such a dialogue the reader is asked to consider what she or he wants from the text. Both the text and a self perform differential replies, perhaps in the form of a question, perhaps an argument, perhaps a misunderstanding. Reading thus begins with a supposition of difference, division, and negotiation. When reading practices are privileged over the intentions of the author or reader, the concern becomes one of thinking through the structures of textuality as opposed to the attributes of biography. This makes possible the disruption of the interpreter/interpreted hierarchy. And so the insistence of such a dialogue is implication not application.

Finally, as a practice, reading provokes a theory of reading, not just a reworking of meaning. How one reads matters. In Felman's words, "There is a constitutive belatedness of the theory over the practice, the theory always trying to catch up with what it was that the practice or the reading, was really doing" (1987, p. 60). Such belatedness, where the recognition of how one reads in terms of what one wants drags behind the investment in the immediacy of gathering meanings, marks uncertainty as a condition of possibility. And in the marking of one's theory of reading one can then begin to study where one's reading breaks down. What might become a problem is the study of one's own theoretical limits.

How, then, does one get to a place where identity is not the primal scene of reading as a repetition but instead a discursive practice, a practice of the self that can exceed the self? In considering the reading practices of Lacan, Felman sketches what she terms 'a new mode of reflexivity' (Haver, 1993). She argues that for interpretations to be critical and hence exceed the impulse to normalize and contain meaning, reading must begin with an acknowledgment of difference within identity and not reduce interpretation to a confirmation or negation of identity. This is a question of reading as alterity through the consideration of the fault lines of identity. The exploration becomes one of analysis of the signifier, not the signified, and hence an analysis of where meaning breaks down for the reader. The problem is to think of reading practices as a means for disrupting inside/outside hierarchies—beginning with a self that reads as a means to exceed that very self. And within such excess one might consider the belatedness of theory. In this way Felman suggests how one might begin to depart from the self in order to think the self as always already divided from itself, as embodying difference and division.

If the problem were posed as how subjection is made from any body and what makes normalcy thinkable in education, then the information campaigns of AIDS education that Patton describes and the hierarchy of identities that Sedgwick worries about might be encountered or produced differently. There might be a decision on the part of those positioned as outside the AIDS pandemic to refuse the proffered grounds of innocence and rationality and hence refuse to identify with the general pubic. What might become suspect are the categorical imperatives and attendant inequalities produced with this campaign. Then, no one is safe from the governmental campaigns. As for Sedgwick's seminar, where the grounds of identity are still confined to mastery and certitude, there might be a decision to refuse these very grounds. Reading might then be one of theorizing reading as always about risking the self, about confronting one's own theory of reading, and about engaging one's own alterity and desire. Then, thinking itself, in classroom spaces, might take the risk of refusing to secure thought and of exposing the danger in the curious insistence on positing foundational claims at all costs (Benjamin, 1995, p. 47). Then no one is safe because the very construct of safety places at risk difference as uncertainty, as indeterminacy, as incompatibility. The problem, then, becomes one of working through ethical relations.

As Felman suggests, if reading practices could begin to read the real as constructed, as necessarily mediated by a self that is always already divided from itself, identity might be encountered as 'never identical to itself,' and hence located, however partially and provincially, in that queer space between what is taken as real and the afterthought of (mis)recognition. Thus a queer pedagogy is not concerned with getting identities right or even having them represented as an end in themselves. The point is to read—in radical ways—the insufficiencies of identity as positivity and to examine and to refuse 'cases of exorbitant normality,' whether such cases take the form of heteronormativity, racisms, gender centrings, ability hierarchies, and so on. And thus one might read identity as a political relation, whether that reading concerns the reader or the read.

These insights into reading practices are impertinent because they begin with an insistence on alterity, the irrevocability of difference within identity, which is to say that unthought of the thought of identity. As a pedagogical practice, reading becomes a practice of constituting the criteria that make the self and that make another both intelligible and unintelligible, an occasion for thought to think against itself. At the same time, reading practices need to be understood as constituting the dialogic, thus requiring something more than the self in order to think the self differently. And because reading practices also produce a theory of reading practices, the act of reading might become more complicated. It might return the subject to the problem of one's own subjection, rethinking the way that self-knowledge becomes, as Foucault explains it, being subject to someone else's control.

V

Now, much of my argument is predicated upon the belief that to recognize difference outside the imperatives of normalcy—that is, beyond the need to render difference through the lens of the same, either through discourses of feelings or discourses of information—requires attention to how one's reading practices as historically, socially, and psychically configured produce particular conceptual needs. My thinking has been influenced by queer theories that mark as a site of subjection the production and valorization of normalcy and by the psychoanalytic attention to the split and desirous subject. Whether cases of exorbitant normality take big forms such as various racisms, heteronormativities, nationalisms, ethnocentricities, Eurocentrism, and colonization or take little forms such as empathy, tolerance, self-esteem, safety, and so on, these cases should become a central problem of educational thought and practice, a central problem of pedagogy. And I raise these dynamics as a question of reading practices, because at the level of the everyday, structures of intelligibility are sustained not only by hegemonic and punishing chains of signification but also, just as significantly, in the way education closes down how the everyday might be imagined and lived, and hence how one becomes a social subject in a place called the classroom.

If reading practices partially structure one's capacity to do something more, to become something otherwise, is there a way for pedagogy to rethink how reading practices are practiced and educated in classroom sites? Are there ways of thinking about proliferating one's identificatory possibilities so that the interest becomes one of theorizing why reading is always about risking oneself, of confronting one's own theory of reading, of signification, and of difference, and of refusing to be the same? What if 'difference' made a difference in how the self encountered the self and in how one encounters one?

In my work on pedagogy, what I want to call my queer pedagogy, I am attempting to exceed such binary oppositions as the tolerant and the tolerated and the oppressed and the oppressor, yet still hold onto an analysis of social difference that can account for how dynamics of subordination and subjection work at the level of the historical, the structural, the epistemological, the conceptual, the social, and the psychic. But such an interest is also one of thinking through an implication that can tolerate a curiosity about one's own otherness, one's own unconscious desires and wishes, one's own negations. My interest is in provoking conditions that might allow for an exploration of unsettling the sediments of what one imagines when one imagines normalcy, what one imagines when one images differences. So I wonder whether identity categories will be helpful in this work if identity depends upon the production of sameness and otherness, dynamics that anchor modes of subjection. And I am thinking that maybe, given the desire for knowledge of difference to make a difference in how social subjects conduct themselves and in how sociality might be imagined and lived, the new questions that must be addressed concern what education, knowledge, identity, and desire have to do with the fashioning of structures of intelligibility and unintelligibility; with what education has to do with the possibilities of proliferating identifications and critiques that exceed identity, yet still hold onto the understanding of identity as a state of emergency. This I take as the beginnings of a queer pedagogy, one that refuses normal practices and practices of normalcy, one that begins with an ethical concern for one's *own* reading practices and what these have to do with the imagining of sociality as more than an effect of the dominant conceptual order. In the queer pedagogy I am attempting, 'the inessentially common' is built from the possibility that reading the world is always already about risking the self, about attempting, on the one hand, to exceed cases of exorbitant normality, and on the other, developing an interest in confounding instituted law.

Notes

1. McLaren's study of the eugenics movement in Canada details the historical shift from defining and containing 'deviancy' to the movement leaders' preoccupation with the fashioning of normalcy through such progressive measures as the introduction of school nursing, hygiene, sex education, and pedagogies directed at white racial improvement. From a different vantage point Foucault's first volume on sexuality traces this shift, whereby constituting normalcy becomes the central strategy of knowledge/power/pleasure.

2. The notion of 'the-subject-presumed-to-know' and 'a passion for ignorance' is discussed in the work of Jacques Lacan. The subject-presumed-to-know desires an omnipotent knowledge. Paradoxically, such a subject is propped up by a passion for ignorance. Lacan theorizes ignorance as a residue of knowledge, not its constitutive outside. Statements of dismissal and dis-implication, such as 'I don't want to know about it' or 'That has nothing to do with me,' support the work of ignorance.

3. See, for example: Felman (1987), Silin (1995), and Sedgwick (1990).

4. The cost of narrating identities is not, in queer theory, a problem of getting identities right. Rather, there is a

significant moment in queer theory that agonizes the conceptualization of identity: how it 'works' as history, how it is narrated as synecdoche, or as a part capable of standing in for the whole, and how its exclusions permit its categorical claims. (See, for example, Sedgwick, 1990.) This mode of questioning owes much to the work of Michel Foucault.

5. The claim of 'perversity' as a marker of identification is quite contradictory in queer theories. Foundationally, the claim draws from the Freudian notion of all sexuality as perverse, as in polymorphous perversity (see Laplanche, 1990). But two kinds of claims about perversity are made in queer theories. On the one hand, perversity works as a means to dispute dominant chains of signification or what D.A. Miller (1992) calls 'not a name but the continual elision of one [that disrupts] a system of connotation' (pp. 24–25). On the other hand, Eve Sedgwick (1992) and Mandy Merck (1993) take up perverse reading practices meant to disassemble the temples of gay and lesbian mythology. Both challenge the essentialist feminist and lesbian claims of identification as issuing from identity. For a debate on the question of whether claims of perversity are political claims, see 'Perversity,' *New Formations: A Journal of Culture/Theory/Politics, 19* (Spring 1993).

6. My use of the term *everyday* has been influenced by the work of Gary Wickham and William Haver (1992). Specifically, I am trying to theorize along with their insight that 'violence against queers is installed not merely in a legal apparatus, but in "daily life" itself, as well as in the objectification, thematization, and valorization of everydayness (as in "family values," for example)' (p. 5). Essentially, such a formulation opens the question of how it becomes conceivable for some folks to have an everyday while other folks become either a special event or a disruption of the everyday.

7. The concept of negation, according to Freud, is a means by which the individual can acknowledge an idea while disclaiming its emotional value or its structuring principle. In Freud's words: 'Negation is a way of taking cognizance of what it repressed; indeed it is already a lifting of the repression, though not, of course, an acceptance of what is repressed. We can see how in this the intellectual function is separated from the affective process' (SE, Vol. 19, pp. 235–239). The recognition of repression does not guarantee a removal of repression. Thus one can happily claim normalcy without considering its affective costs.

8. The paradoxical phrasing—the education of education—is meant to signal education not as if it were simply an originary network of institutions, policies, learning theories, curricular moves, and a social network of subjects. Rather, such a phrasing approaches education as an effect of knowledge/power/pleasure, and thus as caught in larger historical apparatuses to which education responds.

9. Sedgwick (1992).

10. In Joan Copjec's (1989) terms, happiness is both objective and subjective. She clarifies Freud's views of empathy with the following observation: 'If we cannot judge immediately what measure of pain or pleasure belonged to an historical individual, this is not because happiness is subjectivity and we cannot project ourselves into her private mental sphere, but rather because we cannot so easily project ourselves into her objective *social* sphere in order to disarm the categories of thought that constructed her expectations, narcotized her against disappointment, made her obtuse to her own suffering' (p. 228).

11. I find the term *heteronormativity* more interesting than the familiar and often misused *homophobia* because debates about gay and lesbian oppression and desire must move beyond the humanist psychological discourse of individual fear of homosexuality as contagion (and not, coincidentally, the centring of heterosexuality as the normal). The term homophobia rarely ventures into political critiques of how normalcy becomes produced and sexualized as heterosexuality. That is, how sex becomes inserted into normalcy and how normalcy becomes inserted into sex is not an area accessible to the naming of homophobia because the term is centrally given over to the correction of individuated attitude. The term heteronormativity begins to get at how the production of deviancy is intimately tied to the very possibility of normalcy. That is, normalcy can only be intelligible through the construction of its other: the deviant. In such a relation, normalcy must always make itself normal, must always normalize itself. Recent writing in queer theory suggests the problem is not fear of queerness but obsession with normalizing and containing queerness, and, not coincidently, otherness. The odd story is that such mechanisms in actuality, are, about the production of normalcy. (See, for example: Butler (1993); Dollimore (1991); Fuss (1991); Sedgwick (1990); and Warner (1993, "Introduction.")

12. Britzman, 'The Ordeal of Knowledge'; and Patton, *Inventing AIDS*.

13. Cindy Patton's groundbreaking study traces how discourses of information produce the grounds of estrangement in that one might 'know' the facts but not how to relate 'facts' as relevant to the self. In Patton's words: 'Several studies suggest that teenagers and young adults believe that other people acquire HIV infection or develop AIDS through specific and known sets of acts while they perceive their *own* susceptibility to HIV or AIDS to be a matter of chance' (Patton, 1990, p. 109).

References

Agamben, G. (1993). *The coming community* (Michael Hardt, Trans.). Minneapolis: University of Minnesota Press.

Benjamin, J. (1995). *Like subjects, love objects: Essays on recognition and sexual difference.* New Haven, CT: Yale University Press.

Borch-Jacobsen, M. (1982). *The Freudian subject* (Catherine Porter, Trans.). Stanford, CA: Stanford University Press.

Britzman, D.P. (1993). The ordeal of knowledge: Rethinking the possibilities of multicultural education. *The Review of Education, 15,* 123–135.

Butler, J. (1991). Imitation and gender insubordination. In D. Fuss (Ed.), *Inside/out: Lesbian theories, gay theories* (pp. 13–31). New York: Routledge.

Butler, J. (1992). Sexual inversions. In D. Stanton (Ed.), *Discourses of sexuality: From Aristotle to AIDS* (pp. 344–361). Ann Arbor: University of Michigan Press.

Butler, J. (1993). *Bodies that matter: On the discursive limits of 'sex.'* New York: Routledge.

Copjec, J. (1989). Cutting up. In T. Brennan (Ed.), *Between feminism and psychoanalysis* (pp. 227–246). New York: Routledge.

Crimp, D. (1992). Hey, girlfriend! *Social Text, 33,* 2–18.

Delaney, S. (1991). Street talk/straight talk. *Differences: A Journal of Feminist Cultural Studies, 5*(2), 21–38.

Dollimore, J. (1991). *Sexual dissidence: Augustine to Wilde, Freud to Foucault.* Oxford: Oxford University Press.

Duttman, A.G. (1993). What will have been said about AIDS: Some remarks in disorder. *Public, 7,* 95–115.

Edelman, L. (1994). *Homographesis: Essays in gay literary and cultural theory.* New York: Routledge.

Felman, S. (1987). *Jacques Lacan and the adventure of insight: Psychoanalysis in contemporary culture.* Cambridge, MA: Harvard University Press.

Foucault, M. (1990). *History of sexuality* (Vol. I). New York: Vintage Books.

Freud, S. (1925). Negation. In *The complete psychological works of Sigmund Freud* (James Strachey, Trans.; Vol. 19 [1923–1975], pp. 235–239). London: Hogarth Press.

Freud, S. (1975). *Civilization and its discontents* (Joan Riviere, Trans.; Standard ed., 21). London: Hogarth Press. (Original work published 1930)

Fuss, D. (Ed.). (1991). *Inside/out: Lesbian theories, gay theories.* New York and London: Routledge.

Fuss, D. (1995). *Identification papers.* New York: Routledge.

Goldberg, D.T. (1993). *Racist culture: Philosophy and the politics of meaning.* Oxford: Blackwell Publishers.

Golding, S. (1993). Sexual manners. *Public, 8,* 161–168.

Haver, W. (1993). Thinking the thought of that which is strictly speaking unthinkable: On the thematization of alterity in Nishida-Philosophy. *Human Studies, 16,* 177–192.

Laplanche, J. (1990). *Life and death in psychoanalysis* (Jeffery Mehlman, Trans.). Baltimore: The Johns Hopkins University Press.

Lauretis, T. de. (1991). Queer theory: Lesbian and gay sexualities, an introduction. *Differences, 3*(2), iii–xviii.

McLaren, A. (1990). *Our own master race: Eugenics in Canada, 1885–1945.* Toronto: McClelland and Stewart.

Merck, M. (1993). *Perversions: Deviant readings.* London: Verso.

Miller, D.A. (1992). *Bringing out Roland Barthes.* Berkeley: University of California Press.

Patton, C. (1990). *Inventing AIDS.* New York: Routledge.

Phelan, P. (1993). *Unmarked: The politics of performance.* London: Routledge.

Sedgwick, E. (1990). *Epistemology of the closet.* Berkeley and Los Angeles: University of California Press.

Sedgwick, E. (1992). White glasses. *Yale Journal of Criticism, 53*(3), 193–208.

Silin, J. (1995). *Sex, death and the education of children: Our passion for ignorance in the age of AIDS.* New York: Teachers College Press.

Spivak, G.C. (1992). Acting bits/identity talk. *Critical Inquiry, 18*(4), 770–803.

Warner, M. (1993). Introduction. In M. Warner (Ed.), *Fear of a queer planet* (pp. vii–xxxi). Minneapolis: University of Minnesota Press.

Wickham, G., & Haver, W. (1992). Come out, come out wherever you are: A guide for the homoerotically disadvantaged. Unpublished paper.

CHAPTER TWENTY-EIGHT

Making the AIDS Ghostwriters Visible

FRANCISCO IBÁÑEZ-CARRASCO

When I talk about AIDS with graduate students and emerging health researchers in the context of my work with the Universities Without Walls training program for emerging Canadian HIV researchers, I find that they draw on a remarkable amount of scientific information about HIV/AIDS. Digital databases give researchers nearly unfettered access to a wealth of knowledge, and the sheer volume of evidence seems to validate our research—it makes it authoritative. Depending on their home disciplines, students can speak authoritatively about the function of the foreskin in the transmission of HIV, the lack of access to HIV-related medical and social services, the pros and cons of dispensing HIV antiretrovirals as prevention, the criminalization of nondisclosure of HIV, and other topics that represent the complexity of AIDS today. AIDS researchers, educators, and students focus on behaviors (e.g., smoking and living with HIV) and populations (e.g., immigrants from sub-Saharan Africa or urban white gay men). However, the difficulty for researchers of *placing ourselves in this data* is beginning to be recognized in qualitative research (Mantzoukas, 2004; Abma, 2002). How does the researcher's autobiography and subjectivity shape her or his understanding of "unhealthy" sexual behaviors, attitudes, and norms?

In North America, we seem to have progressed seamlessly from health crisis and vociferous AIDS activism to the normalization of HIV as a chronic illness—from public elation to apathy. For people living with HIV (PHAs), particularly gay men in industrialized countries, the stigma of being gay and having brought HIV upon oneself has been rationally dismantled but is still lodged in our collective psyche. The epidemiological picture does not lie: gay men are still engaging in unprotected HIV-transmitting sex and are overrepresented in seroconversion and seroprevalence cases. Age-based trends in HIV transmission are characterizing the epidemiological scenario in North America especially among 15- to 24-year-old youth and adults over 50 years old (UNAIDS, 2010). Overall, gay men continue to drive the epidemic in Canada (PHAC, 2009).

This situation presents an interesting tension for the field of HIV/AIDS research. On the one hand, the complex motivations of gay men living with HIV to engage in sex are obfuscated by researchers and educators: they are too complex to explain. Queer lives and sexual practices may seem to have been liberated in the media, but these practices continue to be awkward for science. On the other hand, some behaviors are studied piecemeal (e.g., how gay men find sex on the Internet, how we use drugs, etc.). However, it has been noted that more disagreeable practices such as "rectal douching" receive limited and often only clinical attention although they have considerable implications for research and sexual health education for young queers (Schilder et al., 2010).

In Canada I meet often with HIV researchers and educators (and here I refer to those who teach researchers), and we talk shop at conferences or in passing. We all seem quite sure of why we are there, doing what we do best: everyone is highly specialized in one aspect of the AIDS epidemic. (Who has time for the vagaries of reflecting upon the overall picture?) We tend to not ask ourselves the question, "What brings us to this research/educational work?" The asking seems distrustful and the answers seem obvious: scientific interest, compassion for women living with HIV in poor regions of the world (many of whom are coerced into the sex trade), the broken family lives and life in poverty suffered by a great number of injection drug users, or sheer altruism. Are the answers as obvious when we ask ourselves about specific groups that do not seem to want to be helped, even when they have reaped the benefits of AIDS exceptionalism in medical, social, and non-profit support services?

Thirty years into the AIDS epidemic, we must make evident the role that researchers and educators from many disciplines play in HIV research and education and consider how our research practices make visible or invisible the work that gay men do. I use the phrase "make visible" to highlight that, as sexual beings, gay men engage in a number of strategies to seek and find sex, and this is work that is often largely ignored as escapist and unproductive—isn't it like watching TV? I use the word "work" advisedly to include seeking and finding sex and integrating these tasks into one's psychological and social life. For gay men, sex is central to the daily work of constituting a complex subjectivity.

The challenge for emerging HIV/AIDS researchers in North America today is to design and implement research agendas and educational programs that both take into account these intricate and often marginalized stories of sexual practices and pay close attention to the research narrative devices utilized to relay those stories (whether qualitative or quantitative, audiovisual or written). This essay focuses on the ghostly place that gay men occupy in social scientific and epidemiological health research and in education. In particular, it focuses on an emerging sexual microculture, that of sex pigs, and how they can make significant aspects of the fourth generation of persons living with HIV visible, including the extent of our complicity in these research accounts and processes. What can be learned from sex pigs? What is manifest in their narratives and nascent folklore? How can sex pigs, and by extension gay men and other stigmatized target groups, be centered and involved in our research and educational efforts? What will we make of the disjuncture between, on the one hand, activism, research, policy, and education and, on the other hand, the often-unsafe behaviors of HIV-positive activists, researchers? In what follows, I offer a preliminary framework for thinking about the opportunity that HIV-positive "sex pigs" and their "pig sex" present for inquiry into the growing in/visibility of gay men in participatory HIV/AIDS research. In the latter half of the paper, I argue that autobiographical self-inquiry and values clarification are necessary points of departure for a new generation of "community engaged scholars."

Who Are the Sex Pigs and Why Should We Care?

Sex pigs are identified as men who practice adventurous sex (fisting, group sex, drugs). A useful definition of the sex pig can be found in Stacey's (2005) research study of the cliché "men are pigs." According to Stacey, "gay men operate in a male sexual economy that grants them greater license to pursue animalistic passions, they subject one another to heightened levels of the tyranny (as well as the titillating and serendipitous pleasures) of the male gaze" (p. 1926). In my view, HIV/AIDS researchers have much to learn from sex pigs, and from our academic ways of positioning sex pigs, and gay men in general, as vectors of the HIV epidemic, while also making them invisible in one extraordinary *trompe-l'œil*. Instead of dragging sex pigs out to be re-victimized, I purposely resensationalize "sex pigs," and the spectacle of "pig sex," because a great deal of our collective queer indigenous sexual knowledge is decanted in the figure of the sex pig: these men are lightning rods for emotionality, excess, exhilaration, envy, and scorn. These complex perceptions of sex pigs come not just from the outside, but also from the inside, of queer communities. In this respect, "pig sex" is an incubator of research questions, an awesome place for taking theoretical risks and experimenting with ideas as vectors of intellectual infection.

Why this interest in sex pigs in the context of education and research? Why focus our research efforts around what is seen by many people as the worst of gay men's behavior? Sex pigs are an important subject of HIV/AIDS research because they represent an integrative repository of the collective memory of gay men (Connerton, 1989). Moreover, sex pigs are sexual "connectors" in an environment where the objectification of gay men is encouraged, promoted, and socially sanctioned, albeit in ambivalent terms. Our careful examination of the intricate practices of sex pigs' sexual networking, and of *how we examine those practices,* has the potential to shape progressive participatory educational research, to instigate a new generation of "community engaged scholars" (Calleson, Jordan, & Seifer, 2005). One could say that "community engaged sluts" preceded community-engaged scholars. Finally, as a complex psycho-socio-sexual phenomenon, pig sex presents abundant opportunities for researchers and educators to reflect upon our methodological and analytical choices.

In the current academic literature on HIV/AIDS, pig sex is barely emerging as a discernible unit of analysis. One has to read in between the lines of systematic reviews of health promotion or HIV prevention interventions for men who have sex with men (MSM) to put together a composite of sex pigs and their actions and motivations. Gleaned from current peer-reviewed literature and anecdotally from my work with frontline prevention/harm reduction workers, I have culled some of the most noticeable characteristics of pig sex. These include an intense and experimental use of illicit drugs and medications to prolong sexual pleasure and reduce sexual inhibitions (Colfax et al., 2010); an eroticization of body cavities (e.g., fisting), fluids (e.g., feltching, pissing), and disfigurement due to lipoatrophy (a form of teratophilia); the use of fantasies of rape, incest, and breeding/insemination as an answer to the enigma of Others' desire (Lacan, 2002); the absence of bodily and symbolic phallic erection resulting from use of hard drugs that fragments sex pigs into body parts, "crystal dicks" (i.e., lack of erection resulting from PnP/party and play, slamming, booty bumps, etc.), and desiring anuses (Dowsett et al., 2008); and the avid use of social media (Graydon, 2007; Grov, 2004). Pig sex, although physical, is not always anchored to a tangible space or a physical body, and in this voyeuristic/exhibitionistic way it is spectacular and ghostly. In an increasingly medicalized society where one has telescopic access to the inner recesses of one's body, its intimate motions, and most esoteric counts (e.g., CD4s, viral loads, etc.), it is not surprising that individuals feel entitled and eager to become intimate with their own bodies even when the final effect can be quite dissociative.

A great deal of the peer-reviewed evidence about gay men who practice unprotected anal intercourse reports a crushing diagnosis of deficits and ailments and mental health illness (e.g., stress, anxiety, and depression), chronic sorrow (Grov et al., 2010; Welles et al., 2009; Kelly et al., 2009; Rees et al., 2004; Stall et al., 2003; Lichtenstein, Laska, & Clair, 2002; Semple et al., 2002), loss of libido or sexual dysfunction for fear of infecting others (Shapiro & Ray, 2007), loss of self-image due to lipoatrophy (Persson, 2005), increased stigmatization (Kavouni et al., 2008; Persson, 2005), coercion (Gavey et al., 2009), fear of aging, and increased risk of coinfection with hepatitis C (Klein et al., 2009). The responses to this catastrophic scenario are often catalogued individually as either adaptive (coping, seeking social support) or maladaptive, such as the abuse of drugs and alcohol, and social isolation (Moskowitz et al., 2009). At the public health and community organizational level and in spite of generalized adherence to safer sex in North America enhanced by the decrease in infectiousness of sexually active HIV-positive gay men due to adherence to antiretroviral treatment, sex pigs are *individually* seen as impervious to HIV prevention. Only sociologists, cultural studies academics, and others in the humanities seem interested in finding positive truths about gay men's status as risk takers, for example the integrative, celebratory, and resisting function of promiscuity, limit experience, bareback sex, and pig sex (Dowsett et al., 2008; Holmes, O'Byrne, & Gastaldo, 2006; Stacey, 2004). All in all, the clinical/epidemiological/individual psychological/public health views and the symbolic/behaviorist/human agency/collective psychology research approaches do not often meet.

Pig sex is too intricate to be explained by mono-disciplinarian studies. Most evidence on sexual radicals is gleaned from clinical, epidemiological, and social scientific studies of specific factors without any attempt to generate integrative theories of gay men's behavior that explain a "gay male subjectivity" (Halperin, 2007; Champagne, 1995). There is a need to reinsert the researcher/educator, her lived experience, biography, values, and motivations into the research/educational project in order to produce integrative theory on sexual radicals.

How do we begin to theorize the ghostly presence of sex pigs in HIV/AIDS research? Sex pigs are a nascent sexual microculture that possesses attributes of many other social groups with radical behaviors (e.g., drug users, fetishists, barebackers). The locations of pig sex and the motivations of sex pigs are nomadic. It might be a subculture in gestation as leatherfolk or skinheads were in the 1990s (Bell et al., 1994). At its clearest, pig sex is a more or less identifiable series of tactical actions in virtual or physical locations. Sex pigs are at times more like a micro sexual flash mob than an organized culture that is externally discernible to others or even internally discernable to the sex pigs themselves. It is said that HIV transmission moves in episodic bursts among particular groups in at-risk populations (Brenner et al., 2008; Fisher et al., 2009). Sex pigs are a subset of individuals with recalcitrant risk-taking behaviors. I speculate that a generation from now this psycho-socio-sexual phenomenon will not be extraordinary, as the use of drugs, virtual sex, and spectacular risk-taking sex is becoming commonplace. Our mission as researchers/educators must not only be to follow trends but also to be prophetic.

This preliminary attempt to sketch the ghostly contours of the sex pig is both theoretical and autobiographical. My research is based upon the previous work of my intellectual mentor, Dr. Suzanne de Castell; I have endeavored to extend her work on queer pedagogy (Bryson & Castell, 1997) to the field of HIV/AIDS research. Over the past ten years, I have also been engaged in community-based research and educational work with HIV-positive gay men. More recently, my research has been informed by my work with the HIV research training program for emerging Canadian HIV researchers, Universities Without Walls at the Ontario HIV Treatment Network (OHTN). Finally, my work in the field of HIV/AIDS research has been shaped by my experience as a person living with

HIV since 1985. This brief résumé enables me to declare my biases and conflicts. Without a declaration of my biography, personal and professional, and what it brings to the research partnership table, I make myself invisible.

Gay Men As Ghostwriters of HIV Research: MSM and GIPA

Social media has thrown gay men into a cynical vanity fair. We are lost in a mob of victims, petty heroes, or celebrities. We all have a reality show, a Facebook page, a tragic or heroic story to tell. We are living increasingly in a parallel reality of avatars and parasocial relations (Donald & Wohl, 1956; Ballantine & Martin, 2005), falling in love with or hating people we think we know intimately. We broadcast ourselves to death contentedly, constantly, and widely in a diasporic transnational Self. It is a reality TV show environment that, in its supernova of pixels, paradoxically enhances invisibility due to sheer saturation and overexposure. The charges leveled against this continuous self-memorializing are indiscretion, betrayal, and outright fraud. This state of affairs has an impact on health research and health education where the main staple of our work is the lived experience of people living with HIV/AIDS. This media spectacularity creates a sort of odd transparency of the Self in the research accounts.

Do you believe what others say about themselves, about their actions and motivations? In the confessional booth of our research instruments—surveys, focus groups, or interviews—do researchers believe the stories of the research subjects? By the same token, do research "subjects" trust what researchers report and what they/we say about them/selves? The standards of proof for the humanities and social sciences seem relative and inadequate. In particular the "evidence of experience" has been put into question, especially when it comes to homosexuality, a fact largely ignored by clinicians, epidemiologists, and public health researchers, who tend to take persons literally and at face value. This institutional gesture often demotes lived experience to a caption of quantitative results, statistics, and graphs. In her landmark essay "The Evidence of Experience," Joan Scott (1997) offers a lucid explanation of what our scientific gaze does to homosexuality as proof of a personhood:

> To put it another way, the evidence of experience, whether conceived through a metaphor of visibility or in any other way that takes meaning as transparent, reproduces rather than contests given ideological systems—those that assume that the facts of history speak for themselves and those that rest on notions of a natural or established opposition between, say, sexual practices and social conventions, or between homosexuality and heterosexuality. (p. 778)

In the material world, the actions, motivations, and emotions of an individual may be startlingly different across ever-shifting social locations, ever-changing opportunities, and constraints. A health-care patient or a public-health case can be a suit-and-tie real-estate agent, a citizen-consumer, and a devout husband to his husband, father to his children, and member of his religious group, and also come in and out of sexualized spaces such as bathhouses or websites. A number of eagerly used acronyms such as MSM and GIPA (Greater Involvement of Persons Living with AIDS) are erasing through shorthand the complex sexual lives of gay men and allowing researchers to abdicate their responsibility to explicate their research positions and theories.

The phrase "men who have sex with men" (MSM), used widely to explain all kinds of male-on-male sexual and emotional behavior, originated in epidemiology as a inoffensive shorthand to force "a conceptual shift in public health from identity-based to behaviorally based notions of sexuality"

(Young & Meyer, 2005, p. 1114). The acronym has not generated "more complex approaches to sexuality" (p. 1145) and is now being contested. Young and Meyer also point out that "by implication MSM and WSW [women who have sex with women] imply absence of community, social networks and relationships" and, most worrisomely, "with this usage, researchers ignore the important task of describing actual sexual behavior, even though this information has greater relevance for public health" (p. 1147). MSM also carries significant arguments regarding public rights, biopolitical identity, and exclusion (Martucci, 2010).

While sex pigs represent a ghostly presence in HIV/AIDS research, a second example of ghost-writing the research narrative is contained in another shorthand expression, that of the greater and meaningful involvement of persons living with AIDS (GIPA and MIPA). GIPA "represents a mobilizing and organizing principle" for inclusion (Morolake, Stephens, & Welbourn, 2009) that requires different conceptualizations and implementation by distinct groups of HIV-positive persons regionally (e.g., the North and South), across the social spectrum, and across sexual minorities. GIPA is being implemented with varying degrees of success due to its most common barriers: HIV-related stigma, health-related challenges, lack of research capacity, trust, and credentialism (Travers et al., 2008).

Paradoxically, MSM and GIPA are two ways in which researchers and educators make invisible the presence of sexual radicals in HIV in Canada today. Indeed, MSM and GIPA make invisible the researchers/educators' own location in the research; it goes without saying that queer researchers/educators are also made invisible in a "covering" gesture, a leftover institutional homophobia (Yoshino, 2006).

In passing, established researchers make invisible their judgments and abdicate any fiduciary responsibility to make judgments and stand by them. A potentially false sense of neutrality in research on/about queers trumps sincerity. In a cultural/media environment that seems to drift inevitably to transparency and where all information can be "leaked," it is to be expected that researchers and their motivations/autobiographies and professional careers enter the fray. Any principle of "greater involvement" as applied to research/education must begin by implicating all of the participants of these projects in autobiographical forms of inquiry. The challenge for researchers and educators is to locate ourselves with/in the research before trying to get the "other" involved and busy designing protocols and courses that still benefit mostly academic careers.

Research Essentials: A Sense of History

In order to understand stigma and discrimination and thus really integrate marginalized sexual groups in our research frameworks, the onus of disclosure in research and education must be shared by researchers, educators, policymakers, members of stakeholder groups, community members, and community leaders. In my view, two elements are central to the formation of the next generation of researchers, educators, students, and engaged research participants. First, emerging researchers need to understand the socio-cultural history of HIV and its place within the overall Western medical and political history of health. Second, researchers need to understand themselves within history. We must engage in self-memorializing forms of reflection on our attitudes, motivations, and movements in pursuing research, especially with highly stigmatized and seemingly less powerful individuals and groups as our research subjects. Only by understanding our history as participants of HIV research (either as academic researchers, community leaders, or mere research subjects) can we truly integrate the lived experience of PHAs into our research stories. This necessity extends to students as well as to a new lesbian, gay, bisexual, transgender, queer, intersex, and two-spirit generation, including sex pigs who do not necessarily know—or feel they need to know—about HIV politics and history.

Not all research is educational (or even provides reliable information to its population of interest), but more often than not, our research methods (i.e., questions arranged linearly in surveys or focus groups), reports, graphs, abstracts, funding grants, and conference presentations are historical. They tell a context-specific story. In research systematic reviews, researchers are expected to map out their search, "comprehensively identify all relevant studies to answer a particular question, and assess the validity (or 'soundness') of each study taking this into account when reaching conclusions" (Petticrew & Roberts, 2005), as well as make the reader aware of all the steps taken, limitations, and emerging categories. Why don't we do this as research/educator teams in HIV/health research? Our choices are often taken for granted or politely understood by our audiences, and our choices carry authority.

For example, we should keep in mind significant landmarks in the history of HIV in North America: Stonewall marks the beginning of a more or less discernible queer liberation project before the advent of HIV in the early 1980s. The universal dispensation of HIV medications and treatment in 1996 in Canada changed the disease from fatal to chronic and episodic. The advent of the Internet changed forever the way individuals relate to each other socially and sexually. In broad strokes, we have moved from an easing of social repression on sex, sexuality, and gender expression in the 1970s to further stigma, shame, denial, and slow public health response during the 1980s. This was followed by AIDS exceptionalism and the strengthening of AIDS service organizations in the 1990s, and the gradual dismantling of ASOs and the growing disconnect of gay men from ASOs (which has been flagged as a potential cofactor for weak networks that may put individuals at higher risk for HIV) (Trussler, 2008). These historical changes have combined with the rise of a sexual apartheid between HIV-positive and HIV-negative gay men—apartheid as powerful as the traditional code of silence of gay men—to result in the criminalization of HIV in Canada and the advent of two scenarios: the aging of PHAs and a silent epidemic of mental health. Where are you located in this timeline? And why does it matter?

Belly up to the Trough! Queer Directions in Interdisciplinary Research

In my pedagogical work with emerging HIV researchers I notice acute interest from students and colleagues in epidemiological accounts of types of sex that may or may not lead to transmission of HIV, hep C, STIs, or other medical harms, and a lack of interest in anthropological and sociological accounts of sexuality (collective and/or individual). Since I started my Master's studies in this field in 1989, I see a routine avoidance of theory and few accounts of how the personal in our research/education work shapes whatever little theory we produce.

Meanwhile, clinicians, epidemiologists, and even social scientists avoid all reflection on their positions with respect to the gay problem and refuse to speculate on it. Also, this political correctness permeates the education of emerging researchers, where students' disinterest in sexuality stems from a misunderstood politeness toward people living with HIV. It must also be pointed out that my colleagues in the field of HIV research are predominantly heterosexual women and men who have been socialized not to discuss the minutiae of gay men's sex and sexuality and emotionality except in clinical tones.

To redress this apprehension toward gay subjectivity, gay sex, and emotionality in our HIV accounts, I propose to reinvigorate memory-work and self-reflexivity among new and emerging HIV researchers. Why not turn the very community-based research techniques that we herald as progressive onto the autobiographical stories of researchers and educators? We might begin by asking ourselves: How did I get here? How was I socialized as a sexual body? How do I divest myself from that sexual body when I am acting as researcher? How do I acquire the privilege and authority to do what I do? And in my research and education, what constitutes solidarity with, complicity with, and betrayal of those people/individuals I study?

If emerging (and established) researchers want to have an impact on the lives of the people we study, shouldn't we also measure the impact that our research choices have on our team as well as on our research subjects/participants (i.e., the people we approach as coinvestigators, and those we exclude, the actual extent of our claim being that getting involved in community-based research empowers participants)? Memory-work, the feminist social constructionist method that "breaks down the barriers between the subject and object of research," includes "everyday experience as the basis of knowledge," and in which "the academic positions herself with the group and becomes a member of the research group . . . thus eliminating the hierarchy of 'experimenter' and 'subject'" (Onyx & Small, 2001, p. 775), is one of the possible pedagogical methodologies to make visible the imbricate relations between researchers and subjects: our motivations, our narrative devices, and our collective/individual development as apprentices in a "community of practice" (Lave & Wenger, 1991).

Indeed, the increasing requirement of knowledge translation and exchange (KTE) by social scientific research funding institutions (Armstrong et al., 2006) should not only be interpreted as disseminating research evidence efficiently throughout and at the end of a research project or as trying to turn every piece of evidence into hard policy changes but should also be interpreted as turning the gaze onto the researcher team, its inner workings, and its achieved degree of interdisciplinarity and self-reflection. Only by looking at ourselves as community-engaged scholars can we become transparent, sincere, and trustworthy to the communities we investigate. Only by looking at ourselves as embodied and situated ongoing learners can we accept that seemingly radical and diasporic clusters of individuals can amount to collective knowledge, skill, and experience—that they have something to teach us and they are not only sources of information. This shift in scientific gaze and positioning makes us reflect on how we learn about our subjects/participants.

In this writing I suggest that the emergence of radical sexual groups in the HIV/health research/education field behooves us to ask questions about how we include others, how we ask questions in research/education, and with what consequences. I suggested that looking at the most puzzling examples of gay male subjectivity should compel us to be intensely self-reflective (e.g., why do I look? what do I bring to my gaze?) and prophetic (e.g., what are groups such as sex pigs signaling about the future of HIV/AIDS research?).

Researchers implicitly or explicitly embed overarching questions in our research. For example, how do licentious sex pigs go about practicing sexual promiscuity? How do they find and identify each other? And what are the causes and consequences of their kinship? As researchers, we should also ask ourselves (ideally prior to going out to investigate others) questions such as:

- How do we find each other or invite each other to research partnerships?
- What constitutes our affinity when we agree on the specific practices or attitudes we want to study? Is it professional opportunism, mere politeness, altruism, or a combination of many motives and strategies?
- How will we take up the GIPA principle in relation to the most intricate and difficult stories of sexual subjectivity?

- How does the researcher's autobiography and subjectivity shape his or her understanding of "unhealthy" sexual behaviors, attitudes, and norms? How do we agree on what we will not study and politely exclude by using acronyms such as MSM?
- What are the causes and consequences of our kinship and choices? What do these choices say about us as a team of researchers?
- How will our team double-check for acceptance, and not mere tolerance, of gay relationships/kinship radically different from heteronormative models?

I have argued in this chapter that the greater involvement of persons with AIDS (GIPA), especially the likes of difficult and recalcitrant gay men such as sex pigs, must start with clarifying the investments, blind spots, and biases of researchers and educators. Our researcher/educator attention is not pure or undivided; it is opportunistic, constrained by career ambitions, the constraints of research funding, or public health and educational policy.

Our emerging HIV researchers manage a great deal of scientific evidence about the lives and practices of gay men, but they do little in the way of integrating this knowledge into comprehensive understandings and theories. My concern is that by the time junior researchers propose clinical interventions, research projects, results, and even policy changes, they have not thought about their own intricate stories of sexuality, and how they are expecting others to tell their stories in the name of research. Universities are producing highly trained researchers with insufficient maturity and reflection on lived experience. These same researchers will transform the lived experience of their research participants into captions and graphs, charts and reports that we all accept literally and at face value. Can researchers risk wondering how our autobiography shapes our engagements with and perceptions of the research subjects?

I have discussed two typical examples of "ghostly presences" in the field of HIV research: the phrase "men who have sex with men" (MSM) and the principle of greater involvement of persons living with AIDS (GIPA). The meaning of these terms must be unpacked because they turn both researchers and researched into AIDS ghostwriters without direct authoring responsibility. By making visible what we do in our clinical, social scientific, and public health accounts, we can design and implement more critical forms of community-engaged scholarship. In addition, I suggest that before starting one more research project on gay men, often underlined by the overarching research question "What do gay men want?" (Halperin, 2007), established and emerging HIV researchers and educators must ask ourselves, "What do we want?" I speculate that the HIV/AIDS stigma will lose its virulence in the next generations, because we don't want other ailments and diseases that we seemingly bring upon ourselves to be equally condemned and neglected. This would be a concrete improvement in the area of health and sexual health. Moreover, contrary to what we all earnestly would like to believe, researchers and educators might be still contributing to the stigma of HIV/AIDS by not changing the archaic ways in which we carry out our science and work together.

I close these preliminary speculations on new directions in HIV/AIDS research and education by proposing two starting points for the ongoing education of researchers. First, established and emerging HIV researchers should become familiar with the history of HIV, which is tantamount to understanding some basic tenets of the Western construction of illness. Second, both established and emerging HIV/AIDS researchers need to engage in autobiographical inquiry on why they have come to be working on HIV research in the first place. Self-reflection has the potential to extend the post-positivistic dialogue that troubles the meaning of objectivity and neutrality in research and education. Self-reflexivity is also a useful tool for bringing together and building the capacity of diverse and interdisciplinary research and educational teams. Self-reflexive research teams may offer more effective, exciting, and engaging opportunities for persons living with HIV to participate and make GIPA a reality. By working toward the inclusion of all participating selves in the research process, researchers and educators must face the same double-bind their subjects/participants do: you are damned if you don't disclose (e.g., HIV nondisclosure is criminalized in Canada), and damned if you disclose too much (it might be belittled as "too much information"). Nevertheless, the work of community-engaged scholarship must begin with researchers exploring our own intricate stories of sexual subjectivity as key stakeholders in the transmission and reception of HIV/AIDS knowledge.

References

Abma, T.A. (2002). Emerging narrative forms of knowledge representation in the health sciences: Two texts in a postmodern context. *Qualitative Health Research, 12*(1), 5–27.

Armstrong, R., Waters, E., Roberts, H., Oliver, S., & Popay, J. (2006). The role and theoretical evolution of knowledge translation and exchange in public health. *Journal of Public Health, 28*(4), 384–389.

Ballantine, Paul W., & Martin, Brett A. S. (2005). Forming parasocial relationships in online communities. *Advances in Consumer Research.* Vol. 32, 197—201.

Bell, D., Binie, J., Cream, J., & Gill, V. (1994). All hyped up and no place to go. *Gender, Place & Culture, 1*(1), 31–47.

Brenner, B. G., Roger, M., Moisi, Daniela D., Oliveira, M., Hardy I., Turgel, R., Charest, H., Routy, J., Wainberg, M., & the Montreal PHI Cohort and HIV Prevention Study Groups. (2008). Transmission Networks of Drug Resistance Acquired in Primary/Early Stage HIV Infection. *AIDS.* 2008 November 30; 22(18): 2509–2515.

Bryson, M., and de Castell, S. (1997). Queer Pedagogy?!: Praxis makes im/perfect. In M. Bryson & S. de Castell (Eds.), *Radical IN<ter>ventions: Identity, politics, and difference/s in educational praxis.* Albany: State University of New York Press.

Calleson D., Jordan, C., & Seifer, S. (2005). Community-engaged scholarship: Is faculty work in communities a true academic enterprise? *Academic Medicine, 80*(4), 317–321.

Champagne, J. (1995). *The ethics of marginality: A new approach to gay studies.* Minneapolis: University of Minnesota Press.

Colfax, G., Santos, G., Chu, P., Vittinghoff, F, Pludderman, A., Kumar, S., & Hart, C. (2010). Amphetamine-group substances and HIV. *Lancet,* 376, 458—74.

Connerton, P. (1989). *How societies remember.* Cambridge: Cambridge University Press.

Dowsett, G., Williams, H., Ventuneac, A., & Carballo-Diéguez, A. (2008). "Take it like a man": Masculinity and barebacking online. *Sexualities, 11*(1/2), 121–141.

Fisher, J.D. & Smith, L. (2009). Secondary prevention of HIV infection: The current state of prevention for positives. *Current Opinion in HIV and AIDS.* 4: 279–287.

Gavey, N., Schmidt, H., Braun, V., Fenaughty, J., & Eremin, M. (2009). Unsafe, unwanted: Sexual coercion as a barrier to safer sex among men who have sex with men. *Journal of Health Psychology, 14*(7), 1021–1026.

Graydon, M. (2007). Don't bother to wrap it: Online Giftgiver and Bugchaser newsgroups, the social impact of gift exchanges and the "carnivalesque." *Culture, Health & Sexuality, 9*(3), 277–292.

Grov, C. (2004). "Make me your death slave": Men who have sex with men and use the Internet to intentionally spread HIV. *Deviant Behaviour, 25*(3), 329–349.

Grov, C., Golub, S.A., Parsons, J.T., Brennan, M., and Karpiak, S.E. (2010). Loneliness and HIV-related stigma explain depression among older HIV-positive adults. *AIDS Care, 22*(5), 630–639.

Halperin, D. (2007). *What do gay men want? An essay on sex, risk, and subjectivity.* Ann Arbor: University of Michigan Press.

Hart, T., Adam, B., Maxwell, J., Mackay, R., Hoe, D., Leahy, R., Co, H., Maticka-Tyndale, E., & Murray, J. (2009). Gay poz sez: A community based counseling intervention for HIV-positive men. Poster presented at the Ontario HIV Treatment Network annual conference.

Holmes, D., O'Byrne, P., & Gastaldo, D. (2006). Raw sex as limit experience: A Foucauldian analysis of unsafe anal sex between men. *Social Theory & Health, 4*, 319–333.

Horton, D. & Wohl R.R. (1956): Mass communication and para-social interaction: Observations on intimacy at a distance, *Psychiatry* 19: 215–29.

Kavouni, A., Catalan J., Brown S., Mandalia, S., & Barton, S.E. (2008). The face of HIV and AIDS: Can we erase the stigma? *AIDS Care, 20*(4), 485–487.

Kelly, B.C., Bimbi, D.S., Izienicki, H., & Parsons, J.T. (2009). Stress and coping among HIV-positive barebackers. *AIDS Behavior, 13*, 792–797.

Klein, M.B., Yang, H., Cohen, J., Conway, B., Cooper, C., Côté, P., Cox, J., Gill, J., Haase, D., Haider, S., Montaner, J., Pick, N., Rachlis, A., Rouleau, D., Sandre, R., Tyndall, M., & Walmsley, S. (2009). Cohort profile: The Canadian HIV-Hepatitis C co-infection cohort study. *International Journal of Epidemiology, 39*(5), 1162–1169.

Lacan, J. (2002). *Écrits: A selection* (A. Sheridan, Trans.). New York: W.W. Norton & Co. (Original work published 1977)

Lave, J., & Wenger, E. (1991). *Situated learning: Legitimate peripheral participation.* New York: Cambridge University Press.

Lichtenstein, B., Laska, M.K., & Clair, J.M. (2002). Chronic sorrow in the HIV-positive patient: Issues of race, gender, and social support. *AIDS Patient Care and STDs, 16*(1), 27–38.

Mantzoukas, S. (2004). Issues of representation within qualitative inquiry. *Qualitative Health Research, 14*(7), 994–1007.

Martucci, J. (2010). Negotiating exclusion: MSM, identity, and blood policy in the age of AIDS. *Social Studies of Science, 40*(2), 215–241.

Morolake, O., Stephens, D., & Welbourn, A. (2009). Greater involvement of people living with HIV in health care. *Journal of the International AIDS Society, 12*(4). Retrieved November 6, 2010, from http://www.jiasociety.org/content/12/1/4

Moskowitz, J.T., Hult, J.R., Bussolari, C., & Acree, M. (2009). What works in coping with HIV? A meta-analysis with implications for coping with serious illness. *Psychological Bulletin, 135*(1), 121–141.

Persson, A. (2005). Facing HIV: Body shape change and the (in)visibility of illness. *Medical Anthropology, 24*(3), 237–264.

Petticrew M., & Roberts, H. (2005). *Systematic reviews in the social sciences: A practical guide.* Oxford: Blackwell Publishing.

PHAC (Public Health Agency of Canada). (2009). HIV/AIDS in Canada: Surveillance report until December 31st 2008. Surveillance and risk assessment division, Centre of Infectious Disease Prevention and Control, Public Health Agency of Canada.

Rees R., Kavanagh J., Burchett, H., Sheperd, J., Brunton, G., Harden, A., Thomas, J., Oliver, S., & Oakley, A. (2004). *HIV health promotion and men who have sex with men (MSM): A systematic review of research relevant to the development and implementation of effective and appropriate interventions.* London: EPPI-Centre, Social Science Research Unit, Institute of Education, University of London.

Schilder, A.J., Treena R., Orchard, C.S., Buchner, S.A., Strathdee, S.A., & Hogg, R.S. (2010, July). Insert discourse: Rectal douching among young HIV-positive and HIV-negative men who have sex with men in Vancouver, Canada. *Sexuality & Culture, 28*, 327–343.

Scott, Joan W. (1997). The evidence of experience. In J. Chandler, A.I. Davidson, & Harry Harootunian (Eds.), *Questions of evidence: Proof, practice, and persuasion across the disciplines.* Chicago: University of Chicago Press.

Semple, S.J., Patterson, T., & Grant, I. (2002). Motivations associated with methamphetamine use among HIV+ men who have sex with men. *Journal of Substance Abuse Treatment, 22*, 149–156.

Shapiro, K., & Ray, S. (2007). Sexual health for people living with HIV. *Reproductive Health Matters, 15* (29 supplement), 67–92.

Stacey, J. (2004). Cruising to Familyland: Gay hypergamy and the rainbow kinship. *Current Sociology, 52*(2), 181–197.

Stacey, J. (2005). The families of man: Gay male intimacy and kinship in a global metropolis. *Signs: Journal of Women in Culture and Society, 30*(3), 1911–1937.

Stall, R., Mill, T.C., Williamson, J., Hart, T., Greenwood, G., Paul, J., Pollack, L., Binson, D., Osmond, D., & Catania,

J. (2003). Association of co-occurring psychosocial health problems and increased vulnerability to HIV/AIDS among urban men who have sex with men. *American Journal of Public Health, 93*(6), 939–942.

Travers, R., Wilson, M.G., Flicker, S., Guta, A., Bereket, T., Mckay, C., van der Meulen, A., Cleverly, S., Dickie, M., Globerman, J., & Rourke, S.B. (2008). The greater involvement of people living with AIDS principle: Theory versus practice in Ontario's HIV/AIDS community-based research sector. *AIDS Care.* 20:6, 615–624.

Trussler, T. (2008). *Sex Now survey report.* Retrieved December 2010 from http://www.cbrc.net/attachments/209_SNIndex07final.pdf

UNAIDS. Uniting the world against AIDS: Young people. Retrieved December 2010 from http://www.unaids.org/bangkok2004/GAR2004_html/GAR2004_07_en.htm

Welles, S.L., Baker, C., Miner, M.H., Brennan, D.J., Jacoby, S., & Rosser, S. (2009). History of childhood sexual abuse and unsafe anal intercourse in a 6-city study of HIV-positive men who have sex with men. *American Journal of Public Health, 99*(6), 1079–1086.

Yoshino, K. (2006). *Covering: The hidden assault on our civil rights.* New York: Random House

Young, R.M., & Meyer, L.H. (2005). The trouble with "MSM" and "WSW": Erasure of the sexual-minority person in public health disclosure: Critical concepts for reaching populations at risk. *American Journal of Public Health, 95*(7), 1144–1149.

CHAPTER TWENTY-NINE

"A Different Idea" in the Sex Education Curriculum

Thinking through the Emotional Experience of Sexuality

BRIAN CASEMORE

Introduction

Sex education calls forth a fundamental process of human subjectivity: the ceaseless and uncertain translation of sexuality into meaning. If sex education conveys knowledge about sexuality and sexual health, it does more than merely transmit information; with the knowledge sex education introduces, it invites consideration of the pleasures and difficulties of living in one's body and developing relationships from within one's embodied subjectivity. Students of sex education must negotiate, both consciously and unconsciously, the question of what they have made and what they will make of the mutable drives, desires, affects, and relationships that constitute their sexuality. Sex education thus frames and intensifies a core process of self-formation—thinking the emotional experience of sexuality—as an educational event.

Recent debates over the sex education curriculum, however, obscure the significance of this educational event. The debates over abstinence have heightened efforts to determine the particular content of sexuality and sexual health education, drawing attention to the boundaries, limits, and comprehensiveness of the curriculum. In this context, curriculum is understood as a specific body of knowledge to be learned, and the foremost pedagogical problem is to impart a prescribed curriculum to students. Determining the known in the absence of the knower, this traditional model of curriculum development and implementation diminishes what a curriculum could provoke in the lives of students in sex education—that is, a particular and complex subjective orientation to sexual knowledge.

Whatever the educational context—school, community organization, online course—sex educators must interpret sexuality and sexual health as a field of knowledge, develop curriculum to make this knowledge available for study and understanding, and engage students in learning the information deemed necessary for sexual health. Yet however comprehensive the knowledge, no sex education curriculum totalizes the conditions and experiences of sexual being that it provokes. Coming to understand one's own sexuality is an eternally incomplete subjective process. Endlessly confronting the otherness of desire—an uninterpretable core of self and sexuality—the learning that sex education compels, therefore, is a counterforce to the synthesis and comprehensiveness of the sex education curriculum. For the student of sex education, this poses the challenge of integrating the split domains of sexuality and schooling. And for the researcher and teacher of sex education, this poses the challenge of conceptualizing curriculum, not as an academic plan or body of knowledge, but as a subjective process that includes self-states and emotional experiences that both require signification and exceed our grasp.

In this essay, I analyze a focus group conversation in which middle school students from Washington, D.C., struggle to express and understand the emotional experience of sex education. Using psychoanalytic theory as a framework, I provide a close reading of the conversation and demonstrate how, through speech, the focus group participants negotiate this complicated emotional terrain. Contributions made by several participants reveal the difficulty of thinking the emotional experience of sexuality, a difficulty manifested in the psychological defenses that shape the conversation: splitting, projection, and idealization. In my analysis, I approach these defenses as expressions of the emotional experience of sex education, as forms of resistance to thinking in sex education, *and* as features of the effort to negotiate new or difficult sexual knowledge.

When focused on information provision, sex education excludes from the curriculum students' complex subjective orientations to sexual knowledge (Sandlos, 2010). In efforts to include emotional life in sex education, both abstinence-only and comprehensive sex education have promoted a search for "knowledge that leads directly and unambiguously to happiness," thus significantly narrowing the emotional landscape of healthy sexuality (Lesko, 2010, p. 282). Given the centrality of uncertainty, anxiety, and loss to desire, sexual identity, and sexual relationships (Gilbert, 2007), severing the more difficult emotional experiences of sexuality from conceptions of sexual health can be read as a defensive splitting of sexuality from formal education or schooling. In my analysis, therefore, I read the nexus of related psychological defenses that appear in the focus group conversation as a reflection of conditions of learning established through curriculum conceptualization and development. Reading the defenses as symptoms of sex education, I argue, can provide insight into the learning particular to sex education and can provide a foundation for critiquing sexual health curricula.

I also consider events of splitting, projection, and idealization more specifically within a psychoanalytic theory of human development. Originating in infancy and intensifying during the physical, sexual, and emotional changes of adolescence, these defenses are typical features of adolescent life and can be read as evidence of the focus group participants' experience of the shifting "centre of gravity" of adolescent identity (Meltzer, 1973/2008). Moreover, this nexus of defenses plays a fundamental role in psychoanalytic accounts of thinking. It is through these defenses that individuals and groups rid themselves of emotional experience necessary for thought, particularly the experience of uncertainty (Britzman, 2003, pp. 97–124). However, rather than suggest that these defenses have forestalled all meaningful thought in the focus group conversation, I take seriously the point that "thinking begins with the dilemmas of 'being able to bear not knowing'" (Bion; cited in Britzman, 2003, p. 100). If splitting, projection, and idealization in the focus group conversation indicate resistance to thought, they also characterize a significant struggle with uncertainty and a profound, if hindered, effort to think new or difficult ideas. I read the conversation, therefore, for fissures in the defenses and for emergent thought about sexuality.

In conditions of troubled communication about sexuality and sexual health, free associative speech can become a pathway to more productive thought (Casemore, 2010). By attending to the free associative speech that accompanies the defenses in the focus group, therefore, we can recognize associations that move toward meaningful thought and inquiry. Recognizing associations as such—that is, as constitutive features of authentic inquiry, inquiry without a predetermined outcome or meaning—and making room for them to be considered and ruminated upon in sex education, I argue, is necessary for supporting students as they navigate the divide between the information in a formal sex education curriculum and their own subjective experiences of sexuality. I therefore offer my manner of attending to these associations as a model for fostering inquiry in sex education conversations.

Recognizing the psychological defenses that emerge in conversation both fosters a sense of the unconscious subject in qualitative research (Hollway & Jefferson, 2000, pp. 19–21) and allows research to take account of unconscious self-states as features of thought and speech (Bollas, 2009b, pp. 14–15). This mode of interpretation, however, involves a risk for the researcher who seeks understanding of the speech of research subjects. If an interpretation of defenses helps deconstruct the imagined fully conscious subject represented in much qualitative research, it also risks becoming a search for "a specific psychodynamic source for a subject's 'choice' of location in discourse" (Frosh, 2007, p. 643). In other words, as researchers employ a psychoanalytic framework with attention to a subject's defenses against anxiety, they risk enacting the position of the omniscient observer, searching for a single underlying cause for a research subject's self-expressions, and "fix[ing] subjectivity in one, predetermined grid" (p. 643).

My analysis, therefore, does not present the defenses as evidence of the focus group participants' unchanging subjective identities or mental states. Splitting, projection, and idealization are taken up instead as inevitable and recurring dimensions of human development—a development that, psychoanalytic theorists argue, unfolds unevenly (Britzman, 2009; Meltzer, 1973/2008; Waddell, 2002). In her account of "uneven development," Britzman suggests that psychological defenses are evidence that development "carries its own traces of antidevelopment" (p. 27). Defenses, she explains, represent a clinging to "a place that no longer exists" (p. 27), an effort to secure the self's position in a tolerable (because familiar), though ineluctably passing, mental state. Defenses arise then to establish a sense of certainty where thoughts, emotions, and desires threaten the sense of one's subjective identity as a "centre of gravity" (Meltzer, 1973/2008). Protecting the self against the unknown, the defenses of splitting, projection, and idealization do indeed forestall insight. As Britzman (2009) explains, they are the very "problem that destroys the mind's capacity to think" (p. 40). But in defending against the difficult and ultimately inexpressible emotional experience of not knowing, splitting, projection, and idealization also illuminate particular conflicts of knowledge, identity, and desire as well as the sense of uncertainty these conflicts introduce. These defenses return what they defend against—difficult emotion and knowledge that might, in the right conditions, be translated into insight. Splitting, projection, and idealization are therefore inevitable and necessary features of an individual's learning to cope with the incompleteness of the self, ways of attaching to self-states that usher conflicts and their meaning into one's future development.

A Focus Group about *Desire*

In the focus group I conducted with middle school students from Washington, D.C., I prompted conversation by screening clips from Julie Gustafson's (2005) documentary film *Desire*. The film follows the lives of five young women growing up in New Orleans, and it includes short autobiographical films the young women made themselves about their desires, relationships, sexualities, and life struggles. The film represents diverse experiences of race, ethnicity, class, sexuality, and schooling. In the three clips I screened for the focus group, the research participants learned about three of the young women depicted in the film: Kimeca, an African American mother of two from the Desire housing project for which the film is named; Peggy, a first-generation Asian American student attending the distinguished Isidore Newman Private High School in New Orleans; and Tiffanie, a teen mother from a working-class suburb of New Orleans, who questions her marriage and sexual identity. Viewing film narratives about Kimeca, Peggy, and Tiffanie, the research participants watched these young women struggle to understand sexuality, relationships, and education. They witnessed Kimeca, Peggy, and Tiffanie communicate with friends, family members, and various authority figures in a range of social, familial, and educational contexts, and they saw them develop, however hesitantly, real authorial power in the framing, recording, and composing of their lives. In the present study, I focus on the research participants' discussion of Kimeca.

The focus group was made up of an all-white class of students from a school dedicated to children with learning disabilities. I chose this group for the research in my effort to explore conversations about sexuality and sexual health representing the voices and milieus of various members of the community. Along with this focus group, for example, I conducted focus groups with Latino/Latina peer sex educators, African American high school students, and race- and age-diverse sex educators. For the present study, I learned from the teacher of the research participants that they frequently discuss how they feel labeled because of their disabilities and marginalized within educational contexts. Many of these students have changed schools several times in their effort to find an environment in which they can learn. The research participants' struggle with a sense of difference emerged in the focus group conversation as they considered race, class, and sexuality experiences different from their own.

I mention this social and educational context to frame the issues of social difference that appear in my analysis of the focus group conversation. The psychological defenses that shaped the conversation clearly aligned with forms of social marginalization, racism in particular. As a white man leading a conversation with an all-white group of students, I was aware that offering images, voices, and narratives of non-white youth for consideration and reflection risked an objectification of the racial "other." I attempted to lessen this risk by showing diverse racial experiences to the focus group and by encouraging deeper and potentially more empathetic reflection when participants drew on racial stereotypes in their discussion of the film. Moreover, by using the film *Desire*, I showed the focus group racially diverse youth engaged in meaningful and effective acts of inquiry and self-representation. In the film clip depicting Kimeca, for example, at one point Kimeca chooses not to speak about herself and instead questions Julie Gustafson, the filmmaker, about her sexual experiences and pregnancies, thus significantly unsettling the authority over representation in the film. With film clips like this one, I attempted to show the racially diverse young women in the film active and agentic in their lives.

In my analysis of this focus group, we can nonetheless see that the conversation aligned with structures of racial marginalization. What most interests me about the conversation is that in conditions of splitting, projection, and idealization that followed embedded perceptions of racial difference, a participant worked against these boundaries of thought to venture "a different idea." In other words, my analysis will show how—in subtle, free associative speech—this participant worked against racial splitting to make room for thought about once-excluded emotional experience, both her own and another's.

Prior to my conversation with the students who participated in the focus group, these youth went through an educational unit on sexuality and sexual health. The curriculum focused on biology, reproduction, contraception, and sexually transmitted infections. In the unit, the students explored a range of issues—loss and mourning, sexual identity, living with AIDS, and the politics of public health, for example—that emerged in their discussion of the film *Common Threads: Stories from the Quilt* (1989), a documentary film about the NAMES Project AIDS Memorial Quilt. Finally, the students also participated in a workshop led by their peers that encouraged recognition and respect for sexual diversity and gender identity.

In the focus group conversation, the research participants struggled to integrate sexual knowledge they acquired from their comprehensive sexual health curriculum with experiences of sexuality represented in and evoked by the film. A clash between the students' curricular knowledge and the emotional experiences of sexuality that the film raised appeared prominently as a splitting of sexuality and education, a projection of unmanageable sexuality onto one of the girls in the film, and an idealization of school knowledge. The focus group participants imagined school knowledge to be stable, coherent, and unfailingly authoritative, and they turned to this imagined realm of complete knowledge to address and contain the inexpressible force of sexuality.

Idealizing Authority, Splitting Sexuality and Schooling

As an initial foray into the effects of splitting, projection, and idealization on the focus group conversation, I want to briefly explore a discussion of sexual orientation that occurred during the focus group warm-up activity. For the warm-up activity, intended to encourage open discussion about the sex education curriculum, I provided the participants with a list of terms and asked them to circle the terms they felt were most relevant to sex education, to cross out the terms they felt were irrelevant to sex education, and to star the terms they feel were difficult for sex education. I then invited the participants to discuss their choices. In the discussion, the participants considered a range of terms—knowledge, birth control, abstinence, protection, curiosity, secret, sexuality, and homosexuality—and they provided specific, often subtle explanations for the relevance and difficulty of these terms for sex education.

The question of the relevance and difficulty of particular concepts in sex education clearly provoked concern in this group about what sex education—as curriculum, pedagogy, and dimension of schooling—could adequately or safely hold. As a result, throughout the warm-up activity, the participants made statements that demonstrated their concern with the authority over knowledge in sex education. The group's discussion of sexual orientation in particular revealed an idealization of knowledge in sex education that, I want to argue, represents a defensive splitting of sexuality, as an emotionally complex dimension of human experience, and schooling, as an imagined authority over knowledge.

Nicole began the discussion of sexual orientation by explaining which terms she had crossed out: "I x-ed out some like sexuality and like homosexual because, even though I know that they play roles in sex education . . . for some reason, I feel like they're not, not kind of, not as important as some of the other things on it. I mean, they're relevant, just not at the forefront for me." Though initially making a claim for the irrelevance of these terms, Nicole ultimately expressed her uncertainty about them. The sense of uncertainty seemed to invite Audrey to state explicitly how sexual orientation should be addressed in the curriculum. Clearly taking non-normative sexual orientation to be the subject at hand, and "expanding on what [Nicole] said," Audrey explained that students "should be informed of what it is and that it's normal in a sense, that it occurs and it's not a bad thing."

With this statement, Audrey framed the purposes of teaching and learning. Though she did not name those who should provide students with information about sexual identities, she implied an authority over knowledge—teachers or schools—who should inform students as students become informed. This framing of education allowed Audrey to address the uncertainty raised by Nicole's reflections on sexual orientation. While Nicole's statement seemed to introduce the emotional risk of not knowing in sex education, Audrey's statement invoked school knowledge and the educational process to situate sexuality safely in the social and educational norm. Where this conversation rendered sexuality unknown, an imagined authority over knowledge assuaged the anxiety of uncertainty. The significance of this dynamic was then made more explicit as Nicole, also invoking an imagined authority over knowledge, returned to the conversation. About the question of knowledge in sex education, she stated simply: "you have to be taught to know what you're going into."

Another student, Matt, then entered the conversation, expressing more definitively the concern with the authority of knowledge in sex education and the need for knowledge to displace uncertainty. In his discussion of sexual orientation, Matt strengthened the case for an authoritative curriculum. He explained:

> I think it's good to know about [sexual orientation] because . . . if you don't know about it, if it's not included in sex ed, there's lots of stereotypes and stuff that come from, like especially homosexuality people, there's all these stereotypes about it. So without the correct knowledge or right understanding you won't know as much about it as you can. You might have stereotypes . . . stereotypes can spawn from a lack of knowledge of [homosexuality].

In his contribution to the conversation, Matt identified conflicts around identity ("stereotypes can spawn from a lack of knowledge of [homosexuality]") while emphasizing the need for "correct knowledge" and "right understanding" in the face of such conflict. In Matt's speech, as with Audrey's, we can hear his engagement with and translation of a progressive, comprehensive sexual health curriculum, one that both encourages respect for sexual diversity and values a student's right to knowledge about sexuality. We hear these students of sex education not only reiterate the content of the curriculum (homosexuality is normal and stereotypes are dangerous) but also argue for the process by which they received this content. Students "should be informed," Audrey explained, and "without the correct knowledge," Matt added, "you won't know as much about it as you can." This demonstration of knowledge and reflection on educational experience exemplified the students' capacities to engage with and integrate knowledge from comprehensive sex education. Yet there is something else at stake here that I would like to bring into focus.

As these students displayed their knowledge of sexual health and argued for an imagined complete educational process, they revealed an idealization of authority—the authority of school knowledge. The idealization of authority is a typical characteristic of adolescent efforts to negotiate the physical, sexual, and emotional upheavals of this period of development (Gilbert, 2007, pp. 53–55; Waddell, 2002, pp. 142–143). Through their speech, therefore, these students not only demonstrated knowledge of curricular content and educational process. They were also working through an emotional attachment to the authority of school knowledge that arises from the loss and longing inherent to development.

While this idealization is typical of adolescence, it is also a feature of the mechanism of splitting, a psychological defense that divides the world and the self into idealized "good" and threatening "bad" elements. A primitive form of managing anxiety, splitting separates sources of pleasure and distress, segregating good and bad objects—both internally and externally—and therefore shaping both perceptions of the external world and the structure of the ego (Feldman, 1992, pp. 74–75). In early development, the infant idealizes sources of nourishment and comfort, identifying "good" parts of the self with those sources and projecting "bad" feelings—pain, lack, disappointment, discomfort—onto others in the outside world. Splitting is essential to the child's development of a sense of being safe and protected. And through parental containment, early severe forms of splitting eventually give way to empathy, altruism, and awareness of the complexity (rather than the simple "goodness" or "badness") of the self and others.

In adolescence, however—with the onset of puberty, new relational and identity conflicts, and the sense of parental holding radically changing—splitting intensifies. "Not only does the other come to be experienced in terms of love and hate, the polarities of which are felt to be irreconcilable," Waddell (2002) explains, "but the self also comes to be experienced in equally extreme terms" (p. 150). Moreover, as conflicts over authority in adolescence replay the dynamics experienced in infancy, splitting again appears as a means of negotiating emotional tumult (Meltzer, 1973/2008). The adolescent shifts between poles of "love and hate, conformity and rebellion . . . hero worship and repudiation" (Gilbert, 2007, p. 54), therefore, as he or she struggles to bring parts of the self into communication and to experience others in their complexity.

If splitting is an essential process in early development and a typical feature of adolescence, it is also, Britzman (2009) argues, "the problem that destroys the mind's capacity to think" (p. 40). Splitting, that is, is a defense against the emotionally difficult experience of uncertainty—the experience of not knowing that must be held internally for thinking to occur. To think reflectively, the adolescent must find environments in which the various parts of the self, in their uncertain relationships, can be held and integrated. The sex educator, therefore, must imagine a curriculum that does more than encourage the adolescent's wish for an absolute authority over knowledge. For as Gilbert (2007) argues, "whenever education appeals to the adolescent's sense of authority, they are conjuring up an unstable and psychically combustible dynamic" (p. 54), a dynamic that is likely to forestall self-integration and thoughtful engagement with the emotional experience of sexuality.

This account of adolescent development illuminates the processes of self-formation that influenced the focus group's effort to negotiate meaning in the tensions between sexuality and schooling. In the focus group conversation, adolescent students managed the uncertainty around the emotional experience of sex education by splitting good and bad knowledge and projecting good knowledge onto the authority of the school. Through this defense, the students reduced the emotional complexity of sex education to a dichotomy of knowledge that allowed them to disclaim their ignorance and their responsibility for knowing. We can, I believe, read the students' splitting of sexuality and schooling as a symptom of comprehensive sex education. When defined solely by the educational purpose of having students acquire correct information about sexuality, sex education obscures the emotional conditions of self-formation that attend the development of sexual knowledge—indeed, the experience of love, hate, anxiety, and loss that are central to sexuality itself. Sex education thus paradoxically splits the experience of sexuality and the development of sexual knowledge. We participate in such splitting, I believe, if we read Matt and Audrey's reiteration of the knowledge they acquired in sex education, and their bolstering of the authority of the source of that knowledge, as evidence of the success of sex education. We miss the underlying emotional context and the potential for deeper inquiry in sex education as well, if we see these students' own splitting of sexuality and schooling as mere compliance with school authority. Understanding that ambivalence—the holding of conflicting emotions—will characterize the adolescent's pathway to genuine intellectual authority, we might hear in their passionate attachment to authority their effort to assuage the anxiety of uncertainty, and thus the potential revolution of thought.

"A Different Idea" in Sex Education

After the warm-up activity, I showed film clips depicting three girls in the film *Desire*. One of the clips I showed features Kimeca Rogers, an 18-year-old mother of two whose struggle to remain in school compels the focus group participants to reenter the tensions between sexuality and schooling. In the clip I screened for the group, Kimeca is first seen playing with her two children. She then introduces herself by providing an account of her two pregnancies in the context of her school experiences. Speaking to Gustafson, she explains:

> Well, what happened was, I was doing good in school till I got pregnant with him. When Jeremy was born, he was premature and they were saying he wasn't going to make it. And I, I live with that every day when I'm with him. And I stopped going to school, and I was in the tenth grade then, so that made me have to repeat the tenth grade again. So, after he got out of the hospital and everything, and I went back to school, while I was repeating the tenth grade, I got pregnant again. I don't know. I just, I don't know what happened. I fell back again.

The film then takes us to Carver High School where Kimeca discusses with the principal, Dr. Lindsey Moore, the possibility of her returning to school and continuing her education. If in her conversation with Gustafson Kimeca is shy in her speech, with Dr. Moore she is taciturn. Dr. Moore asks: "Why, at this point in your life, have you decided to return to school?" He then further inquires: "How many times have you dropped out before now?" Kimeca, clearly nervous, responds: "Twice." Dr. Moore continues, inviting Kimeca to consider the difficulty of her return to school: "So are you familiar with the old saying, three strikes you're out?" Kimeca responds simply: "Yes." Dr. Moore pushes for a more substantial account of Kimeca's interest in returning to school, asking: "So if I give you one more chance, it will probably be your last chance. . . . How do I know you won't drop out again? What assurances can you give us?" Kimeca responds through nervous laughter: "I'm serious."

In a subsequent conversation with Julie Gustafson, Kimeca questions the filmmaker about her children and sexual history, and she discovers that Gustafson had two abortions in her teens. In the conversation that ensues, still struggling with her shyness on camera, Kimeca explains that she doesn't believe in abortion and asks Gustafson: "Do you ever wonder, if you would have had the babies, how they would have grown up and what their goals would have been?" With this question, we hear Kimeca's strongest voice, as this voice invites the filmmaker to enter an emotionally difficult space of thought. Gustafson replies: "I never thought about that before you spoke about it."

In the focus group, I began the conversation about Kimeca by asking what conflicts the participants saw in the film. One participant, Lindsey, captured the sense of repetition in Kimeca's experience. The central conflict, Lindsey explained, is "dropping out and repeating . . . just going over the same, over and over." Nicole stated her understanding that Kimeca may not be able to accept abortion as an option but wondered why Kimeca didn't use birth control. And in Beth's early reflections on the clip, she emphasized Kimeca's sense of uncertainty about having children: "Of course she was confused," Beth insisted, "[about] having kids and taking care of them while redoing tenth grade." As these contributions indicate, in the discussion of Kimeca, the group linked sexuality with the feeling of being stuck and confused, finding in Kimeca a place to contain the anxiety about this troubling link.

This use of Kimeca was further evidenced as Matt reentered the conversation to elaborate on the conflict in her story:

> She's not getting her high school diploma, which for a lot of jobs you need and then just a general educa-
> tion . . . to do stuff in life and have right decisions that are not always about sex ed. I mean school is a big
> thing and if you're dropping out relatively young . . . you're really shutting doors on yourself. So that's a con-
> flict because of the babies that she, there's doors getting shut for her because she can't, she hasn't been able
> to finish high school.

In Matt's speech, we again hear his concern with a strong, authoritative education. While his earlier contribution emphasized the need for correct knowledge about sexuality, in his comments about Kimeca, Matt distinguished general education from sex education, suggesting Kimeca's pregnancies had prevented her from getting an education that will help her make "right decisions" unrelated to sexuality. Having set aside sexuality—concerned as he was about "right decisions that are not always about sex ed"—Matt then struggled to complete his statement about the conflict in Kimeca's life. There is a conflict, he explained, "because of the babies she . . ." and "because she can't. . . ." Matt ultimately resolved these elliptical explanations with the statement that Kimeca had not been able to finish high school. However, because he had set sex education in opposition to the education that will open doors for Kimeca, Matt's struggle to name the force that opposes Kimeca's success in school invites us to consider the difficulty he assigned to sexuality in this moment. At that point in the conversation, sexuality began to take on an increasingly enigmatic character, and the focus group participants attempted to manage its unsettling force by splitting sexuality and education and projecting unwanted aspects of sexuality onto Kimeca.

In the earlier discussion of sexual orientation, the group's splitting of sexuality and schooling initiated discourse about the authority of the school, revealing how splitting can result in the projection of "good" objects and experiences onto another who might serve as a safe or strong holding environment. In the discussion of Kimeca, however, we see more clearly how the adolescent frequently projects uncomfortable experiences or "bad" objects onto another. "This unconscious process of attributing to others what are really aspects of the self," Waddell (2002) explains, "means that somebody else can then become the problem if it is the 'bad' parts of the self that are being projected" (p. 146). In this conversation, Kimeca became "the problem" through which the group attempted to manage anxieties about the relationship between sexuality and schooling.

Here in the heightened tensions of splitting and projection is a crucial interpretive moment for the researcher and teachers in sex education. In these tensions, one will recognize the students' effort to remain wholly separate from the object or other made to contain distressing experiences, an effort that significantly diminishes capacities for self-reflection and empathy. One might also recognize how splitting and projection align with social hierarchies, acting out, for example, fantasies about racial differences. In the focus group's discussion of Kimeca, I became acutely aware of this dynamic, wondering how my presence as a white male researcher in a group of all-white students, may have intensified this racial splitting. I also recognized how the racial splitting was akin to splitting along lines of sex orientation that appeared in other focus groups.

In ways relevant to the research and educational context, one should call attention to the harmfulness, indeed the social and psychical violence, of splitting identities and experiences. One should also analyze the forms of social hatred unconsciously enacted in such splitting. However, in recognizing the harmful effects of splitting and projection, including the ways these defenses forestall thinking, one should not miss the opportunity to take account of and foster the potential and emergent thought of which these defenses are a part. For it is thinking with greater capaciousness—open to the emotion that animates, intensifies, and troubles experience—that enables us to consider more reflectively, less judgmentally, the seemingly unfit experiences of others and ourselves (Young, 1994, pp. 33–52).

In heightened conditions of splitting and projection, when the researcher or educator takes a critical stance that secures the psychological defense or its social implication as the single cause or meaning of subjectivity, he or she participates in a "hermeneutics of transparency" (Moss, 2003, pp. xxx–xxxiii) that acts out the very splitting under critique. Through such a critical stance, one takes the position of the omniscient observer, an imaginary remove from the implications of discourse, thought, and emotion. To remain in contact with the emergent thought in these conditions, the researcher and teacher must take account of, rather than split off, his or her own complex emotional response to the troubling ideas of students and research participants. In doing so, he or she might keep in mind the typicality in adolescence of the defenses of splitting and projection, and consider how

> the projective mode, if not too extreme, may at this stage stem from curiosity about the self as well as from anxiety, and may thus enable someone to investigate and engage with emotional possibilities which are not yet experienced as integrateable into his sense of who he is. (Waddell, 2002, p. 147)

If Kimeca served as a shared point of projection for the participants in the focus group, she also became an/Other from whom they might learn. The group rid themselves of self-states and self-experiences by making Kimeca the container for them. But Kimeca gave them much more than her image. She shared a life narrative, emotional struggles, and courageous efforts to make meaning of those struggles. When directed to such life narratives and the subjective experiences they represent, students can both encounter the complexity of "the other" and reintegrate the parts of themselves they have made the other hold. If the environment in such conditions is flexible enough to enable a return to the parts of the self that have been split off and projected, then re-introjection, indeed thought, may occur. "Parts of the self can be related to in the other," Waddell (2002) explains, "and can then be owned or further disowned by the self" (p. 147). Moreover, through this process, one makes passage from the position of splitting off another's experience to empathy and concern for the welfare of another. To encourage the reintegration of disowned parts of the self, the sex educator can listen patiently to the speech in which expressions of splitting and projection appear, and point to associations—counterthoughts, negations, and juxtapositions—that will allow students to hear their own unconscious lines of inquiry and recognize the lives of others in their complexity.

In the focus group, a chain of associations began that demonstrated the group's effort to negotiate the intractable drive of sexuality. If Beth highlighted the confusion Kimeca would experience raising two children and continuing high school, Anne then introduced the question of the source of this conflict. "She wants to try to finish high school," Anne explained. "She wants to," Anne continued, "but she just like, for some reason, it's happened twice and she can't." In the momentary shift in the subject of Anne's statement—from "she" to "it"—sexuality again appeared as an inexpressible force: "for some reason, it's happened." And Anne links this force to the seeming impossibility of Kimeca's growth: "it's happened . . . and she can't."

Anne implied an inexpressible sexual drive with the phrase "for some reason." Shortly after, however, she responded to the provocation of her own statement, naming this force that disrupts a life. In her statement, she followed the others in the group in their turn to education as an authority that might contain this force. About Kimeca, Anne said:

> It's like if she doesn't believe in abortion and she's always having sex, why not just like—obviously she's not using protection—and so it's just like if you want to continue, you have to stop something. You have to either stop having sex to get the education or, yeah.

To understand the complexity of thought embedded in Anne's contribution to the discussion, I want to listen closely to what this associative speech communicates. If Anne's earlier ambiguous reference to sexuality—"for some reason, it's happened"—conjured up the "disturbing, confusing, [and] disruptive states of mind" characteristic of adolescent sexuality (Waddell, 2002, p. 146), her subsequent statements about Kimeca—"she's always having sex" and "obviously she's not using protection"—projected those states of mind, along with the very thought of sexuality, onto another. Anne thus associated from the thought of an intractable sexual drive through the idea of Kimeca continually involved in sex and ultimately to the idea of protection—that which might serve as a buffer against the drive Anne's speech evoked. In this turn of thought, Kimeca represented those who would refuse protection as Anne projected onto Kimeca a lack of a self-protective impulse, evacuating, it seems, her own drive to put the self at risk.

Having located unwanted aspects of sexuality in Kimeca, Anne then offered a general statement about managing sexuality in the face of one's educational responsibilities: "If you want to continue," she explained, "you have to stop something." This statement refers to two specific actions: continuing school and stopping sex. But the ambiguity of the statement—to continue what? to stop what?—invites other interpretations. The conscious or intentional meaning Anne expressed is that if Kimeca wants to continue in school, she has to stop having unprotected sex. But attending to the ambiguity of the statement, listening to its free associative nature, allows for other meanings to emerge.

First, the ambiguity of "something" raises the question of what *thing* needs to be stopped for Kimeca to continue in school. Must she stop having unprotected sex, getting pregnant, or being sexual altogether? Anne's speaking of sex as "some" unnamable "thing" resonates with earlier circuitous references to sexuality in this conversation, allowing us to hear the "something" to be stopped, not as an action ("stop *having sex*"), but as an inner drive or force, an intractable otherness ("stop some *thing*").

Second, given that this statement is rooted in the logic of splitting, it names its own reversal. "If you want to continue, you have to stop something" can be read as "If you want to continue having sex, you have to stop going to school." The statement thus exposes the logic of splitting at work in the conversation—the imagined mutual exclusiveness of sexuality and education—and the implications of that logic: that to embrace one's sexuality is to eradicate the possibilities of one's education.

Finally, we can hear the meaning of "continue" without an object. In this interpretation, something must be stopped, if one wants to continue—that is, if one wants to go on, to endure, to last or remain in place. Again, the ambiguity of "something" comes into play. What must be stopped for one to endure? Is it sexuality itself? This interpretation compels us to ask in what conditions sexuality is perceived as a threat to one's capacity to go on, to develop, to grow? In what ways does education—

sex education or otherwise—threaten or foster one's sense of continuing, one's sense of being and becoming? If the more conscious meaning of Anne's statement suggests that, to continue, one must stop some aspect of sexuality, what can we make of the underlying logic contained in the reversal—that to continue or endure, one must stop education? Moreover, what are we to make of this juggling of sexuality and education in the work of "going on being" (Epstein, 2002)? Anne's associations invite us—they implore us, it seems—to imagine an education that integrates rather than severs sexuality from learning, growth, and being.

As the conversation continued, these youth suggested that such an education would center the problem and process of thinking the emotional force of sexuality and that it would unfold through an open responsiveness to the unconscious inquiry of others. Such responsiveness appeared as Anne's associations called Beth back into the conversation. Anne moved from an ambiguous idea about sexuality and education—"if you want to continue, you have to stop something"—to a more specific idea about the dangers of sex: "You have to either stop having sex to get the education or, yeah." Yet, as Anne specified her earlier ambiguous statement, naming the two actions, she furthered the ambiguity through an either/or statement that she left incomplete. In Anne's speech, therefore, we hear a rhythm in the movement between knowledge and ambiguity, an ambiguity that functions like a question as it returns to each statement of knowledge. This rhythm exemplifies Bollas's (2009b) argument that "we live . . . within the drive of an infinite question" (p. 142). If in our drive to know we come under the sway of a desire for certainty, a desire for absolute knowledge, free associative speech, our own and others, reminds us that "one may solve one question, but no matter how finite it may seem, the answer will be displaced by latent questions embedded within it" (p. 142). Moreover, from the associations that emerge in the focus group conversation, we learn that an individual's pursuit of an infinite question can be taken up by another.

Anne's incomplete either/or statement, an expression of her infinite question, invited Beth to complete the idea. Returning to the conversation, Beth imagined what would follow the clash between sexuality and schooling in Kimeca's life. "If she does get kicked out of her school," Beth explained, "it'll be hard to make her go to a different school because they may not accept her." From this statement, it is not clear if Beth meant Kimeca will be rejected by the school administration or by the students. In the conversation, I was struck by this ambiguity and asked Beth to explain further. Beth continued, speaking more specifically about the conditions in which Kimeca would be rejected. "Because if she does keep having sex," Beth explained, "the schools will allow that to happen because maybe *somebody else* will get *a different idea* and do it and that just won't have a really good reputation at school."

Beth explained, it seems, that the schools will "allow" Kimeca to be rejected. This was a significant translation of the group's splitting of sexuality and schooling. In Beth's formulation of the problem, the schools would allow an agent other than the school administration—a social agent such as the students or school community—to reject Kimeca because other students—"somebody else"—might get the idea that having sex, or being sexual, is acceptable. Speaking of students' reputations, Beth again identified the social environment as the dominant force and an unsettling of that environment as the threat the group faced. Was Beth describing her identification with some aspect of the group that would allow her to feel protected from sexuality? Was she worried about her own "different idea," the possibility that she might feel compelled to have sex, might translate her sexuality into different ideas, and therefore might be marginalized within the social environment?

In Beth's statement, the idea of a reputation was ambiguous as well. With her statement "that just won't have a really good reputation," she suggested both that others are susceptible to Kimeca's reputation and that sexuality itself, spread through "different idea[s]," would be a troubling force for the reputations of others. Therefore, the "that" in her statement may reference the sex itself that Kimeca is imagined to have in the future. But it may also reference "a different idea," the thought of sexuality threatening to disrupt a social context in which sexuality is split off from education. A different idea about sexuality—thoughts of sexuality or sexuality as thought—Beth seemed to suggest, has no room in school.

As the focus group facilitator, I felt compelled by Beth's talk of "a different idea" to further the inquiry she has begun. I asked Beth to elaborate on the phrase. "You said they would get a different idea. What do you mean?" I asked. Beth explained: "Of the person, they may follow what she was doing, or she may find it really weird, and it'll cause really bad emotions. It would have a really big problem."

This associative turn contained substantial movement in unconscious thought. When I prompted Beth regarding "a different idea," she first explained a risk: students in school might get a different idea "of the person," Kimeca, and "follow what she [is] doing"—that is, they might have sex or be sexual. But getting an idea "of" a person is different from getting an idea "from" a person. Beth's statement suggested both possibilities constitute the problem. Students might get a different idea "of" Kimeca, of who she is—that is, she might be identified as different from the norm—and they might get a different idea "from" her—that is, they might get an idea about *being sexual* from someone they've identified *as sexual*. When it comes to sexuality, these associations suggest, identifying someone "as" risks identifying "with" them. Recognizing another's sexuality, it seems, invites a person to "follow" that sexuality.

However, and most importantly, in her speech, Beth also associated to Kimeca as an agent of thought and a subject of emotion. When she first introduced the phrase "a different idea," Beth stated that "somebody else" was at risk. Others, with whom Beth identified, would be susceptible to Kimeca's sexual thought. But as Beth elaborated on "a different idea," she began to think against the logic of splitting that held Kimeca at a distance from education. About the state of emotional difficulty, Beth explained, "[Kimeca] may find it really weird." This subtle association revealed Kimeca at risk of having, and thus having the power to have, "a different idea." At that point, Beth encountered Kimeca as another who, also troubled by the complexity of her inner life, could not be known with certitude. The "it" in Beth's statement about Kimeca—"she may find *it* really weird, and *it*'ll cause really bad emotions. *It* would have a really big problem"—was also ambiguous. Many meanings emerged. Kimeca may find the experience of marginalization really weird, but she also may be unsettled, like the members of this group, by sexuality, the thought of sexuality, and the emotional experience of sexuality. If, from one perspective, Beth's statement seems fraught with ambiguity, from another, one in which we can attend to the unconscious inquiry in her associative speech, we can hear Beth urging us to consider how students in school "following" Kimeca, how Kimeca facing social marginalization, and how all students experiencing sexuality as thought, as a "different idea," will "cause really bad emotions."

In a conversation structured by the splitting of sexuality and schooling, in which Kimeca serves as the point of projection for unwanted aspects of sexuality, Beth's account of different ideas and bad emotions was subtle but substantial evidence of a drive toward more integrative thought and a greater capacity for empathy. Beth did not merely link ideas and emotions, she negotiated difficult emotional terrain to consider how a range of others—her peers in school and Kimeca—might think of the different ideas embedded in their emotional lives. Beth thus brought Kimeca, one burdened by an unnamable force of sexuality, into the group as a potential thinker and as one who could feel the emotional difficulty of being and thinking in a group. The emotions, Beth insisted, would be the source of "a really big problem," an impossible problem, it seems, but in a slight turn—a free associative turn—she had a different idea *of* Kimeca, followed what Kimeca was doing, and learned a different idea *from* Kimeca: that is, that both the individual and the group struggle with the emotional experience of sexuality and that the meeting of sexuality and education—though troubling—can be imagined.

Conclusion: Free Association in Sex Education

In this essay, I have provided a close reading of a conversation about sexuality and sexual health. With my analytic approach to thought in the focus group, I have demonstrated how we can attend to particular features of unconscious life—like the defenses of splitting, projection, and idealization—and illuminate unconscious lines of inquiry into sexual knowledge and self-formation. In the group engaged with problems of sexual knowledge, a growth in the capacity for hearing unconscious life can serve substantial educational purposes.

If attention to free associative speech and thought develops one's capacity to hear unconscious life, then orienting education to the free associative elements of communication and thinking can both enable students to think through the complex emotional fabric of their experience *and* encourage them to translate emotional difficulties into intellectual and autobiographical inquiry (Casemore, 2010). This argument entails a psychoanalytic conceptualization of sexuality, one that understands sexuality to be inextricable from emotional life, rooted as they both are in the reception and processing of unconscious meaning. If, as Britzman (2000) explains, "the wanderings of sexuality signify excess, more than we may consciously ask for or even want" (p. 33), sexuality is nonetheless "a force that allows the human its capacity for passion, interests, explorations, disappointment, and drama" (p. 37). In the focus group conversation, despite her own conscious purposes, Beth introduced this emotional fact of human sexuality. Sexuality, she demonstrated, compels different ideas with emotional implications.

Thinking the complexity of emotional experience and translating that experience into inquiry, therefore, are educational purposes that center sexuality in the learning process. And it is through a respect for our free associative capacities that we can foster such educational experience. Psychoanalysis teaches us that ideas are overdetermined in meaning, having an apparent unity constituted through an amalgamation of numerous pathways of thought and experience. Moreover, ideas are not only condensations of other thoughts, images, and ideas but also condensations of affect. "A condensation of ideas," Bollas (2009a) explains, "[is] a dense affective experience, as the various different affects evoked by separate ideas are brought into relationship" (p. 42). In psychoanalysis, a patient free-associates to a psychical text: a dream, narrative, or thought, and the proliferation of associations *both* provides a sense of the plenitude of meaning subtending the dream, narrative, or thought *and* dismantles the assumed meaning of that manifest text. Free association, therefore, both elaborates and deconstructs meaning. Given the emotional density of the manifest text it elaborates and deconstructs, the associative process also returns some aspect of this emotional complexity to the fore of experience. "When ideas are gathered into a unity, such as a dream, the unravelling of this compaction through free association," Bollas explains, "will often therefore involve an emotional experience—a 'moving experience' which derives from the lived structure of emotional organization" (p. 42).

Given the emotional complexity of sexuality, and the way it is manifested in conversations about sexuality and sexual health, the sex educator's open listening and patient responsiveness to free association will invite more reflective, integrative, and empathetic thought in sex education. Such listening and responsiveness encourages the inquiry suggested by associations to unfold. We foster such inquiry when we give students opportunities to stay with their associations—in their incompleteness and uncertain relevance—and to pursue their possible meanings. We forestall such inquiry when we insist that all thinking in sex education must lead to some conception of correct thought and behavior. If we approach with generous curiosity the fractured but abundant meaning of free associative speech in sex education, we can foster the development of a richer, more nuanced emotional fabric of educational experience and thus a more thought-provoking and thought-sustaining sexual health curriculum.

References

Bollas, C. (2009a). *The evocative object world.* London: Routledge.

Bollas, C. (2009b). *The infinite question.* London: Routledge.

Britzman, D. (2000). Precocious education. In S. Talburt & S.R. Steinberg (Eds.), *Thinking queer: Sexuality, culture, and education* (pp. 33–59). New York: Peter Lang.

Britzman, D. (2003). *After-education: Anna Freud, Melanie Klein, and psychoanalytic histories of learning.* Albany: State University of New York Press.

Britzman, D. (2009). *The very thought of education: Psychoanalysis and the impossible professions.* Albany: State University of New York Press.

Casemore, B. (2010). Free association in sex education: Understanding sexuality as the flow of thought in conversation and curriculum. *Sex Education: Sexuality, Society and Learning, 10*(3), 309–324.

Epstein, M. (2002). Going on being. *Buddhism and the way of change.* New York: Broadway.

Feldman, M. (1992). Splitting and projective identification. In R. Anderson (Ed.), *Clinical lectures on Klein and Bion* (pp. 74–88). London: Tavistock/Routledge.

Frosh, S. (2007). Disintegrating qualitative research. *Theory and Psychology, 17*(5), 635–653.

Gilbert, J. (2007). Risking a relation: Sex education and adolescent development. *Sex Education: Sexuality, Society and Learning, 7*(1), 47–62.

Gustafson, J. (Director). (2005). *Desire* [Documentary Film]. New York: Women Make Movies.

Hollway, W., & Jefferson, T. (2000). *Doing qualitative research differently.* London: Sage.

Lesko, N. (2010). Feeling abstinent? Feeling comprehensive? Touching the affects of sexuality curricula. *Sex Education: Sexuality, Society and Learning, 10*(3), 281–297.

Meltzer, D. (2008). *Sexual states of mind.* London: Karnac. (Original work published 1973)

Moss, D. (2003). *Hating in the first person plural: Psychoanalytic essays on racism, homophobia, misogyny, and terror.* New York: Other Press.

Sandlos, K. (2010). On the aesthetic difficulties of research on sex education: Toward a methodology of affect. *Sex Education: Sexuality, Society and Learning, 10*(3), 299–308.

Waddell, M. (2002). *Inside lives: Psychoanalysis and the growth of the personality.* New York: Routledge.

Young, R.M. (1994). *Mental space.* London: Process Press.

CHAPTER THIRTY

Christmas Effects

EVE SEDGWICK*

What's "queer"? Here's one train of thought about it. The depressing thing about the Christmas season—isn't it?—is that it's the time when all of the institutions are speaking with one voice. The Church says what the Church says. But the State says the same thing: maybe not (in some ways it hardly matters) in the language of theology, but in the language the State talks: legal holidays, long school hiatus, special postage stamps, and all. And the language of commerce more than chimes in, as consumer purchasing is organized ever more narrowly around the final weeks of the calendar year, the Dow Jones aquiver over Americans' "holiday mood." The media, in turn, fall in triumphally behind the Christmas phalanx: ad swollen magazines have oozing turkeys on the cover, while for the news industry every question turns into the Christmas question—Will hostages be free *for Christmas?* What did the flash flood or mass murder (umpty-ump people killed and maimed) do to those families' *Christmas?* And meanwhile, the pairing "families/Christmas" becomes increasingly tautological, as families more and more constitute themselves according to the schedule, and in the endlessly iterated image, of the holiday itself constituted in the image of "the" family.

The thing hasn't, finally, so much to do with propaganda for Christianity as with propaganda for Christmas itself. They all—religion, state, capital, ideology, domesticity, the discourses of power and legitimacy—line up with each other so neatly once a year, and the monolith so created is a thing one can come to view with unhappy eyes. What if instead there were a practice of valuing the ways in which meanings and institutions can be at loose ends with each other? What if the richest junctures weren't the ones where *everything means the same thing?* Think of that entity "the family," an impacted social space in which all of the following are meant to line up perfectly with each other:

> a surname
> a sexual dyad
> a legal unit based on state-regulated marriage
> a circuit of blood relationships
> a system of companionship and succor

a building
a proscenium between "private" and "public"
an economic unit of earning and taxation
the prime site of economic consumption
the prime site of cultural consumption
a mechanism to produce, care for, and acculturate children
a mechanism for accumulating material goods over several generations
a daily routine
a unit in a community of worship
a site of patriotic formation

and of course the list could go on. Looking at my own life, I see that—probably like most people—I have valued and pursued these various elements of family identity to quite differing degrees (e.g., no use at all for worship, much need of companionship). But what's been consistent in this particular life is an interest in *not* letting very many of these dimensions line up directly with each other at one time. I see it's been a ruling intuition for me that the most productive strategy (intellectually, emotionally) might be, whenever possible, to *dis*articulate them from one another, to *dis*engage them—the bonds of blood, of law, of habitation, of privacy, of companionship, and succor—from the lockstep of their unanimity in the system called "family."

Or think of all the elements that are condensed in the notion of sexual identity, something that the common sense of our time presents as a unitary category. Yet, exerting any pressure at all on "sexual identity," you see that it elements include

your biological (e.g., chromosomal) sex, male or female;
your self-perceived gender assignment, male or female (supposed to be the same as your biological sex);
the preponderance of your traits of personality and appearance, masculine or feminine (supposed to correspond to your sex and gender);
the biological sex of your preferred partner;
the gender assignment of your preferred partner (supposed to be the same as his/her biological sex);
the masculinity or femininity of your preferred partner (supposed to be the opposite[1] of your own);
your self-perception as gay or straight (supposed to correspond to whether your preferred partner is your sex or the opposite);
your preferred partner's self-perception as gay or straight (supposed to be the same as yours);
your procreative choice (supposed to be yes if straight, no if gay);
your preferred sexual act(s) (supposed to be insertive if you are male or masculine, receptive if you are female or feminine);
your most eroticized sexual organs (supposed to correspond to the procreative capabilities of your sex, and to your insertive/receptive assignment);
your sexual fantasies (supposed to be highly congruent with your sexual practice, but stronger in intensity);
your main locus of emotional bonds (supposed to reside in your preferred sexual partner);
your enjoyment of power in sexual relations (supposed to be low if you are female or feminine, high if male or masculine);
the people from whom you learn about your own gender and sex (supposed to correspond to yourself in both respects);
your community of cultural and political identification (supposed to correspond to your own identity);

and again—many more. Even this list is remarkable for the silent presumptions it has to make about a person's sexuality, presumptions that are true only to varying degrees, and for many people not true at all: that everyone "has a sexuality," for instance, and that it is implicated in each person's sense of overall identity in similar ways; that each person's most characteristic erotic expression will be oriented toward another person and not autoerotic; that if it is alloerotic, it will be oriented toward a single partner or kind of partner at a time; that its orientation will not change over time.[2] Normatively, as the parenthetical prescriptions in the list above suggest, it should be possible to deduce anybody's entire set of specs from the initial datum of biological sex alone—if one adds only the normative assumption that "the biological sex of your preferred partner" will be the opposite of one's own. With or without that heterosexist assumption, though, what's striking is the number and *difference* of the dimensions that "sexual identity" is supposed to organize into a seamless and univocal whole.

And if it doesn't?

That's one of the things that "queer" can refer to: the open mesh of possibilities, gaps, overlaps, dissonances and resonances, lapses and excesses of meaning when the constituent elements of anyone's gender, of anyone's sexuality aren't made (or can't be made) to signify monolithically. The experimental linguistic, epistemological, representational, political adventures attaching to the very many of us who may at times be moved to describe ourselves as (among many other possibilities) pushy femmes, radical faeries, fantasists, drags, clones, leatherfolk, ladies in tuxedoes, feminist women or feminist men, masturbators, bulldaggers, divas, Snap! Queens, butch bottoms, storytellers, transsexuals, aunties, wannabes, lesbian-identified men or lesbians who sleep with men, or . . . people able to relish, learn from, and identify with such.

Again, "queer" can mean something different: a lot of the way I have used it so far in this dossier is to denote, almost simply, same-sex sexual object choice, lesbian or gay, whether or not it is organized around multiple criss-crossings of definitional lines. Again given the historical and contemporary force of the prohibitions against *every* same-sex sexual expression, for anyone to disavow those meanings, or to displace them from the term's definitional center, would be to dematerialize any possibility of queerness itself.

At the same time, a lot of the most exciting recent work on "queer" spins the term outward along dimensions that can't be subsumed under gender and sexuality at all: the ways that race, ethnicity, postcolonial nationality criss-cross with these *and other* identity-constituting, identity-fracturing discourses, for example. Intellectuals and artists of color whose sexual self-definition includes "queer"—I think of an Isaac Julien, a Gloria Anzaldúa, a Richard Fung—are using the leverage of "queer" to do a new kind of justice to the fractal intricacies of language, skin, migration, state. Thereby, the gravity (I mean the *gravitas*, the meaning, but also the *center* of gravity) of the term "queer" itself deepens and shifts.

Another telling representational effect. A word so fraught as "queer" is—fraught with so many social and personal histories of exclusion, violence, defiance, excitement—can never only denote; nor even can it only connote; a part of its experimental force as a speech act is the way in which it dramatizes locutionary position itself. Anyone's use of "queer" about themselves means differently from their use of it about someone else. This is true (as it might also be true of "lesbian" or "gay") because of the violently different connotative evaluations that seem to cluster around the category. But "gay" and "lesbian" still present themselves (however delusively) as objective, empirical categories governed by empirical rules of evidence (however contested). "Queer" seems to hinge much more radically and explicitly on a person's undertaking particular, performative acts of self-perception and filiation. A hypothesis worth making explicit: that there are important senses in which "queer" can signify only *when attached to the first person.* One possible corollary: that what it takes—all it takes—to make the description "queer" a true one is the impulsion *to* use it in the first person.

Notes

* Excerpted from the chapter "Queer and Now," *Tendencies* (pp. 5–9). Durham, NC: Duke University Press, 1993.

1. The binary calculus I'm describing here depends on the notion that the male and female sexes are each other's "opposites," but I do want to register a specific demurral against that bit of easy common sense. Under no matter what cultural construction, women and men are more like each other than chalk is like cheese, than ratiocination is like raisins, than up is like down, or than I is like o. The biological, psychological, and cognitive attributes of men overlap with those of women by vastly more than they differ from them.

2. A related list that amplifies some of the issues raised in this one appears in the introduction to *Epistemology of the Closet*, pp. 25–26.

CHAPTER THIRTY-ONE

Feel Tank

Lauren Berlant

For the last few years a project titled Feminism Unfinished has developed a national program of local cells, dedicated to a variety of topics; one of these is Public Feelings.[1] The Chicago group calls itself a feel tank rather than a think tank, only partly as a joke. Comprised of artists and academics, the feel tank is organized around the thought that public spheres are affect worlds at least as much as they are effects of rationality and rationalization. This is a collaborative project, and collaboration is one of our topics. We study theoretical, historical, and aesthetic materials engaged with the affects and emotions. Right now, we are amassing for future research the negative political emotions because most U.S. citizens and occupants have abandoned participating in the political sphere and because many who do, say, merely vote, do it without optimism for the kind of transformative agency that might/ought to have been a possibility. Some of these emotions: detachment, numbness, vagueness, confusion, bravado, exhaustion, apathy, discontent, coolness, hopelessness, and ambivalence.

Our instinct is that these political emotions are often experienced as disconnection, consciousness at a distance. In the tradition of the negative dialectic, but also in other ways, what does it mean to think about the aversive emotions of negativity as kinds of attachment? We have hosted, for example, an International Day of the Politically Depressed. What does it mean to think of negativity not as an effect of bad power but as a way of being critical without consciousness, as we currently understand its cultivated form? How is it possible to think about cultivated subjectivity in the aesthetic sense without implying uplift, progress, or errancy? Situated in our own contradictions, we are also restless, angry, mournful, and strangely optimistic activists of the U.S. political sphere. I close with the slogan that will be on our first cache of T-shirts and stickers: Depressed? . . . It Might Be Political.

Note

1. Feel Tank Chicago has a complex bureaucratic history. It is a cell in a larger system first generated by the collaborative effort of Janet Jakobsen of the Barnard Center for Research on Women and Elizabeth Lapovsky Kennedy of the Department of Women's Studies of the University of Arizona.

Utopia Now, 2007. Mary Patten

Parade, 2004. Lane Relyea

Introduction: Educating to Affirm Life

Sexuality, Politics, and Education

ANGEL RUBIEL GONZALEZ

The oppressed, who have been shaped by the death-affirming climate of oppression, must find through their struggle the way to life-affirming humanization, which does not lie simply in having more to eat. . . .

—FREIRE, 1970/2000, P. 68

. . . in terms of the *content* and *motivation* of power, the 'will-to-live' of the members of a community, or of the *people*, is already the fundamental *material* determination of the definition of political power. That is, politics is an activity that organizes and promotes the production, reproduction, and enhancement of the lives of the members of that community.

—DUSSEL, 2008, P. 14; AUTHOR'S EMPHASIS

Those fighting to situate schooling in relationship to the projects of liberation and democracy have noted the tensions between reforming and fundamentally changing the nature of schools. While some teachers and organizers see schools as potential sites for fostering critical thought and practice, the emerging imperatives of schooling have made such efforts increasingly difficult. Narrow curricular demands, federal funding strings, and free market imperatives have left schools devoid of the dynamism and complexity found in life. This has led to a climate in which questions about our existence in the world, social justice, history, and difference are pushed to the margins in favor of a business model of education that privileges limited skills and operational efficiency. Similar to Freire's (1970/2000) indictment of the banking model of education, I would argue that schooling in our time has become an act of *necrophilia* and not an affirmation of *life*.

While this charge may smack of hyperbole to some, the battle for life through education is made painfully real to those whose interests, needs, and existence are made invisible by systems such as heterosexism, capitalism, and racism. Whether we are speaking of dilapidated classrooms, narrow curricula, or the physical and symbolic violence endured by youth deemed "different," our task as educators, researchers, and administrators is to understand, as Judith Butler (2004) writes, "what maximizes the possibilities for a livable life, what minimizes the possibility of unbearable life or, indeed, social or literal death" (p. 14). While schools surely have a part to play in making life livable, one needs only to study the history of social movements to see that part of the project of redefining the terms of "livability," for a range of communities, has also meant to reimagine the purpose, structure, and location of education.[1] Thus schooling, as one particular form of education within a particular social and historical context, holds possibility but also is limited in its capacity to carry out the full range of educational and political projects necessary in reproducing the life of vast and diverse communities.

Fortunately, this section on *Sexualities Organizing, Activism, and Education* offers a window onto the ways in which those who have met with the limits of schooling have created, participated in, and developed alternative pedagogical spaces from which to reproduce the life of those whom society deems deviant and thus expendable. The collective group of intellectuals, organizers, educators, and parents found in this section allows us to see the possibilities in reorienting the politics of education in the service of affirming an array of gender expressions and sexualities within schools and broader society. In contrast to the current rhetoric of "schooling for competition in the global economy," this section—situated within the context of struggle, personal experiences, pain, and healing—provides a fresh take on the ways we might come to conceive the purpose of education as the ability to affirm *life*. Similar to Enrique Dussel's (2008) invitation to rearticulate politics as "an activity that organizes and promotes the production, reproduction, and enhancement of the lives of the members of that community" (p. 14), these texts allow us to position education in service of the plurality of human life.

The section begins with a spotlight on Gender JUST, an organization based in Chicago dedicated to holding schools accountable to the needs and well-being of queer youth. Deborah B. Gould's case study of ACT UP sheds light on how "the movement's affective, political, and sexual pedagogies" expanded notions of being, politics, feeling and emotion, and as a result challenged their usage both within and outside of lesbian and gay communities. In his analysis of the Black Panther Party, Ronald K. Porter examines the ways in which a need for coalition building created a reflective educational dialogue wherein the sexual politics of the party could be interrogated and rethought. The notion of self-reflexivity, a key component of critical pedagogical thought, continues as Alan Wong examines how theories of panethnicity have the capacity to provide organizers with useful conceptual tools to resist essentialist discourses both outside and within LGBTQ communities. Andrea Gibson artfully and painfully draws out the contradictory truths of personal struggle and world history from which we as educators and students might begin the difficult but necessary conversations to tackle violence in our lives. Drawing from his experiences as an organizer, Sendolo Diaminah discusses what it would mean to move beyond a politics of inclusion and toward a politics of sustainability where the sovereignty of peoples is predicated on an array of resources that are not mutually exclusive such as food, land, ways of being, and learning about the world. Finally, Anayvette Martinez's poem "Luna Boii" reminds us of the pedagogical power that resides in our positions as elders, adults, and parents as we create spaces where gender and sexual fluidity are not merely accepted but celebrated. The section concludes with a poster designed by Jeanette May that provokes us to not simply expand sex education but also to reimagine its purpose and intent.

The political-pedagogical as expressed throughout the works in this section is not reducible to physical survival but also includes protecting ways of being and knowing that have been historically devalued and underappreciated in our society. Thus, the authors of this section send a clear message: the aim of an education accountable to the freedom of *all* is neither to learn mindless facts and figures, nor to create a compliant citizenry. An education accountable to the array of human needs and desires enables us to affirm our humanity *through* our struggles with the contradictions of our lives. As Gloria Anzaldúa (2002) proposed, perhaps a more profound form of knowing through "conocimiento," allows one to acknowledge the potential of the "knowing within" that is gained from experiences of trauma, healing, and struggle. However, Anzaldúa adds that this redefinition of knowing as such is only possible once we are able to step out of the privileged worldviews that we draw on, and in turn define education, politics, and humanity in a more pluralistic fashion.

The essays, manifestos, interviews, and poetry all contribute to Anzaldúa's pedagogical vision through their analysis of the educative outcomes of struggle through organizing, personal experiences, and parenting. These authors enable us to see not only how the politics of education is transformed, but also, as Dussel (2008) suggests, that politics at large be redefined as the "will to live." Moreover, this section challenges us to understand how social movements large and small function to create the physical, ontological, and epistemic spaces to enable participants to stretch the possibilities of what it means to exist as a human being. Ultimately, *Sexualities Organizing, Activism, and Education* provides rich examples, ideas, and alternatives that enable life to become more livable not just for some, but for all.

Note

1. For instance, in the U.S. context, the SNCC Freedom Schools and the Highlander Folk School are prime examples of movements and peoples looking to redefine both schooling and education.

References

Anzaldúa, G.E. (2002). now let us shift . . . the path of conocimiento . . . inner work, public acts. In G.E. Anzaldúa & A. Keating (Eds.), *This bridge we call home: radical visions for transformation*. New York: Routledge.

Butler, J. (2004). *Undoing gender*. New York: Routledge.

Dussel, E. (2008). *20 theses on politics* (G. Ciccariello-Maher, Trans.). Durham, NC: Duke University Press.

Freire, P. (2000). *Pedagogy of the oppressed* (M. Ramos, Trans.). New York: Continuum. (Original work published 1970)

CHAPTER THIRTY-TWO

Queer Youth of Color Organizing for Safe & Affirming Education

Sam Finkelstein, Lucky Mosqueda, Adrian Birrueta, & Eric Kitty

"I'm here representing queer youth with disabilities," shouted Lucky Mosqueda into the bullhorn. "I have been oppressed because of my sexuality and my gender identity, because of my disability and my needs, because of who I am! If Chicago Public Schools had their way, our mouths would continue to be sewn shut!" Lucky is a student at Roosevelt High School in Chicago and a member of Gender JUST, a Chicago-based grassroots organization led by queer youth of color that works for racial and economic justice. Lucky was one of over 70 queer students of color and allies who took over the lobby of Chicago Public Schools on Thursday, April 29, 2010, to demand action on issues of violence and safety in Chicago schools.

The April 29 lobby takeover was the second in a series of escalating direct actions led by Gender JUST youth. After meeting with the district superintendent several times, Gender JUST youth came to the conclusion that the school district does not have a genuine commitment to dealing with the issue of systemic violence in Chicago Public Schools, including harassment from security guards, heterosexist curriculum, and the lack of any formal grievance process. Consequently, Gender JUST developed a direct-action strategy that demanded the implementation of a grievance process for students who experience violence at the hands of the school system. In response, Gender JUST youth have protested outside of the district headquarters, taken over the lobby of the headquarters, occupied the office of the superintendent, and protested at the superintendent's home. "We're going to keep at this," said Adrian Birrueta, another youth leader of Gender JUST. "At this point, it's about building momentum and pressure, expanding our alliances and our base, and generally highlighting the crisis within Chicago Public Schools until they agree to do something about this issue."

While Gender JUST youth have countless stories of youth-on-youth violence or "gay bashing" experienced within Chicago high schools, the primary issue that youth are bringing to the table is that of systemic violence. "If I get beat up by another student who takes offense to my sexuality or my gender identity, more times than not I can get the school to do something about it," explained Eric Kitty of Gender JUST. "But when I get harassed by a security guard at school or if a teacher calls me a 'fag' or something, that's when we lose our voice." At each of the actions, Gender JUST youth testified about experiences of harassment, assault, neglect, and abuse on the part of the educational institution. While the district would like to paint the issue as one of "bullies" or bad students, Gender JUST continuously highlights the role of the school system itself, including violence perpetrated by staff members and a heterosexist curriculum that does not acknowledge the experiences of queer and transgender students.

Gender JUST came together in 2008 after the school district developed an idea for a "Gay High School" as part of the district's Renaissance 2010 plan of gentrifying education through privatization, charter schools, and the closing of schools in low-income communities of color. While Gender JUST youth were split on the question of whether this school would be helpful to queer youth who are at a greater risk of dropping out, the organization was united in its opposition to any policy that privatized education since it ran contrary to the economic justice framework on which Gender JUST was founded. Gender JUST youth did, however, believe that the issue of violence toward queer youth of color needed to be addressed—although it would be better addressed through systemic solutions that improved conditions for all students. Youth came together to discuss the connections of race and poverty to safety, sexuality, and education. Out of these formal discussions, Gender JUST developed a proposal entitled *Solutions for Safe & Affirming Education*. After a series of direct actions to bring the Chicago Public Schools superintendent to the table, youth presented this proposal to CPS leadership at a public forum in June 2009 in front of 200 community allies.

Threaded throughout all of Gender JUST's work is an intersectional framework that acknowledges and values all the many identities that youth bring to their work. As described by Lucky at the April 29 action, youth identify as queer, as people with disabilities, as people of color, and as countless other identities. It is critical for Gender JUST to bring all these identities to the table when developing solutions and strategies.

As a result of this intersectional framework, Gender JUST pushes solutions based on principles of Restorative Justice. Many groups in the traditional "safe schools" model demand harsher punishments and zero tolerance for those who break "anti-bullying" rules. In contrast, Gender JUST youth realized that this doesn't work for them and their communities, who are often disproportionately targeted by the prison-industrial complex and the school-to-prison pipeline. Therefore, in the midst of Gender JUST's campaign for safe and affirming education in Chicago schools, Gender JUST youth adamantly opposed Safe Schools legislation in the Illinois Legislature because it would have reinforced zero-tolerance policies that hurt youth of color.

For Gender JUST youth, issues of sexuality and education boil down to the simple demand of safe, quality, public education for everyone. While Chicago Public Schools has tried to dismiss Gender JUST's demands as minor issues secondary to academics, we reemphasize that what our youth are experiencing is violence. It is clearly an issue of violence when young people are denied critical health information just because of their sexuality; it is violent when school authorities neglect the safety of a group of young people because of their gender identity; it is violent when young people are denied quality education because of their sexuality. It's important that young people hear about their histories in schools, as highlighted by Gender JUST's frequent chant, "Open up the textbooks and you will see, the history you teach don't represent me!"

Gender JUST, Chicago 2010. Gender JUST

CHAPTER THIRTY-THREE

Education in the Streets

ACT UP, Emotion, and New Modes of Being

DEBORAH B. GOULD

Social movements and other activist formations are sites of collective world-making. Organized with the goal of bringing about other realities, they often counter the common sense, the habits of feeling, and the ways of living that prevail in a given time and place. More than challenging what *is,* they offer something else: the ongoing interactions of participants produce sentiments, ideas, values, and practices that manifest and encourage new modes of being. Along with being instrumental to social change, activist spaces are, in that sense, important sites of unlearning and learning.

In this essay I explore the direct-action AIDS activist movement ACT UP as an exemplar of just such an educational site. It certainly was for me. In 1990, after being in graduate school for 3 years, I took a leave of absence, in part because of the urgency I felt about fighting the AIDS crisis but also because I was learning more from being in the streets with ACT UP. I do not wish to elevate that type of learning over what is gained through books and in the classroom; book learning accompanies me in the streets, and my activist knowledges inform my research and teaching, making any rigid separation across these modes of learning untenable. But in an effort to extend our thinking about learning beyond what occurs in formal educational settings and with an eye toward highlighting some of the noninstrumental dimensions of activism, in this essay I focus on the valuable learning that occurs in activist contexts.

I begin with a brief discussion of the environment in which ACT UP operated. Importantly, the movement's affective, political, and sexual pedagogies enacted and authorized ways of feeling and emoting as well as ways of being political and sexual that went against the normative grain in both mainstream society and the more establishment-oriented lesbian and gay community. I continue, then, with a discussion of how ACT UP addressed its environment, focusing especially on the important role played by the emergence of a renewed *queer* sensibility within the movement and beyond.

The Difficulties of Acting Up

Like other social movements in the United States, ACT UP confronted an American ideology of democracy that locates legitimate political activity in the halls of legislatures and in the voting booth and maligns street activism as unnecessary and extreme, a threat to social order.[1] ACT UP also faced a dominant emotional habitus that governs the U.S. American political sphere: in the realm of political conflict, we tend to favor calm, dispassionate discussion over furious outrage expressed by socially marginalized people amassed in the streets.[2] A dimension of ACT UP's context related to its lesbian and gay composition complicated its task even further: the movement operated in a heteronormative society that naturalizes and privileges heterosexuality and classifies sexual and gender minorities as abnormal deviants. Interpellation, to be sure, is a two-way street: to be hailed as a disgusting pervert does not guarantee one's self-understanding as such. But even if we acknowledge that a given interpellation can be met with "consequential disobedience" (Butler, 1993a, p. 122), we also need to recognize the force of that ideological, discursive hailing: although different individuals are affected differently, few if any queers move through a heterosexist world psychically untouched.

With the psychic effects of oppression in mind, I have argued elsewhere that lesbians' and gay men's subordinated position in a heteronormative society and consequent social nonrecognition, even social annihilation, generate ambivalent feelings among lesbians and gay men about self and society. That widely circulating, contradictory constellation of positive and negative affective states—simultaneous self-love and self-doubt, gay pride and gay shame, as well as attraction toward and repulsion from dominant society—has political effects. Combing through dozens of lesbian and gay newspapers and organizational documents from the early 1980s, prior to ACT UP's emergence, I found that that structure of ambivalence significantly shaped lesbians' and gay men's initial understandings of the crisis as well as their collective political responses to it. Lesbian and gay individuals, activists, and organizations repeatedly expressed and evoked feelings like love for their gay brothers and pride about the community's responsible efforts to fight AIDS, as well as shame about gay sexuality and a corollary fear of intensified social rejection; anger about the government's unwillingness to fund research and services was frequently suppressed. That emotional habitus helped to establish, and delimit, a collective political horizon in the first 5 years of the crisis that authorized some forms of activism—e.g., service provision, lobbying, and candlelight vigils—while delegitimizing anything more confrontational that might rock the boat too much and compromise lesbians' and gay men's social acceptability (Gould, 2009a, 2009b).

Famous for its anger, disruptive direct-action activism, and sex-radicalism, ACT UP, then, had its work cut out for it with regard to both mainstream U.S. society and the more establishment-oriented lesbian and gay community. Vital to the movement's success was its affective pedagogy, the work direct-action AIDS activists did—sometimes consciously but usually less purposively—that nourished and extended an emotional habitus that was both amenable to ACT UP's style of confrontational activism and responsive to the contradictory feelings that make up lesbian and gay ambivalence. ACT UP activists marshaled the widespread grief in lesbian and gay communities, linked it to anger, and tethered both sentiments to confrontational AIDS activism; extended the objects of gay pride to include sexual difference and confrontational activism along with care-taking and service provision; and altered the subject and object of shame from gay shame about homosexuality to government shame about its negligent and punitive response to the AIDS crisis. ACT UP's emotional pedagogy offered new ways for lesbians and gay men to feel about themselves, about dominant society, and about political possibilities amid the AIDS crisis, offering a "resolution" of sorts to lesbian and gay ambivalence that emphasized self-love and self-respect over shame and self-doubt, authorized antagonism toward society, eased fear of social rejection, and challenged the desire for acceptance on straight society's terms.[3] Again, AIDS activists for the most part were not consciously and purposively engaging in this "emotion work" (Hochschild, 1979); it is better understood as simply the air we breathed. Intended or not, the new matrix of feelings, expressed repeatedly in the movement's rhetorical and ritual practices, strongly affected how people in lesbian and gay communities felt not only by legitimizing these feelings, but by naming and enacting them and thereby bringing into being and elevating those emotions while suppressing other feeling states.

Crystallizing this alternative set of feelings was a newly politicized *queer* sensibility that emerged within ACT UP and quickly spread to sexual and gender outlaws not directly involved in the movement. In its valorization of angry, confrontational activism as well as gay difference and sex-radicalism, *queer* knit together ACT UP's affective, political, and sexual pedagogies and effectively addressed the movement's complex context. Offering a compelling vision of "how to be gay" in this moment of crisis, it furnished a powerful response to lesbian and gay ambivalence. In what follows, I explore ACT UP through this lens, as the vital site where this new *queer* sensibility emerged and stimulated alternative ways of thinking, feeling, and being in the world for an entire generation of lesbians, gay men, and other sexual and gender outlaws.[4] But first, to understand how striking was the emergence and flowering of this new *queer* sensibility circa 1990, we need to rewind to the early 1980s, the first years of what since has become known as the AIDS epidemic.

Pre-Queer

From our current vantage point where AIDS is no longer considered a "gay disease" and where many people with HIV/AIDS in the United States have access to drugs and are living longer, it is easy to forget the bafflement, terror, and panic that saturated those first years.[5] The magnitude of the health crisis was unclear, but the forecasts were dire. Dozens, then hundreds, and soon thousands of previously healthy gay men were suddenly being diagnosed with mysterious and rare diseases that indicated a breakdown in their immune systems; the mortality rate was unknown, but some thought it might be close to 100 percent. Equally troubling, the diseases seemed to be striking gay men in particular, reinforcing implausible antigay rhetoric that linked disease to gay identity itself. Indeed, along with the medical aspects of AIDS, lesbian and gay communities simultaneously had to face the social and political dimensions of the epidemic. The AIDS crisis unleashed tremendous state and societal homohatred: politicians, pundits, and others demanded quarantines and tattooing the buttocks of gay men; scores of people with AIDS were fired from jobs, evicted from their homes, disowned by families, and in other ways treated as pariahs. Newly elected to the presidency, Ronald Reagan was intent on preserving close relations with leaders of the homophobic religious right; his championing of neoliberal views and policies, including the evisceration of government-funded social services, also immeasurably slowed the government's response. Local and state governments matched the Reagan administration's aggressive indifference to the epidemic by similarly refusing to respond to the crisis. Indeed, by the mid-1980s, it was clear that legislators were focused less on addressing the needs of people who were sick than on proposing and enacting repressive laws. The mysteries, ambiguities, horrors, and devastation of the epidemic, as well as state and societal (non-) responses to it, alarmed and terrified gay men and lesbians, particularly those living in the urban centers most affected by AIDS.

Amid the insecurity and dislocation of the AIDS epidemic, and in the context of vitriolic and homophobic reactions from the state and dominant institutions of mainstream society, sexual and gender minorities had to reconsider who they were and where they fit within society. They furthermore had to consider their relationship to this epidemic: how they should feel about it and how they should respond. What did AIDS reveal about them? How should they approach the question of the relationship between gay sexual practices and these deadly diseases? How would the epidemic and society's views about it affect lesbian and gay communities? To what extent should they identify with and mobilize around this health crisis, given the immense stigma of AIDS?

In a collective and ongoing way—at community meetings, in AIDS organizations, in the pages of community newspapers, through broadsides, safe-sex education materials, calls for volunteers, and in everyday conversations—gay men, lesbians, and other sexual and gender outlaws engaged in a complex process of meaning-making amid chaos. They drew from gay liberationist discourses that criticized dominant heterosexual society, foregrounded gay community self-determination, and celebrated gay sexuality and gay difference, but also, and frequently, from heteronormative discourses that disparaged gay sexuality, gay culture, and the gay community, ideas that were pervasive, albeit usually subterranean, in lesbian and gay communities.

In a context where mainstream discourses construed AIDS as proof of gay deviance, the perplexing and ambiguous nature of AIDS elicited understandings in gay communities that perhaps inevitably were filled with self-blame, shame, and anxiety about social rejection. The following quotations indicate how powerful and widespread within the gay world were homophobic understandings of AIDS in this period. In an explosive manifesto published in November 1982 in New York's gay newspaper, the *New York Native,* two gay men with AIDS blamed the institutions of the gay male sexual culture, and indeed gay men themselves, for the AIDS epidemic:[6]

> Those of us who have lived a life of *excessive promiscuity* on the urban gay circuit of bathhouses, backrooms, balconies, sex clubs, meat racks, and tearooms know who we are.... [W]e have been unwilling or unable to accept responsibility for the role that our own *excessiveness* has played in our present health crisis. But, deep down, we know who we are and we know why we're sick.... *Our lifestyle has created the present epidemic of AIDS among gay men.* (Callen, Berkowitz, & Dworkin 1982, p. 23; emphases mine)[7]

A statement by a gay doctor went even further: "Perhaps we've needed a situation like this to demonstrate what we've known all along: Depravity kills!" (quoted in Bronski, 1982, p. 9). In a 1983 interview in *Newsweek,* Richard Failla, a New York City gay judge, suggested that shame and self-doubt among gay men were widespread: "The psychological impact of AIDS on the gay community is tremendous. It has done more to undermine the feelings of self-esteem than anything [homophobic crusader] Anita Bryant could have ever done. Some people are saying, 'Maybe we are wrong—maybe this is a punishment'" (quoted in Andriote, 1999, p. 70). Writing in 1985, cultural theorist Cindy Patton similarly noted "intense ambivalence" about sexuality among gay men, even affecting those with a strong gay pride:

> Lurking deep in the heart of even the most positive and progressive lesbians and gay men [is] the fear: maybe they are right, homosexuality is death.... Regardless of the medical facts ... there is an inescapable feeling that sex, the thing which to some important degree defines gay identity and community, is the cause of the killing. It is extremely difficult to escape this sex-negative ethos when people are dying of AIDS every day. (Patton, 1985, pp. 6, 16–17)

Sociologist Steven Seidman cites numerous examples from the first years of the crisis of gay men criticizing promiscuity and using AIDS "as a pretext to speak critically about homosexuality and to advocate reforms of the gay subculture" (1988, p. 197; see also Patton, 1985, pp. 107–108, Rofes, 1990, p. 15, and Padgug & Oppenheimer, 1992, p. 261). Not all gay men and lesbians read AIDS as a morality tale with certain 1970s-inspired gay sexual practices as the villains and adoption of straight society's sexual mores as the path to gay redemption, but many did.

The New *Queer* Sensibility

Against that background, the emergence of a new *queer* sensibility was remarkable indeed. And it also wasn't, in the sense that state and societal responses to the AIDS crisis demonstrated all too clearly that the straight world deemed gay men expendable, indeed, better off dead, whether they were assimilated or not. Like ACT UP itself, the new queer sensibility grew out of the political exigencies of the mid-to-late 1980s. By that point, the AIDS epidemic was exploding and the deadly consequences of existing as a despised population were unambiguous and staggering. Also apparent were the repercussions for gay activism of the painful psychic effects of gay oppression, especially a widespread anxiety about acting up. *Queer* not only challenged the vehement homo-hatred that structured state and societal responses to AIDS; it also offered emotional, political, and sexual ways of being that both addressed that anxiety and helped to carve out an exciting alternative world.

Queer: Anger, Political Opposition, Sex-Radicalism

By 1990, to identify as queer was to embrace righteous anger about homophobia and the AIDS crisis and to link that anger to political defiance; it was to feel proud about sexual difference and relatively unconcerned about social acceptance. Rather than an identity, or even an *anti*-identity in the way that queer theory posits, *queer*, in its moment of rebirth circa 1990,[8] might best be understood as an emotive (Reddy, 1997, 2001), an expression of self and collectivity that created and regenerated feelings that were a powerful and alluring response to lesbian and gay ambivalence about self and society: pride about gay difference and about confrontational activism, fury about homo-hatred, antipathy toward heteronormative society, and aspirations to live in a transformed world.[9]

The new queer generation proudly and joyously shook up norms in straight and gay society. ACT UP queers reeroticized sex and catapulted their proud sexual difference into the public realm, challenging the tendency of the gay establishment to downplay gay difference in a bid for mainstream social acceptance. In sociologist Steven Epstein's words, "Queerness connoted a provocative politics of difference—an assertion that those who embraced the identity did not 'fit in' to the dominant culture *or* the mainstream gay and lesbian culture and had no interest in doing so" (Epstein, 1999, p. 61; emphasis his). ACT UP's queer stance also fought the AIDS-era equation of sex with death and made a clear link between confrontational AIDS politics and liberatory sexual politics. ACT UP/Chicago's speech at the 1992 Lesbian and Gay Pride Parade knit the two together:

> Fighting the AIDS epidemic must go hand-in-hand with fighting for queer liberation. And we mean liberation for all queers! Queers of all colors and sexes, leather dykes and drag queens and radical faeries and bulldaggers and dykes on bikes and poofters and fish and studs and butches and femmes and clones from the 1970s and the 1990s. We need to celebrate our sexuality, our erotic innovations created out of this epi-

demic, our fantasies and fetishes, our particular ways of fucking, sucking, and licking. It is our queer love that has made us capable of fighting the insurance industry, the drug companies, the government, the bureaucracies, the gay-bashers, the right-wing zealots, the AIDS crisis. (ACT UP/Chicago, 1992, p. 5)[10]

The new queer sensibility unabashedly drew sex and militant politics together. ACT UP/Chicago member Mary Patten extolled ACT UP's conjoining of the two: "ACT UP combined the red fists of radical 1970s feminism and the New Left with the flaming lips of neo-punk, postmodern, pro-sex queer politics. . . . Red now stood for lips, bodies, and lust as well as anger and rebellion; fists connoted not only street militancy, but sex acts" (Patten, 1998, p. 389).[11]

Queer also spurred a remarkable coming together of lesbians and gay men, dykes and fags. ACT UP/NY member Polly Thistlethwaite spoke about gay men's and lesbians' "passionate respect for each other," recalling in particular how "revered" many lesbians in the movement were: "Faggots were crazy about these girls" (Thistlethwaite, 1993; see also Moore, 2003, p. 4). Jeanne Kracher recalled that gay men's openness about their sexuality had a strong influence on her own sexuality:

> I think for me, one of the earliest memories I have of really feeling like, "Huh, this is interesting, this is something I haven't experienced before, and this is something I better be open to and learn from," was all the sex-positive stuff [in ACT UP]. . . . Sex certainly was never the basis of anything that I had organized around. Certainly not as a feminist. And there was a way that these guys were so expressive about their sexuality, which helped to free me. . . . There was something about being in that crowd that was very freeing, about being a lesbian, about being gay, that this was about sex on a very deep level. (Kracher, 2000)

Ferd Eggan credits lesbians for the movement's embrace of queer sexuality: "I think that one of the reasons why ACT UP and the AIDS movement in general became a movement about gender and sexuality was because of lesbians. And all the advance work that people had been doing during the '80s, like *On Our Backs* [a lesbian sex magazine]" (Eggan, 1999).

Challenging the recent attacks on queer sexuality, gay men brought their highly developed (and much-maligned) sexual cultures to the movement; lesbians brought their experience from the feminist sex wars and the recent renaissance in lesbian sexual experimentation,[12] and both brought an openness about learning from one another in the sexual realm. United (at least temporarily) by their activism, feelings, and sex-radicalism, lesbians and gay men in ACT UP turned to each other as political allies and friends, embracing and even trying on each other's identities. Men in ACT UP/Chicago wore the Women's Caucus "Power Breakfast" T-shirt, which pictured two women engaged in oral sex. Around the country, dykes wore "Big Fag" T-shirts, and fags wore "Big Dyke" T-shirts. Queers embraced gender and sexual fluidity.

Some queer dykes and fags even started having sex with one another (see Black, 1996).[13] That is not to say that ACT UP created an utterly accepting and experimental sexual environment. Men and women having sex together often felt the need to hide their relationships (Cvetkovich, 2003, p. 194). Still, my recollection is that many of us, although somewhat uncomfortable with the "hetero" queer sex going on in our midst, were trying to interrogate our reactions. Zoe Leonard's reflections about the difficulties she faced in being "out" about having sex with a man in ACT UP/NY indicate some of the complexities of sexual ecumenicalism. At the time, she experienced people's attitudes as "small-minded and painful," but she came to an understanding of why these sexual relationships were difficult for some in the movement to accept: "We had created a safe queer space and now there were people having heterosexual sex within that space, occupying that space. I can understand now why that was threatening" (quoted in Cvetkovich, 2003, p. 193). *Queer* had its sexual limits, then, but there was nevertheless an immense opening out toward sexual and gender outlaws of *most* stripes, especially those who were outcasts in the mainstream gay world—drag queens and kings, trannies, S&M practitioners, butches and femmes, bisexuals, leather dykes, nelly boys, public sex lovers, sluts, dykes donning dildos and other sex toy aficionados, man/boy lovers.[14]

While the new queer attitudes about sexuality, society, and politics took shape in the emotionally charged atmosphere of ACT UP meetings and actions, they rapidly spread to people not directly involved in the movement. Along with being a vital social change organization, ACT UP quickly became a site for self-transformation, and as the movement's ethos circulated outside of its boundaries, new ways of thinking, feeling, and being opened up for LGBT folks across the country. To be sure, as a provocation to both gay and straight establishments, ACT UP was often challenged by lesbians and gay men who disputed its representation (in both senses of the word) of the lesbian and gay movement and community. Still, ACT UP's queer sensibility momentarily overturned the gay status quo, effecting sweeping changes in many lesbians' and gay men's sexual and political subjectivities and practices.

The Emotion of Queer

The emotional effects of reclaiming a queer sensibility were perhaps what most attracted lesbians, gay men, and other sexual and gender outlaws to embrace the term as well as the movement from which it grew. The AIDS epidemic had ravaged lesbians' and gay men's already-conflicted feelings about homosexuality. *Queer*, as an emotive, offered a new sensibility that allowed, encouraged, and in a way *enacted*, a changed orientation both to self and to dominant society. ACT UP/NY member Gregg Bordowitz has written eloquently about his need, after testing HIV-positive in 1988, to fight "an internal conclusion that my pleasure had led to my death" (Bordowitz, 2004, p. 126). He describes "the discourse of blame that would judgmentally bring sentence down upon me for getting fucked up the ass, liking it, and getting a fatal disease from it," asking, "Where did this discourse exist?" He answered, "Among the homophobes. Among the right wing. And in my own mind. Sometimes, I believe that my homosexuality is a disease and that I deserve to get sick from it. This thought can overtake me at any time. I think it in my dreams. I hear it in the voices of kind friends and see it in the faces of my relatives. It's always present." But, he writes, "I am not resigned to it. I fight it" (pp. 126–27). *Queer* offered a potent emotive for the fight. Bordowitz suspects that his embrace of ACT UP's queer fashion was primarily about repudiating the shame he felt about his sexuality (Bordowitz, 2002). ACT UP/NY member Peter Staley credits the movement with queering him, both politically—by enticing him to become a confrontational activist—and in terms of his self-understanding and self-presentation: "ACT UP has had a dramatic effect on my life. I left Wall Street altogether and am doing ACT UP activities full-time, getting arrested, and wearing an earring" (Anger, 1988).[15] ACT UP's queerness, along with the feelings of solidarity generated in the movement, encouraged ACT UP/NY member Michelangelo Signorile to embrace his sexuality. "I'd never felt so close to people I worked with. . . . We were putting our bodies on the line for each other, going to jail for each other. I loved these people—and was loved back—in a way I had never known. I was feeling powerful about being gay. Feelings from when I was a child came back. I had longed for people to tell me that being gay was great. My closet was opening. These people were the most out-of-the-closet, in-your-face people in the world" (Signorile, 1993, p. 63). In a context of social nonrecognition, ACT UP's queer sensibility invited and intensified our recognition of ourselves and one another.

Lesbians' and gay men's appropriation of the label *queer*, as with the appropriation of any collective identity or sensibility, entailed both "an affective as well as cognitive mapping of the social world" (Jasper 1998, p. 415). *Queer* valorized anger, defiant politics, and sexual nonconformity and displaced gay shame, self-doubt, fear of rejection, and the desire for social acceptance. As queer theorist Judith Butler has noted:

> The increasing theatricalization of political rage [e.g., in disruptions of politicians' speeches, die-ins, etc.] in response to the killing inattention of public policymakers on the issue of AIDS is allegorized in the recontextualization of "queer" from its place within a homophobic strategy of abjection and annihilation to an insistent and public severing of that interpellation from the effect of shame. To the extent that shame is produced as the stigma not only of AIDS, but also of queerness, where the latter is understood through homophobic causalities as the "cause" and "manifestation" of the illness, theatrical rage is part of the public resistance to that interpellation of shame. (Butler, 1993b, p. 23)

With outrageous, in-your-face, sexy, and angry activism, queers reappropriated *queer*, expurgating it of its shame-inducing power and, in the process, suppressing feelings of shame they might have had. Where mainstream discourses and some prominent lesbian and gay discourses had earlier blamed gay sexuality for AIDS, *queer* valorized non-normative sexuality and, even more, suggested the positive role of gay male sexual culture in the AIDS epidemic. Similar to cultural theorist and ACT UP/NY member Douglas Crimp, who asserted that "it is our promiscuity that will save us" (1987, p. 253),[16] ACT UP/Chicago member Ferd Eggan challenged criticisms that depicted the 1970s as "a death trip of ruttish sexuality and alienation," urging queers to remember that "gay men's sexual networks in particular were the foundation to build the communities that care for each other now" (Eggan, 1988).

As became evident during the feminist "sex wars" that raged during the 1980s, numerous lesbians had already been engaging in a sexual renaissance that foregrounded a multiplicity of sexual pleasures, some of which had been disparaged in some lesbian feminist circles—use of dildos and other sexual accessories, penetrative sex and fisting, S&M, butch/femme, bondage, and use of pornography. The rebirth of *queer* extended these and other lesbian sexual practices, and discussions about them to many more lesbians and marked a new explosion in lesbian sexual experimentation. Celebrations of queer sexuality united lesbians and gay men in a common cause: the fight against the stigmatization of their sexual practices and identities and the fight for sexual liberation. For both lesbians and gay men, characteristics that queers were supposed to be ashamed of now became sources of pride.

Pride in queer sexuality was pronounced, for example, in a demonstration that ACT UP/Atlanta hosted against Georgia's sodomy law. Five hundred activists from ACT UP chapters across the country demonstrated at the Georgia state capitol on the opening day of the legislature in 1990. Holding signs that read "Sodomy: the law is the perversion" and chanting "Suck my dick, lick my clit, sodomy laws are full of shit," demonstrators simulated sex acts as they blocked traffic (Gerber, 1990, p. 1). In response to the governor's description of the action as "repulsive," one demonstrator stated, "it was an audacious affirmation of lesbian and gay *sex*" (quoted in Gerber, 1990, p. 1; emphasis in original). Chip Rowan, an ACT UP/Atlanta organizer of the protest, called the demonstration "a source of strength and pride for gay people in the South who want to take the risk of coming out publicly" (p. 3). After the sodomy action and a demonstration the next day that targeted the Centers for Disease Control, Rowan remarked, "Everywhere we went today and last night, people were applauding us, saying we had to continue this, saying how good ACT UP made them feel" (p. 3). The pride demonstrated in ACT UP actions—whether it attached to queer sexuality or to confrontational activism—was infectious.

The embrace of a queer, anti-assimilationist, and oppositional sensibility also addressed lesbians' and gay men's fears of social rejection: as they themselves were rejecting society, they were less concerned with society's rejection of queers. To feel and express anger was now normative. The queer embrace of defiant activism valorized as rational and indispensable that which mainstream society typically disparaged as irrational, dangerous, and unnecessary. *OutWeek* columnist Nina Reyes registered the psychological and political shift that had occurred through ACT UP and that was propelling this new queer sensibility forward:

> It took us years to realize that in our attempts to check the ravages of AIDS, we had contributed to the repression of our own queer sexuality. We have had to come to terms with the pall of fear that had descended upon our collective psyches, demonizing promiscuity and equating all of our sexual experimentation with death. Then, in 1986, the U.S. Supreme Court affirmed that we have no basic right to our sexual self-expression. . . . When it became clear that AIDS would decimate not only individual queer lives but our sexually queer culture, ACT UP was spawned. The flickering spirit of liberation ignited queer rage, and our community developed a self-consciously sex-positive movement. . . . The AIDS-activist group has rebaptized the liberation impulse. . . . ACT UP erupted into activism with the incendiary passions of individuals united in anger, unwilling to take it anymore. . . . It gave lesbians and gay men who had had enough of the [gay rights] movement's reservation and politesse the chance to fight hard and dirty and without apology. (Reyes, 1990, pp. 41, 44)

In sum, ACT UP's queer sensibility offered an emotionally compelling response to lesbians' and gay men's often contradictory feelings about self and society. Intense affective states of eroticism and sexiness, exuberance and euphoria, pride and self-respect, now attached to the term *queer* and animated identification with and the embrace of both this new sensibility and ACT UP, the site where new queer selves were being publicly and passionately enacted. As a collective identification that embraced opposition and an outsider status, queerness validated those who held radical politics, who refused assimilation, and who celebrated sexual difference.

Conclusion

ACT UP was a place to fight the AIDS crisis, and it was always more than that as well. It was a place where we learned from one another, offering each other, by example, new modes of thinking, feeling, and being. Participants learned to elaborate critiques of the status quo, imagine alternative worlds, express anger, defy authority, experiment sexually, create alternative forms of intimacy, practice non-hierarchical governance and collective self-determination, argue with one another, develop new desires, refashion identities, feel new feelings, and be changed. Vital in this mix was learning to be queer, a knitting together of new emotional, political, and sexual ways of being.

Activist spaces are vital educational sites. Through protests and other manifestations, social movements unravel commonsense knowledges, counter the subtle and not-so-subtle power relations that pervade our lives, and assert that the way things are is not necessarily natural or the way they must or should be. Reminding us that there is nothing inevitable or immutable about a given state of affairs, social movements offer insights that are easily forgotten in periods when social transformation seems impossible, at best distant. Most importantly, activist formations offer alternative ways of understanding and being in the world, an education with the potential for both social and self-transformation. ACT UP offered an education in being queer, and that emotional, political, and sexual education has shaped LGBTQ activism in the years since.

Notes

1. As social movement theorists Frances Fox Piven and Richard Cloward argue, "The ideology of democratic political rights, by emphasizing the availability of legitimate avenues for the redress of grievances, delegitimizes protest" (1992, p. 313).

2. I use the term *emotional habitus* to describe the collective, largely nonconscious, relatively enduring emotional dispositions within a collectivity and members' embodied, axiomatic attitudes and norms about feelings and their expression. The concept guides us to consider how our feelings are bodily and trained, individual and collective, structured and structuring. See Catherine Lutz (1986, 1988) on anxiety about anger in Western societies.

3. To be sure, any such "resolution" would be temporary and unstable insofar as the repressed or submerged sentiments are not actually purged. On the irresolvability of ambivalence, see Freud (1909/1955), Laplanche and Pontalis (1973, p. 28), and Smelser (1998, p. 6).

4. I use the term *generation* not as a marker of age, but as a way to indicate the ascendance at this time of a queer emotional and political sensibility and its widespread influence on sexual and gender outlaws of many ages.

5. The AIDS mortality rate in the United States has declined dramatically since the advent of protease inhibitors in 1996, but the crisis is ongoing in the United States and especially around the world.

6. Because the once-common view that gay male sexuality is innately "perverse" and that gay men brought AIDS on themselves may still have traction, I should note that AIDS is not caused by homosexual sex *per se* or by the so-called "gay lifestyle" but by a virus (HIV) that has a standard disease transmission route. Anyone who engages in any activity with an HIV-positive person where body fluids like blood or semen are exchanged can become infected with HIV. See Crimp (1987, p. 253) and Bérubé (1988, p. 18) for arguments about how promiscuity among gay and bi men actually may have helped to *curtail* HIV transmission.

7. Notably, the manifesto authors wrote a safe-sex booklet in 1983 that challenged the way that anti-gay, anti-sex moralizing was masquerading as medical advice (Berkowitz, Callen, & Dworkin, 1983).

8. I say *re*birth to indicate that the term *queer* was embraced by some sexual and gender outlaws in earlier historical moments (Chauncey, 1995); I focus here only on its usage circa 1990.

9. On the concept of emotives, see Reddy (1997, 2001); I elaborate on the term in Gould (2009b).

10. Full disclosure: I co-wrote this ACT UP/Chicago speech.

11. Patten (1998, p. 405) credits lesbian pornography editor Susie Bright with popularizing the red fists/red lips metaphor as a way to signal the transformation in lesbian identities in the late 1980s and early 1990s.

12. For accounts of the sex wars, see Snitow, Stansell, and Thompson (1983), Vance (1989), and Duggan and Hunter (1995).

13. This phenomenon may have been more frequent on the coasts than in the Midwest. Although some gay men and lesbians had sex with one another in ACT UP/Chicago, we often joked that we were more "conservative" in the Midwest, where girls do it with girls and boys with boys.

14. *Queer* also had its racial and gender limits. Although for some it signified a political stance for radical social transformation, including challenges to white and male supremacy, for others *queer* elevated sexual oppression above all other oppressions. See Barbara Smith (1993) for an analysis of how *queer* became raced as white and gendered as male.

15. Before joining ACT UP/NY, Staley worked as a bond trader. By his own account, he was deeply closeted while working on Wall Street before joining ACT UP. Accessed June 29, 2008, from http://blogs.poz.com/peter/archives/2008/06/peter_staley_ai.html

16. Crimp's reasoning was that promiscuity taught gay men about sexual pleasures and also about the varied ways to seek and attain those pleasures. "It is that psychic preparation, that experimentation, that conscious work on our own sexualities that has allowed many of us to change our sexual behaviors [amid AIDS]" (1987, p. 253).

References

ACT UP/Chicago. (1992, June). Pride speech. Document housed in author's personal ACT UP archive.

Andriote, J.-M. (1999). *Victory deferred: How AIDS changed gay life in America.* Chicago: University of Chicago Press.

Anger, D. (1988, October). On ACT UP. *ARTPAPER,* p. 10. Document housed in the New York Public Library, Manuscripts and Archives Section, ACT UP/New York Records, and in my personal ACT UP archive.

Berkowitz, R., Callen, M., & Dworkin, R. (1983). *How to have sex in an epidemic.* New York: News from the Front Publications. Reprinted in M. Blasius and S. Phelan (1997), pp. 571–574.

Bérubé, A. (1988, Fall). Caught in the storm: AIDS and the meaning of natural disaster. *Out/Look,* 8–19.

Black, K. (1996). *Fighting for life: Lesbians in ACT UP.* M.A. thesis. Department of Sociology, University of Kentucky.

Blasius, M., & Phelan, S. (1997). *We are everywhere: A historical sourcebook of gay and lesbian politics.* New York: Routledge.

Bordowitz, G. (2002, September 3). Interview conducted by Deborah Gould, Chicago, IL. Interview housed in author's personal ACT UP archive.

Bordowitz, G. (2004). *The AIDS crisis is ridiculous and other writings: 1986–2003.* Cambridge, MA: MIT Press.

Bronski, M. (1982, October 9). AIDing our guilt and fear. *Gay Community News,* pp. 8–10.

Butler, J. (1993a). *Bodies that matter: On the discursive limits of "sex."* New York: Routledge.

Butler, J. (1993b). Critically queer. *GLQ, 1,* 17–32.

Callen, M., & Berkowitz, R., with Dworkin, R. (1982, November 8–21). We know who we are: Two gay men declare war on promiscuity. *New York Native,* pp. 23, 25, 27, 29.

Chauncey, G. (1995). *Gay New York: Gender, urban culture, and the making of the gay male world, 1890–1940.* New York: Basic Books.

Crimp, D. (1987). How to have promiscuity in an epidemic. *October, 43,* 237–271.

Cvetkovich, A. (2003). *An archive of feelings: Trauma, sexuality, and lesbian public cultures.* Durham, NC, and London: Duke University Press.

Duggan, L., & Hunter, N.D. (1995). *Sex wars: Sexual dissent and political culture.* New York: Routledge.

Eggan, F. (1988, October 8). PISD off and fighting back. Keynote speech from ACT NOW AIDS Teach-in in Washington. Document housed in author's personal ACT UP archive.

Eggan, F. (1999, October 30). Interview conducted by Deborah Gould, Chicago, IL. Interview housed in author's personal ACT UP archive.

Epstein, S. (1999). Gay and lesbian movements in the United States: Dilemmas of identity, diversity, and political strategy. In B.D. Adam, J.W. Duyvendak, and A. Krouwel (Eds.), *The global emergence of gay and lesbian politics: National imprints of a worldwide movement* (pp. 30–90). Philadelphia, PA: Temple University Press.

Freud, S. (1955). A phobia in a five-year-old boy. In J. Strachey (Ed.), *The standard edition of the complete psychological works of Sigmund Freud* (vol. 10, pp. 3–149). London: Hogarth Press. (Original work published 1909)

Gerber, J. (1990, January 14–20). Southern discomfort: ACT UP/Atlanta hosts two days of protests against sodomy laws and the CDC. *Gay Community News,* pp. 1, 3.

Gould, D. (2009a). The shame of gay pride in early AIDS activism. In D. Halperin and V. Traub (Eds.), *Gay shame* (pp. 221–255). Chicago: University of Chicago Press.

Gould, D. (2009b). *Moving politics: Emotion and ACT UP's fight against AIDS.* Chicago: University of Chicago Press.

Hochschild, A.R. (1979). Emotion work, feeling rules, and social structure. *American Journal of Sociology, 85*(3), 551–575.

Jasper, J.M. (1998). The emotions of protest: Affective and reactive emotions in and around social movements. *Sociological Forum, 13*(3), 397–424.

Kracher, J. (2000, February 15). Interview conducted by Deborah Gould, Chicago, IL. Interview housed in author's personal ACT UP archive.

Laplanche, J., & Pontalis, J.-B. (1973). *The language of psycho-analysis* (D. Nicholson-Smith, Trans.). New York and London: W.W. Norton & Company. (Original work published 1967)

Lutz, C. (1986). Emotion, thought, and estrangement: Emotion as a cultural category. *Cultural Anthropology, 1,* 287–309.

Lutz, C. (1988). *Unnatural emotions: Everyday sentiments on a Micronesian atoll & their challenge to Western theory.* Chicago: University of Chicago Press.

Moore, P. (2003). Interview conducted by ACT UP Oral History Project. Available at www.actuporalhistory.org

Padgug, R.A., & Oppenheimer, G.M. (1992). Riding the tiger: AIDS and the gay community. In E. Fee and D.M. Fox (Eds.), *AIDS: The making of a chronic disease* (pp. 245–278). Berkeley and Los Angeles: University of California Press.

Patten, M. (1998). The thrill is gone: An ACT UP post-mortem (confessions of a former AIDS activist). In D. Bright (Ed.), *The passionate camera* (pp. 385–406). New York: Routledge.

Patton, C. (1985). *Sex and germs: The politics of AIDS.* Boston: South End Press.

Piven, F.F., & Cloward, R.A. (1992). Normalizing collective protest. In A.D. Morris and C.M. Mueller (Eds.), *Frontiers in social movement theory* (pp. 301–325). New Haven, CT: Yale University Press.

Reddy, W.M. (1997). Against constructionism: The historical ethnography of emotions. *Current Anthropology, 38*(3), 327–351.

Reddy, W.M. (2001). *The navigation of feeling.* Cambridge: Cambridge University Press.

Reyes, N. (1990, August 15). Queerly speaking: The three-word title of an essay has hurled the lesbian and gay community into yet another raging controversy. Why has "I hate straights" ignited such a furor? *OutWeek*, pp. 40–42, 44–45.

Rofes, E. (1990, Spring). Gay lib vs. AIDS: Averting civil war in the 1990s. *Out/Look*, 8–17.

Seidman, S. (1988). Transfiguring sexual identity: AIDS & the contemporary construction of homosexuality. *Social Text, 19/20,* 187–205.

Signorile, M. (1993). *Queer in America: Sex, the media, and the closets of power.* New York: Random House.

Smelser, N.J. (1998). The rational and the ambivalent in the social sciences: 1997 presidential address. *American Sociological Review, 63,* 1–16.

Smith, B. (1993, July 5). Queer politics: Where's the revolution? *The Nation*, pp. 12–15.

Snitow, A., Stansell, C., & Thompson, S. (Eds.). (1983). *Powers of desire: The politics of sexuality.* New York: Monthly Review Press.

Thistlethwaite, P. (1993, September 26). Interview conducted by Kate Black. Interview housed at the Lesbian Herstory Archives, Brooklyn, New York.

Vance, C.S. (Ed.). (1989 [1984]). *Pleasure and danger: Exploring female sexuality.* London: Pandora Press.

CHAPTER THIRTY-FOUR

A Rainbow in Black

The Gay Politics of the Black Panther Party

RONALD K. PORTER

We may not have been able to talk about gendered racism; "sexuality" may have still meant sexiness; homophobia, as a word, may not yet have existed; but our practice, I can say in retrospect, was located on a continuum that groped and zigzagged its way toward this moment of deliberation on the pitfalls of nationalism and essentialism.

—DAVIS, 1998, P. 291

In August 1970 Black Panther Party (BPP) cofounder and leader Huey P. Newton published a letter in the party newspaper, *The Black Panther*, that has since been celebrated as an essential writing on gay and lesbian liberation.[1] In "A Letter from Huey to the Revolutionary Brothers and Sisters About the Women's Liberation and Gay Liberation Movements," Newton acknowledged that homosexuals constitute an oppressed group. He urged BPP members to recognize the legitimacy of the Gay Liberation Movement by, for instance, removing derogatory terms against homosexuals from their vocabulary. In statements that illuminated the social status of homosexual persons and articulated a working theory of homophobia, Newton argued that those in the Black Panther Party should transcend a "revolutionary value system" that worked to oppress homosexuals, and that men should be willing to discuss how their hatred of homosexuals stems from their own insecurity and fear of possibly being identified as homosexual. Newton declared, "We haven't said much about the homosexual at all but we must relate to the homosexual movement because it's a real thing. I know through reading, and through my life experience, my observations, that homosexuals are not given freedom and liberty by anyone in the society. Maybe they might be the most oppressed people in the society" (p. 5).

Curiously, Newton's letter has since been simultaneously overlooked and celebrated. While scholars in the areas of African American studies and BPP history have written on topics such as the formation and history of the Black Panther Party (Jones & Jeffries, 1998; Self, 2006; Sing, 1998, 2004; Smith, 1999), the party's survival programs (Abron, 1998), the Oakland Community School

(Huggins & LeBlanc-Ernest, 2009), the political repression of the party (Churchill, 2001; Churchill & Wall, 2002; Jones, 1988; Newton, 1996), and the role of women in the party (K.N. Cleaver, 2001; Jennings, 1998; LeBlanc-Ernest, 1998; Matthews, 1998; Williams, 2006), Newton's letter—and the resulting conversations and Revolutionary People's Constitutional Convention of 1970—have received scant attention. In addition, although there has been increasing interest in the role of women in the Black Panther Party over the past twenty years, very few scholars have written on the multiple forms of masculinity found in the party or the issue of sexuality (Estes, 2005).

Newton's letter has been partially examined in intellectual circles that focus on lesbian, gay, bisexual, transgender, and queer (LGBTQ) social movements and black LGBTQ history. Scholars and activists in these areas invoke the letter not only because of its concern with coalition building among blacks, gays, lesbians, women, and others but also because it has been identified as a pioneering pro-gay statement made by a black political organization (Deitcher, 1995; Grau, n.d.; Teal, 1995). In the words of scholars Carbado, McBride, and Weise (2002):

> Never before had a black civil rights group recognized lesbians and gay men as an oppressed population...facing a struggle for acceptance and equality comparable to that of African Americans. For the first time in the movement's history, blacks sought political coalitions with gay activists based on their similar oppression. (pp. 113–114)

However, while scholars focusing on gay history and social movements have mentioned the Newton letter, they have only done so in passing. The relative dearth of information on this text within black studies circles and the passing glance by LGBTQ historians unfortunately works to obscure not only the historical and theoretical tensions that led to the letter's creation and the response from the Panthers themselves, but also the pedagogical implications of this story. In other words, the story of how Newton and some Panther members critiqued status quo homophobia raises questions regarding how social movements operate as educative spaces, in which participants develop new understandings of their social conditions and new tactics of agitation.

This article takes the Huey P. Newton letter, and the historical/intellectual climate in which it was written, as a useful point of departure to illuminate how the Black Panther Party leadership approached the issue of homosexuality. The letter was written at a critical juncture in the history of multiple liberation movements. In the words of political activist and scholar Angela Y. Davis, "If I recall that moment what strikes me most in hindsight is that there was a certain kind of attentiveness to what we might today call intersectionality" (personal communication, September 8, 2010). To be sure, some in the BPP leadership made an indelible contribution to the LGBTQ movement by considering both the nature and elimination of gay and lesbian oppression. As Rawley Grau (n.d.) points out, the letter was a major breakthrough for the emerging Gay Liberation Movement, which sought to form alliances with progressive and leftist groups following the 1969 Stonewall Riots. The Panther letter appeared to be a welcome mat in the midst of "New Left groups [who] were usually no less homophobic than the rest of the country" (para. 1). Newton's stance on gay liberation represents both a criticism of and departure from the hegemonic heterosexism and homophobia that plagued both the Black Power and Black Nationalist Movements. In addition, his intervention illustrates how social movements can operate with a pedagogical force—via ideological reflection and coalition building—that offers everyone a richer notion of humanity that directly challenges dehumanization in all its forms. In order for some in the Black Panther Party to take up the issue of gay and lesbian oppression, a general openness to the issue had to exist within the ideological framework of the party, and complex coalitions had to be established and maintained between members of the party and persons who were involved in the burgeoning Gay Liberation Movement.

The Black Panther Party: A Historical Context

Born of the turbulent political climate of the late 1960s, the Black Panther Party developed as a direct response to the oppression faced by blacks in Oakland, California. Founding members Huey P. Newton (1995) and Bobby Seale were frustrated with the intellectual posturing of other black political groups that they felt were not truly attentive to the plight of all black persons (pp. 108–109). According to Newton and Seale, victories in civil rights legislation did not appear to directly affect the lives of black people living in the inner city. Newton and Seale wanted an organization imbued in actions that sought to meet the specific needs of black people. In 1966, Newton and Seale drafted the "Black Panther Party Platform and Program." Also known as the Ten Point Program, the document outlined the specific needs of all black people at the time, ending with a summation emphasizing, "We want land, bread, housing, education, clothing, justice and peace." The BPP initiated this program by establishing police patrols in accordance with party platform number seven, which stated, "We want an immediate end to POLICE BRUTALITY and MURDER of black people." The Panthers argued that the police patrols were a form of self-defense to defend the "black community from racist police oppression and brutality" ("October 1966 Black Panther Party Platform and Program," 1968, p. 23). However, members of the Black Panther Party also felt a new form of self-actualization through the taking up of arms in order to defend themselves and their communities. As Newton (1995) emphasized, "With weapons in our hands, we were no longer their [the police's] subjects but their equals" (p. 120). Panthers on patrol carried guns but were also well versed in the law and surveilled the police while remaining completely within the sphere of their rights as citizens.

The Black Panther Party stepped onto the national and international scene as a result of two events. The first occurred in May 1967 at the California State Capitol. The Panthers arrived at the Capitol carrying arms to protest the Mulford Act, a bill directed at stopping their police surveillance program. The protest failed to prevent the passage of the Mulford Act, but media outlets broadcasted images of black men carrying guns to a national audience (Newton, 1995, pp. 150–151). *The New York Times* reported that the group of armed "anti-white" Negroes clad in "black or dark blue berets with bandoliers of shells draped across their shoulders" had invaded the Sacramento legislature ("Armed Negros Protest Gun Bill," 1967). The imagery and language invoked at this event—including the use of guns, hypermasculine and highly heterosexualized men in militaristic uniforms, and supportive black women—worked to assert a politics of blackness through the archetype of heteropatriarchal masculinity. As Elaine Brown (1992), later Chairman of the Black Panther Party, observed during her early involvement in the party, "Guns were the natural accessory of the new black militants, who were determined to claim their manhood 'by any means necessary'" (p. 107). The move made in Sacramento, the assertion of a politics via one's manhood, should not be too surprising (Freire, 2003, pp. 45–46). Black Nationalist and cultural movements occurring during the Black Power era sought to assert ideals that equated political freedom with the assertion of heterosexual and patriarchal masculinity. Nevertheless, in order to even consider the plight of any homosexual population, some members of the Black Panther Party would have to work to transcend this model that equated political action with hypermaleness.

The second event occurred in October 1967, when Huey P. Newton, then BPP Minister of Defense, was arrested and faced capital charges for the killing of Officer John Frey. This incident sparked a highly publicized and international "Free Huey" campaign, which not only further increased Panther membership but also moved the Black Panther Party in the years that followed to build coalitions with other leftist political organizations and individuals, including gay French writer and activist Jean Genet. These developments are critical to an understanding of the Newton letter, because as the Panthers began to gain more exposure and broaden their political base, members of the group also began consider the relevance of other movements. As a result of their growing exposure, the BPP shifted from strictly adhering to a nationalist ideology to an internationalist ideology. According to political activist and scholar George Katsiaficas (2001), "The platform and program were written during the party's black nationalist phase. Still to come were three more phases in the ideological evolution of the BPP: revolutionary nationalist, revolutionary internationalist, and intercommunalist" (p. 144). These differences in ideology are highlighted by the changes in the BPP's stance on various issues between the 1966 founding and the 1970 Revolutionary People's Constitutional Convention. In 1966 the BPP advocated for an end to the robbery of the black community, while in 1970 they argued for the complete abolition of capitalism. In addition, in 1966 the Panthers focused primarily on the rights of black people, and the Ten Point Program is marked by highly masculine rhetoric (there are no fewer than fifteen uses of the words "man" or "men" in the program). By 1970 the Panthers not only sought to produce an International Bill of Rights but also replaced the term "man" with "people," and moved to support both the Women's and Gay Liberation Movements (Katsiaficas, 2001, p. 152). Newton himself claimed that when the Black Panther Party first started in 1966 they considered themselves to be a Black Nationalist organization. However, as time passed, some Panther members began to realize that the concept of nationalism was flawed (Erikson & Newton, 1973, pp. 27–28). This conclusion led to an expansion of the Black Panther Party's activities beyond just the black community toward those striving for a unity of identity. As a result, the Panthers began to identify with other oppressed peoples and to build networks of solidarity with other political movements and organizations, such as the Gay Liberation Front. It is this international perspective, coupled with an evolving political ideology, that opened the space for the Black Panther Party to publicly consider the revolutionary potential of gay and lesbian persons.

Black Nationalism, Masculinity, and the Controversial Gay Subject

In order to understand the process through which the Black Panther Party considered the revolutionary implications of homosexuals as a group, one must begin by exploring the ideology of the broader Black Nationalist Movement. Black Nationalism emerged as a critique of the integrationist strategies of the Civil Rights Movement and advocated enhanced racial dignity, black economic control within communities, and an appreciation of black culture. The Black Nationalist mood, however, was set in masculine tones that disparaged both black women and other perceived threats to black manhood. Davis (2004) worked for the Los Angeles Chapter of the Student Nonviolent Coordinating Committee (SNCC) in 1968. "All the myths about black women surfaced," Davis recalled. "We were trying to control everything, including the men—which meant by extension that we wanted to rob them of their manhood" (p. 181). Women in power were, according to Davis, viewed as "aiding and abetting the enemy, who wanted to see black men weak and unable to hold their own" (p. 181). Scholar E. Frances White (2001) elaborates on Davis's claim by arguing that Black Nationalism worked as a politically charged double-edged sword. On the one hand Black Nationalism operated as an oppositional movement that actively critiqued white supremacy. On the other hand, White argues, this critique was often performed through the construction of conservative "utopian" images of what it means to be black. The construction of an African past and an authentic blackness often reinscribed European and/or oppressive views of history and gender relations (pp. 117–120). Although Black Nationalism purported to do the work of reconstructing black humanity and masculinity, it did so in a constrictive way that upheld conservative notions of familial and gender roles.

Due to the movement's emphasis on the importance of the maintenance of one's manhood, especially in terms of providing for the community and the nation, the homosexual—and especially the black homosexual—remained the ultimate threat within the context of Black Nationalism. In 1968, when the Black Nationalist Movement was at its apex, Eldridge Cleaver (1991), who was the Minister of Information for the Black Panther Party, wrote an essay entitled "Notes on a Native Son," which appeared in his book *Soul on Ice*. Written as a critique of author James Baldwin, Cleaver argued passionately that Baldwin possessed a reverence for white people, while at the same time participating in "the most grueling, agonizing, total hatred of . . . blacks" (p. 124). According to Cleaver's thinking, the black homosexual is a being whose masculinity has been destroyed and whose manhood has been "castrated" by the white man (p. 128). Revealing his true thoughts on the nature of homosexuality, Cleaver stated, "Homosexuality is a sickness, just as are baby-rape or wanting to become head of General Motors" (p. 136). This marginalization of gay black men within the context of Black Nationalism highlights not only a lingering heterosexism but also contradictory thoughts regarding masculinity and gender roles existing within the Black Panther Party itself.

In the preceding statements we see three continual themes regarding Black Nationalism, gender relations, and homosexuality. First, race is defined in such a way that those who are identified as feminists, lesbians, or gay men are excluded from the category of being black. Second, homosexuality is associated with whiteness, and the homosexual is a pathological subject in terms of authentic blackness. Third, the black homosexual is perpetually weak because he is intrinsically linked to the idea of assimilation. It is important to keep in mind how the creation of the Newton letter and discussions concerning homosexuality acted as a departure from the regulatory politics of Black Nationalism occurring both within and beyond the Black Panther Party. It is to this complex approach to homosexuality and the historical climate that created the Newton letter that we will now turn.

Huey P. Newton's Critique and the Revolutionary People's Constitutional Convention of 1970

Forces acting both within and beyond the party would move Newton and members of the BPP leadership to take a concrete stance on the issue of gay liberation.[2] Prior to the emergence of the Gay Liberation Movement and despite Cleaver's homophobic rhetoric, James Baldwin influenced many members of the Black Panther Party, including Newton. According to Davis, Baldwin proved influential due to his openness regarding his sexuality, a posturing that prefigured the Gay Liberation Movement and thus demanded the need for coalition-building tactics that transcended one's racial identity (personal communication, September 8, 2010). In 1969 a group of gay men and transsexuals of color protested in New York's Greenwich Village in response to police harassment ("4 Policemen Hurt in Village Raid," 1969, p. 33). This event, known as the Stonewall Riots, instigated the Gay

Liberation Movement and brought the issue of gay oppression to national, and BPP, attention. The following year, French writer, activist, and homosexual Jean Genet entered the United States to advocate for imprisoned members of the BPP, including Huey P. Newton and Bobby Seale (E. White, 1993, pp. 521–522).

Like Baldwin, Genet's presence would prove influential in bringing the politics of homosexuality to the attention of the Panthers. On the evening of his initial meeting with the Panthers in the United States, Genet went into a bathroom at a hotel where he was staying with BPP Chief of Staff David Hilliard and New York Deputy Information Officer Zayd Shakur to change for the night. He emerged wearing a red silk kimono, which Hilliard immediately interpreted as being a lady's negligee. Genet, insulted by the repeated use of homophobic language by the BPP, then began to scream in French and knock over objects in the room (Sandarg, n.d., p. 57). Davis insists that Genet's actions that evening forced a conversation with the Panthers on the issue of the fluidity of sexuality (Davis & Huggins, 2006; E. White, 1993, p. 529). According to Sandarg, following the incident the Panthers began to offer political education classes on homophobia. Hilliard recalls, "Genet became our educator; he enlightened us and humanized us" (as cited in Sandarg, n.d., p. 58). Genet later asserted that the Panthers sought him out specifically to inform them on the issue of homosexuality following a surge of gay activism "because it was a subject they didn't understand very well." Genet continued, "I sent David [Hilliard] a letter in which I explained to him that, like the color of one's skin, homosexuality was a matter of fate; that it did not depend on us to be or not to be homosexuals" (Démeron, 1972, p. 100). Reports on these events, including Genet's continuous agitation over Panther rhetoric referring to adversaries as "faggots" and "punks," would have a profound influence on imprisoned Panther leader Huey P. Newton (E. White, 1993, p. 527).

Newton was released from prison in August of 1970. That same month he wrote and published "A Letter from Huey to the Revolutionary Brothers and Sisters About the Women's Liberation and Gay Liberation Movements." The letter appeared in the BPP paper, *The Black Panther*, on August 21. In the article Newton acknowledged that women and homosexuals constitute an oppressed group and that there was a need for both the recognition of the Gay Liberation Movement and the purging of derogatory terms against homosexuals from activist vocabulary. He began by arguing that members of the party should move beyond "personal opinions" and "insecurities" in order to build coalitions with the Women's Liberation and Gay Liberation Movements. Newton was fearful of the Black Panther Party reproducing systems of oppression, what he called a "racist type attitude like the White racists use against people because they are black and poor," to further marginalize homosexuals and women (p. 5). He spoke specifically on what he perceived to be the source of patriarchy and homophobia, arguing that women and homosexuals are feared because insecure men perceive that women wish to emasculate them, and that men "want to hit the homosexual in the mouth because we're afraid we might be homosexual" (p. 5).

Focusing on arguments over what makes an individual a homosexual, Newton insisted that he could not provide answers to that question. He stated, "Some people say it's the decadence of capitalism. I don't know whether this is the case; I rather doubt it. But whatever the case is, we know that homosexuality is a fact that exists, and we must understand it in its purest form: That is, a person should have freedom to use his body in whatever way he wants to" (p. 5). Newton then went on to say that while the Panthers should support the Gay Liberation Movement, they should not be averse to criticizing actions taken by gay individuals and groups that were antirevolutionary. Due to the evolution of BPP political ideology, Newton understood that it would be critical to build coalitions between the Black Panther Party and the emergent gay Liberation Movement. Contrary to statements made by Black Nationalists, Newton did not assert that homosexuality *in and of itself* was counterrevolutionary. In fact, he emphasized that a homosexual could in fact possibly be the "most revolutionary" member of a movement. Speaking directly on the need to illuminate the insecurities that result in the disparagement of homosexuals, Newton argued:

> We should be willing to discuss the insecurities that many people have about homosexuality. When I say "insecurities," I mean the fear that they're some kind of threat to our manhood. I can understand this fear. Because of the long conditioning process which builds insecurity in the American male, homosexuality might produce certain hang ups in us. I have hang ups myself about male homosexuality. Where, on the other hand, I have no hang up about female homosexuality. And that's phenomena in itself. I think it's possibly because male homosexuality is a threat to me, maybe, and the females are no threat. (p. 5)

While the article did make very bold statements regarding gay oppression, it only referenced homosexuality occurring outside of the Black Panther Party. Nevertheless, Newton (1970) did take Genet's frustrations to heart, proclaiming, "The terms 'faggot' and 'punk' should be deleted from our vocabulary, and especially we should not attach names normally designed for homosexuals to men who are enemies of the people, such as Nixon or Mitchell" (p. 5). In addition, he continued to argue that revolutionary activists should not isolate the Women's and Gay Liberation Movements. In discussions that took place at Yale University with Erik H. Erikson in 1971, Newton asserted:

> We think it is very important to relate and understand the causes of the oppression of women and gay people. We can see that there are contradictions between the sexes and between homosexuals and heterosexuals, but we believe that these contradictions should be resolved within the community. Too often, so-called revolutionary vanguards have tried to resolve these contradictions by isolating women and gay people, and, of course, this only means that the revolutionary groups have cut themselves off from one of the most powerful and important forces among the people. (Erikson & Newton, 1973, p. 43)

Newton's proclamation, however, was not met without criticism. Ericka Huggins, BPP member and Director of the Oakland School Community Project, reports that while there was an internal backlash against the letter, Newton's intervention led to teach-ins within the party on the issue of homosexuality. While specific information on the content of the political education classes on homosexuality remains sparse, Huggins notes that they certainly provided an open space for party members to share their thoughts on the issue. Huggins adds, "The women really did not have a problem with it, but the men were not down. One man said to me something like, 'I can't believe Huey wrote that. I'm not getting fucked in the ass,' not realizing the memo highlighted social change, not a change in one's sexuality" (personal communication, April 24, 2009). These teach-ins would be pivotal in the Panthers' approach to the issue of homosexuality during the 1970 Revolutionary People's Constitutional Convention. However, the FBI would use the rifts in the BPP concerning homosexuality in order to create divisions within the BPP. According to Sandarg, the following letter was sent to David Hilliard from the San Francisco Federal Bureau of Investigation office:

> Mr. David Hilliard,
> I seen by last week paper that now the Panthers are supposed to relate to c......s. Huey is wrong. Something must have happened to him in prison. Panthers got enough things to do in the Ten Point Program and fighting for niggers without taking up with m......f queers.
> All Power to the People. (p. 58)[3]

While this letter from the FBI was generated to establish derision within the party, it does indeed reflect the sentiments of many members of the Black Panther Party. However, Huggins and Davis argue that Newton's letter was meant to operate as a pedagogical tool that would initiate conversations within the party about homosexuality and that such responses were a natural part of the process in the growth of the Panthers' ideology (Davis, 1998, p. 292; Newton, 1973/2002). In addition, Newton's words were taken seriously within the Gay Liberation Movement itself. Following an increase in police harassment of gays in Manhattan, members of homosexual organizations convened a news conference to publicly protest police repression. An individual at the conference not only stated, "All power to gay people" (an adaptation of the Panther slogan, "Power to the People"), but members also mentioned that Newton had requested that BPP members "try to form a working coalition with the Gay Liberation and Women's Liberation Groups" (Fraser, 1970, p. 28).

A second article written by Newton in 1973 also suggested that his views about homosexuality were evolving. In "Eldridge Cleaver: He is no James Baldwin," Newton criticized Cleaver for his homophobia and sexism in "Notes on a Native Son." In a biting criticism that attempted to debunk Cleaver's definitions of masculinity and manhood and which affirmed Baldwin and Genet's influence, Newton (1973/2002) asserted:

> If only this failed revolutionist had realized and accepted the fact that there is some masculinity in every female and some femininity in every male, perhaps his energies could have been put to better use than constantly convincing himself that he is everyone's superstud. How confused and tortured he must be to equate homosexuality, baby-rape, and the desire to become the head of General Motors. But Cleaver's imagination is not healthy. It is paranoid and self-condemning; it is consumed by a need to be female and white. He is no Baldwin, no Genet. (p. 289)

Because this article was written in 1973, however, it must be examined within the context of the split occurring in the BPP in 1971 over what methods to utilize in the struggle. It is well known that Cleaver and Newton were bitter enemies during this period, and one can interpret this article as being less about homosexuality and more about a lingering political rivalry. Yet, when asked about this article, Huggins commented that Newton's statement exemplified the open attitude he had about issues of sexuality since the founding of the BPP (personal communication, December 1, 2006). Both Genet's reports and Newton's articles clearly illustrate that the Black Panther Party publicly took the issue of homosexuality into account after 1969. While it can be argued that these debates only occurred at the level of BPP leadership, an actual event confirmed that they did have concrete influence on BPP political work.

In 1970 the Black Panther Party convened a special convention in Philadelphia with the purpose of rewriting the U.S. Constitution. This convention, known as the Revolutionary People's Constitutional Convention (RPCC), provided a clear example of how seriously the issue of gay oppression was viewed by the Black Panther Party. *The New York Times* reported that 6,000 people, half of them white, participated in the RPCC along with members of the Women's and Gay Liberation Movements (Delaney, 1970b, p. 13). Katsiaficas (2001), who attended the convention, reported that the event began with a crowd of gay people "chanting and clapping rhythmically: 'Gay, gay power to the gay, gay people! Power to the People! Black, black power to the black, black people! Gay, gay power to the gay, gay people! Power to the People!'" (p. 147). According to *The Black Panther*, recommendations made at the RPCC included the need for proportional representation of women and people of color in government, the replacement of prisons with "community rehabilitation programs," an overhaul of the racist criminal justice system, and the provision of health care and housing to all as a constitutional right. The *Panther* also asserted that, along with these provisions, "Sexual self-determination for women and homosexuals was affirmed" (Rosemarie, 1970, p. 3).

The *New York Times* reported that the RPCC welcomed the participation of individuals from diverse communities, which was a clear departure from the "racial separatism" promoted at meetings held earlier that year by Black Nationalist organizations in Mobile, Alabama, and Atlanta, Georgia. When questioned in a news conference on the inclusion of other liberation movements, Raymond (Masai) Hewitt, BPP deputy Minister of Education, stated, "We feel a move on behalf of any oppressed people is a move in the right direction" (as cited in Delaney, 1970a, p. 57). Zayd Shakur, who had worked closely with Jean Genet, confirmed that recommendations "ranged from self-determination to the end of repression of homosexuals. . . . We moved to make it unconstitutional for one man to oppress another" (as cited in Johnson, 1970, p. 32).[4] Despite its apparent success and a motion to reconvene the convention for ratification in Washington, D.C., the coalitions built at the RPCC collapsed. The reasons behind the dissolution of the coalitions created at the RPCC remain in dispute. According to Katsiaficas (2001), "Rather than allow the insurrectionary impulse to continue, Newton systematically undermined and blunted the revolutionary initiative and aborted the multicultural alliance the Panthers had built as part of the Free Huey Campaign" (p. 154). Huggins argues that the actions taken by Newton were a move to centralize the party in California as a means to prevent the continual political repression of the party (personal communication, December 1, 2006). Whatever the reason behind its undoing, the Revolutionary People's Constitutional Convention represented a moment in history when the Black Panther Party put its rhetorical statements into action and worked directly alongside the Gay Liberation Movement for the liberation of gay and lesbian people.

The history of political social movements in America is riddled with convenient spaces left by those who are not deemed respectable enough to enter into the traditional political and historical canon. At its core, this is inherently a pedagogical issue as often the experiences of marginalized individuals and groups are rendered invisible in both educational curricula and popular historical representations. To be clear, this excavation of the history of the Newton letter is not indended to advocate for a type of multicultural agenda where LGBTQ histories are merely added on to American, African American, Latino, Chicano, Women's, or Asian American history. Rather, my hope is that the lessons learned from Newton's intervention and the Panther response can disturb many of our commonsense understandings of American history, moving us to consider that it is impossible to understand American history without understanding the contributions and struggles of a variety of groups. As Davis (1998) insists, the relative invisibility of the Newton letter, as well as the questions it raises around coalition building and the pedagogical implications of social movements, are directly linked to our own sense of historical legacy. "Such moments as these have been all but eradicated in popular representations today of the black movement of the late sixties and early seventies," writes Davis. She continues, "Young people with 'nationalist' proclivities ought, at least, to have the opportunity to choose which tradition of nationalism they will embrace. How will they position themselves en masse in defense of women's rights and in defense of gay rights if they are not aware of the historical precedents for such positionings?" (p. 292). The excavation of homosexuality in the context of the Black Panther Party reveals a whole host of characters and actions adding both breadth and depth to the black and LGBTQ experience in America. The problems inherent in this issue also illustrate for those blacks involved in struggle and/or celebration that black life has not been comprised solely of a homogenous and/or heterosexual body.

Scholars, educators, and activists can learn from the subtle critique of individualistic identity politics that was at play. For Newton and other members of the Black Panther Party, political action was not so much about identifying struggles with particular bodies as it was about building movements that could sustain action by allowing persons to come out of their own bodies and identify with others. Davis adds, "That was an extremely important moment of promise that foreshadowed what might become possible. One of the problems we have today is that we do not think beyond the body, or the individual, and we assume that in order for something to be valuable to us we must have a direct experience" (personal communication, September 8, 2010). And while the letter may seem obscure, the political debates we currently face regarding race and sexuality may make the letter more relevant now than it was in 1970. As author Jewell Gomez writes, "The importance of Newton's statement lay not in the groundswell of support that it failed to promote, but in its simple recognition that alliances must be formed if social justice is to be attained" (as cited in Grau, n.d., p. 2). Perhaps we can use Newton's intervention as a point of departure to not only talk about LGBTQ histories but also to engage in dialogues in order to understand the complex connections between race and sexuality in today's political climate. Every political organization and movement is wrought with contradiction. Rather than disparage the movement, it is critical that we struggle with and analyze these complexities in order to take the next steps. Looking back at this story one can see the obvious pitfalls of patriarchy, heterosexism, and homophobia. It also reveals how one black political organization was willing to take some strides to move beyond these debilitating factors.

Notes

1. In this article I will be using the terms "homosexual" and "gay" interchangeably due to the usage of both words in Newton's letter and the use of both terms at the time the letter was written. Also, while Newton's letter does take up the Women's Liberation Movement, my primary focus in this article will be his thoughts on gay liberation.

2. Not all Panthers adopted the one-dimensional view of homosexuality espoused by Cleaver and others in the Black Nationalist Movement. While there is very little specific information on homosexuals working within the party, David Hilliard, BPP National Chief of Staff, has asserted:

   There were gay operatives in the Black Panther Party working at the highest levels of leadership. . . . Lesbian relationships were more acceptable in the party than homosexual relations between men. But the uneasiness over gay men was expressed primarily by men, most of whom were insecure with their own sexuality. Still, no one ever asked you to define your sexual orientation. We didn't divide ourselves like that. First and foremost you were a Black Panther (as cited in Carbado, McBride, & Weise, 2002, p. 113).

   While Ericka Huggins has confirmed Hilliard's statement, a deeper exploration of the experiences of lesbian and gay members of the Black Panther Party is beyond the scope of this study (personal communication, December 1, 2006).

3. Robert Sandarg, *Jean Genet in America* (Huey P. Newton Papers, Stanford, CA, series 2 box 60) 58–59. Also see Airtel from Special Agent in Charge, San Francisco, to Director, FBI, August 31, 1970. An airtel is an internal communication typed they same day it is received and forwarded by mail.

4. Unfortunately, Shakur's name, which is correctly spelled Zayd, was incorrectly spelled Zayed by Johnson.

References

Abron, J.M. (1998). "Serving the people": The survival programs of the Black Panther Party. In C.E. Jones (Ed.), *The Black Panther Party reconsidered* (pp. 177–192). Baltimore, MD: Black Classic Press.

Armed Negros protest gun bill. (1967, May 3). *The New York Times.*

Brown, E. (1992). *A taste of power: A black woman's story.* New York: Pantheon.

Carbado, D.W., McBride, D., & Weise, D. (2002). 1950–1980, the protest era: "I dream of your freedom/as my victory." In D.W. Carbado, D. McBride, & D. Weise (Eds.), *Black like us: A century of lesbian, gay, and bisexual African-American fiction* (pp. 107–135). San Francisco: Cleis Press.

Churchill, W. (2001). "To disrupt, discredit and destroy": The FBI's secret war against the Black Panther Party. In G. Katsiaficas & K. Cleaver (Eds.), *Liberation, imagination, and the Black Panther Party* (pp. 78–117). New York: Routledge.

Churchill, W., & Wall, J.V. (2002). *Agents of repression: The FBI's secret wars against the Black Panther Party and the American Indian Movement.* Cambridge, MA: South End Press.

Cleaver, E. (1991). *Soul on ice.* New York: Delta.

Cleaver, K.N. (2001). Women, power, and revolution. In G. Katsiaficas (Ed.), *Liberation, imagination, and the Black Panther Party: A new look at the Panthers and their legacy* (pp. 123–127). New York: Routledge.

Davis, A. (1998). Black nationalism: The sixties and the nineties. In J. James (Ed.), *The Angela Y. Davis reader* (pp. 289–293). Malden, MA: Blackwell Publishing.

Davis, A. (2004). *Angela Davis, an autobiography.* New York: International Publishers.

Davis, A., & Huggins, E. (2006, October 12). *The Black Panther Party, reflections in light of forty years.* Paper presented at the American Studies Association, Oakland, CA.

Deitcher, D. (Ed.). (1995). *The question of equality: Lesbian and gay politics in America since Stonewall.* New York: Scribner.

Delaney, P. (1970a, September 8). Panthers to reconvene in capital to ratify their constitution. *The New York Times,* p. 57.

Delaney, P. (1970b, September 7). Panthers weigh new constitution. *The New York Times,* p. 13.

Démeron, P. (1972). Conversation with Jean Genet. *Oui, 62*–64, 99–102.

Erikson, E.H., & Newton, H.P. (1973). *In search of common ground: Conversations with Erik H. Erikson and Huey P. Newton.* New York: W.W. Norton.

Estes, S. (2005). *I am a man! Race, manhood, and the Civil Rights Movement.* Chapel Hill: University of North Carolina Press.

4 policemen hurt in Village raid. (1969, June 29). *The New York Times,* p. 33.

Fraser, C.G. (1970, August 31). "Gay ghettos" seen as police targets. *The New York Times,* p. 28.

Freire, P. (2003). *Pedagogy of the oppressed.* New York: Continuum.

Grau, R. (n.d.). The "Letter from Huey." Retrieved March 3, 2009, from http://www.planetout.com/news/history/archive/huey.html

Huggins, E., & LeBlanc-Ernest, A.D. (2009). The Black Panther Party's Oakland Community School. In D.F. Gore, J. Theoharis, & K. Woodard (Eds.), *Want to start a revolution? Radical women in the black freedom struggle* (pp. 161–184). New York: New York University Press.

Jennings, R. (1998). Why I joined the party: An Africana womanist reflection. In C.E. Jones (Ed.), *The Black Panther Party reconsidered* (pp. 257–265). Baltimore, MD: Black Classic Press.

Johnson, T.A. (1970, September 9). Theme of black parleys: 3 organizations show divergent views but their members favor Negro unity. *The New York Times,* p. 32.

Jones, C.E. (1988). The political repression of the Black Panther Party 1966–1971: The case of the Oakland Bay area. *Journal of Black Studies, 18*(4), 415–434.

Jones, C.E., & Jeffries, J.L. (1998). "Don't believe the hype": Debunking the Panther mythology. In C.E. Jones (Ed.), *The Black Panther Party reconsidered* (pp. 25–55). Baltimore, MD: Black Classic Press.

Katsiaficas, G. (2001). Organization and movement: The case of the Black Panther Party and the Revolutionary People's Constitutional Convention of 1970. In K. Cleaver & G. Katsiaficas (Eds.), *Liberation, imagination, and the Black Panther Party: A new look at the Panthers and their legacy* (pp. 141–155). New York: Routledge.

LeBlanc-Ernest, A.D. (1998). "The most qualified person to handle the job": Black Panther Party women, 1966–1982. In C.E. Jones (Ed.), *The Black Panther Party reconsidered* (pp. 305–334). Baltimore, MD: Black Classic Press.

Matthews, T. (1998). "No one ever asks what a man's role in the revolution is": Gender and the politics of the Black Panther Party, 1966–1971. In C.E. Jones (Ed.), *The Black Panther Party reconsidered* (pp. 267–304). Baltimore, MD: Black Classic Press.

Newton, H.P. (1970, August 21). A letter from Huey to the revolutionary brothers and sisters about the Women's Liberation and Gay Liberation Movements. *The Black Panther*, p. 5.

Newton, H.P. (1995). *Revolutionary suicide.* New York: Writers and Readers Publishing, Inc.

Newton, H.P. (1996). *War against the Panthers: A study of repression in America.* New York: Harlem River Press.

Newton, H.P. (2002). Eldridge Cleaver: He is no James Baldwin. In D. Hilliard & D. Weise (Eds.), *The Huey P. Newton reader* (pp. 285–289). New York: Seven Stories Press. (Original work published 1973)

October 1966 Black Panther Party platform and program. (1968, November 2). *The Black Panther*, p. 23.

Rosemarie. (1970, September 12). The people and the people alone were the motive force in the making of history of the People's Revolutionary Constitutional Convention Plenary Session! *The Black Panther*, p. 3.

Sandarg, R. (n.d.). *Jean Genet in America.* Unpublished manuscript, Stanford, CA.

Self, R.O. (2006). The Black Panther Party and the long civil rights era. In J. Lazerow & Y. Williams (Eds.), *In search of the Black Panther Party: New perspectives on a revolutionary movement* (pp. 15–55). Durham, NC: Duke University Press.

Sing, N.P. (1998). The Black Panthers and the "underdeveloped country" of the left. In C.E. Jones (Ed.), *The Black Panther Party reconsidered* (pp. 57–105). Baltimore, MD: Black Classic Press.

Sing, N.P. (2004). *Black is a country: Race and the unfinished struggle for democracy.* Cambridge, MA: Harvard University Press.

Smith, J. (1999). *An international history of the Black Panther Party.* New York: Garland.

Teal, D. (1995). *The gay militants: How gay liberation began in America, 1969–1971.* New York: St. Martin's Press.

White, E. (1993). *Genet: A biography.* New York: Knopf.

White, E.F. (2001). *Dark continent of our bodies: Black feminism and the politics of respectability.* Philadelphia: Temple University Press.

Williams, R.Y. (2006). Black women, urban politics, and engendering black power. In P.E. Joseph (Ed.), *The Black Power Movement: Rethinking the Civil Rights–Black Power era* (pp. 79–103). New York: Routledge.

CHAPTER THIRTY-FIVE

Who Is Asian?

Representing a Panethnic Continent in Community Activism

ALAN WONG

Between 2004 and 2009, I served as the coordinator[1] of Gay and Lesbian Asians of Montreal (GLAM), a not-for-profit, volunteer-run community organization that functions as both a social and political support group for local lesbian, gay, bisexual, trans, and queer (LGBTQ) Asians. During my tenure with GLAM, I attempted to broaden its membership in order to attract and be more inclusive of those who I felt were underrepresented in the group. In so doing, one major question surfaced: How could GLAM present itself as a unified Asian voice while still taking into account the diversity of ethnicities that comprised its membership? In other words, what strategies could GLAM employ to accommodate and bridge the various interests of a group of people defined by their continental affiliation without compromising their individual subjectivities? As I pondered this, I realized that coordinating GLAM required thinking outside the proverbial box if we were to grow and become more than just another monolithic social clique in Montreal's LGBTQ scene.

Indeed, when I joined GLAM in early 2003, I immediately took note of its homogeneity. Aside from a couple of female members and a few Caucasian friends and boyfriends of male members, the vast majority of those I encountered were of Chinese origin, whether they had emigrated directly from mainland China, Hong Kong, or Taiwan, or were born into the diaspora, including Canada and many Southeast Asian nations as well as Mauritius. In fact, almost everyone spoke Cantonese, narrowing the identity pool even further. The few that diverged from this ethnic line were predominantly ethnic Vietnamese. Having spoken to several veterans of GLAM, my understanding was that this had been the composition of the organization since its founding 11 years earlier. Thus, while inserting the word "Asian" in its name, GLAM really only represented a certain segment of that population, synecdochically assuming a primarily Chinese identity. Moreover, there were few bisexuals in the organization and no transsexual or transgender members, thus affirming the gender exclusivity of the "GL" in GLAM's name. Finally, almost everyone was in his or her 20s or 30s and, for the most part, middle class socioeconomically. In short, the membership base was quite narrowly defined.

This Chinese dominance within GLAM was evidenced by the group's past involvement in Divers/Cité, Montreal's largest LGBTQ pride celebration.[2] In 2002, GLAM's participation in the parade portion of that event consisted of a float depicting a Chinese junk, an ancient sailing vessel that one would typically find floating in Hong Kong's harbor. In 2003, the GLAM float was awash in large red Chinese lanterns. Furthermore, during Community Day, which is a day set aside for a street fair featuring LGBTQ community groups, volunteers at the GLAM booth were distributing condoms and coupons in traditional red Chinese gift packets and selling glasses of bubble tea, a trendy drink invented and popularized in Taiwan. Anyone exposed to these public displays of Chinese-ness could rightly assume that GLAM catered solely to the interests of Chinese queers.

Other promotional tools conveyed a similar sensibility. When I joined GLAM in early 2003, for example, the homepage of the GLAM website featured a photo of the Chinese junk pride parade float positioned at the top of the homepage alongside the GLAM logo, which features a large fire-ball that could be construed as Chinese due to its similarity in color to the red sails of the junk. In addition, the social events that GLAM organized before I became coordinator centered mostly on Chinese themes and holidays, such as Chinese New Year, to the exclusion of cultural markers of other ethnicities.

Where did that leave Montreal's "other Asians," then? How could the absence of non-East and non-Southeast Asians in GLAM's membership and promotional materials be explained in light of the appearance in its name of the word "Asian"? One could argue that GLAM's intentions had always been to target the LGBTQ Chinese population, given that the group was founded by Chinese Montrealers. There were other mitigating factors, as well, though. First, other organizations in the city served various segments of the Asian population, including Helem, an LGBTQ Lebanese-focused association that also caters to sexual "margin resistors"[3] from other Arab and Islamic national and ethnic cultures based in West Asia, such as Syria and Iran. Moreover, individuals from more religiously or culturally conservative backgrounds may have been too leery of joining *any* LGBTQ group, let alone one that was directed toward their particular ethnicity.

Regardless of the reason, the need for broader representation of the LGBTQ Asian community in a formal organization had to be addressed, as heterosexism and racism were part of the everyday experiences of a wide array of individuals who identified with that intersectional identity. GLAM, as the oldest and most established Asian-oriented LGBTQ group in Montreal, was in the best position to fulfil that need. Thus, after assuming the position of GLAM'S coordinator, I made a concerted effort to reach out to "other" Asian communities that previously had been considered simply "allies." In short, I had to reconsider how the "A" in GLAM has been conceptualized or, as Benedict Anderson (1991) would put it, "*imagined*" (p. 6; author's italics); in other words, I needed to think of Asia as not simply a material, geographic location but as an idea that has been constructed discursively over time in many different ways, complicating my entrenched notions of Asian-ness as being defined by East and Southeast Asian communities. I, as an Asian, had already endured many confining stereotypes throughout my life, particularly in school, where I was viewed as a "model minority," which led to perceptions of me as being not only smart but also quiet, physically and emotionally weak, and, thus, easy to bully. It would be hypocritical of me, as the coordinator of GLAM, to continue to maintain the very limiting parameters of membership as they currently stood, since they would most certainly contribute to further stereotyping of Asians, particularly in the mainstream LGBTQ community, as being comprised of a particular ethnic group or racial phenotype. Therefore, redefining Asian-ness in the GLAM context was about not only reaching out to underrepresented Asian ethnicities but also resisting against the way our identities were being constructed by Montreal's predominantly Eurocentric LGBTQ community—for instance, the local chapter of an international gay organization was founded by a white man who wanted to create a space for non-Asian men to meet Asian men, specifically of the orientalized (Said, 1978), "exotic" variety.

The challenge in "reimagining" one's communitarian identity in broader terms, however, is that many different political, social, and economic forces work to construct such an identity in ways that often benefit colonialist and imperialist interests (see, for example, Said, 1978; Spivak, 1988; Trinh, 1989; and Young, 2001). Discursively, for example, Anderson highlights, among other things, the census and the map as key institutionalized inventions that have "profoundly shaped the way in which the colonial state imagined its dominion" (pp. 163–164). For instance, the 2000 U.S. census categorized its Asian population according to nationalistic character ("Asian Indian" and "Sri Lankan") and ethnicity ("Hmong," "Okinawan," "Iwo Jiman") as well as the indefinable ("Other Asian, unspecified") (Barnes and Bennett, 2002, p. 9). Cartographically, on the other hand, Asians are identified according to territorial boundaries that have been devised by map-makers in the West, according to Anderson, "to put space under the same surveillance which the census-makers were trying to impose on persons" (p. 173). Thus, Western powers have used such instruments as the census and the map to configure and reconfigure the parameters delimiting what constitutes Asia and Asians as a means of monitoring their Asian colonies and subjects and maintaining the geopolitical hegemonic order.

To complicate matters even further, how Asians themselves construct their identities in Western societies often depends on their geographic location. As Richard Fung (1994) notes:

> Whereas in North America, East and Southeast Asians have claimed the term, in Britain, "Asian" is commonly taken to refer to people whose ancestry lies in the Indian subcontinent and Sri Lanka. . . . [N]o matter whether they are born in North America, come from the subcontinent or from the Indian diaspora in Africa, Southeast Asia, the Pacific, or the Caribbean . . . [t]hey are seen to look alike. (p. 163)

With myriad factors working all at once to change and stretch and shrink the limits of Asian-ness, one can see that the Asian is an elusive and confounding being. The consequence of this for a group such as GLAM is that it can develop an identity crisis, in that it throws into question how narrow or broad its reach needs to be with respect to target audience and membership. This was the conundrum I was facing as I attempted to reinvent and reinvigorate the organization.

Tackling this problem demanded a reimagining of Asian identity as one that unites the panoply of cultures found within the discursively defined continent. Stuart Hall (1992) argues that globalization, with all the exposure to different cultural elements that comes with it, has facilitated such a reimagining through the "disembedding" of identities "from specific times, places, histories, and traditions" (p. 303), potentially leading to the "*strengthening* of local identities or to the production of *new identities*" (p. 308; author's italics). Arjun Appadurai (1990) makes a similar argument through his concept of the ethnoscape, which refers to

> the landscape of persons who constitute the shifting world in which we live: tourists, immigrants, refugees, exiles, guestworkers and other moving groups and persons constitute an essential feature of the world, and appear to affect the politics of and between nations to a hitherto unprecedented degree. (p. 297)

As noted here, the fluidity of cultural influences among ethnicities in recent times has had a destabilizing effect on the hegemonic structures that have traditionally pervaded society, leaving the door wide open for what were once thought of as marginalized groups to rise up and assume control over their own destinies. Thus, in this sense, globalization has provided Asians with the opportunity to forge for themselves an identity that is removed from the imposed orientalist imaginary of the colonial powers while still enabling them to retain their individual ethno-nationalist identities.

In attaining this newfound power of self-definition, however, certain new complications have emerged. In particular, Asians are now expected to speak as *authentic* representatives of their ethnicity. In effect, what has transpired is a new essentialization of Asian-ness, taking the imagining of this ideal from the orientalist end of the spectrum and transferring it to the other end, which is just as totalizing and problematic, especially where it concerns engagement in activism. Although, as Gayatri Spivak says in her interview with Sneja Gunew (1990), "there are many subject positions which one must inhabit" when one is "speaking *as*," those that are listening often only absorb what they anticipate to be the truth (p. 60; author's italics). Thus, Gunew concludes, "the whole *notion* of authenticity . . . is one that comes to us constructed by hegemonic voices; and so, what one has to tease out is what is *not* there" (p. 61; author's italics). "Teasing out what is *not* there" can certainly pose a problem for Asians with a public profile in the West who, identified as such, must remain true not only to their own experiences but to the diversity of cultures represented by the word "Asian."

This conundrum of representation is where the deployment of panethnicity had become useful to me as a tool for activism. Yen Le Espiritu (1992) describes "pan-movements" as those that "involve shifts in levels of group identification from smaller boundaries to larger-level affiliations" (p. 2). Panethnicity embodies such a shift, whereby the boundaries of ethnicity become elastic, allowing for the creation of "a politico-cultural collectivity made up of peoples of several, hitherto distinct, tribal or national origins" (p. 2). This concept challenges traditional notions of ethnicity, which have been predominantly based on either primordialist or instrumentalist theories; that is, ethnicity respectively based on either its "sentimental" value in relation to culture and tradition or its utility in instances of economic, political, or social gain (p. 4). "The phenomenon of panethnicity," as Espiritu refers to it, "call[s] attention . . . to the coercively imposed nature of ethnicity, its multiple layers, and the continual creation and re-creation of culture" (p. 5).

This challenge that panethnicity levies against "imposed" characterizations of ethnicity hearkens back to the earlier discussion on Asian-ness as an imposed imagined identity. Adopting panethnicity as a way of looking at ethnicity can lead to the subversion of such imaginings; panethnic groups can seize the categories that they have been coerced into—categories that "[lump] together diverse peoples in a single, expanded 'ethnic' framework" (p. 6)—and appropriate them to their own advantage. As Espiritu (1992) notes, panethnic organizing helps "to mobilize diverse people and to force others to be more responsive to their grievances and agendas" (p. 7). An example of this would be the slaying of Vincent Chin, which gave rise to formation of the American Citizens for Justice (ACJ).[4] However, while the emergence of such pan-Asian advocacy groups has demonstrated the viability and efficacy of pan-Asian collective action, many of these organizations have tended to attract a specific kind of Asian. When the ACJ formed, for example, it was comprised primarily of members of East and Southeast Asian heritage. This, of course, returns us to the question: What about the "other" Asians?

In the United States, some Asian Americans have experienced difficulty gaining acceptance into Asian American panethnicity. Shilpa Davé et al. (2000) contend that, "[w]hile notable exceptions exist, attempts at fostering unity among Asian Americans often exclude South Asian Americans, or treat them as a liminal entity, which is dealt with tokenistically" (p. 71). A variety of factors can be pinpointed as causes of this dichotomy, including disparities in population size, physical dissimilarities, and religious differences, to name a few (pp. 71–72). Moreover, in the current geopolitical climate, many South Asians have been identified more as Muslims associated with Arab populations than as Asians, as evidenced by the many hate crime incidents that reportedly befell the South Asian American population following 9/11. Given the experiences of those Asians whose heritage does not originate in the East or Southeast parts of the continent, how can their exclusion from panethnic Asian community activism be resolved? One could argue that maybe this is as it should be, that the differences between these ethnicities are simply too great to overcome and that perhaps it would be best to let each subgroup look after its own. There might certainly be some validity to this argument. However, there will also be situations where the inclusion of multiple Asian ethnic groups in a panethnic framework can only be beneficial to all parties concerned. Activism in the LGBTQ Asian community would be an instance of this.

Identities based on categories other than and in addition to race and ethnicity make the formation of panethnic collectivities perhaps more complex but also necessary. For example, Rick Bonus and Linda Võ (2002), paraphrasing Eng and Hom (1998), state that "[f]or many Asian American gays and lesbians [sic] today, ethnic-bound communities are not sanctuaries but stifling sites of exclusion where homophobia persists and where they are remarginalized" (p. 9). If this is the case, then LGBTQ Asians face the prospect of being multiply subjugated in terms of their race, ethnicity, and sexuality. A panethnic LGBTQ Asian group, though, will find that it has a stronger voice to promote the concerns of its members to many different communities. Furthermore, its members will be creating a safe space for themselves—a space protected from oppressive forces due to the sheer number of Asian cultures represented in the organization.

Due to these factors, I and other like-minded members of GLAM made a concerted effort to change the perception of the organization as being ethnically one-sided through the implementation of a more panethnic approach to its recruitment and marketing strategies. In 2004, for example, GLAM's float in the Divers/Cité parade featured flags representing more than 25 Asian nations, including Afghanistan, Iraq, Israel, India, Japan, and the Philippines, mounted on bamboo sticks and erected on the wooden platform of an 18-wheel truck. The following year, GLAM's members marched, and even though the design concept had reverted back to showcasing Chinese lanterns, the composition of the marchers was much more diverse, featuring not only Chinese, but also Filipinos, Cambodians, Vietnamese, Arabs, Koreans, and South Asians. In 2009, the GLAM contingent carried signs promoting and celebrating the decision by a judge in New Delhi, India, to strike down the anti-sodomy law in his district. Community Day saw just as diverse a volunteer brigade, pitching not only traditional Chinese calligraphy, but also Indian samosas and Vietnamese spring rolls. Moreover, GLAM's (2005) mission statement was revised to reflect this new panethnic attitude and reality, broadening its definition of "Asian" to include a greater plurality of ethnicities (Mission section).

Another sign of the shifting tide at GLAM was the completion, printing, and publicizing of the GLAM poster project titled "Together Under One Roof" (See Figure 1).

The intention behind the creation of this poster, a collaborative initiative on the part of GLAM, Chinese Family Services of Greater Montreal, and the South Asian Women's Community Centre that was worked on by a committee of Chinese, South Asian, and Jewish LGBTQ men and women, was to raise awareness about LGBTQ issues in different Asian communities in Montreal. The premise was that of an apartment building with eight windows, each one depicting members of a particular Asian culture dealing with a specific LGBTQ issue in their own language, which ran the gamut from Tagalog to Tamil to Vietnamese. Such a project had long been needed, yet this would not have been possible without the panethnic cooperation that went into its production. By uniting organi-

"Together Under One Roof," GLAM Poster Project. Alan Wong

zations representing different Asian ethnic groups as well as volunteers who identified as Asian in diverse ways, the GLAM poster project exemplified the coalitional possibilities of doing panethnic activist work.

The friction that often accompanies relations between LGBTQ Asians and their friends, families, and ethnocultural communities necessitated GLAM's proactive incorporation of this view toward panethnicity; political activism would have been—and would still be—very difficult without this kind of cohesion and collaboration between communities. Also, the risk of an essentializing image of Asian-ness that can contribute to harmful stereotypes, exoticization, and marginalization of GLAM's members in the mainstream LGBTQ community as well as society at large was too great for the organization *not* to go panethnic. These factors—along with an increased feeling among GLAM's members that the organization should be more inclusive if it is going to have "Asian" as part of its name and, thus, its identity—led the group down this path toward greater ethnic diversity.

Ultimately, panethnicity as a tactic for coalition building is to the advantage of all parties in a diverse environment. If representation is to be, as Ella Shohat (1995) states, "less of a burden and more of a collective pleasure and responsibility" (p. 177), then GLAM has certainly been making strides toward this goal through its panethnic approach. Indeed, in 2006, GLAM deployed its panethnic strategy outside of the organization by helping to found Coalition MultiMundo, which brought together almost a dozen Montreal-based LGBTQ ethnic groups and their allies under one banner. Here panethnicity has stretched beyond the continental context exemplified by GLAM to a more global domain, demonstrating that panethnic activism is not only effective but flexible, as well.

Notes

1. To be more precise, I was officially a *co*-coordinator, with one bisexual woman and one gay man each sharing the title with me for approximately one year during my own tenure. However, other commitments prevented them from devoting their full attention to the group.

2. Divers/Cité is a not-for-profit corporation that coordinated the first Pride events in Montreal in 1993, including the parade and community fair, and continued to do so until 2007, when a group comprised of local community members and business leaders formed a new organization called Célébrations LGBTA (the "A" referring to "allosexuel," a term used by the Québécois that has similar connotations to "queer") and assumed the coordination of the parade and community fair (Célébrations de la fierté, 2007, History section).

3. "Margin resistors" is a term I currently use in place of "minorities" to recognize the active role played by those in the margins of society in countering and resisting the blatant and systemic oppressions imposed on them by different hegemonic social, political, cultural, and economic structures.

4. Vincent Chin was a Chinese American in Detroit who was slain by two unemployed white autoworkers in 1982 because they "allegedly mistook him for Japanese" (Espiritu, 1992, p. 7) and "blamed their unemployment on him" (Hall, 2001, p. 17). While upset about Chin's death, it was not until both of his killers received a light sentence of three years' probation and were "fined each a mere $3000" that "Detroit's fragmented Asian American groups [came together] into a united community" (Espiritu, 1992, p. 144). As Espiritu notes, "Although the Chin case started out as a Chinese American issue, it quickly became an Asian American cause," drawing "Japanese, Korean, and Filipino American community representatives" to activist meetings in solidarity with the Chinese American community (p. 145). Out of this collective organizing emerged the ACJ.

References

Anderson, B. (1991). *Imagined communities: Reflections on the origin and spread of nationalism* (2nd ed.). London: Verso.

Appadurai, A. (1990). Disjuncture and difference in the global cultural economy. In M. Featherstone (Ed.), *Global culture: Nationalism, globalization and modernity* (pp. 295–310). London: Sage Publications.

Barnes, J.S., & Bennett, C.E. (2002, February). *The Asian population: 2000.* Retrieved from http://www.census.gov/prod/2002pubs/c2kbr01–16.pdf

Bonus, R., & Trinh Võ, L. Introduction: On intersections and divergences. In L. Trinh Võ & R. Bonus (Eds.), *Contemporary Asian American communities: Intersections and divergences* (pp. 1–24). Philadelphia: Temple University Press.

Célébrations de la fierté. (2007). *History.* Retrieved from http://www.fiertemontrealpride.com/en_history.htm

Davé, S., Dhingra, P., Maira, S., Mazumdar, P., Shankar, L., Singh, J., & Srikanth, R. (2000). De-privileging positions: Indian Americans, South Asian Americans, and the politics of Asian American studies [electronic version]. *Journal of Asian American Studies, 3*(1), 67–100.

Espiritu, Y.L. (1992). *Asian American panethnicity: Bridging institutions and identities.* Philadelphia: Temple University Press.

Fung, R. (1994). Seeing yellow: Asian identities in film and video. In K. Aguilar-San Juan (Ed.), *The state of Asian America: Activism and resistance in the 1990s* (pp. 161–172). Boston: South End Press.

GLAM. (2005, August 11). *Mission.* Retrieved from http://glamontreal.spaces.live.com/

Hall, P.W. (2001). Introduction. In P.W. Hall & V.M. Hwang (Eds.), *Anti-Asian violence in North America: Asian American and Asian Canadian reflections on hate, healing, and resistance* (pp. 1–26). Walnut Creek, CA: AltaMira Press.

Hall, S. (1992). The question of cultural identity. In S. Hall, D. Held, & T. McGrew (Eds.), *Modernity and its futures* (pp. 274–316). Cambridge, UK: Polity.

Eng, D. and Hom, A. (1998). *Queer in Asian America.* Philadelphia, PA: Temple University Press.

Said, E. (1978). *Orientalism.* New York: Pantheon Books.

Shohat, E. (1995). The struggle over representation: Casting, coalitions, and the politics of identification. In R. de la Campa, E.A. Kaplan, & M. Sprinker (Eds.), *Late imperial culture* (pp. 166–178). London: Verso.

Spivak, G. (1988). Can the subaltern speak? In C. Nelson & S. Grossbert (Eds.), *Marxism and the interpretation of culture* (pp. 271–313). Basingstoke, UK: Macmillan Education.

Spivak, G., & Gunew, S. (1990). Questions of multiculturalism. In S. Harasym (Ed.), *The post-colonial critic: Interviews, strategies, dialogues* (pp. 59–66). New York: Routledge.

Trinh, T. M-h. (1989). *Woman, native, other: Writing postcoloniality and feminism.* Bloomington: Indiana University Press.

Young, R.J.C. (2001). *Postcolonialism: An historical introduction.* Oxford, UK; Malden, MA: Blackwell.

"Dive"

Andrea Gibson

All of my love poems are political poems and all of my political poems are love poems in a society where people can be so separated from each other.
—Andrea Gibson

The following poem "Dive" by Andrea Gibson is a political poem since it stands in the tradition of feminist thought that argues that the personal is political. The poem is about the irony of life and about a search for reason and understanding when love, hate and indifference meet. "Dive" also allows us to ponder sexuality in a safe place. A reference to Matthew Shepard shows up in a stream of consciousness and it belongs. When Gibson mentions Shepard she makes the point that death can save lives, only after she confesses her own candidacy for a potential stake burning. Gibson knows her words can hurt or heal so she stands firm on the stage or "meditation mat" with well crafted messages that can be utilized in classrooms to educate as well as entertain. This is art for social justice and another tool in what the great Gil Scott Heron would call our untelevised revolution. More of Andrea's poems can be read or heard at http://www.andreagibson.org.

Forward,

Venus Jones, Author of "She Rose"

Dive

> i often repeat myself
> and the second time's a lie
> i love you
> i love you
> see what i mean i don't
> . . . and i do
> and i'm not talking about a girl i might be kissing on

i'm talking about this world i'm blissing on
and hating
at the exact same time
see life—doesn't rhyme
it's bullets . . . and wind chimes
it's lynchings . . . and birthday parties
it's the rope that ties the noose
and the rope that hangs the backyard swing
it's a boy about to take his life
and with the knife to his wrist
he's thinking of only two things
his father's fist
and his mother's kiss
and he can't stop crying
it's wanting tonight to speak
the most honest poem i've ever spoken in my life
not knowing if that poem should bring you closer
to living or dying
drowning or flying
cause life doesn't rhyme
last night i prayed myself to sleep
woke this morning
to find god's obituary scrolled in tears on my sheets
then walked outside to hear my neighbor
erasing ten thousand years of hard labor
with a single note of his violin
and the sound of the traffic rang like a hymn
as the holiest leaf of autumn fell from a plastic tree limb
beautiful—and ugly
like right now
i'm needing nothing more than for you to hug me
and if you do
i'm gonna scream like a caged bird
see . . . life doesn't rhyme
sometimes love is a vulgar word
sometimes hate calls itself peace on the nightly news
i've heard saints preaching truths
that would have burned me at the stake
i've heard poets tellin lies that made me believe in heaven
sometimes i imagine hitler at seven years old
a paint brush in his hand at school
thinkin what color should i paint my soul
sometimes i remember myself
with track marks on my tongue
from shooting up convictions
that would have hung innocent men from trees
have you ever seen a mother falling to her knees
the day her son dies in a war she voted for
can you imagine how many gay teen-age lives were saved
the day matthew shepherd died

could there have been anything louder
than the noise inside his father's head
when he begged the jury
please don't take the lives of the men
who turned my son's skull to powder
and i know nothing would make my family prouder
than giving up everything i believe in
still nothing keeps me believing
like the sound of my mother breathing
life doesn't rhyme
it's tasting your rapist's breath
on the neck of a woman who loves you more
than anyone has loved you before
then feeling holy as jesus
beneath the hands of a one night stand
who's calling somebody else's name
it's you never feelin more greedy
than when you're handing out dollars to the needy
it's my not eating meat for the last seven years
then seeing the kindest eyes i've ever seen in my life
on the face of a man with a branding iron in his hand
and a beat down baby calf wailing at his feet
it's choking on your beliefs
it's your worst sin saving your fucking life
it's the devil's knife carving holes into you soul
so angels will have a place to make their way inside
life doesn't rhyme
still life is poetry—not math
all the world's a stage
but the stage is a meditation mat
you tilt your head back
you breathe
when your heart is broken you plant seeds in the cracks
and you pray for rain
and you teach your sons and daughters
there are sharks in the water
but the only way to survive
is to breathe deep
and dive

CHAPTER THIRTY-SIX

Gender Sovereignty

SENDOLO DIAMINAH

Introduction

We are living in a time when capitalism is stretching the ecological limits of the planet. We are fast approaching and indeed may have passed "peak oil," which means that we have used up the majority of the earth's oil resources and that we are looking at a steady decline in its availability. The same is true with essential resources such as water. And as the crises of ecology and the economy deepen, capitalism is less and less able to reform itself to adjust to the demands for justice, dignity, and well-being that come from popular movements. And so I have begun talking about this as an era of "peak reform" as well. The challenge facing activists and organizers today is to recognize the nature of this moment and advance from a politics of reform and resistance to a politics of system change and transition. This interview speaks to this need, using the concept of sovereignty to open up our thinking about gender in a way that places queer people on the stage of history so that we can contribute to the process of transformation, liberation, and renewal that our people and the planet so desperately need today.

The idea of sovereignty used in this interview draws heavily from my study of indigenous and Latin American social movements. But it is also deeply informed by my personal experience as a queer, black communist living and organizing in the U.S. South. The idea of gender sovereignty first emerged through my work with Southerners On New Ground, a queer Southern regional organization dedicated to creating change across lines of race, gender, culture, sexuality, class, and ability. This in turn has been informed by conversations with members of Freedom Road Socialist Organization and Movement Generation Justice and Ecology Project about the connections among socialism, ecology, and the transition beyond capitalism. Finally, this piece grows from my everyday work with People's Durham, an organization in North Carolina dedicated to rethinking and transforming democracy and governance.

The Politics of Sovereignty

Sendolo Diaminah: What I mean when I talk about sovereignty is that "we have a different way of being." Those of us who are organizing around the idea of sovereignty are not asking for inclusion within the capitalist system. We're not asking for the so-called benefits of a capitalist system, which is always based on exclusions because it is based on privatizing what was once communal and shared. We're saying no to being incorporated. We're saying yes to a completely different way of being, to a society based on commonality and plurality, not the fundamentalism of markets, religion, and the gender binary. We're not pushing to get in. Why would we want to enmesh ourselves in an economy and a political system that is driving the planet and our species toward destruction?

Instead of thinking of ways that queer people can be integrated into the existing political and economic system, we need to put our energies into the kinds of projects and movements that are building alternatives to capitalism. We need to go beyond rights-based and identity-based movements that don't call into question capitalism and its exploitation of people and the planet. And that doesn't mean that people won't unite to build culture. It doesn't mean that people won't unite to move forward an issue. But the notion that the fundamental basis for the kind of unity we need to achieve system change is going to come through an issue or an identity, or even an amalgamation of these things—that way of viewing things isn't going to move us forward. Our role is to articulate a story, a worldview that embraces all of those things in a common project.

And that common project has to speak to each of our issues and identities and point the way toward ways of living meaningfully with each other in relation to the earth. That's an enormous project. And it is not abstract. People are increasingly unable to produce the food that they need to survive. The cheap energy that our way of life depends on, the way of life that the United States is dependent on, is going away. Our relationships to each other and the planet are changing drastically. If we don't start to change and do things to restore, repair, and transform our society and our relationships, we're in a shitload of trouble. And you can't name an identity or an issue that can take on a project of this kind of transformation alone. It's going to take a renewal of our whole worldview.

Angel Gonzalez: Not only are you proposing criticisms of current or past political strategies or tactics, but you're also proposing a set of categories with which to understand a new way of integrating an anti-capitalist, anti-patriarchal, anti-heterosexist world or politic through the concept of sovereignty. I'm interested to hear more about why the use of sovereignty. Why introduce it in a conversation about the ways we need to move forward in this particular moment?

SD: First, I want to put out that I'm not introducing the concept of sovereignty. I want to be really honest about sovereignty as something that I've taken up as a result of being in relationship to or reading about indigenous people and their movements in the Americas. And in stretching and creatively reshaping the concept I hope to honor and respect these movements. I first got connected with the radical notion of sovereignty through the work of La Via Campesina (2003), which is a global movement of peasants fighting against the destruction of local food security, ecosystems, and economies as a result of the globalization of agriculture. In response to the idea of free trade in agriculture, LVC put out their vision of food sovereignty. Food sovereignty can be defined as "THE RIGHT of all peoples, communities, and countries to define their own agricultural, labor, fishing, food and land policies which are ecologically, socially, economically and culturally appropriate to their unique circumstances. It includes the right to food and to produce food, which means that all people have the right to safe, nutritious and culturally appropriate food and to food-producing resources and the ability to sustain themselves and their societies." (NGO/CSO Forum, 2002).

I had heard of the idea of sovereignty before, but this was a creative and powerful new application of the idea to contemporary issues. It was only later that I learned that indigenous people throughout the Americas have been developing the practice and the idea of liberatory sovereignty for centuries, since colonization and genocide began its assault on indigenous nations. The concept of sovereignty that was being used by these movements wasn't sovereignty in the sense of the nation-state. Rather, liberatory sovereignty, as a value as well as a concept, is about the right of a people to choose its own way of life. At the center of this right to ways of life is the question of territory, relationship to land.

Now, one of things that has happened is that capitalism has defined territory as property, as a form of exclusive ownership. But we need to make a break with that way of thinking. The shift is moving from the idea of who "owns" that space—which really means who has the right to kick other people out and who can exploit it however they want regardless of the consequences—to a notion of the coexistence of different ways of life in shared space. You can have multiple groups of people existing on the same piece of land who are all sovereign and who can claim that same land as territory because their ways of being acknowledge the right of other people to live in relation to that land as they choose. It's like different people living in a house or groups using a community center for different things. It's about relating to space in a way that doesn't destroy the ability of others to also live and grow in that space. And it's not only a question of space, but of economies and of culture. Is there economic sovereignty? Food sovereignty? There are a whole set of interrelated rights which we need to understand as plural sovereignties. And because we're not talking about private property and exclusion we can talk about how these sovereignties, between and among people and the land, can coexist. This is exactly what a vibrant, diverse democracy is about: governing the plurality of sovereignties that overlap in an ecology of self-determination and mutual determination.

When we say a democratic society is based on the sovereignty of the people, we are talking about the basic agreements for how we organize politics, economies, culture, our relationship to the earth. Constitutions are the expression of that, they're the agreements we always go back to and that everything else must be in harmony with. Of course, we shouldn't fetishize or reify a constitution as something above us. We reach these agreements through dialogue, negotiation, and struggle. In a class society a constitution represents the balance of forces. So we're talking about the shared social agreements that are reached and enforced based on who has a voice, who is organized, who has power and is at the table of governance.

The struggle for sovereignty is saying that no political power, no government can claim authority over a people if it does not recognize their inherent rights, their right to determine for themselves their ways of living. And that includes everything from gender to religion. And it means also recognizing the rights of the ecosystem, the rights of the Earth, because there is no humanity and no society without the earth and its ecosystems.

In Latin America, Left governments have called for the rewriting of constitutions as a process for broader sectors of people to talk about what the country's basic agreements should be. And indigenous people, Afro-descendent people, women, LGBTQ people, youth, environmentalists, and so many others have come to the table to redesign governance; to fight so that it is not property and the interests of the powerful, but the sovereignties of the people that are the foundation for society.

Now what about the constitution of the United States? Though this country claims to be the vanguard of democracy, the U.S. constitution is more than 200 years old and was written by genocidal colonizers, slave owners, and landowners in order to protect their power and their property. It enshrines slavery and all but blots out the full sovereignty of the indigenous, people of color, women, queer folks. What a poverty of imagination to think that tinkering within the framework of that document could possibly encompass the sovereignties of all the people who have lived and contributed to the economy, the society, and the culture of this place! We should ask ourselves what it would look like to create processes for popular movements, including queer people, to rewrite the city charters, school board bylaws, and the constitutions of the states and the federal government. What would it look like to set that as a goal for our movements?

Gender Sovereignty against Gender Genocide

AG: Why introduce the category of sovereignty into a conversation about sexuality and gender?

SD: I mentioned how La Via Campesina was able to apply the idea of sovereignty to the rights of small farmers and the rights of people to determine their own land and agricultural policies in the face of resistance to neoliberalism and capitalist globalization of agriculture. Well, we need to do the same thing with the rights of queer people. We need to connect them up with the global struggle against capitalism. We need to talk about gender sovereignty as the right of all individuals, communities, and peoples to define their own genders, the right to our own bodies, including the right to control over our own labor, reproductive abilities, and gender expressions. We need to talk about the right to access of information about our bodies, the right to decision making about our bodies over surgeries and childbirth. And we need to talk about the right to the resources that we need to sustain and develop ourselves as whole people. I think the framework of sovereignty can offer us a powerful tool for rethinking queer struggles and connecting us to global movements struggling for other aspects of sovereignty against capitalism and the fundamentalisms of the right wing that exclude and exploit.

I also think sovereignty is a powerful idea when we talk about gender because the oppression of queer people has historically been connected to the violation of the sovereignty of indigenous and peasant cultures by capitalism, colonialism, and patriarchy. The right of peoples—in particular peoples of color—to determine how they wanted to express, envision, and embody gender was put under attack as part of the colonization process. For example, when the conquistadors came to the Americas, one of the first things they did and documented was killing those whose gender expressions were outside the male/female binary. So when I say gender genocide, I am not being metaphorical. They literally went about wiping out gender alternatives. In fact, according to Catholic religious law, "sodomy" and male homosexuality, if "widespread" and "tolerated" by indigenous peoples, were sins that could give Christian nations the "right to conquest." This was a key part of the debate over whether the indigenous should be enslaved, which was fought between Bartolome de Las Casas and Gonzalo Fernandez de Oviedo (Trexler, 1995, pp. 82–84).

Colonialism also went about transforming the ways that men and women were understood and what their power relations were. Maria Lugones (2007) has an excellent article in which she talks about how the gender system that we have today is the product of colonialism, which created new genders. In societies where anatomy did not determine land ownership or the ability to hold political power, "men" and "women," as they would come to be known under colonialism, did not exist. The imposition of the gender binary and the attachment of power to men and over women were connected processes that went on at the same time as colonialism developed racial categories. So the attacks on queer genders, the subjugation of women, and imperialism were all—and continue to be—interrelated processes by which capitalism has expanded.

There's less literature on the gender systems of enslaved Africans and their transformation through the slave trade, but it's not hard to imagine that there were alternative gender and sexual understandings that were attacked and suppressed along with the destruction of African spiritual systems in the process of the slave trade. How could they not be when slavery enabled so much rape and exploitation? How could the commodification of people, their bodies, and their labor not lead to a transformation of how gender was embodied? When we think about slavery we should also be thinking about the traumatic transformation of ways of thinking and being gendered that were part of the process, were part of that cultural catastrophe. Slavery was part of this essential fact of a concerted attack on different ways of gendered being by colonialism: gender genocide.

And this continues today. We see it in daily harassment and in the economic and psychological consequences of heterosexism, which manifest in the disproportionate homelessness of queer youth, the astronomical unemployment rates of transgender people, and the rates of suicide among our people, particularly our youth (NGLTF, 2007, 2009).

And this isn't just about eliminating queer people. It's about the mutilation of gender with all people in order to force them into the gender binary, the racialized gender binary. And if you don't fit that, whatever doesn't fit will be cut off, beaten, abused, attacked, ridiculed. You might identify as a man, as a black or Latino man. But you didn't get to that identity without a traumatic process of creating that gender, without being teased and tortured into "proper" gender roles. And that process didn't just happen with you. That's a historical process that's part of colonialism, that's part of destroying the sovereignty of a people to decide who they want to be, how they want to relate to each other and the planet, and removing choices through violence, through appropriation of means of production, of bodies, of life. Women go through a similar process, but they are inserted at the bottom of the hierarchy. They are mutilated and forced into a narrow "woman" category and pushed under male genders.

Queer people, in particular queer people of color, have no place in this system. Genocide is a logic that says, "this group of people has no place in the society that we are building and in order for the society that we want to exist, these people need to not exist." The existence of that society depends on continually erasing them. And this erasure is neither just physical nor just cultural or metaphorical. There are actual instances of murder in a very physical way. And there is the ongoing cultural, control mythology that's saying: these people don't exist. That indigenous people are gone, are part of history. That this is our land. That no one else is here, like Israel and Palestine.

Fighting on this edge of gender sovereignty is about fighting for liberated territory for our people. It seeps into everything I do. It's not just something that happens when I'm organizing queer people. It means that when I'm in a space of "my people" I'm doing the work of liberating us from the imposition of a colonial gender system. That we're opening the space for a free expression and a new dialogue about how each of us came to the genders that we're in, and through the stories articulating where we want to be. My fight is to create spaces among my people so that we can choose how we want to be. Do we want to continue domestic violence, queer bashing, isolated men? Are these the gender pathways we want to continue, or do we want something different? My fight is against a system that's pushing on our people to choose either male or female, black or queer—imposing false choices. We want to get beyond the vision they are allowing us and say we have a different way of being.

We need to understand that it isn't a coincidence that the attack on queer people is being mounted by the same right wing that is attacking the environment, workers' rights, immigrants. The joining of the Christian fundamentalists, the market fundamentalists, and the racial fundamentalists is no coincidence. The more capitalism privatizes the collective wealth of our planet and our labor, the more communities are pushed into scarcity and crisis. And when there are no solutions to that crisis, people turn to extremism and are vulnerable to the scapegoating, xenophobic, exclusionary politics put forward by the right wing. As Vandana Shiva says, "exclusions breed extremisms" (2005, pp. 2–4). So we need to take seriously what's happening here, because the genocide that's happening is immense and broad. It's about wiping out those who are no longer useful to the market system, and today that means the majority of the world.

It is our role as queer people to make sure that our voices are among those calling for a different world where no one and no part of life is expendable. As queer people we need to be at the table in shaping the kind of society that we want to have. Our gender sovereignty must be part of designing the new way of living that will replace capitalism.

The Role of Education in Genocide and Sovereignty

AG: It seems to me that the reason why your framing of things in terms of genocide, sovereignty, liberated territories is so relevant to the question of education is that by using this language, it says that unique to notions of power and domination, particularly after colonialism, is not just simply the question of the use of physical force, but the ability to manipulate and dominate in the arenas of knowledge and being. But to do so, one of the greatest technologies developed was the teaching and the internalization of our invisibility and our dehumanization as peoples. To accept gender and these binary categories of sexuality and other things is to accept dehumanization, to accept a mutilated sense of ourselves. This isn't something that folks are born with, but which folks are taught that must continue. So I'm interested in hearing about pedagogy in the negative sense in terms of genocide. But I'm also interested in pedagogy in a positive sense in terms of building sovereignty and liberated territory. How can we mobilize educational projects for sovereignty and liberated territories?

SD: First and ongoing, violence is a form of pedagogy. Genocide is a form of pedagogy. What it hopes to create as an internalized experience are the limits of who we can be and what our relationships can be by announcing "beyond this point is death." Violence is never just some brute force. It never has been. Violence is a political tool used in an attempt to set the boundaries of the possible. That's one pedagogy that we need to be aware of, and it's got the best-funded school system on the planet: the U.S. military. Compare military funding and that of the public school system and it will tell you something about the balance of coercion and consent being used or anticipated on a global scale.

Now, to legitimize that—because it's a terrifying and unsettling fact—control mythologies get created. A huge part of that is erasing the humanity of the people who will be physically erased by violence. Because if you kill a human being that's murder. But you execute an enemy of the state, you don't murder them. And they aren't just to justify the violence of the state, but also of vigilante white racists who kidnap and torture immigrants or the exploitation of immigrant labor. Or the heterosexist vigilantes who kill queer and trans people. The story is that those people are tortured and exploited because they don't belong, they don't deserve to be here. These are the ideas we are taught.

Now let's talk about gender. A tremendous part of our education about gender is being taught that the gender binary is natural. That there are only two sexes and that everyone is either one or the other. Of course, this myth of natural genders is only viable if the actual history of gender formation through genocide, violence, and colonialism is erased. And they also erase the scientific evidence that shows that human beings can't be simply reduced to two "biological sexes." In fact, everything from our hormones to our genitals is diverse and unique. The fact that a certain set of these variations is sometimes capable of childbirth and others of producing semen doesn't mean that "men" and "women" are the natural and only way of defining ourselves. But by naturalizing the gender binary and erasing its history and saying "this is what is," in this myth, queer people, intersex people, trans people—we are all made to disappear. And this teaching of our invisibility is the prerequisite to the violence and discrimination that works toward our physical oppression and erasure. Because we are defined as outside nature and humanity, it becomes justified to violate our sovereignty, our right to our own bodies, desires, and identities.

What about the positive role that education can play? What about the role of pedagogy in the building of pluralist sovereignties? In some ways it's about having these concepts and putting them to work. Sharing them with other people. But more and more I think the place to start is where these concepts come from: lived experience. How can I create a lived experience of sovereignty, liberated territory? Because in that space of liberated territory people can choose and ask questions that come out of their experiences. The concepts are tools for creating lived experience, for opening up liberated territories where we can dialogue across our identities and issues.

And really these concepts are tools for opening our thinking so that we can educate one another, so that we can learn from the diversity of experiences and cultures and bodies and ecosystems that exist on this planet. What I've been trying to get at with all of this is that the struggle for liberation can't just be "activism" in the sense of protesting the things we don't like or organizing for a particular reform. We've got to get beyond this and see our work as queer people and as revolutionaries as learning how to govern collectively and democratically. And we have a lot to learn.

References

Gay American Indians. (1988). *Living the spirit: A gay American Indian anthology.* New York: St. Martin's Press.

Lugones, M. (2007). Heterosexualism and the colonial/modern gender system. *Hypatia, 22*(1), 186–209.

NGLTF. (2007). Lesbian, gay, bisexual and transgender youth: An epidemic of homelessness. Retrieved November 14, 2010, from http://www.thetaskforce.org/reports_and_research/homeless_youth

NGLTF. (2009). National transgender discrimination survey: Preliminary findings. Retrieved November 14, 2010, from http://www.thetaskforce.org/reports_and_research/trans_survey_preliminary_findings

NGO/CSO Forum. (2002, June 13). Food sovereignty: A right for all. Political statement of the NGO/CSO Forum for Food Sovereignty. Rome, Italy. Retrieved November 14, 2010, from: http://www.poptel.org.uk/panap/latest/wfs7.htm

Shiva, V. (2005). *Earth democracy: Justice, sustainability, and peace.* Cambridge: South End Press.

Smith, A. (2006). Heteropatriarchy and the three pillars of white supremacy. In INCITE! Women of Color Against Violence (Ed.), *The color of violence: The INCITE! anthology* (pp. 66–73). Cambridge: South End Press.

Trexler, R.C. (1995). *Sex and conquest: Gendered violence, political order, and the European conquest of the Americas.* Ithaca, NY: Cornell University Press.

La Via Campesina. (2003). Food sovereignty. Retrieved November 14, 2010, from http://www.viacampesina.org/en/index.php?option=com_content&view=article&id=47:food-sovereignty&catid=21:food-sovereignty-and-trade&Itemid=38

"Luna Boii"

Anayvette Martinez

When first approached about submitting a piece for a section of an anthology that examines sexualities in education I was first humbled and thrilled. Yet as more time passed and the deadline loomed I became perplexed at how my work fit in such a category. Sexuality in education? My sexuality in education? And whose education? Mine? My kids?

After wrestling with how this topic relates to my work it suddenly became clear to me that all these possibilities intersect with my own trajectory in education and sexuality, and how I—as a community-scholar, youth worker, educator, director, and mother—live, teach and thrive in my sexuality in the realm of education everyday.

I've been working with youth for over ten years, have been a mother for six years and have been out as a queer high femme of color for nine years. All of this is not coincidental and therefore my sexuality has infused my work in education both personally and privately in all sectors of my life.

Most recently I've worked as a Programs Director at non-profit organizations and at a middle school helping low-income youth of color navigate through a system that often sets them up for failure. As someone who has gone through these same systems I take the work I do personally. As a service provider in my community, my educational theory and practice is guided by my commitment to show-up as my full self, everyday. This means that everyday I show-up as an ex-chola, academic, native community member, organizer, flaming queer, mother of two, and harness my sexuality in how I model anti-oppression work with youth, implement youth development in programming, and build ally-ship with hetero identified youth. My identities and past experiences infuse how I build relationships with my youth, how I create curriculum and ultimately how I teach as an educator. I believe strongly in being out in these spaces because for many youth this will become their reference point for queerness. Youth who are questioning, queer, homophobic or allies, will find that the modeling and growing that happens in working with a strong out adult ally gives them room to challenge hetero-normative structures.

One of the first icebreakers I do with my youth is "Two Truths and One Lie." In this game everyone takes turns guessing which statement out of three is the lie. "I'm Gay" is always one of my statements and there has never been a time where youth don't guess this one as my lie. I have strings of pictures of my kids around my office, and most often in guessing they say "She can't be gay, she has kids" or "She doesn't look gay." I use all these as teaching moments to address my sexuality, the issue of passing and pre-conceived notions of queerness. What results is the beginnings of them realizing the intersections of oppression. Oftentimes they disclose that they have close friends or relatives that are queer, question their own sexuality or they are able to feel solidarity and commonality with someone from their block who is queer.

Throughout 2010 there has been heavy media attention on the onslaught of anti-gay bullying, intimidation, and overall harassment of queer/LGBT youth that has resulted in numerous consecutive suicides this past month. 2010 was an emotional and heart breaking time for queer lives.

We need to pay attention to our youth. I draw strength and energy from my interactions, conversations, and memories with the young people I have worked with over the past 10 years. We must actively challenge each other to be better allies. Let's take ownership of our own learning and become engaged in increasing awareness and acceptance. But our work does not end in just making safe spaces for youth in our classrooms and youth centers. A way to resolve the tension between the liberated spaces we create as educators with our youth and the "real world" is to encourage youth to express the full range of their selves and identities. Furthermore as educators our role is not simply to encourage this but also to support and create the conditions necessary for youth to feel ready to confront the challenges of living in the face of a society that encourages their death through homophobia, heteronormativity and gender binaries. How are we holding these institutions, communities and ourselves accountable? How are we taking into account our straight youth, specifically our young men of color who many times are the perpetuators of the violence?

Much of my work in schools is engaging with young men of color who are already holding on by a string to a school system that is pushing them out. Our approach in creating safety, normalizing and celebrating queerness has to be one that is inclusive of all involved. Further marginalizing a population of youth by labeling them as "bullies" continues the cycle of dumping a group that is already disenfranchised. Bullying is a behavior, not an identity. Our approach must be restorative and multifaceted; recognizing that all youth face violence everyday our response must be to educate, make connections and foster healing that addresses how the multiple systems of oppression we each encounter fail and hurt all of us.

As a queer single mother of color I am blessed to be raising my two children, Lupita and Diego Luna. Since day-one their lives have been infused with cross-gender play. When Lupita received her first doll it was accompanied with a toy truck. Diego Luna's name was chosen for its gender fluidity. In their short lives they have already swum in and out of different stages that explore each and in-between genders, I call them my little gender-renegades. Still I am well aware that although their father and I have made a conscious decision to raise them to not feel constrained by labels, names, and boxes, the real-world has a very different reality waiting for them; some of which they have already experienced.

As a queer mother, educator and youth/social justice worker I am committed to making it better for ALL youth. Beyond my children, the youth I am privileged to work with, and myself, my responsibilities include creating the type of world in which we can all thrive. In that spirit, I offer here a wish for Diego Luna:

Luna Boii

I always think to myself there might come a day where you hate me for this.

But I want you to know that your name was so thoughtfully threaded together by your father and I, woven like bright indigo blue and hot disco pink to give you, with intention, the choice to not feel constrained.

You fell in love with cars and for your whole 2nd year in life you carried them around in your neon colored hello kitty purse . . . opposites to some but the perfect pairing for you, and your ear-to-ear sticky smile would make anyone question why it has to be any other way.

The day *La Senora* who takes care of you expressed her disapproval of your pink colored nails at 3yrs old the look on your face of hurt and confusion pained me—I was angry at her, and then angry at myself because this is now and ten years from today it could be chants of "FAGGOT" at school, on the streets. This is the reality of raising you to bust boxes, yes *mijo,* boys can wear make-up, dresses and heels, and girls can wear suits, raising you to question how/why things have been set-up this way knowing that toe-tapping outside the box can earn you a label, category or sentence.

I want you to know that none of this is meant to make your life harder, but fuller. The world is yours to be who you want to be and all that bullshit, but I know its *harrrrrrrd.* Right now you're a toddler, but you will grow into a young man of color and the weight that comes with that is heavy.

From hibernating in my cocoon for nine months, to soaring as a full fledged *mariposa* today, to whoever you want to be tomorrow, I am here for you and love you unconditionally. I am committed to making a world that is better, safer, bigger—where you, and every other child, can swing freely from butterflyboii to butterflygirl and back, like monkey bars at a favorite playground.

The More We Know about Sex, the Better Our Choices, 1997.
Jeanette May and the Coalition for Positive Sexuality

11-1   A self-help group

Self Help, 1981. Suzann Gage
Published in *A New View of a Woman's Body: A Fully Illustrated Guide by the Federation of Feminist Women's Health Centers*
(New York: Simon & Schuster), this image portrays self-health care activism.

Resource Guide for Educators

TIM BARNETT

My son Tyler's birth certificate lists my partner, Scott Steinkamp, and me as his parents. Biologically, Tyler is the son of Scott and a friend of ours who was, amazingly, willing to help us create a family, in part because she so appreciates the beauty of her own. Scott passed away from brain cancer 3 years ago when Tyler was almost 4 years old, and since that time I have thought long and hard about how to talk to Tyler about issues of reproduction, family, and sexuality. As his non-biological, gay father, how will these issues take on special meaning as I attempt to educate my rapidly growing son? My specific family structure is still unusual, but the complexities we face are far from unique, and, in a sense, we represent the new norm, for every extended family contains an LGBTQ person, a single parent, men trying to balance traditional male roles with parenthood and relationships, children negotiating connections to half-brothers and sisters and multiple "families." As these and other issues make clear, education about sexuality and family has never been more complex and deserves close attention from all educators so that we can give our students what most of us never had: accurate, comprehensive, sensitive information about a wide and growing range of sexual issues.

In this resource guide, you will find practical discussions about how to make your office or classroom more inviting to students seeking information about sexuality along with theoretical inquiries into the nature of identity, power, and knowledge as they relate to sexuality and gender. Both sides of this spectrum are important, as issues from the most mundane to the most theoretical are critical for any educator wishing to provide quality education. We need practical resources, for example, when we meet students who have been assaulted because of their real or perceived sexual or gendered identity. It is our duty to help young people find friendly doctors and advocates and to keep them safe. At the same time, educators from kindergarten to the university must be aware of the theoretical, historical, and cultural work that probes at the source of these moments of violence and the nature of the heterosexist society that tries to envelop all of us: gay and straight, men, women, and transgendered. While physical and emotional violence may seem like forthright legal or medical problems to be addressed by the proper authorities, the theoretical work highlighted in the resources below (and in the essays and images throughout this book) can help us understand the more complex roots, and consequences, of such violence.

As educators we also need to use such knowledge to imagine ways of approaching these issues in our teaching and advising of students on a daily basis and not just when a crisis occurs. Sexuality is already being addressed by students on the playgrounds, in the hallways, and in the cafeteria, and it is important that we find multiple ways to thoughtfully guide students through this maze of information. Parents, advisors, and educators all need to intervene in regular ways as young people navigate various understandings of what it means to be sexual in a world where new understandings of gendered and sexual selves are emerging regularly, alongside new justifications for suppressing those who do not fit traditional norms.

The resources in this guide tackle these questions, among many others, and help students and educators see that sexual education is, by necessity, a widely inclusive field. It is important, for example, that we educate ourselves and our students about the dangerousness of normalizing one form of sexuality—monogamous heterosexuality—at the expense of any other sexuality that does not conform strictly to this norm. We need to follow feminist inquiries into the nature of public v. private and what it really means for the personal to be political. How, that is, have "private" heterosexual lives created a heterosexist public domain in which it becomes ok to ostracize the lives of LGBTQ youth and adults? How can we help students see that all of our most intimate relationships contribute to and evolve out of a public sphere that sanctions these relationships (or not) in the name of religion and "normalcy"—but that, ultimately, our discourse on sexuality is as much about political gain and power as it is about some absolute set of values? How do we help students, educators, and families see that the distinctions we make between what is publicly acceptable for gay and straight youth is a source of discrimination itself? It is our job to help students, all students, see that straight lives are not any more "normal" than queer lives, and we can do so by helping students understand how all of our personal relationships are deeply intertwined in the public world. It is reasonable to ask students to consider, for example, how our understanding of marriage as a state-sanctioned and rewarded institution affects all of us, those who can be married legally and those who cannot. Why is the state involved in our most personal relationships and, in effect, regulating our emotional lives in various ways? How does this issue present a variety of concerns for all?

On a practical note, it is important for teachers to remember that any resource guide such as this one is partial and subject to change. All the websites listed below, for example, have been reviewed and are valid as of March 2011, but, given the nature of the Internet, there is no guarantee that they will be available in coming years. It is also important for educators to compile their own list of local resources to have available when needed. In big cities, this is a comparatively easy task (although one that is often overlooked), as we can look online or in the phone book for Planned Parenthood offices and gay and lesbian centers. Even in small towns, though, it is possible to discover which doctors or religious or social groups are open to honest discussions of sexuality with young people. Word of mouth; LGBTQ chat rooms; progressive political organizations, figures, and churches (a safe bet is always a Unitarian Universalist Church); LGBTQ parents and kids—all of these can serve as potential resources as you negotiate what can be difficult territory in towns with no central public presence for sexual education.

Note: I have divided resources based on what I believe to be their suitability for various age groups, but, since there is no universal standard for what is appropriate for different groups of young people or different communities, it is important that you review any items for their suitability before using them.

Websites

General

- Advocates for Youth, http://www.advocatesforyouth.org/: A comprehensive site that "champions efforts that help young people make informed and responsible decisions about their reproductive and sexual health."
- Al Fatiha, http://www.al-fatiha.org/. A website that advocates respect and support for LGBTQ Muslims. The site is not limited to school-based issues but may be very useful for Muslim students, educators, and others.
- AVERT: AVERTing HIV and AIDS. http://www.avert.org/aids-hiv-prevention.htm. A straightforward site for anyone interested in learning more about HIV, AIDS, and the prevention of both. Includes lesson plans for instructors seeking to include HIV prevention in the curriculum.
- Center for LGBT Education, Outreach & Services, http://www.ithaca.edu/sacl/lgbt/resources/other/. This site provides references for Academic, Education/Advocacy, Family, Health, and Identity issues relevant to teachers and students interested in lgbtq issues.
- Chochmat HaLev (Come Home), http://www.chochmat.org/lgbt-welcoming-resources.html. A resource that attempts to "provide . . . a Jewish space where we can bring our whole beings in all our complexity, enjoying the support and affirmation of our non-queer allies."
- Planned Parenthood, http://www.plannedparenthood.org/info-for-teens/index.asp. Advice about health and sexuality for teens and adults from one of our most important national organizations.
- Trans-Gender Law and Policy Institute, http://www.transgenderlaw.org/ and the Transgender Law Center, http://transgenderlawcenter.org/cms/: These sister web sites (the first based in New England and the second in California) offer legal advice to anyone dealing with issues of gender identity.

Sites Aimed at Teens and Young Adults

- About Gay-Straight Alliances, http://www.lausd.k12.ca.us/lausd/offices/hep/programs/01a.html. Posted by GLSN, this site can help students and teachers develop GSAs and includes everything from sample mission statements to a brief history of these groups.
- GSA Network, http://gsanetwork.org/resources/research-reports/national-research. This site's mission is to empower "youth . . . to fight homophobia and transphobia in schools."
- Positive.Org. http://www.positive.org/Home/index.html. A youth-friendly site advocating an honest, complete sex education for all young people.
- Scarleteen: Sex Education for the Real World. http://www.scarleteen.com/. A 10-year-old site that is the go-to source for sexual advice for many teens because of its matter-of-fact, youth-friendly approach to sexual health.
- Sex, Etc. http://www.sexetc.org/. An award-winning site for and by teens offering straightforward sex education and information about sexual health.
- Youth Action for Sex Education, http://www.freechild.org/reproductiverights.htm. A site valuable for its own contributions and also valuable as it provides many links to some of the most significant sites on teen sexuality on the web.

Sites Aimed at Educators, Parents, and Other Concerned Adults

- American Association of Sex Educators, Counselors, and Therapists, http://www.aasect.org/. A site designed by and for professionals to offer support for educators seeking guidance on issues of sexual education.
- Answer Sex Ed, Honestly. http://answer.rutgers.edu/blog/category/sex-education-resources/. A site developed at Rutgers University that offers a range of information and resources for children's, teens,' and adults' sexual education.
- Consortium of Higher Education LGBT Resource Professionals, http://www.lgbtcampus.org/directory/. A site listing LGBT university resource centers from universities around the country that will be useful to lgbtq youth deciding on higher education or to teachers looking for helpful local resources.
- Family Education, http://life.familyeducation.com/sex/teen/34505.html. A site designed to help parents and other adults talk about sexuality and sexual health issues.
- Gay, Lesbian, Bisexual, Transgender (GLBT) Resources, http://pegasus.cc.ucf.edu/~rgause/glbt.htm. A site from the University of Central Florida that is especially useful for Floridians but includes a great deal for anyone interested in academic resources on queer theory, culture, history, and politics.
- GLSEN, http://www.glsen.org/cgi-bin/iowa/all/antibullying/index.html. Probably the best known and most comprehensive site for LGBTQ educators from a group at the center of the struggle for inclusive, unbiased education. Includes lesson plans, anti-bullying resources, policy information, etc.
- Go Ask Alice! http://www.goaskalice.columbia.edu/. Columbia University's comprehensive site dedicated to sexual health.
- Groundspark: Igniting Change Through Film, http://groundspark.org/. A site that reflects on the ways film can help us understand issues of difference, having to do with LGBTQ issues but also issues of race, ethnicity, etc. Offers a range of films for purchase, including the breakthrough *It's Elementary* (see below).
- Guttmacher Institute, http://www.guttmacher.org/. A site aimed at professionals whose goal is to advance "sexual and reproductive health worldwide through research, policy analysis and public education."
- Hatred in the Hallways: Violence and Discrimination Against Lesbian, Gay, Bisexual and Transgender Students in US Schools, http://www.hrw.org/legacy/reports/2001/uslgbt/. A site dedicated to ending bullying (verbal and physical) in K–12 settings.
- National Youth Advocacy Coalition, http://www.nyacyouth.org/#: A politically based advocacy group seeking to change the external world faced by LGBTQ youth and to help the youth themselves navigate political, social, and personal complexities.
- NCTE Issue Brief: Sexuality Studies, http://www.ncte.org/college/briefs/sexuality. A site published through the National Council of Teachers of English that is directed primarily at instructors who teach literature and writing.
- Parents and Friends of Lesbians and Gays (PFLAG), http://community.pflag.org/Page.aspx?pid=194&srcid=-2. One of the best known advocacy and support groups dedicated to helping parents and allies of LGBTQ people support their loved ones and understand the nature of homophobia in and out of schools.
- Pride Education Network, http://www.pridenet.ca/main.htm. A British Columbia-based site that offers models of workshops for educators interested in creating safe and welcoming schools. This group may be available to work with B.C.-based educators and students, and its website is informative for all.
- Safe Schools Coalition, http://www.safeschoolscoalition.org/RG-teachers_k-12.html. A resource site for educators that includes curricular suggestions and ideas for combating homophobia in the classroom.
- Sex Ed. Library, http://www.sexedlibrary.org/. Touted to be the most comprehensive source of sexual education in the nation, this site is "brought to you by SIECUS (the Sexuality Information and

Education Council of the United States)."

- Sexual Education Resources, http://uscm.med.sc.edu/cdr/sexualeducation.htm. This University of South Carolina site contains, among other things, an important list of resources for youth and educators interested in sexual education for those with disabilities.
- Sex Education Resource List, http://www.frcog.org/pubs/teen/resources/SexEducation.pdf. A list of print resources on sexual education aimed at librarians and educators.
- Voice of the Shuttle: Gender and Sexuality Studies, http://vos.ucsb.edu/browse.asp?id=994. One section of this enormous education site focuses on a variety of academic and theoretical resources for LGBTQ people.

Trans Ally Poster, 2011. Chances/Dances

Trans Ally Card is produced as a form of collaborative community political education by Chances/Dances (a Chicago dance party), Trans Youth Resource and Advocacy (TYRA) a weekly transgender and gender-questioning drop-in program for youth ages 12–24 through Chicago's Howard Brown Health Center's Broadway Youth Center, and Strap-on.org <http://strap-on.org> a queer* positive, trans* positive, sex* positive, girl* positive community message board.

Films

Films Aimed at Grades K–8

Chasnoff, D., & Cohen, H. (Directors & Producers). (1999). *It's elementary: Talking about gay issues in school.* [DVD]. United States: New Day Films. The classic film that looks at young children's responses to gay issues and homophobia.

Chasnoff, D., & Cohen, H.S. (Directors & Producers). (2000). *That's a family.* [DVD]. United States: New Day Films. Children discuss multiple ways of being a family.

Chasnoff, D., Cohen, H.S., & Stilley, K. (Directors & Producers). (2003). *Let's get real.* United States: New Day Films. [DVD]. A look at name calling and bullying in middle schools told by youth.

Chasnoff, D., & Symons, J. (Directors & Producers). (2007). *It's still elementary.* [DVD]. United States: New Day Films. A follow-up on how homophobia and LGBTQ education have fared since the original film.

Lesbian and Gay Parents' Association. (Producers). (1994). *Both my moms' names are Judy: Children of gays and lesbians speak out.* [DVD]. United States: Lesbian and Gay Parents' Association. Children of LGBTQ parents help others understand their issues and concerns.

Marcolina, K., & Grimaldi, L. (Directors & Producers). (2008). *Camp out.* [DVD]. United States: Evolution Media. Teens wrestle with being gay and Christian.

Mayle, P. (Writer). (1985). [DVD]. *Where did I come from?* United States: Goldhil Entertainment. An animated film for young children that explains sex and procreation.

McCaffrey, T. (Director and Producer). (2004). [DVD]. *The birds, the bees, and me: For boys.* United States: Ntoccp. A primer on boys' bodies and sexuality, aimed at pre-teens.

McCaffrey, T. (Director and Producer). (2004). [DVD]. *The birds, the bees, and me: For girls.* United States: Ntoccp. A primer on girls' bodies and sexuality, aimed at pre-teens.

Regan, Melissa. (Director & Producer). (2003). *No dumb question.* [DVD]. United States: Epiphany Productions. Young girls explore their feelings about their transgendered uncle.

Spadola, M. (Director & Producer). (2008). *Our house: Kids of gay and lesbian parents.* [DVD]. United States: First Run Features. Children of LGBTQ parents tell their stories.

Films Aimed at Grades 9–12

A2ZCDS.com (Directors). (2005). *Sex education: Pesky puberty.* [DVD]. United States: Tapeworm. A historic look at the various ways adults tried to educate teens about sexuality in the 1950s.

Barbosa, P., & Lenoir, G. (Directors), & Woman Vision (Producer). (2001). *De colores.* [DVD]. United States: Iron Rod Motion Pictures, Inc. A bilingual look at Latino families and homophobia.

Chasnoff, D. (Director), & Chen, S. (Producer). (2009). *Straight-laced: How gender's got us all tied up.* [DVD]. United States: New Day Films. Teens explore how gender affects all of us, gay and straight, and how gender intersects with sexual identity.

Dunne, G. (Director & Producer). (2001). *Today I found out.* [DVD]. United States: Scenarios USA. Adapted from a teen's essay, this short film considers pregnancy in the lives of teens.

Dupre, J. (Director & Producer), & Tobias, A., Byard, E., Jennings, K., & Huffington, H. (Producers). (1998). *Out of the past: The struggle for gay and lesbian rights in America.* [DVD]. United States: Zeitgeist Pictures. This film considers historic LGBTQ struggles as they connect to one young woman's efforts to start a high school gay-straight alliance.

Jenkins, T. (Director), & Stover, S. (Producer). (2001). *Choices: The good, the bad, the ugly.* United States: Scenarios USA. High school students wrote this film about three teenage boys who are facing issues having to do with relationships, sex, and HIV.

Kheyfets, M., & Hababou, M. (Directors & Producers). (2008). *Teens, sex & health: A comprehensive approach to sex-*

ual education. United States: Revodition. Aimed at older teens, this 4-hour guide provides a great deal of information about sex, sexuality, health, and reproduction.

Koepp, D. (Director), & Swerdlow, E. (Producer). (2004). *All falls down.* [DVD]. United States: Scenarios USA. Written by a 15-year-old, this film examines three young women's choices as they consider how to handle the boys they meet on their way home from school.

Lipschutz, M., & Rosenblatt, R. (Directors & Producers). (2005). [DVD]. *The education of Shelby Knox.* United States: PBS. The story of a young, conservative woman who recognizes the need for honest discussion of sexuality in her community and becomes an activist.

Mosbacher, D., Reid, F., & Rhue, S. (Directors & Producers). (1996). *All God's children.* [DVD]. United States: Woman Vision. An African American response to homophobia.

Prince-Bythewood, G. (Director), & Higgins, B. (Producer). (2006). *Reflections.* [DVD]. United States: Scenarios USA. Written by a teen, this film examines three teen girls as they deal with relationships, sex, and how to protect themselves from HIV.

Simons, L. (Director & Producer). (2000). *Our faces: A film about growing up gay, lesbian, bisexual, transgender.* [DVD]. United States: Education Videos Plus. Youth tell their stories.

Skurnik, J. (Director & Producer). (2010). *I'm just Anneke.* [DVD]. United States: New Day Films. A teen works to establish her own gender identity.

Walton, P. (Director & Producer). (2006). *Gay youth.* [DVD]. United States: New Day Films. A documentary that contrasts the lives of two LGBTQ youths to show the difficulties and possibilities of growing up gay in the United States.

Films Aimed at University Students

Aldrich, G., & Baumgardner, J. (Directors and Producers). *I had an abortion.* (2005). [DVD]. United States: Women Make Movies. A look at several generations of women and their experiences with abortion.

Bull, D., & Mulryan, J. (Directors & Producers). (1996). *Men talk sex.* [DVD]. United States: Fanlight Productions. Men from a variety of backgrounds talk frankly about sex and their lives.

Canner, L. (Director & Producer), & Benello, J.P., Ettinger, W., Helfand, J., & Weiss, M.N. (Producers). (2011). *Orgasm, inc.* United States: Astrea Media. A look into the way the pharmaceutical industry is attempting to exploit women's sexuality in its search for the new "miracle" drug.

Chase, C. (Director & Producer). (1997). *Hermaphrodites speak.* [DVD]. United States: Intersex Society of North America. A ground-breaking work that asks intersex people to talk about their lives and the issues they face.

Chasnoff, S. (Producer & Director). (2009). [DVD]. *HIV: Hey, hey it's viral.* [DVD]. United States: Beyondmedia Education. A sex-positive film produced by youth that looks at HIV prevention and activism.

Chasnoff, S. (Producer & Director), & The Empowered Fe Fe's (Producer). (2005). [DVD]. *Doin' it: Sex, disability & videotape.* [DVD]. United States: Beyondmedia Education. A close look at disability, sexuality, and relationships.

Chiang, S.L. (Director & Producer). (2002). *One + one.* [DVD]. United States: New Day Films. Two couples (one straight and one gay) explore HIV in their lives.

Condon, B. (Director), & Mutrux, G. (Producer). (2004). *Kinsey.* [DVD]. United States: Fox Searchlight. A motion picture based on the life of Alfred Kinsey and his research into sexuality and sex ed.

Cram, B. (Director & Producer), & Schermerhorn, C. (Producer). (1996). *You don't know dick: Courageous hearts of transsexual men.* [DVD]. United States: Berkeley Media, LLC. A critically acclaimed look at the lives of female-to-male (ftm) transsexuals.

De Seve, J. (Director & Producer). (2004). *Tying the knot.* [DVD]. United States: 1,049 Films. An analysis of what is lost by gay couples not allowed to marry.

Finch, N. (Director), & Wall, A., Vachon, C., Faber, G., Hamilton, M., & Caleb, R. (Producers). (1995). *Stonewall.* [DVD]. United States: BBC Warner. A fictionalized look at the famous Stonewall uprisings.

Goldman, M.T. (Director & Producer). (2010). [DVD]. *Subjectified: Nine young women talk about sex.* Women offer personal and in-depth insight into their sexual interests and needs.

Green, N. (Director & Producer). (2005). *Latino beginnings.* [DVD]. United States: LOGO Network. A look at being a minority within a minority through the eyes of LGBTQ Latinos.

Killing us softly: Advertising's image of women, v. 1, 2, 3 & 4. (1979, 1987, & 1999). [DVD]. United States: Cambridge Documentary Films. An exploration of the advertising industry and the ways it sexualizes women.

Kopple, B., Harty, C., Korin, J., & Morales, S. (Directors). (1998). *A century of women 2: Sexuality and social justice.* [DVD]. United States: Turner. A consideration of the intertwined issues of sexuality, reproduction, and justice and some of the many women who have made a difference in these areas.

Krodman, M., & Williams, B. (Directors & Producers). (2006). *Diana.* [DVD]. United States: Media That Matters. A short documentary following a young woman with HIV.

Livingston, J. (Director & Producer), Finch, N., & Davis, L. (Producers). (1990). *Paris is burning.* [DVD]. United States: Miramax Films. A look at race, class, sexuality, and gender in the drag balls of the 1980s.

Rees, D. (Director), & Cooper, N. (Producer). (2007). *Pariah.* [DVD]. United States: New Day Films. A young, black lesbian struggles with her identity and her family.

Riggs, M. (Director & Producer). (1989). *Tongues untied.* [DVD]. United States: Strand Releasing. An examination of the lives and sexuality of gay black men.

Rosenberg, R., & Schiller, G. (Directors & Producers). (1984). *Before Stonewall.* [DVD]. United States: First Run Features. A history of LGBTQ politics before 1969.

Scagliotti, J. (Director), Hunt, D., & Baus, J. (Producers). (2003). *Dangerous living: Coming out in the developing world.* [DVD]. United States: Human Rights Watch Series. One of the first looks at what it means to be openly gay in sexually repressive countries.

Scagliotti, J. (Director), Williams, R., Baus, J., & Hunt, D. (Producers). (1999). *After Stonewall.* [DVD]. United States: First Run Features. A history of LGBTQ politics since 1969.

Sharma, P. (Director & Co-producer). (2007). *A jihad for love.* [DVD]. United States: Halal Films. An analysis of how Muslim beliefs and practices can conflict with being LGBTQ.

Simmons, J. (Director), & Smothers, T. (Producer). (2004–2005). *TransGeneration.* [DVD]. United States: New Video Group. A look at four college-aged students transitioning between genders.

Skurnik, J. (Director & Producer). (2010). *The family journey: Raising gender nonconforming children.* [DVD]. United States: New Day Films. A discussion of the ways families work with transgendered children.

Walton, P. (Director & Producer). (2004). *Liberty: Three stories about life and death.* [DVD]. United States: New Day Films. Lesbian celebrations of life and community in the face of death.

Nomy Lamm, 2009. Richard Downing

The sexualities education-for-justice work of Sins Invalid offers an example of art used to re-frame normative concepts of beauty, identity, sexuality, gender, and more. The group's focus—"that we will be liberated as whole beings"—is ours, as well.

—The Editors

Sins Invalid

Mission and Vision Statements

Sins Invalid is a performance project that incubates and celebrates artists with disabilities, centralizing artists of color and queer and gender-variant artists as communities who have been historically marginalized. Our performance work explores the themes of sexuality, embodiment, and the disabled body. Conceived and led by disabled people of color, we develop and present cutting-edge work where normative paradigms of "normal" and "sexy" are challenged, offering instead a vision of beauty and sexuality inclusive of all individuals and communities.

We define disability broadly to include people with physical impairments, people who belong to a sensory minority, people with emotional disabilities, people with cognitive challenges, and those with chronic/severe illness. We understand the experience of disability to occur within any and all walks of life, with deeply felt connections to all communities impacted by the medicalization of their bodies, including trans, gender variant and intersex people, and others whose bodies do not conform to our culture(s)' notions of "normal" or "functional."

Sins Invalid recognizes that we will be liberated as whole beings—as disabled/as queer/as brown/as black/as genderqueer/as female or male bodied—as we are far greater whole than partitioned. We recognize that our allies emerge from many communities and that demographic identity alone does not determine one's commitment to liberation.

Sins Invalid believes in social and economic justice for all people with disabilities—in lockdowns, in shelters, on the streets, visibly disabled, invisibly disabled, sensory minority, environmentally injured, psychiatric survivors—moving beyond individual legal rights to collective human rights.

Our stories, imbedded in analysis, offer paths from identity politics to unity among all oppressed people, laying a foundation for a collective claim of liberation and beauty.

www.sinsinvalid.org

Print Texts

Academic Research Aimed at Educators

Ashcraft, C. (2008). So much more than "sex ed": Teen sexuality as vehicle for improving academic success and democratic education for diverse youth. *American Educational Research Journal, 45*(3), 631–667.

Beyer, C., Griffin, P., Lee, C., & Waugh, J. (2004). Describing roles that gay-straight alliances play in schools: From individual support to school change. *Journal of Gay & Lesbian Issues in Education, 1*(3), 7–22.

Bishop, H.N., Caraway, C., & Stader, D.L. (2010). A case for legal protection for sexual minority educators. *Clearing House: A Journal of Educational Strategies, Issues and Ideas, 83*(3), 84–88.

Bornstein, K. (1994). *Gender outlaw: On men, women and the rest of us.* New York: Routledge.

Bryson, M.K., & MacIntosh, L.B. (2010). Can we play "fun gay"? Disjuncture and difference, and the precarious mobilities of millennial queer youth narratives. *International Journal of Qualitative Studies in Education* (QSE), *23*(1), 101–124.

Burns, K. (2007). Giving voice, making change: How PFLAG resources can be useful classroom tools. *Journal of Gay & Lesbian Issues in Education, 4*(2), 107–109.

Chauncey, G. (1994). *Gay New York: Gender, urban culture and the making of the gay male world, 1890–1940.* New York: Basic Books.

Comment, K.M. (2009). "Wasn't she a lesbian?" Teaching homoerotic themes in Dickinson and Whitman. *English Journal, 98*(4), 61–66.

Corngold, J. (2011). Misplaced priorities: Gutmann's democratic theory, children's autonomy, and sex education policy. *Studies in Philosophy & Education, 30*(1), 67–84.

DeJean, W. (2007). Out gay and lesbian k–12 educators: A study in radical honesty. *Journal of Gay & Lesbian Issues in Education, 4*(4), 59–72.

D'Emilio, J. (1998). *Sexual politics, sexual communities.* Hyde Park, IL: University of Chicago Press.

D'Emilio, J. (2002). *The world turned: Essays on gay history, politics, and culture.* Durham, NC: Duke University Press.

Duberman, M. (1993). *Stonewall.* New York: Plume.

Elia, J.P., & Eliason, M. (2010). Discourses of exclusion: Sexuality education's silencing of sexual others. *Journal of LGBT Youth, 7*(1), 29–48.

Feinberg, L. (1997). *Transgender warriors: Making history from Joan of Arc to Dennis Rodman.* Boston: Beacon Press.

Feinberg, L. (1999). *Transliberation: Beyond pink or blue.* Boston: Beacon Press.

Formby, E., Hirst, J., Owen, J., Hayter, M., & Stapleton, H. (2010). "Selling it as a holistic health provision and not just about condoms. . . ." Sexual health services in school settings: Current models and their relationship with sex and relationships education policy and provision. *Sex Education: Sexuality, Society and Learning, 10*(4), 423–435.

Goshert, J. (2008). Reproductions of (il)literacy: Gay cultural knowledge and first-year composition pedagogy. *Composition Studies, 36*(1), 11–27.

Haglund, K., & Fehrin, R. (2010). The association of religiosity, sexual education, and parental factors with risky sexual behaviors among adolescents and young adults. *Journal of Religion & Health, 49*(4), 460–472.

Hrabe, F. (2006). Are you dedicated to diversity? Is the welcome mat out? *Alabama Counseling Association Journal, 32*(1), 15–19.

Kilman, C. (2007). "This is why we need a GSA". *Teaching Tolerance, 31*, 30–36.

Letts, W. (2006). I can't even think straight: Queer childhood and adolescence. *Journal of Gay & Lesbian Issues in Education, 3*(2–3), 163–166.

Limmer, M. (2010). Young men, masculinities and sex education. *Sex Education: Sexuality, Society and Learning, 10*(4), 349–358.

McCready, L.T. (2004). Some challenges facing queer youth programs in urban high schools: Racial segregation and de-normalizing whiteness. *Journal of Gay & Lesbian Issues in Education, 1*(3), 37–51.

Meem, D.T., Gibson, M., & Alexander, J. (2009). *Finding out: An introduction to LGBT studies.* Thousand Oaks, CA: Sage Publications.

Miner, J. (2009). How to make your office and institution more transgender friendly. *College & University, 84*(4), 69–72.

O'Higgins, S., & Nic Gabhainn, S. (2010). Youth participation in setting the agenda: Learning outcomes for sex education in Ireland. *Sex Education, 10*(4), 387–403.

Rasmussen, M.L. (2010). Secularism, religion and "progressive" sex education. *Sexualities, 13*(6), 699–712.

Renn, K.A. (2010). LGBT and queer research in higher education: The state and status of the field. *Educational Researcher, 39*(2), 132–141.

Roberts, G., Allan, C., & Wells, K. (2007). Understanding gender identity in k–12 schools. *Journal of Gay & Lesbian Issues in Education, 4*(4), 119–129.

Rodriguez, N.M., & Pinar, W.F. (Eds.). (2007). *Queering straight teachers: Discourse and identity in education.* Complicated Conversation: A Book Series of Curriculum Studies, vol. 22. New York: Peter Lang.

Russell, S.T., Muraco, A., Subramaniam, A., & Laub, C. (2009). Youth empowerment and high school gay-straight alliances. *Journal of Youth and Adolescence, 38*(7), 891–903.

Sadowski, M. (2010). Core values and the identity-supportive classroom: Setting LGBTQ issues within wider frameworks for preservice educators. *Issues in Teacher Education, 19*(2), 53–63.

Sarmiento, L.E., & Vasquez, S.A. (2010). "Abriendo puertas" (opening doors) through writing. *Teacher Educator, 45*(4), 273–286.

Savage, T.A., & Harley, D.A. (2009). A place at the blackboard: Including lesbian, gay, bisexual, transgender, intersex, and queer/questioning issues in the education process. *Multicultural Education, 16*(4), 2–9.

Sinkinson, M. (2009). "Sexuality isn't just about sex:" Pre-service teachers' shifting constructs of sexuality education. *Sex Education, 9*(4), 421–436.

Swango-Wilson, A. (2009). Perception of sex education for individuals with developmental and cognitive disability: A four cohort study. *Sexuality & Disability, 27*(4), 223–228.

Turnbull, T., van Schaik, P., & van Wersch, A. (2010). Adolescents' preferences regarding sex education and relationship education. *Health Education Journal, 69*(3), 277–286.

Walls, N.E., Kane, S.B., & Wisneski, H. (2010). Gay-straight alliances and school experiences of sexual minority youth. *Youth & Society, 41*(3), 307–332.

Watson, L.B., Varjas, K., Meyers, J., & Graybill, E.C. (2010). Gay-straight alliance advisors: Negotiating multiple ecological systems when advocating for LGBTQ youth. *Journal of LGBT Youth, 7*(2), 100–128.

Wilson, K.L., & Wiley, D.C. (2009). Influence of materials on teacher adoption of abstinence-only-until-marriage programs. *Journal of School Health 79*(12), 565–574.

Zain, A.D., & Muhammad, M. (2010). Perceptions of sex education among Muslim adolescents in Canada. *Journal of Muslim Minority Affairs, 30*(3), 391–407.

Fiction, Non-Fiction, Biographies, and Essays for Students (compiled with the assistance of Linda Beaugureau and the 2011 Rainbow Project Committee's 2011 Rainbow List)

K–4

Agell, C. (2010). *The accidental adventures of India McAllister.* New York: Henry Holt & Co. A young girl works to understand her dad and his new boyfriend.

Brannen, S.S. (2008). *Uncle Bobby's wedding.* New York: Putnam. Chloe the guinea pig tries to prepare for her favorite uncle's wedding to his boyfriend James.

Brown, L.K. (2000). *What's the big secret?: Talking about sex with girls and boys.* Boston: Little Brown Books for Young Readers. For pre-schoolers up to age 8, this is a handy guide for discussing issues of gender, love, and relationships.

Bryan, J., Combs, B., & Hosler, D. (2006). *The different dragon.* Annapolis, MD: Two Lives. A boy and his moms explore friendship with dragons as part of their bedtime storytelling.

De Haan, L., & Nijland, S. (2003). *King and king.* Berkeley, CA: Tricycle Press. Two princes meet and fall in love.

Ewert, M., & Ray, R. (2008). *10,000 dresses.* New York: Seven Stories Press. A young boy has dreams of beautiful dresses.

Fierstein, H., & Cole, H. (2005). *The sissy duckling.* New York: Simon and Schuster. A bullied duck proves himself to the others.

Gitchel, S. (2005). *Let's talk about s-e-x: A guide for kids 9 to 12 and their parents.* Minnetonka, MN: The Book Peddlers. A smart guide to talking about sex.

Harris, R.H. (2004). *It's so amazing!: A book about eggs, sperm, birth, babies, and families.* Somerville, MA: Candlewick. A comprehensive guide to reproduction for young children and their parents.

Harris, R.H. (2008). *It's not the stork: A book about girls, boys, babies, bodies, families and friends.* Somerville, MA: Candlewick. This animated book helps children understand some of the relationships between love, sex, and babies.

Hickling, M. (2002). *Boys, girls & body science: A first book about facts of life.* Madeira Park, B.C., Canada: Harbour Publishing. A nurse's sensitive guide for kids about their bodies and reproduction.

Hodel, P. (2010). *Monday hearts for Madalene.* New York: Stewart, Tabori & Chang. Stories of love written in hearts.

Ignatow, A. (2010). *The popularity papers: Research for the social improvement and general betterment of Lydia Goldblatt and Julie Graham-Chang.* New York: Amulet Books. Two girls explore friendship as they make their way through middle school.

Kemp, A. (2010). *Dogs don't do ballet.* New York: Simon & Schuster Children's Publishing. A girl and her dog explore the art of ballet.

Newman, L., & Ferguson, P. (2007). *The boy who cried fabulous.* Berkeley, CA: Tricycle Press. Roger's parents are unsure about whether it's good that he finds so many things "fabulous" until they join him in appreciating the world around him.

Newman, L., & Thompson, C. (2009). *Daddy, papa, and me.* Berkeley, CA: Tricycle Press. Two dads care for their toddler.

Newman, L., & Souza, D. (2009). *Heather has two mommies.* Boston: Alyson Books. Heather discovers multiple possibilities of family, and her friends learn that some kids have two moms.

Newman, L. & Thompson, C. (2009). *Mommy, mama, and me.* Berkeley, CA: Tricycle Press. Two moms care for their new baby.

Parr, T. (2003). *The family book.* New York: Little, Brown Books for Young Readers. A look at the multiple forms families can take.

Parr, T. (2009). *It's okay to be different.* New York: Little, Brown Books for Young Readers. Young children explore difference of all sorts.

Richardson, J., & Parnell, P. (2005). *And Tango makes three.* New York: Simon & Schuster Children's Publishing. The true story of two male penguins who raise their own "baby."

Saltz, G. (2008). *Amazing you!: Getting smart about your private parts.* New York: Puffin. For children up to 6 or 7, this book provides basic information about bodies and sexuality.

Schaefer, V. (1998). *The care & keeping of you: The body book for girls.* Middleton, WI: Pleasant Company Publications. A book designed to help girls from third to sixth grades understand their bodies.

Schwartz, P., & Cappello, D. (2000). *Ten talks parents must have with their children about sex and character.* New York: Hyperion. A book designed to help parents discuss sexuality with children of all ages.

Skeers, L. (2010). *Tutus aren't my style.* New York: Dial. A tomboy considers ballet and tutus.

Skutch, R., & Nienhaus, L. (1997). *Who's in a family?* Berkeley, CA: Tricycle Press. An exploration of multiple kinds of families that eventually asks children to imagine how their family fits into the spectrum.

Wilhoite, M. (1994). *Daddy's roommate.* Boston: Alyson Books. A young boy tries to make sense of his father's relationship with a man.

5–8

Bailey, J. (2004). *Sex, puberty, and all that stuff: A guide to growing up.* Hauppauge, NY: Barron's Educational Series. A humorous, animated guide for ages 11–14.

Blume, J. (2010). *Are you there God? It's me Margaret.* New York: Delacorte Books for Young Readers. The classic story of a middle-schooler worrying about puberty, boys, and fitting in.

Fakhrid-Deen, T., with COLAGE. (2010). *Let's get this straight: The ultimate handbook for youth with LGBTQ parents.* Berkeley, CA: Seal Press. A guide for kids whose parents are gay.

Gravelle, K. (2006). *The period book.* New York: Walker Books for Young Readers.

Gravelle, K., Castro, N., Castro, C., & Leighton, R. (1998). *What's going on down there: Answers to questions boys find*

414 | SECTION 9—"DOING IT": SEXUALITIES IN EDUCATION RESOURCES

hard to ask. New York: Walker Books for Young Readers. A companion book to *The period book* (below), this text helps boys understand puberty.

Howe, J. (2005). *Totally Joe.* New York: Simon and Schuster. A seventh-grader realizes he is gay and things turn out OK.

Madaras, L., & Madaras, A. (2007). *My body, my self for boys* (3rd ed.). New York: Newmarket. A respected guide for boys.

Madaras, L., & Madaras, A. (2007). *My body, my self for girls* (2nd ed.). New York: Newmarket. A respected guide for girls.

Magrs, P. (2003). *Strange boy.* New York: Simon and Schuster. A story of a 10-year-old facing family difficulties and wondering why he likes boys.

McCaughrean, G. (2010). *The death-defying Pepper Roux.* New York: HarperCollins. Adventures on the high seas for a 14-year-old and a cross-dressing friend she meets.

9–12

Basso, M.J. (2003). *The underground guide to teenage sexuality* (2nd ed.). Minneapolis, MN: Fairview Press. A collection of questions that teens are often afraid to ask and answers they need to know.

Beale, E. (2010). *Another life altogether.* New York: Spiegel & Grau. A high school girl struggles with a new school and her new same-sex attractions.

Bell, R. (1998). *Changing bodies, changing lives: A book for teens on sex and relationships* (3rd ed.). New York: Three Rivers Press. A self-described "encyclopedic" collection of information on the sexual and emotional development of teens.

Bergman, S.B. (2009). *The nearest exit may be behind you.* Vancouver, B.C., Canada: Arsenal Pulp Press. Essays from a transgendered perspective.

Boyd, M. *Will.* (2010). New York: Knopf Books for Young Readers. Friendship between a straight jock and a gay member of the band forces both to reconsider masculinity.

Corinna, H. (2007). *S-E-X: The all-you-need-to-know progressive sexuality guide to get you through high school and college.* Jackson, TN: Da Capo Press. A straightforward, comprehensive guide to help teens manage sexuality in their lives.

Daldry, J. (1999). *The teenage guy's survival guide: The real deal on girls, growing up and other guy stuff.* Boston: Little Brown Books for Young Readers. A guide for boys as they approach adulthood.

Diaz, A. (2009). *Of all the stupid things.* New York: Egmont USA. A high school couple both realize they are gay.

Diersch, S. (2010). *Out.* Halifax, NS, Canada: Lorimer. A student must rethink his ideas about sexuality when his brother comes out.

Gallup's modern guide to gay, lesbian & transgender life. (2010). 15 vols. Broomall, PA: Mason Crest Publishers. A series of books discussing the celebrations and challenges of living as an LGBTQ young person.

Garden, N. (1992). *Annie on my mind* (2nd ed.). New York: Aerial Fiction. Two high school girls explore friendship and love.

Green, J., & Levithan, D. (2010). *Will Grayson, Will Grayson.* New York: Dutton Juvenile. Gay and straight 16-year-olds with the same name discover friendship.

Henderson, E., & Armstrong, N. (2007). *100 questions you'd never ask your parents.* Richmond, VA: Henderson. A gynecologist's answer to the questions all teens have but are afraid to ask.

Heron, A. (Ed.). (1995). *Two teenagers in twenty: Writings by gay and lesbian youth.* Boston: Alyson Books. Teens from across the country write about their lives.

Huegel, K. (2003). *GLBTQ: The survival guide for queer and questioning teens.* Minneapolis, MN: Free Spirit Publishing. A solid, informative guide for teens written in a youth-friendly manner.

Hyde, C.R. (2010). *Jumpstart the world.* New York: Knopf Books for Young Readers. A teen falls in love with a neighbor boy who turns out to be transgendered.

Jukes, M. (2002). *The guys' book: An owner's manual (maintenance, safety and operating instructions for teens).* New York: Crown Books for Young Readers. A non-judgmental guide for teenage boys.

Keen, L. (2007). *Out law: What LGBTQ youth should know about their legal rights.* Boston: Beacon Press. A journalist helps teens understand their rights.

Levithan, D. (2003). *Boy meets boy.* New York: Alfred A. Knopf. A work that helps students imagine a world without oppression.

Lowrey, S. (2010). *Kicked out.* Ypsilanti, MI: Homofactus Press. Homeless LGBTQ youth share their stories.

Martin, R. (2010). *Me.* New York: Celebra Hardcover. Ricky Martin tells his story of coming out, being gay and Latino, and giving back.

Peters, J.A. (2003). *Keeping you a secret.* New York: Little, Brown and Co. A high school senior girl falls in love with another, and her world turns upside down.

Peters, J.A. (2004). *Luna.* New York: Little, Brown and Co. A positive portrayal of a transgendered youth.

Rossi, P. de. (2010). *Unbearable lightness.* New York: Atria. Portia de Rossi discusses coming out, her eating disorder, and coming to terms with both.

Sinclair, A. (1994). *Coffee will make you black.* New York: Perennial. A young African American woman explores race and sexuality with humor and spunk.

Webber, C.K. (2010). *Gay, lesbian, bisexual, transgender and questioning teen literature: A guide to reading interests.* Santa Barbara, CA: Libraries Unlimited. A guide to appropriate reading for young people of all ages.

Younger, B. (2009). *Learning curves: Body image and female sexuality in young adult literature.* Lanham, MD: Scarecrow Press, Inc. A critical analysis of the ways young women are depicted in literature.

University

The following fictional texts focus almost exclusively on LGBTQ issues or the intersection of gay and straight issues and are just a few of the books that I have used successfully in a class on LGBTQ literature. There are so many texts that address straight issues having to do with sex, love, and relationships (from Chaucer to Toni Morrison) that I have not tried to list them here. A useful website for educators interested in more fictional materials on LGBTQ issues is The Publishing Triangle's "100 Best Gay and Lesbian Novels" (http://www.publishingtriangle.org/100best.asp).

Anshaw, C. (1992). *Aquamarine.* New York: Pocket Books. One woman's life told in three very distinct ways, all of which involve her unresolved feelings for her first lesbian love.

Baldwin, J. (1956). *Giovanni's room.* New York: Dell Publishing. A young man in Paris questions and explores his sexuality.

Chabon, M. (1989). *The mysteries of Pittsburgh.* New York: Perennial. After college, a young man discovers another side to his sexuality.

Ebershoff, D. (2000). *The Danish girl.* New York: Penguin Books. A fictionalized account of the first known male-to-female transsexual to undergo gender reassignment surgery.

Feinberg, L. (1993). *Stone butch blues.* Ithaca, NY: Firebrand Books. The groundbreaking story of butch lesbian culture in the mid-20th century.

Holleran, A. (2001). *Dancer from the dance.* New York: Perennial. A group of NYC men explore sex, drugs, love, and life in the 1960s.

Kenan, R. (2000). *A visitation of spirits.* New York: Vintage. A story told from multiple perspectives of a gay, southern, black, Christian youth who descends into madness because he cannot reconcile his various identities.

Lorde, A. (1982). *ZAMI: A new spelling of my name.* Berkeley, CA: Crossing Press. A "biomythography" of Audre Lorde's life that also traces lesbian culture in the 1950s.

Merlis, M. (1994). *American studies.* New York: Penguin. A fictional history tracing two men and their alternative ways of being gay at Harvard in the 1940s and 1950s.

Perez, E. (1996). *Gulf dreams.* San Francisco: Aunt Lute Books. A book of love, obsession, feminism, and madness in Latina culture.

Puig, M. (1991). *Kiss of the spider woman.* New York: Vintage International. Two men, one gay and one straight, share a prison cell, politics, movies, and emotions in Argentina.

Rechy, J. (1963). *City of night.* New York: Grove Press, Inc. An explicit look at gay male sexual codes and culture in the mid-20th century.

Rule, J. (1991). *Desert of the heart.* Vancouver, B.C., Canada: Talon Books. A look at women's lesbian identities and relationships in the mid-20th century.

Selvadurai, S. (1994). *Funny boy.* New York: William Morrow. A Sri Lankan "girlie-boy" faces family, political, and sexual conflicts as he comes of age.

Winterson, J. (1985). *Oranges are not the only fruit.* New York: Grove Press. A searing look at fundamentalist Christianity and one girl's sexual longings in Britain.

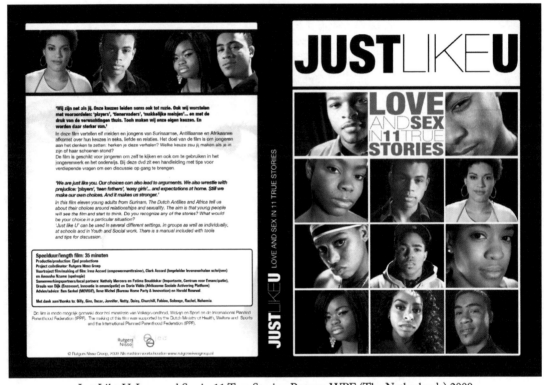

Just Like U. Love and Sex in 11 True Stories, Rutgers WPF (The Netherlands) 2009

Teaching Sexuality and Relationships Education in Multicultural Classrooms in the Netherlands

Daphne van de Bongardt

The Netherlands has a long history of teaching about sexuality issues within formal education. Over the course of the 20th century, the pragmatic Dutch approach has led to a general acceptance of youth sexuality and recognition of young people's need for information. Dutch sexuality education, too, has traditionally had a pragmatic approach, aiming at providing young people with the information they need to be responsible sexually active individuals and focusing on preventing risks (e.g., STIs, HIV/AIDS, unwanted pregnancy, and sexual coercion), as well as enhancing pleasure. The main objective of sexuality education is to support youth with appropriate knowledge, skills, and attitudes to enable them to make their own responsible choices.

Since the 1970s and 1980s Dutch society has become more diverse culturally and religiously through immigration. Today's Dutch classrooms, especially those in the large cities, contain many children, either first, second, or third generation, from countries such as the Netherlands Antilles, Surinam, Morocco, Turkey, Indonesia, Afghanistan, Iraq, Iran, or African countries. In 2010, about one in ten Dutch schools (and almost half of the schools in the large cities) had more than 50% non-Western immigrant students (Statistics Netherlands, 2010).

Teaching sexuality and relationships education in multicultural classrooms requires different approaches than in monocultural classrooms. In response to population shifts, new materials have been developed to assist teachers with discussing sexuality-related topics in culturally diverse classrooms. As one example, in this film called *Just Like U: Love & Sex in 11 True Stories,* 11 young men and women with Surinamese, Antillean, and African backgrounds tell about the personal decisions they made regarding sex, love, and relationships. Through peer examples, it aims to stimulate young people's self-esteem, encouraging them to make their own choices concerning virginity, safe sex, teen pregnancy and parenthood, prostitution, and communication with parents. The DVD, which contains 11 separate film stories (which are also available on the Internet) and a version with English subtitles, can be used by teachers, youth and health care workers, or parents. It comes with a booklet with tips on how to start a reflexive and interactive group discussion after watching the DVD. These materials are produced by Ejed Productions and published by Rutgers WPF (formerly known as Rutgers Nisso Groep) in the Netherlands.

Contributors

THERESE QUINN teaches at the School of the Art Institute of Chicago and writes about the arts and public education and other justice issues. She contributes a column to *Yliopisto*, the magazine of the University of Helsinki, grows gooseberries and poppies, and lives near Lake Michigan.

ERICA R. MEINERS teaches, writes, and organizes in Chicago on a range of justice issues. She works at an open-access public university, Northeastern Illinois University, teaches at other free sites in Chicago, and is an errant fruit canner.

Section 1

CONNIE E. NORTH is a writer, scholar, and media specialist and the author of *Teaching for Social Justice? Voices from the Front Lines*. She holds a Ph.D. in Curriculum and Instruction and Educational Policy Studies and is pursuing an M.S. in counseling.

HEATHER AULT is an artist, graphic designer, and activist engaged in 4000 Years for Choice (www.4000yearsforchoice.com), a project that has exhibited throughout the country. She received her Master's of Fine Arts degree from the University of Illinois at Urbana-Champaign.

JESSICA FIELDS is Associate Professor of Sociology and Research Faculty at the Center for Research and Education on Gender and Sexuality at San Francisco State University. Her book, *Risky Lessons: Sex Education and Social Inequality*, won the 2009 Distinguished Contribution to Scholarship Book Award from the American Sociological Association Section on Race, Gender, and Class.

SHANNON N. KAVANAGH has worked in community-based arts organizations as an educator, artist in residence, and counselor. She is a graduate of the School of the Art Institute of Chicago's art therapy program, and currently lives in Madison, Wisconsin.

MEL MICHELLE LEWIS is a doctoral candidate in women's studies at the University of Maryland and holds an M.S. and an M.A. in women's studies. Her research focuses on Black queer feminist pedagogy and performance.

ELIZABETH J. MEYER is Assistant Professor in the School of Education at California Polytechnic State University in San Luis Obispo, CA, and the author of *Gender, Bullying, and Harassment: Strategies to End Sexism and Homophobia in Schools and Gender and Sexual Diversity in Schools.*

MATTILDA BERNSTEIN SYCAMORE (www.mattildabernsteinsycamore.com) is most recently the editor of *Why Are Faggots So Afraid of Faggots?: Flaming Challenges to Masculinity, Objectification, and the Desire to Conform* and the author of *So Many Ways to Sleep Badly.*

Section 2

LUCY E. BAILEY is an Associate Professor of Social Foundations and Qualitative Inquiry and Associate Director of the Gender and Women's Studies Program at Oklahoma State University. She is the co-editor of *Wanted—Correspondence: Women's Letters to a Union Soldier.*

KAREN GRAVES is Professor of Education at Denison University. She is the author of *And They Were Wonderful Teachers: Florida's Purge of Gay and Lesbian Teachers.*

JACKIE M. BLOUNT is Professor of Educational Policy and Leadership at the Ohio State University. She is author of *Fit to Teach: Same-Sex Desire, Gender, and School Work in the Twentieth Century* and *Destined to Rule the Schools: Women and the Superintendency, 1873–1995.*

WARREN J. BLUMENFELD is Associate Professor in the Department of Curriculum and Instruction at Iowa State University. He is co-editor with Khyati Y. Joshi and Ellen E. Fairchild of *Investigating Christian Privilege and Religious Oppression in the United States.*

CATHERINE A. LUGG is Professor of Education at Rutgers, the State University of New Jersey. Her research interests include the influences of social movements and political ideology on educational politics and policy.

Section 3

ISABEL NUÑEZ is an Associate Professor of Foundations, Social Policy and Research at Concordia University Chicago. Her research interests connect education and the individual psyche, from autobiography and life curriculum to the ideological role of schooling.

BECKY ATKINSON is an Assistant Professor of Educational Leadership and Foundations of Education at the University of Alabama. She has published articles in *Educational Theory, Qualitative Inquiry, Educational Studies,* and the *Journal of Educational Research.*

CAROLYN PAJOR FORD is a high school English teacher in Park Ridge, IL. She is interested in teacher autobiography, reflection, and memoir as curriculum in life and in the classroom.

JANE GALLOP teaches at the University of Wisconsin, Milwaukee. She is the author of eight books, including *Thinking Through the Body* and *Anecdotal Theory*. Her latest book, entitled *The Deaths of the Author*, was published in July 2011.

COYA PAZ BROWNRIGG is a writer, director, and lip gloss connoisseur. She cofounded Teatro Luna and Proyecto Latina and is an Assistant Professor in The Theatre School at DePaul University. Visit her on the web at www.coyapaz.com

ERIC ROFES was a longtime educator and activist who worked on a wide range of progressive social and political justice issues. For over 30 years, his various careers brought together four key elements: teaching, organizing, research, and writing.

Section 4

DARLA LINVILLE is a Research Associate in the Education Program at Colby College. She uses participatory action research to interrogate the discourses about sexuality and gender and young people's identifications with them.

ERICA M. BOAS is a doctoral candidate in the Social and Cultural Studies program at the University of California, Berkeley's Graduate School of Education. Erica Boas teaches and writes about the ways in which schools aid in constructing and conducting social realities.

JACINTA BUNNELL is an artist, writer, and educator living in New York's Hudson Valley. She is the author of three coloring books, including *Girls Are Not Chicks*.

KATHLEEN ELLIOTT is a Visiting Assistant Professor of Educational Studies at Trinity College in Hartford, Connecticut. She conducts ethnographic research on how diverse adolescents negotiate their gender and sexual identities in the context of shifting educational policies and practices.

DAVE GLICK is a Minnesota-based independent consultant specializing in virtual education and school improvement, particularly those serving minority and disenfranchised populations. He is also the Executive Director of GLBTQ Online High School and the co-author of iNACOL's website, "How to Start an Online Program."

JULIE NOVAK is an actor, writer, musician, and visual and performance artist living in New York's beautiful Hudson Valley. She is committed to teaching tolerance and believes that the wisdom of young people can change the world. To hear her music, check out www.myspace.com/guitarsand-hearts.

C.J. PASCOE is an Assistant Professor of Sociology at Colorado College. She researches youth, masculinity, sexuality, and new media. Her book *Dude, You're a Fag* won the American Educational Research Association's Book of the Year Award. Her current research focuses on youth romance practices.

Section 5

JILLIAN C. FORD is an Assistant Professor in the Secondary and Middle Grades Department at Kennesaw State University's Bagwell College of Education. She teaches social foundations courses to pre-service teachers, and her research includes queer youth citizenship, identity, and agency.

KEN JACKSON is a Professional School Counselor in Decatur, Georgia, and a Ph.D. student in Counseling and Student Personnel Services at the University of Georgia. He focuses on diversity, advocacy, and LGBTQ issues in his research and conference presentations.

JANE BRYAN MEEK is an instructor in the Center for Writing and Rhetoric at the University of Mississippi where she also conducts trainings for LGBTQ allies. Her research focuses primarily on queer mentoring networks and youth movements for social justice.

SANDRA J. SCHMIDT is an assistant professor in the Department of Arts and Humanities at Teachers College, Columbia University. She teaches social studies methods and queer theory. Her research interests include critical geography and citizenship in public spaces.

MIKAELA SHELT is a graduate of Agnes Scott College and teaches math and art at a non-profit academy for refugee boys in Clarkston, Georgia (Fugees Family Academy).

ANNELIESE A. SINGH, Ph.D., LPC, is an Assistant Professor at the University of Georgia in the School Counseling program. Her research explores school bullying and violence related to LGBTQQ youth and the resilience strategies of historically marginalized communities.

LUCIA VIDABLE (translator) was born and raised in Argentina. She graduated from Emory University and currently works for housing at Oxford College of Emory University.

Section 6

DR. JUKKA LEHTONEN is a research coordinator for the project "Gender Awareness in Teacher Education," which is funded by the Finnish Ministry of Education and Culture. He works at the Department of Behavioral Sciences at the University of Helsinki, Finland. He has researched and published widely on the issues of sexual and gender diversity and heteronormativity in education and the work environment. His current research interests include non-heterosexual and transgender youth, their educational and career choices, and their experiences of violence and health.

ROLAND SINTOS COLOMA is Assistant Professor of Anti-Racist and Feminist Studies in Globalization and Education. Coloma's interests focus on empire and diaspora, race, gender, and sexuality, history, and theory. He is working on two books, *Subjects of Empire: Modernity and Education in American Philippines,* a history of the public school system in the Philippines under U.S. colonial rule, and *Postcolonial Challenges in Education,* an edited volume that brings together postcolonial education scholars in Canada, the United States, and the U.K.

PETER DANKMEIJER was trained as a teacher. He did research on gay and lesbian teachers in the Netherlands and went on to found EduDivers, the Dutch Expertise Centre on Sexual Diversity in Schools, which develops curricula, offers training, and advises school managers. In 2005, he founded GALE, the Global Alliance for LGBT Education, a network of educators and organizations who work on concrete educational projects.

DR. C.P. GAUSE is an Associate Professor in the Department of Educational Leadership and Cultural Foundations at the University of North Carolina at Greensboro. He is a former public school teacher, social service worker, and K–12 school administrator, and a co-editor of *Keeping the Promise: Essays on Leadership, Democracy and Education.* His research interests include gender and queer studies; black masculinity; cultural studies; critical race theory; critical spirituality; and collaborative activism.

PHAL SOPHAT is the Country Director of Men's Health Social Services in Phnom Penh, Cambodia. He has played an active role in the HIV response in Cambodia since 1999, and has lectured at various domestic universities on sexual health and human rights issues. Phal Sophat has worked with the MSM Secretariat in Cambodia and is a member of the National Technical Working Group on HIV/AIDS and MSM, and the Country Coordination Mechanism for the Global Fund in Cambodia. He is a board member of the Purple Sky Network based in Thailand.

SILJA RAJANDER has researched school choice with an interest in the discursive production of space and identity. She has worked in the area of gender and HIV with the UN and with various networks and community organisations in Cambodia. She currently teaches qualitative research at the Royal University of Phnom Penh, and continues her involvement in the HIV response through her work with the Cambodian Community of Women Living with HIV/AIDS. Her present research interests include educational choice and the production of social vulnerability.

DR. JAY POOLE is Visiting Assistant Professor in the Department of Social Work in the School of Human Environmental Sciences at the University of North Carolina at Greensboro. He has a background in clinical social work practice focused on mental health and substance abuse services and as a social work educator. His interests include gender and queer studies, and social work practice and aging. His work has appeared in the journals *Social Work, Brightlights, Forum on Public Policy,* and the *Michigan Family Review.*

DIANE RICHARDSON is Professor of Sociology at Newcastle University. She has written extensively about gender and sexuality and, with Vicki Robinson, co-edited *Introducing Gender and Women's Studies.* She is editing a new book series, Genders and Sexualities in the Social Sciences, for Palgrave Macmillan, and working on a forthcoming book, with Surya Monro, *Sexuality, Diversity and Social Change* (also with Palgrave Macmillan), based on findings from a recent Economic and Social Research Council (ESRC) project on Sexualities Equalities Initiatives.

IRINA SCHMITT is a lector at the Centre for Gender Studies, Lund University, Sweden. She is interested in queer and feminist thinking and work, both at the desk and in the classroom, and at the intersection of academic and "everyday" knowledge. Currently she is doing research about "rainbow children"—children growing up with LGBTTIQ parents—and their experiences in school, and on teachers' knowledges about and strategies toward LGBTTIQ children and young people.

Section 7

KARYN SANDLOS is an Assistant Professor of Art Education at the School of the Art Institute of Chicago (SAIC). She is a co-investigator on the 3-year study "The Emotional Geography of Sex Education: Toward a Revitalized Curriculum." Recent publications include *Sex Education: Sexuality, Society and Learning* and a contribution to *The Journal of Sexuality, Research and Social Policy.*

DEBORAH BRITZMAN is Distinguished Research Professor at York University and a prolific author. Widely known for her published work in bringing psychoanalysis to discussions of contemporary pedagogy, teacher education, social inequality, and problems of intolerance and historical crisis, her most recent books are *The Very Thought of Education: Psychoanalysis and the Impossible Professions* and *Freud and Education.*

BRIAN CASEMORE is an Assistant Professor of Curriculum & Pedagogy in the Department of Curriculum & Pedagogy at the George Washington University. He conducts psychoanalytic research on the emotional geography of conversations in sex education.

SUNIL GUPTA is an artist, curator and writer. His work has explored narratives of contemporary gay life in India and other parts of the world; tackled issues of gender and sexuality; and documented his own experiences living with AIDS.

BARBARA HAMMER is a visual artist working primarily in film and video; her works include *Dyketactics* (1974) and *Nitrate Kisses* (1992). Her most recent work is an experimental film on cancer and hope, *A Horse Is Not a Metaphor.* The memoir *HAMMER! Making Movies Out of Sex and Life* (CUNY Feminist Press, 2010) will coincide with retrospectives at the Museum of Modern Art in New York City, the Reina Sophia in Madrid, and the Tate Modern in London. www.barbarahammer.com

FRANCISCO IBÁÑEZ-CARRASCO is an AIDS activist, teacher, researcher, and founder of Universities Without Walls, a national training program for emerging HIV researchers. He completed his Ph.D. in Education at Simon Fraser University in 1999, and his research interests include community-based research, gay men's sexuality, and rehabilitation in the context of HIV. He is the winner of the 2010 Award of Excellence of the Canadian Working Group on HIV and Rehabilitation (CWGHR).

ISAAC JULIEN was nominated for the Turner Prize in 2001 for his film *The Long Road to Mazatlán.* Earlier works include *Frantz Fanon: Black Skin, White Mask, Young Soul Rebels,* and the acclaimed poetic documentary *Looking for Langston.* He is a Visiting Professor at the Whitney Museum of American Arts. www.isaacjulien.com

MARY PATTEN is a visual artist, video-maker, writer, educator, occasional curator, and political activist. In all her work, she seeks to address collisions as well as alignments between the worlds of "politics" and art-making. She is an Associate Professor in the Film, Video, New Media, and Animation Department at the School of the Art Institute of Chicago, where she has been teaching since 1993.

LANE RELYEA is a critic living in Chicago, where he teaches at Northwestern University in the Department of Art Theory & Practice. His book *DIY Culture Industry: Social Networks, Signifying Practices and Other Instrumentalizations of Everyday Life* is forthcoming from MIT Press.

EVE KOSOFSKY SEDGWICK (1950–2009) was a leading scholar in queer theory and literary studies, and a Distinguished Professor of English at the CUNY Graduate Center. Her numerous books include *Epistemology of the Closet* and *Novel Gazing: Queer Readings in Fiction.*

LAUREN BERLANT teaches English at the University of Chicago. Recent work related to affect, politics, and aesthetics includes *The Queen of America Goes to Washington City* and *The Female Complaint.* Her book *Cruel Optimism* is forthcoming. She can also be found at supervalentthought.wordpress.com

Section 8

ANGEL RUBIEL GONZALEZ is a doctoral candidate in the Social and Cultural Studies in Education program at the University of California, Berkeley. His research interests include transnational feminisms, theories of coloniality/decoloniality, and the social and cultural dimensions of education. At present his work focuses on the historical, philosophical, and sociological development of U.S. masculinity and its relationship to the existential struggles of young Black and Latino men in contemporary U.S. society.

SENDOLO DIAMINAH (aka Lola) is a black, queer communist living and organizing in Durham, NC. Sendolo is a member of Freedom Road Socialist Organization and an organizer with People's Durham.

Gender JUST (chapter authored by members Sam Finkelstein, Lucky Mosqueda, Adrian Birrueta, and Eric Kitty) is a grassroots organization led by queer, transgender, and gender non-conforming young people building power and developing leadership by organizing through a racial, economic, and gender justice framework.

ANDREA GIBSON is the winner of the 2008 Women's World Poetry Slam and has placed third in the world on two International Poetry Slam stages. Andrea's first book, *Pole Dancing to Gospel Hymns,* won the DIY Poetry Book of the Year and was nominated for the Pushcart Prize. Gibson has been showcased on Free Speech TV, the BBC, Air America, CSPAN, and NPR, and was featured in the documentary *Slam Planet.*

DEBORAH GOULD is an Assistant Professor in the Department of Sociology at the University of California, Santa Cruz. She is the author of *Moving Politics: Emotion and ACT UP's Fight Against AIDS.* She was involved in ACT UP for many years as well as Queer to the Left, and is a founding member of the art/activist/research collaborative group Feel Tank Chicago.

VENUS JONES's poetry has appeared in *Poet Lore,* U.K.'s *X Magazine, Spoken Vizions* and anthologies including *How I Freed My Soul, A Time to Rhyme,* and *A Generation Defining Itself,* and she's an Austin International Poetry Slam finalist. She's also a former MTV correspondent, the author of *She Rose,* and a two-time Onyx Award nominee. Visit www.venusjones.com

ANAYVETTE MARTINEZ is a GuaNica High-Femme QSMOC (Queer Single Mother of Color) of two little rambunctious nene's, Theory-Enthusiast, passionate baker/lover/spoken text artist/youthworker and eternal nerd who *hearts* making escandalo and manifesting theory into barrio praxis. She's currently employed at LYRIC as the Programs Director of Community Building and believes deeply in youth development and queer youth advocacy.

JEANETTE MAY is an artist and activist currently living in Brooklyn, New York. She is a founding member of the Coalition for Positive Sexuality, a grass-roots organization dedicated to providing teens with a frank, positive, and empowering sex education.

RONALD K. PORTER is a doctoral candidate in the Social and Cultural Studies in Education program, with a designated emphasis in critical theory, at the University of California, Berkeley. His research interests include African American educational thought and critical theories of race, gender, and sexuality. His dissertation research traces the intellectual history of African American educational thought, looking specifically at the work of W.E.B. Du Bois, Alain Locke, and James Baldwin.

ALAN WONG is a community activist and Ph.D. candidate in the Special Individualized Program at Concordia University in Montreal, Quebec, Canada. His scholarly and social justice work focuses on the intersections of race, ethnicity, gender, and sexual identity.

Section 9: Resources Section

TIMOTHY BARNETT is an Associate Professor of English at Northeastern Illinois University who specializes in composition, rhetoric, critical literacy, and LGBTQ studies. His research looks at the way reading, writing, and language help to maintain and/or refigure the status quo.

SUZANN GAGE played a pivotal role in the Federation of Feminist Health Centers as a volunteer lay health worker and later as the lead illustrator for their publication *A New View of a Woman's Body*. Gage now runs Progressive Health Services in San Diego, California, as an OB/GYN nurse practitioner.

CHANCES/DANCES is a Chicago dance party. TYRA (Trans Youth Resource and Advocacy) is a weekly transgender and gender-questioning drop-in program for youth ages 12 to 24. TYRA is a program of Howard Brown Health Center's Broadway Youth Center located in Chicago. Strap-on.org (http://strap-on.org) is a queer* positive, trans* positive, sex* positive, girl* positive community message board.

DAPHNE VAN DE BONGARDT (MSc) has a background in sociology and educational sciences and specializes in gender and sexuality issues. She has done research at the University of Amsterdam on sexuality education, planned lesbian families, and first-time sexual experiences of same-sex attracted youth. Currently a Ph.D. student at Utrecht University, she conducts research within "Project STARS," a large-scale longitudinal study on relational and sexual development of Dutch adolescents, specifically investigating the influence of parenting and peers.

SINS INVALID is a San Francisco-based performance project that incubates and celebrates artists with disabilities, centralizing artists of color and queer and gender-variant artists as communities who have been historically marginalized. Conceived and led by Patricia (Patty) Berne and Leroy F. Moore, Jr., Sins Invalid develops and presents work by artists in all creative genres. Sinsinvalid.org

NOMY LAMM is a writer, musician, and activist whose work has been featured in magazines (*Ms., Punk Planet, Make/Shift*), anthologies (*Listen Up, Body Outlaws,* and, most recently, *Word Warriors and Working Sex*), and onstage across the United States. She has toured with Sister Spit, the Sex Workers Art Show, and the cabaret showcase Dr. Frockrocket's Menagerie and Medicine Show.

Studies in the Postmodern Theory of Education

General Editor
Shirley R. Steinberg

Counterpoints publishes the most compelling and imaginative books being written in education today. Grounded on the theoretical advances in criticalism, feminism, and postmodernism in the last two decades of the twentieth century, Counterpoints engages the meaning of these innovations in various forms of educational expression. Committed to the proposition that theoretical literature should be accessible to a variety of audiences, the series insists that its authors avoid esoteric and jargonistic languages that transform educational scholarship into an elite discourse for the initiated. Scholarly work matters only to the degree it affects consciousness and practice at multiple sites. Counterpoints' editorial policy is based on these principles and the ability of scholars to break new ground, to open new conversations, to go where educators have never gone before.

For additional information about this series or for the submission of manuscripts, please contact:

> Shirley R. Steinberg
> c/o Peter Lang Publishing, Inc.
> 29 Broadway, 18th floor
> New York, New York 10006

To order other books in this series, please contact our Customer Service Department:

> (800) 770-LANG (within the U.S.)
> (212) 647-7706 (outside the U.S.)
> (212) 647-7707 FAX

Or browse online by series:
> www.peterlang.com